School

An Introduction to Education

Edward S. Ebert II
Coker College

Richard C. Culyer III
Coker College

THOMSON
WADSWORTH

Australia · Brazil · Canada · Mexico · Singapore · Spain · United Kingdom · United States

THOMSON

WADSWORTH

School: An Introduction to Education
Edward S. Ebert II and Richard C. Culyer III

Education Editor: Dan Alpert
Development Editor: Tangelique Williams
Assistant Editor: Ann Lee Richards
Editorial Assistant: Stephanie Rue
Technology Project Manager: Julie Aguilar
Marketing Manager: Karin Sandberg
Marketing Assistant: Teresa Jessen
Marketing Communications Manager: Shemika Britt
Project Manager, Editorial Production: Trudy Brown
Creative Director: Rob Hugel
Art Director: Maria Epes
Print Buyer: Doreen Suruki

Permissions Editor: Bob Kauser
Production Service: Lachina Publishing Services
Text Designer: Cheryl Carrington
Photo Researcher: Robin Samper
Copy Editor: Christy Goldfinch
Cover Designer: Liz Harasymczuk
Cover Image: © WireImageStock/Masterfile; Stockbyte/Getty Images;
    Jack Hollingsworth/Getty Images; Ryan McVay/Getty Images;
    SW Productions/Getty Images; Kevin Peterson/Getty Images;
    Vicky Kasala/Getty Images
Compositor: Lachina Publishing Services
Text and Cover Printer: Courier Corporation, Kendallville

Library of Congress Control Number: 2006937356

ISBN-13: 978-0-534-52465-4
ISBN-10: 0-534-52465-6

Thomson Higher Education
10 Davis Drive
Belmont, CA 94002-3098
USA

For more information about our products, contact us at:
Thomson Learning Academic Resource Center
1-800-423-0563

For permission to use material from this text or product, submit
a request online at **http://www.thomsonrights.com**

Any additional questions about permissions can be submitted
by e-mail to **thomsonrights@thomson.com.**

The authors are pleased to dedicate this book to all teachers who bring the world to their students each and every day.

Brief Contents

Unit One: The Profession   1

CHAPTER 1	The Teacher	2
CHAPTER 2	The Strategic Nature of Teaching	30
CHAPTER 3	Student Diversity	56
CHAPTER 4	Becoming a Teacher	102

Unit Two: Curriculum, Management, and Assessment   149

CHAPTER 5	Understanding Curriculum	150
CHAPTER 6	Contemporary Curricula: Influences and Standards	180
CHAPTER 7	Classroom Pragmatics	212

Unit Three: The Institution of Education   251

CHAPTER 8	A History of American Education	252
CHAPTER 9	Philosophy and Education	286
CHAPTER 10	Ethics in Education and Matters of Law	316
CHAPTER 11	Education: Purpose, Organization, Governance, and Funding	358

Unit Four: Challenges for Today and Tomorrow   397

CHAPTER 12	Social Issues Affecting Students and Schools	398
CHAPTER 13	Reform Efforts and the Professional Educator	424
CHAPTER 14	Innovations and the Future	452

Contents

List of Features   xii

Preface   xv

Acknowledgments   xviii

Preface to Unit I   1

Unit One: The Profession   1

CHAPTER 1   The Teacher   2

Introduction   4
You, the Teacher   4
Pedagogy   6
     The Art of Teaching   7
     The Science of Teaching   9
Pedagogical Competencies   10
     Purpose   11
     Content   14
     Communication Skills   17
     Professional Development   22
Conclusion   25
     Key Terms   25
Educational Engineering   25
     Case Studies in Education   25
Designing the School of the Future   27
Praxis Practice   28

CHAPTER 2   The Strategic Nature of Teaching   30

Introduction   32
The Strategic Nature of Teaching   33
Facilitating Learning   33
     Arranging Experiences   34
     Instructional Techniques   37
     Monitoring and Flexibility   48
Modeling   49
     Are Teachers Role Models?   49
     Are Teachers Role Models
         Away from School?   51
Conclusion   52
     Key Terms   52
Educational Engineering   53
     Case Studies in Education   53
Designing the School of the Future   54
Praxis Practice   55

CHAPTER 3   Student Diversity   56

Introduction   58
General Ways in Which Students Differ   59
     Culture, Ethnicity, and Race   59
     Religion   69
     Gender   69
     Language   71
     Motivation   74
     Academic Self-Concept   75
     Temperament   75
     Learning Styles   79
     Reading Ability   79
Learning, Sensory, and Physical Diversity   80
     Perspectives on Intelligence   81
     Meeting the Needs of Students
         with Cognitive Exceptionalities   83
     Learning Disorders   87
     Sensory Aspects of Student Diversity   92
     A Perspective of Empathy   96
Conclusion   97
     Key Terms   97
Educational Engineering   97
     Case Studies in Education   97
Designing the School of the Future   99
Praxis Practice   100

CHAPTER 4   Becoming a Teacher   102

Introduction   105
Earning a License to Teach   105

Accreditation of the Teacher
  Education Program   105
National Influences on Teacher
  Education   107
Traditional Teacher Education Programs   109
Alternative Teacher Education Programs   118
Where Teachers Teach   121
  Teaching in Public Schools   121
  Teaching in Private Schools   121
  Teaching in Charter Schools   122
  Using Your Teacher Licensure
    in Other Fields   123
Getting a Job as a Teacher   124
  Teaching Positions   124
  Tools for Getting Hired   125
Teachers and Salary   127
What to Expect as a New Teacher   127
Development as a Teacher   130
  Performance Appraisals   130
  Professional Development   130
Professional Organizations and Affiliations   132
  Generalized Organizations
    for Professional Educators   132
  Subject Area Organizations   133
  Administrative/Supervisory
    Organizations   134
  Research-Oriented Organizations   135
  Freestanding Publications   136
  Special Service Organizations   138
Conclusion   138
  Key Terms   139
Educational Engineering   139
  Case Studies in Education   139
Designing the School of the Future   140
Praxis Practice   141

Unit Workshop I   **142**

Preface to Unit II   **149**

Unit Two: Curriculum, Management, and Assesment   149

CHAPTER 5   Understanding Curriculum   **150**

Introduction   152
Understanding "Curriculum"   153
  Defining "Curriculum"   153

The Purpose of Curriculum   156
The Four Curricula   157
Perspectives of Curricula   162
  The Cognitive and Affective
    Perspectives   163
  The Cognitive Perspective   163
  The Affective Perspective   169
Conclusion   175
  Key Terms   176
Educational Engineering   176
  Case Studies in Education   176
Designing the School of the Future   178
Praxis Practice   179

CHAPTER 6   Contemporary Curricula: Influences and Standards   **180**

Introduction   182
Influences on the Curriculum   183
  Parents and the Schools   183
  Special Interest Groups   184
  State Legislatures   185
  The Schools   186
  Textbooks   188
Emerging Standards   190
  Mathematics   193
  Science   194
  Language Arts   195
  Social Studies   196
  Foreign Languages   197
  The Arts   197
  Physical Education   198
  Vocational/Technology/
    Computer Education   199
Issues in Curriculum   200
  Testing   200
  A National Curriculum?   202
  Emergent Literacy Programs   204
  School Uniforms   206
Conclusion   208
  Key Terms   209
Educational Engineering   209
  Case Studies in Education   209
Designing the School of the Future   210
Praxis Practice   211

CHAPTER 7   Classroom Pragmatics   **212**

Introduction   215
Assessment   215
  The Aims of Assessment   215

Standardized and Classroom Assessment   216
Assessment as Part of Instruction   218
Assigning Grades   220
Classroom Management   224
Some Perspectives on Classroom
Management   225
Keys to Successful Classroom
Management   228
Establishing a Learning Environment   233
Noninstructional Tasks and Responsibilities   240
Outside of the Classroom   240
Committee Work   240
Planning for a Substitute Teacher   241
Conclusion   242
Key Terms   243
Educational Engineering   243
Case Studies in Education   243
Designing the School of the Future   244
Praxis Practice   245

Unit Workshop II   **246**

Preface to Unit III   **251**

Unit Three: The Institution of Education   251

CHAPTER 8   **A History of American Education**   **252**

Introduction   254
The Emerging Need for Education   254
The Ancient Greeks   254
The Ancient Romans   256
The European Middle Ages   258
Education in America   259
The New World (1600s)   259
The New Nation (1700s)   262
Developing an Educational System for a New
Nation (1800s)   265
Education in 20th-Century America   273
The First 50 Years of the 20th Century   274
The Second Half of the 20th Century   278
Conclusion   281
Key Terms   282
Educational Engineering   282
Case Studies in Education   282
Designing the School of the Future   283
Praxis Practice   284

CHAPTER 9   **Philosophy and Education**   **286**

Introduction   288
Developing Your Philosophical Perspective   289
More Philosophical Perspectives   289
Conceptual Clusters of Philosophical
Questions   290
Metaphysics   290
Axiology   291
Epistemology   292
Logic   293
Schools of Philosophy   293
Idealism   294
Realism   295
Pragmatism   298
Existentialism   300
Philosophies in Schools   301
Perennialism   302
Essentialism   303
Progressivism   305
Social Reconstructionism   306
Psychology: The Pragmatics of Philosophy   308
Behaviorism   308
Humanism   309
Constructivism   310
Conclusion   311
Key Terms   313
Educational Engineering   313
Case Studies in Education   313
Designing the School of the Future   315
Praxis Practice   315

CHAPTER 10   **Ethics in Education and Matters of Law**   **316**

Introduction   318
Ethics   319
Morals, Ethics, and Laws   319
You as an Ethical Person   319
You as an Ethical Teacher   322
A Code of Ethics for
the Teaching Profession   323
Teachers and the Law   325
The Teacher and the Protection
of Due Process   326
Employment: Contracts, Tenure,
and Dismissal   326
Tort Law and Teacher Liability   328
Reporting Child Abuse   329
Reasonable Force   330

Copyright Laws   331
Freedom of Expression   332
Lifestyle   334
Private Sexual Behavior   335
Conduct with Students   335
Students and the Law   336
The Student and Due Process   336
Suspension and Expulsion   336
Corporal Punishment   337
Freedom of Speech   340
Sexual Harassment   341
Records and Students' Right to Privacy   342
Schools and Religion   343
Prayer in the Public Schools   343
Religious Instruction in Public Schools   344
Public Funds for Parochial Schools   344
Religious Clubs/Prayer Groups   344
Federal Law   344
Higher Education   345
Elementary and Secondary Schools   345
Civil Rights   346
Exceptional Education   347
Compensatory Education   349
School Subjects and Topics   351
Information and Research   351
Challenges to the Law   353
Conclusion   355
Key Terms   356
Educational Engineering   356
Case Studies in Education   356
Designing the School of the Future   357
Praxis Practice   357

CHAPTER 11 Education: Purpose, Organization, Governance, and Funding   358

Introduction   360
An Overview of Schools: Purpose,
Grade Levels, and Options   361
Purpose of Schools   361
School Levels   362
Purpose of Each Level   365
School Options   368
The Federal Role in Education   371
The State Role in Education   372
Characteristics of State Control   372
The Governor   373

State Superintendent and the Board of
Education   373
"Grading" the Schools   374
Education and the State Legislature   374
Judicial Influence   375
The Local Role in Education   375
The Local School Board   375
Superintendent of Schools   376
District Personnel   376
Building-Level Administration   378
Financing Education   381
The Federal Role   381
The State Role   383
The Local Role   385
Channeling Funds to the Schools   385
Conclusion   388
Key Terms   389
Educational Engineering   389
Case Studies in Education   389
Designing the School of the Future   390
Praxis Practice   390

Unit Workshop III   **391**

Preface to Unit IV   **397**

Unit Four: Challenges for Today and Tomorrow   397

CHAPTER 12 Social Issues Affecting Students and Schools   398

Introduction   400
Socioeconomic Issues   401
Family Structure   401
"At-Risk" Students   404
Poverty   406
Homelessness   407
Child Abuse and Neglect   411
The Society in Which We Live   413
Issues Facing Children and Adolescents   413
Substance Abuse   413
School Violence and Vandalism   414
Teen Pregnancy   416
Adolescent Suicide   417
Other Societal Influences on Social
Development   418

Conclusion   420
    Key Terms   421
Educational Engineering   421
    Case Studies in Education   421
Designing a School of the Future   423
Praxis Practice   423

CHAPTER 13 **Reform Efforts and the Professional Educator**   **424**

Introduction   426
Change and Reform   427
The Reform Model   429
    Higher Education: The Reform
       Model Finds a Home   429
    Business: Who Will Blink First?   430
    Politics: The Assumption of Expertise   432
    Parents   434
A Brief Look at Some Reforms
   and Interventions   435
    Reforms   436
    Interventions   438
What Makes a Reform Effort Exemplary?   441
    Category I: The Need for the Program   442
    Category II: The Nature of the Program   443
    Category III: Implementation   445
Conclusion   448
    Key Terms   449
Educational Engineering   449
    Case Studies in Education   449
Designing the School of the Future   451
Praxis Practice   451

CHAPTER 14 **Innovations and the Future**   **452**

Introduction   455
Understanding "Technology"   455
Technology Past and Present   456
    Technology in the Schools   456
    Technology Issues   459

Technology and Tomorrow   461
    Logistical Innovations   461
    Instructional Innovations   472
Fiscal Education   481
    Funding Education   481
    Economic Education   482
The Global Community   483
Conclusion   484
    Key Terms   485
Educational Engineering   485
    Case Studies in Education   485
Designing the School of the Future   487
    Near Vision   487
    Distant Vision   487
Praxis Practice   487

Unit Workshop IV   **488**

Appendix A: Case Studies in Education   **493**

Appendix B: Designing a School of the Future   **499**

Appendix C: State Departments of Education   **501**

Appendix D: The Praxis Series   **507**

Appendix E: Answer Key for Unit Workshop Quizzes   **509**

Glossary   **513**

References   **521**

Subject Index   **541**

Name Index   **552**

List of Features

Ice Breakers

I Want to Be a Teacher Like . . .	3
Challenging Your Students to Think	31
What's Your Style?	57
First Year	103
What Did *You* Learn About?	151
A Standards Sampler	181
How Should You Be Graded?	213
Meet the Folks!	253
What Is Your Philosophical Disposition?	287
Are You Legal?	317
It Costs *How* Much?	359
A Short (and Fictional) Family History	399
Have You Been Reformed?	425
Let's Get Creative!	453

Activities

Activity 1.1:	Why Teach?	6
Activity 1.2:	Field Observation Activity—A Philosophy of Teaching	12
Activity 1.3:	Examining Attitudes and Styles	14
Activity 1.4:	Go Online! Coursework and the Teacher	16
Activity 2.1:	Go Online! PCs and Teaching Machines	36
Activity 2.2:	Developing Inference Questions	44
Activity 2.3:	Applying the Various Instructional Techniques	46
Activity 2.4:	Field Observation Activity—Observing How Teachers Adjust	48
Activity 2.5:	Go Online! Are Teachers Role Models?	50
Activity 3.1:	Field Observation Activity—Observing Student Demeanor	78
Activity 3.2:	Identifying Student Differences	81
Activity 3.3:	Go Online! Requirements for Admission to Gifted/Talented Programs	87
Activity 3.4:	Sitting in Their Place	96
Activity 4.1:	Field Observation Activity— Relating Your Coursework to Your Observations	113
Activity 4.2:	Go Online! Comparing Certification Requirements	120
Activity 4.3:	Go Online! Considering Alternative Certification Programs	122
Activity 4.4:	Go Online! Exploring Professional Organizations	136
Activity 5.1:	Class Discussion to Define Curriculum	154
Activity 5.2:	The Tyler Rationale: Answering Fundamental Curriculum Questions	157
Activity 5.3:	Field Observation Activity—The Explicit Curriculum	158
Activity 5.4:	Go Online! Redesigning the Extra-Curriculum	161
Activity 6.1:	Field Observation Activity—Attending a Meeting of the Legislature or School Board	185
Activity 6.2:	Evaluating Textbooks	188
Activity 6.3:	Go Online! Considering the Pros and Cons of Issues in Education	200
Activity 7.1:	Go Online! An "A" for Effort	222
Activity 7.2:	Gain Scores or Mastery of Objectives?	223
Activity 7.3:	Rules in the Classroom	229
Activity 7.4:	Field Observation Activity—Identifying Classroom Procedures	230

Activity 7.5:   What Teachers Will Say about Working with Parents   241
Activity 8.1:   Assessing the Themes   259
Activity 8.2:   Go Online! What Was Teaching Like Then?   264
Activity 8.3:   Field Observation Activity—The New Issues and the Old   280
Activity 9.1:   Go Online! A Brief Look at Eastern Philosophy   297
Activity 9.2:   Identifying Long-Lasting Consequences   299
Activity 9.3:   Who Is Most Represented in a Perennialist Curriculum?   304
Activity 9.4:   Field Observation Activity—Behaviorism in the
Contemporary Classroom   309
Activity 10.1: If Not Now, When?   321
Activity 10.2: Field Observation Activity—Should All Teachers
Affirm an Oath of Ethical Conduct?   325
Activity 10.3: Go Online! Researching Federal Law   349
Activity 10.4: Go Online! Researching Court Rulings Concerning Education   353
Activity 11.1: Field Observation Activity—The Purpose of School   363
Activity 11.2: Go Online! Who's Who? Education Officials in Your State   373
Activity 11.3: Go Online! Who's Who on the Local Level?   381
Activity 11.4: State and Local Education Expenditures in Your Hometown   387
Activity 12.1: Field Observation Activity—Talk with School Officials   410
Activity 12.2: Go Online! Possible Interventions   418
Activity 13.1: Reforms You Have Known   428
Activity 13.2: Field Observation Activity—Interviewing the Decision Makers   435
Activity 13.3: Go Online! Evaluating a Reform Effort   447
Activity 14.1: Field Observation Activity—Computers in the Schools
and in Your Class   460
Activity 14.2: Identifying Common Characteristics of Schools and Their Campuses   462
Activity 14.3: Go Online! Around the Curriculum in 180 Days   470
Activity 14.4: Janus in the Classroom: Considering the Past and the Future   473
Activity 14.5: What Are the Experiences of Life That Should Be
Experiences of School?   477
Activity 14.6: From a Node to Nations: The Global Creative
Problem-Solving Consortium   478

In Their Own Words

Feature 8.1:   Aristotle   257
Feature 8.2:   W. E. B. DuBois   268
Feature 8.3:   Horace Mann   271
Feature 8.4:   John Dewey   275
Feature 8.5:   Maria Montessori   277
Feature 9.1:   Robert Maynard Hutchins   302
Feature 10.1: Chief Justice Earl Warren Writes the Opinion of
the Supreme Court in *Brown v. Board of Education*   338
Feature 14.1: Bill Gates Discusses Education and Technology   475

Teacher Testimonials

Feature 1.1:   A Student Teacher's Experience   8
Feature 2.1:   Lynette Turman Provides Insights from 40 Years of Teaching   42
Feature 3.1:   Student Diversity   64
Feature 4.1:   Getting Certified to Teach   110

Feature 5.1:   The Teacher's Curriculum   164
Feature 6.1:   The Impact of Teachers on Curriculum   192
Feature 7.1:   On Classroom Management   226
Feature 11.1: The Care and Feeding of the Principal   378
Feature 12.1: Unique Challenges and Opportunities   408
Feature 13.1: Education Reform and the Teacher   438

Preface

■ Empowerment

Welcome to the beginning of your studies toward becoming a teacher. While reading through these pages and progressing through the teacher education program, you will find that teaching is a dynamic and complex profession. Therefore, this book has been written not only with the intention of telling you *about* education but also to *empower* you as a professional educator and instructional leader. To do this, we must draw out *your* thinking rather than simply expecting you to read a book and assimilate what it has to say. Perhaps a brief story will help to explain just what I mean.

When I was in seventh and eighth grades, one of my teachers was in her first and second year of teaching. I have to admit that we gave her a pretty rough time during that first year. It was not malicious by any means, but my classmates and I were perhaps a bit more rambunctious than a first-year teacher was ready to face. No doubt she often said to herself, "They didn't tell me about this in college!"

My particular story, however, is about an incident on one of the last days in her class during my eighth-grade year. I was in my typical seat—last row, last column, over by the window—as Miss Agostino was returning our term papers. She commented that if we wanted to read a very well-written paper, one that was mechanically sound, we should read Vicki's. That sounded familiar. But she then went on to say that if we wanted to read "a really interesting paper, a paper that had something to say," we should read . . . Eddie's. There was an audible gasp in the room. Most audible of the gasps was mine. At that moment the paper arrived at my desk. There was a large A emblazoned on the cover page. My classmates turned and looked at me in disbelief as I stared at the graded paper. In my mind's eye I can still see that page.

I was not a terrible student but certainly not an outstanding one. As far as I was concerned, school was simply the place where kids had to be during the day. I was just there. A major part of my ambivalence toward school was that I disliked writing papers that received uninspiring grades merely for errors of grammar and punctuation. This time, and it was the first time that I can recall, a teacher had valued my *thinking*.

It would be difficult for me to express how much of an effect that one act has had on my life. No, it's not the reason that I became a teacher, but when Miss Agostino recognized the ideas in that paper she *empowered* me as a thinker. What I had to say had merit. I often refer to that event when telling students of education that they need to empower the children (of any age) in their classrooms. A sure way to foster student thinking is to find merit in their ideas. Finding that merit, however obscure it may be, is what makes a teacher a professional.

Miss Agostino never knew that on that last day of her second year of teaching she had touched someone for a lifetime. Unfortunately, that's part of the territory that goes along with teaching. She probably taught for a number of years, got married, maybe raised a family. Perhaps she enjoyed a long and rewarding career as an educator. What is important now, however, is that *you* are at the threshold of preparing to have the same effect on some child. Someone is waiting to be empowered by *you*. That's pretty exciting, isn't it? It certainly is, and we want to help!

You will likely discuss "teacher empowerment" during your teacher education program. This refers to bringing the considerable talents of teachers to discussions and decision making across all levels of organized education. We believe that the future of education depends upon teachers rising to a new level of professionalism and expanding their influence beyond the confines of the classroom. This does not minimize the teaching part at all, but instead broadens the teacher's influence. We want you to understand that organized education needs your insight and your expertise in all facets of providing an education to children and young people. We want you to become an instructional leader whose talents are brought to bear in the classroom, in the conference room, with curriculum committees, with community committees, and as a key player—an acknowledged expert—in the planning of school.

It takes no great stretch of the imagination to realize that before long humankind may begin to colonize new worlds. Prominent political figures early in the 21st century have already expressed a vision for establishing a base on the moon. How will educational systems be established for the families who first venture some 200,000 miles from Earth? Who will go? Will we send the best and brightest to extend the reach of our species? Will we send the incorrigible as exiles to a distant prison? Will we send those who are so dissatisfied with the state of affairs in their own land that existence in a harsh and difficult environment is a price worth paying to hold to one's beliefs (i.e., history repeating itself)? Or will it simply be folks like you and me—adventuresome, inquiring, seeking to understand more than we understand now? Whatever the circumstances, a system of organized education can be expected to emerge. Will it be significantly different from what we know of as "education" today? Should it be?

Even if your career as an educator is entirely on terra firma, education will prove to be a vibrant endeavor that will continue to evolve to accommodate the challenges of the new millennium. Educational reform on the national, state, district, and building levels is an ongoing concern. What are the lessons that should be remembered as new schools are established or old schools changed? What mistakes have been made that we don't want to perpetuate? What efforts have failed but perhaps could succeed with appropriate correction?

So many questions! Rather than considering education as a historian or as a technician, we urge you to be an active participant as a creative problem solver: an *educational engineer*. We want you to see yourself as part of what energizes education. See yourself as becoming a teacher *and* an instructional leader among educators. A new century is upon us, and the frontiers are even more fantastic than those faced hundreds of years ago by the Native Americans, the Pilgrims, the immigrants, the burgeoning populace of a new nation. Use this book as your thinkbook, rather than just as a textbook, for writing the new story of education—for a new world—wherever that world may be.

How Shall We Go About It?

It has been said that teachers, and in particular elementary school teachers, are the most practical example of a liberal arts education. That's because teachers must have knowledge of many things. After all, students see the teacher as the source for answers to all questions. Students will ask their teachers about schoolwork, about what they heard on TV, and about personal problems and issues. Because teachers must have knowledge of many things, *School* discusses a wide range of topics including history, philosophy, U.S. government, instructional practices, sociology and psychology of the learner, a solid consideration of the future, and a unique chapter about a unique facet of education: education reform. We want you to understand that education in all aspects is an enterprise that needs dynamic and broadly educated people.

Our intention is to empower you as a thinker by engaging you in many critical and creative thinking opportunities. Effective teachers are adept at both of these thinking skills, and this book has been designed to help you exercise and develop your abilities. To accomplish this, numerous activities are provided throughout the book. These are designed to encourage additional and open-ended consideration of the topic. The activities rarely look for one specific answer, but instead offer you a chance to explore ideas in the directions that your own interests will take you. Each chapter will begin with questions to think about as you read, and you will also find a brief activity to help get your higher-order thinking skills in gear. We call these activities Ice Breakers because they are intended to help overcome that about-to-read-a-chapter inertia. Additionally, questions are often asked within the text. You don't have to write out answers to all of these questions, but we want to demonstrate to you that the topics presented here are topics that you should think about and consider in terms of your own perspective and opinions.

At the end of each chapter and each unit you will find two specialized sets of activities. Each provides a conceptual strand that is maintained throughout the book. One strand, Case Studies in Education, will exercise your critical thinking through a look at education from the context of an individual student. You begin by selecting a student from the six brief biographies in Appendix A: Case Studies in Education. If you follow along with this strand, you will gather more and more information about that student with each chapter that you read. By the end of the term, you will have compiled a case study about the child that reflects personal likes and dislikes, family background, standardized test scores, classroom achievement, goals and aspirations, and many other perspectives. It is an exercise intended to introduce you to the depth of those people who will one day be your students.

The other strand, Designing the School of the Future, focuses on the larger institution of education. Here you will find opportunities to foster your creative thinking abilities as you consider education as you have known it and then "design" a school for the new millennium. Either working alone or with a group, with this exercise you will consider each section of the text and think of it in terms of an organized system of education. What sort of philosophy should underlie education? What are the goals of an institution of education? What part, if any, should teachers play beyond classroom instruction? How should schools be funded? How could the schools themselves become centers for innovation? These are just some of the questions you may wish to entertain. When you are finished, you should have a much deeper understanding of this grand experiment we call . . . *school.*

We hope that you will accept this book as your formal invitation to become a professional educator. If so, empowerment as an instructional leader begins with you right now. So, let's get started!

Edward S. Ebert II
Professor of Education
Coker College
eebert@coker.edu

Acknowledgments

It's a very long way from the first few ideas for a new book to the finished product. The two names on the front cover do not come close to reflecting the number of people who have been very much involved in making it all happen. We would like to acknowledge and thank the many individuals who worked diligently to make it possible for you to read *School: An Introduction to Education*.

We are grateful to our many colleagues in education who reviewed various drafts of the manuscript. This process began when there was only a chapter or two on paper and continued through the development and refinement of the completed work. The reviewers typically saw just the plain, double-spaced text on a page without the colorful charts or interesting photographs. They concentrated on what was written, how it was written, and where it appeared in the overall scheme of the book. They provided valuable insights and perspectives that we used to compile a textbook that would provide you with the most effective educational experience possible. We want to thank each of the reviewers for constructive comments and suggestions:

Alice A. Amonette, Volunteer State Community College
Gloria Ayot, Eastern Washington University
Rebekah Baker, Anderson University
Jim Barta, Utah State University
Heather Boylan, Metropolitan State College of Denver
John Bruno, Florida State University
Patricia Clow, Brevard College
Allan F. Cook, University of Illinois at Springfield
Thomas Dickinson, DePauw University
A. Keith Dils, King's College
Suzanne Eckes, Indiana University
Tom Fiegan, Dakota State University
Kathy Finkle, Black Hills State University
S. Kay Gandy, Western Kentucky University
Winston T. Gittens, Southwest Minnesota State University
Larry Glover, Fisk University
Joy Goodrich, Virginia Union University
Katherine K. Gratto, University of Florida
Ramona A. Hall, Cameron University
Randy Hall, Auburn University, Montgomery
Wayne Heim, Susquehanna University
Dwight Holliday, Murray State University
Wanda Hutchinson, Athens State University
Hal E. Jenkins II, Mississippi University for Women
Emile Johnson, Lindenwood University
Donna W. Jorgensen, Rowan University
June Lemke, Gonzaga University
Melissa Luedtke, St. Mary's University
Mark Malisa, University of Wisconsin, La-Crosse
Gregory M. Martin, Lynchburg College

James McKernan, Eastern Carolina University
Arturo Montiel, South Texas Community College
Andrew Mullen, Westmont College
Steven W. Neill, Emporia State University
A. K. Nur-Hussen, Grambling State University
Gary N. Oakes, Simmons College
Robert Oprandy, University of the Pacific
Marybeth Peeples, Marietta College
Jeff Piquette, Colorado State University, Pueblo
Sandy Rakes-Pedersen, Delta State University
Marlene Reed, Southern Arkansas University
Dutchie Riggsby, Columbus State University
Judy Roberts, Hanover College
John Ross, Virginia Polytechnic Institute and State University
Robert Shkorupa, Community College of Southern Nevada
Kayla Simmer, St. Bonaventure University
Edythe J. Smith, Santa Fe Community College
Sister Catherine Stewart, Mount Mercy College
Jeff A. Thomas, University of Southern Indiana
Jay Tieger, Florida Atlantic University
James Van Patten, Florida Atlanta University
Doreen Vieitez, Joliet Junior College
Brian P. Yusko, Cleveland State University
Ronal L. Zigler, Pennsylvania State University, Abington

We wish to thank the teachers and staff at Pontiac Elementary School, the Chesterfield County School District, and the Highline Public School District for their enthusiastic assistance. This book includes a number of features that were contributed by teachers and administrators. We are indebted to these educators for graciously agreeing to contribute and for adding a special dimension with their words. The Teacher Testimonials were written by the following people:

Garland "Joe" Waddilove	Lynette Turman
Cheryl Larson	Megan Brenna-Holmes
Clint Wright	Sally Huguley
Beth Elliott	David Blackmon
Julie Allen	Richard Puffer

The Case Studies in Education were compiled by:

Sharon Moser	Joe Albin
Susan Sturgis	Tara Thompson

Original artwork was contributed by Jim Boden.

We also want to express our appreciation to some of the many people who worked directly for or in conjunction with the publisher in the development of our book. Thanks go to Dianne Lindsay of Wadsworth/Thomson Learning for moving our initial conversations into a proposal and ultimately a project. We are grateful to Trudy Brown, our project manager at Wadsworth, for keeping things on track once the book moved past the manuscript phase. It has been a pleasure to work with Lori Kozey, our project manager at Lachina Publishing Services, and we appreciate her attention to detail. Through Lori, we worked with Christy Goldfinch, one stickler of a copy editor! She did an outstanding job.

In particular, we want to thank Tangelique Williams-Suggs, our development editor, and Dan Alpert, our editor, at Wadsworth/Thomson Learning. Their vision has guided the development of this book throughout the roller-coaster experiences that comprise writing and publishing. Tangelique has been involved in this project since the very beginning, which alone is worthy of praise, but has also been an even-keel influence all along the way. Dan has brought a broad perspective and deep understanding of educational publishing to the development of this book. We're not going to tell you that we agreed about everything, but we will tell you that Dan was always willing to take the time to find our common ground. And we thank him very much for that.

In closing, Ed would like to thank Dave Walker for the advice he offered a number of years ago. Those few words have helped to overcome many an obstacle. And finally, we want to thank our wives, Christine Ebert and Gail Culyer, for their unending love, support, assistance, caring, and . . . patience.

Edward S. Ebert II
Richard C. Culyer III
January 2007

The Profession

Keys to Learning

The four chapters of Unit I discuss the teaching profession in terms of the personal, and interpersonal, aspects of teaching. Taken together, these four chapters will help you to consider your "fit" with this dynamic, and demanding, profession:

Chapter 1, The Teacher, addresses characteristics and competencies of those who would teach other people's children. It will discuss finding your personal philosophy and describe the various groups of people with whom teachers must communicate. Students are just one of those groups!

Chapter 2, The Strategic Nature of Teaching, demonstrates that there are many dimensions to what ultimately comes across to a classroom of students as "a lesson." There is a strategy and a plan that incorporates all a teacher knows about instruction.

Chapter 3, Student Diversity, looks at the complex nature of your future students. Before even getting to the topic of subject matter, teachers must understand that their students differ from one another in many ways and for many reasons. You may gain a greater appreciation for teachers as "psychologists" by the time you finish studying this chapter.

Chapter 4, Becoming a Teacher, introduces you not only to the general process of becoming a teacher, but also to the world of continuing education and professional development that is expected of teachers.

1

The Teacher

Make the chapter work for you with CPR²:

Conceptualize   Here are the major themes you will encounter in this chapter:

1. Teaching can be conceptualized as both an art and a science.
2. Teachers understand that there is a purpose to what they do.
3. Teachers have skills in both the static content and the dynamic content of teaching.
4. Teachers communicate with students, parents, colleagues, and the community.
5. Professional development is part of a teacher's commitment to lifelong learning.

Preview   Read the chapter headings; look at any figures, tables, and activities; and read through the items in the conclusion.

Activity 1.1:   Why Teach?
Activity 1.2:   Field Observation Activity— A Philosophy of Teaching
Activity 1.3:   Examining Attitudes and Styles
Activity 1.4:   Go Online! Coursework and the Teacher

Read   Now read through the chapter. Mark or highlight information that you consider to be especially important or about which you have a question.

Reflect   Consider these questions as you read: What is your philosophy of teaching? How would you explain the difference between static and dynamic content?

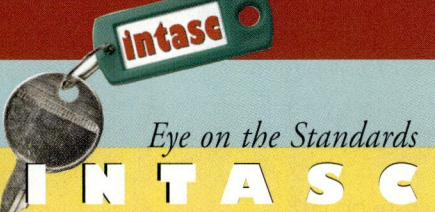
The following standards from the Interstate New Teacher Assessment and Support Consortium (INTASC) will be addressed in this chapter. As you read the chapter, consider how teacher competence and professional development are tied to these principles.

Principle 1 The teacher understands the central concepts, tools of inquiry, and structures of the discipline(s) he or she teaches and can create learning experiences that make these aspects of subject matter meaningful for students.

Principle 3 The teacher understands how students differ in their approaches to learning and creates instructional opportunities that are adapted to diverse learners.

Principle 4 The teacher understands and uses a variety of instructional strategies to encourage students' development of critical thinking, problem solving, and performance skills.

Principle 5 The teacher uses an understanding of individual and group motivation and behavior to create a learning environment that encourages positive social interaction, active engagement in learning, and self-motivation.

Principle 6 The teacher uses knowledge of effective verbal, nonverbal, and media communication techniques to foster active inquiry, collaboration, and supportive interaction in the classroom.

Principle 7 The teacher plans instruction based upon knowledge of subject matter, students, the community, and curriculum goals.

Principle 9 The teacher is a reflective practitioner who continually evaluates the effects of his/her choices and actions on others (students, parents, and other professionals in the learning community) and who actively seeks out opportunities to grow professionally.

Principle 10 The teacher fosters relationships with school colleagues, parents, and agencies in the larger community to support students' learning and well-being.

ice breakers

I Want to Be a Teacher Like . . .

Take a moment to think about the person or persons you would like to emulate as a teacher. Perhaps a particular teacher really left an impression on you. Or perhaps several people together represent "the best" of what it means to be a teacher. Whether you describe one person or build a composite is up to you. We've provided examples of descriptors to help you get going.

Describe your best teacher with regard to each of these attributes:

Attitude (likes to laugh / all business / really interested in learning / maintains a professional distance):

_____

_____

Teaching Ability (expects students to do the learning / could explain any topic clearly / could make any topic interesting / very organized and methodical):

_____

_____

Appearance (kind of looked like a student—related to who I was / very prim and proper / always dressed very well / didn't seem to emphasize appearance):

_____

_____

Wisdom (had a thorough knowledge of the topic—and kept all discussions on that level / I could ask her about anything—she had a wide range of knowledge / had a deep understanding for what I was going through and how to deal with things):

_____

_____

The Intangibles (made me feel good about myself / never seemed flustered, never seemed like she had a bad day / everyone had worth / earning her trust was important to me):

_____

_____

The attitudes we form about people, places, and events can stay with us all of our lives. By the time you finished reading the title for this Ice Breaker, you had probably already recalled the teacher you want to emulate, or at least started to put together a list of the several people that you would consider.

Now that you have some descriptors listed, you need to ask yourself several important questions:

1. Does this describe the person I am?

2. Does this describe the person I could become?

3. Most important of all, does this describe the person I want to be?

Think carefully about your responses, and return to these questions as you work your way through this book. After all, one day another student will complete this activity, and it will be *you* that he or she is describing!

> *"You will always be my teacher."*
> *Xia Qingfeng, speaking to his professor after graduation*

■ Introduction

Reflect for a moment on some of your classroom experiences. What did a teacher have to know for you to feel that she was competent? Perhaps at the time you didn't think in terms of "competence," so you could also ask yourself: What made a teacher a good teacher? For example, it was probably important that she "knew her stuff," right? Maybe it was important to you that the teacher could explain things clearly, or that she showed enthusiasm for the topic. Some students will say that the best teachers were the ones who were hard on them, while others contend it was the teachers who gave them those few extra points "for effort" when they needed them. Whatever your perspective, obviously a teacher had to be proficient in a number of different aspects to strike you as being "good." Research (Fermanich, 2002) makes the same point. There is an "important link between teacher quality and the academic success of students" (p. 49). Moreover, research funded by the Office of Juvenile Justice and Delinquency Prevention (Lewis, 1998) finds that "School success is the most important factor that helps at-risk youth overcome factors that drag them down" (p. 71).

In this chapter we will consider three topics that help define the teacher: reasons for teaching, teaching as both an art and as a science, and pedagogical competencies. As you might suspect, there is much more to being a teacher than just handing out worksheets and reading from a teacher's edition of the textbook. The three categories discussed in this chapter embrace philosophy, psychology, and knowledge of subject matter. All of these interact in an infinite number of ways to yield the diversity of teaching styles that you have experienced in your own education. Did you realize that teachers were so complex? They are, and that complexity begins with the reasons people become teachers.

■ You, the Teacher

If you are enrolled in an introductory or a foundations of education course, you have likely considered being a teacher for some time. This isn't like taking History 101 or a required biology class; it is the first step in a program of study that leads to certification as a professional. You may not know where, and you certainly don't know who (though they're out there, you can be sure, waiting for the day when they will walk into *your classroom*), but you do know that you might like to teach. So, let's consider the reasons people teach.

Professors in education programs often hear students say they want to teach because they love children. Or perhaps their mother or father—or both—are teachers. Maybe they were inspired by their second-grade teacher, and so they've always known that teaching is what they wanted to do. Well, these are good reasons, valid reasons, but in all honesty they are only good enough to get you past the first day or two of field service or the other internship experiences that you will have as part of your education program. If you are truly resolute, reasons such as these might even carry you through your student teaching semester, but then watch out! These cautions are not intended to dissuade you from teaching. Teaching is the right path for many, but let's be certain it is the right path for *you*.

If you love children, you could work with a day-care facility, as an after-school tutor, as a counselor, or perhaps at a museum or other organization that provides educational experiences for children. In all of these instances, you would have the opportunity to interact with young people without the demands of a teacher-education program and the stresses and strains of teaching all day, every day.

If your parents or your Aunt Millie or your brothers and sisters are teachers, that might not be the best reason to commit to this career. Because this wonderful use of your life will demand everything you have to offer, the decision to teach must be *your* choice, not someone else's. However, if you want to teach because your parents or your Aunt Millie or your brothers and sisters have convinced you that teaching is the most rewarding thing they have ever done, that's another story. Then you can certainly consider whether teaching offers the sorts of rewards that would interest you. In her study of a group of successful urban teachers, Nieto (2003) found they were committed to teaching, loved their students and their subject matter, had hope and faith in their students, collaborated with their colleagues, and believed they could influence the future. Does that sound like the person you are, the teacher you could become? Activity 1.1 will provide you with an opportunity to consider your reasons for teaching.

Considerable research has been done to identify some of the reasons that people become teachers (Rust, 1991; Toch, 1996). It may surprise you to find that though "summer vacations" is a familiar one, it is not one of the *primary* motivations. That's good to know for several reasons. One, as most teachers will tell you, is that summertime is typically spent in a different mode of school preparation. Teachers often attend summer classes for recertification or advanced degrees, and they certainly spend a considerable amount of time planning and preparing for the upcoming year. Not only does this include work for their own classroom assignment, but it may also involve meetings with other teachers and school administrators to discuss schoolwide plans and programs. Teaching is definitely not a profession that ends each day when the children go home, or even at the close of the school year. Rather, it stays on your mind—challenging you. Over the years, we have asked many students why they want to be teachers. Figure 1.1 lists some of the typical responses.

Teachers work with other people's children, which requires a deep understanding of the teaching profession.

Courtesy of Guilherme Cunha

Just to be fair, we should mention research that attempts to explain why teachers *leave* the profession (Toch, 1996). For instance, a national survey of teachers (Ingersoll, 2002) identified five major sources of dissatisfaction: low salaries, lack of support from school administrators, discipline problems, lack of student maturation, and lack of influence over decision making. A study conducted by the Harvard University Graduate School of Education's Project on the Next Generation of Teachers concluded that "[l]ast-minute hiring of educators and lack of meaningful support for such hires once in the classroom contribute to high rates of educator attrition" (Helgeson, 2003). Nearly one-half of beginning teachers leave within five years (McCann, Johannessen, & Ricca, 2005). Furthermore, teachers who leave the profession early tend to be those who were the best candidates for becoming professional teachers (Gordon & Maxey, 2000).

On a more philosophical note, keep in mind that teachers represent the bridge between what the world is and what the world will become. In *My Pedagogic Creed,* John Dewey (1897) argued that education does not prepare an individual for life, it *is* life. And he was correct. School is where children spend much of their young lives, and it is where teachers spend their careers. The life experiences of formal education are specifically intended to *prepare* the student for the life experiences to come. So, the teacher's challenge, every day, is to take the lessons of the past and make them relevant in the present *and* useful in a future yet unknown. Indeed, your ability to adjust to ever-changing circumstances and undesirable or unexpected situations—we call it resilience—is essential if you plan to make teaching your life's work (Bobok, 2002). Do you see yourself enjoying a profession that involves so much flexibility? If so, teaching may certainly be for you!

■ Pedagogy

pedagogy The art and science of teaching children.

The term **pedagogy** refers to the art and science of teaching. In particular, it refers to the teaching of children. However, whether you will be teaching children, adolescents (who don't like to be called children), or adults, some sort of pedagogy will underlie all of your efforts. The ability to shape and articulate the components of your own pedagogy contributes to your professional standing. Most likely, that pedagogy will represent a blend of art and science.

I love working with children.

I LIKE HAVING THE SUMMER OFF.

I want to turn kids on to learning.

My guidance counselor said I'd be good at it.

I want to make a difference in people's lives.

It's a respectable job.

The money is good.

It seems like a fun thing to do.

It's better than working at a discount store.

My guidance counselor said teachers would always have a job.

I like science.

I like the hours. We get off at 3:00.

My mother is a teacher.

Why be a teacher's aide when I can do the same amount of work and make a whole lot more money?

I LOVE KIDS.

It gives me a chance to coach.

I hear state jobs have good benefits and retirement plans.

I like to write, but I don't think I can make a living doing that.

I need a less stressful job. (This was from a lawyer choosing teaching as a second career. He lasted less than two months.)

I can't think of anything else I'd like to do.

You have to teach before you can be a principal.

Figure 1.1

Some reasons why people teach.

The *art* of teaching is concerned with one's philosophy, style, and attitude toward providing educational experiences for children. The *science* of teaching involves an understanding of the psychology behind the task of providing appropriate educational experiences that might accomplish various instructional goals. Does all of this sound just a bit overwhelming? It might, because in fact it refers to something very personal and very difficult to express.

Perhaps an example would help here. Within a given culture, the practice of medicine is based upon a core body of knowledge. That information is derived through the *science* of medicine. When a patient is treated, "sound medical practice" is based upon that core body of knowledge. Observations and investigations that have been made over many years enable a physician to diagnose a particular condition based upon the symptoms presented.

However, both in diagnosis and in treatment, physicians will be quick to tell you that medicine is not an exact science. Working with people to determine a given ailment is not entirely scientific because patients are often unable to provide a "scientific" explanation of their problem or the events that led to it. Too, a physician may instruct a patient to do something as a remedy, yet the patient, having no understanding of how or why the remedy should work, is less than duly diligent. Evaluating symptoms, monitoring the effects of the treatment, combining that information with expectations, and reassuring the patient about the results are all outside of the strict controls of science. It is at this point that another facet of medicine comes into play. The interpersonal aspect, as you've likely learned through your own experiences with physicians, is very much an *art*. Similarly, teaching is a combination of a core body of knowledge and the use of interpersonal skills; there is a science to it, and also an art.

The Art of Teaching

A common misconception among students of education is that if they pass the required courses, everything will work when they enter the classroom. As satisfying as that would be, the interpersonal element comes into play. The students you will read about in this book or in any of your other classes are not your future students. The students you will work with are unique in time and in the environment in which you actually encounter them. Your teacher education program can prepare you for what things will be "like," but it is only a representation of the reality you will experience. You can be *prepared,* but ultimately you will have to observe, assess, and adjust on your own.

This does not mean that teachers are "born" to it. While some people do seem to have a knack for teaching, what they really have is a talent for communicating. Who can knock a nice knack like that? Yet, teaching in a school requires more than just being a good communicator. It requires being able to teach some very specific information and skills under some rather specific conditions of time, place, and available materials.

That's where the art of teaching lies. Individuals must combine content knowledge and teaching skills (information that can be learned) with their own abilities, characteristics, and personality (qualities that they bring to the task) to develop what will ultimately be their own pedagogical style. That's why you have never had two teachers who were just alike. It may even be that two of your favorite teachers were not at all alike. Yet despite their differences, their pedagogies were equally sound.

Developing the artistry of teaching can be very demanding. Students of education are well advised to keep journals of their experiences in the classroom and to reflect on what transpires. They also need to be accomplished evaluators of their own performance. Rather than simply going to a classroom and "helping" a student or two, pre-service teachers need to decide in advance what they want to do, try it, and *reflect* on what happened. Over the course of a teacher education program, students should avail themselves of every opportunity to assume the role of a teacher and to try various styles, techniques, and strategies as appropriate. This is a very personal endeavor, for each individual has to decide what feels most

Teacher Testimonial

Feature 1.1   A Student Teacher's Experience

As I began my student teaching experience, I recall feeling a combination of emotions. I was eager and apprehensive. I had positive expectations both for myself and for "my" students. I had studied the stage theories of development, cognitive learning theories and styles, devising and using objectives, and assessment strategies. I had received training in all of the elementary content areas: mathematics, reading, science, and social studies. I felt well prepared, yet I was still troubled. The learning needs of these children were real, and their success (or failure) would depend on my competence as a teacher!

With limited responsibilities and a supervising teacher in the classroom, the first few weeks went mostly as expected. In fact, I had become weary of simply observing and occasionally teaching a lesson monitored by the cooperating teacher. I was impatient to begin making my own impact on instruction and the success of these students.

It was during the second phase of the student teaching experience, when I started taking on responsibility for more and more of the entire day, that the problems arose. The classroom behavior of these students had never been good, but now it was getting steadily worse. I found that my fourth graders were largely uninterested in the subject matter and were much more interested in their social concerns than in their academic success. Incidents of misbehavior in class began occupying much of my time. From the perspective of my personal history and environment, I believed that students should be able to develop self-control on their own accord. I tended to ignore misbehavior as much as possible, hoping that it would go away. I anticipated that, as the students learned that I truly believed in them and was competent in the elementary curriculum, their conduct would improve and we would begin to make progress. Yes, this was naive.

I began to question my competence as a teacher, and it began to show. My supervising professor noticed

Courtesy of David Ottenstein Photography

If you look closely at this photograph, you will see examples of both the art and the science of teaching that help to provide students with quality educational experiences.

comfortable and effective. Most important of all is for students of education to realize that the art of teaching doesn't just "happen"; it requires thoughtful development and practice.

The Science of Teaching

The science of teaching will be the focus of your teacher education program. Though your professors will foster your personal style, the formal emphasis will be on the science, and there is a lot of science to know.

Education undergoes continuing research, analysis, reform, intervention, and evaluation. Aside from decisions about the content to be taught, there is extensive literature about topics such as the *sociology* of teaching, *psychology* (of the learner, of the group, of being evaluated, of being retained, and so on), and the *philosophy* underlying why we have public schools, as well as the *economics* and cost efficiency of educational institutions. You are not entering a profession that lacks formal, empirical research. Though you may not have come to grips with all of these areas of concern (at least not yet), you should know *and understand* many of the currently accepted professional philosophies about educating other people's children. As you continue your studies, you will find that few of your friends in other majors will have the breadth of understanding that you will develop along the way to becoming a teacher.

my frustration, continually expressed his confidence in me, and encouraged me to take a proactive stance. Together we devised a plan. Previously, I had been primarily confined to the front of the room as if on stage. My first step was to begin "working the crowd." I became more mobile within the room and would use proximity to a student as a technique for preventing the student's impulse to be disruptive. Next, we worked on building a classroom structure. In addition to general rules that spelled out overall expectations for good work and good behavior, we established specific routines and procedures such as handing in papers, getting into small groups, and lining up quietly. Finally, I worked on staying calm and staying strong.

I learned that classroom management must come before instruction for learning to be effective. I became more consistent in addressing off-task behavior. I found that the "look," along with a firm chin and a wrinkled brow, was more effective at correcting disruptive behavior than verbally nagging students.

At the end of the semester I realized that I had "turned the corner" and would indeed be successful. In fact, I was excited to learn that the district would be hiring me immediately. I was to replace my cooperating teacher for the spring semester, as she was transferring to another position within the district. I would have the same class for another semester! Actually, what I was to have was an opportunity to finish the work that I had started with this challenging class. I can honestly say that I was anxious for the opportunity. As it turned out, the students' performance on the district's standardized tests in the spring was satisfactory, but what was rewarding for me was that I had succeeded in stimulating their desire to learn.

Joe Waddilove still teaches at that same elementary school, L. W. Conder. In 2003 he became certified by the National Board for Professional Teaching Standards. ■

Acknowledging that there is a science to teaching is easy enough. More difficult is developing a real understanding of that science. When it comes to education, the stakes are higher because a certified teacher is given the responsibility for teaching other people's children. Simply knowing the information, the science of teaching, is not enough. The National Board for Professional Teaching Standards (1997) proposes five standards for accomplished teachers:

1. Teachers are committed to students and learning.
2. Teachers know the subjects they teach and how to teach those subjects to students.
3. Teachers are responsible for managing and monitoring student learning.
4. Teachers think systematically about their practice and learn from experience.
5. Teachers are members of learning communities.

Notice that items 2, 3, and 4 address the particular knowledge and skills that teachers should possess. However, the standards also speak to commitment, reflection, learning from experience, and membership in learning communities. That's where the understanding part comes in.

■ Pedagogical Competencies

To help you consider and develop your own pedagogical style, we will look at pedagogical competencies in terms of four components: purpose, content, communication, and professional development (Table 1.1). This does not represent the only way of approaching your personal pedagogical style, but at this stage in your progress toward becoming a teacher we believe it will be useful.

Since there are many levels of teaching and many subjects that can be taught, it should not surprise you that each of these four categories can be applied in dif-

Table 1.1   The Four Pedagogical Competencies
Purpose
The philosophy, attitude, and style that a person brings to the task of teaching.
Content
Static Content is the curriculum that teachers are responsible for teaching. It is static because it doesn't change from day to day with the mood of the students or events in the school environment. **Dynamic Content** is the knowledge and skills about teaching that a teacher uses to do the teaching. This can change at any time based on what is happening in the immediate environment. A teacher must know how to monitor and adjust throughout the day as well as know the procedure for presenting a lesson.
Communication Skills
Teachers must be prepared to communicate effectively with four very different audiences: students, colleagues, parents, and the community at large.
Professional Development
Teachers are lifelong learners. They do additional coursework in their discipline, take classes in other areas of interest, mentor new teachers, and take part in research activities.

ferent ways to different people with different educational responsibilities. Purpose, for example, is concerned with three topics: an individual's personal *philosophy* of education, the *attitude* that is brought to the task, and the particular *style of interaction* with students. Content, particularly for the elementary school teacher, involves a broad range of knowledge. For secondary teachers, content is more narrowly defined but requires considerably greater depth. Communication skills addresses the four main **constituencies** (students, parents, colleagues, and community members) with which a teacher is involved. And finally, there is an area that you may not have thought about much: professional development. In this regard you will find that teachers are themselves learners, mentors to other teachers, and front-line researchers in their discipline.

constituencies Those groups of people to whom educators are responsible. They include students, parents, the community in general, the school administration, and their colleagues.

Purpose

The first of the four pedagogical competencies that we will consider is *purpose*. The question here is not why people become teachers, but rather what *you* expect to accomplish by teaching. Though this question has philosophical undertones, it also includes a personal consideration of your attitude toward working in the classroom and the particular style that you will use in your interaction with students.

Philosophy

Chapter 9 discusses various philosophies of education, and you may find one there that fits with your own thinking. Or perhaps you already have your own philosophy of what education is all about, and you can integrate that into your personal expression of the art of teaching. However, Chapter 9 focuses on what *society* wishes to accomplish through a formal system of education. Our concern here is with your *personal* perspective.

Begin by asking yourself what you want to accomplish as an educator. For instance, love of children is not a philosophy of education. As indicated earlier, there are many occupations that you could pursue simply because you love being around children. What is it that you hope to accomplish as a teacher?

Some people have a philosophy that children possess an innate sense of curiosity and wonder and so feel that a teacher should encourage children to pursue those inquiries. Such people see themselves as channeling human energy for personally and socially productive purposes. Others might focus on society and its future, believing that societies need citizens who share a common set of values and who see the world in a coherent, and even evolving, way. People must speak the same language to interact in ways that promote the health and well-being of the society at large. They teach so that these goals might be realized.

You've likely heard the phrase "children are our most valuable resource." From a personal perspective, some might see teaching as a way of protecting their own interests. That is, it is possible that the six-year-old in your first-grade class will become president of the United States while you are enjoying your retirement years. Teach that child well! On a more altruistic level, some might want to be part of the efforts to bring out the best in all people and help children build worthwhile lives.

These certainly sound like lofty aims. Some sort of philosophy, a perspective that gives meaning to human enterprise, underlies virtually all of them. Practically speaking, an articulated philosophy is the foundation upon which an individual's life work can be built. So challenge yourself to express your own philosophy of education. In an interview (Sikorski, 2004), James H. Korn, a noted and respected educator, asserted, "Every teacher has a philosophy, but getting it out where you

Field Observation

ACTIVITY 1.2   A Philosophy of Teaching

At this early point in your teacher education program, what is your philosophy of teaching?

1. Write a statement of your philosophy of education addressing the following questions: Why should there be formal systems of education? What should they accomplish? What is your place within that system?

2. Now talk to several of your classmates. In addition to the first two questions in item 1, ask them what they think a teacher's responsibility is within formal education. (*Note:* When conducting interviews such as this, do not be judgmental about a person's response. You've asked for their opinion, so don't challenge it once it's given.)

3. Interview one or two teachers as you did with your classmates in item 2. Speak with teachers in grades K–12, if possible. If you don't have access to classroom teachers, ask one or two of your professors these same questions.

4. Compare your original philosophy statement with what you have found from your friends and teachers. How do their perspectives relate to your own? If you want to rewrite your philosophy statement at this time, do so. If not, explain how the additional information you've obtained has supported your original statement.

can see it and show it to others helps you to understand why you do what you do as a teacher. More importantly, it allows you to become aware of inconsistencies in what you believe and what you do" (p. 74). What will be accomplished because *you* became an educator, and why is it important? Ask your professors to explain their philosophy of education. Ask the teachers with whom you interact in the K–12 setting. Be sensitive, however. Ask only for what people are willing to offer, and don't presume to judge the efficacy of anyone's philosophy. The objective of such an exercise is not to challenge other people, but to understand your own philosophy behind educating other people's children. Though your philosophy may change with experience, at any given time it will be the basis for all you do in education. Activity 1.2 will give you the opportunity to begin considering your own philosophy of teaching.

Attitude

Teachers, like everyone else, have an attitude. However, the attitude referred to here is not a matter of good mood/bad mood. It is the attitude brought to the task of teaching. A teacher's attitude follows from what she hopes to accomplish as stated in her philosophy of education. Students, parents, and colleagues will define teachers in part by the professional attitude that guides their work. Obviously, it would be advantageous for anyone considering a career in education to make her personal and professional attitudes as consistent as possible. Strong (2002) suggests that this "dual attitude" characterizes effective teachers. Here's a list of some teacher attitudes. Have you ever encountered any of these?

- Don't smile until Christmas.
- If I can reach just one child, I'll consider my career worthwhile.
- Learning is supposed to be fun.

- Summer camp is supposed to be fun; school is work.
- My students and I are partners in learning.
- I can learn as much from my students as they can from me.
- My job is to present information; it's their job to learn it.
- When it is all said and done, either they learned it or they didn't.
- I want to be their friend.
- I'm a role model.
- I'm their teacher, not their role model.

This is not an exhaustive list of teachers' attitudes, of course, but it does demonstrate that there are many different perspectives. Very few professions can accommodate such a range of individual approaches to such a specific task. Yet if you take any item from this list, you will find that arguments can be made for and against each position.

For example, you have probably heard some educators say that if they can reach just one child, the effort will have been worthwhile. That is a difficult position to argue against. Suppose one child is thus saved from a life of crime. Or perhaps one child will someday invent a tool or make a discovery that benefits civilization. Indeed, the prospect of reaching that one student could make each student/teacher interaction a very important event.

On the other hand, if you needed a lawyer to defend you in some legal battle, chances are that you would not hire an attorney whose attitude is "If I can win just one case, my career will have been worthwhile." (If you do, be sure to ask if she has won a case yet.) The same would be true if you needed medical attention. Would you seek out a physician who would be fulfilled if she could ease just one person's suffering? Or what of an engineer who aspired to design and build just one bridge that stood up?

Each of the items on the list can be addressed in this manner. In the final analysis, "attitude" is a function of who you are, and it will affect who you are as a teacher.

Style

If you feel comfortable with the reasons you want to teach and with your own attitude toward teaching, a third aspect to consider is your *style* of interacting with students. A teaching style is the result of integrating teaching strategies with one's own personality. For example, consider a teacher whose philosophy of education is that schools are indispensable because it is through schools that society passes its knowledge from one generation to the next. This same person's attitude toward teaching could be that it is her job to present that information to students in class. A lecture-oriented style of teaching might fit this individual well. Of course, in the elementary grades there is not much lecture, but a visit to the teacher's classroom might reveal this teacher doing a vast amount of the talking.

Another teacher may feel that school is the process through which children learn the rules and regulations of society and, hopefully, the higher value of observing those rules. Her attitude may then be that an optimum learning environment is one that is established around a strong set of class rules. Such a teacher's style may be very controlling, insistent on only the most obedient behavior.

Still other teachers may see school as an organized effort to allow children to explore and understand the world around them. These teachers may bring to their classrooms an attitude that values inquiry and discovery, arranging experiences that rely less on lecture and much more on students' engagement with the subject matter. They may take an investigative approach to the topic rather than expecting to be seen as experts. Their particular style may also be more tolerant of noise in the classroom.

You can see from these few examples that certain teaching styles match better with some grade levels than with others. To a degree you may be able to adjust your style to the grade level you wish to teach. However, you might consider your personal choices in each of these three areas (philosophy, attitude, and style) and then match your traits to the grade level that would benefit most from such a combination.

Programs in teacher education rarely address the pedagogical competency of purpose as a specific instructional objective. Students often feel their way through introductory courses, as well as practicum or internship experiences, expecting that things will suddenly "make sense." This pedagogical concern, however, provides the raw materials for making sense of it all. Spending time considering these characteristics does not mean that they can never be changed. The fact is that education is such a dynamic enterprise that one should expect to make changes as a career progresses. It may be surprising, however, to discover how much staying power a well-thought-out philosophy has. There may be no more valuable advice to offer as you strive to become a *professional* educator than to heed Socrates' classic admonition, "Know thyself!" Use Activity 1.3 to consider differences in attitudes and styles.

Content

With regard to the teaching profession, "content" competency can be viewed as having two dimensions. One relates to your knowledge of the subject(s) you will teach. This is an obvious indicator of your professionalism, for it is easily observed and evaluated. We characterize the body of knowledge to be taught as the **static content;** you might think of it as the "what" of teaching, that is, *what* you teach.

static content The curriculum that teachers are responsible for teaching. It is static because it doesn't change.

ACTIVITY 1.3
Examining Attitudes and Styles

Activity 1.2 focused on your philosophy of teaching. Now, consider the attitude and style that you might bring to teaching.

1. Watch several of your professors. They all differ in attitude and in style. It is not necessary to name names in this exercise, so just label them as Professors A, B, and C.

2. Write a general statement about each professor's attitude in the class. Do they seem to believe that responsibility for learning rests with the student, or do they make certain that students understand? Does education seem to be a means to an end, or is education treated as a part of life, as an extension of what it means to be human?

3. Note each professor's style. This may be easier to observe than attitude. Do they prefer lectures or discussion? Demonstrations or student activities? Is humor involved, or is class very business-like?

4. Finally, consider your own attitude and style. How do they compare with what you have observed? Was there one professor who seemed to have an attitude and style that you would like to develop, or did you find that you liked the attitude of one but the style of another? How would you explain the attitude and style that you would like to bring to teaching?

dynamic content The knowledge and skills that a teacher uses to do the teaching. This can change at any time based on what is happening in the immediate environment.

The second dimension, **dynamic content,** is the knowledge of *how* to teach. It is concerned with what teachers need to know to be able to teach: knowledge of child growth and development, the psychology of learning, personality development, appropriate instructional techniques, and classroom management.

Static Content Competency

The required level of subject-area knowledge is not the same for elementary school teachers as it is for secondary teachers. Both the range and the depth of content mastery are different depending upon the age and cognitive level of the students being addressed. In either case, however, children, parents, and administrators are quick to note lapses in content competency. The expectations for a teacher's command of content knowledge are undergoing significant scrutiny by virtue of the No Child Left Behind Act of 2001 (NCLB), a revision of the Elementary and Secondary Education Act of 1965. NCLB sets federal standards both for teachers and paraprofessionals working in the public schools. Though the requirements for new teachers are somewhat different from those for teachers already in the classroom, all teachers must now meet the standards for being considered "highly qualified" under the NCLB (Robelen, 2002).

Elementary Content As mentioned earlier, an elementary-level teacher may well be the most practical example of a liberal arts education. What does that mean? It means that at some time, to some degree, someone is going to ask you questions and come to you for advice that will tap the entire range of your knowledge. You might be prepared to begin a math lesson with your third graders, but their minds are on last night's TV news reports about terrible things happening to people in a country whose name they can't quite pronounce. They will ask you about it because you are the teacher—and the teacher knows everything. They won't need a detailed political analysis of foreign border disputes or ethnic or religious differences, but they will need a response that makes enough sense to put their minds at ease.

With regard to academics, elementary teachers are responsible for everything from the teaching of reading to scientific inquiry. Programs leading to elementary certification emphasize broad experiences in the liberal arts and rarely require advanced coursework in any content area. But elementary teachers do need significant amounts of coursework in the "methods" courses. These courses focus not on content but on techniques for teaching a particular subject area, such as reading, language arts, mathematics, science, and social studies. Increasingly, efforts are being made to integrate the teaching of these basic subject areas. Science as a subject area, in particular, holds great promise for such interdisciplinary instruction since the course of scientific inquiry brings each of the other content areas into play.

Indeed, teachers are practical expressions of a liberal arts education because they can expect to discuss matters of science, mathematics, language, politics, geography, social issues, and philosophy—and all at a moment's notice. You should not be intimidated by this expectation. On the contrary, the interaction with young minds working to make sense of the world around them and challenging you to take part in that process is what keeps many teachers vibrant and, shall we say, young.

Secondary Content Secondary teachers will get the sort of "out of field" questions discussed above as well. You may be very good at teaching 10th-grade biology, but there will be some student who just seems to "connect" with you and wants more. That student will want to talk with you about philosophy or politics or—to keep it "in field"—about the bio-ethics of cloning animals or human beings. True, a teacher can discourage off-topic conversation but you must realize that students see the teacher as more than just an instructor. That is to be expected since the implied function of school is that one person teaches something of value to another. In such instances, bonds are formed.

Secondary teachers do substantially more coursework within a specific content area as part of their programs, but they do not need as wide a range of teaching skills as do the elementary teachers (that is, skills in the teaching of different subject areas). Course requirements for secondary teachers are more content-focused than methods-focused. Chapter 4, Becoming a Teacher, will consider course requirements in greater detail. Activity 1.4 will provide an opportunity to take a closer look at course requirements and the debate over content knowledge versus pedagogy.

Dynamic Content Competency

We have discussed static content in terms of the actual subject matter to be taught. *Dynamic content,* on the other hand, is the information and skills that a teacher uses to do the teaching, and so is concerned with *how* to teach. Shulman (in Darling-Hammond & Bransford, Eds., 2005) says that a "pedagogical content knowledge—the ability to make subject matter knowledge accessible to students—is developed by combining an understanding of content with an understanding of learner's needs and perspectives" (p. 56). We refer to it as *dynamic content competency* to emphasize that while this aspect of a teacher's work may be part of instructional planning, much of it comes into play *during* the presentation of a lesson. *Planning* refers to the expectations of a situation; *dynamic competency* refers to working effectively with the reality of the experience and being able to adjust appropriately to those circumstances.

When students are focused on what the teacher is saying during a lesson, all of the monitoring and adjusting that a teacher does throughout the class may go unseen. Whether working with a classroom full of students or one-on-one, the teacher watches faces, listens for reactions, and looks for signs of understanding or lack of understanding. A teacher ought never rely on the student response when she asks, "Are there any questions?" For many reasons, students often let these

Go Online!

ACTIVITY 1.4   Coursework and the Teacher

The requirement for content knowledge versus education methods is a current debate in teacher education. Some argue that with a sufficient knowledge base, virtually anyone can teach. Others argue that with sufficient teaching skills, an individual can teach anything.

1. Compare the course requirements for elementary certification and for secondary certification at your institution. How are they similar? How do they differ? What benefits, or problems, do you see with the differences between programs?

2. Use the Internet to locate the most current information about the debate over content knowledge versus pedagogy. Search terms such as "alternative teacher certification" or "teaching credentials" will get you started. Based on the information you find, do you support the position that anyone with adequate knowledge can teach, or that anyone with enough teaching skills can teach anything? Perhaps your opinion is somewhere in the middle. If so, explain your perspective on the issue.

opportunities for further explanation go by. It is up to the teacher to observe both the obvious and the subtle reactions of students throughout the lesson and decide whether to go over something again, rephrase what was said, or move on.

Dynamic content competency is drawn from a number of disciplines, disciplines that often seem to overlap. For instance, teachers must understand patterns of human development. This might include a consideration of Piaget's model of cognitive development (1926, 1985) and the taxonomies of educational objectives: cognitive, affective, and psychomotor domains (Bloom et al., 1956; Krathwohl et al., 1964; Simpson, 1972), as well as Freudian (1974) and Eriksonian (1950, 1968) views of personality development. Cultural values and experiences can also have a pronounced effect on what happens in the classroom. The physical condition of the students at the time (hungry, tired, uncomfortable because of the heat or the cold) can be a major factor in the success or failure of the lesson. An awareness of Maslow's hierarchy of needs (1954) will help a teacher understand the dynamics within the classroom. And, of course, the style of presentation itself (e.g., expository, inquiry, drill and practice) will have an effect on the lesson.

Perhaps you have seen these elements at work. Have you ever been in a class in which the teacher was missing all the signs from the students, or was choosing to ignore them, as a lesson simply fell apart? Student teachers often find themselves in such a situation while being evaluated during a lesson. Their feeling is that if a lesson plan has been written out, they are obligated to proceed with the plan no matter what happens in the class. If you have ever seen this happen (with a new teacher or an experienced one), then you have seen someone who is oblivious to the premise of dynamic content competency. In most cases teachers in such a situation realized that the lesson was not going well. That means that they were indeed monitoring what was happening. The mistake they made, however, was in not *adjusting* (that's the dynamic part) to what was going on.

The work of Jean Piaget (1926, 1985) sheds some light on what is happening. Piaget suggested that knowledge itself is dynamic. People build knowledge as they integrate new information with what they already know. They must do this to adjust to what's going on in the environment (for example, the classroom) to make sense of it and to function within it. Why do we have to adapt to the environment? Because the environment has no intention of adapting to us. Teachers who understand this basic premise know that monitoring during a class is not enough. Teachers must be able to monitor *and adjust* accordingly. They must be able to apply knowledge about how people learn before, *during,* and after instruction. For an effective teacher the static content is the easy part (though by no means a trivial part); the real challenge is in becoming highly proficient in terms of dynamic content competency.

Communication Skills

Have you ever noticed that some people are easier to talk to than others? Maybe your best friend understands everything you say, but other people are never as quick to pick up your meaning. It's also likely that you speak to your teachers differently than you do to your friends. You communicate differently with different people. On any given day, teachers must communicate with four distinct constituencies: students, parents, colleagues, and the community at large. Each of these groups attends to and interprets communications in different ways. To a degree they speak "different languages," and, without a doubt, the *rules* for speaking with various constituencies differ. In all cases, however, it is the teacher's responsibility to communicate effectively and to determine whether or not understanding has been achieved.

Communicating with Students

The vast majority of a teacher's work involves communicating with students. Interestingly, this type of communication is the most susceptible to long-term misunderstandings. There are several factors at work here. For one, children often feel that they cannot challenge what a teacher says. The teacher represents the established authority, and so students integrate what has been presented into their understanding to the greatest degree possible. Since it is unlikely that the teacher will engage every student in a detailed discussion of the topic, misconceptions that develop might never be identified. As a result, it is not uncommon for teachers to assume that children understand what was "taught" and for children to assume that what they learned is what the teacher meant.

Clearly, communication skills between students and teachers have multiple dimensions. An effective teacher communicates expectations (Stronge, 2002). It is also the teacher's responsibility to present information in a manner appropriate to the cognitive level of the students. That may involve rephrasing complex ideas in simpler terms. Or it may involve finding several ways to express the same idea. Consistent and deliberate monitoring of students' understanding is also the teacher's responsibility. There is no mistaking the fact that effectively communicating with students is a skill that must be acquired and *practiced*.

Communicating with Parents

Perhaps even more so than with students, the watchword for communicating with parents is *listen*. The parent's involvement with a teacher is often due to a particular event or problem. In all cases there is an intermediary between the parent and teacher who has interests of her own (that is, the student). The result is that parents typically come to a meeting with the teacher armed with a child's perspective of the situation. That's not always bad, but it's rarely the complete story. For a teacher, effective communication begins with listening to the parent's perspective.

Million (2003) suggests that there are several techniques that teachers should develop to facilitate good communication with parents. For instance, in an initial meeting with a parent, listening to the parent's perspective of the child's strengths, weaknesses, and needs forms the foundation for future effective communication with that parent. In problem situations, parents may ask questions such as: Are you being fair to my child? Is my child really the instigator of the problem? What have you done to provoke my child? What steps have you taken to discipline my child? It is the teacher's responsibility to avoid being defensive and instead listen, keep a professional perspective, and work to resolve the situation with the best interests of the student in mind. Stevens and Tollafield (2003) advise teachers to recognize that since 21 percent of parents can't read and 6 percent have no phones, invitations to meet should be delivered in a variety of ways. They also stress the importance of pre-planning with a clear focus, documenting information, following up conferences, and considering parents as partners.

A teacher's interaction with parents does not always involve discipline problems. Sending notes home or placing calls to parents to indicate progress and positive behaviors would be an excellent practice to develop. Home visits, general letters at the beginning of the year and periodically as appropriate, regular informational newsletters, and parent meetings such as Open House are other avenues for parent-teacher communication.

The teacher's responsibility is to clearly explain the child's progress through school. However, parents are not likely to be fluent in educational terminology, and they similarly may not understand district policies and expectations. The test scores and work samples that a teacher brings to the conference may be just so

For a teacher, good communication begins with being a good listener.

many pieces of paper to the parent. So, what *does* a z score or percentile rank mean? What do the student's work samples indicate? How can the teacher demonstrate in tangible terms that these samples indicate progress or lack thereof?

The keys in both the problem situation and the collaborative one are listening to what the parents have to say, communicating in their language, and monitoring (much as is done in class) to establish whether all parties understand each other. This last item cannot be overemphasized. When a parent conference draws to an end, the parent is not likely to ask the teacher to summarize and review what has been discussed. From the parent's perspective, this would be like saying that she was unable to understand the child's teacher. Just as classroom assessment is part of the teaching profession, assessing whether parent and teacher understand each other is the teacher's responsibility.

Clear and open communication is important because, as research has clearly established, parent involvement is linked to student achievement. For example, Lazar & Slostad (1999) have found that parent involvement programs provide many benefits, such as improved student motivation, increased long-term achievement, decreased dropout rates, and more parent support of the school. What do teachers want parents to do? Initiate contacts with and be involved in the school, monitor homework, teach study skills, set expectations for student behavior, support the teacher and the school, emphasize reading, respond to school communications, and be sure their children get a healthy diet and enough sleep (Boers, 2002). It is helpful to keep in mind a broader perspective of the value of parents. Not only can teachers assist parents with parenting skills, but they can foster two-way communication, encourage parents to become involved in (not "do") children's homework, encourage volunteerism and participation in school activities, and help them to become aware of community resources and opportunities (Epstein & Jansorn, 2004).

Communicating with Colleagues

Still another constituency with whom teachers communicate are their own colleagues. The National Staff Development Council recommends that 25 percent of a teacher's work time be spent in collaborating with and learning from one's colleagues (Lewis, 1999). Collegial interaction can take many forms, including working with fellow teachers on grade level, communicating with resource teachers or teachers on grade levels that students will be coming from or moving to, working with staff personnel, and interacting with the building-level administrators. While it is hoped that all of these groups see themselves as members of the same team so communication can be somewhat more relaxed, there is nonetheless the inescapable fact that while all groups should be treated with respect, there are nuances for establishing the lines of communication with each.

Administrators   Though all educators work toward the goal of providing the best possible educational experience for each child, the fact remains that administrative concerns and faculty concerns are two different matters. Administrators are typically the point of contact for angry parents, the bearers of bad budget news, and the guardians of district policy for the curriculum. A teacher's most frequent communication with administrators will be with principals, assistant principals, and grade or department chairs in her own building. The communication skills that come into play are different from that of the other constituencies we have discussed.

Keep in mind that this discussion is focusing on "official" communication. A school may have an atmosphere of collegiality that extends across faculty, staff, and administrative lines. But that atmosphere has at least two limitations: It is likely a characteristic of the particular school (rather than extending district-wide), and it does not erase the fact that teachers and administrators have different responsibilities. The bottom line is, the building-level administrator decides what will transpire in that school. And that decision-making authority is to be respected.

Unlike conversations with parents, the conversations between teacher and administrator can be expected to be rich with educational terms. Discussions about academic achievement will make extensive use of assessment terms and their accompanying scores, instructional techniques, intervention strategies, curriculum plans, and educational policies. Procedural matters will focus on district policies and state requirements. Disciplinary situations will involve evidence, documentation, explanations of what was done—and why—and what contact, if any, has thus far been made with parents or other caregivers. All of these situations require that the teacher communicate in a manner that allows the administrator to make decisions, contacts, and recommendations that facilitate the work of the school.

Perhaps you are beginning to understand that the range of communication skills that a teacher needs is nearly to the point of speaking several languages. In fact, the analogy to a foreign language might not be very far off. The teacher is essentially saying the same things to several different groups in several different, and appropriate, ways. One other point to remember as we discuss communicating with people about a student's performance in school is the importance of respecting the confidentiality of student records. The files are available to parents until the student reaches age 18, at which time the student has free access to the records (Zirkel, 2001, 2003).

Faculty   Like conversations with administrators, a teacher's conversations with fellow faculty members may involve a lot of educational terminology. The difference is that conversations between faculty members are characterized by a closely shared perception of the work situation. Teacher-to-teacher discussions are based on a mutual understanding of the stresses and strains of working with students, parents, administrators, and staff. Teachers will help each other with educational issues ranging from decorating the classroom to curriculum development. It is not unusual for a closely knit cadre of teachers to have an end-of-the-year party, away from school, where they will *still* talk about school and teaching. This can be a very special sort of communication.

Staff   Effective teachers are well aware that one of the key elements that allows them to "shut the door and teach" is the work of staff personnel at the school and district levels. These people, typically underappreciated and overworked, are the ones who keep everything else running. Office staff, resource workers, medical staff, custodians, and food service workers all contribute to making the school run smoothly enough that the teacher can concentrate on teaching. Communicating with these people also takes special skills.

Unlike communication with administrators or fellow teachers, educational terminology is not of particular importance in conversations with staff personnel. In fact, the primary skills to bring to this facet of conversing are diplomacy and understanding. Diplomacy comes into play because an emergency in one teacher's situation does not necessarily constitute an emergency in terms of the staff workers' responsibilities. This means the teacher has to enter into the discussion understanding that her problem is not the only issue to be addressed. Understanding is important because staff workers are responsible for an entire school, and so the broad demands on their time have to be taken into account. A teacher who understands that she is not the only teacher in the building, who identifies needs before they become problems, who facilitates the work of the staff by doing her own work correctly (for instance, filling out and submitting requisitions), and who maintains a friendly and helpful attitude will establish good and productive communications in this regard.

Communicating with the Community

All of this, and there are still others with whom teachers need to communicate! Each of the groups considered thus far represent what might be called building-level communications. Even the matter of talking with parents is typically handled by phone from a teacher's workroom or with conferences held at the school. But sometimes a teacher needs to speak with people away from her home turf. Aside from being approached by parents in an informal way, there are times when teachers are seeking support for classroom activities and times when they act as education professionals representing their school. As ever, these situations require attention to a unique set of considerations.

Representing the School There are a variety of situations in which a teacher may represent the school. Local news agencies writing a report about schools may ask a teacher for an opinion. Or they may have heard of some interesting project or activity that a teacher is conducting in class and want to write a newspaper article or brief newscast story about it. In such instances, a teacher must understand that even though it is her opinion or work that has been highlighted, readers/viewers see her as representing the school district at large.

Similarly, teachers often speak to various community groups and to audiences at conventions sponsored by educational organizations. Organizations such as the National Science Teachers Association (NSTA), the National Council for Teachers of Mathematics (NCTM), and the International Reading Association (IRA), to name just a very few, sponsor state, regional, and national conventions each year that draw tens of thousands of participants. Many of the presenters at these conferences are classroom teachers.

No matter the circumstances, whether participating in a one-on-one interview or making a presentation to a hundred colleagues, when a teacher steps outside of the cloistered world of her own school she is representing a much larger entity. To that end, a teacher's communication skills then require, for lack of a better term, a political nature. Every time a teacher speaks publicly or to the press, her thoughts and ideas can potentially be taken out of context. Nothing that a person can do will change this fact, but it is prudent to avoid making comments that can be misinterpreted. That is to say, teachers—understanding that they represent the school as well as themselves—must take care not to disparage themselves or their colleagues and not to imply that their views necessarily represent the opinions of their school and their colleagues.

Seeking Support At times, teachers need materials or other resources that do not fall into the normal realm of educational supplies. Items in this category can range from a box of 500 drinking straws for a "tower building" activity in science, to arranging a field trip to a local business, to asking people from various walks of life to speak to the class. In these situations, the people with whom the teacher communicates are not interested in gain scores or grade equivalencies. Whether or not they have a child in that class, the topic of discussion is not one of academic standing or discipline problems. And, instead of purchasing products or services, the teacher is asking for donations of time or materials to the school.

Asking people for such assistance requires explaining clearly and plainly what the needs are and why they are educationally valuable. Just as important is the ability to communicate in a pleasant and positive manner that acknowledges that these people are not obligated to agree to the request. People might turn down the request for any number of reasons, and a teacher's parting words should leave the door open for a request at another time rather than vent frustration.

Professional Development

professional development
Activities in which educators engage to expand their knowledge, skills, and general competence or contribute to the profession (e.g., engaging in research, mentoring, reading professionally, taking courses, attending conferences).

The fourth area of pedagogical competence that we offer is **professional development.** Physicians and attorneys refer to their work as a "practice" because with each patient and each case they are improving their ability to work within their respective disciplines. For whatever reason, teaching is not usually referred to as a practice, but it remains true that with each experience of working with students, teachers refine their skills. Professional development is intended to improve one's abilities as an educator. The three categories under the heading of professional development are concerned with continued learning, mentoring, and research. Taken together, these three areas of professional development represent a teacher's activities directed toward being a part of, and contributor to, the discipline of education.

As Learners

Teachers pursue professional development as learners in a number of ways. Chief among them is by completing additional coursework. Teacher certification carries with it the requirement for recertification. To accomplish this, within a defined period of time teachers are required to complete a minimum number of college-level courses that are approved for recertification credit. Though these hours do not have to be offered for graduate-level credit, many teachers meet some of their recertification requirements while pursuing advanced degrees. Obviously, the approved courses (whether undergraduate or graduate) will be in areas that relate to teaching. Another advantage to continuing education is that teacher salaries are often keyed to hours earned toward graduate degrees. Approximately 42 percent of teachers have at least a master's degree (Digest of Education Statistics 2001, 2002). And you thought you would be through studying and learning in four years?

Some professional development opportunities do not involve course work and are not tied to recertification or degree programs. For example, school districts often provide "in-service" programs and workshops for teachers at their schools. In-service refers to teachers already working in the classroom, as opposed to students of education (who are typically referred to as "pre-service" teachers).

Teachers are learners too.

© Able Stock/Index Stock Imagery

In-service programs can be as narrowly or broadly focused as a district desires. Some districts offer a range of weekend, summertime, or after-school courses, taught by teachers or by others from outside of the district. Such programs may offer workshops in gardening techniques, a particular type of literature, or sign language. The intent is not to increase the teachers' subject area knowledge as much as it is to keep the teachers *learning*—and along with learning comes the awareness of what it's like to learn. That awareness, and the vitality found with learning something new, is taken back to their own classrooms.

Districts may also adopt a theme for in-service programs to be conducted throughout the school year. In the first days of the school year, a program featuring a national speaker on behavior management or a particular program that the district has adopted may be conducted for all faculty members. Throughout the school year several more in-service days may be devoted to further development of the topic. In our current environment, and likely for some years to come, programs in the use of computer technology will be certain to occupy many in-service agendas. Programs in drug awareness, zero-tolerance policies, and child abuse indicators are prevalent in the schools today. It is important to note that student achievement is not significantly related to *time* spent in professional development but to the *content* of the sessions (Garet, Porter, Desimone, Birman, & Yoon, 2001; Wenglinski, 2000). Even more productive is the concept of program development, in which a comprehensive effort is directed toward initiating and implementing coordinated school-wide plans to meet the needs of all students (Culyer, 2002).

As Mentors

As if it's not enough that teachers work with students all day long, and perhaps even conduct an occasional workshop or in-service program, at times teachers also teach other teachers. This special type of one-on-one educational experience is called **mentoring.** It is not the same as regular teaching, and it is not something for which one can be trained. To be successful at this particular type of teaching, the mentor must possess, among other things, patience, experience, and a knowledge of teaching that goes deeper than the mere mechanics of instruction. Not everyone can be an effective mentor.

mentoring The process by which an experienced educator helps a less experienced educator in some aspect of teaching or professional development in a one-on-one setting.

For a new teacher, the first day of school flies through the classroom door at full speed. All of the tasks required and the expectations held for the classroom teacher begin at once. There is no "easing" one's way into it. Don't be discouraged by this, for it is the way of all professions. Every airplane pilot once took to the air alone without the aid of an instructor for the first time. Of course it is also true that a pilot's first solo flight is not made with a planeload of people, whereas you will face an entire class as *the person in charge.* It can be a little overwhelming. In fact, the entire first year is such an indoctrination that many teacher education programs are designing formal mentoring programs to assist their graduates through that experience. Research indicates (Zepeda & Ponticell, 1996), for instance, that first-year teachers who learn how experienced teachers develop the "classroom emotional climate" become better able to manage their own classrooms. Likewise, teachers who were supported by administrators maintained their high initial enthusiasm (Khmelkov, 2000).

So what do mentors do in all of this? The purpose of mentoring is to provide a new teacher with guidance and advice as she works her way through the initial stages of being a professional. The mentor does not teach someone *how* to teach as much as to teach her *about* teaching in the full context of the task. This provides the new teacher with insights gained by the mentor through years of experience as a classroom teacher. But it is still more than that, for the mentor literally has "been there, done that, bought the T-shirt" and so can commiserate with the beginning teacher. All the while, the mentor is aware that the experiences being faced both by the teacher and the mentor have never been faced before with these children, in this situation, on this day. So it is a learning experience for both individuals—a shared experience. There's just no other way to say it: Teaching is a dynamic profession.

How does a mentor go about accomplishing this mini-miracle? A truly accomplished mentor is a patient listener who provides guidance through advice based on experience. A mentor who understands the nature of learning realizes that the new teacher is free to accept or reject that advice. It is not a matter of doing things the same way that the more experienced teacher does them. Rather, mentoring provides an individual with an opportunity to find her own style with the benefit of another's insights.

As Researchers

There was a time when many teacher education programs at larger institutions used "lab schools" as part of their instructional and research functions. These schools, operated under the auspices of the various universities, used innovative instructional approaches under controlled conditions. Those days are past, but with the emergence of professional development schools (PDS) (Darling-Hammond, 1996), a teacher education model that focuses on a collaboration between a university and a public school, and the National Education Association's Teacher Education Initiative (Major & Pines, 1999), classrooms are increasingly seen as valuable research territory for education improvement. The close collaboration in a PDS model has allowed teachers to act as researchers in those efforts rather than just being participants in someone else's study. Indeed, a study published by the National Council for Accreditation of Teacher Education (NCATE) concluded that student achievement is greater in professional development schools than in typical public schools (Teitel, 2001).

The "teacher as researcher" idea is one that has significant advantages for all concerned. As an active partner in research efforts, the teacher raises her own level of professionalism by helping to contribute to the accumulated body of knowledge regarding education. Without doubt, new insights are developed about teaching and learning. Teachers may also become involved in grant-writing activities and presentations at professional conferences. Universities benefit by increased cooperation and by being able to carry out their studies with less disruption to the normal atmosphere of the classroom.

Participating in classroom-based research is not for everybody. We are not suggesting that all teachers are, or should be, expected to engage in this sort of professional development. However, a "teacher as researcher" collaboration offers professional development that differs from coursework and mentoring in that it specifically focuses on bringing new knowledge to the enterprise of education. Of course, the development of new knowledge is not enough—it must be disseminated. Speaking at conferences and writing and publishing research findings offer teachers a new and rewarding outlet for their creative and intellectual expertise.

The pedagogical competencies of purpose, content, communication, and professional development manifest themselves in many different ways. It can be seen that even apart from instructional strategies and matters of classroom behavior, an effective teacher is a complex individual. Few other occupations, professional or otherwise, require so much of their practitioners. Yet effective teachers are able to find their own combinations of these four competencies and can integrate them seamlessly. As you consider the teachers you've known and the teachers you now work with, try to identify these competencies. Some teachers will be stronger in communication than they are in content. Some will clearly have a philosophy guiding their work. Others will always seem to be leading the efforts of teachers in workshops or new programs or perhaps in completing higher degrees. All will have definite strengths and weaknesses. Reflect on your own competency level in each area as well. Based on your observations and reflections, what sort of teacher do you want to be? Which of these competencies have you identified as your strengths? Which are weaknesses? How might you develop your strengths and overcome your weaknesses?

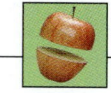

Conclusion

This chapter has considered what it means to be a teacher from the perspectives of motivation, teaching as an art and as a science, and the four dimensions of pedagogical competency. The picture that emerges reveals the teacher as a multidimensional individual who puts a wide range of knowledge to very practical use. The presentation of subject matter is just one portion that contributes to the totality of an effective teacher.

1. There are many motivations to teach. Common themes are service to others and helping people realize their own potential.
2. Teaching is both an art and a science. Effective teachers know this and have carefully developed their expertise in each of the two domains.
3. The science of teaching is based upon the work of researchers, practitioners, philosophers, and a host of other disciplines searching for the best combination of theory and practice to help people learn.
4. The art of teaching is developed through careful practice and honest reflection. It can be fascinating to learn from a teacher who has found an appropriate balance between the two.
5. *Purpose* is concerned with philosophy, attitude, and style, and is often the most difficult of the four pedagogical competencies to express.
6. *Content* is also a multidimensional concern. Static content is provided to the teacher by the state, district, and school. Dynamic content is an ongoing application of all that pre-service teachers learn throughout a teacher education program and improve upon through the practice of teaching.
7. *Communication skills* are the stock in trade of teachers. Teachers regularly communicate with four distinct constituencies: students, parents, colleagues, and the community.
8. *Professional development* is the ongoing education of teachers. Whether in formal or informal situations, teachers are lifelong learners. Most educators have an insatiable desire to learn new things—and not just in the one or several subject areas they teach.
9. Teachers can, and should, contribute to the accumulated body of educational knowledge as researchers.

Key Terms

pedagogy	static content	professional development
constituencies	dynamic content	mentoring

Educational Engineering

Case Studies in Education

Case Studies in Education provides you the opportunity to compile an educational record for a particular student and to maintain a journal of your opinions, concerns, and suggestions for providing that student with the best possible educational opportunity. Each chapter will provide you with more information about the student in the context of the particular chapter. You will also be provided with

questions and activities to address in your journal. Of course, your journal is your own, and so feel free to go beyond the questions we provide.

Turn to Case Studies in Education in Appendix A to find six case studies of students ranging from kindergarten through high school. Read the brief descriptions, and then select a student to follow as you continue through this book. You will also find instructions for beginning an Educational Record of the student you have chosen and suggestions for setting up your journal. Then return here and enter the information provided for your student. You can then proceed to consider the questions provided.

	Type of Person the Student Responds To	The Student's Academic Demeanor	Parents' Perspective of the School
Davon	Davon responds to a teacher who provides structure and consistency in the classroom. He needs to be spoken to in a quiet tone.	Davon is an average student. He has difficulty making connections to things discussed in school because of his limited life experiences.	The mother does not communicate with the teacher, respond to notes, or attend parent conferences. She rushes phone conversations to get off the phone quickly.
Andy	Andy responds best to authoritative teachers. His ADHD requires a firm hand in order to keep him on task, but he "shuts down" when yelled at.	Andy is of low-average intelligence. Oral language development is adequate but written language development is well below average. Joins in discussions and brings wide background knowledge to the classroom. Resists reading due to his difficulty in decoding words.	Lives with grandparents. Has lived with mother but says he is more comfortable living in his grandparents' home. Grandmother attends conferences but had him moved to different classes due to conflicts with teachers. Discontinued his ADHD medication because of side effects. Reluctantly resumed when his schoolwork declined.
Judith	Authoritative teachers are best for her. Authoritarian teachers cause her to "shut down." Since she is easily distracted, permissive teachers find it difficult to keep her on task.	Judith is a below-average student in all subject areas. She does not often connect what occurs in class to the world outside of school. However, she actively takes part in educational activities.	The parents are supportive but seem to be unaware of how to contribute to her development. They attend open-house events but engage in little conversation with the teachers.
Tiffany	Tiffany responds well to an authoritarian teacher because she is always seeking direction and specific instructions. Tiffany wants to please adults and is always seeking their input. However, Tiffany has a very hard time taking her own initiative with projects if expectations are not clearly stated.	Tiffany is very sharp. She constantly seeks academic stimulation and craves the stress and challenges of higher-level work. She's been labeled as "Gifted and Talented" since the third grade. She does make connections drawing upon events from her family or social situations. However, her connections are primarily based on previous school years and academic experiences.	Tiffany's parents have been very supportive of her academic success and teachers. They are proud of the school and the gains she has made academically. They do have concerns with Tiffany's social and emotional growth. However, they address this issue collaboratively with the school and have not "blamed" the teachers or school for this problem.
Sam	Sam responds positively to authoritative teachers. He is most successful when he is in a structured environment where he can focus his energies and know what is expected of him.	Sam functions in the Low Average intellectual range. He is actively engaged in educational tasks and is very persistent. He makes connections between things taught in school, though is slow to process information. Often needs reteaching.	The mother is supportive of the school and the teachers. She does not take the initiative, but is very cooperative when the school communicates with her about Sam. Can be instrumental in Sam's academic success.

(Continued on next page)

Bao

Bao doesn't like conflict, and so prefers teachers who have good classroom control, yet are personal and warm. Authoritative teachers are her favorites; if such teachers also happen to be friendly and open, all the better. Bao works hard in these classes because she wants to make these teachers happy and because she feels safe.

Bao is an above-average student. She can be actively engaged or detached, depending on the atmosphere of the class. Even in her more difficult subjects, she does well if she enjoys the style of teaching and the people in the class; her grades drop in even her best subjects if she feels threatened by the teacher or other students. When pressed, Bao makes connections in class, but she prefers to let others make the connections, which she then has little problem comprehending.

Bao's parents support the school, and the few times a teacher has called home, they have made it clear to Bao that such phone calls are unacceptable. (This is partly why Bao avoids her teachers' attention.) In this Bao's parents are very traditional; they feel her teachers are absolute authorities, and would never question the school.

1. How will the reasons that have brought you to the possibility of a teaching career serve the needs of your student? How will working with your student meet the personal needs you wish to fill by becoming a teacher?

2. Of the four pedagogical competencies discussed in the chapter, which ones do you perceive as strengths and which do you perceive as areas of weakness that might need to be developed to best serve your student? How will your expertise in each area affect the academic, social, and emotional development of the particular student you are considering?

Designing the School of the Future

This activity strand appears at the end of each chapter and after each unit in the Unit Workshop feature. Though the mention of "school" typically brings an image of buildings and classrooms to mind, you will find that there are many considerations to be discussed before we ever get to the point of drawing floor plans. Schools will, however, change as time goes by. As professionals in education, we want you to take part in that change rather than simply being changed by the process. That is why we have provided this particular feature in the book.

Turn to Designing a School of the Future in Appendix B. There you will find detailed directions for beginning a notebook that will hold your plan for the school of the future. One of your first decisions is whether you want to consider the design of a school five, 10, 20, or 50 years in the future. The choice is yours. Some people are more comfortable with the near term, and others like to look farther down the road. In either case, the point is not to predict the future but instead to take part in the evolution of school. When you have completed the introductory steps in Appendix B, return here and begin by addressing the following questions as Part I of your plan.

1. This chapter has discussed that teaching is both an art and a science. As education continues to develop, which of these two aspects should be emphasized? In your school of the future, will teachers be "education scientists" or "education artists" or some combination of the two? Explain the combination that you think would provide the best education to students.

2. What would be your expectations of a teacher for each of the four pedagogical competencies discussed in the chapter? For instance, it has become necessary for teachers to be more effective communicators with parents than historically was the case. Would you expect that in the school of the future

teachers need to be more adept at communicating with business people in the community at large? Address each of the competencies in this way. (*Note:* You will find in Chapter 10 that the No Child Left Behind Act is already addressing the area of "content.")

3. Based on your responses in items 1 and 2, write a job advertisement for a teaching position in the school you are designing. Would many people qualify at this time? If so, are you saying that teaching qualifications will remain the same in the future as they are today?

 ## Praxis Practice

Many states will require that you successfully complete the Praxis Series of examinations to qualify for certification. One or more of those tests will be subject-area tests. Another, which has a more practical orientation, will be the Principles of Learning and Teaching (PLT) examination that is appropriate for your certification area.

Completing the Quick Check Quizzes for Chapter 1 in the Unit Workshop will give you practice with the multiple-choice format of the PLT. The Case Studies in Education and Designing a School of the Future activities will help prepare you for exercises that require reading a scenario and providing short answers to questions asking what you might do in such a situation.

The Strategic Nature of Teaching

CPr²

Make the chapter work for you with CPR²:

Conceptualize   Here are the major themes you will encounter in this chapter:

1. There is a strategic nature to teaching.
2. Teachers facilitate learning by arranging educational experiences, selecting and utilizing appropriate instructional techniques, and monitoring student progress.
3. Flexibility is a key trait among effective teachers.
4. Teachers are role models for their students.

Preview   Read the chapter headings; look at any figures, tables, and activities; and read through the items in the conclusion.

Activity 2.1:   Go Online! PCs and Teaching Machines

Activity 2.2:   Developing Inference Questions

Activity 2.3:   Applying the Various Instructional Techniques

Activity 2.4:   Field Observation Activity– Observing How Teachers Adjust

Activity 2.5:   Go Online! Are Teachers Role Models?

Read   Now read through the chapter. Mark or highlight information that you consider to be especially important or about which you have a question.

Reflect   Consider these questions as you read: How would you "bring the world" to your students? Are teachers responsible for being role models when away from school?

Photo: Courtesy of David Ottenstein Photography

Eye on the Standards
INTASC

The following standards from the Interstate New Teacher Assessment and Support Consortium (INTASC) will be addressed in this chapter. As you read the chapter, consider how effective teaching strategies are tied to these principles.

Principle 1 The teacher understands the central concepts, tools of inquiry, and structures of the discipline(s) he or she teaches and can create learning experiences that make these aspects of subject matter meaningful for students.

Principle 2 The teacher understands how children learn and develop, and can provide learning opportunities that support their intellectual, social, and personal development.

Principle 3 The teacher understands how students differ in their approaches to learning and creates instructional opportunities that are adapted to diverse learners.

Principle 4 The teacher understands and uses a variety of instructional strategies to encourage students' development of critical thinking, problem solving, and performance skills.

Principle 5 The teacher uses an understanding of individual and group motivation and behavior to create a learning environment that encourages positive social interaction, active engagement in learning, and self-motivation.

Principle 6 The teacher uses knowledge of effective verbal, nonverbal, and media communication techniques to foster active inquiry, collaboration, and supportive interaction in the classroom.

Principle 7 The teacher plans instruction based upon knowledge of subject matter, students, the community, and curriculum goals.

Principle 8 The teacher understands and uses formal and informal assessment strategies to evaluate and ensure the continuous intellectual, social and physical development of the learner.

ice breakers

Challenging Your Students to Think

Number the eight categories of instructional techniques represented below in the order that you think progresses from the least sophisticated level of thinking required of the student to the most sophisticated. When you have arranged them, consider which levels of thinking are the least often used and which are the most often used in the typical educational life of a student.

Courtesy of Bill Lisenby

Inquiry: _____

Courtesy of David Ottenstein Photography

Discussion: _____

Courtesy of David Ottenstein Photography

Direct Instruction: _____

© PureStock/Index Stock Imagery

Discovery Learning: _____

Courtesy of Becky Stovall

Drill and Practice: _____

Courtesy of David Ottenstein Photography

Lecture: _____

Courtesy of Bill Lisenby

Mental Modeling: _____

Courtesy of Guilherme Cunha

Question and Answer: _____

This chapter will discuss, among other things, eight general categories of instructional techniques that teachers use. We will present a taxonomy that organizes those techniques from the least sophisticated thinking required of the student (and the most input required from the teacher) to the most sophisticated thinking required of the student (and the least input from the teacher). All thinking is sophisticated to one degree or another but, as you will see, the transition from teacher-focused techniques to student-focused techniques requires increasingly greater cognitive demands of the students. Here's the order of the taxonomy that we will present:

Direct Instruction: 1

Drill and Practice: 2

Lecture: 3

Question and Answer: 4

Discussion: 5

Mental Modeling: 6

Discovery Learning: 7

Inquiry: 8

> *"If you can read this, thank a teacher."*
>
> *Anonymous*

■ Introduction

In Chapter 1 we discussed the person who would be a teacher. Our discussion now turns to the manner in which teachers go about the task of providing educational experiences for their students. This will not be a lesson in *how* to teach, but it will introduce you to a wide range of instructional possibilities—because there are many ways to go about teaching a lesson. The instructors at your particular college or university likely have their own preferences in that regard, and so your studies will concentrate on those techniques. However, virtually any topic in education has a number of major themes running throughout its multiple dimensions. This chapter will address three instructional aspects of the teaching process in particular: strategy, facilitating learning, and modeling.

The topics of this chapter should provide you with some provocative food for thought and discussion as you consider what is involved in being an effective teacher. Avail yourself of the opportunity to ask your professors, the teachers where you do your in-school observations, and of course your friends for their opinions on the questions raised in this chapter. The diversity of opinions on any educational issue may astound you!

■ The Strategic Nature of Teaching

strategy A means of coordinating the implementation of a set of procedures. A strategy combines subject matter, techniques, and the skills for implementing instruction.

The next time you sit in class, watch your professor as he walks into the room. It is likely that he enters with some information that he wants you to know before you leave. However, the information itself is just one aspect of the dynamic event that is about to take place. In addition to information, your professor likely has a **strategy** for teaching the course. That strategy includes a number of components such as techniques for teaching, methods for monitoring the students' understanding, ideas for activities to enrich understanding, and of course a means for assessing whether they have acquired the information (Tomlinson, 2000; Deshler, Ellis, & Lenz, 1996). Lecture or otherwise, "information" is just part of the strategy that a professor brings to each class session.

Strategy refers to the art of planning some course of action *and* coordinating the implementation of that plan. It represents a broader view of the overall goal. The strategic nature of teaching requires an understanding of the bigger picture of what is to occur during a lesson or during an entire year. For example, the syllabus for the course you are taking right now represents a plan for the semester. That syllabus probably stays pretty much the same from class to class (if more than one section is being offered at a time) and semester to semester. However, different combinations of students may move along at different rates or respond better to different teaching styles. In such a case a professor may adjust his *strategy* for reaching his goal even though the basic plan (syllabus) remains the same.

A teacher is more than a technician. The strategist is responsible for combining content (subject matter), technique, and resources to provide an effective learning experience. This responsibility is what will make you a professional rather than a technician or a teacher's aide. In essence, an educational strategy must (1) identify what is to be accomplished, (2) detail how it will get done, (3) specify how to assess the results, and (4) account for the means (either in terms of the teacher's capabilities or other resources) for putting the plan into action (Figure 2.1).

■ Facilitating Learning

The teacher's challenge is to accumulate a set of "tools" that when properly implemented will contribute to an overall strategy for accomplishing the learning of identified content. We have chosen to organize those tools, the elements of a strategy, into the categories of (1) arranging experiences, (2) instructional techniques, and (3) monitoring and flexibility. You may have noticed that we haven't included

Figure 2.1

The Components of an
Educational Strategy

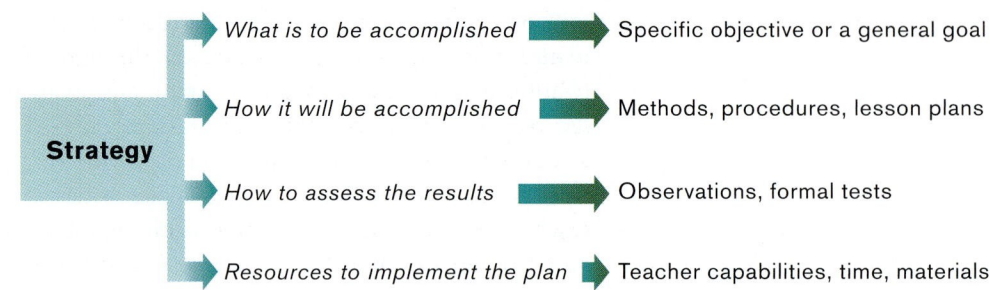

"subject matter" as one of the tools. This is because the teacher uses the tools, or elements of a strategy, to bring subject matter and students together in an experience that facilitates learning. Therefore, subject matter is not a tool per se, but more like the material from which the experience is fashioned, much like a carpenter uses tools to work with the wood that eventually becomes a house.

Simply being in possession of the knowledge that we want students to acquire is not sufficient for effective teaching. You might think of it in terms of painting a house: Having a can of paint does not get the house painted. Something else—a big something else—has to happen to get the paint from the can onto the house. In education, that big something else is what the teacher does to facilitate learning. If we take the perspective that learning is something that occurs *within* a student, then the role of a teacher can only be to facilitate that process. The teacher arranges experiences and materials in a manner that will *enable* a student to learn a particular lesson.

Arranging Experiences

The essence of teaching is arranging experiences from which students can learn. A lecture may seem a rather dry and passive approach, but it is nonetheless an experience that someone determined would be the most appropriate means of presenting information in that particular situation. Another teacher may choose to use videotapes or other media to present information. Yet another teacher favors an approach that more actively engages the students. There are merits to each, but all are a matter of the teacher trying to engage students in learning situations.

The sections that follow discuss four broad categories of experiences: classroom lessons, multimedia, guest speakers, and field trips. Though there may well be an infinite number of ways to combine variations of these approaches, there are several trends that you should watch for. One is the degree to which the teacher is directly involved in providing instruction. Another is the movement from the specialized atmosphere of the typical classroom, which metaphorically brings the world to the students, all the way to experiences provided in a real-world context, in essence taking the students to the world.

Classroom Lessons

By classroom lessons we mean those experiences most typically associated with teaching school. In this situation a teacher works with one or more students in a classroom environment. As states and school districts struggle to bring class sizes to an effective level, a typical classroom has 20–30 students. Depending on the district's policy on ability grouping, all students in your classroom might be classified on the same grade level (which is not the same thing as being on the same grade level academically). Some districts use regrouping plans that bring students from other grade levels to a teacher's class for instruction in particular subjects such as reading or math. In any case, classroom lessons represent a format in which a teacher brings knowledge, culture, and the world at large to the students. The contributions of scientists, mathematicians, authors, composers, artists, and all the rest are represented as passages in books, class discussions, activities, and discrete assignments to be completed.

It is no wonder that students, elementary students in particular, think of their teachers as "knowing everything." Though by middle school and high school much of this reverence is lost, there is nonetheless a certain mystique associated with being the individual who brings new knowledge to the classroom day in and day out. That, of course, is the romantic aspect of being a teacher. The responsibilities that come along with this are formidable.

The teacher must account for everything that will be necessary for the presentation of that lesson. If special skills are required for any aspect of the presentation (for example, working with hazardous materials in a science demonstration), they are skills the teacher needs to possess. The autonomy of working with your own classroom can be empowering, and the sense of accomplishment for completing a well-presented lesson leads to pride in a job well done. However, even the best teacher can become tired of hauling the world (let alone the universe!) into class every day, and so there are other ways that teachers can augment some of these classroom lessons.

Multimedia Presentations

Years ago, we referred to *multimedia* as AV (audio-visual) equipment. Among the marvelous machinery of the times were record players (what?), 16mm movie projectors, filmstrip projectors (the high-tech ones had a built-in tape recorder and advanced the film automatically), and the overhead projector. Interestingly enough, the only one to make the transition into the 21st century—and even enjoy a renaissance—has been that plain old overhead projector. Perhaps as an example of Ockham's razor—that is, all things being held equal, the simplest answer is probably correct—the simplest machine was the one with enough flexibility to adapt to a new age (Cambourne, 2001). There's a lesson in there somewhere for all of us.

"Technology" is a ubiquitous term in our new millennium. By no means has technology supplanted the teacher, but instructional materials that make use of a wide range of electronic media are increasingly available. Books and encyclopedias on CD-ROM allow full-text searching of documents and files. Television (broadcast, satellite, and closed-circuit), VCRs, and DVDs not only bring high-quality presentations into the classroom but also allow students to engage in interactive projects to collect information from all around the world. Even so, the teacher remains as the ringmaster.

A key difference between high tech of today and high tech of days gone by is the heavy reliance on computer-based systems. Teachers must be well versed in the use of technology in the classroom; fortunately, most education students today are already computer literate. Rather than starting from scratch, as the previous generation of teachers had to do, you may simply need to "transition" from the basic skills of word processing and game playing to computer-based record-keeping, spreadsheets, interactive investigations, and so forth.

Used effectively, multimedia allows the teacher to bring a more accurate representation of the real world to the classroom setting. It also allows students to interact with the sights and sounds of historic events, scientific inquiry, and self-expression in matters academic or artistic. Activity 2.1 will provide you an opportunity to examine how "high tech" has developed over the years.

Go Online!

Activity 2.1   PCs and Teaching Machines

Computers and educational software have had a tremendous impact on education. Some programs are effective in providing drill and practice routines. Others make historic events and prominent individuals more "real" by presenting digitized images and sound from important events. Computers, however, are simply realizing the potential that was first seen with "teaching machines."

1. Use the Internet to find out more about the original teaching machines. Use search terms such as "teaching machines" and "B. F. Skinner" to get started.

2. Based on what you have found, why do you think the teaching machines didn't catch on?

3. What capabilities does the computer offer that makes the idea of teaching machines more practical today?

4. What do you envision as the next generation of computer technology as an instructional tool?

Guest Speakers

On the continuum moving from representations of the real world to the real world itself, next on the scale is bringing guest speakers to the classroom. Having a real person in the classroom is bringing life outside of the school inside. A teacher wants to seek out organizations and individuals who can offer significant insights about a topic under consideration in the class. Even though guest speakers don't come with all the bells and whistles of a slick multimedia presentation, it is nonetheless invaluable in our increasingly "electronic" and "interactive" age for children to have the opportunity to speak with actual people.

Many guest speakers are well versed in the requirements of being "teacher for a day" and come prepared to inform and dazzle. Others are flattered by your request and are full of good intentions, but do not know how to seize and hold the attention of a classroom full of students. They may need your assistance to carry off the experience successfully. *Note:* It is always, always a good idea to have something else planned in case the speaker finishes early or cancels at the last minute. Being prepared for that contingency is part of the strategy.

Guest speakers help to bring the world to the students.

Courtesy of Guilherme Cunha

Field Trips

There comes a time when no amount of pushing and shoving will fit the real world into a classroom. At this point the only alternative, if the experience is to occur, is to take the students to the world. Field trips to a museum, an assembly plant, nature study areas, or other specialized environments can provide students with rich experiences that simply could not be duplicated in the classroom.

Field trips have fallen into disfavor in recent years. This is not because of the efficacy of the experience but rather because of the logistics, expense, and liability involved in moving large numbers of students away from the relatively safe confines of the school. Without question, these very concerns have given rise to the explosion of multimedia presentations available to educators. Those multimedia products can also serve a role by providing background and context to students before the trip. You may want to read "School Trips without a Hitch" for specific recommendations about how to prepare for, conduct, and follow up on field trips (Patterson & Fiscus, 2000).

Don't forget, the real world is not far away. Sometimes the "field" you need is just outside the door. That is, try to overcome the feeling that all things educational must happen within the walls of your classroom. Science, art, mathematics, and even history can be found just outside of the school building, and still on school grounds, in the "real world."

As a teacher conceptualizes a lesson, it tends to emerge as one form or another of the four situations just described (classroom lesson, multimedia presentation, guest speaker, field trip). The interesting pattern to note is the inverse relationship between the frequency of each type of experience and exposure to the real world. Thinking back over your own past (and present) classroom situations, you may find that the vast majority of your educational experiences were presented in terms of classroom lessons. To a lesser degree your teachers incorporated various multimedia presentations and activities to enhance the experience. To an even lesser degree, people from the community and specialized services were brought in to speak with you. And you can probably count the number of field trips that you ever took. Since school is all about preparing students for the world in which they will live, it is an intriguing paradox that the most basic practice within organized education (classroom lessons) is the furthest removed from that world. Many factors play into this, not the least of which are matters of efficiency and economy. That is what makes this a specialized challenge of the classroom teacher: arranging educational experiences within the classroom that students can find relevant outside of the classroom. Table 2.1 summarizes the general categories of instructional experiences.

Instructional Techniques

Having decided the basic format for an educational experience, a teacher must next choose the appropriate instructional technique. Generally speaking, there are eight categories of techniques from which a teacher might choose. As has previously been the case, the teacher may well determine that a combination of techniques would be most appropriate.

Table 2.1	The General Categories of Instructional Experiences
Instructional Experience	**Value for Students**
Classroom Lessons	Bring experiences and knowledge to the students.
Multimedia Presentations	Bring depictions of people and events to the classroom. Can also provide instructional experiences.
Guest Speakers	Bring expertise, knowledge, and insight from people who represent particular skills, abilities, and responsibilities (for example, local political figures)
Field Trips	Take students to the real-world experience in its natural environment (that is, away from the classroom)

In the discussion below, we have ordered these eight techniques in terms of increasing sophistication of the thinking required of students. This is not to say that any one of the techniques is inappropriate for particular ages. After all, you can probably remember being "lectured to" by your parents at one time or another in your life, and you likely discovered some things on your own even as a young child. However, when planning educational experiences, teachers need to identify the level of cognitive processing they want to engage, and select the technique that best encourages that level of thinking (Lasley, Matczynski, & Rowley, 2002). They should also consider the relationship of instructional strategy to student retention of information. Issues such as the developmental level of the students, the instructional venue (indoors, outdoors, individual desks, tables and chairs for group work, etc.), and the subject matter to be presented must also be considered.

Our list of techniques parallels Bloom's taxonomy, described in *Taxonomy of Educational Objectives Handbook I: Cognitive Domain* (Bloom et al., 1956). The taxonomy begins with the least sophisticated level of processing, that being the recall of knowledge and facts, and progresses to the highest level, thinking that involves evaluative processes (See Figure 2.2). After reading through the descriptions of these eight approaches, compare them to Bloom's taxonomy to see how a teacher might select one technique or another based upon the level of thinking he wishes to encourage.

Direct Instruction

direct instruction A means of delivering instruction by specifically explaining or demonstrating a skill and having the students attempt to replicate it.

In **direct instruction,** the teacher specifically explains or demonstrates a skill and the student attempts to replicate it. We list it as the lowest level of our taxonomy of instructional techniques because very little abstraction is involved, though that does not mean the task is a simple one. As children struggle to reproduce the letters of the alphabet, they need all the concentration and control they can muster.

Figure 2.2

Bloom's Taxonomy

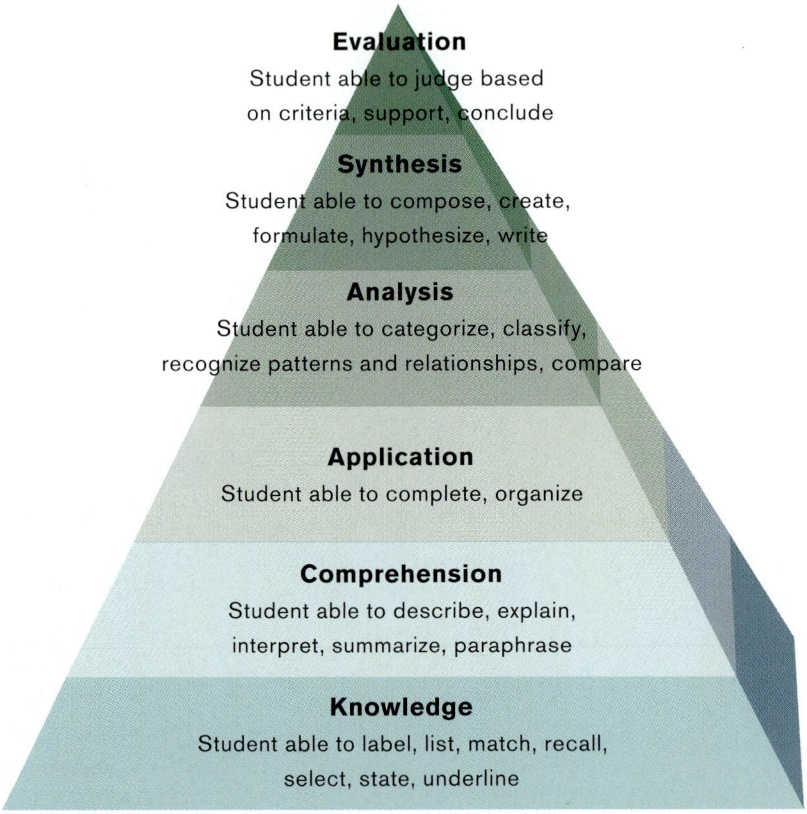

Evaluation
Student able to judge based
on criteria, support, conclude

Synthesis
Student able to compose, create,
formulate, hypothesize, write

Analysis
Student able to categorize, classify,
recognize patterns and relationships, compare

Application
Student able to complete, organize

Comprehension
Student able to describe, explain,
interpret, summarize, paraphrase

Knowledge
Student able to label, list, match, recall,
select, state, underline

Courtesy of Bill Lisenby

Similarly, the middle school student performing the steps of an experiment can be fully focused and intent. Nonetheless, the demands for deep understanding and recombining of information are minimal in direct instruction. The emphasis is clearly on the acquiring of information or procedural skills. A review of 34 comparative studies found results significantly favoring direct instruction for the acquisition of information or skills 64 percent of the time and non-direct instruction 1 percent of the time. The remaining studies showed non-significant results (Directing Direct Instruction, 1997). It is important to note, as does Rosenshine (1983), that direct instruction is most applicable for young learners, slow learners, and older learners when the material is new, difficult, or hierarchically arranged.

Teachers choose from a repertoire of instructional techniques when working with students. Of those discussed in the text, which might be in use in this situation?

drill and practice An instructional technique that emphasizes the repetition of previously learned information or skills to hone the skill or provide a strong cognitive link to the information to improve remembering it.

Drill and Practice

One level up from direct instruction is **drill and practice.** Though it might seem that this technique is even more rote than direct instruction, the implication is that something has already been learned, or at least been presented, and now the emphasis is on repetition to hone the skill or provide a strong link to the information to improve remembering it.

This particular technique does not emphasize abstraction or the synthesis of new understanding. Your own experience with "times tables" is an example of drill and practice. You were not learning much mathematical theory as you memorized those products; the emphasis was on providing you with basic information that you would later use in a variety of mathematical situations.

lecture An instructional technique in which the teacher takes the active role of providing information while students take a more passive role by listening. Characterized by limited dialogue between teacher and student.

Lecture

The mainstay of a traditional college education, **lecture** shows up third in our instructional technique hierarchy. What does that tell you about the thinking that lectures require of a student? We are by no means denigrating the lecture approach, but the simple fact is that lectures in their pure form serve only to impart information in a one-way verbal transaction.

Of course, many times teachers will follow up a lecture with some sort of discussion session. We are not suggesting that this does not happen; however, it does not always occur. A lecture can be presented without any opportunity for an intellectual exchange between student and teacher (see the anecdote in Figure 2.3). Its strength is that a large amount of information can be provided to a large group of people in a short amount of time with a concomitant "personal" touch. Its weakness, pedagogically speaking, is that the instructor, not the student, does the work.

reflection The process of thinking critically about experiences or observations and making connections with other ideas and/or drawing inferences for further consideration.

question and answer Instructional technique in which the teacher poses questions soliciting content-specific responses from the student.

Question and Answer

At this point we begin considering techniques that actually require **reflection** on the part of the student and thus involve evaluation and the synthesis of new information, the two highest levels of Bloom's taxonomy. Reflection requires that a student receive information and then consider it with regard to his own experiences and interpretations. The **question and answer** technique supposes that to some degree the teacher and the student share a common body of knowledge. This does

Figure 2.3

The Lecture

> There is an anecdote told of a prestigious professor who lectured at a prestigious university. However, due to his busy schedule, he would tape record his lectures. A graduate assistant would then bring the tape to the lecture hall, and the students would listen to the tape and take notes.
>
> One day the professor decided to provide the students with a treat and deliver the lecture in person. "I don't think that would be a good idea, sir," advised the graduate assistant. "Your schedule is much too busy. Perhaps next week?"
>
> "Nonsense," replied the professor, and the two left for the lecture hall. Upon their arrival the professor found no students. Instead, on each chair in the auditorium was a tape recorder waiting to tape the day's lecture!

not mean that the student has the same depth of knowledge or understanding, but there are sufficient common elements to allow the student and teacher to consider the topic in a two-way exchange. Each party must be prepared to consider the topic from the other's perspective.

There are several approaches to using the question-and-answer technique. In one approach, the students may question the teacher. The teacher needs to be sufficiently knowledgeable of the subject matter to provide appropriate responses without knowing the questions in advance or having the opportunity to research the answers. You're probably thinking that this is no trick at all since the teacher knows a lot more than the "kids" in the class. However, sometimes those "kids" are middle school or high school students who may well possess information about a topic that the teacher does not. For instance, a student with an interest in World War I aviation may know quite a bit about the emergence of aerial warfare in the early part of the 20th century. A teacher cannot have all of the answers, but *being prepared to deal with the unexpected is part of being a teacher,* not something that happens once in awhile.

Don't get the idea that those elementary school children are any less likely to stump the teacher. Children come to school thinking about the same questions that they have heard their parents discuss at home. They may not always understand those questions, but the idea of asking the teacher for an answer is typically considered a good one. In November of 2000, the United States experienced a most unusual presidential election. Questions of the electoral college, popular vote, vote counting and not counting, legal issues, and even the United States Supreme Court swirled around the determination of the country's president. What would you say to a third grader who asked why some people did not want to count all of the votes?

The other side of question and answer is the situation in which the teacher asks questions of the students. You are certainly familiar with this approach! However, our concern now is with the reason for those questions. One purpose is to give the students practice with the recall (and perhaps application) of particular information. Another is to assess the students' acquisition of particular information. In either of these cases, techniques such as providing think-time (Gambrell, 1983) and challenging initial responses will improve the use of question-and-answer sessions. Indeed, in her classic study of the effects of wait time, Mary Budd Rowe (1978) found that providing students additional time to think increased the number and quality of responses and decreased discipline situations.

divergent thinking The process of taking information and creating new ideas or adapting it in original (to the thinker) ways.

convergent thinking The process of taking one or more sources of information and drawing conclusions about their characteristics (perhaps similarities or differences) or implications.

Yet a third purpose for the use of this instructional technique is to stimulate thought and encourage **divergent thinking** (as opposed to the **convergent thinking** of the previous two examples). When using question and answer, the teacher is challenging students to apply prior knowledge and then use that as a basis for synthesizing new knowledge. As you review Bloom's taxonomy (1956), you will find that synthesis is a level of thinking near the top of the taxonomy. The challenge presented to the teacher is that when such questions are asked, a wide range of answers is likely. The teacher must be prepared for whatever might come along, and this includes finding ways to identify merit in virtually any response. If a teacher is willing to open up the classroom to divergent thinking and the opinions of the students, then he must be ready to help students formulate and reformulate their ideas without diminishing the value of the original idea. Asking students for their opinions and then telling them they are wrong is one of the surest ways to bring original thinking in the classroom to a halt. Conversely, the amount of innovative and creative thinking that a teacher can initiate, in virtually any subject area, is empowering both for students and teachers.

Discussion

discussion Involves the interchange of ideas. With this approach a teacher hopes to develop greater depth of ideas and to foster the manipulation of information for solving problems rather than just the acquisition of knowledge.

A step higher on our taxonomy of instructional techniques is **discussion.** This differs from the previous level in that neither the teacher nor the student "holds the upper hand." This situation concerns a very different treatment of knowledge from the ones described thus far. Discussions involve the interchange of ideas. With this approach a teacher hopes to develop greater depth of ideas and perhaps to foster the manipulation of information for solving problems rather than just the acquisition of knowledge.

Some might argue that "discussion" is not the most appropriate term for what teachers wish to accomplish. In fact, discussion does refer more to the debating of points of view, whereas *dialogue* refers to an exchange of ideas. In either case, the instructional intent is to take students beyond "just the facts" and to engage them in a more poignant treatment of the subject matter.

Admittedly, engaging student thinking in this manner is sometimes difficult to do, but that's why the other techniques exist. However, we want to encourage you to find ways within any subject to draw your students further up the taxonomy. If you are teaching algebra and can provide a discussion opportunity with an enrichment activity about "the beauty of mathematics," then by all means make the effort to give your students that experience.

Courtesy of Becky Stovall

Discussions, no matter what the grade level, encourage the exchange of ideas. All participants benefit.

Mental Modeling

mental modeling A technique used to foster students' ability to direct their own learning. It involves careful modeling of the cognitive processes required to solve problems.

Mental modeling (Culyer, 1987) and a variation of it, the "I Wonder. . ." model (Bentley, Ebert, & Ebert, 2000) are techniques specifically intended to enhance students' ability to direct their own learning by modeling the use of cognitive processes in the solving of some problem. This might sound "elementary" at first, and it is quite effective when working with young children, but it is a process that you may well have been exposed to in your secondary—and now tertiary—educational experiences.

Teacher Testimonial

Feature 2.1   Lynette Turman Provides Insights from 40 Years of Teaching

What would I say to someone just starting out in teaching? It's funny, though I've been teaching for a few years now, that's something that I have to stop and think about for a while.

You need to know that during the first three years you have to kill yourself: to work hard and apply everything you've learned and know. If it doesn't work, reflect on it to see if you can change it to make it work. If not, dump it. But know that the extra amount of time you put into teaching in the first three years will benefit your students and make it easier for you later on. It gets easier.

OK, it's never easy, but it gets easier and no two days are ever the same. After decades of teaching, I am busier now than I have ever been. Keep in mind, however, that things are very different today. When I started teaching, "computer" was not a term we even discussed. And changes happen almost daily during your career. Yet this is also what keeps you young at heart.

As a Student Teacher

You have to really observe what your supervising teacher is doing good *and* bad. Write it down! Once you get into class you will forget unless you have written it down. For example, where do you keep the attendance cards, how do you take attendance, what do you do with the cards afterwards? You have to know how to do transitions—that is, moving from one subject or activity to another, or coming into the room and getting started on work, or going outside and coming back in.

With Children

I often hear new teachers say, "If I could touch just one life, it will all be worth it." Well, maybe, but I'd like you to approach *each* child as being the one you are going to touch, whose life is going to be better for having had you

as a teacher. I think that way you'll come out with a better record than one out of several hundred or several thousand.

You have to look at each child as an individual. Try to make your own connection with him and don't rely on what past teachers have said about the child. You also need to understand the physical and emotional limits of your students so that you can get them to perform at their very best in an appropriate manner.

I believe that you have to teach what you love and what you are enthusiastic about so your enthusiasm can become contagious. That, frequently, is what will stay with a child. Figure out a way to bring the things you love into the curriculum so that you will have joy in teaching and your children will have joy in learning. If you are a photographer, teach kids about photography. If you're a dancer, do dance. Find a way to incorporate it into the curriculum. And by the way, always carry a dictionary, and don't ever be afraid to say that you were wrong and to correct yourself in front of the students. And no matter what you hear in college or in some professional development workshop, *always* take advantage of teachable moments! When you are holding the students' curiosity and wonder in your hands, it's time to deviate from the plan, because you have the opportunity to make learning relevant in the real world of a child. The teachable moment is that time in a teacher's and a student's life when all of the planets have lined up to facilitate learning. It's like a key sliding smoothly into a lock, moving all the tumblers into position, and just waiting for someone to turn the key and unlock something new and wonderful. You've heard the phrase *carpe diem*—seize the day—well, I'm telling you that as a teacher you need to be quicker than that; you need to seize the *moment!*

For example, during an elementary school lesson about using maps a teacher might say, "I'd like to find my way to Sarah's house. I know the address, but I don't know how to get there from the school. I think I'll use the map of our city to find the way there. First I'll check the street index to find out where to look on the map. Then I'll use the numbers from the index to find the street." In this way a teacher demonstrates how to sequence steps and put information to work in solving a problem. Students are then able to practice the same procedure.

The "I Wonder. . ." model uses the same approach, though in the context of science education. Bentley, Ebert, & Ebert (2000) consider this to be one of the best ways of initiating the information-seeking process. As thinking is an otherwise unobservable process, this technique attempts to *verbalize* the thinking that goes on. Here's an example from *The Natural Investigator* that a teacher might use with elementary level children:

About Parents

Parents really want the same thing for their children that you do. Learn how to make them your partner in educating their/"your" children. Keep them informed of the good things their children are doing. Ask for their help in the classroom, if possible. And let parents know what a good job they're doing with their children! Let the children know too! Always give positive feedback both to parents and children.

Administration

Do your paperwork well and on time. You are frequently judged by the administrative staff by the quality of your paperwork. You may not like hearing that, but it is the reality of the situation. And it's not such a terrible thing. Completing the paperwork demonstrates a job well done and a professional attitude.

The most important person in the school is the principal. The principal needs to be aware of the good things you're doing. Invite her in when you think you're going to be doing something special. It takes some pressure off of the teacher and helps get the principal to support you.

And What about "Me"?

I suppose that I've been going on and on about what a teacher should know and what a teacher should do. But you probably want to know *why* a teacher should do all of this. There are, after all, easier ways to make a living. It won't take you years of teaching to understand these feelings, but I can promise you that they are worth the effort it takes to experience them. Here are some of the things that don't show up in a paycheck, but can absolutely make my day no matter how hectic it's been:

- Seeing a child accomplish something
- A compliment from a peer or administrator/staff
- A compliment from a parent
- Watching your students perform well for an assembly or physical activity
- A visit by a former student that brings positive feedback
- Teaching multiple children in a family (or the children of the children you've taught)
- Seeing a child take pride in something he's done or created in your classroom
- Seeing a child improve her grade or progress from a lower reading or math group to a higher one
- Seeing a child shine in one area even though he is having problems in other areas
- Becoming friends with the wonderful people in the profession—you make lifelong friends because you have so much in common
- Seeing your kids grown up, remembering you and thanking you
- Realizing that you are learning something new every day, as are your students

What other profession gives you all of that? You are just starting out on the journey toward becoming a teacher, but as these experiences ultimately become yours as well, you will understand that they are, well, *priceless.* Teachers who stay in teaching do so because they love teaching. It's not for the money, it's because they want to be the best teacher in the whole wide world!

Lynette Turman was an elementary school teacher with the Los Angeles Unified School District for 40 years. For 28 years she has also been instructing prospective teachers at California State University–Dominguez Hills. ■

This morning I looked outside and noticed that it wasn't very sunny. I observed lots of gray clouds. I wondered if it was going to rain today. I could have just carried an umbrella in case it did rain and not thought about it anymore. However, I was planning to wear my new shoes, and I really didn't want to get them wet and dirty the first time I wore them. So I checked the newspaper and the weather channel. The paper predicted . . . . (p. 127)

In this scenario, the children are exposed to the steps of listing observations, formulating a question, and identifying possible sources of information. These steps are not confined to elementary instruction, and you can probably think of experiences on the college level in which the professor has provided an analogous example. For instance, in college-level science courses you are encouraged to go through the same three steps. Your chemistry professor probably will talk you through conducting an experiment as instruction for preparing for what might occur.

Mental modeling is a powerful technique that is on a high cognitive level. Precisely for that reason, it is something that you should try to use with your students at every opportunity. But practice first! The keys to using this technique are modeling thinking that your students can understand and then providing them with immediate opportunities to apply what they have learned. Having your students explain their own mental models or "I wonder . . ." models aloud will help clarify the process for them and allow you to assess their understanding. Activity 2.2 (from Culyer, 1989) will give you some practice in developing this skill.

discovery learning An approach to instruction that focuses on students' personal experiences as the foundation for conceptual development. Students are expected and assisted to use their prior knowledge as a basis for making inferences and drawing conclusions.

Discovery

Discovery learning is an approach to instruction that focuses on students' personal experiences as the foundation for conceptual development. It is unlikely that children will walk into your classroom with all of the necessary experiences that relate to the concepts you want to teach. So your challenge is to *provide* your students with the experiences they need in the context of discovery—allowing them

---

ACTIVITY 2.2
Developing Inference Questions

Read the following passage and answer the questions that follow. Explain how you figured out the answer. The first question is done for you.

> My teacher this year expected us to correct all of the mistakes we made in our schoolwork. When we missed examples on our homework, we had to rework them. We had to learn to spell any words we wrote wrong. If we missed math problems, we had to do them over too. If we labeled our maps wrong, she gave us another sheet and told us to start over.
>
> Some people lost their papers before they corrected their errors. My teacher made them do the whole thing over. You can bet we learned a lesson from that experience.
>
> On my report card for the first nine weeks I made a lot of low grades. That was the term I lost a lot of my papers. For the last three terms I made all A's and B's. I always returned my corrected papers the day after I got them. I also had a loose-leaf notebook with sections for each of my subjects in school.
>
> My parents are going to talk to the principal later this week. I know it's not about me. It's about my brother, who is a year younger than I am. He doesn't want them to go, of course. You know why.

1. In paragraph 2, what lesson did the student learn? (The mental model: I can tell the student learned a

lot of things, but I have to think just about paragraph 2. The last sentence in that paragraph tells about learning a lesson from *that* experience. The experience was losing papers and having to do them over. I've never learned a lesson from losing papers, but I think I would learn something if I had to do them over. The thing I would learn is not to lose them or to do the work over right away. That's the answer that makes the most sense to me and is likely to be true. How do I know that I'm right? Because most students would not want to have to do their work a second time.)

Now answer questions 2 through 8, remembering to tell, by mental modeling, how you determined your response.

2. What does the teacher think of schooling?

3. What grade or grade range was the student most likely in?

4. When did the student correct mistakes on the papers?

5. Why did the writer have a notebook with a section for each subject?

6. What are the parents going to say to the principal?

7. Why doesn't the brother want them to go?

8. What kind of student is the brother?

to find the information for themselves by virtue of some activity you have provided. The students in your class will then share a common experience that you can develop as it relates to the concept under consideration. In essence, we are cheating just a bit because, from an instructional perspective, the children will discover what we *want* them to discover. It's new to them, of course, but it is all part of the strategy for the teacher.

Throughout life, whether in school or out, children seek to make sense of the world around them. To greater or lesser degrees, they are successful. The conclusions that a child draws may not be scientifically accurate, expressed in a grammatically correct manner, or mathematically defensible, but for the child they make sense. These are situations in which the child made observations and found satisfactory answers. Most importantly, the child came to his own conclusions rather than simply being told or shown that such and such is the case. The meaningful answers were those that the child discovered and conceptualized on his own.

Discovery learning channels the natural inquisitiveness of children (and the natural inquisitiveness that remains in adults) by providing structure to the experience without restricting the *thinking*. That is, unlike the science experiments that you did in high school that were "wrong" if they didn't come out the way the book said they should, discovery learning encourages children to engage in the activity and document what does happen.

Even with structured activities in the classroom, 20 students will experience the activity in 20 different ways. Because of that, for discovery learning to be pedagogically sound it must be structured beyond the discovery phase of the exercise. Such a structure, or framework, is intended to clarify the experience in terms of the concept being taught. The four-phase learning cycle in Figure 2.4 (from Atkins & Karplus, 1962) offers one such framework.

Inquiry

inquiry A sophisticated technique that attempts to engage students in generating relevant and meaningful questions about the topic under consideration.

We have placed **inquiry** at the highest level of our taxonomy because it not only involves the use of prior knowledge and the discovery of new knowledge, it also involves *generating the question* to be answered. It is no coincidence that the tendency to ask questions is characteristic of children as well as of adults at the top of their professions. Scientists, professors, writers, politicians, and others are people who frame questions and then go about finding solutions. Children, with that natural curiosity, also are compelled to ask questions, and they take delight in finding answers. The task for professional educators is to channel that inquisitiveness to be

Figure 2.4

The Four-Phase Learning Cycle

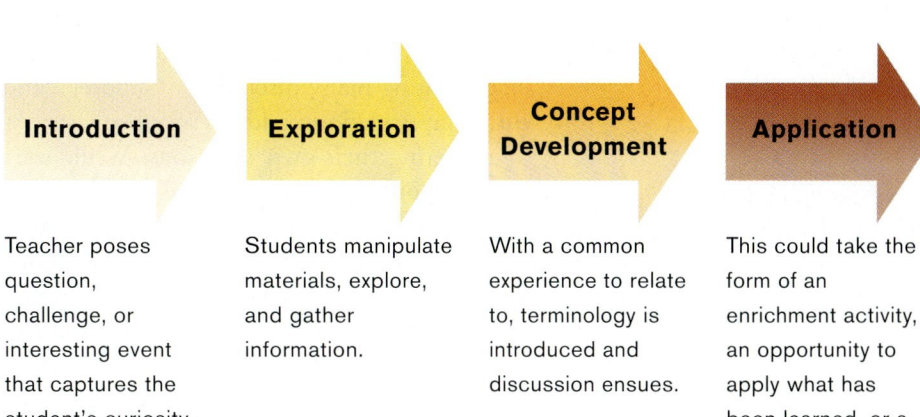

Introduction	Exploration	Concept Development	Application
Teacher poses question, challenge, or interesting event that captures the student's curiosity.	Students manipulate materials, explore, and gather information.	With a common experience to relate to, terminology is introduced and discussion ensues.	This could take the form of an enrichment activity, an opportunity to apply what has been learned, or a test to assess learning.

ACTIVITY 2.3
Applying the Various Instructional Techniques

This activity is best conducted during classroom observation. However, if you are not currently in an observation, practicum, or field service, complete this activity with regard to your college classes.

1. Observe several different teachers (or professors) and identify their instructional techniques. If you see a combination of techniques in one lesson, be sure to note each. The techniques discussed in the chapter are listed below:

Direct instruction	Drill and practice	Lecture	Question and answer
Discussion	Mental modeling	Inquiry	Discovery learning

2. Of the different instructional techniques you observed, was there one that you preferred? If so, what about it did you like?

3. Choose one of the classes you observed and explain how the lesson would be conducted using a different instructional technique. What might the new technique accomplish in terms of student involvement in the lesson? What advantages and disadvantages do you see to changing from the observed technique to the new technique?

---

beneficial to the individual and perhaps even to the world at large. Suddenly our discussion has come a long way from rudimentary direct instruction. Teaching changes lives, and it changes the world!

The teacher who uses an inquiry approach has a considerable amount of preparation to do and also must be prepared to teach the students how to use inquiry. A student using inquiry must be guided to frame a question in a manner that can be investigated. For example, what would your response be if a child were to ask, "Why do birds fly?" Would you say that birds fly because it's faster than walking? Because they enjoy being in the air? Just *because? Why* birds fly is a legitimate question but one likely to be addressed by theologians or philosophers. Perhaps your student will take on that consideration one day. For now, a more appropriate question might be "*How* do birds fly?" This is a question that can be investigated in the context of school. Students could even investigate what factors allow one type of bird to fly faster or higher than another or, in the case of ostriches and chickens, not at all. Helping to frame an appropriate question, without diminishing the validity of the initial question, is a primary challenge the teacher faces.

One strength of the inquiry approach is that it can integrate the curriculum by incorporating many disciplines. Children can read, write, calculate, engage in scientific investigations, address social concerns, and utilize the arts, all in the context of answering their own questions. While the amount of lecturing that a teacher does is significantly reduced, the intellectual challenge for a teacher preparing and conducting such activities is considerable, and considerably rewarding.

A teacher may use combinations of all of the techniques we have discussed in the course of a single lesson. A lesson plan may begin with a question-and-answer session that stimulates student interest and thinking, proceed to a discovery learning experience, and conclude with a discussion of what was learned. It is important for you to understand that teaching is a task that requires considerable instructional flexibility, and we still have not even considered the topic of knowing the subject matter!

The obvious implication of our taxonomy of instructional techniques is that before a teacher selects from these various techniques, he must first be in command of each. The not-so-obvious fact is that as simple as some of these techniques may sound, implementing them as part of an overall strategy is something that has to be practiced. These techniques do, in fact, represent a repertoire of skills for teaching. See Activity 2.3, Applying the Various Instructional Techniques, for an opportunity to take a single topic and fashion a presentation using a variety of these approaches. Which of them seem to best suit your own style?

Before we leave the topic of instructional techniques, consider one other aspect of the taxonomy we have provided. You may have already noticed that the first three levels represent approaches in which the teacher does the most talking or directing of student activity. The middle two levels transition to a dialogic approach in which the teacher and student share more of a partnership. The teacher continues to direct the activity, if only by having planned the whole experience, but the exchange of ideas is of central concern with these levels.

But what happens as we move to mental modeling and the levels beyond? Do you see how the emphasis changes now to the thinking that students will do? At these levels students are not only investigating academic topics but ultimately are asking their own questions and finding ways to seek answers and solve problems. You have probably heard that education is a process that seeks to develop lifelong learners. The teacher who uses all levels of the taxonomy with an eye toward leading students to these highest levels and allowing them to develop their critical and creative thinking abilities will be the teacher whose students develop that love of learning that we all wish to impart. Figure 2.5 summarizes the taxonomy of instructional techniques.

Figure 2.5

The Taxonomy of Instructional Techniques

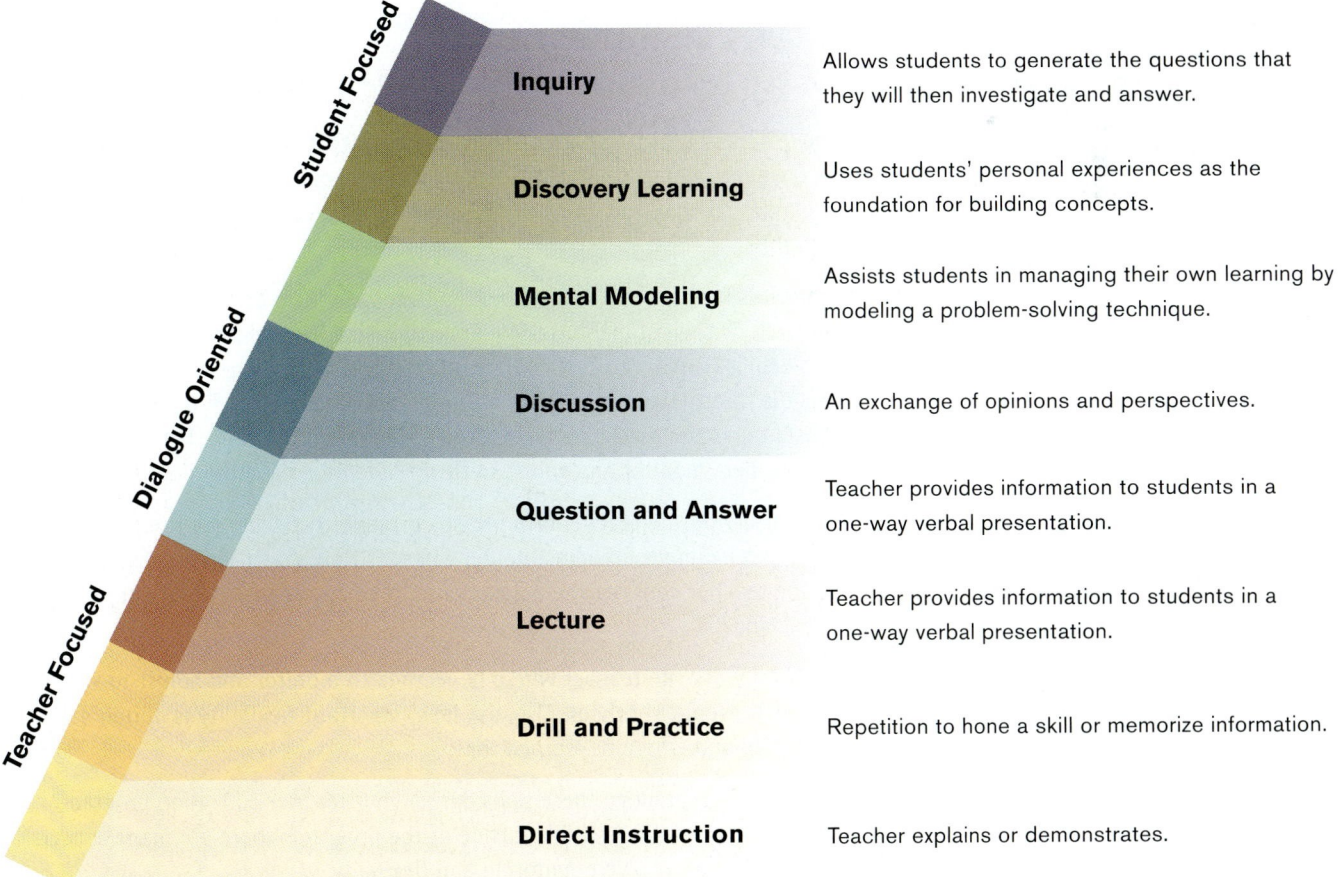

Inquiry	Allows students to generate the questions that they will then investigate and answer.
Discovery Learning	Uses students' personal experiences as the foundation for building concepts.
Mental Modeling	Assists students in managing their own learning by modeling a problem-solving technique.
Discussion	An exchange of opinions and perspectives.
Question and Answer	Teacher provides information to students in a one-way verbal presentation.
Lecture	Teacher provides information to students in a one-way verbal presentation.
Drill and Practice	Repetition to hone a skill or memorize information.
Direct Instruction	Teacher explains or demonstrates.

Student Focused · Dialogue Oriented · Teacher Focused

Monitoring and Flexibility

Facilitating learning requires extensive preparation of educational plans. Deciding upon a format for arranging the educational experience and selecting the most appropriate technique(s) for presenting the lesson constitutes the foundation work that any teacher must do to present a lesson. In the course of your own educational experiences you have been in classes with teachers who have prepared this founda-

monitoring Observing student academic and social behavior, both individually and collectively, during a variety of activities.

Courtesy of Guilherme Cunha

tion to greater or lesser degrees, and no doubt you have been able to tell the difference. Key to becoming an effective teacher will be your ability to make the concerns we have discussed here a part of your typical routine for planning educational experiences.

The good news is that a foundation based upon what has been presented thus far will assist the development of effective educational opportunities for your students. The bad news (and it's really not bad news, just some additional news) is that there are two more considerations to keep in mind. One of those is **monitoring.**

It would be foolish for us to suggest that you can put together a plan that simply could not fail. Teaching is an interpersonal concern, and you simply cannot know for certain the attitudes, moods, and recent experiences that your students will bring to the classroom on any given day. Therefore, as you implement the plan that you've developed, it will also be necessary to mon-

Effective monitoring not only tells a teacher what the students are doing but also helps the teacher decide how best to proceed with a lesson.

 Field Observation

ACTIVITY 2.4   **Observing How Teachers Adjust**

If you have access to a school classroom, this activity will be easy to accomplish. If you don't, we recommend that you sit in on a class on campus that is not one of your regular classes so that you can pay attention to the *teaching* rather than what is being *taught.*

1. Strange as it may seem, teachers often become a little anxious when people who are not their students sit in class and take a lot of notes. So, before the class begins, explain to the teacher what you will be doing. In this activity the object is to observe things that happen in class and to watch as the teacher adjusts to circumstances. Even if it seems as though "nothing happened" that day, teachers monitor and adjust to their students on a continuous basis.

2. After observing the teacher or professor, arrange to discuss your notes with him. What examples of adjusting did you see? How major did it seem to you? Did the teacher consider the adjustments to be out of the ordinary or just part of teaching?

3. Specifically ask the teacher where he learned to monitor and adjust to students and events at school. Also, ask how important flexibility is during a school day and where he learned that.

4. How could you practice these skills during your teacher education program? *Note:* Don't be afraid to think outside of the program—there are many aspects of your life that involve monitoring and flexibility.

itor the progress of that lesson. Is it going smoothly? Are the students receptive? Do they appear to be learning? Is this experience appropriate? Is this technique working? Are there student needs that you did not account for adequately? And all of this, of course, is something you do while also teaching the lesson.

flexibility The ability to make adaptations or major changes in diagnostic, instructional, or evaluative procedures based on an awareness of student behavior. It depends on careful monitoring.

Whether or not the monitoring you do is effective will be represented in terms of the adjustments *you* make. **Flexibility** is a virtue that all effective teachers have cultivated to a high degree. For example, if you get into a car and turn the key, only to be met by that dreaded silence of a dead battery, no amount of turning the key will overcome the basic facts. You'll have to do something else to start the car, or find alternative transportation, or cancel your plans. So too with teaching. If the information you receive from monitoring indicates that changes need to be made, it is imperative that (1) you are willing to make them and (2) you are capable of making them. A lesson that isn't working is lost time. It's that simple.

Flexibility is what saves the day. You may even find yourself in a situation in which discontinuing the lesson and moving on to something else will be an appropriate course of action. Put that instructional time to efficient use and devise another strategy for teaching the lesson that just couldn't take off. Monitoring and flexibility are the tools a teacher uses to maintain the momentum of learning. It takes a keen eye to observe how teachers monitor and adjust during a lesson. Follow the format provided in Activity 2.4, Observing How Teachers Adjust, in order to see this subtle skill in action.

■ Modeling

Modeling? How does that figure into a strategy for teaching? Well, that's a good question. Think back for a moment to one or two of your best teachers. Did you ever notice that he never seemed to have a bad day? His dog never died. Stress was not a problem. He never had sour milk in his breakfast cereal. And though you may have come to class a time or two with tales of woe explaining why your homework wasn't done, you got the feeling that those calamities never seemed to befall him. Well, it just wasn't true. Teachers are people, and they have the same problems that other people have. However, as with folks in show business, when it's time for class to begin, personal problems, concerns, sadnesses (and sometimes gladnesses) are left outside. The class must go on!

Are Teachers Role Models?

role models Those who engage in personal and professional behavior that provides an opportunity for students to observe desirable characteristics in practice.

What is really happening here involves an undeniable aspect of teaching: Teachers are **role models.** At the very least they model an attitude toward learning that includes the joy of discovery as well as an understanding of how difficult discovery can be. They model the idea that learning is worthwhile. Your best teachers made dull subjects (were there any dull subjects?) come alive by virtue of their enthusiasm for what they were doing. It is likely that few, if any, of your really good teachers modeled despair, discontent, and disinterest. And that left an impression on you, didn't it? We include role modeling as an education strategy because as a teacher you will teach lessons to students simply as a function of who you are. Students, to varying degrees, will want to be like you. Those desires will be based on the model that you provide every time you interact with them in school or away from the classroom.

We qualified our comments by saying "at the very least" these are things modeled by teachers. We did that because the debate over teachers as role models is by

Go Online!

ACTIVITY 2.5   Are Teachers Role Models?

There are at least two aspects to the question of teachers as role models. One is whether they are responsible for modeling particular behaviors, attitudes, and beliefs at school. Another is whether they are responsible for being role models for the students away from school.

1. What attitudes, behaviors, and beliefs do you think schools should expect their teachers to model?

2. Should teachers be expected to model these behaviors on their own time and away from school? What is your opinion?

3. Take a poll in your class with regard to items 1 and 2. Is there a consensus among your classmates? If there is, summarize the opinion of the class as a "policy statement." Don't be surprised, however, if opinions differ and consensus is difficult to achieve.

4. Use the Internet to find current commentary on this issue. Search terms such as "teachers as role models" will get you started. How does the information you have found affect the opinion that you began with? How does it compare with the thinking in your class?

no means insignificant. Activity 2.5, Are Teachers Role Models?, asks you to take a position and then investigate the opposing point of view because from either perspective you would not be alone. The question of whether teachers are role models, and, if so, what they should model is one that has evolved with the progress of our open and multiethnic culture.

Take a look at the teacher's contract presented in Figure 2.6. This is not a piece of fiction but rather the expectations for a young teacher entering the profession around 1915. The contract was reprinted in *The Cracker Barrel Journal* (Fall 1995).

The items about starting the fire and scrubbing the floor regularly may not be germane to our discussion, but the items about how the teacher was to conduct herself, in and out of school, certainly are. From American education's Puritan beginnings as Bible-study lessons taught by the preacher's wife, appropriate behavior and moral principles have been integral to the message of formal education.

Your actions as a teacher, your beliefs, sense of humor, self-discipline, bearing, and demeanor are all lessons that are presented to students throughout the educational experience. Albert Bandura's landmark work with social learning theory (1986) places great emphasis on the impact of observing and imitating a model in the development of behaviors. We can expect that children will imitate and internalize those behaviors that they observe as being valued and rewarded. For example, if it seems that a teacher who acts in a particular manner is well-liked by students and colleagues, the student will likely imitate those observed behaviors. This is reflected in the expectations that schools have for their teachers.

As a teacher in a public or private school, you can anticipate that the school will expect you to model behaviors such as self-control, good grooming, a good work ethic (valuing work, punctuality, preparedness, following the rules, etc.), and placing a value on learning. Furthermore, you may also be expected to model ideologies such as being pro-democracy, accepting of cultural diversity, and maintain-

A Teacher's Contract in the Good Old Days

Truly, the lifestyle of a school teacher has changed radically. For example, a 1915 teacher's magazine listed the following rules of conduct for teachers of that day.

- You will not marry during the term of the contract.
- You are not to keep company with men.
- You must be home between the hours of 8 p.m. and 6 a.m. unless attending a school function.
- You may not loiter downtown in any of the ice cream stores.
- You may not travel beyond the city limits unless you have the permission of the chairman of the board.
- You may not ride in a carriage or automobile with any man unless he is your father or brother.
- You may not smoke cigarettes.
- You may under no circumstances dye your hair.
- You must wear at least two petticoats.
- Your dresses must not be shorter than two inches above your ankle.

To keep the school room neat and clean, you must, scrub the floor at least once a week with hot, soapy water, clean the blackboards at least once a day, start the fire at 7 a.m. so the room will be warm at 8 a.m.

Figure 2.6

Teacher Contract

ing a high moral standard. Whether or not explicitly stated within the curriculum, these are lessons that schools bring to the students. The teacher who encourages his students not to recite the Pledge of Allegiance, albeit on defensible grounds, will likely find himself at odds with the district and the community. The teacher who habitually arrives late for work probably will not have his contract renewed. Teachers are not expected to be surrogate parents, but they are—without question—role models of one sort or another to their students.

Are Teachers Role Models Away from School?

There is another compelling side to the role-model issue, and it is one that we cannot resolve in a few pages of this text. However, it is an issue that you must include in your consideration of a teaching profession. The simple version of the question is: Are teachers role models *away* from school? Based on what has been presented thus far, the obvious answer is "yes." Students—and this applies to students anywhere along the educational continuum—delight in seeing their teachers away from school. Their expectations, however, remain the same. Seeing the teacher who is always neatly dressed at school now loading bags of mulch into his car at the local gardening shop will be a cognitive stretch for the child. Since gardening is not something on the list of improper behaviors in a child's mind, the experience will likely just require a cognitive assimilation. This could actually be a good expansion of the child's view of the world.

However, seeing a teacher purchase alcoholic beverages at the local grocery store or appearing tipsy at a community function will leave a different impression.

The question, therefore, is whether teachers are *responsible* for modeling particular behaviors even when away from school? Is this a fair expectation?

Whether or not it is fair, you will find that the expectation is widely held. Many a teacher has lost his job because of behavior completely removed from school, but which the community does not endorse as appropriate for an educator. This is a delicate issue that involves one's personal rights as well as the concerns of a community (society) that has entrusted its children to the influence of the teachers it has hired. Keep in mind, as you consider this issue, that children typically do not get involved in the philosophical and political aspects of these deliberations. The teacher is "the teacher."

Perhaps a personal experience (which will also explain the quotation beginning Chapter 1) will demonstrate this point. While teaching in China one semester, we found that both in class and away from campus, graduate students typically displayed utmost courtesy toward their professors. They would hold doors open, wait for the professor to be served in a restaurant before being served themselves, and so on. There came a time, however, when the semester had ended and the students had graduated from the program. While walking into a restaurant one day to celebrate graduation, one of the students hastened to open the door for the professor, and the others waited for him to enter the building. The professor said, "You are graduates now, and we're colleagues. You need not wait for me." Without hesitation, the student at the door quietly said, "You will always be my teacher." There is something very special about being a teacher.

 Conclusion

Our look at the practice of teaching has emphasized the following major points.

1. Effective teaching includes a strategic nature that involves techniques for facilitating learning, monitoring and flexibility, and modeling.
2. The four approaches to arranging instructional experiences to bring the world to the classroom are classroom lessons, multimedia presentations, guest speakers, and field trips.
3. When designing appropriate lessons, teachers choose from eight instructional techniques: direct instruction, drill and practice, lecture, question and answer, discussion, mental modeling, discovery, and inquiry.
4. Part of any teacher's strategic repertoire is the ability to monitor the progress of the class and the flexibility to make adjustments based on those observations.
5. Teachers are, to one degree or another, role models. The question of how much responsibility a teacher bears for being a role model away from school relates to one's concept of professional ethics.

Key Terms

strategy	question and answer	discovery learning
direct instruction	divergent thinking	inquiry
drill and practice	convergent thinking	monitoring
lecture	discussion	flexibility
reflection	mental modeling	role models

Educational Engineering

Case Studies in Education

Enter the information from the following table into the Educational Record for the student you are studying.

	Instructional Techniques to Which the Child Responds	**Response to Role Models**
Davon	Davon responds to hands-on activities and is a super listener both in whole group and small group settings. He listens well during instruction and is quick to answer and share what he knows. You can hear how proud he is of himself in his tone as he eagerly shouts out answers.	Davon is not easily influenced by his peers. He shows a natural desire to be successful and have his peers notice. He shares with his peers and looks for acceptance from them. He appears to try to win his peers over by lending a helping hand without being asked.
Andy	Andy states that he learns best while listening but this is not the case. Has difficulty focusing on discussion and directions. Works well in small groups but has to be monitored to stay on task. Peer tutor provides extra support and modeling Andy needs to complete assignments.	Andy is easily influenced by his peers. He feeds off of the disruptive behaviors of several students in his classroom. Regardless of that, he desires to please his teachers and is contrite when in trouble.
Judith	Judith responds best to hands-on situations. She prefers to work with others, though the feeling is not necessarily mutual. Extensive repetition helps her to memorize, though it does not necessarily equate with understanding.	Judith imitates peer behaviors that might lead to acceptance. She respects her teachers and quickly senses which teachers will respond to her with warmth.
Tiffany	Tiffany prefers working alone and becomes anxious in partner or team activities. When in groups, she is viewed as bossy and uncooperative with other students. She gets upset and emotional when she feels her statements are not being acknowledged.	Tiffany's role models are primarily teachers she has had in class. She believes that whatever the teacher says is the absolute truth and never disagrees. She holds most teachers in the highest regard and will defend them to other students. She will repeat phrases and dialogue that she has heard from teachers and argue with anyone who may disagree with her point of view.
Sam	Sam has developed compensatory skills to adapt to various instructional techniques. The most effective teaching strategy for him is a multisensory approach. He is most productive and concentrates best when working alone with minimal distractions.	Sam responds well to positive role models and is not easily misled or influenced by others. He has a strong sense of right and wrong, and no history of behavior problems in school. If he anticipates a potential problem with a classmate, he will consult with a teacher or other adult about his concern.
Bao	Bao is extremely social, so she always prefers to work with friends. In groups, she tends to talk about irrelevant topics while doing all the work, and then allows her group members to copy her work. She also does well with independent work, but dislikes most hands-on learning because she dislikes having to construct meaning. She enjoys lectures because she likes to take notes and has strong recall of information that is given to her.	Bao does imitate those she admires, but always chooses role models that are "safe" and unquestionable. Therefore she emulates teachers, peers, adults, and pop icons who are popular but innocuous, and steers clear of ones who drink, do drugs, are sexually permissive, or challenge the status quo.

1. Based on the information provided, to which of the instructional techniques does your student best respond? Which of the instructional techniques discussed in the chapter do you feel most suit your own style and personality? Do your preferences match well with the learning preferences of your student? If they do, do you think you should expand your student's learning styles, or should you stick to his or her preferences as they are? If your preferences and your student's do not match, how might you strengthen your abilities in the techniques your student prefers?

2. Unlike learning instructional techniques, role modeling is something that is very much a part of who you are as a person. Not all students will see you as a model of the person they want to become, but many will to one degree or another. From what you have learned about your student and what you know of yourself at this early point in your teaching career, what will this student learn from you beyond academics? If you saw this student at the grocery store or in a shopping mall, would you maintain your "teacher" demeanor? What responsibility, if any, do you feel to be a role model for this student?

Designing the School of the Future

The sorts of experiences that a school will provide to its students, the instructional techniques that characterize the school and its teachers, and the attitudes, behaviors, and beliefs that the teachers model all coalesce to form the "culture" of a school. You can sense elements of that culture immediately upon entering a school. Some schools are bright and inviting while others can be dark and difficult to navigate. As you consider the school of the future, decide how the topics discussed in this chapter will characterize your school. "The whole is greater than the sum of its parts" is an excellent description of schools.

1. How will your school "bring the world" to its students? To what degree will your school rely on (a) classroom instruction, (b) multimedia presentations, (c) guest speakers, and (d) field trips? What other experiences should be included but don't fall within these four categories? Which, if any, of the categories for arranging educational experiences could you completely do without? Write a *vision statement* (that is, a statement of what your school aspires to become) that addresses the manner in which your school will address these four categories.

2. Will your school be characterized by particular instructional techniques, or will that be left to the individual teacher? For instance, some schools are inquiry-based, and so all teachers utilize an inquiry approach for all subjects. Other schools may emphasize direct instruction along with drill and practice. Colleges and universities, of course, traditionally emphasize lecture. What will be the situation in your school of the future? Explain the reasoning behind whatever approach you decide to take. What will be the educational benefits to the students of using the technique(s) you have identified? As an administrator, would you hire teachers based on their ability to use those particular techniques?

3. As the final component in establishing the basic theme or culture of your school, what will be your expectations of teachers with regard to role modeling? Remember, the attitudes, behaviors, and beliefs that teachers model are typically not part of the lessons students must learn for graduation. So, role

modeling becomes a matter of regional or local values. Would you hire (and perhaps fire) teachers based on the role model they present? Would you deny a job to a qualified teacher because he does not "look" the way you want teachers to look? What will people in the community say when they speak of the teachers at your school?

Praxis Practice

Many states will require that you successfully complete the Praxis Series of examinations to qualify for certification. One or more of those tests will be subject-area tests. Another, which has a more practical orientation, will be the Principles of Learning and Teaching (PLT) examination that is appropriate for your certification area.

Completing the Quick Check Quizzes for Chapter 2 in the Unit Workshop will give you practice with the multiple-choice format of the PLT. The Case Studies in Education and Designing a School of the Future activities will help prepare you for exercises that require reading a scenario and providing short answers to questions asking what you might do in such a situation.

3

Student Diversity

Photo: © Blend Images/SuperStock

Eye on the Standards
INTASC

ice breakers

What's Your Style?

To get some insight about your learning style, read the statements below and circle the number for each one that seems to describe you. You can circle as many as you like.

1. You stare into space while trying to think of an answer.
2. You like to record information and play it until you learn it.
3. As a child you traced or copied letters to learn them.
4. You learn a lot by listening as other people provide information.
5. You remember things by singing (for example, the alphabet song or new songs).
6. On a test you can "see" where the information is in a book.
7. You jot down ideas to remember them (and even after misplacing the paper, you still remember some of them).
8. You hear a song and remember interesting or repeated parts of the words or music.
9. You remember information by saying it aloud (for example, poetry, the Gettysburg Address).
10. You close your eyes to "see" something in your mind.
11. You like to draw or paint.
12. You practice talking aloud when preparing a speech or comments to someone.
13. You notice many features in a picture, graph, diagram, or other illustration.
14. You like to sketch out written math problems.
15. You pay attention to and follow oral directions well.
16. You talk to yourself as you do something (for example, verbalizing the steps to be accomplished).
17. Instead of reading a story, you prefer to hear it discussed by the group.
18. You proofread your work by reading it aloud.
19. In math you follow the written examples for solving a problem.
20. You write a word you can't spell to see what your hand "says."

21. You like to learn by reading.

22. You remember things better if you write them down.

23. You remember a new term or idea when a teacher explains it.

24. You read difficult material aloud to help you to understand it.

Use the guide below to identify your strongest learning preferences. Circle the item numbers that you marked from the list of statements. Then count up the number of circled items you have in each category. Your strongest preference will be for the style that has the most circled items. You may find that you have strong preferences in two or more categories.

Preference	Visual	Auditory	Kinesthetic	Vocalic
Items:	1 6 10 13 19 21	2 4 8 15 17 23	3 7 11 14 20 22	5 9 12 16 18 24
Number of circled items:				

This chapter will discuss learning preferences and many other factors that account for the diversity among students.

> *Treat students as individuals whose identities are complex and unique.*
> *R. Freeland (1998)*

■ Introduction

diversity The ways in which individuals and groups differ from each other.

Have you ever found anyone who was exactly like you? Of course not. Even though there may be some people who are a little like you or even a lot like you, the fact remains that you are unique. A set of special qualities and characteristics is what makes each of us special and makes the world a richer place.

As a teacher you will encounter **diversity** in the classroom, just as you did (and do) as a student. The difference is that you will be on the other side of the desk, and the challenges and opportunities will be different in some ways. One of your most important challenges will be in coming face to face with the many ways in which students differ. Recognizing and appreciating those differences is important if you are to provide learning opportunities that are compatible with students' needs. To illustrate, in a report entitled *The Schools We Have: The Schools We Want*, James Nehring (1992) summarizes, "We assume . . . that all kids are the same. . . . We force all kids through the same mold. If there is one thing on which both research and common sense agree, it is that kids are not the same" (p. 156). A joint position statement of the International Reading Association and the National Association for the Education of Young Children (1998) makes the same point: Experienced teachers throughout the United States report that the children they teach today are more diverse in their backgrounds, experiences, and abilities than were those they taught in the past (pp. 196–197). Even siblings differ, sometimes dramatically.

■ General Ways in Which Students Differ

Let's consider just a few of the many ways in which your students will differ. Hopefully you will consider these differences as you study subject area and methods courses, for you should understand that one size doesn't fit all.

Culture, Ethnicity, and Race

Often the first things that come to mind when discussing student diversity are differences in culture, ethnicity, and race. As you will discover in this chapter, these are just a few of many factors that will make each of your students unique. However, appreciating and accommodating differences in this category are particularly important within our diverse American culture.

culture The values, attitudes, and beliefs that influence the behavior and the traditions of a people. They are social, not biological, dimensions.

Culture represents the values, attitudes, and beliefs that influence the behavior and the traditions of a people. Notice that these are social, not biological, dimensions. Even though people often label others according to physical features, culture is actually a matter of commonly held ideas. A chief purpose of schooling has been passing on the traditions of the society. Education has been the means by which people came to understand their heritage and the attitudes, behaviors, and beliefs the society valued.

In the United States, however, many cultures are represented within our American culture. As a result, diversity is also considered in terms of *race,* though that word is a misnomer. If you check with the biology professor on your campus you will find that among human beings there is only one race—*homo sapiens.* The differences you were thinking of as race are actually differences of **ethnicity.** James Banks (1994) defines ethnicity as a sense of common identity based upon common ancestral background and the sharing of common values and beliefs. That sounds a lot like culture, though *ancestral background* implies another dimension. In discussing ethnic minorities, Banks (1997) qualifies the definition to say that ethnicity involves "unique physical and/or cultural characteristics that enable individuals who belong to other ethnic groups to identify its members easily, often for discriminatory purposes" (p. 66). That same biology professor whom we mentioned a moment ago will probably go on to say that there is actually more biological diversity *within* an ethnicity than there is *across* ethnicities. The bottom line? We are far more alike than we are different.

ethnicity Sense of common identity based upon common ancestral background and the sharing of common values and beliefs.

Seen in a broader perspective, these definitions show that while a culture *might* be characterized by a particular ethnicity, one culture (such as the American culture) could actually include people from many ethnicities. The result is a culture that has been evolving since the United States was founded. There are several metaphors that try to explain our unique culture. Two of the most prevalent are the *melting pot* and the *salad bowl.*

The period 1820–1920 was one in which America wrestled mightily with the overwhelming desire of people to emigrate from their home countries in favor of a life in the United States. Laws were written and rewritten (and some, thankfully, repealed) to control the influx, which at one point reached as many as a million people per year. And through the early part of the 20th century up to the years following World War I, people came to America *to become Americans.* The metaphor was that the United States was a cultural melting pot. In this view, many cultures combined to form a new culture. That new culture, though often changing—evolving—was distinctly different from the cultures that went into the mix. More

multiculturalism The social psychology perspective of how various cultural groups interface with each other.

cultural pluralism Acceptance of and interaction between multiple cultures in one society.

importantly, becoming an American meant relinquishing much of one's prior culture (though not their heritage) to become a part of this new culture.

In the latter half of the 20th century and with great acceleration in the past 25 years, the metaphor has changed as the U.S. Constitution has stood the test of time and been interpreted in light of many unique and unanticipated circumstances. The emerging cultural conscience shifted from the desire to *be* American in favor of being of another culture *in* America. The "salad bowl" metaphor came into vogue, and the social psychology of **multiculturalism** was born. The salad bowl has an identity as a particular sort of salad, but the various ingredients do not lose their individual identity as a result of being mixed with the other ingredients. The salad bowl metaphor more recently came to reflect the notion of **cultural pluralism,** the acceptance of and interaction between multiple cultures in one society.

The history of education in the United States has been greatly influenced by a predominantly Caucasian Western European perspective on culture. As a result, the mission of schools in the 19th century and early 20th century tended toward "Americanizing" students by overcoming cultural characteristics reflective of minority ethnic populations. Though contemporary schools seek to promote, value, and integrate the various cultures into all phases of the curriculum (curriculum will be considered in detail in Chapters 5 and 6), you can see from Table 3.1 that as late as the year 2000 there existed an overwhelming disparity in ethnic representation between teachers and students. Unfortunately, minorities are not entering the profession in sufficiently large numbers to change the demographics shown in the table (Duarte, 2000).

Moreover, by 2003 the Census Bureau noted that 18 percent of the students enrolled in school were Hispanic, and that it was the fastest-growing school population (Rolon, 2005). Meier (2003) noted that "by the year 2020 students of color will represent the majority of students in 18 states including California, Texas, Florida, and New Mexico."

All of this has implications for your work as a teacher, for in the 21st century it is necessary for you to do more than just "appreciate" the diverse cultures that will be represented in your classroom. The multiethnic nature of the school population will require that you *understand* how culture affects the way children learn. No, this is not a discussion of the biological functioning of the brain but instead a matter of how different cultures engage in social interactions.

For example, Native American children tend to speak softly and avoid looking authority figures in the eye (Manning & Baruth, 1996). The classroom teacher who is not attuned to this and demands that her students "speak up" and "look at me when I'm talking to you" is not necessarily encountering a recalcitrant child. It could simply be that the child has been taught to demonstrate respect for the teacher in another way. Many behaviors could be misinterpreted by a teacher who

Table 3.1	Ethnic Representation in Public Schools 1999–2000	
Ethnicity	**Percentage of Teachers**	**Percentage of Students**
White, non-Hispanic	84.32%	61.2%
Black, non-Hispanic	7.58	17.2
Hispanic	5.63	16.3
Asian or Pacific Islander	1.61	4.1
American Indian or Alaska Native	0.86	1.2

(Digest of Education Statistics, 2002, 2003, pp. 58, 80)

is insensitive to cultural differences among students; this applies to teachers of any ethnic background. Let's consider some aspects of the broad range of ethnic diversity among students. We must caution you, however, not to take this overview of cultural diversity as a descriptor for every child who enters your classroom. For instance, the African American population accounts for approximately 13 percent of the national population, yet within that 13 percent there exists wide cultural and ancestral diversity. Similarly, a reference to a "Western European" perspective refers to people of many different nationalities and cultural origins. No matter what ethnicity one speaks of, each child is a unique individual.

African American Students

The cultural background that African American students bring to the classroom is a complex blend of ancestral heritage, hundreds of years of enslavement in this country, and more than a century of struggle to realize equal opportunity and membership in the society we live in today. Without question, this must be expected to have an effect on both identity development and achievement of young people within a system founded on a Western European curriculum.

Franklin (1992) notes that years of enslavement and oppression (pre– and post–American Civil War) have left the African American culture with a set of core values: resistance, freedom, self-determination, and education. Each of these values plays a part in school achievement and in the approach to school taken by many African Americans.

Though not confined only to the African American population, by about third grade African American students, particularly males, begin to show signs of underachievement, especially in math and science. Steele (1992) suggests that "blacks begin school with test scores that are fairly close to the test scores of whites their age. The longer they stay in school, however, the more they fall behind. . . . This pattern holds true for the middle class nearly as much as in the lower class. . . . [S]omething depresses black achievement at every level of preparation, even the highest" (pp. 68–69).

Whether this "something" happens *in* school or *as the result* of school is difficult to say. Jacqueline Jordan Irvine (1991) suggests that black students encounter a lack of *cultural synchronization,* an incompatibility between their own cultural norms and those they encounter within the school. Both the curriculum of the public schools and the culture within the school provide an experience more in keeping with that of the white majority than with that of any ethnic minority. The result: African American students may feel disenfranchised and detached from the "message" and values of school.

Add to this context the finding that in the past decade, the percentage of African-American students enrolled in predominantly white schools has markedly decreased. For instance, the percentage of African-Americans attending schools with white majorities decreased from 43 percent in 1988 to 35 percent in 2000. New York and Illinois were the most segregated states for African-Americans while Kentucky and Washington were the most integrated. Hispanic enrollment in predominantly minority schools increased from 42 percent attending minority schools in 1968 to 80 percent at the present time. For Hispanics, New York and California are the most segregated, and Wyoming and Ohio are the most integrated. This trend is referred to as resegregation (Orfield & Lee, 2004).

Nevertheless, in 21st-century curriculum materials you will find a far greater emphasis on the role that individuals from various ethnicities play and have played in the progress of our nation than would have been the case as recently as a decade ago. Still, culture—even school culture—is slow to change, and a school culture that truly infuses the diversity of ethnicities into the curriculum can evolve only slowly.

Combined with the approach of *acknowledging* diversity rather than *embracing* it, there are cultural traits that can be met with disapproval by teachers. Patricia Marshall (2002) refers to

> language patterns and personal presentation style as reflected in attire, body movements, and/or behavior patterns. Also, aspects of the cognitive/learning style predominant among black students often are incompatible with the preferred instructional styles of most teachers. For example, the information processing mode most common for Blacks emphasizes active and cooperative learning patterns whereas teachers traditionally focus on more individually oriented instruction. (p. 93)

To counteract the lack of cultural synchronization, Marshall (2002) suggests five measures teachers can take when working with African American students:

1. **Believe that all students can succeed.** This would seem an obvious expectation for teachers, but statistics indicate that African American students tend to be overrepresented in special education classes and underrepresented in programs for the academically gifted (Marshall, 2002). Teachers may assume below-average intelligence for African American students who perform below grade level on standardized achievement tests or who fail to acquire appropriate academic skills (note that the problem here is a perception of *poor general intelligence* based on academic performance—an assumption of intellectual capacity that is not based on appropriate diagnostic testing). Maintaining the belief that all children can succeed will encourage teachers to find the most appropriate instructional methods for each child rather than making unwarranted assumptions about ability.

2. **Promote multidimensional student development.** The essence of this suggestion is that teachers make the content of instruction relevant to the lives of the students in the classroom. This is likely something you have heard before, but the key point here is that much of the curriculum, the culture, of school can be seen as more relevant to one ethnic group than to another. The teacher is the catalyst through which the message must be made relevant to all students or—perhaps more precisely—to each student.

3. **Use cooperative learning activities.** As opposed to the more typical competition-based activities, cooperative activities encourage students to work toward common goals while demonstrating individual knowledge and abilities. One example of a cooperative activity is giving choral responses to questions posed by the teacher. This technique actively involves students and does so in a cooperative atmosphere.

4. **Recognize that no knowledge is sacrosanct.** Particularly in a curriculum that could offer conflicting cultural messages, students should be encouraged to critically consider knowledge, explanations, and the representation of events.

5. **Respect teaching as a profession and as an art.** Such teachers use a wide range of instructional techniques that actively engage students in the process of learning.

Certainly, you have noticed that these recommendations are sound for working with *all* students. What you may not have considered is that a teacher may well draw upon these skills and perspectives within a single classroom and during a single lesson to address the needs of each student appropriately and effectively.

Native American Students

As we consider the Native American culture, keep in mind that these are a people who neither were brought into a culture different from their own nor emigrated from another culture to become American. Rather, the Native American culture has been suppressed by a foreign people who were on foreign soil. Representations of "Indians" in the American culture have glorified the white conquest of an indigent nation and romanticized the Native Americans' place in our national history. Thus, they are a people who have no reason to give up their own culture in order to become something else.

It is difficult to shine a positive light on what was done to Native Americans over the past 400 years just as it is difficult to find a positive light on the treatment of other minority ethnic populations in our American history. Arthur Schlesinger (1998) writes: "We must face the shameful fact: historically America has been a racist nation. White Americans began as a people so arrogant in convictions of racial superiority that they felt licensed to kill red people, to enslave black people, and to import yellow and brown people for peon labor" (p. 18). Though the past cannot be undone, the eventual history of the 21st century can be very much affected by the lessons you learn from the past and by your subsequent work in the classroom.

Many Native American students consider the tribe or nation to which they belong as the primary referent for their identities and values. Deyhle (1995) suggests that in the Navajo culture, success is gauged in terms of the extent of intact family relationships, the degree to which one's work enhances the family and community, and group—as opposed to individual—accomplishment. These values are contrary to those of the Anglo population, which emphasizes individualism in terms of credentials, work, and prosperity. Deyhle writes, "Navajos have a more humble view of 'individual choice' which acknowledges both the dependence of the individual on the group and the importance of the extended family" (p. 425).

Given this situation, it is to be expected that Native American students could face the same lack of cultural synchronization that other groups do. Such children may not wish to be singled out within the classroom. They see themselves as equals with other students rather than being driven to achieve to a higher level. They may frequently use nonverbal means to express themselves (Chavers, 2000), thus being put off by the extensive verbal orientation characteristic of schools. (*Note:* Verbal ability—particularly written ability—is a challenge for many students. In this context, however, we specifically refer to a cultural *preference* for nonverbal communication that finds itself at odds with the typical school emphasis.)

By the third or fourth grade Native American students begin to decline academically compared with white students. Butterfield (1983) notes that the children "become quiet, withdrawn, and do not participate verbally in classroom activities" (p. 51). Not surprisingly, the dropout rate among Native Americans is very high. Differences in teaching strategies, combined with the disparity between "school culture" and Native American culture, are primary factors contributing to the dropout rate.

Successful teachers of Native American children will be attuned to teaching practices that complement the students' cultural background and will also be aware of the stereotypical way

The Native American culture emphasizes family and community rather than the individual.

© Spencer Grant/PhotoEdit

that "Indians" are often characterized in the curriculum. According to Marshall (2002): "The overall goal of successful school programs and teachers is to prepare Native American students for interactions within the larger society while at the same time encouraging them to maintain alliances with their own communities" (p. 208). To do this, teachers should demonstrate their respect for the Native American culture and use interaction patterns in their teaching that exemplify Native American cultural values. For example, teachers might direct questions to the group rather than to specific individuals and, similarly, temper praise that would single out students from the greater classroom community.

Asian Americans and Pacific Islander Students

As long ago as 1980 the U.S. Census Bureau used the name Asian Pacific Islander to identify the ethnic group often referred to as Asian Americans. The fastest growing segment of the U.S. population, Asian Pacific Americans represent a very wide range of regions and national origins. Trueba et al. (1993) identifies the following groups and their constituents:

East Asians: Chinese, Japanese, Korean, Filipino

Pacific Islanders: Fijian, Guamanian, Hawaiian, Marshall Islander, Melanesian, Paluauan, Samoan, Tahitian, Tongan, Trukese, Yapese

Southeast Asians: Hmong, Indonesian, Khmer, Lao, Malayan, Mien, Singaporean, Thai, Vietnamese

South Asians: Bangladeshi, Bhuanese, Burmese, Indian, Nepali, Pakistani, Sri Lankan, Sikimese.

Teacher Testimonial

Feature 3.1   Student Diversity

I didn't mean to lie. When asked if I was experienced in teaching diverse students, I said yes. I realized what diversity really meant, however, when I faced my fifth-grade class in Burkina Faso, West Africa. Our school of 100 students had over 40 nationalities represented. My class of 16 had students from Korea, Ghana, Germany, The Netherlands, France, the United States, Belgium, England, Israel, Nigeria, and Ethiopia. They held many different religious beliefs, had traveled all over the world, and had attended schools in many countries. Excited about teaching overseas, I didn't realize that the challenges to come would affect my entire teaching career.

Among the first things that struck me was the inappropriateness of the content of the textbook materials. The reading stories reminded me of *Leave it to Beaver* episodes that were not at all like the lives my students led, and the story problems in math seemed to be about life on a different planet. Africa was very different from Iowa. Compared to the wondrously diverse and culturally stimulating world my students experienced on a daily basis, the textbooks seemed boring and irrelevant. So, we turned to the library for books that suited their interests. Students brought in materials from their home countries and translated them for the class. We created our own readings and made up our own story problems and daily oral language sentences. We explored what was going on in Africa, Europe, and Asia during the American Revolution, the Roaring Twenties, the Great Depression, and the Vietnam War. Keeping to the school curriculum, we tailored the content to the interests and experiences of the students.

Finding ways to make the content more relevant to the students was exciting. What wasn't so easy was dealing with the cultural differences. Having never been out of the United States before, I had much to learn. I learned what hand to use when greeting my students and their parents. After I became frustrated at a student who refused to look me in the eyes, he taught me that he was looking down as a sign of respect. I learned to deal with the bold way some of my students were taught to deal with authority and the quiet reserved way of others. I soon learned to see each one as an individual with different beliefs, customs, and learned behaviors.

As you can see, just saying "Asian American" is to characterize this ethnicity in very general terms.

Asian Pacific Americans compose about 3 percent of the student population in U.S. schools (Poon-McBrayer & Garcia, 2000). In Hawaii, these students represent the majority of the school enrollment, and in California they constitute the second largest group after Hispanics (Gordon, 2000; Trueba et al., 1993). As you might expect, these students bring cultural values to the American scene that differ in some regards from the "traditional" western European values so prevalent in U.S. schools.

Asian Pacific American students often come from homes that promote reverence and respect for parents and other persons in authority, conformity, obedience, promotion of group goals over individual interests, humility, and "face-saving" (endeavoring to avoid dishonor). These students might also be expected to have a group orientation, connectedness with others, and interdependence rather than an inclination toward independence (Asakawa & Csikzentmihalyi, 2000; Uba, cited in Lecca et al., 1998). The influence of the family is also felt by students as the expectations for achievement in school can be very high. You will see evidence of this in Feature 3.1 as Cheryl Larson describes her experiences teaching in an international school. Education can be very much a family matter.

In the classroom, cultural behaviors of these students can be misinterpreted by teachers who are not attuned to such diversity (Cheng, 1987; Mathews, 2000). For example, students who do not readily ask for more information from teachers or who do not ask questions may be perceived as shy and passive. This may be the case for some students, but for others it may simply reflect respect for the authority of teachers. While teaching for a semester in China, one of your authors found

As the parents of my students found respectful ways to share their expectations, it was Kim's mother who taught me the most. She came in one day after school and bowed low to me. I had learned to bow back respectfully and greet her appropriately. When she apologized for Kim's poor performance on a test (97 percent), I explained that this was a very good grade and that I would gladly work with him to master this subject completely. That did not seem to satisfy her. I felt that I had misunderstood something, that I had caused her to feel like an unsuccessful parent. When I talked with another colleague I learned that in Korea, the mothers were held responsible for a student's success. They were required to teach their child the subject so when the child came to school, he or she could get all the answers correct. My offer of help implied that she could not do her job well. Fortunately, I was able to address this misunderstanding and work with her to balance the Korean and American philosophies of responsibility.

There was much more to what I had learned in Iowa about learning styles and diversity than I had ever thought possible. Now, having moved back to the United States and teaching at the college and elementary level, I can honestly say that every day I apply and extend what I learned in Burkina so many years ago. When I look at the students in my class, I know to look past the surface. I may not have 7 different countries represented, but still, no two children are alike. I need to constantly relate the content to their interests, experiences, learning styles, and needs. I learned to listen to each of them and find out their beliefs and customs. I learned to talk with their parents—not simply send home newsletters and discipline cards—but to sit with them and have conversations about what they wanted for their children. There are so many lessons of student diversity from that first year, and each contributes to the quality of my teaching every day.

Cheryl Larson, Ph.D., has taught in the International School of Ouagadougou, Burkina Faso, West Africa; the Singapore-American School, Singapore; and in the Richland Two School District of Columbia, South Carolina. She is now on the faculty at the College of Charleston, Charleston, South Carolina. ■

that students expected to have very little dialogue with the professor during a class. Instead, the professor was to speak and the students were to listen. This was in stark contrast to the American professor's inclination to encourage discussion and debate. The students' disconcerting reluctance to speak in class was out of respect for the teacher rather than being meant as disrespect. It was interesting, however, that outside of class the students were eager to spend time with the professor discussing all sorts of matters.

Teachers' misreading of cultural behaviors can also include the perception that Asian Pacific American students lack initiative and are unsociable (Cheng, 1987). This, however, may be a matter of a student's limited English verbal ability. The difficulty with acquisition of a second language (bilingual educators suggest it can take four to seven years to develop fluency), especially if the home environment continues to use the native language, can drive students toward subjects that are not verbally dependent, such as science and mathematics.

Of course there is no crime in becoming fluent in science or math, but it should not be at the expense of developing interpersonal communication skills. Rather than drawing us together, the failure to develop communication skills can factionalize ethnic groups. Chao (1992) explains that when teachers fail to learn the correct pronunciation of students' names or when students anglicize their names to make it easier for teachers, a divide begins to develop that disaffirms the student's native culture relative to the culture of the school. In the above story about teaching in China, the professor went to great lengths to learn the proper pronunciation of each student's name as quickly as possible. The pleasant surprise for the professor was that many students commented that they appreciated his effort.

In the classroom it is important for teachers of Asian Pacific American students to recognize that student behavior and student achievement can have cultural implications. Often these students are faced with two cultures; that of the school and that at home. Helping to bridge that gap can be very much a part of the work of a teacher. As we have found with other ethnic groups, the avoidance of stereotypical cultural representations and a respect for the personal dignity and integrity of each child are essential first steps to establishing a culture-friendly learning environment.

Hispanic/Latino(a) American Students

"Hispanic" typically refers to a culture or group whose ancestors at one time were heavily influenced by the rule of colonial Spain. "Latino" specifically applies to the geographical region of Latin America. For comprehensiveness, we will use the term "Hispanic/Latino(a)."

It is predicted that by the year 2050 the percentage of Hispanic/Latino(a) students will account for nearly 25 percent of the overall K–12 population (President's Advisory Commission, 2000). In fact, projections called for Hispanic enrollment to become the largest minority group in the United States, exceeding the number of African-Americans by 2005 (Yaden et al., 2000). That projection became reality in 2004.

English language acquisition is a primary issue for Hispanic/Latino(a) students. For many students, Spanish is the primary language spoken in the home. Marshall (2002) suggests, "Moreover, because they tend to reside and develop their most meaningful interpersonal relationships in largely poor and ethnically segregated communities, most Mexicans, Chicano/as, Puerto Ricans, and so on tend to value the retention of their Spanish-speaking skills" (p.172). In such cases, language is a matter of personal and cultural identity. Indeed, there are cities in the Southeast and Southwest that conduct all of their business in Spanish. Such local governments still must communicate with the state and federal government in English, but day-to-day functioning is carried out in Spanish. As you might expect, this can cause a problem for schools. Which way should they go? Should the public schools in such areas be conducted in Spanish, or should English be the required language for public education in the United States?

Many students do acquire *conversational* language skills in two years or less, but as we have seen before, *academic* language proficiency can take considerably longer to develop (Anderson, 1995; Carrasquillo, 1991; Garcia, 1993; Krashen, 1996). Consequently, we find that by age 9, Hispanic/Latino(a) students often lag behind Anglos in reading, mathematics, and science, and by age 13 they are on average two years behind. In addition, Hispanic/Latino(a) American students are reported to have the highest dropout rates of all students in schools (President's Advisory Commission, 1996; *School practices,* 2000).

English as a Second Language (ESL) Any program designed to teach English to nonspeakers of English while providing instruction in the various areas of the curriculum.

The debate continues with regard to how best to educate English language learners (ELL). **English as a Second Language (ESL)** programs as we know them in the schools were first developed by the military during World War II. There are many versions of ESL programs. Marshall (2002) cites the following orientations as common to the public schools:

1. *Sheltered English,* in which all lessons are also English language lessons.
2. *Immersion English,* in which students are taught in English but may converse with their teachers in their native language.
3. *Submersion English,* in which students are taught entirely in English.
4. *Structured immersion,* in which students may speak a second language though English is the primary language for instruction.

Do any of these sound familiar from the schools you attended? It may be that the foreign language department at your college or university offers sections that use the immersion or submersion approach to learning another language.

Providing effective instruction for children who speak a language different from your own will always be challenging. Even if you speak another language, you will likely need some assistance with this aspect of instruction. However, overcoming the cultural incongruity mentioned with regard to other ethnic groups will also be an issue when working with Hispanic/Latino(a) students.

Language may not be the only culprit placing students at risk for failure in schools. Other "indexes of vulnerability" found among Hispanic/Latino(a) students who are having academic difficulty include low family income, poverty, high percentage of female-headed households, and high rates of functional illiteracy (Garcia, 1995). Do not take this as an indictment of the entire ethnic group. Nor does this suggest that only this group is vulnerable to these influences. Instead, understand that these points of vulnerability have been found among Hispanic/Latino(a) students who *do* have academic difficulty.

White American Students

The diversity of the white American population is evidenced across dimensions such as economic status, religious affiliation, education, and political influence. But whites represent diverse ethnic ancestries as well. Indeed, the Bureau of the Census defines the white population as persons of European, Middle Eastern, and North African origins. Taken together they represent the majority ethnic population in the United States.

Historically, the collective values of the white American population have had the greatest influence on the nation's schools and the work of teachers. Commonly referred to as the mainstream worldview, these values, expectations, and assumptions have influenced public schooling from curricula to teacher-student interactions. Chief among these values are (1) an emphasis on individual rights over group interests, (2) one's ability to control and plan for the future, (3) competition as a motivator, and (4) equal opportunity without the stipulation of equal end results (Alba, 1990; Carter and Parks, 1992; Gans, 1988; Kluckhohn & Strodtbeck, 1961). This is not to say that other ethnic groups do not embrace these values as well, but this underlying worldview is identified most closely with the collective white population.

The importance of ethnicity as an ancestral identity, however, seems to have faded for the average white American (Alba, 1990). With the possible exception of special occasions (e.g., parades, festivals) most whites are likely to consider themselves simply as being American. White American students currently constitute more than 62% of the overall U.S. student population (Digest of Education Statistics, 2002, 2003). They are no longer the majority in California schools, and will soon be a minority in Texas schools, but they have maintained majority status in the rest of the nation (Rosenblatt & Helfand, 2001; Yardley, 2001). Yet as majority or minority, to this point, white adolescents typically do not perceive ethnicity or race as an important factor in their lives. Because the set of cultural norms that affects their lives is drawn from the mainstream worldview, most white adolescents never experience the cultural encounters that might cause their nonwhite peers to explore their own ethnic and racial identities.

In an increasingly multicultural society, it becomes increasingly important that students be able to appreciate diversity as *reflecting components of a whole* rather than as demonstrating differences from a vague conceptualization of what constitutes the cultural norm. Multicultural content infused into the curriculum can be utilized to create vicarious contact between white adolescents and nonwhites, and teachers should generate opportunities for students from culturally diverse backgrounds to work with each other. This provides students with meaningful interpersonal experiences, challenging them to rethink preconceived notions they might hold about those who differ from themselves. Simply adding in "cultural awareness" classroom activities and lessons, on the other hand, serves to factionalize both whites and nonwhites by presenting the nonwhite culture as that which differs from the normal (white) culture.

It is very likely that in the decades to come, success with the teaching of students of all ethnicities will require not only measures of academic achievement (note: because standardized tests are statistically oriented around an average, that average is most representative of the majority—in this case, the white American population) but also some indicator of the student's ability to succeed as a member of a society that truly strives for equity and justice for all its citizens.

■   ■   ■

We hope that you have noticed certain themes throughout our discussion of ethnic diversity:

1. All children need to know that the cultural underpinnings of their identity are valued and not subservient to any other culture.
2. All children need to feel valued for themselves within the classroom.
3. Children are served best by teachers who are committed to the child's success.
4. Classrooms and teaching materials should not be culturally sterile but instead be infused with an appreciation of the strength that ethnic diversity brings to our "American" culture.

Clearly, given just the five general ethnic subdivisions of Native American, African American, Caucasian, Hispanic, and Asian American, a classroom teacher has a con-

Table 3.2	Percentage Enrollment in Public Elementary and Secondary Schools by Race/Ethnicity				
Year	White	Black	Hispanic	Asian /Pacific Islander	Native American
1999	62.1%	17.2%	15.6%	4.0%	1.2%
1986	70.4	16.1	9.9	2.8	0.9

(Digest of Education Statistics, 2002, 2003, p. 58)

siderable challenge to address when designing appropriate educational experiences. Table 3.2 shows that the percentage of minority enrollment between 1986 and 1999 has increased significantly (the percentage of Hispanic students has increased by nearly two-thirds) while the percentage of white enrollment has decreased (Digest of Education Statistics, 2003).

Religion

Religion is not only a part of culture, it is a very powerful part. As recently as 2003 an Alabama Supreme Court Chief Justice, Judge Roy Moore, was removed from the bench because he refused to have a stone sculpture depicting the Ten Commandments removed from the courthouse lobby. Even with a strong and sincere effort to make school a more culturally friendly place, religion (in the sense of practicing a religion, not in the sense of discussing one) typically is not a part of the curriculum.

Yet a classroom teacher must consider the impact of religious beliefs on the classroom. For example, some parents do not allow their children to take part in any celebrations at school. This includes not only events with a religious overtone (for instance, a Christmas party), but also birthday celebrations. So, if you are planning to bring in treats each time one of your students has a birthday, some students may have to be somewhere else during that time. These students, however, will still be your responsibility. You may also have students who dress in accordance with their religious beliefs; students who miss class in observance of religious holidays (and you will have to provide some way of making up work missed); and students whose religious beliefs may be in opposition to particular subject area content.

Teachers cannot be aware of every nuance of religious belief that might be represented in the classroom. However, as a teacher you must not devalue another's religious beliefs or observations because they differ from your own or from the mainstream in your community. Your role as a teacher will never be to pass judgment on a religious perspective, nor to indicate that your own convictions are superior, but instead to demonstrate that in your community of learners, tolerance and considering other perspectives are of value.

What examples of the social aspect of gender can you identify in this picture?

© HIRB/Index Stock Imgery

Gender

Of all the categories of student diversity, gender is likely the most enigmatic. In sorting this out we will consider the difference between *gender* and *sex*, sexual stereotyping, and cognitive differences between the sexes.

Distinctions of Gender and Sex

gender The social aspect of sexuality: behaviors that are considered masculine or feminine.

Gender refers to the *social* aspect of sexuality, that is, behaviors that are considered masculine or feminine. The social forces that teach gender specific behaviors and expectations are prevalent from birth. Names given to boys and girls have a social context that implies gender. The way children are dressed implies gender. Activities in which boys engage versus those in which girls engage, even the way that they are taught to interact with other people, are all gender-bound. We say gender-bound because none of these examples has any biological basis.

sex A biological distinction between male and female.

However, when people speak of the different physical and cognitive abilities of boys and girls in school, gender is not the issue. The issue is **sex,** the *biological* distinctions of male or female. For example, do males and females learn differently as a function of being male or female? For our discussion, the focus is on how these distinctions and expectations are treated in the classroom.

gender bias/sexism Preferential treatment toward or discrimination against individuals or groups based on their gender or sex.

Few people would argue against providing educational opportunities to boys and girls in an atmosphere that is free of **gender bias** or **sexism.** That is, neither group should be given preferential treatment or be discriminated against based on gender or sex. For example, it would be biased to allow aggressive behavior (or extremely active behavior) in boys while simultaneously expecting the girls to be quiet and demure.

Sexual Stereotyping

sexual stereotyping The expectation that males should fill particular roles while females fill other roles.

Similarly, boys and girls should not be directed to particular career paths based on **sexual stereotyping** (the expectation that males fill particular roles and females fill others) when in fact sexuality has no bearing on the job. A typical example of this has been directing females to become nurses while directing males to become doctors.

Cognitive Differences between Boys and Girls

What if there *are* distinctions to be made between the society's expectations for masculine and feminine behavior (remember, the school represents and teaches society's values) and between the native abilities of each sex? For instance, Carol Gilligan's pioneering work suggests that women prefer learning through first-hand observation and that they are more likely to personalize knowledge than men are (1982). With regard to moral reasoning, she found that while males value following rules and law, females value relationships and caring. So, are there legitimate differences between the sexes that should be addressed? Or are these differences social in nature, the result of the forces that people are exposed to throughout their lives? If that is the case, it might be appropriate to avoid sending different messages to boys and girls.

For the past several decades, considerable funding has gone into educational research and instructional programs to encourage females to pursue careers in science and mathematics. Perhaps those efforts have had an effect. Willingham and Cole (1997) examined the standardized tests and college placement exams of 15 million students in the fourth, eighth, and 12th grades. They found that the performance differences between the sexes was minimal. No picture emerged of one sex excelling over the other. The average performance difference across all subjects, they found, "is essentially zero." Does this mean that Gilligan's findings do represent social effects on learning rather than biological distinctions? What is your opinion?

Gender and sexuality have been an issue throughout our country's history. It is not resolved at this point, and the increased visibility of alternative lifestyles and sexual orientations ensures that it will continue as an issue. In the meantime, it would be appropriate for classroom teachers to

- Avoid imposing sexual stereotyping,
- Promote collaboration between boys and girls, and
- Make all subjects equally accessible to both sexes.

Language

Language Use

You will notice significant differences in language usage even among your students for whom English is their native language. At one end of the spectrum are youngsters who have neither traveled beyond their local communities nor developed an awareness of the structures and interrelationships of their immediate surroundings. These students possess impoverished or "different" vocabularies (street language, for instance), poor "formal learning" skills, and inadequate and inaccurate academic concepts. Poverty rather than culture or ethnicity is the predominant connection with low levels of achievement (Jencks & Phillips, 1998; Payne, 1998).

At the other end of the spectrum, some students may possess a rather sophisticated grammar and vocabulary. These students typically speak in complete standard-language sentences and verbally communicate with their peers and any number of adults on a variety of topics. It is likely that their parents read and talk to them and introduce them to a variety of cultural experiences, both vicarious and direct.

Why is this important for the teacher? It is important because these language differences are based on environmental concerns that then lead to diversity among students. That is, rather than English as a second language, we are discussing the differences in language-use ability that arise from the background experiences of individual students. You will notice significant differences in language usage even among your students for whom English is their native language.

English as a Second Language (ESL) and Limited English Proficiency (LEP)

Elsewhere we have discussed various ways of envisioning the increasing heterogeneity of our society. In this section, we will consider briefly two aspects as they relate to students who speak a home language other than English. Although there is some disagreement about the interpretations, let's begin by defining some terms in layman's language.

ESL, *English as a second language,* refers to English being taught to native speakers of other languages. Another term often used is ESOL, which stands for *English for speakers of other languages.* You may also hear or see TESOL, *teaching English to speakers of other languages.* In each case, the referent is a person (in our case, a student) whose first language at home is something other than English. The range is broad, everything from a bilingual household in which two languages are spoken by one or both parents to a household where no adult (and perhaps no one) speaks English.

Another term with which you will soon become familiar is LEP, or *limited English proficiency.* A student identified as LEP can be someone who speaks no English at all or a student who knows a few words of "playground language" but not the complex English that characterizes texts and other formal print materials.

When you are studying achievement test data (and you will spend considerable time doing so), you will encounter the term ELL. This represents *English language learners* and is specifically used when the No Child Left Behind Act, Reading First projects, and Adequate Yearly Progress (AYP) are considered. More on that later in this section.

© Paul Conklin/PhotoEdit

Providing instruction to students for whom English is a second language is a challenge that the schools address.

In terms of the instruction that is provided for students for whom English is (or will become) a second language, there are several concepts you should know. With *language immersion,* all instruction is in English. The assumption is that students need to be immersed in English all day long, much as they would if they visited (another) foreign country. Another approach is to provide a pull-out program during which English language learners receive separate instruction, often on basic skills. Another approach is to provide initial instruction in the students' native language, thus delaying the introduction of English instruction.

An alternative concept is *bilingual education,* in which instruction is provided daily in both English and the student's native tongue. The topic of immersion or delayed English or bilingual education has been, and probably will continue to be, controversial (Gilroy, October 23, 2001; Shannon & Milian, Fall, 2002).

Some Demographic Data for English Language Learners

Now, why should you care about the controversy or, for that matter, about teaching students whose first language is not English? The first reason is that, as a teacher, you are professionally responsible for providing the highest possible quality of instruction to *all* of your students. National origin, ethnicity, culture, gender, level of cognitive functioning, and other differences are not acceptable excuses for dereliction of duty. The second reason you should be actively interested in the topic is that you will almost certainly have in your classroom a number of children with limited English proficiency. How many will you have? That depends. How diverse will your classroom be? That also depends. If you teach in a state or area with a high concentration of speakers of other languages, you may have a majority of your class who speak a primary language other than English.

According to the National Center for Education Statistics (Digest of Education Statistics 2004, 2005), 17 percent of students speak a language other than English at home. That translates (no pun intended) into an average of four students in a class of 24. Three of those four children, on average, are Hispanic (Diversity Data, n.d.). That percentage is increasing every year (National Clearinghouse for Bilingual Education, 2002), and you, as a first-year teacher, are likely to have more of these students than are the veteran teachers. After all, you will have just graduated, knowing the latest strategies for helping these students, and you will surely speak a second language much better than a teacher who graduated 20 or 30 years ago when taking a foreign language was not nearly so "hot" an issue. The bad news is, that while 41 percent of teachers have students with limited English proficiency in their classrooms, only 12.5 percent of those teachers have had as much as eight hours of specialized training (NCELA, 2002). By the way, almost two-thirds of students with limited English proficiency were born in the United States. In the year 2000, the United States census determined that 3.4 million of these children spoke English poorly or not at all (Black, 2005). Some of them are headed for your class. At the present rate, by the year 2044, when you will be a veteran teacher, the majority of the students will be minority-language speakers (Crawford, 2002).

Are you wondering, "Who are these children?" Good question. Nearly 85 percent of them come from non-European countries, with the preponderance arriving from Asia and Latin America. Of the immigrant group, 20 percent come from Mexico, and 5 to 7 percent come from China, India, and the Philippines (Federation for American Immigration Reform, 2006). Census data indicate large numbers of students who speak Vietnamese, Russian, Arabic, and French Creole. Imagine a class with just four students with limited English proficiency, and then consider what you might need to do if they represented four different languages. One can easily encounter such situations in California, New York, and Chicago, but don't think it's different if you teach in a rural area. Many of these students live in those areas (Black, 2005).

Of course, no one is really sure how many children with limited English proficiency there are in the United States. For instance, in 1990, Florida schools reported approximately 84,000, but the census records showed 113,000. On the other side of the record, Michigan educators reported 37,000 such students while the census listed only 28,000 (Crawford, 2002).

What do we know about the achievement of these students? First of all, Hispanic students from low socioeconomic backgrounds average two years lower in achievement on the National Assessment of Education Progress (NAEP) by the fourth grade and fall farther behind the Caucasian achievement level as they go through middle and high school (White-Clark, 2005). Abedi and Dietel (2004) point out that ELL students often perform 20 to 30 percentage points lower than other students and that their progress shows "little improvement over many years" (p. 782). However, ELL students are not a homogeneous group. Chinese students in one study performed far higher on science and reading subtests than did Hispanic students. Mathews (2000) also cautions us not to view students from different areas as culturally homogeneous. A broad label can lead to misinterpretations of student actions and achievement.

Teacher and School Expectations

Now that you have a general idea of the population we are considering in this section, let's look at some of the legal aspects and see how they relate to you as an individual and your school as a collective entity. Like almost every other child in your school, a student whose first language is something other than English is affected by a number of laws and regulations, everything from those promulgated by the principal or superintendent or district school board to those established by state and federal agencies and Congress itself. Chapter 10, Ethics in Education and Matters of Law, includes a number of specifics. We will concern ourselves here with just a few prime examples of the parameters under which you will operate.

By far the compelling force in this new century is the federal government's No Child Left Behind Act. Besides its requirement that teachers be "highly qualified" and that schools be "graded" according to the accomplishments of the student body, the law requires annual testing in reading and math in grades 3 through 8 and at least once in high school. The expectation is that all students will perform at grade level by 2014. At almost the halfway mark (the bill was signed into law in 2002), the easy part of the progress has already been made. That is, students who were close to the expectation have generally been able to meet the standard. However, if 75 percent of your class achieves at grade level, that is not acceptable to the government. The mandated figure is 100 percent, and each state was required to establish a graduated scale for each year or cluster of years to end with a target of 100 percent achievement in the final year. Thus, Adequate Yearly Progress (AYP) reports are issued to each school each summer, and schools must meet the expectations. The expectations are the same for all subgroups of students (e.g., English language learners, minority students, students living in poverty, students with learning exceptionalities). In a given year, for instance, a state might require that 59 percent of every subgroup meet the grade-level standard in reading and 64 percent of every subgroup meet the standard in math. While that is doable for some subgroups, it is often impossible for English language learners and for students with exceptionalities. Both groups diverge from the "standard" population, the first because of a language difference and the second because of a cognitive issue. However, both groups are treated just the same as any other subgroup.

Imagine, for instance, your students who enter school with limited English proficiency. Some researchers contend they need five to eight years to learn the academic English needed to perform well in school (Black, 2005). Hakuta's study (reported in Gilroy, 2001) found that children need three to five years to acquire oral proficiency and four to seven years to acquire academic English proficiency. Collier and Thomas (1999) note that one reason English language learners take five to seven years to "catch up" is that the other students are not standing still. They are continuing to make progress.

The law does provide for a three-year "grace period" while students acquire proficiency in written language. (On a case-by-case basis, the time can be extended up to two more years.) In the meantime, the students must be assessed in English language acquisition (No Child Left Behind, February 17, 2005). However, for many in education the period of time is considered far too brief.

Teaching English Language Learners

How will you teach these students? Like a number of other aspects of the curriculum, this is one over which you have no control. Your state or district school board (not the federal government) will make that determination. In many states, a pull-out program removes students from their classrooms for part of a day to be instructed by an ESL teacher. This has met with objections by Mohr, who advocates "strong bilingual programs . . . [with] . . . a language-oriented and challenging academic curriculum" (2004). The one thing you are responsible for is student achievement, whether your school has a pull-out program or whether you have in your classroom for part of the day a paraprofessional (who hopefully speaks the predominant non-English language).

You generally will be expected to use grade-level texts and "adapt" the material to the needs of the students (but that will apply to native English speakers too). You will probably be discouraged or prohibited from retaining these students if a language difference is the major issue. You may even be required to put an eight-year-old immigrant who has never been in school (because in her country one had to own a pair of shoes to attend class) into third grade with the various expectations at that grade level. So now is a great time for you to begin thinking about how you plan to address the needs of these special students.

Motivation

Students vary greatly in their degree of motivation. Some children arrive at school without purpose, without concern for the intellectual, social, behavioral, ethical, and physical objectives of the school. For them, school may be just something to be endured until the time arrives when state statutes allow a long-awaited reprieve.

Yet classes also contain students who are highly motivated to achieve and who do so on their own power. For them, a teacher serves not as a goad or potential source of punishment, not as an adult to be pleased by diligently applying themselves, but

Courtesy of Becky Stovall

Lessons that engage students' minds tap their motivation to explore.

as a resource person who helps provide direction and guidance and then fades into the shadows. Hopefully you fall into the latter category, especially since you will expect that of your students. It may well be that the range of individual differences in motivation is much wider and far more significant than any of the other categories discussed so far, if only because it is affected by so many factors.

As you study more about educational psychology you will find that motivation is *an intrinsic desire to accomplish some task.* What that means is that motivation comes from within. As a teacher, you can provide students with a *reason* to do something (a grade, aversive consequences, as a personal favor), but whether or not the student is motivated by your reason is determined by that student. The art of teaching comes into play as you try to find the reasons that ignite an intrinsic desire toward achievement. It is an art because what motivates one child is not necessarily a motivator for another child.

Academic Self-Concept

One of the most significant and overlooked differences in people is that of academic (as opposed to other types of) self-concept. Much of what children learn or fail to learn may be influenced by their academic self-concepts. Pupils who have become accustomed to succeeding and who feel academically competent are generally successful in a variety of scholastic activities. Those who become accustomed to failure and who feel academically inferior tend to fail in scholastic endeavors. Interestingly, these children tend to perform as they have done in the past, and, what may be more significant, they tend to accept their performances as inevitable.

People typically reflect the academic concepts others have of them. Research (Rosenthal & Jacobson, 1968) indicates that when teachers and classmates consider a child in a positive manner, he or she tends to develop self-confidence and react as the group seems to expect. Conversely, when teachers and fellow classmates consider a pupil in a negative manner, the student begins to mirror their prejudices and react in the way they expect. Thus we have the spiral that is often referred to as a self-fulfilling prophecy. Good and Brophy (1994) put it this way: "Sometimes our expectations about people cause us to treat them in ways that make them respond just as we expected they would" (p. 87). Children profit from high but reasonable expectations. That is, such expectations are appropriate for each student.

Temperament

She's got a great personality. He's so friendly. What do you mean when you make those statements about the wide range of temperaments that children can exhibit? Like economic, intellectual, and social characteristics, aspects related to the development of personality are clearly interrelated. Emotional differences are inextricably intertwined with other aspects of student development. You will study these topics in considerable detail in your human growth and development course(s). For our purposes, let us briefly consider selected aspects of emotional development that will affect classroom management and student participation in the life of your classroom. Some of these facets are anger, happiness, sadness, level of confidence, introversion or extroversion, novelty, and competition or cooperation. In his best-seller, *Emotional Intelligence,* Daniel Goleman (1995) discusses, among other topics, impulse control, which relates to social competence, enthusiasm, persistence, motivation, and morality. Do you see some of the connections between the two lists?

Anger

You have seen *angry* students, possibly many of them. You have been angry yourself. While transitory or low-grade anger can be managed by someone with a healthy emotional outlook and experience, sometimes anger becomes a controlling factor, even the focal point, in a student's life. Sometimes peers and teachers minimize the circumstances or try to ignore them. Yet self-contained anger is destructive to everyone in the learning community. It can simmer for a long time, or it can explode over what appears to be an unrelated event. A second grader misses a simple question and overturns his desk, runs around the room shouting obscenities, and throws books off the shelves. A middle school student puts his head on his desk and covers himself with his jacket. A high school student gets into a fight in the hall when someone accidentally bumps him. You may not be able to solve all of the problems in the lives of these children, but you can become part of the solution rather than part of the problem simply by the manner in which you respond to a child's temperament.

A student teacher of ours had an experience that exemplifies what we mean. The student teacher (now a certified teacher) decided to become a teacher following a career in the U.S. Navy. She has traveled the world and experienced many facets of human behavior. In this particular incident at school (fifth grade), a boy was not completing an in-class assignment. The student teacher brought this to his attention, at which time the student proceeded to yell and scream, stomp around the room, and referred to the student teacher in terms that we can't mention here. When he stopped, the student teacher asked if he was done. He said, "Yeah. I suppose you want to send me to the office now." She quietly replied, "No, I want you to sit down and finish your work." Stunned by her calm reaction, the student complied and she had no difficulties with him for the remainder of the semester!

Happiness

You will also have students who seem to be naturally *happy.* For whatever reason, they are able to take whatever comes along and remain upbeat and positive. They smile and enjoy laughter, willingly engage in conversation, and are anxious to share their experiences with you. These are the children of whom you'll be saying, "If I could just have a classroom full of students like her!" Perhaps it would be nice to have an entire class of such students. The surprise, however, is that you would then become sensitive to other differences between the students. A pleasant demeanor can be a pleasure to work with, but what will make you a professional educator is your ability to effectively bring your compassion and pedagogical expertise to the needs of each child.

Sadness

Unfortunately, some of your students may have a generally *sad* demeanor. The burdens they carry, whether arising from the circumstances of their life or their own willing assumption of them, nevertheless give them an abundance of emotional baggage that colors everything that happens. Some of them will be temporarily stressed, others chronically depressed. Some of them will be quiet and perhaps escape your notice. Studies (Weinberg et al., 1995) show that between 60 percent and 80 percent of students who are identified as learning disabled and who are failing in school also meet the criteria for depression.

Confidence

How much *confidence* do you have? You probably will respond by saying "It depends." And, that's the correct, if vague, answer. Think about some of the classes you have taken recently or are taking right now. Do some people raise questions, voluntarily participate in discussion, stand up for their points of view even when others disagree? We often say those people have the courage of their convictions. Yet you know of others who are so lacking in confidence that they are unwilling to attempt homework, study for tests, or complete projects. The excuse you will often hear is "I can't. . . . It's too hard." Yet these same students may demonstrate considerable confidence on the ball court, in a recital, or amid friends. If you lack self-confidence, perhaps around adults but not children, you can understand that your students may lack confidence and fear embarrassment in some settings but not in others. You will see one side of them in class. They may, however, have another side of which you need to become aware. If you are self-confident, you should not forget that others have a different emotional frame of mind that will require your understanding.

Introverts and Extroverts

In a related vein, consider the tendency of some students to be *introverts* while others are *extroverts*. A painfully shy student may be very embarrassed when you issue a simple compliment. She may talk to the desk rather than to you. She may do well on tests but poorly on oral discussions. You must be careful not to ignore or prejudge the introvert, and you must be extremely vigilant so as not to allow the extrovert to monopolize the discussion. He (more boys than girls) may demand to participate by blurting out responses or waving a hand wildly or getting partly out of his seat. Some primary children raise their hands to answer questions the teacher has not yet finished asking!

Introversion and extroversion represent individual cognitive and/or social styles. It is not your task to change a student from one style to another, but simply to help them moderate their style to make the best use of the educational opportunities you provide.

Appreciation of Novelty

You will find that some students respond positively to *novelty*. That is, they like to encounter new situations, new ways of doing things, new types of activities. Many educators will advise you to make your class come alive by sometimes doing things in different ways. At the same time, you should be aware that some students respond negatively to novel situations. They like the security of doing things the same way. As you will learn in our discussion of classroom management (see Chapter 7), and will likely study further in your program, some students need the structure of desks in rows and columns, clear-cut assignments and due dates, and a concise idea of your expectations. Other students will relish the opportunity to pursue your assignments in the context of their own personal interests and may function very well in small-group arrangements of desks.

Chances are slim that you will have a class that is entirely one way or the other in this regard. Your task will be to find the appropriate balance. Novelty is the appreciation of change, and change is a fact of life. So rather than thinking of this temperament (acceptance of or fear of novel situations) as an either/or situation, think of what will be an *acceptable* level of novelty in your classroom. For instance, some teachers might put posters on the ceiling of their classroom. This encourages the development of observation skills. Some students see the posters on the ceiling and are stimulated by the novelty of it. Others don't have to look up if they would rather not. For the same reasons, other teachers change the decorations in the classroom regularly. In either case the teachers would not post assignments on the ceiling or change the locations of important information—that level of novelty would be unacceptable for some students. Find the balance. It can actually be an intellectually stimulating exercise for the teacher!

Competitiveness

Some students are highly *competitive,* both with themselves and with others. If you tell certain students that they cannot achieve a particular task, they will agree and abandon the attempt. Other students will rise to the challenge and prove you wrong. You need to know which students respond to such challenges and which ones respond far better to encouragement. "You can do this; I know you can. And, I'm going to help you get it done."

Of course, you also know students who are much more in the *cooperative* mode. They work well together on common goals and rejoice when their friends do well. You will have to establish a classroom community in which there is a healthy blend of cooperation and competition. Activity 3.1 will provide an opportunity to watch for differences in temperament among students. Whether you use this as a Field Observation activity or in one of your own courses, it should prove to be an interesting exercise.

Field Observation

ACTIVITY 3.1   Observing Student Demeanor

Now that you've read about some of the differences in temperament that you might see in class, take a moment to watch for it. If you are taking part in a clinical internship or school observation, use the students in that class for your observations. If you aren't observing out in the schools, you could use one of your own classes on campus. In either case, keep in mind that you are looking for differences in personality or temperament, not trying to identify particular students. Therefore, your records for this activity need not include names of people.

1.   Make a seating chart for the class you are observing, and then number each student rather than using names.

2.   Prepare a data table. Across the top list the categories: angry, happy, sad, confident, introvert, extrovert, competitive, and cooperative. These are the characteristics discussed in the text. We did not include novelty because it might be difficult for you to observe a student's reaction to novelty in one class session. You can add or delete characteristics as you wish.

3.   Number down the side of your table for as many students as there are in class.

4.   During a typical class period (it's important that the students in the class do not know what you are trying to observe) observe the students' demeanor and put a check mark in the applicable boxes. A student could have several check marks.

5.   Now analyze the data and draw conclusions. How many different temperaments did you identify? Is there a trend in the data? That is, are most (or many) of the students of one disposition or another? What do the data tell you about working with these students if it were your class?

Learning Styles

A popular perspective on student diversity and learning is that of **learning styles.** Though there is some debate about this topic, you can read positive reviews of learning styles (e.g., visual, auditory, tactile/kinesthetic, field-dependent, field-independent, impulsive, and reflective) by consulting publications by Dunn (1995, 2001), Dunn et al. (1995), Carbo (1996), and Barbe and Swassing (1988).

You may already be familiar with the basic categories of learning preferences:

Visual—These students prefer to see things (maps, charts, a problem written out).

Auditory—For these students, processing is facilitated by hearing things and through discussion.

Tactile/Kinesthetic—For these students, movement is very important (writing, actually going through the movements of an activity, manipulating materials).

Vocalic—This refers to talking oneself through something (counting out loud, repeating a phone number aloud, verbalizing the steps in some process or procedure).

Most people indicate a preference for some combination of these styles rather than just one. As you continue through your teacher education program, you will learn to design lessons that address multiple learning styles. For example, in the courses you are taking now it is likely that your professor lectures to the class or engages the class in dialogue (auditory and vocalic) while also writing key points on the board or projecting them on a screen (visual) during which time you take notes (tactile/kinesthetic). In this way, you are using multiple learning styles in combination.

Reading Ability

Regardless of the grade you teach, your students will have a wide range of individual differences in reading ability (Allington, 1975; Burmeister, 1978). Riley (1996) notes that in kindergarten it is common to find a five-year range in children's literacy-related capabilities. (*Note: Literacy* is a more inclusive term than *reading* in that it includes reading comprehension as well as simply recognizing words.) While some children enter school able to sing or recite the alphabet and read a few words or simple books or, on occasion, more complex texts (Jackson, 1991), others arrive without possessing the basic skills, concepts, attitudes, and strategies essential for successfully encountering a multitude of learning tasks. Efforts to teach children with such deficiencies to read will simply prove frustrating to both the teacher and the students. As Lewis (2005) notes, "The fact that a substantial gap in readiness for learning exists in kindergarten and that it stems primarily from income and race is a stark challenge for the best-intentioned teachers and school leaders" (p. 179). When we consider that 8 percent of kindergarten children speak no English (August & Hakuta, 1997), the challenge increases. That percentage of students from homes in which English is not spoken by the adults remains consistent all the way through high school. In 11 states, 15 percent or more of the students speak a non-English language at home (Report of the United States Bureau of the Census, 1998). It is obvious that the diversity among students with regard to reading ability, even within a classroom, can have a considerable effect on the way a teacher plans and presents a lesson.

Table 3.3	Summary of General Ways in Which Students Differ	
Culture/Ethnicity	Religion	Gender
Language	Motivation	Self-Concept
Temperament	Learning Styles	Reading Ability

While the range of individual differences in reading ability is quite broad at kindergarten, it becomes even more so as one ascends the educational ladder (Harris & Sipay, 1980). At the fifth-grade level, for example, a typical class may contain pupils with almost no reading ability as well as some operating well into the high school level. According to the National Center for Education Statistics, two-thirds of the adolescents in 2003 were "struggling to read proficiently" (Biancarosa, 2005, p.16). In grade 12, even though some of the poorest readers have dropped out, the range typically goes from grade 2 or 3 to advanced college. Furthermore, a study of 26,000 adults found that 4 percent of college graduates were functionally illiterate and 15 percent could not function in a sophisticated work environment (McGuiness, 1997). Interestingly, in life after high school, a national survey of adults ages 18–25 found that two-thirds or more of every group—Hispanic, black, white, and Asian—admitted that they "could have paid a lot more attention and worked harder" in high school (Schroeder, 2005, p. 73). Hmmm . . .

Ironically, in 1913, the United States Bureau of Education reported that illiteracy was "doomed. A few years more and there will not be a vestige of it left" (in Johnston, 1978, p. 562). Changing social conditions as well as the increasing standards of literacy during the past 90 years have left millions of adults illiterate or semi-literate. One challenge to the schools as an organization and to you as a professional is to help students become more literate each year.

When we consider the ever-increasing level used to define a literate adult, it is interesting to note that in 1900, the ability to write one's name identified the person as literate. By the mid-1930s, a literate person was one who had attended at least three years of school. In 1947, the Census Bureau set the bar at fifth grade, and in 1970 the United States Office of Education adjusted the bar to ninth grade. Today the bar is high school completion (Gordon & Gordon, 2003). Table 3.3 provides a listing of the general ways in which students differ that have been discussed in this section. Activity 3.2 will provide you with an opportunity to identify and appreciate the diversity that exists within a classroom of students.

■ Learning, Sensory, and Physical Diversity

Discussions of learning, sensory, and physical diversity once referred to students that many students in the "normal" population never saw. Today our perspective toward *students with exceptionalities* is to bring them fully into the educational experience, for "exceptional education" embraces a broad range of capabilities and literally millions of children. The old philosophy of separation has been replaced with a philosophy of inclusion that seeks to bring such children into the general education program at every opportunity. Even more important is the attitude of providing positive support—an emphasis on a child's abilities rather than on a child's disabilities—which affirms the child's rightful place as a member of the general education population.

> **ACTIVITY 3.2**
> **Identifying Student Differences**
>
> It might be best to use one of your classes for this exercise rather than one of students in a local school. As a student teacher you will need to identify the differences among your students. At this point, however, some may see such an activity as an invasion of privacy.
>
> 1. Choose one of your classes for this exercise. You need not list students by name because this activity is addressing diversity as it appears within the class, not as a matter of identifying individual students.
>
> 2. What cultures are represented in your class? Do some students consider themselves "American" while others prefer a hyphenated descriptor such as Hispanic-American, Irish-American, or African-American? What are the implications within your class for the range of cultures that are represented?
>
> 3. Do you notice a difference in behavior in class between males and females? Is one group more or less vocal than the other? Does your professor have to call on one group more than the other in order to get participation in class?
>
> 4. As you consider your classmates, are there some who appear more confident of themselves than others do? Are either of these groups consistently correct or incorrect when they respond to questions in class? What about your self-concept as it is demonstrated in class? Do you speak up or do you prefer to speak only if called upon? How does a student's self-concept affect the way the professor interacts with that student?
>
> 5. Ask your professor about her perception of the diversity in your class and how it affects the way she conducts the class.

Our introductory look at exceptionalities will address three areas:

- **Intelligence,** which, with regard to exceptionalities, can include children with cognitive difficulties and children with heightened cognitive abilities.
- **Learning disorders,** which can range from difficulty with learning to difficulty with focusing attention so as to learn.
- **Sensory and physical disabilities,** which, as with learning disorders, do not imply cognitive impairment.

It is extremely important for you to understand that an exceptionality in any one of these three areas does not imply an exceptionality in another area. Individual children may have overlapping circumstances or they may not. We group these topics together only because all have an underlying neurological or neurophysiological component.

Perspectives on Intelligence

Throughout the life span people differ with regard to intelligence. There is no age at which all people are on the same intellectual level either as a starting point or as a level of attainment. Thus, you can expect that the students in your classroom will represent a range of intellectual ability. For the most part, that range will be fairly narrow. Students with IQ scores (which will be only one of many diagnostic scores considered) below 70 or above approximately 130 will be those who receive various services as *exceptional children,* children whose cognitive or physical needs require services outside of the scope of the traditional classroom.

intelligence An individual's capacity to learn from experience and to adapt to the environment (Sternberg & Powell). It differs from academic achievement, knowledge, and skillful ability in one domain or another.

What is **intelligence**? Attempts to define the term have generated much debate, but "intelligence" is generally agreed to be an individual's capacity to learn from experience and to adapt to the environment (Sternberg & Powell, 1983). Note that this is not the same thing as academic achievement, knowledge, or skillful ability in one area or another. Intelligence is broader and more abstract than the idea of "knowing things." You might think of it as a measure of cognitive potential (at a given point in time) rather than as an intellectual limit.

IQ Ratings

Though it has long been acknowledged, and even legislated, that an IQ score alone is an insufficient indicator for making instructional decisions for students, it is certainly among the key indicators. Thus we can place our discussion in a broader context by using IQ data to establish approximate benchmarks. Let's begin with a brief look at intelligence testing.

The Beginning of Intelligence Testing In 1905 the minister of public education in Paris commissioned Alfred Binet and Theophile Simon to construct a test of intellectual ability. The intent was to identify school children who would likely be unsuccessful in school. These children would be provided with special classes. Binet feared that such a test would ultimately label children in terms of intelligence, a fear that proved all too true. Nonetheless, he and Simon developed a test that consisted of 30 problems arranged in increasing order of difficulty.

In 1916, Lewis Terman of Stanford University revised the Binet-Simon test (Terman, 1926). The new Stanford-Binet test had three important differences from the original test. First, items themselves had been changed and the test made easier to administer. Second, the test was standardized (determining the results to be expected from a given population) on a large American population of approximately 1,000 children and 400 adults. Finally, results of the test were reported as a score called the **intelligence quotient,** or **IQ.**

intelligence quotient (IQ) The relationship between a person's mental age and his or her chronological age. A score of 100 (or a range from 85 to 115) is considered "average."

The Intelligence Quotient (IQ) To determine IQ the examiner took the child's mental age as determined by the test and divided it by the child's chronological age. The quotient was then multiplied by 100 (to remove decimal values). So, a seven-year-old child with a mental age of 7 would have an IQ of 100:

$$\text{MA/CA} \times 100 = \text{IQ}$$
$$7/7 \times 100 = 100$$

An IQ score of 100 signified that the mental and chronological ages were the same, and so represented "normal."

Deviation IQ Over the years, dissatisfaction grew with the idea of reducing one's intellectual capacity to a single score. Subsequent intelligence tests, notably those designed by David Wechsler, obtained an overall score but did so on the basis of several sub-scores within the test.

Wechsler (1975) argued that intelligence, like other characteristics, was *normally distributed* in the general population. That means we can expect that within a population, scores on intelligence tests would fall along a normal, or bell-shaped, curve. Most people would score right around the average. Some people will be a little above average and others a little below. Fewer still would score toward the extremes representing mental retardation at one end and giftedness or genius at the other (see Figure 3.1). In this perspective, intelligence is seen as a function of the degree to which one deviates from the average. This view has replaced the use of mental age versus chronological age.

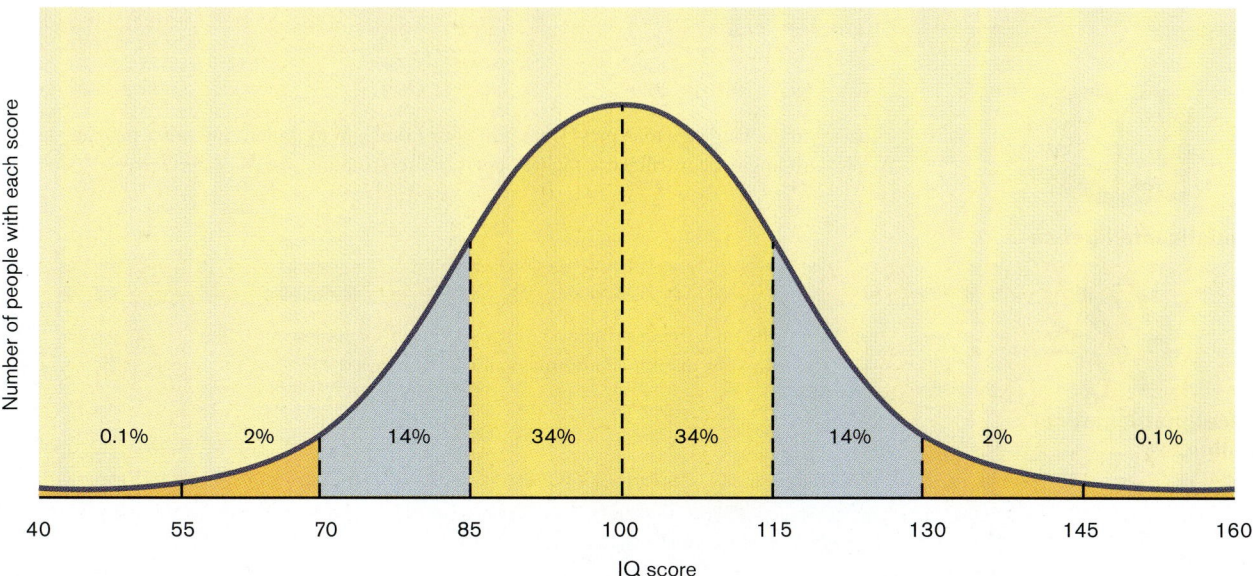

Figure 3.1

Normal Curve Representing Distribution of Intelligence Scores

The Theory of Multiple Intelligences

Another interesting approach to the construct of intelligence is the theoretical framework proposed by Howard Gardner (1983). He identified seven intelligences: linguistic, logical-mathematical, spatial, bodily kinesthetic, musical, interpersonal, and intrapersonal. Later he added an eighth intelligence: naturalistic (1999). Gardner's approach to intelligence broadens the previous perspective considerably. For one thing, Gardner's list includes physical ability (bodily-kinesthetic). For another, it goes far beyond the notion that intelligence should be considered in terms of the traditional categories of verbal and mathematical reasoning. Nor does Gardner's approach confine an individual to strength in just one category. For instance, a concert pianist can be expected to have exceptional abilities in the musical *and* bodily-kinesthetic categories. Which categories in Figure 3.2 represent your strengths and weaknesses?

Meeting the Needs of Students with Cognitive Exceptionalities

Students with cognitive exceptionalities on either end of the scale present particular challenges for the classroom teacher. While we will introduce you to the topics of mental retardation and gifted/talented functioning, an in-depth discussion is beyond the scope of this introductory text. Indeed, you may one day complete entire courses in exceptionalities, and perhaps even a degree program in exceptional education. For an excellent introduction to exceptionalities, see *Special Education in Contemporary Society: An Introduction to Exceptionality,* by Richard M. Gargiulo (2006).

Mental Retardation

Defining mental retardation has been a difficult task, confounded by stereotypical images of individuals with mental retardation. The American Association on Mental Retardation (AAMR) has been the leader in the development and refinement of the concept of mental retardation. In 2002 the AAMR issued its tenth and most recent definition:

Intelligence	Characteristics
Linguistic intelligence	Capacity to use language to express what's on your mind and to understand other people. People with linguistic intelligence include poets, writers, orators, speakers, and lawyers.
Logical-mathematical intelligence	Understands the underlying principles of some kind of a causal system, like the way a scientist or a logician does, or manipulate numbers, quantities, and operations, the way a mathematician does.
Spatial intelligence	The ability to represent the spatial world internally in your mind—the way a sailor or airplane pilot navigates the large spatial world or the way a chess player or sculptor represents a more circumscribed spatial world.
Bodily kinesthetic intelligence	The capacity to use your whole body or parts of your body—your hand, your fingers, your arms—to solve a problem, make something, or put on some kind of a production. Examples include athletes or performing artists.
Musical intelligence	The capacity to think in music, to be able to hear patterns, recognize them, remember them, and perhaps manipulate them.
Interpersonal intelligence	Understanding other people. It's an ability we all need but is at a premium if you are a teacher, clinician, salesperson, or politician.
Intrapersonal intelligence	Understanding yourself, knowing who you are, what you can do, what you want to do, how you react to things, which things to avoid, and which things to gravitate toward.
Naturalistic intelligence	The human ability to discriminate among living things (plants, animals) as well as sensitivity to other features of the natural world (clouds, rock configurations).

Figure 3.2   Gardner Explains the Eight Areas of Intelligence

From Checkley, K. (September 1977), The First Seven . . . and the Eighth: A Conversation with Howard Gardner. *Educational Leadership 55* (1), 8–13. Reprinted by permission. The Association for Supervision and Curriculum Development is a worldwide community of educators advocating sound policies and sharing best practices to achieve the success of each learner. To learn more, visit ASCD at www.ascd.org.

Mental retardation is a disability characterized by significant limitations both in intellectual functioning and in adaptive behavior as expressed in conceptual, social, and practical adaptive skills. This disability originates before age 18. (Luckasson et al., 2002, p. 1)

The five assumptions to be considered when applying the definition are as follows:

- Limitations in present functioning must be considered within the context of community environments typical of the individual's age, peers, and culture.
- Valid assessment considers cultural and linguistic diversity as well as differences in communication, sensory, motor, and behavioral factors.
- Within an individual, limitations often coexist with strengths.
- An important purpose of describing limitations is to develop a profile of needed supports.
- With appropriate personalized supports over a sustained period, the life functioning of the person with mental retardation will generally improve. (Luckasson et al., 2002, p. 1)

Courtesy of Bill Lisenby

The child with special needs also has individual strengths. The effective teacher will provide support that taps these strengths and builds upon them.

Notice that the five assumptions stress the context of community environments, recognition of the individual's strengths, needed support, and the expectation of improving the individual's life functioning. These proactive and positive perspectives are reflective of Gargiulo's belief "that children and adults with mental retardation are first and foremost people who are more like their non-retarded counterparts than they are different" (2006, p. 146).

Classification and Prevalence of Mental Retardation Various classification systems have been used to categorize degrees of mental retardation. One of the most prevalent systems is based on a measure of intellectual deficits and related impairments in adaptive behavior. Table 3.4 lists the four categories of impairment with their related Wechsler IQ scores.

A system that has often been used in education since the 1960s is based on expected or anticipated educational accomplishments (Gargiulo, 2006). Children with cognitive impairments are classified in one of two groups: educable mentally retarded (EMR) or trainable mentally retarded (TMR). "Educable" (with IQs ranging from about 50–55 to 70–75) implies that the individual may have some

Table 3.4	Classification of Mental Retardation as a Function of Measured Intelligence (Wechsler Scale)	
	Classification Level	**Measured IQ**
	Mild Retardation	55–70
	Moderate Retardation	40–55
	Severe Retardation	25–40
	Profound Retardation	Under 25

limited academic potential. "Trainable" (IQs ranging from about 35–40 to 50–55) implies that the student likely does not have a capacity for learning but could be trained for nonacademic tasks. A key difficulty with this system is the presumption of limited or no ability to learn. Many in education would tend to embrace that all children, given the proper support, are capable of learning.

The current system of classification refers to levels of support rather than to levels of deficiency. This scheme, published by the AAMR in 1992, identifies four support levels:

- **Intermittent**—Supports provided on an as-needed or episodic basis.
- **Limited**—Supports characterized by consistency over time, though time limited.
- **Extensive**—Supports involving regular involvement (such as day to day) in at least some environments (such as work or home) and not time-limited.
- **Pervasive**—Supports characterized by constancy and intensity and provided across all environments. (Adapted from Mental Retardation: Definition, Classification, and Systems of Supports, 10th ed., Washington, DC: American Association on Mental Retardation, p. 152.)

During the 2000–2001 school year, approximately 613,000 children between the ages of 6 and 21 were identified as mentally retarded and were receiving special education services (U.S. Department of Education, 2002). This represents approximately 1 percent of the total school-age population. In addition, U.S. Department of Education (2002) statistics indicate that 25,600 preschoolers were identified as being mentally retarded.

Educational Considerations Effective instructional programs for students with mental retardation need to be individualized, comprehensive, and functional. As with all students, the goal is to develop individuals who can be independent and self-sufficient. For students with mental retardation, however, there may need to be less emphasis on academic learning and greater emphasis on life skills.

One way to address the future needs of these students is with a *functional curriculum*. This approach emphasizes the life skills that will be necessary for day-to-day living and reflects the environment in which they will live. *Functional academics* are the skills (such as making change and reading/following directions) that individuals will need to be self-sufficient. For instruction to be most effective, it should occur as much as possible in natural settings rather than as simulations (Browder & Snell, 2000).

New technologies offer valuable possibilities for individuals with mental retardation. Computers and specialized hardware and software are examples of *instructional technology* that can support teaching and learning. *Assistive technologies* are those that can increase, maintain, or improve the functional capabilities of individuals with disabilities.

Gifted and Talented Programs

An IQ score of approximately 130 is often used as the lower limit for giftedness. However, the number used in a school district to assign students to classes for the gifted and talented depends on the pool of applicants. If 20 students are to be selected, the cutoff score may be raised or lowered to correspond to the desired class size. Thus, in a school district that serves a large number of low achievers, a qualifying score might be well below 130. In another setting that same score might be insufficient because a number of students score well beyond that point. Of course, other factors are also included in making that determination, but numerical scores

Go Online!

ACTIVITY 3.3 Requirements for Admission to Gifted/Talented Programs

Most schools have a program for their gifted/talented students. The programs have all sorts of names, some of which are acronyms. The requirements can differ significantly from district to district.

1. Access the Web site for the National Association for Gifted Children (NAGC) at www.nagc.org. The NAGC issues policy statements from time to time, and among them is a statement about the identification of gifted students. What are their recommendations?

2. Contact two area school districts and find out the their requirements for admission to the gifted/talented program. (It is best to contact separate school districts rather than schools within a district since district policy may dictate to all schools.) You can access district Web sites or call and ask to speak with the curriculum coordinator.

3. Compare the information you have received from all three organizations. Do they all use the same criteria? Chances are good that there will be variations. If so, what are those variations? Which of the three sets of criteria do you see as being the most appropriate?

---

are usually considered as one "safe" way of decreasing the size of the original pool of applicants because they reflect objective scores on a standardized test.

Gardner's "multiple intelligences" perspective is also used to identify giftedness. The benefit of this perspective is that average or even below average functioning in one area does not preclude performance on a gifted level in another. This leads us to a consideration of just what is meant by gifted and talented.

gifted and talented Students who show evidence of high performance capability in areas such as intellectual, creative, artistic, or leadership capacity, or in specific academic fields, and who require services or activities not ordinarily provided by the school in order to fully develop such capabilities (United States Congress).

Although the terms **gifted and talented** are often used in tandem, they represent different dimensions of the human condition. A person can be gifted but not talented or can be talented but not gifted. Of course, it is possible to be both. So how is "gifted and talented" defined? Congress (Title IV—H.R. 5, 1988, pp. 227–228) defines it as

> evidence of high performance capability in areas such as intellectual, creative, artistic, or leadership capacity, or in specific academic fields, and who require services or activities not ordinarily provided by the school in order to fully develop such capabilities.

The gifted student has superior intelligence; the talented student shows unusually high ability in some special field of knowledge (Feldhusen, 2000). Gifted and talented children need differentiated programs because they learn rapidly, reason well, use logic, are verbally fluent, or demonstrate advanced achievement. Some of these children are handicapped and require special programs to enable them to achieve their potentials (Weintraub, 2000). An investigation into the various admission requirements to programs for the gifted and talented would be a useful exercise. See Activity 3.3 for some guidance.

Learning Disorders

The discussion so far has considered student diversity in terms of cognitive functioning that can be represented as IQ scores. Other situations also relate to psychological processes, yet are not a function of IQ per se.

Learning Disabilities

learning disability A disorder in one or more of the basic psychological processes involved in understanding or in using language, either spoken or written, which manifests itself in imperfect ability to listen, think, speak, read, write, spell, or do mathematical calculations (Individuals with Disabilities Education Act).

The term **learning disability** as defined by the Individuals with Disabilities Education Act (IDEA), which was reauthorized by the U.S. Congress in 2004, refers to "a disorder in one or more of the basic psychological processes involved in understanding or in using language, either spoken or written, which manifests itself in imperfect ability to listen, think, speak, read, write, spell, or do mathematical calculations" (20 U.S.C., Sec. 1400). A study based on two surveys conducted by the U.S. Department of Education (Coutinho, Oswald, & Best, 2002) found that students classified as learning disabled were most likely to live in poverty, be minorities, or be males. Indeed, boys are three to five times as likely as girls to be diagnosed as learning disabled (Young & Brozo, 2001). The disorders include conditions such as perceptual disabilities, brain injury, minimal brain dysfunction, dyslexia, and developmental aphasia. They do not include "a learning problem that is primarily the result of visual, hearing, or motor disabilities, of mental retardation, of emotional disturbance, or of environmental, cultural, or economic disadvantage" (Turnbull & Cilley, 1999). Notice in the last sentence the conditions that eliminate a person's impairment from consideration. Visual, hearing, and motor disabilities are special conditions but are not *learning disabilities.* The language of IDEA thus provides both inclusionary and exclusionary terminology for the learning disabled classification.

The IDEA definition is not embraced by all professionals in the field, however. In 1988 the National Joint Committee on Learning Disabilities (NJCLD) adopted a definition that identified several important characteristics. First, the condition is heterogeneous. This means that the condition can vary or manifest itself differently in different people. Next, the NJCLD definition states that students with learning disabilities *may* also demonstrate social and behavioral difficulties. Third, learning disabilities occur across the life span. That is, it is a condition that is not outgrown at some point. And finally, the cause of the condition is *intrinsic* rather than resulting from cultural influences or poor instruction.

Combining the two definitions, most states and school districts require that students meet three criteria to be classified as learning disabled (Mercer, Jordan, Allsop, & Mercer, 1996):

1. **Inclusionary criterion:** There must exist a severe discrepancy between the student's perceived potential and actual achievement as measured by appropriate assessment instruments.
2. **Exclusionary criterion:** The learning disability cannot result primarily from a visual or hearing impairment, mental retardation, serious emotional disturbance, or cultural differences.
3. **Need criterion:** There is a demonstrated need for special education services without which the student's learning will be compromised.

You should be cautious in your approach to possible learning disability situations. First of all, teachers are not certified or qualified to diagnose such conditions.

Table 3.5	Summary of Learning Disorders
Disorder	**Prevalence**
Specific Learning Disability	Approximately 50% of all children with disabilities served under IDEA
AD/HD	Approximately 3–7% of the school-age population
Emotional or Behavioral Disorder	Approximately 1% of the school-age population
Autism	Approximately 7.5 per 10,000 children

Thus, you should avoid telling parents that a student has a particular impairment. Your professional role is to make keen observations, document them, reflect on alternative possible causes, and then, if the situation demands it, refer the student to the appropriate personnel in your school (school guidance counselor, school psychologist) without labeling the student. Only an interdisciplinary team (on which you may participate) can make such a determination. The process is lengthy and is spelled out in the federal statutes.

A second point to keep in mind is that a specific learning disability is not to be confused with mental impairments. In general, a person with a specific learning disability possesses at least average ability. Based on some intelligence tests administered to determine the cognitive functioning of a student, the average range is 85–115. Thus, students with learning disabilities are presumed to be at least average in ability. The presence of a specific learning disability neither presumes below average intellectual function nor precludes functioning on a gifted level.

Third, as part of the specific learning disability, these students may function quite well in some psychological aspects, leading you to conclude falsely that if they would work harder, they would do much better in the impaired area. While motivation and effort are possible negative factors, the cause may be psychological. A specific learning disability is often accompanied by frustration, especially when the student believes she has already tried really hard.

Among students with disabilities, students with a specific learning disability are most likely to take part in the general education curriculum. As a classroom teacher, you will have students with learning disabilities **mainstreamed** in your class at least part of the school day and possibly all day long. If you are an exceptional-education teacher, you will have these students in your class part of the time unless you work in a "pull in" arrangement whereby you work with your students in their regular classes. This is frequently referred to as part of the **inclusion** model, which seeks to keep children with special needs in the regular classroom throughout the day. In either situation, you will be part of a partnership working together to help students derive maximum educational benefit.

Two approaches to improving the educational opportunities for students with learning disabilities are the use of learning strategies (Deshler, 1998) and direct instruction (Engelmann, 1991). Learning strategies assist students in learning techniques for acquiring, storing, and remembering information. Direct instruction provides highly structured, scripted programs that gradually move from a teacher-guided to a student-guided format.

Autism

As compared to students with other disabilities, students with **autism** are among those least often included in general education classes. This disorder occurs in approximately 7.5 children per 10,000 (Fombonne, 1999), and it affects about four times as many males as females.

When children were diagnosed with autism in the mid-20th century, it was often noted that they generally seemed to have well-educated and successful parents who were "cold" in their emotional relationships with their children. The misconception that autism was the result of parental emotional distancing was dispelled in the 1970s when it was determined that the condition was the result of a brain or biochemical dysfunction occurring before, during, or after birth (autism typically shows up by age 3). In 1977 the National Society for Autistic Children (which is now known as the Autism Society of America) issued the following statement: "No known factors in the psychological environment of a child have been shown to cause autism."

mainstream An approach to integrating students with special needs into the general education population.

inclusion A model in which an exceptional-education teacher provides assistance in a regular classroom to a student who has been identified as having a disability identified by one of the related laws.

autism A developmental disability that significantly affects a child's verbal and nonverbal communication, social interaction, and educational performance (Individuals with Disabilities Education Act).

The Individuals with Disabilities Education Act (IDEA) defines autism as a developmental disorder that significantly affects a child's verbal and nonverbal communication, social interaction, and educational performance. A child cannot, however, be classified as autistic if the poor educational performance can be attributed primarily to serious emotional disturbance.

The two most common barriers that children with autism face in the general education classroom setting are problem behaviors and atypical social development. Problem behaviors in the classroom could be such things as rocking back and forth constantly or self-injurious behaviors such as biting or head banging. Antisocial behaviors may include biting other students or echolalia—repeating what someone else has just said (which other students may misinterpret as taunting or teasing). Interventions with these situations often take the form of *positive behavior support.* This is closely akin to behavior modification techniques that seek to provide positive reinforcement for appropriate behaviors and to ignore inappropriate behaviors (to the extent possible).

An advantage of positive behavior support is that it can be used for all children rather than just with a particular population. It has three components: (1) *universal support,* a program instituted throughout the school; (2) *group support,* which addresses problem behaviors occurring in small groups of 10–15 students; and (3) the most intense version, *individual support,* which provides support for a single student by eliminating inappropriate behaviors through group or universal support interventions. In all cases, the intent is to replace the problem behavior with the appropriate behavior and to teach students to use appropriate social skills.

Attention Deficit/Hyperactivity Disorder

It is likely that as a classroom teacher you will have one or two students in your class who just can't seem to focus on what's going on or, alternatively, who just can't seem to settle down long enough to find out what's going on. Before losing your temper and becoming upset with the students, consider that such behaviors may fall into the category of **Attention Deficit/Hyperactivity Disorder** (AD/HD). These children would love to be able to focus or to settle down, but for some reason it is just not within their control. According to the American Psychiatric Association (2000), approximately 3 to 7 percent of the school-age population have some form of AD/HD. Notice that unlike statistics we have presented for other disorders, this is not 3 to 7 percent of students with some sort of cognitive disorder; this is 3 to 7 percent of the entire school-age population. That's a lot of students! Of these students, the prevalence of AD/HD in boys to girls is about 3 to 1 (American Academy of Pediatrics, 2000).

IDEA does not list AD/HD as a major category but rather subsumes it under the heading of Other Health Impairments. The American Psychiatric Association (2000) offers this definition:

> The essential feature of Attention-Deficit/Hyperactivity Disorder is a persistent pattern of inattention and/or hyperactivity-impulsivity that is more frequently displayed and severe than is typically observed in individuals at a comparable level of development (p. 85).

For a student to be diagnosed with AD/HD, the symptoms must be manifested before age 7, continue for at least six months, and occur in at least two social settings, such as at school *and* at home. Of course, not all students classified as AD/HD are hyperactive and attention-deficit. Some students may be hypoactive, that is, very slow to respond.

In the past, AD/HD in children has been blamed on, among other things, too much sugar in the diet, food sensitivity, allergies, and poor parenting. Research has

Attention Deficit/Hyperactivity Disorder (ADHD) A persistent pattern of inattention and/or hyperactivity-impulsivity that is more frequently displayed and severe than is typically observed in individuals at a comparable level of development (American Psychiatric Association).

indicated that such environmental causes are not at fault (Baren, 1994; Barkley, 2000, 1998; Hoover & Milich, 1994). Instead, medical technology has shed light on a variety of possible causes that can occur before, during, and just after birth.

As a classroom teacher you should be aware of behaviors that can be associated with AD/HD. AD/HD has three subtypes: Predominantly Inattentive (IN), Predominantly Hyperactive-Impulsive (HI), and Combined (CB). As a classroom teacher you should be aware that these behaviors can interfere with learning development and social experiences. Your first task will be to see the student apart from the behavior and so avoid becoming frustrated over behaviors the child is struggling to control. Next, it will be important for you to coach, model, and role play appropriate behaviors with the child and to reinforce appropriate behaviors (Roan, 1994). With regard to academics, Shank (2002) recommends keeping these seven words in mind: relevance, novelty, variety, choices, activity, challenge, and feedback. Orienting your planning around these terms can involve everything from the timing of lessons to the writing of behavior contracts and the recognition of appropriate achievement.

Emotional or Behavioral Disorders

emotional/behavioral disorder
A condition exhibiting one or more of the specific characteristics over a long time and to a marked degree that adversely affect a student's educational performance.

Of all the cognitive differences we have discussed so far, the category of **emotional/behavioral disorders** is perhaps the most difficult to pin down. We've all been upset or anxious about a situation at some point and may have even engaged in an activity or two that we knew was not the right thing to do, but does that constitute an emotional or behavioral disorder? No, an isolated instance does not a disorder make, yet the prevalence of such disorders is likely much higher than you may expect. There are some 469,000 students with emotional or behavioral disorders in the United States (Digest of Education Statistics, 2002). That represents approximately 1 percent of the entire school-age population, or 1 out of every 100 students. It has been estimated by some experts that the rate is closer to 9 or 10 percent (Walker, Zeller, Close, Webber, & Gresham, 1999).

As we found with Attention-Deficit/Hyperactivity Disorder, the definition for emotional and behavioral disorders provided in the Individuals with Disabilities Education Act (IDEA) differs from that proposed by many mental health professionals. The IDEA definition for this disorder, which qualifies an individual to receive services under the Act, is as follows:

(i) The term emotional disturbance refers to a condition exhibiting one or more of the following characteristics over a long time and to a marked degree that adversely affects a student's educational performance:

(A) An inability to learn that cannot be explained by intellectual, sensory, or other health factors.

(B) An inability to build or maintain satisfactory interpersonal relationships with peers and teachers.

(C) Inappropriate types of behavior or feelings under normal circumstances.

(D) A general pervasive mood of unhappiness or depression.

(E) A tendency to develop physical symptoms or fears associated with personal or school problems.

(ii) The term includes schizophrenia.

The term does not apply to children who are socially maladjusted unless it is determined that they have an emotional disturbance. [34 C.F.R., sec 300.7 (c)(4) (1999)]

A key distinction between this definition and the broader view lies in the reference to "socially maladjusted" and its cause. For instance, a youngster may join a gang because of peer pressure. This would be considered an environmental influence and not entitle the child to services as part of the Act. However, IDEA *would* provide services if, by contrast, the child chose gang membership as a result of an emotional disorder. The quandary is that in the latter case the child receives special educational services whereas in the former case (the example being gang membership as the result of peer pressure) the child is considered as a delinquent to be punished.

Emotional disorders can be classified according to the following conditions (American Psychiatric Association, 2000): (1) anxiety disorders, (2) mood disorders, (3) oppositional defiant disorder, (4) conduct disorders, and (5) schizophrenia. Anxiety disorders are further subdivided into the following categories: phobias, generalized anxiety disorder, panic disorder, obsessive-compulsive disorder, eating disorder, and post-traumatic stress disorder. Mood disorders can also be subdivided as follows: emotion, motivation, physical well-being, and thoughts. Again, keep in mind that as emotional disorders these conditions are pervasive rather than just "being in a mood" for a short period of time.

Behavioral disorders are often thought of in terms of externalizing behaviors and internalizing behaviors. In the classroom, *externalizing behaviors* are those such as acting out and not complying with instructions. You have likely witnessed this on more than one occasion throughout your own school experiences. Now that you are more aware of it, you may notice it during field service or classroom observation experiences. *Internalizing behaviors* may be a little more difficult to spot. They include depression, withdrawal, anxiety, obsessions, and compulsions. Because these behaviors typically do not interfere with the overall functioning of the classroom, they are more likely to be overlooked or to fade into the background.

An important theme that has developed in addressing the needs of students identified with emotional or behavioral disorders is that of strength-based interventions (Brendtro, Long, & Brown, 2000). This approach seeks to assist students by building on their strengths rather than emphasizing their problems. Teachers are advised to provide learning environments that are structured and predictable and to provide positive interactions with the students. The building of skills in self-management, problem solving, and conflict resolution will be of significant value to these students.

Sensory Aspects of Student Diversity

Physical impairments can have a pronounced effect on learning. For that reason, we wish to consider some of the more common conditions that can be expected to affect your work as a classroom teacher. A number of conditions are classified in this category. Among the most common are visual sensory disability, auditory sensory disability, and physical and health impairments (Digest of Education Statistics, 2003).

Visual Sensory Disability

It is difficult to determine just how many children have visual impairments that interfere with their learning because the diagnosis and reporting of visual disorders varies considerably from state to state, and even among local educational agencies. We do know that in the 2000–2001 school year approximately 25,000 children received special education services as a result of visual disorders (Digest of Education Statistics, 2003). However, it is estimated that one out of four school-age children have undiagnosed vision problems significant enough to affect their performance in school and in life. In at-risk populations, such as children born in poverty, this percentage is likely to be much higher (American Foundation for Vision Awareness, 2002; Gould & Gould, 2003). Keep in mind as you read this section that (1) the visual disorders discussed here do not refer to simple matters of visual acuity that are accommodated with corrective lenses, and (2) a student with visual impairment would need substantial assistance to read the words you are reading now.

The definition of visual impairment in IDEA is "an impairment in vision that, even with correction, adversely affects a child's educational performance. The term includes both partial sight and blindness" (34 C.F.R., sec. 300.7 [13]). The key element of this definition is that the impairment interferes with learning. Within the category of visual impairment, individuals can be further classified with regard to their ability to use their vision and their reliance on tactile means (for example, the use of braille materials) for learning (Lewis & Allman, 2000):

1. **Low vision** students can read print though they may require optical aids.
2. **Functionally blind** students may be able to navigate their environment with their vision but rely on braille materials for printed communication.
3. **Totally blind** students do not receive visual input. They rely on auditory and tactile means to interact with their environment.

Visual impairments do not determine what a child can learn, but instead how the child will learn. As a classroom teacher you will likely find yourself to be a member of a collaborative team that augments instruction and instructional materials to meet the needs of these students. In general, accommodating those needs will entail (1) adapted methods for accessing print, (2) instruction that is adapted to increase the meaningfulness of experiences, (3) providing opportunities to use technology that is appropriate, and (4) providing specialized instructional materials (Turnbull, Turnbull, Shank, & Smith, 2004).

Auditory Sensory Disability

In the school year 2000–2001, approximately 1.1 percent of children receiving special education services were those with hearing impairments. That represents approximately 70,000 children (Digest of Education Statistics, 2003). The actual number of children with some degree of hearing loss may be greater, because many children with hearing impairments may be classified under other disability categories. Indeed, the American Speech-Language-Hearing Association (ASHA) contends that 83 out of every 1,000 children have an "educationally significant hearing loss" (Black, 2003), which could represent millions of children.

Hearing loss can have profound effects on a child's development. You have likely closed your eyes at one time or another and imagined what it would be like if you could not see the world around you. As difficult as that would be, deafness can even more dramatically remove one from the surrounding environment. You would likely be surprised by how difficult communication becomes and, in particular, how difficult the learning of language becomes in the absence of sound.

While there are a number of causes of hearing loss, one that is readily preventable relates to environmental noise. Protection is advised for anyone exposed to noise at the 85 decibel level or higher. A lawn mower produces 90 decibels, and a leaf blower creates 100 decibels, just barely below the level at which the Occupational Safety and Health Administration (OSHA) requires protection devices (Wolkomir & Wolkomir, 2001).

Hearing loss is typically graded as follows:

Normal No impact on communication.

Slight Faint speech is difficult to understand in noisy environments.

Mild Classroom discussions are difficult to follow. Faint or distant speech is difficult to understand.

Moderate Conversational speech can be heard only at close distances.

Moderate-Severe Only loud and clear conversational speech can be heard.

Severe Conversational speech cannot be heard unless very loud. Speech is not always intelligible.

Profound Conversational speech cannot be heard. Speech may not be developed at all. (Turnbull, Turnbull, Shank, & Smith, 2004, p. 428)

A child in your classroom who appears to have difficulty hearing may benefit by being moved closer to the source of conversation. However, working with children with deafness or hearing loss will likely require substantial adaptive measures. The next time you go to class, consider how much of what is said is off-hand or dependent upon auditory clues for interpretation (that is, vocal inflections or perhaps a contrived whisper as if something is secret). Students with hearing impairments would find it very difficult to keep up with such cues. Difficulties with communication can, in fact, be the source of negative self-esteem issues for these children as well.

Relatively few classroom teachers are trained in the use of American Sign Language (ASL), and so communication as part of the general education classroom may well involve ancillary personnel to perform this function (though it may be worthwhile for prospective teachers to gain at least rudimentary capability with ASL). Other approaches to working with children with deafness or hearing loss can involve *oral/aural* methods, which require students to use speech, speech reading (you might know this as "lip reading"), and auditory skills for communication. *Total communication* refers to methods that incorporate oral/aural methods along with ASL at the same time, though this is often considered somewhat unrealistic for a mainstream classroom.

Physical and Health Impairments

Children who are physically challenged provide you with a responsibility that cannot be ignored. For example, when one of your authors was teaching middle school, he had a student in class with cerebral palsy. The youngster could not speak well, nor could he manipulate a pen or pencil. However, he was capable of responding to what happened in class (for example, he could answer test ques-

Table 3.6 Summary of Physical Aspects of Diversity (2000–2001)	
Impairment	**Prevalence**
Visual Impairments	Approximately 25,000 students
Hearing Impairments	Approximately 70,000 students
Physical and Health Impairments	Approximately 72,000 students

tions). To accommodate this young man, we built a flat box that had a marker attached to a moving arm. The student could crank the marker into position to mark an answer on a paper, and then push the marker down to leave a mark. The result was that, "on his own," he was able to take part in an activity that most students take for granted.

Approximately 72,000 children received services in the 2000–2001 school year to address *physical and health impairments* that interfere with learning. The Individuals with Disabilities Education Act (IDEA) has established four categories through which students with physical or other health impairments may qualify for special education services:

- **Orthopedic impairment**—this refers to a severe orthopedic impairment that interferes with a child's educational performance (e.g., clubfoot, absence of some member, poliomyelitis, bone tuberculosis, cerebral palsy, amputations, fractures, or burns that cause contractures).
- **Traumatic Brain Injury**—this category refers to an acquired injury to the brain that is caused by an external physical force, resulting in a total or partial functional disability or psychosocial impairment, or both, adversely affecting educational performance. The term does not apply to brain injuries that are congenital or degenerative, or those induced by birth trauma.
- **Multiple disabilities**—refers to concomitant impairments (e.g., mental retardation and blindness, or mental retardation and an orthopedic impairment), the combination of which causes such severe educational needs that they cannot be accommodated in special programs solely for one of the impairments. Note: the category does not include deaf-blindness as a multiple disability.
- **Other health impairments**—this refers to having limited strength, vitality, or alertness and can include a heightened alertness to stimuli resulting in a limited alertness to the educational environment that:
  (i) Is due to chronic or acute health problems such as asthma, attention deficit disorder or attention deficit hyperactivity disorder, diabetes, epilepsy, a heart condition, hemophilia, lead poisoning, leukemia, nephritis, rheumatic fever, and sickle cell anemia; and
  (ii) Adversely affects a child's educational performance.
  (34 C.F.R. 300.7(a) Public Law 105-17 [1999])

As you can see, this category can cover a very wide range of disabling conditions. You might also note that unlike some other categories addressed by IDEA, there is less emphasis on the congenital nature of the disability and more emphasis on the tendency of the condition to impede educational performance. Thus you can see that children who might not receive services under the Act in one category may qualify in another category. Similarly, a child may qualify in several categories.

Within the scope of an introduction to the teaching profession, we cannot address all of the ways that your work as a general classroom teacher or as an exceptional-education teacher might be affected given the range of physical disabilities you might encounter. However, we can tell you that as of the 1999–2000 school year, 94 percent of students with physical disabilities attended regular schools (Digest of Education Statistics, 2003). For the majority of these students you will not need to adapt the curriculum. What will typically be required will be adaptations for student mobility, for communication, or both. Table 3.6 provides a summary of the prevalence of the categories of physical diversity that have been discussed.

It is worth noting that at least 10 percent of American children suffer from some form of chronic illness, including asthma, allergies, diabetes, and epilepsy

Courtesy of Bill Lisenby

According to IDEA, qualified general and special educators must meet the special needs of students with physical or health disabilities in a public school setting.

(Students with Chronic Illnesses, 2003). You should be aware that particularly at the middle and high school levels, as many as 12 percent of the students may suffer from depression (with gay and bisexual students and Native Americans at highest risk); 1.3 percent will attempt suicide each year (Cash, 2003; Vail, 2005). Likewise, at the middle or high school level, you may encounter a student with an eating disorder, most commonly anorexia nervosa (refusing to maintain a healthy body weight, either by eating very little or by binge-eating and then inducing vomiting) and bulimia nervosa (characterized by fasting, excessive exercise, self-induced vomiting, and/or misuse of laxatives and diuretics). The students are usually female (Keca & Cook-Cottone, 2005). You will want to become familiar with family, student, school, and school district responsibilities as they relate to preventing, detecting, reporting, and dealing with these situations.

A Perspective of Empathy

This leads us to refer to *empathy*, the ability to put oneself in the shoes of another person. One principal whom we know asked his teachers at the end of the day to sit in the desk of a student who seemed to be troubled. Teachers were encouraged to reflect on the conditions that contributed to the behavior (academic or social or emotional) and attempt to create classroom environments that were more conducive to good mental health. Not only are we teachers called upon to empathize with our students, we also demonstrate compassion by actively encouraging our students to do the same with their peers. Use Activity 3.4 as an opportunity to empathize with someone else's situation.

ACTIVITY 3.4
Sitting in Their Place

This activity is one of reflection and introspection. We mentioned a principal who asked that teachers sit at the desk of a student who had had difficulty that day. Though a very simple exercise, we want to encourage you to try this. This is not an activity to write up and turn in for credit. This one needs to be done sometime during your semester when it feels "right."

1. At some time during the semester you will be in a class during which things just don't go well for some student. As you notice that situation unfolding during the class, be attentive to those things you can observe.

2. When the class ends, and the other students have departed, try sitting in that person's seat and consider what unrecognized factors could have contributed to the events in class. The seat you choose to take may even be that of the professor. This exercise is intended to help you understand that diversity does not always come along with a clear label on it. Sometimes you have to recognize that something is happening and be willing to consider what might be motivating the behavior.

Conclusion

As you have seen, diversity is a very, very broad topic, perhaps even broader than you had thought. An understanding of student diversity and ways to accommodate that diversity makes the work of a classroom teacher a truly specialized concern. What implications have you drawn from your study of this chapter? Here are some of the major points that were made.

1. Teachers need to be aware of cultural/ethnic differences among students and to develop a greater appreciation for those differences.
2. Teachers need to be aware of students' physical, social, and emotional needs and to establish and maintain contact with colleagues and others whose expertise can assist in meeting them.
3. Creating conditions that make it possible for students to make progress (both academically and socially) is part of a teacher's responsibility.
4. Provide a rich learning environment differentiated to the extent possible.
5. Sexual stereotyping prevents children from maximizing their potential.
6. Cognitive differences between students include intelligence (as measured by IQ) and psychological impairments such as specific learning disabilities and autism.
7. Physical aspects of student diversity can include visual impairments, hearing loss or deafness, and a wide range of physical disabilities.
8. Children (and adults) will display a wide range of temperaments in their social interactions. Among these are anger, happiness, sadness, level of confidence, introversion or extroversion, acceptance of novelty, and competition or cooperation.

Key Terms

diversity	intelligence
culture	intelligence quotient (IQ)
ethnicity	gifted and talented
multiculturalism	learning disability
cultural pluralism	mainstream
English as a Second Language (ESL)	inclusion
gender	autism
sex	Attention Deficit/Hyperactivity
gender bias/sexism	Disorder (ADHD)
sexual stereotyping	emotional/behavioral disorder
learning styles	

Educational Engineering

Case Studies in Education

Enter the information from the following table into the Educational Record for the student you are studying.

	Child's IQ Score	Child's Self-Concept	Cultural/Cognitive Concerns
Davon	Davon's IQ score is probably 100. (There are no standardized test scores for a kindergarten student.) He learns quickly but at times has difficulty due to his lack of life experiences.	Davon is secure in his abilities. Very reserved unless provoked—then quick to react. Confident in his ability to learn. Approaches new tasks enthusiastically. Has some difficulty getting along with his peers and expressing emotions appropriately.	Davon's receptive and expressive language should be taken into consideration when working with him, as well as dialect. He was not enrolled in a compensatory preschool program such as Head Start.
Andy	According to private analysis, Andy has an approximate deviation IQ of 87. He falls within the 25th percentile of students his age in the area of fluency and the 38th percentile for comprehension. Math ability is higher, with a score at the 58th percentile on his second-grade standardized test.	Andy's self-concept seems related to the subject he is working on. He is very hesitant in the language arts areas, but much more confident in math. He participates well in small groups but almost refuses to read orally.	Andy exhibits negativity toward African Americans. During a lesson concerning an African American girl dealing with racism in the 1960s, Andy stated, "It would be nice if there were no black people in school." Has been referred to the Intervention Assistance Team for evaluation for his difficulties with reading and writing. Will be tested for learning disabilities. Is reading two years below grade level. Receives supplemental reading instruction three times per week and attends before-school tutoring one hour per week.
Judith	Last measured IQ score was 80. Percentile rank on standardized tests: English: 47% Verbal, 41% Reading; Math: 25%	Difficult to say. Either Judith's self-concept is strong (at least at school) or she is doing an incredible job of blocking out the treatment she gets from other students. Given opportunities to succeed, her self-concept could become very strong.	Judith's cultural background is similar to many children in this school. An only child. Low SES environment. Parents are not detached, but there is a lack of emotional interaction throughout the family. Subsistence is a higher priority.
Tiffany	Tiffany's IQ during her evaluation report for her individualized education plan during her sixth-grade year was 141. The state guideline considers a student with a score of 130 or higher as Gifted and Talented.	Tiffany feels superior to other students. She feels that if she is not understood it is due to the other person's immaturity or lack of intelligence. Tiffany concludes that she is correct in most of her beliefs and actions and that most intelligent people would agree with her. She knows she is not considered popular, but appears to ignore other perceptions and opinions she might hear about her. She is proud to be her own person.	Tiffany has been labeled Gifted and Talented since third grade. She has been included in seminar groups and extension activity groups since fourth grade. She is planning to seek accelerated academic classes as they become available at the secondary level.

(Continued on next page)

Sam	On the Wechsler Scale for Children—Third Edition, Sam's Verbal Scale score was in the 8th percentile and Performance Scale score was in the 18th percentile. On the Wechsler Individual Achievement Test, Sam's scores were as follows: Basic Reading—5th percentile; Spelling—2nd percentile; Numerical Operations—2nd percentile; and Written Expression—2nd percentile.	Sam is well aware of his learning problems. His frustration sometimes manifests itself as anger but he is receptive to one-on-one teacher intervention. He is resilient and self-directed and does not appear to view himself as inferior.	Cognitively, Sam falls in the Low Average range of intellectual ability. His educational achievement in reading, written language, and math is severely discrepant from his intellectual potential, resulting in a diagnosis of specific learning disabilities in these three areas. Consequently, he is entitled to and receives special education services.
Bao	Bao scores in the upper 80s for English language skills, and in the lower 80s for math. She works very diligently on tests; hence she scores higher on them than her grades indicate. Her folder lists her IQ as 110, which puts her in the upper end of the first standard deviation above average.	Bao is uncomfortable with her background. Her classmates and teachers call her Katy; and at home, she responds to her parents in English. She is not at all ashamed of her culture or heritage, but perceives a difference between herself and being truly "American" despite living here since she was 3 years old. Being Asian hasn't been an issue at school. She's a cheerleader and member of Future Business Leaders of America.	Bao is averse to conflict and will only rarely voice an unpopular opinion. When teachers try to press her, she usually gets embarrassed and grows quieter. There are no special cognitive considerations involved with her education.

1. What does the combination of your student's IQ and test scores and information about self-concept tell you about working with this student? What challenges might it present for you?

2. When you consider the information provided about the student's family life, what expectations would you have for the child's behavior in school? What do you see as your greatest strengths and weaknesses for working with this particular child? Are there cultural factors of which you need to become aware?

 # Designing the School of the Future

There are those in education who argue that trying to consider how education might be in the future is not a valuable exercise because the work of educators is in the present. However, as you have seen from this chapter, there are cultural and ethnic influences that are dynamic and therefore changing. Those changes will mean changes for education as well. You cannot be expected to design a school that anticipates the changes to come, but it is possible for you to consider a design that can adjust as changes come about within the society at large.

1. As you consider a school for the future, what will the emphasis be in terms of what you have encountered in this chapter? That is, will your school focus on the "Americanization" of students that characterized the beginning of the 20th century? Or will your emphasis be on the cultural pluralism that characterizes the beginning of the 21st century? Provide an argument to support your decision.

2. The past has seen separate programs for special-needs students and mainstreaming programs that bring them into the regular classroom as much as possible. Now there is a movement toward full inclusion, which would do away with special programs entirely. What approach do you think schools in the future should take?

3. An important concern in education has always been the messages that children receive at home versus the messages they receive at school. How can a school of the future address these mixed messages? Will your school have a "parents' school" component that explains to parents the messages that the school will be trying to teach? Your approach to student diversity may well be what makes your plans for a school of the future unique in today's world.

 ## Praxis Practice

Many states will require that you successfully complete the Praxis Series of examinations to qualify for certification. One or more of those tests will be subject-area tests. Another, which has a more practical orientation, will be the Principles of Learning and Teaching (PLT) examination that is appropriate for your certification area.

Completing the Quick Check Quizzes for Chapter 3 in the Unit Workshop will give you practice with the multiple-choice format of the PLT. The Case Studies in Education and Designing a School of the Future activities will help prepare you for exercises that require reading a scenario and providing short answers to questions asking what you might do in such a situation.

4

Becoming a Teacher

Make the chapter work for you with CPR[2]:

Conceptualize Here are the major themes you will encounter in this chapter:

1. Each state has its own requirements for teacher certification.
2. Initial certification can follow traditional or alternative routes.
3. There is an increasing emphasis on national standards for teacher qualifications.
4. Professional organizations represent the interests of teachers and the teaching profession.

Preview Read the chapter headings; look at any figures, tables, and activities; and read through the items in the conclusion.

Activity 4.1: Field Observation Activity– Relating Your Coursework to Your Observations

Activity 4.2: Go Online! Comparing Certification Requirements

Activity 4.3: Go Online! Considering Alternative Certification Programs

Activity 4.4: Go Online! Exploring Professional Organizations

Read Now read through the chapter. Mark or highlight information that you consider to be especially important or about which you have a question.

Reflect Consider these questions as you read: What are your state's requirements for certification? Which professional organizations would best represent your professional interests?

Photo: Courtesy of Bill Lisenby

The following standards from the Interstate New Teacher Assessment and Support Consortium (INTASC) will be addressed in this chapter. As you read the chapter, consider how preparing to become a teacher is tied to these principles.

Principle 1 The teacher understands the central concepts, tools of inquiry, and structures of the discipline(s) he or she teaches and can create learning experiences that make these aspects of subject matter meaningful for students.

Principle 9 The teacher is a reflective practitioner who continually evaluates the effects of his/her choices and actions on others (students, parents, and other professionals in the learning community) and who actively seeks out opportunities to grow professionally.

Principle 10 The teacher fosters relationships with school colleagues, parents, and agencies in the larger community to support students' learning and well-being.

ice breakers

First Year

The first-year teacher pictured here has completed an approved teacher education program, holds a valid license, and is teaching in his certification area. Check each item below that could be said of him based on this information and on what you see in the photograph.

Courtesy of E. S. Ebert

❑ The lowest grade this class could be is kindergarten, and the highest is eighth grade.

❑ He has completed student teaching.

❑ His teaching credential is honored in all 50 states.

❑ The National Board for Professional Teaching Standards issued his license.

❑ He is responsible for teaching only one subject.

❑ The program from which he graduated recommended him for certification.

❑ He has never been convicted of a felony.

❑ The United States Department of Education issued his license.

❑ He is a member of his state's professional teacher organization.

❑ Parents can feel confident that he has passed the required state certification exams.

❑ The lowest grade this class could be is kindergarten, and the highest is eighth grade.
Probably true. These children appear to be older than preschoolers and younger than high school students.

❑ He has completed student teaching.
True. To earn a license to teach, students must complete a period of clinical internship known as student teaching.

❑ His teaching credential is honored in all 50 states.
False. His credential will be recognized only by states that have reciprocal agreements with the licensing state.

❑ The National Board for Professional Teaching Standards issued his license.
False. The NBPTS does not license teachers. It offers a voluntary advanced certification.

❑ He is responsible for teaching all academic subjects.
True. As an elementary school teacher he can be expected to teach all academic subjects.

❑ The program from which he graduated recommended him for certification.
True. The Teacher Education Program that he completes must recommend to the state that he is qualified to be licensed and certified.

❑ He has never been convicted of a felony.
Probably true. A background check is required for certification. A felony conviction could disqualify him from receiving a license.

❑ The United States Department of Education issued his license.
False. The federal government is not responsible for licensing or certifying teachers.

❑ He is a member of a professional teacher organization.
This depends upon whether teachers in his state are required to join a union. If not, membership in professional organizations is optional.

❑ Parents can feel confident that he has passed the required state certification exams.
True. Successful completion of state-mandated teacher certification examinations is a prerequisite to receiving a teaching credential.

A license attests that someone meets standards designed to protect the public; a certificate attests to satisfactory completion of a preparation program; accreditation attests that a program meets conditions deemed necessary by the profession. The three together, attended to separately, provide the best assurance we now have that a teacher is competent.

John I. Goodlad (1990)

■ Introduction

What qualities did you expect your teachers in elementary and secondary school to possess? How well qualified did you consider them to be? With the increasing emphasis on standards for students and teachers, what qualifications do you think the public has a right to expect from its teachers in general and you specifically? These questions are important because they offer you a chance to reflect on your current status as a teacher candidate and to decide how to achieve your goals. Accreditation standards, certification requirements, and the work of professional associations help to ensure that teachers are well prepared for the task at hand.

■ Earning a License to Teach

Programs leading to certification as a professional teacher are complex and rigorous. Though each state is responsible for establishing standards and requirements, there are considerable national influences that can affect the program that you ultimately complete. In this section, we look at the accreditation of teacher education programs, national influences on teacher education, and, finally, traditional and alternative teacher education programs.

accreditation agency An organization, most notably the National Council for Accreditation of Teacher Education, that certifies that an institution's teacher preparation program has met a series of rigorous standards.

Accreditation of the Teacher Education Program

Many states designate an **accreditation agency** for teacher education programs. An accreditation agency sets the standards for teacher education programs. Your state may have adopted the standards of a particular agency, or it may have developed its own. In either case, the colleges and universities offering teacher education programs must meet those standards if they wish to be an "accredited program." In most cases, states will certify only those who graduate from approved programs.

The most prevalent of the accreditation agencies is the National Council for Accreditation of Teacher Education (NCATE). As of 2005, 25 states use the NCATE standards for teacher education programs ("Type of partnership," November 4, 2005), so let's consider their six standards (Professional Standards for the Accreditation of Schools, Colleges, and Departments of Education, 2002):

Courtesy of Bill Lisenby

This teacher must graduate from an accredited teacher education program to be eligible for licensure and certification. Ask your professor about the accreditation standards of your program.

Standard 1: Candidates preparing to work in schools as teachers or other professional school personnel know and demonstrate the content, pedagogical, and professional knowledge, skills, and dispositions necessary to help all students learn. Assessments indicate that candidates meet professional, state, and institutional standards.

You are the candidate. The dispositions you must demonstrate are such qualities as attitudes, interests, and values related to learning. Assessments include those prepared by a professor, a textbook author, and state or national tests. Assessments also include projects, presentations, and demonstrations. Some are noted by educators' observations of your work in elementary, middle, or high school settings.

> **Standard 2:** The unit has an assessment system that collects and analyzes data on applicant qualifications, candidate and graduate performance, and unit operations to evaluate the unit and its progress.

You are not just a number. What you do is constantly evaluated to see if you measure up to expectations. Your department or college of education is responsible for noting your progress or lack thereof.

> **Standard 3:** The unit and its school partners design, implement, and evaluate field experience and clinical practice so that teacher candidates and other school personnel develop and demonstrate the knowledge, skills, and dispositions necessary to help all students learn.

student teaching A culminating experience in a teacher education program that provides an extended opportunity for the prospective teacher to assume fuller responsibility, under the guidance of the supervising teacher, for providing instruction to an entire class.

clinical experience Experience during which a prospective teacher engages in classroom activities by observing, assisting a teacher and students, or participating in other educational activities. Sometimes called *field service* or *internships*.

You may think of *clinical practice* as **student teaching.** Beginning with field observations, internships, or practica, your professors and the schools work together to provide a series of **clinical experiences** that gradually increase in complexity (e.g., observing and then teaching, working with individuals and later with groups and an entire class, teaching basic skills and later higher-order thinking skills).

> **Standard 4:** The unit designs, implements, and evaluates curriculum and experiences for candidates to acquire and apply the knowledge, skills, and dispositions necessary to help all students learn. These experiences include working with diverse higher education and school faculty, diverse candidates, and diverse students in P-12 schools.

P–12 refers to pre-kindergarten through grade 12. Of course, you may not be expected to work with the entire range of ages and grades unless your major is P–12 in scope (such as music, art, physical education, and exceptional education). Someone majoring in high school English will be involved just with grades 9–12 or possibly 7–12. The diversity issue relates to working effectively with a wide variety of people at all ages involved in education.

> **Standard 5:** Faculty are qualified and model best professional practices in scholarship, service, and teaching, including the assessment of their own effectiveness as related to candidate performance; they also collaborate with colleagues in the disciplines and schools. The unit systematically evaluates faculty on performance and facilitates professional development.

Your professors engage in considerable professional work that you do not see. They may write books or articles, consult with schools or school districts, and speak at local, state, national, or international conferences. They may serve on institutional committees and the faculty senate of the institution, and they may be involved in a variety of community programs. They are evaluated regularly, both by students and their peers. Like you, they too are accountable.

> **Standard 6:** The unit has the leadership, authority, budget, personnel, facilities, and resources, including information technology resources, for the preparation of candidates to meet professional, state, and institutional standards.

This standard simply states the expectation that your institution will have the personnel and material resources to provide you with an education that will allow you to distinguish yourself as you strive to accomplish the varied objectives of your education program. You will use the resources available at the library/information center, technology center, and curriculum laboratory of materials related to the schools. From time to time there may be guest speakers on education issues and opportunities for you to attend (and even speak at) professional conferences.

So there you have it. There is a reason, *a good reason,* for what you are asked to do as a teacher candidate. The reason is not just that the accrediting agency requires it. The reason is that best practice demands it, and the students in our schools are entitled to the best that we have to offer.

reciprocity The act of accepting in one state the credentials issued in another state.

It often happens that students study in one state and move to another state to teach. When states execute reciprocal agreements (referred to as **reciprocity**) with other states, graduates can take their degrees and certifications across state boundaries, usually being required only to take a state-mandated test or perhaps a course such as state history.

National Influences on Teacher Education

INTASC

In 1987, the Council of Chief State School Officers began to develop a set of guidelines that would bring consistency to the teacher certification process across the country. The result of this initiative was a collaboration between state education agencies, institutions of higher education, and national education organizations that formed the Interstate New Teacher Assessment and Support Consortium (INTASC). Since that time, INTASC has worked to establish performance standards for the assessment of beginning teachers. The standards are based on six core principles. Each of the principles is discussed in terms of the knowledge, dispositions (attitudes), and performances (skills) that teachers should possess. The principles are as follows:

Principle 1: The teacher understands the central concepts, tools of inquiry, and structures of the discipline(s) he or she teaches and can create learning experiences that make these aspects of subject matter meaningful for students.

Principle 2: The teacher understands how children learn and develop and can provide learning opportunities that support their intellectual, social, and personal development.

Principle 3: The teacher understands how students differ in their approaches to learning and creates instructional opportunities that are adapted to diverse learners.

Principle 4: The teacher understands and uses a variety of instructional strategies to encourage students' development of critical thinking, problem solving, and performance skills.

Principle 5: The teacher uses an understanding of individual and group motivation and behavior to create a learning environment that encourages positive social interaction, active engagement in learning, and self-motivation.

Principle 6: The teacher uses knowledge of effective verbal, non-verbal, and media communication techniques to foster active inquiry, collaboration, and supportive interaction in the classroom. (Interstate New Teacher Assessment and Support Consortium, 1991)

No Child Left Behind (NCLB)

The next initiative for us to consider is easily the most far-reaching of certification requirements, those mandated by Public Law 107-110, the No Child Left Behind Act, signed into law in January 2002. While the act consists of many aspects, we are considering here only those regulations that relate to certification and licensure. That part of the law required that all teachers be "highly qualified" by the end of the 2005–2006 school year. Teachers can be certified as "highly qualified" by securing state certification and obtaining a teaching license. However, there are some additional considerations. For instance, if special education teachers who teach several subjects are not certified in each area, they are judged "not highly qualified." The same is true for middle school teachers in grades 7 and 8 who have elementary certification (unless they have passed a middle school test in the subject area they teach). New secondary teachers (but not the current ones, who are "grandfathered in") must have either a major in their field or pass a content test ("The Law: What It Is, And Isn't," 2003).

The requirements that one be "highly qualified" do not apply to teachers in charter schools or to alternatively certified teachers. Currently they also do not apply to public schools that do not receive funding under P. L. 107-110. But if you seek employment at a school supported by Title I funds (about two-thirds of all schools in the country receive these federal funds, which are allocated based on student enrollment and poverty levels), you must be highly qualified to be hired.

In terms of licensure and certification, if you have full certification (no emergency waiver for a critical needs area, no temporary or provisional certificate), and have passed the state licensing tests, you're home free. If you're a new elementary teacher, you must pass a licensing test that covers reading, writing, math, and other elementary curriculum areas. If you're a new middle school or high school teacher, you must have an academic major or "coursework equivalent to a major" in each subject area you teach (or an advanced certificate or graduate degree in each such area) *or* pass a licensing test in each of those subject areas ("Are You Highly Qualified Under NCLB?" 2003). And, of course, you will be observed by trained educators during your first year of teaching (using the state-mandated observation instrument). The Secretary of Education periodically issues updated interpretations of the regulations, so the "rules" may change slightly from time to time.

As you can readily tell, these more-stringent regulations will prevent teachers from teaching out of field, that is, teaching courses for which they are not certified (e.g., a coach with a physical education degree teaching social studies, a science teacher teaching some math courses). There has been considerable concern about teachers being assigned to teach courses for which they may not even have a minor. *All Talk, No Action* (2002), a survey of thousands of teachers, found that the percentage of core courses taught by teachers without minors in the subjects increased from 21.8 percent in 1993–1994 to 24 percent in 1999–2000. According to a National Education Association Fact Sheet on Teacher Quality, nearly 28 percent of teachers teach out of field ("The Opportunity to Excel: Executive Summary," 2001). The findings by subject area are diverse: 48 percent of foreign language teachers and 71 percent of bilingual education teachers lacked the appropriate major and certification (Seastrom, et al., 2002). You may expect this situation to change as the call for teachers to be certified as "highly qualified" permeates the licensure and education of teachers.

The third initiative comes into play after you have completed your initial certification. Once certified, you will need to take additional courses only to renew your certificate or to add other areas of certification (e.g., add early childhood to elementary certification, add science to math certification) or to increase the level of certification (e.g., from bachelor's degree to master's degree). To add on areas of certification, the state department of education will identify the coursework and the examinations you must take. Then, depending on the regulations in your state, you take the courses, pass the test, and apply for the **add-on certification.** This procedure applies whether you are adding on credentials in teaching or in administration and supervision or some other non-classroom major (e.g., guidance counselor, media specialist).

add-on certification The addition of one or more areas of additional certification. It requires the successful completion of additional coursework and a passing score on the corresponding standardized achievement test such as Praxis.

In some states and some districts, your salary will increase after you complete a certain number of additional hours of coursework beyond a bachelor's degree. This can be an incentive to begin your master's program. Even now, over 50 percent of teachers hold a master's degree ("Status of the American Public School Teacher," 2003; "Teachers and ESPs—By the Numbers," 2003). Since a master's degree is rapidly becoming a common level of certification for teachers, not to mention a requirement for supervisors and administrators, you should start thinking along this line.

Traditional Teacher Education Programs

Each state establishes requirements for teacher education programs. The state education agency is your final source for information about certification (see Appendix D for a listing of state departments of education/certification agencies with their Web site URLs). State requirements for teacher certification include both traditional programs and the more recent alternative avenues to teaching. We will consider each of the possibilities but with an emphasis on the more traditional approach to certification.

license A document that certifies that the holder has successfully completed an education program in one or more areas of education.

certification The process one undergoes (e.g., in an elementary or secondary education program) to obtain a teaching license.

Certification terminology can be a bit confusing. The terms **license** and **certification** are often used interchangeably. In education, a *license* will authorize you to teach. The *certification* on that license will indicate the program you completed (for example, elementary education or secondary reading) and thus *what* you are prepared to teach. You might think of the license as a document and certification as the process you go through to obtain that document. For example, you may have a license to drive. That's the document. If you examine that document, you will find a designation indicating what you have been trained to drive—car, motorcycle, trucks of various types. Those designations represent your certifications. A teacher, therefore, can be licensed to teach in a particular state and have one or more certifications attached to that license.

Coursework

certification examination A standardized achievement test, frequently from the Praxis series, that prospective teachers must pass prior to their receiving certification.

general education A program of courses that almost every college and university student is required to take (except for those who enter with International Baccalaureate or advanced placement credits earned in high school or who exempt courses by passing placement tests).

In traditional programs, coursework includes (1) general education, (2) professional education, and (3) areas of specialization related to the student's major. The coursework is followed by a clinical internship (student teaching experience), often of 60 school days (12 full weeks). About the same time, prospective teachers take one or more **certification examinations** as required by the state for the grade levels and subject areas in which they desire to be certified.

The three categories of coursework are the same regardless of whether you attend a liberal arts institution or a college or university that focuses more on preparing students for specific vocations and professions. **General education** includes courses that almost everyone is required to take (except for students who enter college with International Baccalaureate (IB) credit or advanced placement (AP) credit earned in high school or who pass college placement tests). General education courses include mathematics, English, social studies, science, physical

Teacher Testimonial

Feature 4.1: Getting Certified to Teach

My teacher certification experience was a little different than most of the people I went to school with. I'm from Montana but wanted to go away from home for college. I chose to attend a school in South Carolina. So, my initial certification was in South Carolina, where I also did my first three years of teaching. After that I returned "home" and had to obtain certification to be able to teach in Montana. Fortunately for me, all it took was some additional paperwork. I understand, however, that different states might have special requirements for certification in their state. It doesn't prevent you from going to college away from your home state, but if you are in a situation like mine it would be a good idea to check with the certification offices in both states just to be aware of what the expectations will be.

In most cases, becoming a state certified teacher is a matter of completing an approved teacher education program (that is, approved by the state) and then submitting all of the correct paperwork. This isn't anything tricky, but it can easily get messed up when something is missing. When I graduated from school in South Carolina, the state asked for a standard application, which included an official college transcript, the recommendation for certification from the teacher education program, Praxis II test scores (your state may use a different test), and fingerprints for a criminal background check. From what I understand, the background check is something that is more often done prior to student teaching in many states nowadays.

During my student teaching semester, I was also enrolled in a student teaching seminar. We met every day for two weeks before beginning student teaching and then after school once a week or every couple of weeks during the semester. Our professor gave us explicit directions on how to complete this process, and a local police officer even came into our class one afternoon to take our fingerprints. Then, before we knew it, student teaching and four years of studying to become a teacher were over! My provisional certificate, good for one year, came through the mail.

During my first year of teaching, I was evaluated according to the S.T.E.P. program in my school district. All districts have some version of this; the names differ not only from state to state but even from district to district. In all of them, however, the idea is to evaluate and assist teachers through those first years of having full responsibility for a classroom of students all day, every day. Other first-year teachers in my district were asked to complete a long-range plan and other such things for this program. But, honestly, this step of the certification process was very stress-free and easy for me because my professor had us complete the exact same process during the student teaching semester. I felt very confident in what I was doing the first year of teaching (in regards to the S.T.E.P.

---

education, and fine arts. Some institutions require other courses such as religion, computer science, and foreign language. Some institutions require proficiency tests to identify the specific level of course (usually in math, English, computer science, and foreign language) that a student must take.

Some courses are offered on a pass/fail (or credit/no credit) basis or require passing an exit exam to receive credit. Some general education courses are required while others may be selected from several options within a broad category.

professional education A program of education courses that provide overviews of topics important for prospective teachers.

specialization courses Courses that focus on the teaching of particular subjects or other topics related to curriculum and instruction.

methods courses Courses that address diagnostic, instructional, and evaluation strategies as they relate to specific subjects (e.g., reading, math, science).

Professional education courses are usually general in nature but provide excellent overviews of important information for prospective teachers. Examples of these courses are Introduction to Education (or Foundations of Education), Human Growth and Development, and general, not specific, methods courses. Some professional education courses lay the foundation for subsequent specific courses, and others serve as summary (or capstone) courses.

Specialization courses include specific **methods courses** in such areas as elementary reading, middle school math methods, early childhood methods, methods of teaching secondary social studies, classroom management, and children's literature methods. Depending on your institution, there may be courses such as classroom management, science methods, social studies methods, language arts methods, and so on. These courses attempt to prepare prospective teachers for the

program) because of this. I don't know whether every teacher education program does this, but you might want to ask the folks at your school about how well the student teaching seminar will match up with the expectations of local school districts. All I can tell you is that I was much better prepared than some other first-year teachers in my school who had attended different colleges from mine. And just between you and me, there's plenty of stuff to deal with in your first year of teaching without having to learn how to prepare things like a long-range plan at the same time! After completing the first year of the S.T.E.P. program, I received my five-year certificate in the mail.

In South Carolina teachers are required to complete six hours of advanced coursework every three years to maintain certification. The requirements probably differ from one state to another, but this is how teachers get started on (and finish) master's degrees. Also, nowadays there's the option of pursuing National Board Certification.

I moved back to my home state of Montana three years after completing college and contacted the Office of Public Instruction (OPI) to request information on the certification process. I was directed to our state Web site and was able to download all of the necessary paperwork. Besides the application materials, I was required to send fingerprints for a criminal background check, an official copy of my college transcript, and a small fee. Within a few weeks I received a five-year certificate, which allowed me to teach anywhere in the state, including the rural school where I taught for two years.

A last thought—don't underestimate your school's field service or clinical internship experiences. Some people enter a teacher education program without any classroom experience. These opportunities to observe teachers and students in the classroom give teacher education students a realistic view of the career. At my college we began our observations with the very first education course in our freshman year. Though I wasn't so crazy about it at the time (it could be a hassle getting to and from a local school and not be late for classes back on campus), it gave me a really good exposure to school life. I know other college students who did not get into classrooms until their junior or senior year. They didn't get the same range of experiences that I had in my program. But even worse, some people found out after three years of majoring in education that they didn't really like being in the schools! So take advantage of the observation experiences your program provides. You will also find that those supervising teachers can be great resources, and most are more than willing to answer any questions and give both positive and negative feedback.

Megan Brenna-Holmes has been teaching for five years. In only her third year of teaching she was named Teacher of the Year in her school. ■

day-to-day realities of the classroom. Some colleges and universities have field service/internships attached to each of the specialization courses; more frequently there are separate internship courses or practica during which students apply what they have learned as they work with full classes of students in their major.

Professional education and specialization courses include objectives keyed to state or national accreditation standards. Generally there are requirements (e.g., tests, constructed projects, classroom presentations, lesson plans, papers, internships with reaction/reflection logs) based on the objectives. Thus, both you and your professor have an ongoing record of your progress.

Typically there is a flexible outline of projected semesters or quarters for taking general education classes. Many professional education and specialization courses follow a prescribed series of prerequisites. For instance, Introduction to Education usually is the first education course, and Human Growth and Development either follows or is taken concurrently. Likewise, a math methods course may follow completion of the general education mathematics requirement, and a secondary reading course may follow the completion of several content courses in the student's major. The system of prerequisites for some professional education and specialization courses helps to ensure consistency of content and avoid unnecessary gaps in students' backgrounds.

Field Observation

Field observation (which might also be called field service or experience) is another vital component of your teacher preparation programs. Whether you participate in field service in separate courses or as integral parts of professional education and specialization courses, you will want to take full advantage of the unique opportunities these experiences provide for preparing you for student teaching and for teaching itself. While some of your classmates may view field service as just another assignment to be completed and checked off, perceptive students use the opportunities to expand their education horizons and increase their professional expertise.

If you haven't already learned that teaching involves the completion of a myriad of forms, you soon will. Before you enter the schools, you will be expected to complete certain forms and perhaps be checked for communicable diseases such as tuberculosis. You may also be required to be fingerprinted so your previous record (if any) can be noted. Be sure to complete the forms candidly. Furthermore, when submitting final documents at the end of a term, be certain your records are accurate. Professors and staff people check those forms, and you do not want to be accused of falsifying information. Unfortunately, those events do occur occasionally. When you are unsure of a situation, ask questions.

Field observations offer invaluable opportunities to interact with teachers and students in a classroom setting.

© Jonathan Nourok/PhotoEdit

In many ways what you do in a field service experience foreshadows your student teaching assignment. What you learn early on will prove most helpful. There are three possible outcomes, in particular, that you might watch for:

You may have already decided on a major. That is, you know you want to teach high school English or middle school math or perhaps kindergarten. Your experience in field service may convince you otherwise. Perhaps you discover that you don't feel comfortable working with students of a certain age, or perhaps you decide that you really don't like to teach grammar and therefore decide against becoming an English teacher. One student we know entered college as an English education major, switched to elementary education after her first field service, and changed to early childhood after several subsequent field services. She graduated and became an excellent kindergarten teacher. Field service experiences changed the direction of her teaching career.

Another possible outcome: You may discover that teaching is not something you want to do for the next 30 to 40 years. In *The Canterbury Tales,* Chaucer wrote of one of the characters, "Gladly would he learn, and gladly teach." Perhaps only the first part of that quotation applies to you. That's fine. But to be sure one unhappy placement doesn't lead you to a too-hasty judgment, get a second opinion (in your next education course or as a volunteer). If you then decide to make a mid-course correction, you can be sure it is the right decision for you.

The third outcome is that you may realize your anticipated major is just right for you. You relate to the students at that age level, and you enjoy presenting the content relevant to your subject area or grade.

It has been said that the more you put into an experience, the more you get out of it. That's a universal truth, one well worth pondering and applying. What can you do during your field service experience that will prepare you to become the best educator possible? Here are some suggestions.

Relate Your Coursework to Your Field Observations When your professor makes recommendations ("Teachers should . . .") or offers guidelines or principles ("Effective teachers . . ."), note the extent to which the teacher uses them and decide how you would employ them as a teacher. Your introductory course is not merely a class to be completed; it's a window of opportunity that opens onto the world in which you will spend most of your professional life (see Activity 4.1). Relate the ideas you learn. Adapt the information you receive. When appropriate, adopt the practices you are taught. When necessary, create new strategies or solutions based on well-founded principles and research.

Learn about the Teacher and the Students What is the teacher's preparation? How long has he taught this subject or grade level? What background and interests does he bring to the class—travel to foreign countries, a collection of subject-related pictures or objects, classroom research, National Board certification? What do you need to know about the students? How do you deal with the 10–15 percent who have chronic conditions such as asthma, allergies, diabetes, and epilepsy (Students with Chronic Illnesses: Guidance for Families, Schools, and Students, April, 2003)? What are their levels of achievement, academic backgrounds, interests? Which ones have been identified as having exceptionalities? What are the ethnic compositions and the economic status of the class? Who are the new students, the shy ones, the clowns, the bullies? What would you do about them?

As you become familiar with the wide range of individual differences (refer to Chapter 3), you can follow the students throughout the quarter or semester if you

 Field Observation

ACTIVITY 4.1: Relating Your Coursework to Your Observations

If you are observing in a school now, use this activity in that setting. Otherwise, adapt this activity for your college classes.

1. Consider what you have been discussing in class thus far. Don't confine your thinking to this chapter, but to all the topics that have been discussed throughout the course. Write a list of the five most important things you've heard/read/discussed about being a teacher. You might list things such as compassion toward students, or teaching style, or the static and dynamic competencies we discussed in Chapter 1. List whatever has struck you as being really important.

2. In your field placement class (alternatively, select one of the courses you are enrolled in, or ask to sit in on another class so you can devote your attention to this activity), specifically watch for examples of each of the five items you have listed. Also note how the class seemed to respond to each item.

3. Consider your observations in terms of your expectations. Did things happen as you had anticipated? Did you see opportunities to have done things differently? Did students respond better to some things than others?

4. Write a summary of what you observed. Share it in your Introduction to Education class as a discussion starter and compare your observations with those of your classmates. What does this exercise say about the perspective of education as presented in class and what is occurring in the schools? Do they match? Do they differ?

schedule your observation sessions to encompass the entire term. While you might be tempted to "hurry up and get it done," that defeats the purpose of the experience and diminishes or negates the potential value.

In the middle school or high school, you will probably visit the same class each day so you can become familiar with the teacher, the students, the curriculum, and the instructional procedures. At the elementary level, you should try (as best as your schedule permits) to observe at different times of the day so you can see the wide range of curriculum for which a self-contained teacher is responsible. Varied observation times are especially appropriate for education courses that are not subject specific. In elementary language arts or science methods courses, you will necessarily observe at the same time each day, but in more general courses (such as Introduction to Education and Human Growth and Development) you should try to observe at different time periods if possible.

Learn about the Curriculum   Ask to borrow (or at least to look at) teachers' editions of textbooks and support materials (e.g., workbooks, manipulatives, transparencies, videos, curriculum guides, state and district requirements, and computer software). Review sample lesson plans, teacher-prepared and commercially prepared handouts (e.g., study guides), and tests. Read periodic newsletters and general letters to parents. If you can borrow a student copy of a text, read the immediately preceding lesson and the following one so you know what is to be taught, what students already have learned (hopefully!), and what they will study next. To the extent possible, be as prepared as the teacher and students should be.

This does not mean that you are now prepared to be a teacher. On occasion, you may be asked to assume responsibility for teaching an individual or group or even the entire class. While any of these possibilities may be appropriate, they should be preceded by careful preparation. For instance, you will need to become familiar with the teacher's procedures (both in terms of instruction and management) so there is no confusion between two different sets of strategies and expectations. Your initial instructional opportunities are not the time to become creative. That can come later.

To make the individual, group, or class instruction most productive, you must know your content and the teacher's procedures. If necessary for either of you to feel comfortable, discuss the proposed plans before they occur. As time passes and your competence increases, this step may become less important. One caution: You should not be expected to conduct a group or class session in the absence of the teacher. On occasion, a teacher may wish to leave you in charge of the classroom "for a few minutes" for what may be an appropriate mission (e.g., talk to a specialized teacher about a particular student, secure needed materials from the media center). While you may be willing to accommodate the teacher, for legal reasons doing so is not appropriate. There is the issue of professional responsibility, and you should politely refuse the request.

Examine the Policy Handbook   Obtain a copy of the school or district's policy handbook and read the parts that seem appropriate to your current situation. (Eventually, everything in the handbook will apply to you.) At a minimum, read the expectations for teachers, including dress code, specific procedures (signing in, signing out, calling in when absent), forbidden practices (such as chewing gum and bringing food to class), and general expectations.

Pay special attention to the section on professionalism. From time to time you will be privy to confidential information about students. The comments, whether fact or opinion, are private, not public, information, so you are expected not to comment on them or share them except possibly in disguised form (e.g., changed names, grades, schools) in a professional context such as a discussion in one of your classes or in a private conference with a professor. In no case should the privileged information be divulged in a dormitory or among friends. Doing so violates students' rights of privacy and could result in some unpleasant consequences.

As you reflect on the professionalism comments in the handbook, remember that while you may disagree with its contents, the handbook contains a description of rules and procedures rather than negotiable suggestions. As guests of the schools, we amiably adhere to their standards. Later, as teachers, we follow them professionally until they are changed.

You will find it to your advantage to arrive early (before the bell rings to signal changes in class) and stay until the end of the period in middle and high school. In elementary school, you can usually obtain a daily schedule indicating the approximate time that a teacher conducts certain classes. (Some administrators expect teachers to adhere faithfully to the posted schedule; others are less concerned about that issue. As a result of the No Child Left Behind Act, long reading blocks, for example, are likely to adhere to prescribed schedules.) When possible, arrive before the morning bell in the elementary school so you can see how the day begins. Observing at 9:00 each day, for instance, doesn't reveal how the teacher establishes the expectations for the day or how he sets the tone for the class.

If at all possible, you should make arrangements at some point in your teacher preparation program to observe on the first and second days of school, for those are crucial periods of time. One high school math teacher had 38 students in Algebra I on the first day of school. Most of them were rowdy, still in vacation mode. The teacher administered a pre-test and found that the majority of them could not add and subtract two four-digit numbers or solve 3/4 + 5/6. That evening she called 25 parents, spending five minutes with each noting the students' need for additional help, explaining her willingness to tutor before and after school, and asking for student cooperation because of the large class size. Several parents expressed appreciation for the calls. As you can imagine, the entire class was very well behaved the following day. Sometimes the little things make a big difference. If you don't begin observations until a month after school begins, you miss seeing everything a teacher does to set the stage for learning.

Record/React/Reflect Reacting and reflecting depend on careful observations that are recorded in an organized and timely manner (that is, before the inevitable loss of precise information). Be prepared with a notebook and with specific plans to observe certain components of a lesson. Perhaps you want to note how effectively time is used, or how often each member of the class is involved in a discussion, or what strategies a teacher uses to present a lesson. In the first example you may need a stopwatch, in the second a seating chart, in the third an awareness of the components of the lesson plan. Simply wandering into a classroom and sitting quietly is hardly a quality observation experience.

Once you have recorded your information, you can, at your leisure, react to the observations. What did you like or dislike? What did you consider appropriate or inappropriate? What seemed to be missing? What should have been omitted? It's helpful to react from the perspective of the observer (you) and sometimes from the participants (the students). You were comfortable; were they cold? You were interested in the lesson; were they bored? You understood the lesson; were they confused? You were relaxed and alert; were they upset or sleepy?

Now you are ready to reflect. What worked? Why did it work? Maybe you can observe the reason(s); maybe you need to ask the teacher. What did not work? Why do you think it didn't work? If you can phrase your question sensitively, your teacher may be able to offer some valuable insights. What would you have done in certain situations? Remember that it is far easier to sit in the back of the room and offer reams of advice than it is to carry them out in the context of an energetic or lethargic group of students. When reflecting, consider how much preparation would be involved if you were designing the lesson and how the information would be delivered. So be reasonable, be practical, be thoughtful. Remember student limitations—and yours.

Portfolio Preparation

portfolio A visual and physical record of achievement.

Now is an ideal time for you to begin developing your **portfolio,** which is a visual and physical record of achievement (Nidds & McGerald, January 1997). Since the development of a portfolio is not one of those required courses, you may wonder why you should go to all of this trouble. First of all, a comprehensive portfolio documents your activities and achievements, keeping them organized and available when you need them (e.g., when going to a job interview). Second, your institution's accreditation program will likely expect you to have a portfolio, and your teacher education program will probably require it. Third, it prepares you to use portfolios as part of assessing the progress and performance of your students. One caution: If you wait until you are required to present your portfolio in your teacher education program, you will spend far more time and be far more frustrated than if you start now by securing the containers that will hold your documents and thinking about the possible contents as they relate to your areas of interest. Portfolios will be discussed in more detail later in this chapter.

Courtesy of E. S. Ebert

Student teachers are mentored by their supervising teachers.

Student Teaching

Your student teaching experience will typically occur during your last college or university term. As noted earlier, it usually consists of at least 60 full days in one school setting or, especially in the case of double majors, a split placement of two 30-day segments. At the elementary level, the placement typically involves one classroom teacher. At the middle and high school levels, several teachers may be involved. In any case, placement occurs in a public rather than a private institution, and the supervising teacher generally possesses special state or district certification to serve as a mentor.

Student teaching is the penultimate college-based experience toward which your coursework and field service experiences have been directed. Where there are gaps in your educational background, you should continue to overcome them. Some of the previous suggestions related to making effective use of field service experiences are highly applicable for student teaching as well. In addition, there are other aspects to consider.

Request a Teacher and a School Placement That Further Your Career Objectives

For instance, you may want to consider student teaching in a school in which you would like to be employed. Perhaps you have participated in field service there. Perhaps the school is close to your home. Perhaps it has the kind of students with whom you would like to work. (Some people want to teach high-achieving students; others prefer working with at-risk populations.) Perhaps you know an administrator or some teachers at a particular school.

professional development schools
Public schools that function in close cooperation with a college or university's teacher education program. Many prospective teachers do their field service/practicum/internship and student teaching in the professional development school.

critical needs area (1) A professional area (e.g., mathematics, exceptional education) in which there is a shortage of teachers. (2) A geographical area (e.g., rural, inner city) in which it is difficult to secure sufficient numbers of certified and qualified teachers.

If you live in an area in which teaching jobs are scarce, your student teaching placement becomes even more important. However, if your area of the country has a surplus of teachers, your selection of a school may not contribute to your obtaining a local position (although it may result in excellent references). Then, too, you may not have the luxury of requesting a school. Some colleges and universities are affiliated with **professional development schools** that assume responsibility for many student teachers. These schools tend to have higher levels of student achievement than typical public schools (Teitel, 2001). Other schools may not be available because they have no teachers certified to supervise in your subject area or preferred grade level.

It is worth noting at this point that some teaching degrees are much more in demand than others. While the specifics vary from one geographical location to another, in general there is an abundance of secondary social studies teachers and physical education teachers. There are great shortages of exceptional education teachers and teachers of chemistry, physics, and math. In these subjects you have an excellent chance to locate a satisfactory position if you meet all of the employers' other requirements. You will often hear educators talk about **critical needs areas.** You will want to find out if your major is a critical need. It may entitle you to additional compensation in the form of a signing bonus or partial payment of moving expenses or eventual forgiveness of some of your college or university loans.

Requesting a particular supervising teacher can be very effective, for you will likely be most comfortable and effective if the two of you are philosophically and personally compatible. Indeed, you may wish to do student teaching with a teacher who directed one of your field service experiences. However, public school administrators often prefer to make the selection based on their own needs, and the staff at your institution may be justifiably sensitive to this issue. Nevertheless, you won't know what can be done unless you ask.

Obtain as Much Information as You Can about the Student Teaching Experience before You Begin Your first source will be a handbook used at your institution. Read it. Take notes or highlight it or underline it. Study it. When you have your orientation meeting with the supervising teacher, pay special attention to the information that is provided. This is a good time to request textbooks, curriculum guides, district and state standards, the policy handbook, class schedule(s), and roll(s). You should also find out whether you should follow your teacher's lead in every matter or whether you can make adaptations based on what you learned in your coursework and field service. Many teachers are eager to learn about "new methods," but they also are held accountable for student achievement, and that responsibility trumps your preferences to the contrary. Professional development schools often work closely with institutions of higher learning and therefore are more likely to provide opportunities for you to try new methods.

Obviously you will remind yourself of the discussions in this chapter related to your field service and will discuss proposed lessons before you present them. Ask your supervising teacher for feedback about the appropriateness of the content, the pacing of the lessons, and the strategies used for presenting the information.

Typically one begins student teaching by observing the class(es) for a week or so. During this time you will learn students' names, the seating chart, the class schedule, the routines, the general curriculum outline, and the expectations the school may have of you and your work. Next you will assume responsibility for instructing one class (one subject in elementary school or one period in middle or high school). By midterm you will have assumed responsibility for the entire day, and your supervising teacher may spend part of the day in the class but also considerable time away so you can be totally on your own. You will still need to discuss lesson plans with your supervising teacher, both before and after you present them.

As a part of the discussion, remember to record, react, and reflect. Learn to recognize your own challenges rather than wait for someone else to point them out.

After several weeks of full-time teaching, you may begin to return the classes, one at a time, to the teacher. At the end of the term, you may have an opportunity to observe in other classes (same or different subjects or grades, or the media center, or specialized personnel such as speech therapist, bilingual education instructor, exceptional education teacher). Take advantage of these opportunities; as a classroom teacher, you may never have this experience.

Legal Issues

Regardless of your major, you need to determine whether you are legally eligible for eventual certification. For instance, if you have been convicted of something more serious than a moving traffic violation, you should immediately request a conference with the chairperson of the department or college of education. During the conference you should be absolutely forthright. If you're ineligible, you need to know it now. Likewise, you need to know the conditions under which you might become ineligible at some point subsequent to your conference. We have heard of teachers whose certificates have been "pulled" during the school year (because of the authority's oversight in checking) and of teachers and administrators who have been required to forfeit their credentials (including their retirement benefits) for crimes ranging from embezzlement to falsifying standardized achievement test results to having improper relations with students. A word to the wise should be sufficient.

Alternative Teacher Education Programs

There are students (non-education majors) who graduate and later decide to teach. Perhaps they were unable to find a job. Perhaps they found a job that proved to be less than satisfying. Perhaps they finished a career in the military or some other field and were really too young to retire. Perhaps they realized that teaching is what they really wanted to do in the first place. These "second career" teachers make a lateral entry into the profession by passing a teaching examination and agreeing to take education courses on their own time during the first year or so of their employment. In any case, they often begin teaching before being fully certified. Indeed, a study conducted by the United States Department of Education found that only 65 percent of teachers with three or fewer years of experience were fully certified ("Teacher Quality: A Report on the Preparation and Qualifications of Public School Teachers," 1999). That is rapidly changing.

alternative certification
Certification that does not include study in a teacher preparation program. It may involve on-the-job coursework or, at a minimum, passing a test in the subject area to be taught, with the person having a college or university degree in any field.

Alternative certification is an issue with its pros and its cons ("Should Second-Career New Teachers Be Required to Take Methods Courses Before Starting Work?" 2001). One advantage of alternative certification is that it provides a number of teachers to help fill the critical need in some geographical areas and in some critical needs subjects. A second advantage is that these teachers often possess additional skills and a broader perspective of life acquired during their previous employment.

An obvious disadvantage of alternative certification is that the teaching profession was not the person's original commitment. That in itself is not a crime. But as a result, the person has not had a *comprehensive* introduction to coursework and to a variety of organized field service experiences. Thus, the person may know little about human development, specific skills, instructional strategies, and classroom management. Likewise, the person may have little awareness of how a school functions and the multifaceted expectations of teachers. For instance, one lawyer closed his office, became a fifth-grade teacher, and, one month into the school year, notified the principal that he needed a secretary to handle his paperwork. Appalled that no such assistance was available, he resigned before mid-year.

As you would expect, teachers who proceed through the traditional education program "demonstrate stronger classroom management skills and can better relate content to the needs and interests of students" (Stronge, 2002, p. 6). Fully prepared and certified teachers also "have a greater impact on gains in student learning than do uncertified or provisionally certified teachers, especially with minority populations and in urban and rural settings" (Stronge, 2002, p. 7). Alternatively prepared and certified teachers "tend to have a limited view of curriculum; lack understandings of student ability and motivation; experience difficulty translating content knowledge into meaningful information for students to understand; plan instruction less effectively; and tend not to learn about teaching through their experiences" (Laczko-Kerr & Berliner, 2003, p. 37). Furthermore, one fairly recent study (Lewis, 2002) found that of 8,000 alternative-route teachers placed in one federal program (Teach for America, the most well-known alternative certification program), only 2,000 remained in the program. That is an extremely low retention rate. No wonder Arthur Wise, president of the National Council for Accreditation of Teacher Education (NCATE), has urged policymakers not to create regulations that result in "placing unqualified, unprepared individuals in classrooms" (Lewis, 2002, p. 69).

Some traditional students who are unable to pass the coursework or the mandated examinations may decide to teach in a private school or a charter school. Both institutions are permitted to accept as teachers people who have not fulfilled all of the traditional requirements. Actually, public schools are able to do the same, and 10 percent to 30 percent of new teachers begin public school service without full certification (Stronge, 2002, p. 7).

Certification Exams for Pre-Service Teachers: The Praxis

Forty-five states require testing as part of the certification process (Digest of Education Statistics 2002, 2003). Of those, the vast majority now use the Praxis Series: Professional Assessments for Beginning Teachers developed by Educational Testing Service (ETS). The **Praxis series** (*praxis* means putting theory into practice) has three components: Praxis I, II, and III.

Depending on your institution's accreditation requirements, you may begin the certification examination process during your freshman or sophomore year with a test such as the Praxis I, which tests basic skills in reading, math, and writing (composition). Currently, 36 states require such tests of basic skills (Digest of Education Statistics 2002, 2003). If your scores equal or exceed the required scores, you then apply for admission to the teacher education program and continue to work on other requirements such as coursework and grade point average. If you do not achieve the minimum passing score on one or more components of the test, you can take them over (although the institution, accreditation agency, or state may limit the number of times you can do so). While the cutoff (passing) scores are not particularly high—usually below the 50th percentile, meaning you can score in the bottom half of the norming sample of the test and still pass—a number of students have difficulty with one or more sections, depending on their background strengths. If you suspect you have a problem, you should seek immediate assistance: self-study books (check your bookstore), tutorial assistance provided by the institution, computer software programs, or additional coursework. The more serious your problem, the sooner you should seek help and the more diligent you should be in addressing your challenge. Being "pretty good" is not good enough for a teacher. The profession expects more. Remember that we're talking about your career here, not just another test. By the way, research indicates that "teachers' scores on verbal ability tests . . . have a direct positive relationship with student achievement" (Stronge, 2002).

Praxis series A series of three tests developed by Educational Testing Service (ETS). Prospective teachers take these tests at various points in their professional preparation program.

During your junior or senior year, you may take professional examinations; Praxis II is a common one. These tests focus on various aspects of your professional development such as subject matter and professional knowledge. You will also be required to pass these tests to become certified in your field. In addition, the Praxis II has a third component, the Principles of Learning Test (PLT). A performance-based test, the PLT is typically completed during or after student teaching. There are three versions: K–6, 5–9, and 7–12.

The Praxis III component of the Praxis Series is a performance-based assessment system that is often used during a teacher's induction year (first year in teaching). Some states have their own version of induction-year assessments that, in fact, extend to the first two or three years of employment. These programs help new teachers work through deficiencies that the district and state feel can be remediated.

Most of the Praxis I and II examinations can be taken on paper or on the computer. Generally they are offered two or three times per year, which means your graduation or certification can be delayed if one of your scores is unsatisfactory. In large measure, your excellent performance in your classes and in field service should contribute greatly to earning passing scores on these tests. Conversely, low grades in education courses and haphazard field service experiences may foreshadow problems with the tests.

By the time you successfully complete the coursework in general education, professional education, and area(s) of specialization, the field service requirements, student teaching, and the various exams, you will be ready to be certified. You and your institution will complete the paperwork, and the state will issue a teaching license good for a specified number of years (often five). To renew it, you will need to take additional coursework, so don't consider your graduation as the end of your education. It's just a milestone along your academic journey. After all, how much can a person really learn in a few short years? By the way, you may be interested in knowing that research shows "a positive relationship exists between student achievement and how recently an experienced teacher took part in a professional development opportunity such as a conference, workshop, or graduate class" (Stronge, 2002, p. 6).

Go Online!
ACTIVITY 4.2: Comparing Certification Requirements

The Internet makes a comparison of teaching certification requirements in various states an easy task. Appendix C lists the URLs for departments of education/certification agencies for all states. Use that information for the following items:

1. Locate the URL for your state and one other state (perhaps one where you might teach or your home state if you're away at school). Select a certification level of interest (such as middle school) and a secondary area (such as English or chemistry, or a K-12 area such as art or physical education).

2. Use the Internet to find the certification requirements in your selected states and areas of interest.

3. How do the two states differ? Do they require, as some do, that teachers have a course in that state's history? What are the differences in terms of field experiences prior to or during student teaching?

4. Do you believe certification requirements should be standard for all states in the country? What would be the advantages and disadvantages of such a system?

Don't worry if you don't have a job by the time school starts. The Harvard University Graduate School of Education's Project on the Next Generation of Teachers found in its survey that 33 percent of districts' new teachers were hired after the first day of school (Helgeson, 2003). Activity 4.2 will give you an opportunity to research certification requirements for different states.

■ Where Teachers Teach

Teaching in Public Schools

Approximately 48.5 million students were enrolled in public pre-kindergarten through grade 12 in 2005. The recent increases in enrollment are attributed to immigration and the "baby boom echo," baby boomers having children (Livingston, 2006). About 90 percent of students are enrolled in public schools (Characteristics, 2004). The percentages of racial and ethnic minorities are increasing, from 22 percent in 1972 to 43 percent in 2004, most of that attributed to increased enrollment of Hispanics. Correspondingly, white enrollment has decreased from 78 percent to 53 percent over the same time period (see Figure 4.1). Thus, the demographics are changing as the enrollment continues to increase. Beginning in 2003, minority public school students were in the majority in the western part of the United States (Livingston, 2006).

Teaching in Private Schools

Private schools are an option for someone who has not completed an approved program for certification. A large number of these institutions are parochial (particularly Roman Catholic), although the percentage of students enrolled in those schools has decreased while the percentage enrolled in conservative Christian and non-sectarian private schools has increased (Livingston, 2006). Some private

Figure 4.1

Changes in Enrollment in Public Schools

(Livingston, 2006)
Note: Percentages may not total 100 due to rounding.

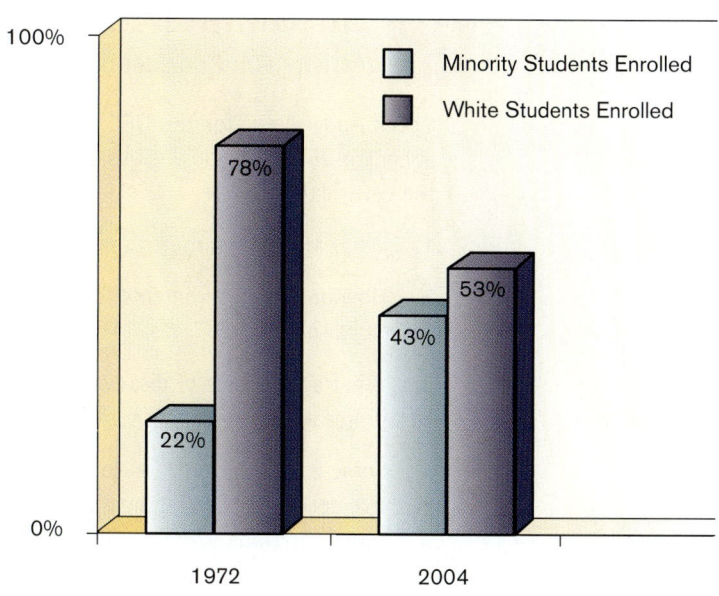

schools are academically exclusive, requiring demonstrated student competence as a criterion for admission. Because private schools are subject primarily to the control of their own trustees or board of directors, they often employ noncertified teachers or teachers who possess certification in areas other than the ones they are assigned to teach. Thus, a former business teacher might teach first grade or a part-time accountant teach math.

All of this is not to disparage alternative programs, and certainly not the successful candidates that emerge from such programs. However, as a pre-professional, you should consider whether alternative programs are necessarily good for the profession. If an alternative program is just as rigorous as a traditional program, then there is no problem. Of course, if it were, there would be no need for an alternative route. The question then is whether there are sufficiently compelling reasons to allow certification in the absence of a rigorous program. Would you like to work in a tall building designed by an architect who graduated from a "fast track" program? Would you prefer that a surgeon who didn't do all of the traditional med-school program because he was a career-changer perform an operation on one of your family members? Activity 4.3 may help you prepare an informed opinion on this issue.

Teaching in Charter Schools

charter school A public school formed or reconstituted to deal either with special concerns of a community (e.g., providing a back-to-basics, technology, or fine arts emphasis) or with a particular group (e.g., at risk of dropping out, exceptional education) or to secure a greater degree of school and local control.

site-based management The legal ability of a school to conduct its own governance, subject to specific local, state, and federal requirements. Charter schools are an example of site-based management.

Charter schools are public schools that have been formed or reconstituted to deal either with special concerns of a community (e.g., providing a back-to-basics, technology, or fine arts emphasis) or with a particular group (e.g., at risk of dropping out, exceptional education). Or, a charter school may simply provide a greater degree of school and local control, for instance by parents and teachers. In one common scenario, a public school desiring to become a charter school submits an operational plan, including a proposed curriculum, to the school board or university or nonprofit group authorized to issue a charter (see Viadero, 2003), which may approve, reject, or return it for additional information. If eventually rejected, the school authorities (having support from both the teachers and the school's clientele) often have recourse to the state department of education.

When approved, the public school (now called a charter school) has much more latitude in what might be called **site-based management** than it did previously.

 Go Online!

Activity 4.3: Considering Alternative Certification Programs

Check Appendix C for the URL for the state department of education/certification agency in the state you wish to become certified. On the Web site, find the page for the certification office.

1. What alternative routes to teacher certification are available in your state?

2. How do the requirements for alternative certifications differ from the traditional program?

3. What advantages or disadvantages do you see to alternative certification programs as compared with a traditional program?

4. Some educators, such as John I. Goodlad (1990), maintain that where alternative certification programs are available, they undermine the value of a traditional program. What is your opinion of this?

Charter schools like this one in Santa Barbara, California, are given more freedom in curriculum decisions, but are still responsible for children's achievement on state required standardized tests.

Courtesy of Becky Stovall

Working under a board of directors, the principal has control over the budget and can allocate funds in the way he deems most appropriate for the school. He also has much more flexibility in hiring personnel. However, the school must still comply with most federal regulations and must still administer the required achievement tests. A charter school that does not accept funds under the No Child Left Behind Act (2002) may hire a college or university graduate who is uncertified or is certified in a different field. This does not mean that all charter school teachers are uncertified; 57 percent do possess certification ("Charter Experience," 2003). It is just that charter schools have more flexibility in employing teachers.

What do we know about the 2,700 charter schools? They enroll 700,000 students in 36 states and the District of Columbia. The teachers tend to be younger and less experienced than teachers in traditional public schools ("Charter Experience," 2003). According to a study by the Brookings Institution, charter school students tend to lag about six months to a full year below their peers in public schools ("Charters Fall Short," 2002). Furthermore, data collected by the National Assessment of Education Progress (NAEP) in conjunction with the 2003 NAEP assessment showed no ethnic differences between the public and charter schools, and the white/minority achievement gap was just as large (Bracey, 2005). A follow-up study intended to determine whether the lower achievement scores occurred because charter schools serve a larger percentage of low-income students found that explanation to be incorrect. Instead, the study found that some charter schools were effective, others ineffective (Carnoy, Jacobsen, Mishel, & Rothstein, 2005).

Using Your Teacher Licensure in Other Fields

It may be that you complete an approved program and decide not to pursue a classroom teaching position. Your teaching credential then becomes a basis for expanding your qualifications. For instance, you may decide to become a media specialist or a guidance counselor or a school psychologist. First you must find a college or university that provides the relevant program; someone there will apprise you of the proper steps to follow and the agencies (e.g., State Department of Education) to contact. These steps will also be appropriate if, after several years of teaching, you decide to change positions. At that point, your options are a little greater. For example, to become an administrator, you must have completed several years of successful teaching. So, if you have any long-term aspirations, now is the right time to ask questions and to ask your advisor to help you choose electives that can be applied to additional areas. You probably know that having licensure in two areas increases your opportunities for employment ("Teachers—Kindergarten, Elementary, and Secondary," 2006).

Getting a Job as a Teacher

Teaching Positions

Even if you are one of those students who takes more than four years to complete an undergraduate major, and that means 75 percent of your class (Kennen & Lopez, 2005), you will want to use your time wisely and get the most out of your time spent as an undergraduate. As a prospective teacher, you are interested in knowing about the job market and its influences, the location of teaching positions for your major, and strategies for securing that all-important first job.

Current Demographics

What are the major factors affecting the number of teaching positions? At first, you might conclude that they are artifacts of increased numbers of students or of teacher retirements. However, neither answer provides the complete picture. Also important are teacher decisions to leave the profession or, because of job dissatisfaction, to teach elsewhere (the "revolving door" factor). Research has shown that teachers with high scores on licensure tests, SAT, and NTE are more likely to leave the profession (Ingersoll, 2003). When we discuss the teacher shortage, it is also important to remember that only 58 percent of the students who earned teaching degrees in 1993 had begun to teach by 1997 (Henke, Chen, & Geis, 2000).

The annual rate of teacher turnover is about 14–15 percent, and approximately 40–50 percent of all new teachers leave the profession by the end of their fifth year. Reasons for job dissatisfaction include low salary, lack of administrative support, student discipline problems and lack of motivation, and lack of teacher influence in the decision-making process (Ingersoll, 2003).

Where Are Teachers Needed?

Of course, you are interested in your teaching position. If you are majoring in secondary special education, math, science, or foreign language, you will be pleased to note that large percentages of high schools report difficulty in filling those positions. Math, science, and elementary special education positions have high turnover rates. On the other hand, turnover rates in English are low, and rates in social studies are very low (Ingersoll, 2003). Because of the distribution of student enrollment, the employment growth for secondary teachers is more rapid than for kindergarten and elementary school teachers ("Teachers—Kindergarten, Elementary, and Secondary," 2006).

In general, teaching positions can be found almost everywhere. In some cases, school districts have even sought out teachers from other countries. Geographically, turnover rates are quite high in high-poverty schools compared with more affluent schools. Indeed, in terms of teacher turnover (and thus opportunities for you), there appears to be more difference within each state than there is from state to state (Ingersoll, 2003). California and Florida need bilingual teachers and teachers prepared to teach English as a second language, and urban school districts have difficulty filling positions ("Teachers—Kindergarten, Elementary, and Secondary," 2006).

Thus, the jobs likely are available, but not necessarily in the particular school or district which you prefer and perhaps not teaching the level of a subject (e.g., math or English) or specific aspect of a subject (e.g., world history versus American history or calculus versus basic math) that you had hoped for. You may even need to relocate to get the best fit for you. In any case, you will need a job, and there are some important steps you can take to increase the chances of your finding that special position.

Tools for Getting Hired

Resume and Application

The application and your resume are the first two documents a school or district will see, so let's begin at this point. Someone once wrote that success favors the prepared person. Your total school record will have much to do with getting an interview in your ideal location. How well you impress your college or university teachers and public school educators with whom you work will have much to do with the recommendations you receive. How well you write when you complete your application is important. Poor grammar and spelling and even lack of neatness may eliminate you from consideration. So you will want to be prepared to write clearly and correctly and to list in organized fashion the specific goals, experiences, and personal and professional qualities you have to offer. Your institution may provide a workshop in writing resumes. You may also wish to consult some of the excellent Internet resources such as the Purdue Placement Manual, http://purdue .placementmanual.com/education (Education Resume, 2006). It suggests including the following in your resume:

- Name and contact information
- Education background
- Teaching experience
- Other employment information
- Teaching or career objective
- Related activities and interests

One comment and one sample suggestion indicate the tenor of the manual. The comment: The typical administrator spends 25 seconds scanning a resume before deciding whether to consider it further. The suggestion: While you are in the interviewing stage, do not use cute personal messages on your answering machine.

Portfolio

Earlier in this chapter we pointed out some important reasons for establishing and maintaining a portfolio. How you organize it and the types of artifacts you include will reflect the nature of your major and your experiences. For instance, you can display term papers, descriptions of projects or experiments, musical compositions, and performance programs in folders. You can house artistic creations or examples of materials you have developed in boxes or display cases. You can enter data on computer disks or present audio- or videotapes of a performance. You can include grade reports and letters of recommendation in notebooks. You will want to be neat and well organized (with a table of contents). Be sure to date each item; comparing artifacts is one way of demonstrating progress.

Once again, there are abundant resources to which you can refer. For instance, Takona (2003) contends in a document from the ERIC Clearinghouse on Assessment and Evaluation that portfolio development as an ongoing process is intended to involve (1) collection of material, (2) reflection on the implication and progress of the document, (3) reduction (selecting the most significant examples), and (4) developing the means of displaying the elements of the portfolio.

Networking and Finding Openings

How do you find a job? On occasion, opportunity will come knocking at your door. Perhaps you do such an outstanding job in your student teaching that the principal offers you a position even before you graduate. It does happen. Or perhaps one of your professors or some other acquaintance knows of an opening and feels you are an appropriate candidate.

On the other hand, you typically have to follow the adage: Seek and ye shall find. Most school districts participate in job fairs, usually in the spring, and they are well advertised. Read the announcements on your education bulletin board or the e-mail announcements from your college or department. Since you are computer literate, you can use a Google search to locate information on job fairs in any state in the country.

Obviously you will not want to limit yourself to places you can travel. In that case, you have yet another choice. That is to access the Web site of a school district in which you might be interested. Vacancies usually are posted very promptly. You might wish to make a telephone call and explore the possibility of submitting your resume and application in the hope that the district will decide to pay your expenses to an interview, perhaps on the condition that you accept a position if it is offered. The process of exploring a variety of alternatives takes some time, but it is time well spent if you want to find a job that will fit your specific requirements.

Interviewing Skills

At this point, the wind will be blowing in your favor. However, there are some decisive steps you must take to increase your chances of finding and accepting the dream job. You will surely dress appropriately, arrive on time, and be prepared to ask good questions as well as to answer the types of questions that administrators and personnel directors are likely to raise (What do you like about this school? What is your philosophy of education? What important professional books have you read? Why did you like them? What excellent experiences have you had? What unsatisfying experiences have you had? What would you do in a specified situation? What are your greatest strengths? What are your greatest weaknesses? Why should we hire you instead of someone else?).

An interview with a school administrator will be your first formal opportunity to demonstrate your ability to communicate.

Writing for the National Middle School Association, Burgess and Lorain (2006) recommend that you write your philosophy and the questions that you expect to be asked and then write your answers as a way of identifying aspects which need more consideration. Another piece of advice: Be sure you know something about the school before you arrive. You can check the school's Web site for this

Courtesy of David Ottenstein Photography

information. Look at the interviewer. Use humor and smile when appropriate. Sit up straight. (Does this sound like your mother talking to you? Sorry, but she's right.) Use an illustration from your experience. Admit it when you don't know the answer. Interviewers have an abundance of experience. They will know if you're trying to fake a response. Of course, you will not ask about such matters as salary and fringe benefits until an offer is made. That offer might come on the spot, or it might be several weeks or a month longer; school personnel have last-minute vacancies caused by delayed resignations and unexpected increased enrollments.

At the end of the interview, you will surely be given an opportunity to ask questions. Now is a good time to ask about something that would have a major impact on your morale if you and the administration disagreed on philosophy. For instance, you might believe strongly that some children need lower-level textbooks if they are to make satisfactory progress. The administration may require the use of grade-level texts with all students. You need to know that before you accept a position. Or perhaps the school divides students into high, average, and low classes, and you are adamantly opposed to this (even if you weren't assigned the low group). So ask. Be prepared to defend your position if the interviewer asks what you think. It is appropriate to ask if you would be permitted to borrow a set of textbooks and the policy handbook if you were hired. It is also appropriate to ask when you might hear from the school.

Within 24 hours of the interview, write a thank you note and mail it immediately. Not only is it the courteous thing to do, it just might tilt the balance when two candidates seem somewhat similarly qualified.

■ Teachers and Salary

base salary The minimum amount of money that is paid to an educator based on his or her certification(s), job description, and years of experience.

The state legislature determines the **base salary** of public school teachers. This figure is often supplemented by the local district as a function of its own tax base. Thus, districts with high property taxes and substantial commercial interests will pay teachers more than a district in the same state with a lower tax base. Other factors influencing salaries are additional coursework beyond the baccalaureate degree, attainment of an advanced degree, and national certification. Table 4.1 lists average estimated annual salaries for teachers by state. Note that the table represents *average* salaries, not salaries for beginning teachers.

■ What to Expect as a New Teacher

When you enter your first teaching job, you will leave behind your "carefree" days as a college or university student. Suddenly you will be legally responsible for the safety and instruction of one or more classes of students, and you will be expected to conduct yourself as a professional, even if students and parents behave in ways that irritate you. You will assume responsibility for providing high-quality instruction every day, realizing that you are establishing a reputation that will characterize you throughout the community, even among people you may never meet.

Expect considerable pressure to increase student achievement even in circumstances that are far beyond your control (e.g., frequent student absenteeism, lack of family support and student motivation, low levels of cognitive functioning or various learning disabilities). Interestingly, a recent national survey conducted by public agenda and focusing on 18–25 year olds found that 51 percent of African-

Table 4.1 Average Salaries of Public School Teachers for 2004

State	Average Salary	State	Average Salary
U.S. Average	**$46,752**		
Alabama	38,325	Montana	$37,184
Alaska	51,736	Nebraska	38,352
Arizona	41,843	Nevada	42,254
Arkansas	39,314	New Hampshire	42,689
California	56,444	New Jersey	55,592
Colorado	43,319	New Mexico	38,067
Connecticut	57,337	New York	55,181
Delaware	49,366	North Carolina	43,211
District of Columbia	57,009	North Dakota	34,441
Florida	40,604	Ohio	47,482
Georgia	45,988	Oklahoma	35,061
Hawaii	45,479	Oregon	49,169
Idaho	41,080	Pennsylvania	51,835
Illinois	54,230	Rhode Island	52,261
Indiana	45,791	South Carolina	41,162
Iowa	39,432	South Dakota	33,236
Kansas	38,623	Tennessee	40,318
Kentucky	40,240	Texas	40,476
Louisiana	37,918	Utah	38,976
Maine	39,864	Vermont	42,007
Maryland	50,261	Virginia	43,655
Massachusetts	53,181	Washington	45,434
Michigan	54,412	West Virginia	38,461
Minnesota	45,375	Wisconsin	42,882
Mississippi	35,684	Wyoming	39,532
Missouri	38,006		

Source: National Education Association

Americans, 44 percent of Asian-Americans, 42 percent of Hispanics, and 37 percent of whites said teachers should have done more to prepare them for college (see Figure 4.2). At the same time, however, 69 percent of African-Americans, 75 percent of Asian-Americans, 75 percent of Hispanics, and 65 percent of whites said they could have worked harder and paid more attention (Schroeder, 2005).

You will be responsible for regularly assessing learning and for grading. This means you will need to document your activities on a daily basis and be prepared to defend your decisions. Some parents will be happy with B's, some will be furious. Some will challenge your assignments, homework, and grading system (e.g., Why didn't you count that assignment? Why did you count something else so much? What can he do to "pull up" the grade that's been earned? He needs an A or B to get into college. He's worked so hard. You don't understand the stress she's under.). Some will complain that you didn't inform them of a problem early in the term. Knowing that some people will go straight to the principal or district office or school board member, you will want to keep your principal fully informed of any likely problems so that he can provide you with support should the need arise. Otherwise, he will seem uninformed, which doesn't help your cause.

Some will complain that you are "picking on" their children because they represent a different ethnic or racial group from yours. Some will contend you favor the girls (or boys) or that you are more lenient with high achievers or the socially elite. The charges may not be true, but you should be prepared to be confronted, either openly or indirectly (through your superiors). Stay focused when it comes to parents: Studies show their involvement has a positive effect on learning (Darling & Westberg, 2004).

Figure 4.2

High School Students' Perception of Their Preparation for College

(Schroeder, 2005)

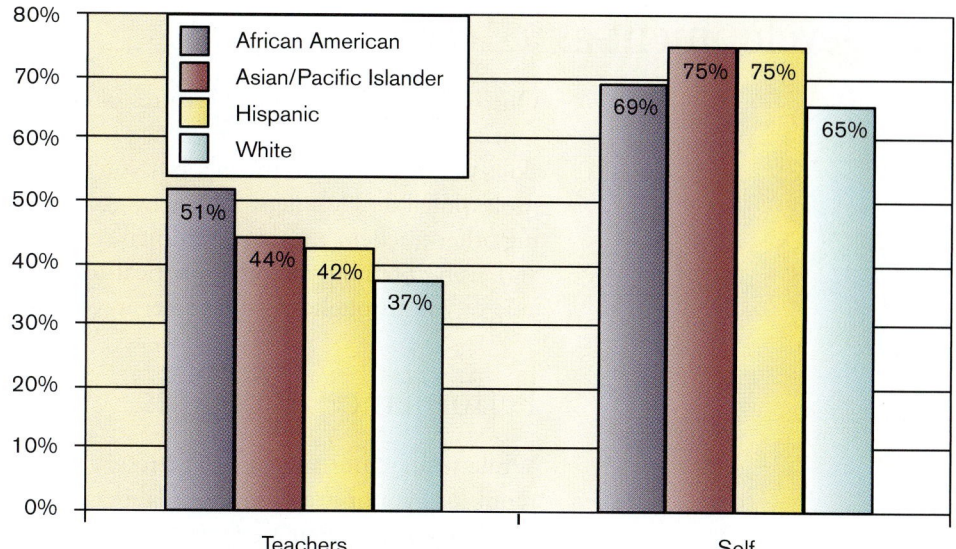

Teachers = Students who felt their teachers could have done a better job of preparing them

Self = Students who felt they could have done a better job of preparing themselves

Expect some committee work and other school assignments such as bulletin board displays and duty (e.g., hall, bus, cafeteria). Expect some before- and after-school activities (e.g., parent conferences and meetings with some of your colleagues, PTA or PTO meetings, staff development sessions, and responsibilities such as operating the concession stand or taking up tickets at ball games). Being a new teacher does not exempt you from these responsibilities.

You will be expected to use your own initiative and to work independently. If you need instructional materials, contact your school secretary or department chairperson, and be specific about your requests. Do you need supplies or equipment? If funds are not available, you can ask businesses to donate the items. You can write a grant (check with your district grant writer, with your State Department of Education, and Internet resources). Indeed, your principal may encourage all teachers to write small grants.

On the positive side, you can expect great satisfaction when you are able to assist students in learning more than they have before, and you will have both students and parents who greatly appreciate your commitment, compassion, and increasing competence. As you work with other educators in addressing school issues, you will enjoy the sense of accomplishment that you are contributing to the overall development of the learning environment. Teaching can be the best learning experience of all (far better than the college classroom because it is hands-on) if you reflect on your experiences, your activities, and your decisions, and learn from your mistakes. Learning begins when you admit your mistakes and consider alternative strategies.

Student and teacher success is most likely to occur when you work collaboratively with your colleagues (as in a community of learners) in addressing the challenges of education (Dearman & Alber, 2005), especially when those collaborations focus on aligning classroom instructional goals with those of the school and district (Standards for Staff Development, Revised Edition, 2001).

When you begin your second year of teaching, you should not be the same educator you were when you first entered the classroom. You will have grown immeasurably and therefore be on a lifelong path to do a better job in changing the lives of students.

■ Development as a Teacher

One of the most distinctive features of education is that the learning never stops. Once you become a certified teacher, you will not only be evaluated in terms of the skills that you bring to the job, but you will also be expected to continue your own professional development. This advanced learning could take the form of mentoring other teachers, earning additional certifications, completing additional degrees, and even obtaining national certification. There will be many opportunities available to you throughout your career in education.

Performance Appraisals

While you are not an actor or actress, you are constantly a performer in the classroom (or gym or music room or laboratory). Although your students are continuously appraising your performance, the appraisals you may fear the most come from your administrators and supervisors. There are two types, both of which are very important. The first type is informal. In some schools, usually elementary, a principal or assistant principal pops into each class for a few moments every day, often at the very beginning to determine if teachers are initiating the day's activities promptly. Administrators are more likely to spend additional time with new teachers and with teachers having discipline or instructional problems. Veteran (and even new) teachers who are well on the way to mastering their craft receive fewer visits. Observers develop a composite of each teacher's effectiveness as a result of these visits, and, as time goes on, adjust the amount of time they spend with each teacher.

Then there are the formal appraisals. Each school district has a policy outlining appraisal procedures. In general, you will be notified ahead of time and will be given a copy of the observation instrument. Normally you will have had a chance to ask questions about various items on the list. The administrator will observe the lesson and later meet with you to discuss the session. You will have an opportunity to clarify information and even challenge the findings. You will be asked to sign a document to show that you attended the debriefing session; your signature does not necessarily mean that you agree with the comments.

If your formal appraisals are not deemed satisfactory, you may be given a professional development plan intended to improve aspects of your performance. You should seek feedback from each major appraisal and thus use it as a benchmark for growing professionally. Remember that teachers appraise the performance of students, principals appraise the performance of teachers, district office staff appraise the performance of principals, and the school board appraises the performance of the superintendent. Thus, you are one part of the broad process of accountability.

Professional Development

Graduation exercises are often referred to as commencement, which means "beginning" rather than "ending." Thus, your entry into the profession simply involves another type of lifelong learning. Today's expectations of schools make this continuous progress far more important than it was perceived to be a generation or more ago.

Being a Mentor

In Chapter 1 we discussed the good possibility that in your first year of teaching you will be assigned a mentor. Pay close attention to the guidance that colleague provides and to the manner in which he provides it. Before long, and probably much sooner than you expect, you will be assigned as the mentor for a "beginning" teacher.

The activities in which you will engage as a mentor are the same ones that your mentor should use. Boston's mentoring program (2001) recommends $1\frac{1}{2}$ to 2 hours per week of after-school face-to-face contact. The mentor should be a school leader and an effective educator (Denmark & Podsen, 2000). Suggestions for providing mentoring assistance include initiating the first contact, establishing a supportive climate by orienting the teacher to the school, introducing the new person to key faculty members, conveying expectations such as relating the curriculum frameworks to student learning, and encouraging a respect for diversity (Boston's Mentoring Program, 2001; Denmark & Podsen, Fall 2000).

It is important to share strategies, perhaps on a classroom management checklist with items such as focusing student on-task behavior, ensuring smooth transition times, distributing materials, and giving clear directions. Besides observing in the new teacher's class, the mentor should model both class lessons and the reflective thinking that accompany them (Denmark & Podsen, 2000). Remember there is a strong connection between mentoring programs and teacher retention after year five (Smith & Ingersoll (2003).

Continuing Coursework and Earning Advanced Degrees

Over the course of your career, you are likely to earn one or more advanced degrees. So it's back to school you go. Over 57 percent of U.S. teachers hold at least one advanced degree (compared with 23 percent in 1961). Furthermore, 77 percent participate in professional development relating to their specialty, and 35 percent engage in school-sponsored professional development during the summer (Status of the American Public School Teacher, 2003).

Becoming a National Board–Certified Teacher

National Board for Professional Teaching Standards (NBPTS)
A national organization that establishes rigorous standards by which teachers can be certified by demonstrating exemplary classroom performance and reflecting critically on the effectiveness of their curriculum and instruction strategies and the needs of diverse learners.

Perhaps the most well-known advanced certification involves the **National Board for Professional Teaching Standards (NBPTS).** Many states encourage teachers to obtain National Board Certification by offering financial incentives, sometimes up to $10,000 per year for 10 years. School districts often provide part of the cost (currently $2,300) of applying for this certification and carrying out the studies required for approval. As of 2006, all states and the District of Columbia had enacted legislation providing such incentives or provided recognition for obtaining National Board Certification (NBPTS, 2003). The process is rigorous and time-consuming but offers teachers an opportunity to showcase their skills and to serve as mentors to other teachers as well. Five percent of teachers hold National Board Certification ("Teachers and ESPs—By the Numbers," 2003). However, the distribution by ethnicity is skewed; 13 percent of the applicants are black teachers, but only 4 percent receive National Board certification. The research study was unable to identify the cause of the disparity (Blair, 2003). Another thought-provoking study, albeit a small one (and the only one of its type), investigated the effectiveness of National Board–certified teachers in improving student achievement in their elementary classrooms in Tennessee. All 16 teachers were rated as average in that regard. The reason for the finding remains unclear, and a panel has been convened to study the findings (Stone, 2003).

The mission of the National Board for Professional Teaching Standards is "to advance the quality of teaching and learning by":

- maintaining high and rigorous standards for what accomplished teachers should know and be able to do,
- providing a national voluntary system certifying teachers who meet these standards, and advocating related education reforms to integrate national board certification in American education and to capitalize on the expertise of national board certification. (NBPTS, 2003)

The standards are based on five propositions:

1. Teachers are committed to students and learning.
2. Teachers know the subjects they teach and how to teach those subjects to students.
3. Teachers are responsible for managing and monitoring student learning.
4. Teachers think systematically about their practice and learn from experience.
5. Teachers are members of learning communities. (NBPTS, 1997)

Do those five propositions sound remarkably similar to the topics we have been discussing in this chapter (and in other chapters as well)? Does board certification make a difference in the lives of students? The Accomplished Teaching Validation Study (2000) did find that National Board–certified teachers scored significantly higher than their peers on 11 of 13 indicators of academic excellence, but whether this correlates with improved student achievement remains to be seen.

■ Professional Organizations and Affiliations

One of the ways in which you can continue your professional development is by becoming involved in various organizations that relate either generally or specifically to your areas of interest. Such organizations can be classified as subject area, administrative/supervisory, research-based, general organizations, free-standing publications, and special services organizations. Some organizations are so comprehensive that they could be classified into several categories.

Generalized Organizations for Professional Educators

Some organizations are general in nature. Two in particular that you should be aware of are the National Education Association (NEA) and the American Federation of Teachers (AFT). Both of these organizations have long histories in the United States and exert considerable influence on behalf of teachers.

The National Education Association (NEA)

National Education Association (NEA) The largest (with over 2,000,000 members) professional association for teachers, administrators, and other school personnel.

Housed in the nation's capital, the **National Education Association (NEA)** was founded in 1857 as the National Teacher's Society. In 1870 it officially became the National Education Association. It is the largest professional association for teachers, administrators, and other school personnel. As of 2003, its membership is well in excess of 2 million people, making it the larger of the two organizations (the American Federation of Teachers has approximately 900,000 members). It also boasts more than 13,500 local affiliates. Both the national and the state organizations have annual conferences. The national organization publishes *NEA Today* and cooperates with other organizations to publish books, such as the three-volume series *What Works (in the Elementary School, Middle School, High School)* in conjunction with the National Staff Development Council.

The NEA's charter states that its goals are "to elevate the character and advance the interests of the profession of teaching and to promote the cause of education in the United States." As you will find in Chapter 8, the National Education Association has taken this role very seriously from the beginning. In the late 19th century and early 20th century the NEA was a leader in the examination of schooling in this country. The Code of Ethics of the Education Profession (see Chapter 10, Ethics in Education and Matters of Law) adopted in 1975 is founded upon principles of commitment to students *and* to the profession. It has also published a Bill of Rights for Student Teachers (see Figure 4.3). Today, it is a powerful political representative of its membership with active lobbying at the state and national level. The NEA also takes part in collective bargaining on behalf of teachers, thus bringing an element of unionism to the organization.

The American Federation of Teachers (AFT)

American Federation of Teachers (AFT) A teacher's union formed in 1916. It is part of the American Federation of Labor/Congress of Industrial Organizations (AFL/CIO) umbrella. Its membership, while nationwide, is more concentrated in large population centers in the North.

The **American Federation of Teachers (AFT)** is a teacher's union formed in 1916. It falls under the American Federation of Labor/Congress of Industrial Organizations (AFL/CIO) umbrella. Its membership is concentrated in large population centers in the North but is found in all areas of the country. Unlike the NEA, the AFT is not open to administrators. Its focus has always been on improving the lot of classroom teachers, a task it has pursued relentlessly over the years.

It was in the 1960s that the organization emerged as a force for teachers when one of its affiliates, the United Federation of Teachers, became the bargaining agent for the teachers of New York City. In the time since, the AFT has come to represent teachers in many major metropolitan areas. The organization has taken an aggressive stance on salaries and benefits for teachers, and has used strikes and the threat of strikes to advance its agenda.

As recently as 1998 the NEA membership rejected a proposal to merge with the AFT. Both organizations are staunch advocates of education; however, the AFT's focus on the teacher and the NEA's broader focus on education as a whole has kept the two organizations separate. Issues of educational reform and control can find the two organizations ideologically at odds.

Parent–Teacher Organizations (PTO)

parent–teacher organization (PTO) A school-based organization that attempts to strengthen the relationship between parents and the school by promoting open communication and activities involving the joint participation of parents and teachers.

Though a different enterprise than organizations such as the NEA and the AFT, **parent–teacher organizations (PTO)** can wield considerable power on the all-important local level. These organizations are far less formal than the NEA and the AFT, but they bring together the two constituencies that interact with children at the local school every day: parents and teachers (as well as building-level administrators). In PTOs the concerns are with matters in and around the local school. There can still be ideological differences between people, but the issues are neither abstract nor so broad as to be unmanageable. PTOs often help schools find funding for local school projects, demonstrate an appreciation for the teachers and administrators in their schools, and, more importantly, provide an open line of communication between the school and the people it serves. Activity 4.4 will provide you with an opportunity to explore some of the professional organizations that may be of interest to you.

Subject Area Organizations

Almost all curriculum areas are represented by one or more professional associations. Most of these are national, but the more populated areas may also have local associations. Many organizations encourage student membership. The organizations mentioned in our discussion are national (and sometimes international) in scope. Your state likely has similar professional organizations made up of educators in that state. Often these state-level associations are affiliates of the national organization.

Professional organizations typically sponsor regional and national conferences and provide assistance to educators, representation in the federal legislative process for issues related to the discipline, opportunities for professional growth, and even such benefits as legal counsel and group rates on insurance. Additionally, each

As a citizen, a student, and a future member of the teaching profession, the individual student teacher has the right;

1. To freedom from unfair discrimination in admission to student teaching and in all aspects of the field experience. Student teachers shall not be denied or removed from an assignment because of race, color, creed, sex, age, national origin, marital status, political or religious beliefs, social or cultural background, or sexual orientation. Nor shall their application be denied because of physical handicap unless it is clear that such handicap will prevent or seriously inhibit their carrying out the duties of the assignment.

2. To be informed in advance of the standards of eligibility for student teaching and of the criteria and procedures for evaluation of his or her classroom performance.

3. To be consulted in advance and have effective voice in decisions regarding assignment, with respect to subject, grade level, school, and cooperating teacher.

4. To be assigned to a cooperating teacher who volunteers to work with the student-teaching program, who is fully qualified to do so, and is appropriately remunerated for the work and given sufficient time to carry out its responsibilities.

5. To be reimbursed by the college or university for any financial hardship caused by the student-teaching assignment; for example, for the costs of traveling excessive distances to the cooperating school district, or for the expenses incurred when the student teacher is assigned to a location so remote from his or her college/university that it is necessary to establish residence there, in addition to the college or university residence.

6. To be informed, prior to the student-teaching period, of all relevant policies and practices of the cooperating school district, including those regarding personnel, curriculum, student requirements, and student-teaching program.

7. To confidentiality of records. Except with the express permission of the student teacher, the college or university shall transmit to the cooperating school district only those student records that are clearly necessary to protect the health and welfare of the student teacher, the cooperating teacher, the students, and others in the cooperating school. All persons having access to the records of student teachers shall respect the confidentiality of those records, as required by law.

8. To be admitted to student teaching and to remain in the student-teaching assignment in the absence of a showing of just cause for termination or transfer through fair and impartial proceedings.

9. To a student-teaching environment that encourages creativity and initiative. The student teacher shall have the opportunity, under the perceptive supervision of the cooperating teacher, to develop his or her own techniques of teaching.

10. To a student-teaching environment that encourages the free exploration of ideas and issues as appropriate to the maturity of the students and the topics being studied.

11. To carry out the student-teaching assignment in an atmosphere conducive to learning and to have authority under supervision of the cooperating teacher, to use reasonable means to preserve the learning environment and protect the health and safety of students, the student teacher, and others.

Figure 4.3

NEA Bill of Rights
for Student Teachers

organization publishes one or more journals to keep members informed of issues and developments.

You can attend regional and national conferences to get a feel for the organization, and we encourage you to attend at least one during your teacher education program. Eventually, you may find yourself presenting lectures, demonstrations, or workshops at the conferences. Table 4.2 lists several of the largest organizations along with the journals they publish and the URL for contacting them online. Many of these organizations also publish professional books.

Administrative/Supervisory Organizations

Administrative/supervisory organizations are also available to increase your professional knowledge. While you may presently be interested in a teaching career, many educators eventually decide to become administrators or supervisors. Whether you harbor those intentions or not, you should find the publications helpful for providing a different perspective on education topics. Some sample organizations include those in Table 4.3.

12. To participate, with the cooperating teacher and college/university supervisor, in planning the student-teaching schedule to include in addition to work with the assigned cooperating teacher, observation of other classes, attendance at professional meetings, and involvement, as appropriate, in extracurricular activities that will enrich and broaden the range of the field experience.

13. To be assigned to duties that are relevant to the student teacher's learning experience. Student teachers shall not be required to act as substitute teacher or teacher aide, nor to handle any non-teaching duties that are not part of the cooperating teacher's duties.

14. To request transfer in the event of prolonged illness of, or serious personality conflict with the cooperating teacher and to have that request given favorable consideration without damage to any party's personal or professional status.

15. To a cessation of student-teaching responsibilities in the event and for the duration of a teacher strike at the cooperating school or school district to which the student teacher is assigned. If the strike is a prolonged one, the college or university has the responsibility to reassign the student teacher to another school district.

16. To the same liability protection as is provided by the school district for regularly employed certified teachers.

17. To influence the development and continuing evaluation and improvement of the student teacher program, including the formulation and systematic review of standards of student teacher eligibility, and criteria and procedures of student teacher evaluation. Such influence shall be maintained through representation of student teachers and recent graduates of the student-teacher program on committees established to accomplish these purposes.

18. To frequent planning and evaluative discussions with the cooperating teacher.

19. To systematic, effective supervision by the college/university supervisor. Such supervision shall include (1) regularly scheduled classroom observations of sufficient frequency and length to permit thorough insight into the strengths and weaknesses of the student teacher's performance; (2) conferences with the college/university supervisor immediately following observation, or as soon thereafter as possible, to discuss results of observation; (3) regularly scheduled three-way evaluation conferences among student teacher, college supervisor, and cooperating teacher, to ensure that the student teacher is fully apprised of his or her progress and is given substantive assistance in assessing and remedying the weaknesses and reinforcing the strengths of his or her performance.

20. To see, sign, and affix written responses to evaluations of his or her classroom performance.

21. To an equitable and orderly means of resolving grievances relating to the student-teaching assignment. The college/university grievance procedure shall incorporate due process guarantees, including the right to be informed in writing of the reasons for any adverse action regarding his or her assignment, and to appeal any such action, with the right to have both student and teacher representation on committees formulated to hear and adjudicate student teacher grievances.

22. To be free to join on- or off-campus organizations, and to enjoy privacy and freedom of lifestyle and conscience in out-of-school activities, unless it is clearly evident that those activities have a harmful effect on the student teacher's classroom performance.   −National Education Association (1977)

Research-Oriented Organizations

Research-oriented organizations can provide an abundance of information, particularly if you are interested in keeping up with the literature and research on topics related to education (and you should be).

Phi Delta Kappa (PDK) has a national headquarters in Bloomington, Indiana, and state and local affiliates. If you maintain excellent grades, you may be invited to become a member. The *Phi Delta Kappan* journal is a major source of research related to current topics in education. PDK also publishes Fastbacks, short research summaries on well over 100 topics. They are somewhat similar to the Topic Packs published by ASCD.

Kappa Delta Pi (KDP) is a national honorary society consisting of 60,000 members drawn from the top 10 percent of people entering education. Membership is by invitation only and is first available to rising college juniors with a grade point average of at least 3.0 on a 4.0 scale. The organization, which is dedicated to scholarship and excellence in education, has 550 chapters and a fairly extensive publishing program, including *New Teacher Advocate,* a quarterly newsletter of practical materials for beginning teachers.

Go Online!

ACTIVITY 4.4: **Exploring Professional Organizations**

No matter your educational interests, more than one professional organization is seeking your membership. The organizations discussed in the text are national organizations. Many of them have state-level affiliates. There are also state and local organizations that do not have national affiliations. You can likely get representatives of national and state organizations to visit your class. You could also attend one of their conferences and see just what they're all about.

1. Select two of the organizations listed in the text and visit their Web sites. Do they offer student memberships (reduced rates for college students)? Does one seem to fit your needs and interests better than the other? What services do they offer to their membership? When will their next regional or national conference be? Where?

2. Now use the Internet to locate the teacher organizations in your state. Don't be surprised if there is more than one. Visit each. What differences can you find between the organizations? Is there a difference in services they provide? Is there a political or ideological difference between the organizations? When will the next state organization conference be held? Where?

3. If possible, talk to a few classroom teachers about the organizations to which they belong. Do they recommend membership? What benefits do they see to membership? If you don't have ready access to a local school, ask these questions of your college professors. Not only are professors typically members of professional organizations, but they are frequently active participants and presenters at conferences.

Freestanding Publications

Some education publications are not directly related to professional associations. They include the following.

Elementary School Journal, published by the University of Chicago Press since 1900, is a research publication that features long articles on four or five topics (except when it has themed issues on one topic). Each issue focuses on research and practice related to school learning and teaching in elementary and middle school.

Education Digest, published by Prakken Publications, reprints condensed articles from other journals. Busy professionals often find this publication a clearinghouse for reading a variety of magazines that may not be readily available.

Education Week is, as the title suggests, a weekly publication. It features articles on major events throughout the nation and uses a highly readable newspaper format.

Instructor, published by Scholastic, is a popular magazine with practical ideas ready-made for teachers in the elementary grades.

Teaching Pre-K-8, Teacher, and Early Childhood Today are but three of a number of popular magazines available from Magazineline in

Table 4.2	Subject Area Professional Organizations
Professional Organization	**Journal(s)**
International Reading Association (IRA) http://www.reading.org	*The Reading Teacher, Journal of Adolescent & Adult Literacy, Reading Research Quarterly*
National Council of Teachers of English (NCTE) http://www.ncte.org	*Language Arts, Voices from the Middle, English Journal*
National Council of Teachers of Mathematics (NCTM) http://www.nctm.org	*Teaching Children Mathematics, Mathematics Teaching in the Middle School, Mathematics Teacher*
National Science Teachers Association (NSTA) http://www.nsta.org	*Science & Children, Science Scope, The Science Teacher*
National Council for the Social Studies (NCSS) http://www.ncss.org	*Social Studies and the Young Learner, Middle Level Learning, Theories and Research in Social Education*
National Art Education Association http://www.naea-reston.org	*Art Instruction*
American Alliance for Health, Physical Education, Recreation, and Dance http://www.aahperd.org	*Journal of Physical Education, Recreation,& Dance*
National Association for Music Education http://www.menc.org	*Music Educators Journal, Teaching Music, Journal of Research in Music Education*
National Association for the Education of Young Children http://www.naeyc.org	*Young Children, Early Childhood Research Quarterly*
Association for Childhood Education International http://www.acei.org	*Childhood Education*
Council for Exceptional Children http://www.cec.sped.org	*Exceptional Children, Teaching Exceptional Children*

Table 4.3	Administrative/Supervisory Professional Organizations
Professional Organization	**Journal(s)/Publication(s)**
Association for Supervision and Curriculum Development http://www.ascd.org	*Educational Leadership, Topic Packs*
National Association of Elementary School Principals http://www.naesp.org	*Principal*
National Association of Secondary School Principals http://www.nassp.org	*Principal Leadership*

Lansing, Michigan. Each of these focuses on practical information for early childhood and elementary teachers.

Journal of Learning Disabilities is a quarterly publication focusing on one aspect of special education. It is published by Pro-ed (Austin, Texas), which also publishes tests, texts, and student materials for special education classes.

Mailbox Teacher, published in Greensboro, North Carolina, is a practical ideas magazine for teachers in kindergarten through grade 6. Some of the activity pages can be photocopied. The *Mailbox Bookbag,* a teacher's idea magazine for children's literature, features ideas and activities for primary and intermediate grades.

Media and Methods, published in Philadelphia, features activities and recommendations related to various types of media.

Special Service Organizations

Special services organizations may provide assistance to schools, conduct conferences, or publish monographs and books on key topics of current concern. The United States Department of Education, for example, provides all three types of services; it also funds twelve research and development centers located throughout the country. Each center focuses on one topic. The twelve research centers, with URLs for contacting them, are listed in Table 4.4.

Educational Resources Information Center (ERIC), another special services organization, consists of 16 regular clearinghouses, each focusing on a different aspect of education (e.g., Disabilities and Gifted Education, Assessment and Evaluation, Social Studies/Social Science Education). There are also ten adjunct clearinghouses on various topics (e.g., Early Intervention and Early Childhood Special Education, ESL, Literacy Education). Educators interested in learning more about a particular topic can access AskERIC on the Internet.

Table 4.4	U.S. Department of Education Research and Development Sites by Topic
Topic	**Internet URL**
Adult Literacy and Learning	http://www.ncsall.gse.harvard.edu/
Assessment	http://cresst96.cse.ucla.edu
At-Risk Students	http://www.csos.jhu.edu/crespar/index.htm
Early Learning	http://www.fpg.unc.edu/~ncedl/
English	http://cela/albany.edu
Gifted Education	http://www.gifted.uconn.edu/nrcgt.html
Mathematics and Science	http://www.wcer.wisc.edu/ncisla
Postsecondary Education	http://www.stanford.edu/group/ncpi/index.html
Reading	http://www.ciera.org
Reform Policy	http://www.cpre.org/index_js.htm
Student Diversity	http://www.crede.org
Teaching Policy	http://depts.washington.edu/ctpmail

Conclusion

This chapter has provided a basis for understanding the expectations of new teachers and the requirements for obtaining licensure and certification as a professional educator. We have also introduced discussion of national influences on the initial certification of teachers and an overview of professional organizations in support of education.

Here are some of the main points from the chapter.

1. Each state determines its certification requirements, though there is increasing momentum for consistency among guidelines used throughout the country.
2. Teacher certification typically falls into two categories: traditional programs and alternative certification programs.
3. Traditional programs can be expected to include liberal arts coursework as well as education-specific courses and field experiences.
4. Praxis I for entry into a teacher education program and Praxis II taken at the end of a program are the primary teacher certification examinations in use today.
5. The Interstate New Teacher Assessment and Support Consortium (INTASC) has established guidelines for initial certification of teachers.

6. The National Board for Professional Teaching Standards (NBPTS) has established an advance level of certification for practicing teachers.

7. Professional education organizations offer a wide range of services to teachers, as well as offering professional development through journals and conferences and providing education advocacy in local, state, and national issues.

Key Terms

accreditation agency	professional development schools
student teaching	critical needs area
clinical experience	alternative certification
reciprocity	Praxis series
add-on certification	charter school
license	site-based management
certification	base salary
certification examination	National Board for Professional
general education	Teaching Standards (NBPTS)
professional education	National Education Association (NEA)
specialization courses	American Federation of Teachers (AFT)
methods courses	Parent–Teacher Organizations (PTO)
portfolio	

Educational Engineering

Case Studies in Education

Enter the information from the table below into the Educational Record for the student you are studying.

	Quality of Teachers in Child's Educational Experience	Quality of Schools in Child's Educational Experience
Davon	This is Davon's first school experience though he has attended day care. Clashes with adults if they use a negative style of disciplining. It sends him into a downhill spiral, from which he has difficulty recovering. Responds to positive statements to guide his behavior.	Davon's current school experience is excellent. His previous day-care experiences were below average.
Andy	Andy reports that his second-grade teacher was his "best" teacher because she was nice. She made the decision to promote Andy despite his difficulties in reading because of his recent diagnosis of ADHD. As far as having a "bad" teacher in the past, it's hard to make a determination. Andy's grandmother influenced his reaction to his first kindergarten teacher by having him moved to another classroom. She also intervened in her other grandson's placement in first grade. Thus, Andy has been promoted year after year in spite of being substantially deficient in reading and writing. In the third grade he must pass his state's comprehensive assessment test to be promoted. It appears unlikely that he will.	Andy attended pre-K through second grade in this community before coming to this school, which houses third through fifth grades. His previous elementary school, while considered to be a good school with good teachers, does not have the same philosophy concerning reading education as the school he now attends. His previous school does not value the comprehension component of the reading curriculum as highly as the decoding of text. The culture of this school is that comprehension comes later; the emphasis of their curricula is phonics. Children are deemed "good readers" if they are good decoders of text.

(Continued on next page)

Judith	Some teachers have commented about Judith's body odor, even in front of other students, saying things like, "Be sure to get a shower after P.E., OK?" She doesn't respond negatively but says little and avoids these teachers. Several teachers in the last few years have befriended her, but nothing has extended to her situation beyond school.	Judith's entire educational career has been in the same district. The school serves a large ethnic population of African-Americans, Hispanics, and Asian-Americans. However, the district is well supported by the presence of petroleum industry corporations. "Excellent" might be a stretch, but the schools are definitely above average.
Tiffany	**Tiffany** Tiffany appreciates all her teachers. She takes their word as fact and does everything she can to meet and exceed expectations and get as much praise as she can from the teachers. Known as a teacher's pet, she enjoys helping the classroom teacher. She has been known to ask teachers for permission to stay after school or inside from recess to help them organize, to work on projects, and to complete extra work.	Tiffany's educational experiences have always been excellent. She loves school and the work assigned. She views assignments and projects as challenges and always strives to exceed expectations.
Sam	Sam has had some very skilled teachers as evidenced by his progression to a general education class by the fourth grade. He continues to receive special education support. He is in a diploma-track program and scheduled to graduate in the upcoming year. The collaboration between special education and general education teachers has been critical to his progress.	Sam's educational experiences prior to and including this year (junior year) have been in average to above average schools. The quality of education, however, has been as dependent on the skill of individual teachers as it has on the overall rating of the school.
Bao	Bao herself would never be able to call a teacher "bad"—that would be too direct a judgment for her to make. Her Language Arts/Social Studies core teacher in middle school was especially strong, and Bao thoroughly enjoyed her two years with him. However, though she worked extremely hard and earned an A– in this class at the end of eighth grade, she did not carry this passion with her to other classes or on to high school.	Bao's elementary and middle schools were average—most teachers cared about teaching and students, but the funding in the district is too low to allow for any really outstanding services, equipment, or facilities. Her high school is considered excellent, in part because it is a magnet school for the district's International Baccalaureate program, of which Bao is not a part.

1. The quality of the teachers your student has encountered can be affected by many factors. One, of course, is the teacher education programs that these people completed. Based on the information about your student's teachers, what recommendations would you make about the education of teachers? What aspects of the program you are entering will prepare you to be one of the best teachers that a student such as this one has had?

2. As with the individual teacher, many factors can affect the quality of the school and the overall educational experience. However, we can look to the quality of teachers within a school as an indicator of the consistency (good, bad, or "up and down") of a student's experience with school. From the information given, what comments could you make about the overall qualifications of the teachers in those schools? Where would you fit into the picture you have described?

 # Designing the School of the Future

In designing your school of the future it will be difficult to account for the certification programs that the state sanctions. John I. Goodlad (1990) suggests that states should be in the teacher licensure business as a protection for the children in the schools, but not in the certification business that prescribes what students must study on the way to licensure. Item 1 below provides you the opportunity to consider the future of education from Goodlad's perspective. Item 2 lets you consider how your school of the future will address inconsistencies in teacher education if the current licensure and certification process remains relatively intact.

1. Let's suppose that in the future professional educators will direct the preparation of teachers as other professions such as medicine and law do today. It is reasonable that candidates will still have to be licensed by the state.

   a. What program would you design for the preparation of teachers? At this point in your own education, your thinking is probably not constrained by "tradition," so feel free to consider what knowledge and skills you believe a teacher should possess. What content knowledge would you require? What skills of teaching would have to be demonstrated before a license was issued? Would you require an internship or residency as in the medical profession?

   b. How does your plan compare and contrast with the program being offered at your institution and required by the state in which you wish to be certified? Which plan would you prefer, and why?

2. Suppose that the school of the future does not have control over the preparation of teachers. Nonetheless, you want your students to have a consistently strong educational experience. What measures would become the standard procedure to help ensure a quality school? The questions below might help you get started:

   a. Would new teachers be required to demonstrate proficiency in the classroom *before* being hired?

   b. Will teachers be able to earn tenure (that is, they cannot be fired except under special circumstances)?

   c. Will there be a standard of performance that must be met to continue employment?

   d. How will outstanding teaching be recognized or rewarded?

 # Praxis Practice

Many states will require that you successfully complete the Praxis Series of examinations to qualify for certification. One or more of those tests will be subject-area tests. Another, which has a more practical orientation, will be the Principles of Learning and Teaching (PLT) examination that is appropriate for your certification area.

Completing the Quick Check Quizzes for Chapter 4 in the Unit Workshop will give you practice with the multiple choice format of the PLT. The Case Studies in Education and Designing a School of the Future activities will help prepare you for exercises that require reading a scenario and providing short answers to questions asking what you might do in such a situation.

Educational Engineering

The four chapters of Unit I have discussed the teacher, teaching, diversity among students, and the process that prepares you to become a professional teacher. The common theme has been a look at the two primary players in the classroom: the teacher and the student. Our look at diversity emphasized that each child is unique and that education is not a "one size fits all" proposition. Our look at teachers focused on motivations to teach and the pedagogical competencies, communication skills, and teaching techniques and styles that teachers must possess, and the expectations for licensure and certification that educational agencies have established for teachers. The following activities should help you find your place in this emerging picture.

Case Studies

1. Write a paragraph to yourself—not for anyone else to read, just for yourself—that describes the child you have chosen for your case study, based on the information you have compiled through the chapters of Unit I. How would you describe the person you have encountered? What sort of cultural, intellectual, and physical needs does this child have that the teacher must meet?

2. Now write a second paragraph. This time, consider the sort of teacher and the best teaching environment for this child. Your focus here is on describing what sort of *teacher* the child needs.

3. In a third paragraph, consider whether the credentialing process as you have studied it here will provide this child with the appropriate sort of teacher. Is anything missing? Are this child's needs accommodated through the requirements for licensure?

4. One final paragraph: Do you see yourself becoming the teacher this student needs? Is it in you? Or would your talents and abilities be better utilized with a different type of student? What can you do as part of your teacher education program to become the teacher this student is waiting for?

5. No, not another paragraph. This time, a title. Use *Being a Teacher for Each Student* as the title for this collection of paragraphs.

Designing the School of the Future

By now you should have decided how far in the future you are looking as you design this new school. You also should have made a number of decisions about the sorts of people, in terms of character and competencies, that will become the faculty of your school. For these next exercises, let's use the title *The Foundation*.

1. Begin by writing a slogan for your school. This exercise is really more difficult than it sounds at first. Your challenge is to build a single sentence that describes your teachers, the teaching focus of your school, the students, and your expectations for professionalism. To top it all off, the slogan needs to be something that people can understand and latch on to, something in which they want to be involved.

2. Now that you have a slogan, write an article for the op-ed page of the local newspaper that describes this new school to the community. In essence, you are laying the foundation for public support of this new direction. The article should be 500–1000 words long (that's just two to four double-spaced, typed pages). You can organize it any way you'd like, but you should include explanations of the need for a new school (or just a different, better, or stronger school), the sorts of teachers that it will employ, the instructional focus (for example, inquiry, discovery, lecture, direct instruction), and how teachers will be prepared and licensed. Ideally, work through several drafts of this article and have the drafts reviewed by your professor. A quality piece could actually be submitted to your local newspaper for publication. This is an article of ideas, and ideas are seeds of new thinking.

 **Quick Check**

Answer keys with page references are in Appendix E.

Chapter 1

1. In a 2003 study of urban teachers, Nieto identified several characteristics of successful teachers. Which of the following was *not* among the findings?
   a. They were committed to teaching.
   b. They preferred working independently of their colleagues.
   c. They were passionate about the subject matter itself.
   d. They believed they could influence the future.

2. The term *pedagogy* encompasses which of the following perspectives?
   a. Making the distinction between the art of teaching and the science of teaching.
   b. Blending the art and science of teaching.
   c. Teaching is an art.
   d. Teaching is a science.

3. The National Board for Professional Teaching Standards supports each of the following propositions *except:*
   a. Teachers are responsible for managing and monitoring student learning.
   b. Teachers are members of learning communities.
   c. Teachers can teach any subject if their foundation skills are strong.
   d. Teachers are committed to students and their learning.

4. Which of the following four pedagogical competencies is most closely related with the style of interacting with students that a teacher brings to the classroom?

   a. purpose
   b. content
   c. communication skills
   d. professional development

5. According to James H. Korn, articulating your philosophy helps you to do which of the following?
   a. become aware of inconsistencies between what you believe and what you do
   b. compare your style with other teachers around you to establish consistency
   c. explain to your students "who you are"
   d. identify inconsistencies between the curriculum and your sense of purpose

6. Which statement is the best example of static content competency?
   a. The depth of content knowledge required of elementary and secondary teachers is substantially the same.
   b. Due to the sophistication of older students, secondary teachers are expected to have greater depth and breadth of static content competency.
   c. Elementary teachers do not need the same level of static content competency as do secondary teachers.
   d. Elementary teachers need a greater breadth of static content competency across subject areas while secondary teachers need greater depth in a particular subject area.

7. Which of the following examples best exemplifies dynamic content competency?
   a. A teacher recognizes that subject matter would

be too difficult for her students and so removes it from a lesson plan.

b. A teacher notices that students do not understand a concept and so finds another way to explain it before moving on.

c. A teacher checks the Internet to find the most up-to-date information about a topic in technology.

d. After grading a test, a teacher drops a question that no one answered correctly.

8. According to the text, which of the following is true of a teacher's communication skills?

a. An effective teacher understands that different constituencies speak different "languages."

b. It is the teacher's responsibility to see that all constituencies know the terms that educators use to communicate about progress in school.

c. An effective teacher knows educational terminology very well.

d. There is little difference between communicating with one constituency or another because all have the same goals in mind.

9. Teachers engage in professional development in all of the following categories *except:*

a. as learners

b. as mentors

c. as school board members

d. as researchers

10. Professional development refers most closely to which of the following statements?

a. Professional development refers to finding ways to extend a teacher's influence beyond the classroom.

b. Teachers work as mentors to save the district money that would have been spent on training.

c. It has been shown that the amount of time teachers spend in professional development is directly related to student achievement.

d. Professional development represents a teacher's activities toward being a part of, and a contributor to, the discipline of education.

Chapter 2

1. Which statement best describes the strategic nature of teaching?

a. Teaching requires planning some course of action *and* coordinating the implementation of that plan.

b. Without a lesson plan, a teacher has lost the battle before it is begun.

c. Students need a teacher who can lead them.

d. Achieving goals and objectives requires a plan.

2. The topic of facilitating learning addresses each of the following *except:*

a. arranging experiences

b. monitoring and flexibility

c. certification requirements

d. instructional techniques

3. The various methods of arranging learning experiences refer to which of the following?

a. Interpreting world events in a manner appropriate for students.

b. Bringing the world and its experiences to the students.

c. Sequencing lessons from most basic to most sophisticated.

d. Scheduling each subject area appropriately throughout a school week.

4. The text suggests that the most common educational experience has which relationship with the real world?

a. It offers the closest relationship with real-world experiences.

b. It is furthest removed from real-world experiences.

c. It parallels real-world experiences.

d. It specifically shields students from the realities of world experiences.

5. The taxonomy of instructional techniques is arranged in which order?

a. drill and practice, direct instruction, lecture, question and answer, discussion, mental modeling, inquiry, discovery learning

b. direct instruction, drill and practice, lecture, question and answer, discussion, mental modeling, discovery learning, inquiry

c. drill and practice, direct instruction, lecture, discussion, question and answer, mental modeling, inquiry, discovery learning

d. discovery learning, inquiry, mental modeling, discussion, question and answer, drill and practice, direct instruction, lecture

6. Which of the following instructional techniques use students' personal experiences as the foundation for building concepts?

a. mental modeling
b. inquiry
c. discussion
d. discovery learning

7. Which of the following represents the three divisions of the taxonomy of instructional techniques?
   a. teacher focused, dialogue oriented, student focused
   b. teacher focused, individual focused, student focused
   c. lower-order instruction, mid-range instruction, higher-order instruction
   d. skills, content knowledge, abstractions

8. In terms of facilitating learning, monitoring refers to which of the following?
   a. an ongoing assessment of the progress of a lesson
   b. assessment of student achievement
   c. watching a class during the administration of a standardized test
   d. assigning jobs to the students

9. A teacher demonstrating instructional flexibility during a class exhibits which of the following?
   a. ability to talk about tangential topics during a lesson
   b. willingness to make changes when things aren't working as planned
   c. willingness and ability to make changes in an instructional plan
   d. awareness that if the lesson continues the students will eventually understand

10. According to Bandura, which of the following is true of teachers?
    a. They are models only for those children who choose them as a model.
    b. Teachers are effective models at school, but that does not extend beyond the classroom.
    c. The development of behaviors does not rely on observing a model such as a teacher.
    d. The emphasis placed on observing and imitating models indicates that teachers are models in and out of school.

Chapter 3

1. Which of the following terms most closely refers to the values, attitudes, and beliefs that influence the behavior and traditions of a people?
   a. customs
   b. ethnicity
   c. culture
   d. race

2. Which of the following most closely refers to a sense of common identity based upon common ancestral background, the sharing of common values and beliefs, and unique physical and/or cultural characteristics that enable individuals who belong to one group to identify its members easily?
   a. heritage
   b. ethnicity
   c. race
   d. culture

3. Which of the following social metaphors most closely reflects the idea of multiculturalism?
   a. the salad bowl
   b. the fog
   c. the melting pot
   d. the filing cabinet

4. According to Franklin, which of the following ethnic groups embraces the core values of resistance, freedom, self-determination, and education?
   a. African-American
   b. Caucasian
   c. Hispanic/Latino(a)
   d. Asian Pacific American

5. Jacqueline Jordan refers to the compatibility between one's own cultural norms and those encountered within the school as which of the following?
   a. overt racial integration
   b. ethnic equilibration
   c. cultural distancing
   d. cultural synchronization

6. According to Deyhle, which of the following groups is most likely to equate success with the extent of intact family relationships, the degree to which one's work enhances the family and community, and group—as opposed to individual—accomplishment?
   a. African American
   b. Caucasian
   c. Native American
   d. Asian Pacific American

7. Which of the following groups is most likely to value reverence and respect for parents and other persons in authority, conformity, obedience, and the promotion of group goals over individual interests?
   a. African American
   b. Caucasian
   c. Native American
   d. Asian Pacific American

8. Which of the following would be an example of sexual stereotyping?
   a. providing physical education classes that combine boys and girls
   b. offering boys basketball and girls basketball teams
   c. tolerating aggressive behavior in girls but expecting boys to act like "gentlemen"
   d. directing boys toward careers as physicians and girls toward careers as nurses

9. A student who needs to work with manipulatives or to actually perform the steps in a process to understand it is likely to have a preference for which of the following learning styles?
   a. tactile/kinesthetic
   b. visual
   c. auditory
   d. vocalic

10. The term "intelligence" is generally agreed to mean which of the following?
   a. the breadth of knowledge one has about a given topic
   b. the extent of knowledge one has across a broad spectrum of topics and experiences
   c. an individual's capacity to learn from experience and to adapt to the environment
   d. the ability to perform mathematical and logical operations with a high degree of accuracy

Chapter 4

1. Which of the following represents the final source for information about teacher certification requirements?
   a. Director of Teacher Education in your school's Education Department
   b. State education agency in your state
   c. National Council for Accreditation of Teacher Education (NCATE)
   d. U.S. Department of Education

2. "Clinical experiences" refers to each of the following *except:*
   a. practicums
   b. field service
   c. coursework in teaching methods
   d. student teaching

3. Reciprocal certification agreements, sometimes referred to as reciprocity, refer to which of the following?
   a. being able to transfer education course credits from one institution to another
   b. forgiveness of student loans for teaching in disadvantaged areas
   c. teacher exchange programs that allow new teachers to work in diverse settings
   d. agreements among states to recognize teaching credentials from other states

4. Coursework reflecting a liberal arts perspective is clustered under which of the following headings?
   a. General Education
   b. Professional Education
   c. Specialization Courses
   d. Clinical Experiences

5. The most widely used series of teacher certification examinations are known as which of the following?
   a. National Teacher Examination (NTE)
   b. Praxis Series
   c. Board of Regents Educational Examination Series
   d. National Boards for Teacher Examination

6. Which of the following is cited as an advantage of alternative certification programs?
   a. Candidates tend to bring a stronger academic background to teaching.
   b. Candidates have a greater commitment to teaching because it represents a second career.
   c. It is more cost efficient to prepare a teacher who already possesses a degree.
   d. Such candidates often possess additional skills and a broader perspective of life.

7. Which of the following represents a collaboration between state education agencies, institutions of higher education, and national organizations to develop performance standards for beginning teachers?

a. National Council for the Accreditation of Teacher Education (NCATE)
b. National Board for Professional Teaching Standards (NBPTS)
c. Interstate New Teacher Assessment and Support Consortium (INTASC)
d. National Education Agency (NEA)

8. Federal legislation requiring teachers to be certified as "highly qualified" in the discipline they teach is referred to as which of the following?
a. The Education for All Children Act
b. The No Child Left Behind Act
c. The Excellence in Education Act
d. Title IX

9. Which of the following offers a voluntary program leading to advanced certification for teachers?
a. National Council for the Accreditation of Teacher Education (NCATE)
b. National Education Agency (NEA)
c. Interstate New Teacher Assessment and Support Consortium (INTASC)
d. National Board for Professional Teaching Standards (NBPTS)

10. A Bill of Rights for Student Teachers has been adopted by which of the following professional organizations?
a. National Education Association (NEA)
b. American Federation of Teachers (AFT)
c. Parent-Teacher Organization (PTO)
d. Association for Supervision and Curriculum Development (ASCD)

Curriculum, Management, and Assessment

The chapters of Unit II discuss three aspects of education that are part of a teacher's everyday life but are not instructional responsibilities. Curriculum is such an expansive topic that it will be covered in two chapters. Classroom management and assessment of student learning are topics that we refer to as *classroom pragmatics*. They are practical issues with which a teacher needs considerable expertise.

Chapter 5, Understanding Curriculum, looks at curriculum from a broad perspective. This discussion is concerned with what curriculum is, types of curriculum, and perspectives on curriculum design. You have probably had little exposure to this aspect of curriculum.

Chapter 6, Contemporary Curricula: Influences and Standards, will likely be more familiar to you. The chapter discusses the major players influencing what is to be taught in school, the various subject areas and the standards that are driving them, and some of the issues in curriculum that you may one day help to resolve.

Chapter 7, Classroom Pragmatics, is unique to this textbook. The two major topics within this chapter, classroom management and assessment of student learning, are areas that beginning teachers often feel most concerned about. We do not provide Chapter 7 as a course in either of these very important aspects of being a professional educator, but rather to introduce you, at the beginning of your teacher education experience, to these critical components of the work that teachers do.

5

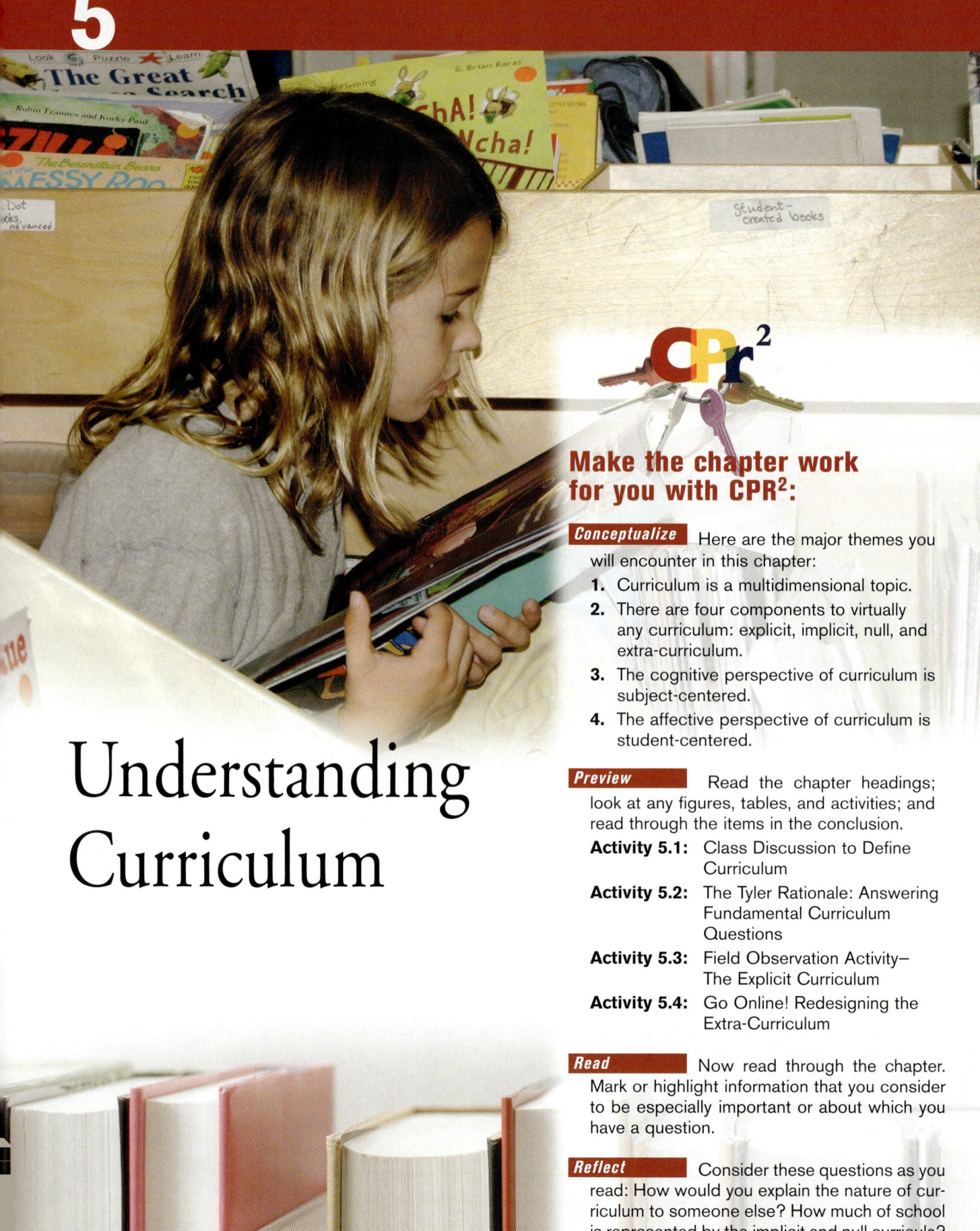

Understanding Curriculum

Make the chapter work for you with CPR²:

Conceptualize Here are the major themes you will encounter in this chapter:

1. Curriculum is a multidimensional topic.
2. There are four components to virtually any curriculum: explicit, implicit, null, and extra-curriculum.
3. The cognitive perspective of curriculum is subject-centered.
4. The affective perspective of curriculum is student-centered.

Preview Read the chapter headings; look at any figures, tables, and activities; and read through the items in the conclusion.

Activity 5.1: Class Discussion to Define Curriculum

Activity 5.2: The Tyler Rationale: Answering Fundamental Curriculum Questions

Activity 5.3: Field Observation Activity— The Explicit Curriculum

Activity 5.4: Go Online! Redesigning the Extra-Curriculum

Read Now read through the chapter. Mark or highlight information that you consider to be especially important or about which you have a question.

Reflect Consider these questions as you read: How would you explain the nature of curriculum to someone else? How much of school is represented by the implicit and null curricula?

Photo: Courtesy of Becky Stovall

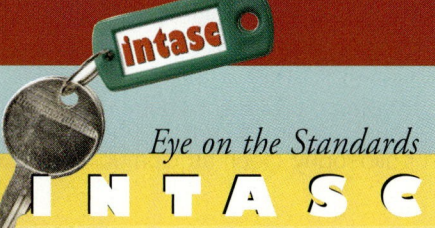

The following standards from the Interstate New Teacher Assessment and Support Consortium (INTASC) will be addressed in this chapter. As you read the chapter, consider how school curriculum is tied to these principles.

Principle 1 The teacher understands the central concepts, tools of inquiry, and structures of the discipline(s) he or she teaches and can create learning experiences that make these aspects of subject matter meaningful for students.

Principle 3 The teacher understands how students differ in their approaches to learning and creates instructional opportunities that are adapted to diverse learners.

Principle 4 The teacher understands and uses a variety of instructional strategies to encourage students' development of critical thinking, problem solving, and performance skills.

Principle 5 The teacher uses an understanding of individual and group motivation and behavior to create a learning environment that encourages positive social interaction, active engagement in learning, and self-motivation.

Principle 7 The teacher plans instruction based upon knowledge of subject matter, students, the community, and curriculum goals.

ice breakers

What Did *You* Learn About?

Read through the list of topics below. You will probably recognize some of them as topics you learned about in classes you had during your K–12 education. Other items might be things you learned about through interacting with teachers and other students, through participation in extracurricular activities, or just by being a part of the school culture. Still other items may not have come up at all during your schooling.

Mark each item 1, 2, or 3 as follows:

1. if it is something that you actually studied in one or more of your classes. These items would be the sort of things for which you took tests and received grades.

2. if it is something you learned by being in school. Examples might include being responsible for your own actions, team work and cooperation, allegiance (to school, community, state, or nation).

3. for items that as far as you know were not discussed in school (aside from just coming up in conversation). This could include such things as controversial topics and issues or even the study of foreign cultures and beliefs.

_____ 1. Math facts and computation skills.

_____ 2. There were some books that the school did not allow in the library.

_____ 3. The need for following the rules.

_____ 4. Some teachers who taught the same subject emphasized different topics; one may have omitted topics in her class though another teacher discussed them in his class.

_____ 5. Boys are better suited to some skills and professions and girls for others.

_____ 6. Respect for authority.

_____ 7. The various means (other than abstinence) for birth control.

_____ 8. English composition and grammar.

_____ 9. Patriotism.

_____ 10. The value of a traditional family structure.

_____ 11. Social structuring (for example, it was more prestigious to be a senior in high school than to be a freshman).

_____ 12. In science, teaching the theory of evolution and the philosophy of creationism.

_____ 13. The benefits of an alternative lifestyle (for example, communal living, nontraditional sexual orientations, civil disobedience).

_____ 14. An in-depth study of Eastern philosophy (such as Confucianism or Daoism).

_____ 15. Lessons in physical fitness and good health.

_____ 16. The structure and function of the United States government.

_____ 17. Study of Western literature such as the works of Herman Melville, Charles Dickens, and William Shakespeare.

_____ 18. Planets and organization of our solar system.

The items that you marked with a "1" represent the *explicit curriculum,* the topics and skills that the school specifically seeks to teach by way of classroom instruction and the educational materials they use.

Items marked with a "2" represent elements of the *implicit curriculum.* These are the lessons you learned that were a part of the "culture" of the school and the community that it represented. Though you did not take classes in things such as teamwork and cooperation, it was likely encouraged throughout your K–12 education.

Another version of curriculum is that of the *null curriculum.* You marked these items with a "3." This represents the topics and ideas that the school, as an agent of its constituents, *excludes* from the curriculum. For instance, in some communities the teaching of evolution is excluded because it is contrary to the prevailing view of creation held in that community. Other examples can be found in the emphasis on Western culture and literature to the virtual, if not real, exclusion of studies centered on the wisdom and literature of Eastern cultures. When considering what elements a curriculum should contain, you must seriously consider the positive and negative aspects of specifically excluding particular topics.

> *To teach the ways of one's own community has always been and still remains the essence of the education of our children, who enter neither a tribal culture nor a transcendent world culture but a national literate culture.*
>
> *E. D. Hirsch Jr. (1988)*

■ Introduction

Seems as though you've been in school all of your life, doesn't it? Given that, you probably think of what goes on in school as not only the norm, the way it is, but also as if it's always been that way. Yet the reality is that curriculum is constantly evolving. As we will see in this chapter, many influences affect a school's curriculum. In virtually all cases these are influences that change with the times. Therefore, we can expect the curriculum to change as well.

Which of the many influences has the greatest effect on the curriculum? That is impossible to determine. It's possible that the folks who had the most significant impact on the American educational curriculum in the last five decades were a group of Soviet scientists working away on a basketball-sized satellite back in the 1950s. The launch of Sputnik (the first man-made satellite) initiated the spending of unprecedented amounts of federal money for the revision of school curricula in math and science, specifically so that we might catch up with and surpass the technological achievements of the Russians. In fact, it was the National Defense Education Act (NDEA) of 1958 that appropriated nearly a billion dollars primarily for math and science curriculum reform efforts. In the time since, the funding emphasis has switched to other subject areas in accord with the prevailing social climate and has lost some of its original furor, but the use of *federal* taxpayer dollars to support educational research and development continues despite the fact that education is each *state's* responsibility. Do you suppose those Soviet scientists had any idea, as Sputnik rocketed into Earth orbit, that they were launching a tumultuous period of educational reform in the United States? Likely not, but it is fascinating to consider the factors that determine what children will and will not be taught in school.

Our look at curriculum is intended to help you see the depth and breadth of this fundamental aspect of organized education. The issues that arise when discussing curriculum are issues that can be divisive in communities, states, and the nation. They include questions of school prayer, uniforms, and the suitability of certain books in the library. We cannot resolve these issues within the pages of this chapter, but since you will one day be in the middle of the debate, we hope that this chapter will provide you with an appreciation of what curriculum is, who develops it, and what some of the issues are in contemporary curriculum discussions.

■ Understanding "Curriculum"

There is considerable discussion these days about requiring public school children to wear uniforms to school or to prohibit the wearing of clothing that displays "culturally offensive" messages. Are these "rules" part of the curriculum? Did the high school *you* attended have a dress code? Was that part of the curriculum? How about the food served in the cafeteria? Many schools today are removing soda machines and no longer offering sugary beverages for sale because they are not considered to have nutritional value. And what of the offering of "ethnic" foods? Is this part of the curriculum? How about the teaching of, or not teaching, evolution as a topic in science classes, or the removal of books considered to represent "new age" philosophy from the library bookshelves? Which of these issues enter into determining what constitutes curriculum—the message of the school? Before continuing with our discussion of curriculum, use Activity 5.1 to consider what it means to you.

Defining "Curriculum"

curriculum The program by which a school meets its educational goals. It includes planned as well as unplanned experiences and involves the means and materials with which students interact.

For our discussion, let's begin with a broad definition for *curriculum* and then examine just what it might mean. Specifically in an educational setting, **curriculum** refers to the means and materials with which students will interact for the purpose of achieving identified educational outcomes. There is much more to it than that, and since you are to be a professional educator it is important that you have a deeper understanding of all that "curriculum" might entail.

> **ACTIVITY 5.1**
> **Class Discussion to Define Curriculum**
>
> You have spent many years experiencing various education curricula. How would you define "curriculum"? Is your definition the same as that of your classmates? Try to come to a definition that you can all agree upon. Note that as you try to define curriculum, you will be tempted to list the subjects or activities that represent the curriculum. That is acceptable as long as you can explain what that particular collection of courses was intended to accomplish.

trivium In medieval Europe, an educational curriculum based upon the study of grammar, rhetoric, and logic.

quadrivium The study of four subjects—arithmetic, geometry, music, and astronomy—in the medieval university.

Arising in medieval Europe was the **trivium,** an educational curriculum based upon the study of grammar, rhetoric, and logic. The later **quadrivium** (referring to four subjects rather than three as represented by the trivium) emphasized the study of arithmetic, geometry, music, and astronomy. Does any of this sound like what you have experienced during your formal education? To a degree it should sound familiar. The emphasis on single subjects (such as those identified in the trivium and quadrivium) persists even today. Very likely you moved from classroom to classroom, particularly throughout your secondary education, studying a different subject with each teacher. Yet there still was more to your education. Perhaps you participated in athletics, or the band, or clubs, or student government, or made the choice *not* to participate in any extracurricular activities. All of these (including the option not to participate) are part of what we might call the contemporary curriculum. But there is more to it.

Some in education would say that the curriculum consists of all the *planned experiences* that the school offers as part of its educational responsibility. Others contend that the curriculum includes not only the planned but the *unplanned experiences* as well. For example, incidents of violence that have occurred at a number of schools across the nation are hardly a planned component of the curriculum. However, the manner in which violence is addressed before, during, and after the actual event sends a definite message about how people in our culture interact and how the laws of our nation are applied. Let's add in here that events of great joy and accomplishment are also powerfully charged as lifelong experiences. Since schools are expected to take a particular perspective on all events that take place within their jurisdiction, we might say that the curriculum *does* include unplanned experiences as well.

Another perspective suggests that curriculum involves "organized" experiences rather than planned because any event must flow of its own accord, the outcome not being certain beforehand. For instance, competitions, whether academic or athletic, can be organized, but the outcomes will depend on a myriad of factors that cannot be planned. Which brings us to the notion of emphasizing *outcomes* versus *experiences.* From this perspective the focus is on what the schools are supposed to accomplish with the students. The curriculum, therefore, will be that program by which the school meets its educational goals.

This shift to the notion of *outcomes* is very much in keeping with the current movement toward *accountability* in the public schools, that is, the perspective that there are indeed specific things that the schools are supposed to accomplish with children. District personnel, school administrators, and teachers are to be held accountable for ensuring that those objectives are met. Where does all of this leave us? It leaves us with an enormous task that cannot be overestimated. E. D. Hirsch Jr. (1988) has written, "During recent decades Americans have hesitated to make a decision about the specific knowledge that children need to learn in school" (p. 19) and "There is a pressing need for clarity about our educational priorities"

(p. 25). Curriculum is indeed much more than the idea of specific subjects as represented by the trivium or the quadrivium. It requires extensive planning and organizing that incorporates built-in flexibility. It must have a clear purpose as well as a structure that allows for the fact that all classrooms are composed of *individual* children. And, as we will see in the next section, it can be characterized not only by what it *does* include but also by what it intentionally *excludes*.

So, if in a challenging situation you should happen to be asked what "curriculum" means, what should you say? First, consider what you and your classmates determined in Activity 5.1. Second, keep in mind that while much of the message of school is strikingly similar throughout the country, there are differences from state to state—and even between regions within a state. Curricula are always intended to serve a particular constituency, and you likely know the constituency where you live or wish to teach better than we do. Third, from a broader perspective, we suggest that you think of "curriculum" as we defined it earlier in this chapter: as the means and materials with which students will interact for the purpose of achieving identified educational outcomes. "Materials" refers to the identified subjects and topics to be presented to the students, and the various media formats in which those topics are presented (books, videos, computer software, etc.). "Means" refers to the strategies teachers use to foster interest, expand perspectives, and encourage learning. Modeling, investigating, and even drill and practice are among the methods a teacher could consider for stimulating inquiry, creative and critical thinking, and attitudes of persistence and respect. In combination, the materials and means represent the curriculum.

The definition offered is necessarily flexible but specific on a couple of points. One is that there must be *clearly identified desired outcomes*. That doesn't mean that all students reach the mark in the same amount of time, but that everybody knows what the mark is—whether it's a particular level of achievement in mathematics or the ability to function as a contributing member of the community. Articulated purposes, goals, and objectives underlie sound instruction *and* assessment. Similarly, they underlie sound curriculum design. As Anderson and Krathwohl (2001) have noted, the more specific the learning experience, the more well-defined the objectives should be.

A key element of the definition we have suggested is that the curriculum is only that part of the plan that *directly affects* students. Anything in the plan that does not reach the students constitutes an educational wish, but not a curriculum. Rutherford and Ahlgren (1990) argue in *Science for All Americans* that "the present curricula in science and mathematics are overstuffed and undernourished" (p. viii).

Textbooks are designed to support the curriculum that a school has chosen to present.

Courtesy of Bill Lisenby

That is, there is too much information and not enough depth. This results from years of tinkering with curricula that may have originally represented sound educational objectives. Almost half a century ago Bruner (1960) wrote, "Many curricula are originally planned with a guiding idea much like the one set forth here. But as curricula are actually executed, as they grow and change, they often lose their original form and suffer a relapse into a certain shapelessness" (p. 54). A chapter that is not addressed in class and for whose content the students are not held responsible is not part of the curriculum—even if it was part of someone's "plan."

Our definition represents a somewhat philosophical perspective of curriculum.

However, as you continue with your consideration of curriculum and all other issues in education, remember that you cannot divorce the student from the the concept of curriculum. Curriculum—however grand the plans may be—can only be that portion of the plan that actually reaches the student. Planning that keeps that point in focus can be expected to result in a more focused curriculum.

The Purpose of Curriculum

We have said that "curriculum" refers to the means and materials with which the student interacts. To determine what will constitute those means and materials, we must decide what we want the curriculum to yield. What will constitute the "educated" individual in our society? In other words, what purpose does the curriculum serve?

At first glance the answer seems rather obvious: A prepared course of study yields people educated in a particular, desired way. The things that teachers teach represent what the larger society wants children to learn. But beyond teaching reading and writing, what *are* the necessary things that they should be taught? Is it really necessary to teach science? Does teaching mathematics really lead to logical thinking, or does it just provide students with some basic computational skills that may or may not come in handy sometime? You may feel that answering questions like these is not a teacher's responsibility, but rest assured that at some point a parent will ask them of you. Once you become a teacher, you will be the representative of "the curriculum" to whom parents and students turn for answers.

From its beginnings in the Colonies as lessons in reading and Bible study, to the secular emphasis on grammar, rhetoric, and logic, to the efforts to make education more "relevant" in the real world, curriculum has responded to prevailing social issues, concerns, and priorities. Surveys conducted by the Committee for Economic Development and by the College Board have indicated that employers look for three traits in school graduates: an ability to learn, literacy, and a positive attitude toward work (Committee for Economic Development, 1985).

Authors such as Theodore Sizer (1985) and Mortimer Adler (1982, 1983) are more specific in their expectations, advocating an emphasis on intellectual development. Perhaps most prescriptive of all is the call for a focus on cultural literacy, that is, those things that "every American needs to know" (Hirsch, 1988).

Another perspective involves emphasizing "character education." The Center for Advancement of Ethics and Character, an organization that sees the school curriculum as lacking in moral authority and ethical language to the point of being sterile and meaningless, looks for a "return" of American values to the school curriculum. Did you ever receive a grade in school for "good citizenship" or something similar? You can imagine how sticky this issue could be. For instance, an English teacher may want her students to read Thoreau's *On Civil Disobedience,* yet obedience to the laws of the land is an ethical trait that citizens are supposed to possess. How might a teacher balance the message with the expectation?

Add into this debate the question of *time* and a paradoxical question that could stump philosophers for decades comes into view. That is, for what time should schools prepare their students: the present or the future? Without doubt, education as we have known it has been based on the past and directed toward practical applications. It is true that high school seniors, college bound or not, will likely be putting their skills to work within days or weeks of graduation. In such a case a reasonable argument can be made that education should focus on today's world, today's needs, and today's expectations of public school graduates.

Yet we also need to consider the youngster on his first day of kindergarten. That child is beginning an educational odyssey that will occupy nearly a decade and a half. Is it reasonable to assume that in more than a decade the needs of the community, nation, and world may be different than they are today? Will there be new ways of communicating, of doing business, of building buildings, and of repairing automobiles? Likely, the answers to these sample questions will be *yes*. The challenge is in designing a curriculum for a future as yet unknown. Are there fundamental skills and basic knowledge that essentially remain unchanged from generation to generation; if so, should that be the emphasis of the school experience? Is it the case that intellectual development prepares one to acquire any skill and to assimilate and accommodate a dynamic knowledge base?

We ask all of these questions not to undermine your desire to be a teacher. On the contrary, we ask you to consider these questions so that you may become an extraordinary teacher, so that you may grasp what Jerome Bruner refers to as the "structure" of education to the point that subject matter is just one component of that framework. Despite the issues that face contemporary education, there has never been a time so dynamic as now to become a teacher.

In true American form, education is all about opportunity. The curriculum provides opportunities, and the teacher does her best to guide the students through those opportunities in a manner that helps to accomplish a desired goal. But a school cannot predetermine the educational experiences that a student will have. Rather, the school provides the opportunity that could result in an experience of value to the student. Whatever the parameters are or may one day be, the purpose of the curriculum is to prepare the student to thrive within the society as it is— and that includes *the capacity for positive change and growth*. Activity 5.2 will provide you with an opportunity to consider the purpose of a curriculum using the questions posed in the Tyler rationale.

The Four Curricula

As we look now to the structure of curriculum, we find that there are essentially four curricula at work in most educational settings. These four are the explicit, implicit, null, and extra, or co-curriculum. You are probably familiar with the notions of explicit curriculum and extracurricular activities. The real intrigue of curriculum debate and design comes into play with the implicit and null curricula.

ACTIVITY 5.2:
The Tyler Rationale: Answering Fundamental Curriculum Questions

Though first proposed in 1949, the questions asked in the Tyler rationale still provide a good starting point for curriculum design. How would you answer each of the following questions? Do your classmates' answers agree with yours? (*Note:* We have asked several times now if you find agreement among you and your classmates. We ask this because a curriculum has to represent the educational desires of many people. Finding agreement among your classmates now will be good practice for finding agreement among larger groups later.)

1. What educational purposes should the school seek to attain?

2. What educational experiences can be provided that are likely to attain these purposes?

3. How can these educational experiences be effectively organized?

4. How can we determine whether these purposes are being attained?

(Tyler, 1949, p. 1)

The Explicit Curriculum

explicit curriculum The subjects that will be taught, the identified "mission" of the school, and the knowledge and skills that the school expects successful students to acquire.

Explicit means "obvious" or "apparent," and that's just what the **explicit curriculum** is all about. This facet of the school curriculum is concerned with the subjects that will be taught, the identified "mission" of the school, and the knowledge and skills that the school expects successful students to acquire. If you speak with an administrator at the school where you do your observations or practicum work and ask about the curriculum, it is this publicly announced (and publicly sanctioned) message of the school that will be explained to you.

The explicit curriculum can be discussed in terms of time on task, contact hours, or Carnegie units (high school credit courses). It can be qualified in terms of specific observable, measurable learning objectives. Each year when students complete the district- or state-adopted achievement tests, two dimensions of the educational process are being measured: the school's success in effectively teaching the explicit curriculum and the students' success in learning it. Activity 5.3 is an opportunity for you to consider your own educational experience in terms of the explicit curriculum.

The Implicit Curriculum

implicit curriculum The lessons that arise from the culture of the school and the behaviors, attitudes, and expectations that characterize that culture.

There are other things included in the message of school that are not typically part of the explicit curriculum. Sometimes referred to as the "hidden curriculum," the **implicit curriculum** refers to the lessons that arise from the culture of the school and the behaviors, attitudes, and expectations that characterize that culture. While good citizenship may be part of the explicit curriculum, a particular ethos that promotes multiethnic acceptance and cooperation may also characterize a particular school. This is not to say that parents, teachers, and administrators sat around a table and said, "Hey, let's promote acceptance of diverse ethnic values in the context of the American experience." That would be nice, of course, but it would fall into the category of the explicit curriculum. What is at work in an implicit curriculum is that by virtue of a high multiethnic enrollment a particular school may have a "culture" of multiethnic cooperation. Another school, "isolated" in that its enrollment is primarily that of one ethnic group, would develop a different sort of culture.

Field Observation

ACTIVITY 5.3: The Explicit Curriculum

For this activity consider either the curriculum you experienced in high school or that of the local school if you are doing observations as part of this course. After you have answered each question, discuss your perspective with a classroom teacher. How do your perspectives agree and differ?

1. What subjects are offered as part of the explicit curriculum?

2. What skills are all students supposed to acquire by completing the curriculum?

3. What knowledge or literacy should the student possess by completing the curriculum?

4. Have you listed any character traits in questions 1–3? If so, is it explicitly stated in writing that students in that school will learn or acquire those traits?

5. What is your opinion of the curriculum you have been detailing? Are you in agreement with its goals? Is the school successful in enabling the students to reach those goals?

As you can imagine, any social system is bound to develop a culture of its own that values certain behaviors, attitudes, and even skills and knowledge. Schools, too, are unique social systems. Even individual schools within a district that share a common *explicit* curriculum can differ greatly with regard to the *implicit* curriculum. This is not an altogether bad situation, but to a great degree the implicit curriculum is subjected to less scrutiny than is the explicit curriculum. On occasion it is worthwhile to consider the implicit messages that are being transmitted and to consider whether they should be perpetuated.

There are other aspects to the implicit curriculum, and interestingly enough it is the students who pick up on these messages. When next you visit a school, notice how the classrooms and common areas are decorated. These decorations will demonstrate what the implicit curriculum of the school values. Watch the children to see how they interact with each other within the class and throughout the building. Is there an emphasis on how students are to walk through the halls? Does the school display student work throughout the building? Is there an unwritten rule that children are to be seen and not heard? All of these contribute to a very particular message sent to students about expectations, demands, and codes of conduct.

If you want to investigate the notion of the implicit curriculum further, speak with some elementary school students. Ask them what is required to get good grades or the approval of the teacher. Then don't be surprised when rather than telling you about studying for an hour every night or completing homework correctly, they tell you things like "sit up straight" or "be quiet in class" or "be on time." The implicit curriculum, difficult as it is to identify and articulate, is something that students understand very quickly. Jerome Bruner (1960) speaks of the need to address intuitive understanding of a subject in order to learn increasingly sophisticated aspects of that subject. Well, here is a practical example of intuitive understanding. When young children explain the expectations for a student in school, it will likely be the implicit curriculum that they discuss.

The Null Curriculum

null curriculum The options students are not afforded; the perspectives they may never know about, much less be able to use; the concepts and skills that are not a part of their intellectual repertoire (Eisner).

Just as compelling as the notion of the implicit curriculum is Eisner's (1994) concept of the **null curriculum.** This aspect of curriculum refers to "the options students are not afforded, the perspectives they may never know about, much less be able to use, the concepts and skills that are not a part of their intellectual repertoire" (p. 106–07). The teaching of evolution provides an example. For more than 75 years this topic has been an issue of debate. The decision by individual states or school districts within states not to include evolution within its explicit curriculum places it in the category of the *null curriculum*. In other words, the decision to exclude particular topics or subjects from a curriculum nonetheless affects the curriculum by its very omission.

Sex education is another contemporary example. The degree to which it should be included in the school curriculum has long been debated, and the newer issues of gender orientation, alternative lifestyles, and alternative family configurations—just to mention a few—exemplify how exclusion from the explicit or implicit curriculum, and thus inclusion in the null curriculum, affects the overall educational experience. Keep in mind that these are not minor issues or issues of limited public awareness.

Other aspects of the null curriculum are important for curriculum designers to consider as they fashion the educational programs of the new century. Artistic activity, creative endeavor, imagination, inventiveness, innovation, and the solving of ill-structured problems (the most prevalent of real-life problems) receive little emphasis in the traditional explicit curriculum and are often the first to go when budgets are being trimmed. It is an interesting paradox that our country has succeeded by innovation and risk-taking, yet these traits are not fostered within the curriculum to the same degree as conformity, procedure, and discipline. As Eisner states, "We teach what we teach largely out of habit, and in the process neglect areas of study that could prove to be exceedingly useful to students" (1994, p. 103). The future of education is wide open with electronic access to information but is equally restrained by the firewalling of electronic access in the name of the null curriculum. Another paradox? Yes, another. Yet the great excitement of the possibilities lies in the potential for adding greater *depth* to the explicit curriculum. That is, if schools were to address issues from the null curriculum, the explicit curriculum would become richer.

Extracurricular Programs

extra-curriculum All of the school-sponsored programs (e.g., athletics, band) that are intended to supplement the academic aspect of the school experience.

The fourth aspect of curriculum is that of the **extra-curriculum** or *co-curriculum*. This curriculum represents all of those school-sponsored programs that are intended to supplement the academic aspect of the school experience. Athletics, music, drama, student government, clubs, and student organizations are all extracurricular activities. In contrast to the explicit curriculum, participation in these activities is purely voluntary and does not contribute to grades or credits earned. Extracurricular activities are open to all, though participation often depends on skill level.

By the early years of the 1990s, more than 80 percent of all high school seniors participated in extracurricular activities. In particular, students from smaller schools and students with stronger academic backgrounds tended to participate. Holland and Andre (1987) suggest that the value of extracurricular activities extends beyond school. Their findings indicate that

1. Extracurricular activities enhance student self-esteem.
2. Athletics, in particular, improves race relations.
3. Participating students tend to have higher SAT scores and grades.
4. Involvement is related to high career aspirations. (pp. 437–66)

Not everybody agrees, however, that the extra-curriculum serves a worthwhile purpose. Bradford Brown (1988) suggests that the effects of participation in extracurric-

Organized school activities represent elements of the extra-curriculum. What lessons can you identify from the extra-curriculum?

Courtesy of Bill Lisenby

ular activities are "probably positive" but are modest at best. Just as students from smaller schools are more likely to be involved, the research also indicates that students from larger schools are less likely to participate. Even more to the point, students who could most benefit from involvement tend to shy away from such such programs.

We might also question the "dream" aspect of extracurricular activities, particularly in terms of athletics. It is often said that sports are what keep many youngsters in school. The aspirations for professional careers are the stuff of which rags-to-riches movies are made. Yet of the more than 5 million students competing in varsity sports, only 1 out of 50 will play for a college team. And of those, only 1 out of 100 male athletes will play for a professional sports team. It is not surprising that critics of the extra-curriculum, such as Gifford and Dean (1990), question the academic value of programs that do little to prepare students for achievement tests, exit exams, and college entrance exams.

This brief look at extracurricular activities is not intended to suggest that they should simply be banished from the schools. However, with the considerable amount of money that goes into some programs and the dearth of funds made available to others (in particular, academically oriented programs), one must question whether the "traditional" extracurricular structure is working to achieve best purposes. Perhaps a worthwhile exercise would be designing an organizational system that (1) integrates the extra programs into the academic program, (2) allows the academic program to become more engaging, (3) opens extracurricular programs to a wider range of participation, and (4) does not allow the abdication of parental responsibility by providing extended "child care" and prefabricated social and intellectual stimulation. Use Activity 5.4 to further explore the issues of the

Go Online!

ACTIVITY 5.4: Redesigning the Extra-Curriculum

Extracurricular activities represent an interesting concern in schools. The very name "extra" curricular indicates that they are *not* part of the graduation requirements of an education program. Yet it is also true that applications for college, scholarships, and employment often ask about a student's extracurricular activities. In addition, they are often cited as "the reason that a child attends school" and as free after-school programs. So how do we make best use of this part of the curriculum? Use the Internet to find the information that will help you answer the following questions.

1. What percentage of students are engaged in extracurricular activities? Approximately how much money is allocated to extracurricular activities? *Note:* You might want to identify a particular level of school such as elementary, middle, or high school.

2. What are the 10 most popular activities? Considering the entire student population of a school, do you think these activities represent the best use of education funds? Why or why not?

3. Should *all* students be required to engage in *some* extracurricular activity? If not, write an editorial or commentary (something that would be suitable for a local newspaper) defending the current use of funds for extracurricular activities. Alternatively, write an editorial that would support either eliminating extracurricular programs or redesigning them to involve the entire student body. You will be able to find support for either position if you use the Internet to search "extracurricular activities in public schools."

Figure 5.1

The Four Curricula
The program offered to students in school is very complex. There are actually four curricula affecting the students throughout the experience:

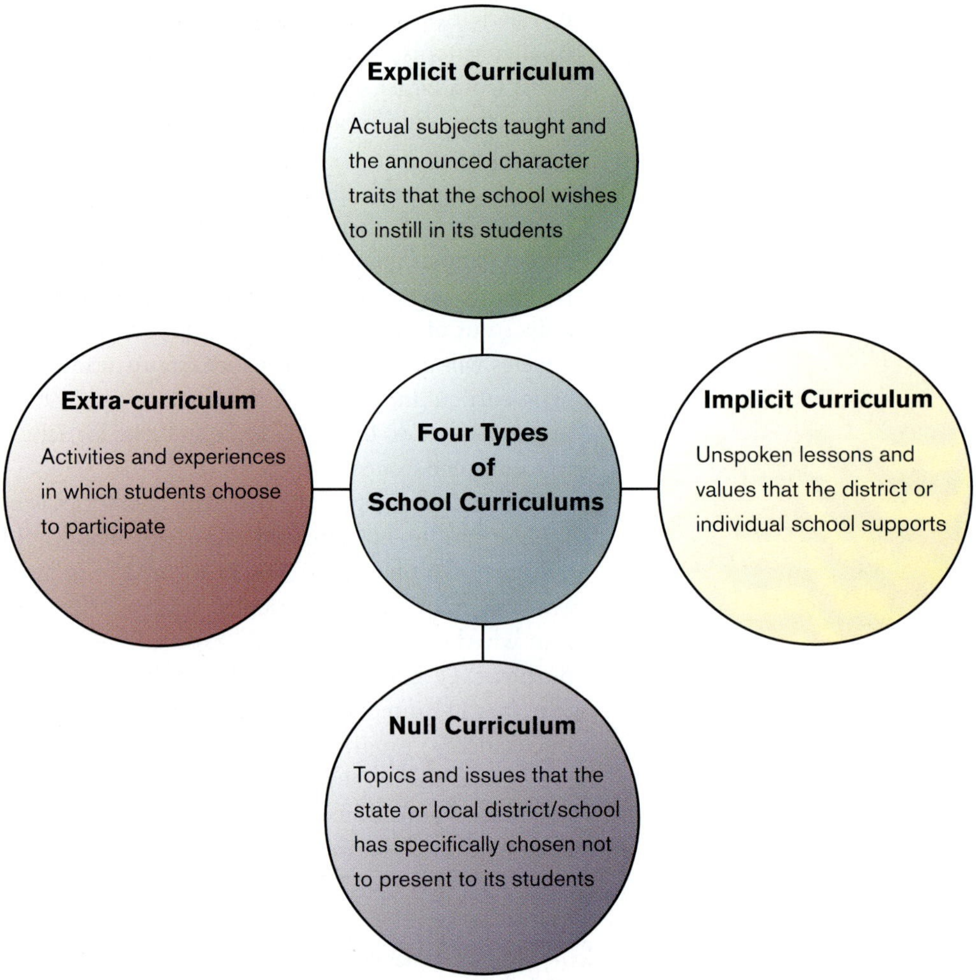

Explicit Curriculum

Actual subjects taught and the announced character traits that the school wishes to instill in its students

Extra-curriculum

Activities and experiences in which students choose to participate

Four Types of School Curriculums

Implicit Curriculum

Unspoken lessons and values that the district or individual school supports

Null Curriculum

Topics and issues that the state or local district/school has specifically chosen not to present to its students

extracurriculum. Having conducted your research, what recommendations would you make about this aspect of the curriculum? Figure 5.1 will provide you with a summary of the four types of curriculum we have discussed.

Perspectives of Curricula

Suppose you wanted to buy an automobile. You would expect the vehicle to have a chassis, a power plant, four wheels (with tires, of course), the necessary controls to operate the vehicle, and the ability to get you from one place to another. Those characteristics would, in general, represent what we think of as an automobile. But you know that there are millions of cars out there, and they differ in many ways. Color, power, styling, and sound systems are just some of the aspects of cars that would make *your* car unique. We are in a similar situation as we now discuss the different perspectives that can characterize a curriculum.

We know that the "curriculum" is really four curricula in a relationship that represents the socially sanctioned skills, knowledge, attitudes, and behaviors that the school is charged with teaching to its students. But that can essentially be said of any curriculum at any school; indeed, there are thousands of curricula across the country, each reflecting their own state, district, and local concerns and values. So, we need to turn our attention to the philosophies and perspectives, the "colors and sound systems" that make the various K–12 curricula unique.

It should be admitted that this discussion is reflective of an ongoing debate in education. Rather than being able to tell you what curriculum is, we hope to provide you with a deep enough understanding of curriculum so that *you* may engage in the debate and assist in developing solutions to educational issues wherever you work as a teacher. You will find that older philosophies get replaced with newer philosophies, which sometimes get replaced again by the older philosophies. Traditional perspectives get replaced by more radical perspectives that eventually become traditional perspectives only to one day be replaced by a new and radical perspective. But there are often trends that can be found just beneath the surface.

The Cognitive and Affective Perspectives

subject-centered curriculum A curriculum that emphasizes the subjects that all students should learn.

Two dominant perspectives of curriculum have occupied the educational spotlight, though more often than not they are embroiled in a struggle to find a common ground. One perspective is the **subject-centered curriculum,** the oldest curricular format in the Western world, dating back to classical Greece and Rome. The other is the **student-centered curriculum,** which first found favor through the work of John Dewey and later enjoyed a resurgence in popularity beginning in the latter 1960s. Because any curriculum must ultimately center on the student, we are going to borrow from the results of the White House Conferences on Education that occurred in 1956 and 1964 and adopt the terms *cognitive* (which takes an objective "thinking skills" perspective) and *affective* (which adopts a subjective perspective emphasizing attitudes and personal meaning) to distinguish between the two approaches. Most versions of curricular design fall into one category or the other. Of course, there will also be those variations that attempt to reconcile the differences and find the *golden mean,* as Aristotle centuries ago advised that we do.

student-centered curriculum A curriculum that emphasizes the natural interests and curiosity of the child.

The Cognitive Perspective

cognitive perspective The aspect of the curriculum that focuses on the acquisition of knowledge.

The **cognitive perspective** focuses on the acquisition of knowledge. To that end, curricula are typically divided among several distinct subject-matter areas. In the elementary school the different subjects are taught at scheduled times each day, with reading and math typically scheduled in the morning when students are believed to be most alert. In the secondary curriculum, students typically move from one room to another for different subjects. In either case, each subject is taught in isolation with its own facts, skills, and lessons to be learned.

The Subject-Centered Curriculum

This particular approach has been prominent in the American public school system for well over 100 years. Its origins can be traced to the work of William Harris in the 1870s. As superintendent of the St. Louis school system, Harris established a subject-centered curriculum in the classical tradition. Over the years, despite variations in course offerings and changing social priorities, this curricular structure has remained largely unchanged. The "basics," those subjects that many still believe all children should learn, continue to hold their place in the daily schedule. To a degree this can be attributed to the *perennialist* view that the best of the past, the important thinking, writing, and literature, is just as pertinent to the present.

The subject-centered approach is an efficient system from a logistical standpoint in that it requires little or no cooperation between teachers in different disciplines. Because the subjects remain separate, textbooks in any particular discipline can be updated without concern for the way information in one discipline might affect that of another. For instance, cloning can be addressed in a biology textbook without concern for the social and ethical ramifications that would be pertinent to a course in social studies or civics.

As you can see, the subject-centered approach lends itself well to a logical—we could even say *linear*—consideration of any particular discipline. The curriculum can be easily organized so that subjects are treated with increasing sophistication. That is, what one learns at an earlier level is the foundation for the next level. However, facilitating a *transfer of learning* (for instance, recognizing that what was learned in fourth grade can be applied in fifth grade) falls more into the *affective* perspective of curriculum design and, unfortunately, is often neglected when the emphasis is on the *cognitive* approach. The very efficiency of the subject-centered approach may be its downfall in this particular regard. It is so easy to package materials to be "grade-level specific" that the curriculum actually becomes rather rigid. Adjusting to factors such as learning style, rates of learning, and even rates of development is not easily managed and therefore is often not attempted.

The rigidity and linearity of the subject-centered curriculum is both a blessing and a curse. On the one hand, the subject-centered approach specifies a knowledge base and provides a solid platform for those who believe that there is a core of knowledge that all students should know. On the other hand, while the subject-centered approach can champion the cause of the common culture, it often does so at the expense of individual styles. A further criticism is that it fails to develop critical thinking or individual creative abilities. This, as is so often the case, is the

Teacher Testimonial

Feature 5.1   The Teacher's Curriculum

I have found over many years in education that curriculum is a very strange animal. You have probably read that there are various types of curricula, such as the explicit curriculum and what is often referred to as the "hidden" curriculum. But I also think there is another sort, something you might call "the teacher's curriculum."

As an administrator on the district level, I encounter many different teachers across the entire range of kindergarten through to teachers of high school seniors. No matter what the level or the background of the teachers, those whom I would consider to be effective teachers share these same underlying themes of the teacher's curriculum. Here are the elements that comprise that curriculum:

Preparation
"If we fail to plan we will plan to fail." You've likely heard that phrase before. It is essential, however, in the effective presentation of whatever curriculum a school might offer. Every effective classroom teacher has a plan of action to cover the day's agenda. In fact, the best teachers always overprepare so they don't have to sweat when things go wrong.

Passion
Getting up every morning and coming to school is not enough. Great teachers are genuinely excited about teaching and learning, and they pass that enthusiasm over to the students. Effective teachers love what they do and everyone will know it. This is something that you may not have considered before as "curriculum," but can you see how a teacher's passion for education (or the lack of it) can affect all of the teaching and learning that goes on?

Parent Communication
Parent communication is an essential part of the teacher's curriculum! Parents must be kept aware of what is essential for the success of their child. An effective teacher sees parent involvement as part of the whole teaching process. It is not something that is done on the side or just on an "as needed" basis. Rather, it is a part of the mix just as teaching materials and assessments are.

Partnerships
Partnerships are key to the success of an effective classroom teacher. You will not succeed by yourself. Think about it. You work with a classroom full of other people—your success must be contingent on the way you work with

basis for an interesting question. At this point in our discussion, would you say that it is more important for children to absorb and memorize many facts and discrete bits of information, or to be able to develop skills in the manipulation and use of information? Or, just so you don't think that we are trying to corral your thinking, does the question imply a false dichotomy?

Core Curriculum

core curriculum A curriculum that emphasizes a particular body of knowledge within the subject areas that all students should learn.

We alluded to the notion of a **core curriculum** in the previous section. Like subject-centered curriculum, core curriculum emphasizes the acquisition of a particular body of knowledge. We include it on the cognitive side of our discussion because its proponents argue that *all* students should know this body of knowledge. However, as Ornstein and Levine (1997) have pointed out, the term has been used in various ways. One version emphasizes an interdisciplinary approach that shows how diverse subjects relate. The other approach focuses on all students experiencing a common body of required subjects. Additionally, over the years there has been some discussion of how the body of knowledge is to be presented to students. It could be possible for a core curriculum to be student-centered rather than subject-centered. However, in a student-centered approach the students themselves have considerable input into what they will learn because it will be based on their individual interests. Despite these variations, the emphasis is on the acquisition of information. For that reason, we find it more appropriate to think of a core curriculum as being centered around the information that all students are to acquire.

others. In the teacher's curriculum it is understood that it will take many people to help build an effective classroom. We must include all stakeholders, community, coworkers, business partners, and parents in the education of children.

Purpose
Purpose is vital to the effective teacher. If you are going to teach other people's children, you must be able to focus on why you're there. Nothing should interfere with your heart-driven purpose. Be true to your own principles and keep your heart close to the masterpiece of effective instruction. There are plenty of jobs that can be done based purely on some acquired skill. But teaching requires skill, knowledge, and commitment—that is, the feeling within yourself that you are not only teaching, but you are also there for a higher purpose.

Priorities
Be mindful of why you wanted to teach and what is most important. There are many things that teachers do and that they must attend to. The simple fact is that not everything can be done at once, nor can it all be done in a single day. Acquire the ability to sort and prioritize the many things you are expected to accomplish in a day.

Putting Children First
Always put the children first. There will be times when your principal is pressuring you for a report or for grades or whatever. An effective teacher communicates to the students not only that he or she needs to complete something else first, but specifically that he or she will return to that student's needs immediately. If you (the teacher) don't care about the students first, then you should question whether this is the best career choice for you. It's that simple.

I've clustered all of these characteristics under the heading of "curriculum" because they are separate components that must be specifically brought together. In and of themselves they present a message, a lesson to be learned, to students without even getting to a discussion of content and subject matter. I encourage you to spend some time considering this variation on the topic of curriculum. There probably won't be a test about this in your class, so it's something that you should just take the time to think about on your own. I hope that you can see these elements as part of the curriculum that *you* will bring to your students.

Dr. Clint Wright is a former high school English and social studies teacher. He now serves as Superintendent of the Lake Wales Charter School District in Polk County, Florida. ∎

The most recent movement behind this idea has come from the somewhat controversial work of E. D. Hirsch Jr. (1988, 1996) and his associates. Hirsch includes more contributions of women and various ethnic groups in his compilation of what all students should know than has been typical in educational materials. Though they definitely suggest that there are specific things that all children should know, Hirsch and his colleagues argue that it is the knowing of these things that allows effective communication within the culture. Perhaps you can understand why the notion of core curriculum sometimes crosses over into the affective domain; the learning is very much knowledge oriented, but the outcome is a matter of cultural value and understanding. Nonetheless, a third grader sitting down to a day of educational delight in a core curriculum environment had better be ready to take plenty of notes and to read them over and over before the next test.

Mastery Learning

mastery learning A series of educational practices based on the belief that given appropriate instruction and sufficient study time, almost all students can meet the specified learning standards.

The **mastery learning** approach to curriculum began with the work of John Carroll (1963). This approach, developed further by James Block (1971) and Benjamin Bloom (1976), addresses the criticisms about the subject-centered curriculum. We keep mastery learning here in the cognitive camp, because as you will see, it does not undermine the philosophy of there being specific information that children must learn. The emphasis is on enabling all children to learn that specified information despite differences in learning abilities—particularly in their individual *rates* of learning.

Underlying the mastery learning perspective is an awareness that not all children learn at the same rate. Yet a typical problem with a subject-centered curriculum is its rigidity and linearity. The curriculum essentially assumes that all children will progress along the educational continuum together. You should have no trouble thinking of a time when you understood what the teacher was presenting long before anyone else in the class did. Or perhaps there was a time when you could not seem to grasp a particular concept at all. From the mastery learning perspective, the problem was that some students needed more time than others to learn a given lesson.

Bloom has pointed out that the problem is that all students are essentially provided with the same amount of instruction, the same quality of instruction (despite individual differences), and the same amount of time available for the instruction. Some students, obviously, will do just fine with this. Others, however, need an adjustment in one or more of the three factors. In essence, what we might consider as "failure" on the part of the student is actually a failure of the curriculum. Adjusting the instruction in terms of quantity, quality, or both as well as adjusting the amount of time a student has to work with a given topic will allow for eventual mastery. So the *content* of the curriculum is not a problem, just some elements of the presentation.

Though the mastery learning theme makes obvious sense, implementing a system of mastery learning is not an easy task. Remember, the subject-centered approach tends to keep all students on the same page and moves them along at the same rate, and this works well with the traditional perspective of placing students in grade levels based on age. The grades children earn tend to reflect their capacity to learn in the specified time rather than their capacity to learn. Mastery learning opens up the possibility, theoretically, that in a class of 25 students the teacher could have students on 25 different pages. Interestingly enough, mastery learning may well represent an instructional technique that was simply ahead of its time in terms of instructional delivery systems. As you read the list below (from Hyman &

Cohen, 1979), note the degree to which the recommendations for implementing a mastery learning approach seem to foreshadow the instructional applications of computer technology.

1. Define instructional objectives so that teacher and student know where they are and what must be accomplished.
2. Provide immediate feedback to learners.
3. Set the level of instruction so that learners are maximally successful.
4. Divide the instruction into small, self-contained modules.
5. Provide positive feedback to reinforce appropriate responses.

(Hyman & Cohen, 1979)

The ideas behind mastery learning seem basic enough, yet perhaps the real lesson that we learn (in terms of looking at formal education) is that the traditional approach of one teacher working with a classroom of students still represents the mind-set of what school is all about. Even something as malleable as curriculum can have characteristics that are exceedingly resistant to change. As one who is just now entering the profession of teaching, you may find it interesting to watch for the effect of computers on classroom instruction over the next decade. Do you think there will be significant change?

Outcome-Based Education

outcome-based education (OBE) The practice of establishing the specific expected outcomes of education.

This approach to curriculum reform is known by several names: **outcome-based education (OBE)**, competency-based education (CBE), and performance-based education (PBE). By any name, this approach seeks to organize the curriculum by identifying what students are supposed to accomplish. With that in mind, you should be able to see how this relates to the mastery learning approach. Proponents of mastery learning and those of OBE would maintain that learning goals must be clearly defined. Generally speaking, this refers to learning specific pieces of knowledge. OBE is intended to allow students to learn at higher levels by clearly setting the standard that must be reached. Evaluation becomes a simple matter because the student either reaches the standard or she does not. Given enough time (the mastery learning perspective), all students could be expected to succeed if they know what standard is expected. Paradoxically, the realistic constraints of time, educational funding, and the desire of parents to see their children succeed can lead to the establishment of standards that represent minimal competency. That is, curriculum designers would have to identify those things that *all* students must know in order to move to the next grade or to graduate from high school, as the case may be. In that situation, students know that they must reach a particular mark in order to proceed, and so there is little incentive to reach a mark any higher. Outcome-based education may, in that regard, lead to achievement at a low level rather than at a higher level. This particular paradox aside, the message of outcome-based education is an important one. Meaningful curricular reform will require that decisions are made as to what the school is supposed to accomplish and what a student who successfully completes the school program should know and be able to do.

Computers in Education

computer-assisted instruction (CAI) The use of computers to deliver pre-programmed instructional tasks.

Computer-assisted instruction (CAI), a term coined by Patrick Suppes (1968), is still searching for its place within the structure of elementary and secondary schooling. The tremendous increase in data storage capability along with sophisticated programming, allowing for *branching programs* rather than the earlier *linear programming,* has made computer-assisted instruction much more practical.

Courtesy of Guilherme Cunha

In the years ahead, computer and other electronic technologies can be expected to become an integral component of educational activities from teaching to student research and creativity.

computer-managed instruction (CMI) The use of software that helps track grades and manage other clerical aspects of the teacher's role.

However, two major obstacles to a meaningful use of computers for facilitating day-to-day instruction are funding to allow for purchasing machines, and stabilizing the technology so that this year's purchase of equipment and software is not obsolete by next year. The first obstacle is the traditional nemesis of publicly funded schools. Some districts will be able to overcome this barrier while others are still trying to get current copies of adopted textbooks. The second obstacle could be an opportunity for an entrepreneurial individual with the stamina to resolve the many issues that come into play.

However, it would be patently unfair to dismiss computer technology from our discussion simply because of those impediments. As with any other instructional perspective, CAI has merit as an idea that can be developed, and its potential is tremendous. We can easily accept the notion that as long as the power is on, the computer is an incredibly patient tutor. As a monitor of student progress, CAI offers the potential of moving a student ahead based upon actual achievement. But CAI can also return the student to a lower level when progress is not being made. When that is the case, it can be done without any sighs of exasperation that a teacher might unconsciously display. The computer can also keep track of patterns of correct and incorrect responses and provide a record of work done. And lest we make all of this sound too electromechanical, computer capabilities at this time can offer high-quality video and audio to accompany lessons. Without question, these capabilities can exceed those of the best textbooks.

Neither is it true that keyboarding skills necessarily limit the use of computers. Scanners, probes, the omnipresent mouse, and touch-screen capabilities increase the input options. CAI can also make use of the wide range of modifications and adaptations that allow students with physical limitations to access the same materials as any other child. As we will discuss in Chapter 14, computers need not be seen as dehumanizing education any more than books have dehumanized it. With appropriate educational opportunities for pre-service teachers and the stabilization of educational technology products, computers in the classroom could become a valuable extension of the *teacher's* educational expertise.

Computer-managed instruction (CMI) is slowly working its way into practice. Programs that can record student grades, calculate averages, and monitor attendance patterns may eventually take some of the paperwork pressure off of teachers. That additional time can then be put into instruction. The concern exists, of course, that electronic data can be lost or altered. No doubt, there was a stone carver at one time who, upon being shown a piece of paper, said, "That's great, but just wait till there's a fire." All of the electronic bugs have not been worked out of the computer applications to education. However, we might well expect that before long attendance will be keyed in to the main office rather than written on slips of paper to be picked up each class period. It is not unreasonable to assume that one day when a new student arrives in your classroom, you will be able to download all of the records from her previous teacher on the other side of the country. You are probably accustomed to the presence of computers in your life. Now, begin considering what computers could do for your professional teaching. Table 5.1 summarizes the approaches we have discussed in the cognitive perspective.

Table 5.1	The Cognitive Perspective of Curriculum (Typically Subject-Centered)	
Subject-Centered Curriculum	Emphasizes the subjects that all students should learn.	
Core Curriculum	Emphasizes a particular body of knowledge within the subject areas that all students should learn.	
Mastery Learning	Sets a standard that must be met and allows time to meet that standard.	
Outcome-Based Education	Establishes the specific expected outcomes of education.	
Computer-Assisted Instruction	Using computers to deliver pre-programmed instructional tasks.	
Computer-Managed Instruction	Using software to track grades and help with other administrative aspects of the teacher's job.	

The Affective Perspective

In 1956 *The Taxonomy of Educational Objectives: Cognitive Domain* emerged as the result of the first White House Conference on Education. Eight years later, in response to what was perceived as an overemphasis on a facts-and-figures, factorylike approach to education, the second White House Conference on Education took place. The result was the *Taxonomy of Educational Objectives: Affective Domain.* The cognitive domain is concerned with levels of thinking (the taxonomy begins with *knowledge* and rises to the most sophisticated level, *evaluation*). The affective domain is concerned with feeling and valuing. The schools, it was believed, should not only present information to students but should also help them see the value of that information and to concern themselves with matters more "human" than the mere acquisition of facts.

The Student-Centered Curriculum

The idea of a student-centered curriculum, though it enjoyed new popularity with the affective movement of the mid-1960s, was by no means a new idea. In the late 1700s the pragmatist philosopher Jean Jacques Rousseau advocated childhood self-expression as the basis for an educational approach to circumvent the corrupting influence of society. Rousseau's perspective, as expressed in his 1762 work *Emile*, may have been a bit extreme when viewed in the context of a system that would serve the more than 50 million students in the schools today. However, the notion that the education of a child can be served by capitalizing on the natural interests of the child bears further consideration. After all, even at this point in your life you are much more likely to learn something that interests you than some subject you study only to fulfill a program requirement.

In contemporary American education, it was John Dewey (1859–1952) who attempted to bring the student-centered concept into a more practical alignment with the subject-matter that the society at large believed children should know. Dewey's work came to prominence in the early part of the twentieth century, then lost its luster for various reasons, only to find new acceptance as the **affective perspective** gained in popularity during the decades of the 1960s and 1970s.

The notion of child-centered education uses subject matter as the context around which student growth and development will be facilitated. That, of course, entails at least two considerations. One is what subjects will be taught to foster that development. The other consideration is a determination of what we, as a society, want to develop in our children. Dewey tried to balance these two considerations by couching education in terms of the child's life and the society's needs. A key observation in understanding Dewey's perspective is his idea that school does not prepare one for life, it *is* life. Thus, if we want children to learn to function in a democratic society we must offer them opportunities to exercise democratic policies

affective perspective The aspect of the curriculum that emphasizes feeling and valuing.

(were you on the student council in high school?). If we can identify pro-social behaviors that we wish to develop in children, we must then put children in situations that provide opportunities to act in desired ways.

Dewey's pragmatist philosophy evolved into the Progressive Education movement. Unfortunately, in the first half of the twentieth century progressivism came to be known as a curriculum based upon juvenile desires, even to the point that children were choosing the courses they would study. Not surprisingly, there arose a discernible lack of academic rigor that continued its decline into the somewhat sleepy post-war national consciousness until Sputnik made its way into Earth orbit in 1957. Along the way even Dewey disagreed with many of the experiments in curriculum that were carried out in the name of progressivism.

The pragmatic thrust had been that children come to school with natural inquisitiveness and curiosity in the context of their own place in the world. Education should seize the opportunity offered when children are naturally eager to learn about the world in which they live. However, Progressivism (note the capital "P") as *an educational reform movement* failed to provide the balance of content and context for which Dewey had argued. Yet it goes without question that progressivism as a personal and institutional philosophy of education has had, and continues to have, considerable influence over pedagogy and curriculum. We may one day see the promise of progressivism fulfilled as its modern-day proponents work to resolve the issues that so divided the initial reform efforts.

Humanistic Education

As the cognitive emphasis of the 1950s and early 1960s waned, curriculum again returned to an emphasis on the *humanistic* aspect of education. **Humanism** seeks to bring an element of value and meaning to education, and to move away from the notion of education as the mere dissemination of information. Building on the work of psychologists Carl Rogers (1983) and Abraham Maslow (1987), curriculum designers again sought to make the factual content of education meaningful in the context of human values such as honesty, cooperation, and individual uniqueness. It is here that we find the impetus toward *values-centered education,* also referred to as **character education.** Efforts in this regard introduce moral and ethical issues into the curriculum along with the traditional subject matter.

A discussion of values, character, or ethics as part of the educational curriculum should bring to mind the four separate curriculum components we presented previously: explicit, implicit, null, and extra-curriculum. The emphasis of the explicit curriculum continues to fall on discrete subject areas such as reading and mathematics. Yet values and character are very much in the province of the implicit curriculum. In a country such as the United States with its blend of diverse social, cultural, and religious perspectives, deciding which values should be taught in the public school becomes problematic.

To a degree, extracurricular activities have been touted as fostering character education. Ideas of teamwork, delayed gratification, planning, and persistence have permeated activities, both athletic and academic. Yet even here we see mixed signals. That is, the affective approach of cooperation may be seen by students as being at cross-purposes to the competition-based economic system upon which our country functions.

Nonetheless, as Maslow (1943) demonstrates through his Hierarchy of Needs (Figure 5.2), people are not inclined to focus on high-level tasks such as academic learning unless lower-level humanistic needs are first satisfied. A child who comes to school hungry is concerned more with getting something to eat than she is with learning vocabulary words. A high school student is first concerned with being accepted by her peers and only secondarily concerned with titration experiments in chemistry.

humanism A philosophy that emphasizes the value and meaning of education rather than the mere dissemination and acquisition of facts.

character education The introduction of moral and ethical issues into the curriculum along with the traditional subject matter.

Figure 5.2

Maslow's Hierarchy of Needs

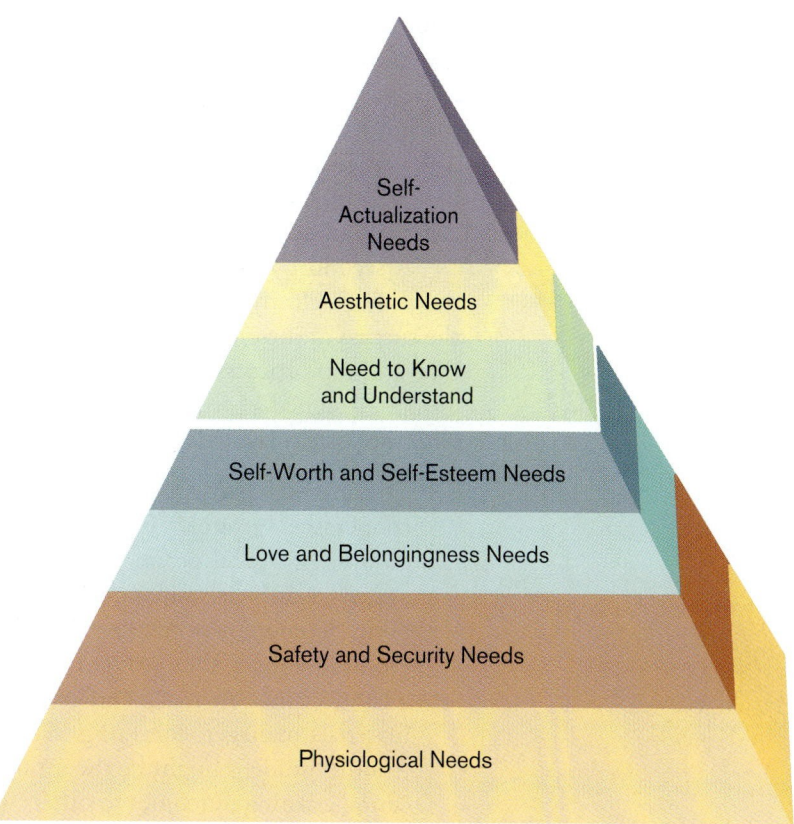

Humanism in education is not an unreasonable expectation. The message is that the school must address both the cognitive and the humanistic (affective) aspects of development if the child is to be successful. This considerably broadens the role of the school. Have your answers to the activities in this chapter been broad enough to account for this wide range of human needs?

Cooperative Learning

cooperative learning A philosophy and set of practices in which heterogeneous groups of students work together on clearly defined and meaningful goals.

A discussion of humanism leads logically to a discussion of the **cooperative learning** perspective because cooperative learning is intended to address the issues that humanists raise. The more traditional competitive structure in virtually all facets of the school experience (academics and extracurricular experiences) tends to divide the school population into high achievers and low achievers. When such factions exist, tension and sometimes hostility between and within the various groups is a typical result. Cooperative learning represents an attempt to address and diminish those problems (Johnson & Johnson, 1986; Slavin, 1988; Slavin, 1989). Therefore, we include the cooperative learning approach under the heading of affective perspectives because it does not change the content being offered to the students and is intended to improve achievement by addressing attitudes.

People often think of cooperative learning as occurring any time students work together in groups. In fact, there is considerably more structure to cooperative learning than might be readily apparent. First, cooperative groups are not just clusters of friends working together. Instead, the teacher assigns the membership of each group so that there exists a *heterogeneous* mix of ability levels within the group. Slavin (1988) defines cooperative learning as "a set of instructional methods in which students work in small, mixed-ability learning groups. The students in each group are responsible not only for learning the material being taught in class, but also for helping their group mates learn" (p. 9). Grouping all of the top-level students together and all of the lower-level students together in a separate group would only promote the distinctions that a typical competitive arrangement establishes. The philosophy of a heterogeneous cooperative group is that the lower-level student is brought up to a higher level by working with a peer on a higher level. The higher-level student is taken to a greater degree of subject matter understanding by having to articulate the information in her own words and in ways understandable to her peers.

A second consideration for successful cooperative learning is that the group must have a clearly defined and meaningful goal. Success is then keyed not only to the success of the group but also to each individual's learning within the group. So that a group's success is not attributed to just one student, each member of the group is assigned a specific task. These tasks can take various forms and can change with the particular exercise. For example, Sunal and Haas (2005) explain it this way:

> The method used in grouping students is important to the success of cooperative groups. Teachers plan heterogeneous, small cooperative groups. A typical group includes four students: one high achiever, two average achievers, and one low achiever. Leadership responsibilities for both the content of the lesson and the success of the group belong to all group members. One student might be the group recorder, writing down what decisions are made and keeping notes. Another student might be the materials manager, collecting the materials needed and organizing them. Another student might be the group spokesperson in charge of communicating learning outcomes to others. One more student might be the group organizer, making sure that everyone has a chance to contribute to the discussion and that each person has a clear task to do. Roles usually alternate over time among members of the group. (p. 139)

It is important to note, however, that even in this arrangement each individual is responsible for understanding the final results of the group's work. Division of labor does not release any individual from accomplishing the academic task assigned to the group. Proponents of cooperative learning (e.g., Slavin, 1995; Johnson & Johnson, 1998; Nieto, 2000) argue that such an approach builds self-esteem, trust, teamwork, and mutual acceptance. In addition, this approach seems particularly valuable for raising the achievement levels of **at-risk students.**

at-risk students Students who are achieving sufficiently below their potential and/or grade level so as to be unable to acquire the competence needed to function in the larger society.

Opponents contend that cooperative learning can give some students the opportunity to receive credit for work not done (that is, group accountability takes precedence over individual accountability) and that it is not the responsibility of students to teach students. In their view, the higher-level student could achieve even more if not held back by the pace of lower-level students. This dilemma poses some intriguing questions in terms of curriculum design. For instance, is it preferable that all students succeed together at a lower level, since living in a society requires cooperation, or that they learn the lessons of competition, which encourage some to achieve at higher levels, since that is the way our social system is organized? What would your opinion be as a curriculum designer?

Broad Fields Curriculum

broad fields curriculum Also known as integrated, or fused curriculum, it attempts to make logical connections among various subject areas and encourage the application of the information to real-life situations.

Proponents of the **broad fields curriculum,** also known as the *integrated curriculum* or the *fused curriculum,* argue that one of the primary problems with the subject-centered approach is that the interconnectedness of subject areas is lost. To a degree this is true. In fact, from a behavioristic perspective we can see it happen on a regular basis. A common example is when a student learns a particular lesson in one subject, for instance in math, but fails to apply that learning to a real-life situation that calls for it. For instance, suppose you needed to cut down a tree. The problem is that it has to fall in the direction of a nearby street and you don't want it to wind up blocking the traffic. How can you tell where the top of the tree will fall? You probably were exposed to a simple technique in geometry that would tell you almost exactly where the treetop would fall no matter how tall the tree. Do you know it? Would you know to apply it in this situation?

The point is that the typical approach of teaching subjects in isolation conditions students to learn the information in isolation; thus they fail to make connections between subjects and situations. The integrated curriculum overcomes this tendency by combining several subjects so that the interrelationships are part of the study itself. Social studies is an example of combining history, sociology, geography, economics, and civics to present the practical meaning behind the isolated facts. Language arts is another example of organization in terms of the broad fields curriculum. Ernest Boyer (1995) recommends that the curriculum be organized around eight "core commonalities": The Life Cycle, The Use of Symbols, Membership in Groups, A Sense of Time and Space, Response to the Aesthetic, Connections to Nature, Producing and Consuming, and Living with Purpose.

It is interesting that the concept of "core" materials shows up both in the cognitive (core content) and the affective (core commonalities) perspectives of curriculum. Proponents of the broad fields curriculum contend that it provides for the easy integration of subject matter, offers a useful context for the presentation of knowledge, facilitates the development of understanding and appreciation, and fosters development of critical thinking more so than the memorization of facts. On the other side of the aisle, the opponents argue that combining courses does not guarantee that useful integration of information will take place. In fact, what one might expect is an overall watering down of the curriculum that leaves the student with a general idea of too broad a picture and very little specific information about anything.

Problem Solving, the Relevant Curriculum, and Inquiry

The consideration of affective perspectives becomes even more sophisticated as we consider curricular formats that focus on *problem solving, relevancy, and inquiry.* Most interesting at this point is that problem solving and inquiry, in particular, are very much cognitive processes. Yet it is their use in making the curriculum relevant to the student's world that places them in our affective category. That is, they serve to give the subject matter meaning in a greater context than the subject matter itself.

Cooperative, collaborative work can foster the development of problem solving skills as students search for solutions.

Courtesy of Bill Lisenby

At first you might think that problem solving has long been part and parcel of what goes on in school. After all, your courses in mathematics, physics, and chemistry focused on equations and numerical manipulations over and over. Those exercises, however, are more representative of "solution finding" than of problem solving as we are discussing it here. In those cases there was one correct answer to the "problem" you were given. There existed a great degree of structure to the problem, and there was a particular formula or equation that you were supposed to apply. Activities such as these represent *well-defined* problems.

By contrast, the activities that characterize a problem-solving curriculum are closer to what are called *ill-defined* problems. In this scenario there are skills that can be applied in working toward a solution as well as a particular genre of information (for instance, problems in science or problems in social studies), but there is not necessarily *one* correct or appropriate answer to the problem. Rather, a logically defensible answer or a creatively appropriate answer is required. The emphasis of such a curriculum is clearly on the *process* of reaching a solution along with the incorporation of knowledge and principles presented in class. Through this process students can be expected to use skills of observing, interpreting, classifying, evaluating, and decision making.

The impetus of a problem-solving perspective can come from one of at least two places. The teacher can assign the problem to be solved and perhaps provide some parameters within which the activity will take place. The activity is then driven by the students' own thinking—a situation that typically generates much more interest on the part of the student. Such an approach facilitates making connections between what is studied in school and how it can be applied in the real world. Students can practice and apply their skills by working with the very problems they hear and read about all the time. Activities that focus on the environment or on intercultural and intracultural issues are among the many topics that a problem-solving approach could use to integrate the various disciplines within the curriculum into a meaningful and relevant educational opportunity.

An *inquiry* approach is another variation of a problem-solving curriculum. In this case students are encouraged to formulate questions and to then discover the answers to their questions by using the problem-solving, critical thinking, and creative thinking skills we have been discussing. Within any discipline, students learn to question things just as practitioners within that field would question their own observations.

For example, when studying science, students often simply read and memorize scientific facts and perform highly structured scientific "experiments." In an inquiry-based approach, students would think like scientists and do the things that scientists do. That is, their lessons would begin with a question that would then be answered by systematically applying the thinking skills that a scientist would use (e.g., observation, prediction, inference, classification, communication, measurement) organized into a particular investigative form (e.g., documenting, generating models, inventing, experimenting, learning by trial and error, reflecting, prediction testing).

Clearly, answering one's own questions has much more meaning than answering questions that someone else has provided. The inquiry approach to a problem-solving curriculum format can bring a tremendous amount of excitement to classroom activities. It takes considerable expertise and preparation for a teacher to provide such situations, but it is a joy for a teacher to watch a classroom full of students engaged in the meaningful educational activities that can be offered.

Activity Curriculum

activity curriculum The designing of educational experiences based on the interests of particular students at a particular time.

The **activity curriculum** is typically seen as being an extreme version of the student-centered curriculum perspective. Sometimes attributed to Dewey, it is more accurately a variation offered by one of his colleagues, William Kilpatrick (1918). The activity curriculum calls for designing education based on the particular interests of particular children at a particular time. Preplanning of a curriculum is not possible. Planning is done only after assessing the interests of the children who will be involved. The plans for children this year may bear little resemblance to those that were carried out with the children a year before or that will be carried out in coming years. Thus, we must expect that the curriculum changes on a continuing basis.

In its favor it can be said that an activity curriculum would indeed hinge on the interests of the students who will be learning, so we might anticipate that enthusiasm will be high. We might also anticipate that the lessons will hold considerable relevance from the perspective of the child. However, several key concerns do arise. First, we must question the source of children's interests given the extent to which they will determine the curriculum. Though not an issue for Kilpatrick or Dewey, the influence of electronic media and entertainment has likely changed the way students would respond to an interests assessment. Are these influences appropriate for determining what should be taught in schools?

Second, changing a curriculum from year to year may be feasible for a private school with a limited enrollment; however, it is an impractical model for a system that serves more than 50 million students. That is not to say that our current system is ideal, but curriculum designers must keep practicality in mind, for there are limits to the resources schools must draw upon.

For the third concern we return to the unanswered questions mentioned earlier. Are there things that the society at large expects all children to know? If so, an activity curriculum as described circumvents those expectations. From a pragmatist perspective, children need not be seen as "passive receptors of knowledge," but still there may well be a more effective balance of the interests of children and the interests of the society that raises those children. Table 5.2 provides you with a summary of the affective perspective we have discussed.

Table 5.2	The Affective Perspective of Curriculum (Typically Student-Centered)
Student-Centered Curriculum	Emphasizes the natural interests and curiosity of the child.
Humanistic Education	Seeks to bring elements of value and meaning to education.
Cooperative Learning	Establishes academically heterogeneous groups of students and downplays competition.
Broad Fields Curriculum	Integrates the subject areas to find the broader meaning.
Problem Solving and Inquiry	Makes the curriculum more relevant to the student by providing real problems to solve and topics to investigate.
Activity Curriculum	Designs a particular curriculum for a particular child at a particular time. Problematic for working with the millions of students enrolled in the public school system.

STOP Conclusion

Had you realized that curriculum could have so many variations? Take some time to reflect on the issues that have been raised. The questions of curriculum that we have discussed in a foundational sense become even more complex as we move to a consideration of curriculum as found in the schools today. Here are some of the chapter highlights to keep in mind:

1. The curriculum includes the "means and materials with which students will interact" as part of an educational program.
2. Curriculum designers begin by attempting to answer questions such as those found in the Tyler Rationale.
3. The explicit curriculum is concerned with the subjects that will be taught, the identified "mission" of the school, and the knowledge and skills that the school expects successful students to acquire.

4. The implicit curriculum refers to the lessons that arise from the culture of the school and the behaviors, attitudes, and expectations that characterize that culture.

5. The decision by individual states or school districts within states *not* to include a topic within its explicit curriculum provides an example of the *null curriculum.*

6. The extra or co-curriculum represents school-sponsored programs that supplement the academic aspect of the school experience.

7. The cognitive perspective of curriculum focuses on the acquisition of knowledge, and curricula are typically divided among several distinct subject-matter areas.

8. The affective perspective is concerned with feeling and valuing and maintains that the schools should not merely present information.

Key Terms

curriculum

trivium

quadrivium

explicit curriculum

implicit curriculum

null curriculum

extra-curriculum

subject-centered curriculum

student-centered curriculum

cognitive perspective

core curriculum

mastery learning

outcome-based education (OBE)

computer-assisted instruction (CAI)

computer-managed instruction (CMI)

affective perspective

humanism

character education

cooperative learning

at-risk students

broad fields education

activity curriculum

 # Educational Engineering

 ## Case Studies in Education

Enter the information from the table below into the Educational Record for the student you are studying.

	Child's Participation in Extracurricular Activities	Child's Preference for Structured versus Independent Work	Child's Preference for Mastery or Inquiry
Davon	Not applicable.	Davon gets especially excited participating in math games. Loves to write, though his fine motor development is below average, which makes this task difficult. Has learned all letters of the alphabet and letter sounds and uses this knowledge in writing.	Davon works diligently in all subject areas and wants to share the work he does.

Andy	Andy does not participate in extracurricular activities.	Andy definitely prefers a curriculum that is inquiry based. His broad background experiences provide an opportunity for him to excel in discussion.	Given his ability to excel in oral discussions, Andy does not have a proclivity to master subjects. He is happy to "get by" with the least amount of effort.
Judith	Judith participates in no extracurricular activities. Programs of a social rather than competitive nature would be of value to her.	Judith would prefer a student-centered curriculum because it involves more active participation. She may benefit more, however, from a subject-centered curriculum with lots of drill and practice.	With regard to schoolwork, Judith just tries to get through. It is simply a task that has to be accomplished and has no value beyond pleasing the teacher.
Tiffany	Since elementary school, Tiffany's parents and teachers have tried to involve her in as many activities as possible. She tries them for a few days or weeks and then decides she does not like the activities. She has gone through more than 15 different sports, dance groups (ballet, jazz, etc.), and school activities (band, orchestra, art enrichment, etc.). She showed remote interest in the reading club but quit because she thought the books were too easy and that no one liked her.	Tiffany thrives on a curriculum that is subject-centered. The more content she can learn, the better. She does not like to be the center of attention or develop her own ideas. She needs direction and a saturation of knowledge. The most common analogy Tiffany's teachers and parents use is that Tiffany is like a sponge. She loves the content and craves the knowledge!	Tiffany is extremely driven to master content. Her teacher has reported that she began sobbing during class when the content was too abstract for her. In fact, she has been given to loud outbursts followed by withdrawal quite frequently during physical science, which is not her strongest area.
Sam	Extracurricular activity participation has been very important to Sam. Though not one of the "stars," he attends all practices and competitions of the cross country and track teams and takes great pride in being a member of the team.	Sam has a definite preference for a subject-centered curriculum. He is not inquisitive but instead is a concrete thinker who does best when he knows exactly what to do. He relies on being taught specific information and skills.	Sam is not always able to master a subject but does well enough to pass his classes—usually with a C or better. Conscientious about his work (and so will question a grade with which he disagrees) but is not inclined to investigate topics.
Bao	Because extracurricular activities are fun, social, and status-giving, Bao is active in Future Business Leaders of America and on the cheer squad.	Bao vastly prefers subject-centered curriculum, and does better on multiple-choice tests than on essays. She is skilled with fact recall, and dislikes inquiry-driven education because there is (often) no right or wrong answer.	Bao is interested in maintaining her 3.1 grade point average. She does not independently seek out the big picture, instead viewing success in school as a clean discipline record, involvement in activities, and good grades. Neither mastering subjects nor investigating topics is relevant to her, because they don't have the extrinsic value that her GPA carries.

1. How does the child's participation in extracurricular activities affect his or her performance in school? What would be the consequence if this child did not have the opportunity to participate in such activities? As this child's classroom teacher, how could you make extracurricular activities relevant to classroom work, or, if the student is not involved in such activities, based on what you know, are there activities that you would recommend?

2. Consider these general statements: A child who favors an emphasis on mastery learning may tend to become frustrated with minor mistakes and thus focus on "correctly completing the assignment" more than on learning from the assignment. A child who favors the inquiry approach may fail to understand the consequences of minor mistakes along the way and thus complete assignments that are not as concise as they should be. How do these statements apply to the child you are studying? As a teacher, how could you influence the situation of your student to overcome these concerns?

3. As you consider what you know about the student you are following, would you favor a subject-centered or a student-centered approach to the curriculum? Explain your answer.

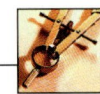# Designing the School of the Future

The answer to the questions of curriculum will provide the foundation for much of what eventually emerges as your plan for a school of the future. By now you should have decided whether you are planning a school for 5 years from now, 20, or 50. Projecting into the future is always difficult, but even if you were designing a curriculum for next year, the basic questions would still remain to be answered.

1. Consider these two questions from the Tyler Rationale (see page 157) and answer each for the school you are designing. Keep in mind that these are two fundamental questions that will require you to consider a wide range of concerns and possibilities. Think carefully, for the people who make these decisions are making decisions for thousands, if not millions, of students.
   a. What educational purposes should the school seek to attain?
   b. What educational experiences can be provided that are likely to attain these purposes?

2. What part will extracurricular activities play in your school? For example, will some activity be required of all students? Will athletics be intramural rather than interscholastic? Will they be specifically tied to the academic mission of the school?

3. How will the null curriculum be represented in your school of the future? For example, are there things that you think should not be taught in school? Are there topics that are widely known but still too controversial for school children on all levels? You might keep in mind that as recently as 1987 (*Edwards v. Aguillard*), the issue of teaching creationism along with evolution was challenged in the U.S. Supreme Court. In this case a Louisiana law requiring the teaching of creationism whenever evolution was taught was struck down. This law was an interesting approach to the null curriculum, for rather than forbidding the teaching of one perspective, it instead required the teaching of another as well. Is there no place for a null curriculum in the school of the future, or must a null curriculum always exist? Explain your thinking.

Praxis Practice

Many states will require that you successfully complete the Praxis Series of examinations to qualify for certification. One or more of those tests will be subject-area tests. Another, which has a more practical orientation, will be the Principles of Learning and Teaching (PLT) examination that is appropriate for your certification area.

Completing the Quick Check Quizzes for Chapter 5 in the Unit Workshop will give you practice with the multiple choice format of the PLT. The Case Studies in Education and Designing a School of the Future activities will help prepare you for exercises that require reading a scenario and providing short answers to questions asking what you might do in such a situation.

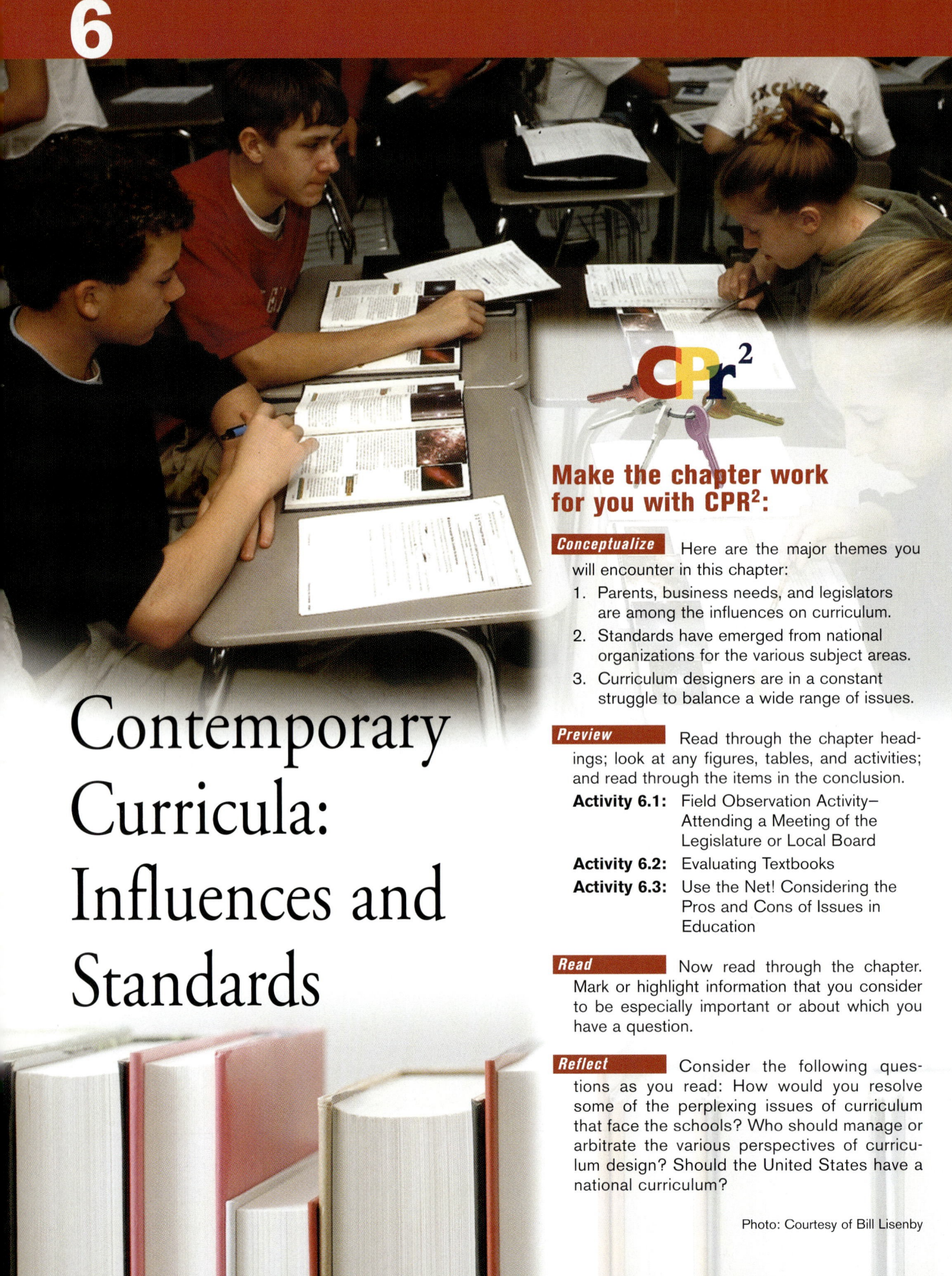

Contemporary Curricula: Influences and Standards

Make the chapter work for you with CPR²:

Conceptualize   Here are the major themes you will encounter in this chapter:

1. Parents, business needs, and legislators are among the influences on curriculum.
2. Standards have emerged from national organizations for the various subject areas.
3. Curriculum designers are in a constant struggle to balance a wide range of issues.

Preview   Read through the chapter headings; look at any figures, tables, and activities; and read through the items in the conclusion.

Activity 6.1:   Field Observation Activity— Attending a Meeting of the Legislature or Local Board

Activity 6.2:   Evaluating Textbooks

Activity 6.3:   Use the Net! Considering the Pros and Cons of Issues in Education

Read   Now read through the chapter. Mark or highlight information that you consider to be especially important or about which you have a question.

Reflect   Consider the following questions as you read: How would you resolve some of the perplexing issues of curriculum that face the schools? Who should manage or arbitrate the various perspectives of curriculum design? Should the United States have a national curriculum?

Photo: Courtesy of Bill Lisenby

ice breakers

A Standards Sampler

In this chapter you will be introduced to academic standards for the various content areas. Here's a sampler of questions taken from state standards across the country. See how you do!

1. When an electric fan is running, most of the incoming electrical energy changes into which kind of energy?
   a. heat energy
   b. light energy
   c. mechanical energy
   d. sound energy

2. Which of the following organisms have the *greatest* effect on an ecosystem because of the changes they make to their environment?
   a. bees building a hive in a hollow tree
   b. wasps building a nest in a leafy bush
   c. beavers building a dam across a stream
   d. fish digging a burrow on a river bottom

3. Jon is 8 years old. His brother, Tom, is 2 years older than Jon, and their brother, Henry, is twice as old as Tom. Which number sentence could be used to find h, Henry's age?
   a. $8 \times 2 = h$
   b. $(8 + 2) \times 2 = h$
   c. $(8 + 2) \div 2 = h$
   d. $8 \times 2 \div 2 = h$

4. 2, 18, 9, 54, 6, 27, 3, and 1 are the 8 factors of which number?
   a. 18
   b. 24
   c. 54
   d. 27

5. Edmund Halley, an *astronomer* in the late 1600s, was very interested in comets. The origin of the word *astronomer* is the Greek root *astro* meaning
   a. comet.
   b. light.
   c. mystery.
   d. star.

6. The word *distracted* is derived from the Latin root *tract,* meaning "to draw." Based on this information, the reader can tell that the literal meaning of *to distract* is
   a. to be unhappy with.
   b. to draw poorly.
   c. to draw away.
   d. to be confused.

7. In today's economy the United States
   a. has achieved a favorable balance of trade.
   b. has about equal amounts of imports and exports.
   c. has more exports than imports.
   d. has more imports than exports.

8. Which two continents would a person 100 miles in space directly above the South Pole not be able to see?
   a. Australia and Europe
   b. Africa and North America
   c. Asia and Africa
   d. Europe and North America

Here are the answers for the questions on the previous page. How did you do?

1. c	3. b	5. d	7. d
2. c	4. c	6. c	8. d

Many tests use several reading passages for the Language Arts questions. You may also have noticed an emphasis on word problems and problem-solving situations. All of the questions in our sampler were taken from fifth grade and seventh grade standardized tests. Has the curriculum changed since you were in these grades? Take a look at the rest of this chapter to see how various forces influence the curriculum that is presented to students.

Sources:
Science (questions 1 and 2): Massachusetts Comprehensive Assessment System (MCAS) 2004, Grade 5, Science and Technology/Engineering
Mathematics (questions 3 and 4): Texas Assessment of Knowledge and Skills (TAKS) 2004, Grade 5, Mathematics
Language Arts (questions 5 and 6): California Standards Test—2003–2004, Standardized Testing and Reporting (STAR) Program, Grade 5, ELA
Social Studies (questions 7 and 8): Illinois Standards Achievement Test (ISAT) 2001, Grade 7, Social Science

> *We need to face the fact that our whole society needs to be held accountable for providing healthy children ready to learn, as our schools are for delivering quality instruction.*
>
> *David Berliner (2002, p. 988)*

■ Introduction

With so many dimensions and variations of curriculum, there must be a lot of people influencing decisions about what will be taught. The institution of education in the United States answers to many masters. Parents, legislators, special interest groups, and various aspects of the school all have a voice in what eventually reaches children in the classroom. Not surprisingly, all of these voices are rarely unified and frequently they are in stark opposition. You need not attend a session of your state legislature during a debate concerning educational issues to witness this (though it would be a valuable experience for all beginning teachers), for debates just as passionate can be experienced at a meeting of your local school board. If at all possible, avail yourself of the opportunity to attend a school board meeting. Although you typically cannot address the board without having first been placed on the agenda, the meeting itself (for a public school) is open to the public.

■ Influences on the Curriculum

As we look at the various influences on the educational curriculum, our discussion will begin with the narrowest view (parents concerned about their child's education) and widen to the broadest perspective (influences of the popular culture). We do not propose that any perspective is superior or inferior to any other, simply that the different perspectives see a different picture of what we know of as school.

Parents and the Schools

Parents can be the most impassioned of influences on the educational curriculum. Particularly on the local level, parents can, and do, have a profound effect on what is taught in the school. Admittedly, their perspective tends to be narrow in that their chief concern is with their own children in school at the given time. Nonetheless, every parent of a school-age child has a vested interest in what happens between the morning bell and the dismissal bell. In terms of numbers, aside from the students, parents represent the largest constituency with a direct interest in the school.

Parents can have an impact on the curriculum of a school by formal or informal means. By "formal" we are referring to participation as school board members or in parent organizations such as Parent Teacher Associations (PTAs). As school board members—which usually are locally elected positions—parents can have direct influence on the district's curriculum. Though curriculum in a local district is largely derived from the guidelines or frameworks handed down by state departments of education, the finer points of what actually occurs in a given school are determined by the board.

School boards, of course, have a limited number of members. Organizations such as the PTA provide the opportunity for greater numbers of parents to speak with a unified voice. Parent-teacher organizations usually serve as support groups for schools by raising funds or contributing time and labor for school projects. However, when volatile issues sweep through a community, school boards need to be attuned to the opinions of a parents' organization.

Parents can also affect curriculum through more informal means. Some parents believe they can speak to the board more frankly from the podium rather than being confined by the "politics" of being an elected board member. There is considerable truth to this position. Short of slander or libel, individuals in the community are free to raise topics and press issues that they deem important without worrying about offending voters. If people agree with them, fine. If people disagree, well, that's also acceptable. An elected official, however, must have more guarded opinions and must express them more carefully.

Though parents can make their opinions known in discussion with other parents, in conversation with their child's teacher, through dialogue with the principal, or with the district superintendent, addressing the board of education is an

local education agency A separate school district responsible for administering the education program for a county, city, or other local education unit.

appeal to the top level of the **local education agency.** This contact often concerns the curriculum categories discussed in the previous chapter: explicit, implicit, null, and extra-curriculum. For example, Sheurer and Parkay (1992) have noted that in a one-year period, one-half of Florida school districts received complaints about the curriculum. These complaints included the undermining of family values, overemphasizing globalism, underemphasizing patriotism, teaching taboo subjects such as Satanism and sex, and the increasing use of profanity and obscenity. The teaching of evolution continues to be debated. The underrepresentation of minorities in history textbooks has long been an issue that parents bring to their local school boards. We increasingly see attempts to ban various books from school libraries—and this runs the gamut from children's fairy tales and Harry Potter to the perennial complaints over *Catcher in the Rye*.

The influence of parents cannot be discounted. But it must also be considered as the double-edged sword that it represents. Though virtually all parents have the best interests of their own children at heart, school is a socializing and enculturating experience that must serve the needs of our pluralistic society. Balancing these two interests will always be an issue. An effective system of education cannot exclude any constituency, but it does require that all constituencies come to agreement on clearly articulated decisions.

Special Interest Groups

There are issues that transcend local boundaries and touch a nerve in communities throughout the country. In these cases, the voices of parents combine into groups that feel their interests have, to one degree or another, been disenfranchised from the process of curriculum development. Most notable in the United States are religious groups that endeavor to have their perspective represented in the curriculum. But groups such as these are by no means the only examples of **special interest groups.** Organizations such as People for the American Way advocate a liberal agenda that specifically seeks to counter what they see as the extremist right influence. In our increasingly diversified country we can also find organizations that represent the interests of various cultures, ethnicities, and non-Christian religions.

special interest groups Groups that adovcate and lobby for a particular direction, focus, or policy. A group may represent the interests of a particular culture, ethnicity, or religious group and may address issues from a liberal or conservative perspective.

Special interest groups are valuable in that they represent the ability of the American people to speak out loudly about their wants and needs, and to inform decision-making bodies about perspectives that might not have been considered adequately. As consciousness-raising enterprises, special interest groups serve a worthwhile function in an ever-changing social environment.

However, the perspective of a special interest group is, almost by definition, a narrow one. There is some *special* interest that the group promotes and has either found lacking or has found its opposite thriving in the curriculum. For instance, Joel Spring (2000) cites the following complaints against the content of books used in the schools as represented in more than 300 censorship cases during 1995–1996:

- Sexual content—44 percent of the complaints
- Offensive language or profanity—24 percent
- Anti-Christian or endorsement of another religion—18 percent
- Objections to historical interpretations, environmentalism, feminism, discussions of government, and other issues—14 percent (p. 237)

Spring goes on to say that 41 percent of the complaints were successful. Special interest groups can have a strong effect on what goes on at school. The schools are ultimately faced with at least two critical questions: Whose special interest do we represent, and is that representation equitable for *all* students?

State Legislatures

Public schools are political entities in that they are funded by taxpayer dollars and governed by the respective states and their designated state agencies. That means that our discussion of influences on the curriculum takes an important change of direction: The emphasis is now on children in general rather than someone's child in particular. This is because legislators must concern themselves with what is best

Parents can have a direct impact on schools and curricula.

© Jeff Greenberg/PhotoEdit

for *all* children. Certainly, most parents and organizations would argue that their perspective is not only good for all children but is indeed the *right* perspective. Of course, if there were unanimity on the particular point there would have been no need for a special interest group. Legislators are supposed to take a more reasoned, comprehensive, and balanced look at educational issues (see Activity 6.1).

The legislative input can be seen in at least three ways. At the most basic level, it is the legislature that allocates the funds for the education budget. For better or worse, having control of the money endows the holder with a considerable amount of input regarding how that money will be spent. Next, as an institution of our social system, much of what occurs in the school is a matter of law, and those laws

Field Observation

ACTIVITY 6.1 Attending a Meeting of the Legislature or School Board

1. If you live in or near your state capital, it would be a valuable experience for you to attend a legislative session and watch your state legislators in action. Contact your local representative and find out how close you can get to observing a debate on educational issues (this would most likely be a budget debate). Alternatively, invite your local representative to visit your class and discuss education legislation.

2. Another valuable experience would be to attend a meeting of the school board of your local education agency. Some meetings are certainly more interesting than others, but becoming aware of how a school board functions is worthwhile for all teachers. Meetings are open to the public (unless the board is meeting in executive session). Contact the local district office to find out when the next meeting will be held and to obtain a copy of the agenda for that meeting. You will not be able to address the board during the meeting unless you have requested to be on the agenda. However, many boards provide time during the meeting for comments from the audience. Perhaps you and your class could formulate a question or two regarding the curriculum issues discussed in this chapter.

3. After attending either of the sessions described above, be sure to chronicle your impressions and opinions of what you have observed. If your professor requires that you keep a reflective journal during the semester, that would be an ideal place to write out your thoughts about the experience.

are passed by the state legislature. Though recommendations concerning testing policies, teacher certification requirements, and aspects of the explicit curriculum are offered from the state's department of education, they nonetheless must pass through legislative scrutiny and ultimately receive the legislature's approval. Finally, the legislature influences the direction that the state's department of education takes—that is, it influences the priorities and, to a considerable degree, the philosophy that will underlie the activities of the agency. As you can imagine, it is important to elect individuals who will best serve the needs of education in our diversified society.

An additional concern that speaks more directly to contemporary curricula is that political administrations serve at the pleasure of the voters. That means that it is likely that the administration in office when a child begins kindergarten will no longer be in office when that child graduates from high school. The contemporary curriculum, therefore, is at best a function of the tone of the administration in office at any given time.

The Schools

The schools influence the contemporary curriculum as well. As is the case with changing political leadership, various aspects of the school enterprise affect what eventually becomes the actual curriculum of the day. A key difference between the school's influence and that of the legislature is that school personnel see children every day. Though legislators can discuss education-related issues with an eye toward the greater good of all children, they do so on their own terms and on their own schedule. School personnel know that funding and curriculum decisions take time, but children are in school now. Therefore, their influence revolves around both the philosophical picture of what schools should accomplish *and* the practical picture of what to do with the students today.

Think back to one of the schools you attended. Was the school organized in the traditional way with a long hallway flanked by individual classrooms? Perhaps you had a large room that served as a cafeteria and as an assembly area. The physical facility influences the type of curriculum that will be offered. For example, a traditional layout is not readily suited to an "open classroom" plan. Similarly, the length of the school day and year as well as that of the class periods will have an effect on the curriculum to be delivered. Even the lighting of the school will affect the curriculum, particularly the implicit curriculum. For instance, a school that has bright and cheery hallways tends to foster a similar attitude among the students. Another school with dark and strictly "functional" hallways may produce quiet and conforming students. Influences such as these are readily observed in your field experience or practicum placements. If at all possible, try to visit different schools during your teacher education program and compare and contrast the various environments you encounter. See whether you can identify a relationship between the physical facility and the tone of the school.

The competencies of the teaching faculty have a strong effect on the curriculum that reaches the students. An obvious example is that of technology. If the faculty of a particular school are comfortable with the use of computer technology, it is likely to appear as a regular component of instruction. On the other hand, if the teachers do not understand computer software that would work with their classes, it will not matter how many computers are provided or how much money the district is willing to spend—the computer equipment will likely sit idle in a corner of the room.

Another example of faculty impact relates to the philosophy that individual teachers and the faculty as a whole bring to instruction. Lecture-oriented and inquiry-oriented curricula, for example, require significantly different instructional expertise. To a degree it could be argued that both of these sample concerns (technological literacy and instructional technique/philosophy) are functions of the administration in that administrators can hire personnel with (or without) particular skills. Nonetheless, once the faculty is substantially in place it takes on an identity of its own, and the characteristics that define that identity will also define the curriculum that the school presents. As a practical matter you might want to keep this in mind when the time comes to interview for a teaching position. Rather than accepting a job at any school that says yes to your application, you might want to ask whether your talents and strengths are a good match with those of the school.

standardized testing The use of norm-referenced tests to determine the performance of individual students, the grade and school achievement levels, and the progress of students from one year to the next (spring to spring or fall to spring administrations).

Standardized testing is yet another major influence on contemporary curricula. You will hear much about testing (both standardized and teacher designed) through the course of your teacher education program. As states become increasingly concerned with what is presently referred to as "accountability in education" and with the federal requirement of testing in reading and math in grades 3–8 (under Public Law 107-110, the No Child Left Behind Act of 2001), the number of tests given to students can be expected to dominate much of curricular thinking. The National Commission on Testing and Public Policy has estimated that more than 125 million tests are given in elementary and secondary schools each year. Keep in mind that the total school-age population in the United States is in the range of 55 million. At this time, 42 states require achievement testing beginning as early as the first grade.

Testing is a complex and controversial issue. Proponents of extensive testing programs can argue with credibility that education will always remain "hit or miss" if data are not collected to show where the successes and failures occur within the curriculum. Further, if high school diplomas, for example, are to have any credibility they must be able to represent academic achievement to a particular level of mastery.

Used properly, standardized tests can provide districts, states, and the nation with worthwhile data for guiding curriculum design and development. Unfortunately, as Edward Fiske argues (1991), standardized tests "measure the wrong things in the wrong way for the wrong reasons" (p. 117). Indeed, it is not uncommon for schools and teachers to place tremendous emphasis on preparation for the standardized tests that their students will complete. As the accountability movement gains momentum, decisions regarding school funding and the hiring of teaching personnel are tied to the results of those tests. Yet many factors can influence a student's performance on these examinations—not the least of which is the stress the students begin to feel because of the pressure the school is explicitly and implicitly applying.

Assessment experts such as Stiggins (2001) argue that in terms of individual achievement of specific curricular goals, the most useful measure is that of teacher-designed tests. Such tests are tailored to the actual students in class and the actual learning experiences that were provided. Standardized tests are useful for obtaining a broader picture of student achievement in a school or district. Depending upon the particular test administered, students can be compared with other students around the state or nation, or areas of relative strength or weakness with regard to specific criteria can be identified.

A final school-related influence on contemporary curricula is that extension of school beyond the 12th grade: college. College and university entrance requirements and their expectations of academic preparation of incoming students influences the curriculum of the K–12 schools. This influence will be a function of the proximity of college opportunities and the expectations of the parents in the community. If the local constituency expects their children to go on to college after high school, the school will be pressured to provide a college preparatory course of study in tune with the academic requirements of the colleges their students are most likely to attend. This alignment of high school and college expectations does much to facilitate the educative process (Conley, 2005). In other geographical areas, under other circumstances, this emphasis on academics and curriculum alignment may not be as important a curricular influence.

Textbooks

With all the time you've spent reading textbooks you probably never stopped to think about how they influence the curriculum. The typical expectation is that someone came up with a curriculum and then someone else wrote a book to go along with it. That, however, is not necessarily so. According to a number of college textbooks on education, the textbook pretty much determines the K–12 curriculum. That might be a bit of an overstatement, but as you will see, it is only a slight exaggeration.

How can it be that textbooks drive the curriculum, you ask? After all, we have no national curriculum, so textbooks can differ from state to state. The textbook business is a very big business, a multibillion-dollar business. That makes sense given that there are millions and millions of children in school and almost every one of them has not one but several textbooks. Clearly it would not be good business for textbook publishers to try publishing 50 different sets of books—each of which will have to compete for adoption or acceptance in any given state. Also, it is easier for states to select from the available textbooks rather than writing all of their own materials. So to a degree it is a two-way street. Activity 6.2 will provide you with an opportunity to take a critical look at some textbooks.

The result is that the states that represent the greatest possible business for the publishers can have tremendous influence over the content of the books. Those states are essentially two: California and Texas. These two states alone represent approximately 20 percent of the textbook market. Publishers, therefore, attempt to satisfy the curricular wishes of these two major markets and then sell those books to the rest of the nation as well. The curriculum in many states is subsequently drawn from those textbooks. We have no official national curriculum, but the curriculum in many states is largely derived from the Texas and California curricula.

ACTIVITY 6.2
Evaluating Textbooks

Either as an exercise in your Introduction to Education class or in another area of study in which you have an interest, conduct an evaluation of textbooks that could be adopted for the class. It is likely that your professor (or the professor for another class you choose to use) has several different textbooks on the topic that could be used for this activity. First, discuss the class syllabus with your professor to find out what requirements he has. Then develop a list of evaluation criteria to guide your selection. If this is done as a class activity, it might be worthwhile for the entire class to decide upon the evaluation criteria and for the entire class to review the same texts. Working in smaller teams, you can review the texts, make your decisions, and then see whether the other teams came to the same conclusions. If they didn't, what does that tell you about the textbook adoption process?

e-publishing Electronic publishing that enables each state to custom-tailor text materials to its specific interests.

It will be interesting to see how the textbook publishing industry adapts to our increasingly electronic environment. **E-publishing** may well allow states to pick and choose curriculum topics and have them combined into a custom textbook. This raises a whole host of questions, as you might imagine. For instance, will the states' ability to choose their own instructional materials lessen whatever "national" orientation exists now in education? If curricula vary greatly from state to state, will families lose some of the mobility that Americans enjoy? Would you want to be required to repeat a grade simply because your family moved from one state to another and your new home had substantially different curriculum requirements?

Aside from the economic circumstances that give some states more control over textbook content than others (and one cannot blame large states for exercising such control in the best interests of their children), some see other negative consequences to the textbook development and dissemination process in the United States. Many critics claim that the homogenization of textbooks leads to materials that are "dumbed down" in order to suit as broad an audience as possible. Michael Kirst (1984) sees contemporary texts as "dull, drained of excitement, and diluted in content" (p. 21). As textbooks are written for a national audience, discussion of local issues and community concerns are necessarily excluded. Since in many states the series must be approved by textbook adoption committees, publishers tend to avoid controversial or politically charged issues (though as you know, exclusion of issues can also affect the educational experience vis-à-vis the null curriculum). And because the books must be used by a wide range of students, writing tends to be directed toward an average reading level. Each of these represents what we might call ancillary academic issues. But content issues arise as well.

In an effort to be all things to all people, textbook publishers seek to include as much subject-area content in a book as possible. The result is a tremendous amount of information with little depth or explanation about any of it. Did you ever "read" a chapter in a high school text by just skimming the bold headings, section summaries, and the chapter summary? Some textbooks (you are likely to see this in your college-level texts) often include marginal notes that summarize individual paragraphs. If this is the case, you can expect that the book has attempted to "overstuff" the pages between the front and back cover. As a reference book, this would not be a problem. However, a textbook is supposed to provide *depth* and stimulate *intellectual inquiry.*

adoption states Those states that narrow the list of eligible textbooks to a small number (usually five or fewer) and require school districts to select materials from that list.

In states that are not **adoption states,** groups of teachers on the various grade levels review available textbooks in their specialty areas and make recommendations to textbook committees on the local level, who make the final selections. Private schools might similarly select their textbooks though they also keep an eye toward the books sanctioned by the accrediting agency in that state.

More than 20 states in the country are adoption states (see Figure 6.1). In these states, adoption committees review textbooks and compile a list of textbooks for adoption. Individual school districts then select their books from the list of state-approved books. Whether the books are approved first at the state level or the local level, the work is typically carried out by committees.

Critics of the adoption process argue that review committees typically have insufficient financial support for the task, an insufficient amount of time to complete the work effectively, and insufficient qualifications for making such determinations. Connie Muther (1985) suggests that "adoption states, special interest groups, and readability formulas have all contributed to produce textbooks designed by committee, written by committee, and selected by committee to please all and offend none" (p. 48). If you consider the scope of textbook selection you will readily understand this criticism. Aside from the issues of state influence on content and the writing of textbooks to serve the widest possible audience, the adoption

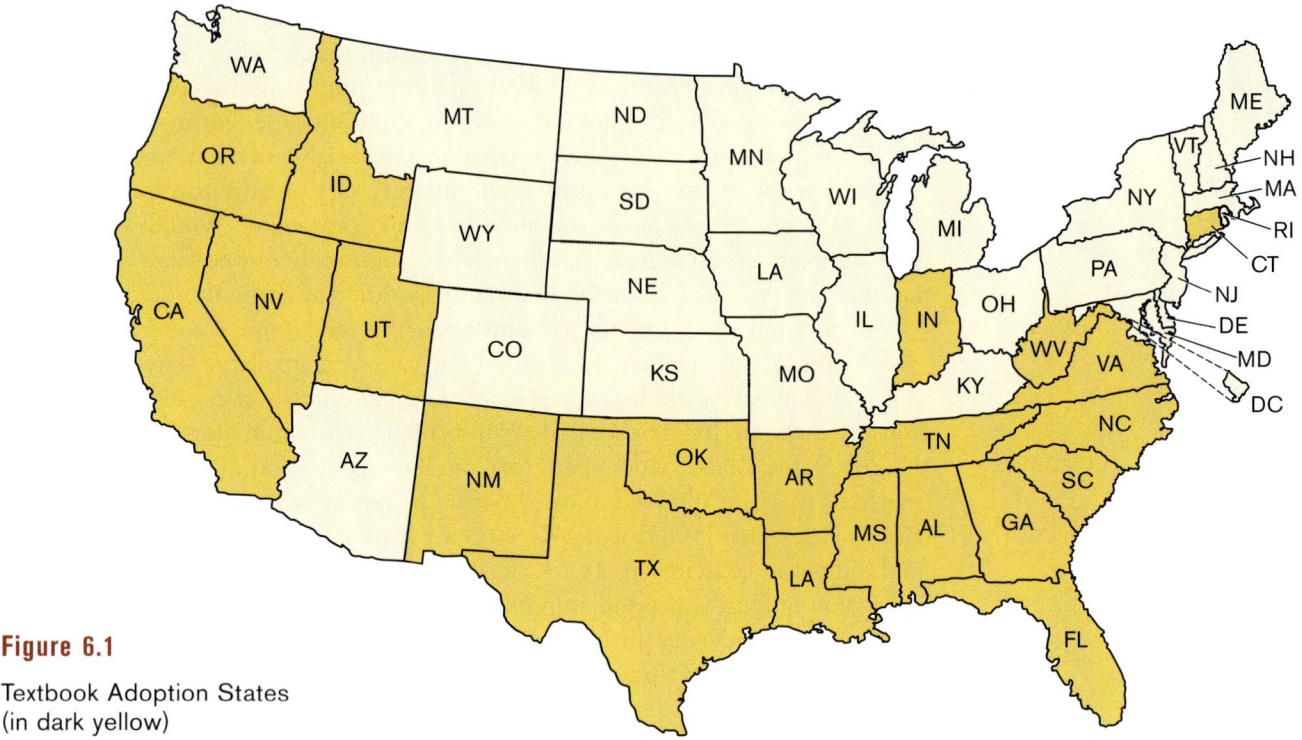

Figure 6.1

Textbook Adoption States
(in dark yellow)

process alone is one that could be expected to involve tremendous amounts of time and considerable expertise beyond simply knowing the subject-area.

For example, suppose you were asked to serve on an adoption committee as the pre-service teacher representative. Let's assume that you have three textbooks to review in the area of social studies. Given the constraints on your time already (remember, your daily responsibilities do not cease) do you think you will read each book cover to cover and thoroughly evaluate each book? Will you then take the time to compare your three evaluations and develop a rubric of some sort that will balance out the relative strengths and weaknesses of each textbook in order to identify the most appropriate text for the school to purchase? How about pedagogy? To what degree will that affect your evaluation? Pictures? Are activities more important than content? How about the binding? Is it durable enough to last through the punishment it will receive from schoolchildren? And what of the content? Will you check the citations and references? Is it up-to-date? Are important issues addressed? How about ancillary materials—are there teacher's guides and test banks? Should there be? So many questions! Table 6.1 provides a summary of the influences on curriculum that we have discussed.

■ Emerging Standards

From the settlements to the colonies to the states, schools have existed in one form or another from the advent of our national history. However, as the responsibility of each individual state, curriculum has lacked a national cohesiveness even though it has developed a significant national "sameness." The tension between forces advocating state control and those advocating a national orientation has resulted in the fragmented though purposeful approach to curriculum design that has been discussed throughout this chapter. Nonetheless, it could be argued that in this arrangement we have the best of both worlds. That is, the sovereignty of the

INTASC Principles by Chapter

Principles	Chapters													
	1	2	3	4	5	6	7	8	9	10	11	12	13	14
Principle #1: The teacher understands the central concepts, tools of inquiry, and structures of the discipline(s) he or she teaches and can create learning experiences that make these aspects of subject matter meaningful for students.	X	X	X	X	X	X			X			X	X	X
Principle #2: The teacher understands how children learn and develop, and can provide learning opportunities that support their intellectual, social, and personal development.	X	X			X	X		X			X	X		
Principle #3: The teacher understands how students differ in their approaches to learning and creates instructional opportunities that are adapted to diverse learners.	X	X	X		X	X	X	X	X	X		X	X	
Principle #4: The teacher understands and uses a variety of instructional strategies to encourage students' development of critical thinking, problem solving, and performance skills.	X	X			X		X							X
Principle #5: The teacher uses an understanding of individual and group motivation and behavior to create a learning environment that encourages positive social interaction, active engagement in learning, and self-motivation.	X	X	X		X	X	X	X	X	X		X		X
Principle #6: The teacher uses knowledge of effective verbal, nonverbal, and media communication techniques to foster active inquiry, collaboration, and supportive interaction in the classroom.	X	X	X									X		X
Principle #7: The teacher plans instruction based upon knowledge of subject matter, students, the community, and curriculum goals.	X	X			X	X				X	X	X	X	X
Principle #8: The teacher understands and uses formal and informal assessment strategies to evaluate and ensure the continuous intellectual, social and physical development of the learner.	X					X								
Principle #9: The teacher is a reflective practitioner who continually evaluates the effects of his/her choices and actions on others (students, parents, and other professionals in the learning community) and who actively seeks out opportunities to grow professionally.	X				X		X		X	X	X		X	X
Principle #10: The teacher fosters relationships with school colleagues, parents, and agencies in the larger community to support students' learning and well-being.	X		X	X					X		X	X	X	X

Table 6.1	Influences on the Contemporary Curriculum

Parents

Parents' chief concern is with their own children in school at the current time.

Parent influence can include participation as school board members or in parent organizations such as Parent Teacher Association (PTA).

Some parents feel that they can speak to the board more frankly from the podium rather than as a board member.

Special Interest Groups

Parents combine into groups that feel their interests have, to some degree, been disenfranchised.

Such groups can provide the American people with the ability to speak out loudly about their wants, needs, and concerns.

Legislators

Legislators must concern themselves with what is best for *all* children.

Control of the budget allows a considerable amount of input regarding how that money will be spent.

The legislature can influence the priorities and philosophy of the state's department of education.

Curriculum is a function of the vision of the administration in office at any given time.

School

School personnel see children on a regular basis.

The physical facility influences the type of curriculum that will be offered; for example, self-contained classrooms as opposed to an "open concept."

Competencies of the teaching faculty influence how the curriculum is presented.

The philosophy that individual teachers and the faculty as a whole bring to instruction is apparent in the presentation of the curriculum.

Standardized testing can affect how the curriculum is presented.

College and university entrance requirements can affect the curriculum that will be offered.

Textbooks

Some experts feel that textbooks determine the K–12 curriculum.

States that represent the greatest business for publishers have tremendous influence over the content of the books.

Insufficient financial support for the task of textbook evaluation, insufficient time to complete the work effectively, and insufficient qualifications for making such determinations affect the content of textbooks and ultimately the curriculum.

states—a key element of our political foundation—remains intact at the same time that there exists a degree of educational consistency from sea to shining sea. Still, some wonder whether this has been the most expedient process for the development of a high-quality system of formal education.

The development of national educational standards has emerged from national organizations including

- National Council of Teachers of Mathematics (NCTM)
- American Association for the Advancement of Science (AAAS)
- The National Science Teachers Association (NSTA)

The lessons and experiences that students have in school increasingly reflect a standards-based curriculum.

Courtesy of Bill Lisenby

- National Council for the Social Studies (NCSS)
- National Center for History in the Schools (NCHS)
- American Council on the Teaching of Foreign Languages (ACTFL)
- National Council of Teachers of English (NCTE)
- National Association for Sport and Physical Education (NASPE).

professional organization A group of educators organized to promote a particular interest. A group may be general in scope (for example, the National Education Association) or subject-specific (for example, the National Science Teachers Association).

In many cases these organizations represent the **professional organizations** for educators in that discipline. In all cases, the standards are voluntary. States may wish to adopt all or some of the standards of any given discipline. They may amend the standards to emphasize or de-emphasize a particular topic or strand. However, the hallmark of these efforts at developing standards is that they represent a non-political approach to identifying the important concepts and knowledge of a particular discipline. This is by no means to say that the standards have not intro-

Teacher Testimonial

Feature 6.1   The Impact of Teachers on Curriculum

Like many issues in education, there is no scarcity of opinions about curriculum. Throughout your teaching career, many groups will want to influence not just what is taught in your classroom, but how you teach it. This will range from the teacher next door to the micromanaging legislator who helps make a state law that a particular lesson must be taught on a particular day in every classroom in the state. The current standards movement, both at the state and federal levels, coupled with high-stakes testing, is the latest mandate influencing classroom curriculum decision making.

While many groups vie for a greater say in curriculum decisions, no group has more influence over what is taught in your classroom than you. Certainly, curriculum standards, textbook adoptions, school board decisions, building administrators, university professors, and myriad other interest groups will have an impact on

your decision making as an educator. However, the day-to-day teaching and learning occurring within the four walls of the classroom comes down to what you decide will be the curriculum objectives and instructional approach. Classroom teachers are the final conduits through which all curriculum decisions must flow. No one knows better than you how students in your class respond to the material put before them, and, in this regard, classroom teaching is much like being in private practice. However, this practice is not so private that there will not be many interested in the outcome of your curriculum decisions—from concerned parents to the district administrator who tracks the Adequate Yearly Progress of subgroups designated by the No Child Left Behind Act.

With attention on accountability at both the state and federal levels, it behooves each teacher to maintain

duced new controversy, but simply to acknowledge that practitioners in the given subject area were responsible for deriving the standards. In a sense, it represents American initiative at its best.

Some believe that the development of these guidelines represents just one more step toward the eventual establishment of nationally imposed standards. That remains as a matter for speculation. Others (e.g., King-Sears, 2001) maintain that standards clarify the curriculum and provide a guide for selecting instructional content. Something you can consider right now is the degree to which the separate development of standards contributes to the subject-centered curriculum. Then again, with clearly articulated standards in hand perhaps it will fall to another generation of educators—*your* generation—to weave those standards into an integrated curriculum that emphasizes the relationship between subjects and the world at large.

The academic disciplines are taught on many levels and by virtue of many course offerings. There are, however, eight major categories of academics that serve as the basis of the contemporary curriculum: math, language arts (including reading, writing, grammar, literature), science (increasingly including technology and the social impact of science), social studies (including history, geography, political science, economics, sociology, psychology, and anthropology), foreign language, the arts, physical education (including physical, mental, and emotional health, sexuality, nutrition, substance abuse, and prevention and control of disease), and vocational education (including career awareness, job training, and school-to-work education). We will introduce each of these subject areas and then provide the conceptual strands recommended by the current standards.

Mathematics

In 1989 the National Council of Teachers of Mathematics (NCTM) released curriculum and assessment standards that enjoyed wide acceptance by teachers around the country. As opposed to more traditional drill and practice, the standards

an active interest in curriculum discussions at all levels. It's easy to become so immersed in daily classroom and school occurrences that you pay little attention to political undercurrents until they emerge as mandates that directly affect your classroom practice. To be too busy or reluctant to become actively involved means you defer some of your authority and responsibility as the frontline practitioner.

Active involvement can mean as little as volunteering to serve on a textbook adoption committee or reading the daily newspaper to regularly attending school board or legislative committee meetings. Professional organizations are excellent channels for the latest developments in curriculum discussions, and the Internet gives you ready access to national education organizations and media reports.

Perhaps you can encourage your colleagues to maintain regular communication with your local school board members or elected officials. Dialogue during calm periods builds the kind of trust and respect that goes a long way during more controversial times.

Having worked in the political arena for many years, I believe teachers forget how powerful a thoughtful letter to a local elected official on a current school issue can be. After all, you see each day what many officials know only in the abstract. As the professional educator, you can provide the insight and real world experience to a proposal that they have only seen on paper. The greatest influence on curriculum is not the signature of the governor or the bang of the legislative gavel; it's the quiet click of your closing classroom door.

Sally Huguley teaches the Gifted/Talented program at Pontiac Elementary School. Prior to becoming a teacher she was a journalist and speech writer for the Honorable Richard Riley, former Secretary of Education, during his years as governor of South Carolina. ■

This photo shows a number of mathematics standards being addressed. Which items from the content standards and the process standards can you identify?

Courtesy of David Ottenstein Photography

emphasized reasoning, problem solving, communication, technology, and the practical applications of mathematical concepts. The newer Standards 2000 emphasizes five mathematical content standards and five mathematical processes for the acquisition and use of mathematical knowledge. The standards recommended by NCTM have been adopted in over 40 states.

The Content Standards	**The Process Standards**
1. Number and Operations	1. Problem Solving
2. Algebra	2. Reasoning and Proof
3. Geometry	3. Communication
4. Measurement	4. Connections
5. Data Analysis and Probability	5. Representation

Science

The science standards developed through a somewhat circuitous route. As you will recall, the science curriculum (and math as well) garnered significant public attention in the late 1950s. The ensuing development efforts concentrated on the development of science curricula rather than on the development of standards for the teaching of science. The National Science Education Standards, released in 1996, were developed by the National Research Council of the National Academy of Sciences. Their work followed the preparatory work done by the American Association for the Advancement of Science. Also involved was the National Science Teachers Association's Scope, Sequence, and Coordination Project. The National Science Education Standards emphasize learning through investigation and inquiry rather than presenting science as an isolated compendium of facts and figures to be memorized.

The Three Content Areas

1. Physical Science
2. Life Science
3. Earth and Space Science

The Five Additional Content Areas

1. Unifying Concepts and Processes in Science
   a. Systems, order, and organization
   b. Evidence, models, and explanation
   c. Change, constancy, and measurement
   d. Evolution and equilibrium
   e. Form and function
2. Science as Inquiry
   a. Abilities necessary to do scientific inquiry
   b. Understanding about scientific inquiry
3. Science and Technology
4. Science in Personal and Social Perspectives
5. History and Nature of Science

Language Arts

Without question, the teaching of reading is the most basic of all the basics presented in school. Yet the teaching of reading is perhaps the most controversial of all subject areas in terms of pedagogy. The range of instructional approaches is varied, and proponents of any particular approach tend to give little credence to other techniques. The two most prevalent camps within reading instruction appear to be phonics and whole-language (though whole-language is in itself a philosophy of instruction). A combination of the two approaches is referred to as a balanced approach to reading instruction and is the concept advocated by the International Reading Association. In 1996 the International Reading Association in collaboration with the National Council of Teachers of English released national standards for English-Language Arts.

The National Standards for English and Language Arts

1. Students read a wide range of print and nonprint texts to build an understanding of texts, of themselves, and of the cultures of the United States and the world; to acquire new information; to respond to the needs and demands of society and the workplace; and for personal fulfillment. Among these texts are fiction and nonfiction, classic and contemporary works.
2. Students read a wide range of literature from many periods in many genres to build an understanding of the many dimensions (e.g., philosophical, ethical, aesthetic) of human experience.
3. Students apply a wide range of strategies to comprehend, interpret, evaluate, and appreciate texts. They draw on their prior experience, their interactions with other readers and writers, their knowledge of word meaning and of other texts, their word identification strategies, and their understanding of textual features (e.g., sound-letter correspondence, sentence structure, context, graphics).
4. Students adjust their use of spoken, written, and visual language (e.g., conventions, style, vocabulary) to communicate effectively with a variety of audiences and for different purposes.
5. Students employ a wide range of strategies as they write and use different writing process elements appropriately to communicate with different audiences for a variety of purposes.

6. Students apply knowledge of language structure, language conventions (e.g., spelling and punctuation), media techniques, figurative language, and genre to create, critique, and discuss print and nonprint texts.

7. Students conduct research on issues and interests by generating ideas and questions and by posing problems. They gather, evaluate, and synthesize data from a variety of sources (e.g., print and nonprint texts, artifacts, people) to communicate their discoveries in ways that suit their purpose and audience.

8. Students use a variety of technological and information resources (e.g., libraries, databases, computer networks, video) to gather and synthesize information and to create and communicate knowledge.

9. Students develop an understanding of and respect for diversity in language use, patterns, and dialects across cultures, ethnic groups, geographic regions, and social roles.

10. Students whose first language is not English make use of their first language to develop competency in the English language arts and to develop understanding of content across the curriculum.

11. Students participate as knowledgeable, reflective, creative, and critical members of a variety of literacy communities.

12. Students use spoken, written, and visual language to accomplish their own purposes (e.g., for learning, enjoyment, persuasion, and the exchange of information).

Social Studies

As is the case with language arts, social studies is not a discipline in itself but rather a collection of disciplines. Different grade levels, particularly in terms of bulk divisions of the K–12 experience (elementary, middle, high school) will emphasize different disciplines within the social studies. For example, the lower elementary grades focus on family and community. Upper elementary and middle school transitions into history, geography, and civics. U.S. history, government, and more narrowly focused courses in world history, sociology, economics, and so forth can be found on the high school level. Current issues in the social studies revolve around the relative inclusion or exclusion of minorities and non-Western cultural perspectives in the curriculum. Given our brief national heritage and burgeoning ethnic diversity one can expect that debates on these issues will begin to yield a less Eurocentric presentation of social studies topics as curriculum materials develop over the next decade. In 1994 the National Council for the Social Studies released these 10 strands for national standards.

Expectations of Excellence: Curriculum Standards for Social Studies

1. Culture and cultural diversity
2. Human beings' views of themselves over time
3. People, places, and environments
4. Individual development and identity
5. Interactions among individuals, groups, and institutions
6. How structures of power, authority, and governance are changed
7. The production, distribution, and consumption of goods and services
8. Relationships among science, technology, and society
9. Global interdependence
10. Citizenship in a democratic society

Foreign Languages

There was a time when Americans expected the world to come to them. In many respects it did. English was the language of business, and without major markets speaking a foreign language along the country's borders, U.S. citizens had no particular need for learning a second or third language.

Prior to World War II, foreign language study in the schools focused on reading and writing. But in the postwar years the new audio-lingual approach to language education came into vogue and the emphasis switched to speaking and listening. Still, the study of foreign language was required but not emphasized. In 1980 only 5 percent of high school students continued their studies of a foreign language beyond two years. Today, of the 40 percent of students who take foreign language courses, most are enrolled in one of only three languages: Spanish, French, and German. In 1996 the American Council on the Teaching of Foreign Languages stated:

> Language and communication are at the heart of the human experience. The United States must educate students who are linguistically and culturally equipped to communicate in a pluralistic American society and abroad.

The council recommended standards of foreign language instruction that addressed the "five C's of foreign language education." They are

Communication: Communicate in languages other than English.

Cultures: Gain knowledge and understanding of other cultures.

Connections: Connect with other disciplines and acquire information.

Comparisons: Develop insight into the nature of language and culture.

Communities: Participate in multilingual communities at home and around the world.

The Arts

The four comprehensive arts are dance, theater, music, and the visual arts. Within the context of these four areas, programs in the arts seek to develop an ability to create art, an understanding of art in its cultural context, and an aesthetic appreciation of the various art forms. Most prevalent of the programs in the arts is music, likely because it serves as a group activity. That is, the band or choir in a school can accommodate a large number of students under the direction of one teacher. Even so, in times of budgetary cutbacks or another round of "back to basics" in the curriculum, programs in the arts are often first to suffer. A clear example was during the movement for curricular reform in science and math during the early 1960s. As the social climate changed in the 1970s programs in the arts began to reemerge. That momentum has continued to the point that in our current magnet-school environment, schools—particularly in larger metropolitan areas—are likely to have a school dedicated to an emphasis on the fine arts.

In 1994, a panel of artists, educators, and business representatives recommended voluntary standards for the arts curriculum. The standards indicated that by the time a student graduates from high school he should have developed a basic level of competency in each of the four following disciplines: dance, music, theater, and visual arts.

Artistic creation is just one aspect of the art education standards.

Courtesy of Becky Stovall

Standards for the Four Comprehensive Arts

1. Students should be able to communicate at a basic level in the four arts disciplines—dance, music, theater, and the visual arts. This includes knowledge and skills in the use of the basic vocabularies, materials, tools, techniques, and intellectual methods of each arts discipline.
2. They should be able to communicate proficiently in at least one art form, including the ability to define and solve artistic problems with insight, reason, and technical proficiency.
3. They should be able to develop and present basic analyses of works of art from structural, historical, and cultural perspectives, and from combinations of those perspectives. This includes the ability to understand and evaluate work in the various arts disciplines.
4. They should have an informed acquaintance with exemplary works of art from a variety of cultures and historical periods, and a basic understanding of historical development in the arts disciplines, across the arts as a whole, and within cultures.
5. They should be able to relate various types of arts knowledge and skills within and across the arts disciplines. This includes mixing and matching competencies and understandings in art-making, history and culture, and analysis in any arts-related project.

Physical Education

Over the years, fairly or not, physical education has been the target of two complaints: It is not particularly physical, and it is not education. Due to the metamorphosis of PE from calisthenics to its emphasis on competitive sports, programs in physical education were destined to attract the students with athletic ability and to discourage students whose skills were not up to the challenge.

During the 1970s and 1980s a change began to occur in physical education programs. Not the least of these was Title IX in 1972, which required that physical education classes be coeducational. Much gender segregation even within coed classes persists today. However, the scope of physical education has expanded to encourage the use of lifelong sports, which are less gender-specific, to maintain physical fitness and more rigorously address issues of health, disease prevention, human growth and development, and combating substance abuse. You will notice in the standards of the National Association for Sport and Physical Education that neither individual nor team competition is mentioned at all when describing the *physically educated student:*

Physical Education Standards

1. Demonstrates competency in many movement forms and proficiency in a few movement forms
2. Applies movement concepts and principles to the learning and development of motor skills
3. Exhibits a physically active lifestyle
4. Achieves and maintains a health-enhancing level of physical fitness
5. Demonstrates responsible personal and social behavior in physical activity settings
6. Demonstrates understanding and respect for differences among people in physical activity settings
7. Understands that physical activity provides opportunities for enjoyment, challenge, self-expression, and social interaction

Vocational/Technology/Computer Education

Like the arts, and to an extent physical education, vocational education is an aspect of the curriculum that is very much affected by prevailing social attitudes. The dialogue over vocational training as part of a public school has been hotly debated for decades and will likely continue in that manner for some time to come. Once again, the critical question is the purpose of school: Is it to prepare students to enter productive citizenship with the ability to learn, or is it to prepare students to take positions in the workforce with skills learned at school?

Though the nation will always need farmers, mechanics, carpenters, and a myriad of other service-industry workers, the shift in the economy from industrial to information processing will affect the offerings of vocational programs throughout the country. Not only will the shift affect job training, but computer training of a general nature may be expected to become so indispensable that it leaves the vocational aspect of education and becomes part of the "academic" track for all students.

Two newer variations of the vocational theme have appeared on the educational scene. One is a concerted effort at what might be called "pre-vocational education" directed at middle school students. Most typical of districts with strong vocational/career education centers, these programs are intended to start middle school students thinking about vocational training in the high school and the coursework that would lead to successful completion of such programs. The other variation is the national movement toward "tech-prep" or "school-to-work" programs. Targeted most specifically for the non-college-bound student, these programs prepare students to transition into the workforce by spending time during their final two years of high school working with local businesses and industries. Alternatively, they prepare students to enter two-year postsecondary training programs.

The scope of vocational education is undeniably broad. Though standards do exist, they are representative of the many specific categories in particular (e.g., manufacturing, mechanical, and agricultural). If you would like more information about standards in this area, you may wish to access the National Center for Research in Vocational Education. The Center itself (housed at the University of California at Berkeley) closed in December 1999. However, a Web site (http://vocserve.berkeley.edu) is maintained with this and other information pertaining to vocational education.

■ Issues in Curriculum

You now know that many issues in education await fresh minds and fresh perspectives to help sort out the best course of action for educating children. In this part of the chapter we present just a handful of those issues with arguments pro and con for each. We encourage you to look over the topics before reading each section and decide what your position is at this time. Then read the sections and see whether your perspective is strengthened or perhaps changed to some degree. Similarly, discuss these issues with your classmates to see whether as a cohort you have relative agreement. Activity 6.3 will help you to organize and broaden your research on this topics.

Testing

In 2001 the federal government mandated achievement testing in reading for grades 3–8 through the No Child Left Behind Act. That requirement adds another layer of tests to the ones students already take, both at the elementary levels and in middle and secondary schools. Proponents and opponents of achievement testing as it currently exists raise serious questions and concerns. A few of the issues are considered next. What additional ones can you raise?

The Pro Point of View

1. State and federal agencies need a yardstick to determine whether education funds are being well spent and whether the changes that the funds are intended to institute significantly affect progress rates. Indeed, academic

Go Online!

ACTIVITY 6.3 Considering the Pros and Cons of Issues in Education

In this chapter we provide arguments in favor of and opposed to several issues in education. These points will not be sufficient to resolve the issues, but they should be enough to start you on the way to forming your opinion on the matters. There are several ways in which you can proceed.

1. Review the points that are raised for one of the issues that you find interesting.
   a. What is your initial perspective on the issue? Are you in favor or opposed?
   b. Now take the opposite view. Use the Internet to find more information about the issue and then write a cogent opinion statement supporting the opposite perspective from yours. Why? So that you will be better able to appreciate that those who oppose your opinion may also have a valid argument.

2. Use these issues as the basis for class debates.
   a. Select an issue that interests you, read the points that we provide, and then decide what your position is on the issue. A classmate of yours should take the opposing view.
   b. Use the Internet to locate the most current arguments that support your position. Prepare an argument that can be presented in class as a debate with the classmate taking the opposing side.
   c. Let the rest of the class act as the school board that must decide which position to adopt. A simple vote from the class is not sufficient. Someone on the "board" must explain why one argument proved more convincing.

progress of students during the past two decades appears to have stagnated, and periodic multigrade testing is essential to determine whether funding leads to more positive student outcomes. This argument represents the *professional accountability* issue.

2. Anecdotal reports, promotion rates, graduation rates, school grades, and the like are insufficient barometers for documenting student progress. Comparative data based on field testing with nationally developed norms are necessary to ensure that student progress is accurately measured. Standardized tests provide high-quality, consistent data to ensure that high levels of growth actually occur. This is the *verification* issue.

3. Schools need information from standardized achievement tests to evaluate their academic programs and to determine what changes are appropriate. Achievement tests can identify patterns at various grade levels in a variety of subject areas. With disaggregate analysis, the tests can reveal strengths and weaknesses among special subpopulations such as students from diverse economic backgrounds, minorities, and students with exceptionalities. Achievement tests can also provide analyses of school and individual student performance according to sub-skills and processes tested in the assessment programs. This argument is the *equal opportunity to learn* issue.

4. Students and teachers who know they will be tested are more likely to focus on the academic skills that are tested, and thus the quality of education is likely to be enhanced. This is also a *professional accountability* issue.

5. Schools and teachers need reliable information to communicate student and school progress to the community in general and specifically to parents and other caregivers. Positive information can engender community support for, among other things, bond issues for buildings and increased salaries for teachers. This is the *public relations* issue.

The Con Point of View

1. Standardized achievement tests tend to drive the curriculum. That is, they encourage schools to teach the content of the test. Thus, the curriculum is determined not by the local or state education community based on what is most appropriate for the students but by the content prescribed by the publishers of the assessment devices. This is the *local control of education* issue.

2. Teaching to the test discourages significant activities that are not "covered" by the test. For instance, having students write articles on events in the colonial era for a class-produced newspaper is likely to be sacrificed for additional study of the Townsend Act, the Molasses Act, and the Battle of Bunker (actually Breeds) Hill. This is the *importance of curriculum activities* issue.

3. Teachers spend large amounts of time preparing students to "bubble in" answers to multiple-choice tests. Indeed, in the two months before an achievement test is to be administered, many teachers "stop teaching" and start assigning practice sheets by the ream. The result is a greatly diminished amount of teaching time, which in turn decreases the likelihood of increased achievement. Any test gains may be the result of the practice in taking tests, not because students have a better education. This is the *use and value of teaching to the test* issue.

4. Since achievement test data are norm-referenced, there must be 50 students above the mean for every 50 students who score below it (Culyer, 1984). Likewise, for every high-achieving school there must be a low-performing school with a similar number of students. In essence, for every "successful"

school, there must of necessity be an "unsuccessful" school. Some schools must always be "losers," regardless of how much progress they make. This is the *guaranteed failure* issue.

5. Achievement tests do not take into consideration demographic factors that are widely recognized as contributing to student outcome differences. Thus, a school with a large clientele from professional families almost certainly will show much more academic growth than will a school with significant numbers of single-parent, low-income, non-English-speaking families. As a result, the data from "deficient" schools do not provide even the semblance of accuracy. Moreover, if both schools make one year of gain, the result still remains: The "professional family" school is successful, and the "blue collar" school is not. This is the *predetermined results* issue.

6. Because achievement tests are timed, they discriminate against children who are slow or methodical or poor readers. Because these tests are typically multiple-choice, they yield inflated scores that differ from child to child, depending on the number of lucky guesses made. This is the *accuracy of information* issue.

A National Curriculum?

The Constitution of the United States does not mention education. According to some scholars, education thus comes under the clause that grants to the states and local agencies powers not expressly delegated to the federal government. An alternate interpretation of the Constitution is that education properly belongs under the article that relates to the power of Congress to "provide for the common welfare" of the people. Herein lies a basis for the differences between those who advocate a national curriculum and those who oppose it. Think about the sample issues identified next. What additional perspectives can you add?

All in Favor Say Aye

1. Research over many decades has clearly demonstrated that the quality of educational opportunities differs from school to school and from geographic region to region. For example, students in the southeastern region of the United States have long averaged lower achievement scores on standardized tests, regardless of which tests were administered. To more closely equalize educational opportunities, the federal government, working in conjunction with the states, should develop a comprehensive outline of the goals, objectives of education, and expectations at each grade level and for each major subject, such as reading, writing, and mathematics. The resulting curriculum would come much closer to providing equal educational opportunities to all children, regardless of student backgrounds, environmental circumstances, and geographic location. This is the *equity* issue.

2. A norm-referenced nationwide assessment test (the National Assessment of Educational Progress, or NAEP) has been used for over three decades to provide valuable information about student achievement. Referred to as the nation's report card, these tests are administered according to a carefully planned schedule such that every major curriculum area is assessed periodically among students at ages 9, 13, and 17 (roughly equal to the end of elementary, middle, and high school). Results of these tests clearly point to the need for a national curriculum. This is the *case for a national curriculum.*

As a result of the No Child Left Behind Act, all states participate in the NAEP sampling. Thus, a national assessment tool that provides longitudinal data (e.g., reading scores for eight-year-olds remained stable from 1992 to 2003, and math scores increased considerably from 1990 to 2003 in both grades 4 and 8) is already in place (The Nation's Report Card: Mathematics Highlights, 2004; The Nation's Report Card: Reading Highlights, 2003). However, 17-year-olds in 2004 scored about the same in reading as the 1971 cohort (NAEP 2004 Trends in Academic Progress, 2004). The NAEP can therefore be used to note trends and identify relative levels of performance. This is the *curriculum assessment* issue.

3. A major component of NAEP is its series of questions to students and teachers about aspects possibly related to academic progress. Thus, questions about the amount of time students spend doing homework, watching television, and reading for fun are also included. When quantitative data are correlated with levels of student academic achievement, they provide guidance to classroom teachers as well as to policymakers. Likewise, information about demographic characteristics of students, school, and community facilitates the development of appropriate policies at the federal level. These are the *demographic and cultural* issues related to policy development.

4. Research informs us that there is a considerable mismatch between the curriculum that is taught and the content that is assessed. Under these circumstances, one cannot determine the effectiveness of the school experience, either at the local or the national level. Unfortunately, local and district staff typically lack the expertise and time to ensure congruence between the curriculum and the assessment measures. Even if they did, changing circumstances would soon require that the congruence issue be revisited. New developments in curriculum and instruction and new (syntheses of) research require periodic changes in curriculum and therefore in the assessment measures. Only the federal government can marshal the resources (funding and expertise in curriculum development and assessment) to provide individual schools with the measurement tools they need to assess the effectiveness of their efforts. This is the *continuous congruence between curriculum and assessment* issue.

5. National data relative to the effectiveness of the school's curriculum can be helpful to policymakers who need to make educational decisions and allocate funds where they are most needed. Likewise, schools require useful data as they engage in program development. This is a *child benefit* issue.

6. The public is best served and is most supportive when it is assured that its schools have a "world class" curriculum that adequately prepares students for life in a society in which change is the most obvious constant. This is the *community support of schools* issue.

All Opposed Say Nay

1. Education is a local issue and a local responsibility. If the founders of our country had intended to provide federal control over education, they would have said so explicitly in the United States Constitution. No national curriculum can meet the needs of a diverse society that is becoming more heterogeneous each year. A national curriculum appropriate for an affluent suburban community would be totally inappropriate for an inner-city area with a large proportion of children for whom English is a

second language. No across-the-board curriculum can encompass the needs of all types of students. This is the *local control based on local needs* issue.

2. Less than 10 percent of the money allocated to schools is provided by the federal government. Those who pay the bills (that is, people at the state and local levels) should exercise jurisdiction over the schools. This is the *financial accountability and responsibility* issue.

3. If there were a national curriculum and hence a national test such as the NAEP, the curriculum would need to be established first and then a test developed to match its objectives and content. Those who advocate a national curriculum based on a national test have the sequence backward. As discussed in (1), no national curriculum fits state and local needs, either current or in the future. Attempting to develop a national curriculum to increase achievement test results is putting the cart before the horse. This is the *"tail wagging the dog"* issue.

4. Tests cannot measure such objectives as character development, social responsibility, and "worthy use of leisure time." A national curriculum would deemphasize such desirable qualities and overemphasize items that lend themselves to multiple-choice tests. (Recent experiences in several states reveal that open-ended questions are not scored adequately—and perhaps cannot be.) Many teachers give short shrift to handwriting, science, and social studies "because they are not tested." Some districts decrease offerings in the fine arts because of budgetary constraints. A national curriculum likely would reduce curriculum to bits and pieces of easily measured but relatively insignificant learning outcomes.

5. A national curriculum likely would be based on recommendations disseminated by the learned societies (e.g., National Council of Teachers of Mathematics, National Science Teachers Association) or by a small number of large states (such as California and Texas). Yet all of these organizations and political entities have changed direction from time to time, sometimes proceeding along paths completely inconsistent with their previous courses. One must question whether it is desirable to subject an entire nation to a set of recommendations that may put all of the children at risk. These are the *trend of the moment* and the *tyranny of the majority* issues.

6. A national curriculum likely would manifest itself in unrealistic standards that would result in increased academic failure and dropouts. Not everyone, for instance, needs to study algebra, even a watered-down version. Current teachers whose students are unable to meet that graduation requirement either find creative ways to circumvent the intent of the course or teach an intellectually honest class that results in large-scale student failures. This is the *unrealistic expectations* issue.

Emergent Literacy Programs

By far the most controversial debate on curriculum issues focuses on various aspects of literacy, especially at the beginning stages. Unlike other topics, which have only one issue that is the primary focus of a pro and con discussion, emergent literacy programs have a multitude of issues. The one considered here is the "great debate" over the role of phonics as opposed to whole language, often recast as phonics versus literature-based instruction. Several definitions may set the stage for the pro and con positions.

Courtesy of Guilherme Cunha

Standards dictate *what* a student should be able to do. *How* they learn to do it can be a matter of great debate, such as the question of whether to use a phonics or a whole language approach to the teaching of reading. Do you have an opinion?

Phonics (also called letter-sound associations or phoneme-grapheme correspondences) is considered by some educators as a body of generalizations or rules about letters and the sounds they represent. Others discuss phonics as a method of teaching, either starting with individual letters and sounds and progressing to whole words (*buh* plus *a* plus *tuh* equals *bat*) or starting with whole words (*bat*) and breaking them down into their individual sounds. The first way is called part-to-whole, or synthetic phonics; the second way is whole-to-part, or analytic phonics.

Whole language has been defined in numerous ways, with the common thread being a philosophy rather than a set of instructional strategies (Altwerger, Edelsky, & Flores, 1987). The philosophy advocates learning to read by reading, just as one learns to talk by talking. Skills are taught as needed and in the context of written text. Like whole language, literature-based instruction uses trade books, usually fiction, rather than basal reading texts. The approach is child-centered rather than textbook- or curriculum-centered.

Consider the following perspectives and decide what additional issues you believe should be raised.

Phonics as a Means of Facilitating Emergent Literacy

1. Although there are exceptions, English is an alphabetic language with letters representing sounds. Thus, mastering the written language requires learning the common letter-sound associations.
2. Research indicates that good readers have mastered the letter-sound associations (Report of the National Reading Panel, 2000), knowledge that enables them to decode most words they are likely to encounter in print. Children who learn to sound out words become good readers.
3. Much practice is necessary for children to acquire the letter-sound associations. These relationships should be taught early and learned thoroughly. Decodable stories that children can read help them appreciate the value of phonics and succeed in early reading.
4. Whole language deemphasizes skills because they are taught only when a child needs them—and different children need them at different times. The most time-efficient method is to teach the letter-sound associations to all children simultaneously so they will be ready to use the phonic elements when they encounter them in new words.
5. The incidental teaching of skills that characterizes whole language and the "skills as needed" approach of literature-based instruction typically result in "accidental" rather than carefully planned teaching. The research indicates that direct instruction of the basics is a highly effective means of facilitating emergent literacy.
6. While it is true that children learn to talk by talking, it is not true that they learn to read just by reading. They must be taught to read. Talking and reading are two different language processes. What is true of one is not necessarily true of the other.

7. Literature-based texts have too many difficult words. Even when children can pronounce the words, they don't necessarily know what the words mean, and that interferes with comprehension. Furthermore, the number of new words in a story is far too large to preteach and, even if they could be pretaught, the words are not reinforced enough for mastery to occur because the next literature-based text has many different difficult new words and insufficient practice for the ones included in the previous text.

8. Providing one literature text for all members of a class ensures that some children will have assignments and expectations that exceed their capabilities. Average and below average children have difficulty keeping up with their peers when reading the difficult high-quality literature.

Whole Language or Literature-Based Instruction as a Means for Facilitating Emergent Literacy

1. Phonics is a boring way of teaching and involves rote memory of a large number of isolated sounds, hardly a way to entice young learners to engage in reading.

2. Exposing children to the best writing encourages them to want to read. Children like good quality literature.

3. Children learn to read by reading, not by doing worksheets or sounding out words. They learn to read by being immersed in reading activities. The more they read, the better they get.

4. Children need full-length texts, not the dull short stories found in basal reading series.

5. Learning the sounds does not make one a good reader. Comprehension is the most important aspect of reading, and children do not acquire understanding by reading selections with phrases such as "Dan can fan a cat. Dan sat on a hat. Dan sat on a cat. Can a cat fan Dan?"

6. Studies show that 10 percent to 30 percent of children do not learn well from a phonics approach (McGuiness, 1997). They lack either phonemic awareness or a strong sensory approach.

7. Since children differ, it should be obvious that not all of them need certain phonics skills. Furthermore, even when they do, why should they learn the skills at a time when they don't need to apply them? How will they remember them without that practice? Whole-class phonics teaching is not developmentally appropriate.

8. Children who learn by a phonics approach often become slow readers who laboriously sound out words, have difficulty blending parts of words, and word call rather than comprehend the text.

School Uniforms

School uniforms? Is that a curriculum issue? It is if you think back to Chapter 5, Understanding Curriculum. In that chapter we discussed a perspective of curriculum known as the implicit or hidden curriculum. The wearing of uniforms is more than just a fashion statement. Like other controversial issues, the debate over whether to require students to wear uniforms is one that excites emotions and poses a number of interesting perspectives. Unlike some of the other issues, it has only a few major contentions, but those viewpoints clearly are contentious. As you consider this issue, try to identify some of the lessons that the wearing of uniforms teaches. For example, do you think uniforms represent a lesson in conformity or community, discipline or singularity of purpose, a reflection of intellectual sameness or a movement away from the distractions that interfere with individual intellectual achievement? Can you think of additional perspectives to add to either point of view?

The Pro Position

1. The term "school uniform" is really a misnomer. In actual practice the term typically refers to a dress code that provides many options about the clothes children wear to school. It is not uncommon for a school to have more than one dozen alternatives of the "school uniform." Thus, even when we use the term "school uniform," what we really are referring to is a dress code, which schools already have in some form. This is the *definition* issue.

2. Requiring school uniforms diminishes the obvious financial differences among the children's families. Without uniforms, wealthy children may wear designer outfits while poorer children may have fewer and lower-quality clothes. These disparities cause numerous problems, with more advantaged children sometimes making fun of their classmates. This is the *economic parity* issue.

3. Requiring school uniforms can decrease distractions that interfere with learning. These distractions include gang colors, low-hanging jeans, raunchy visuals or language, midriff-baring blouses, and short shorts. When students are required to dress neatly and appropriately, clothing-caused distractions are minimized and students can focus on the academics. Students who wear school uniforms are more likely to focus on acceptable academic and social behavior. Usually the school colors or an emblem are included to foster school spirit. Typically there is a concomitant decrease in behavior problems. This is the *discipline and school safety* issue.

4. School uniforms cost less than most clothing because schools and school districts can contract with businesses to provide quality outfits at a reasonable cost. Schools can also maintain a clothing closet consisting of items that students have outgrown. These clothes can be distributed to students from economically less advantaged homes. Likewise, new uniforms can also be purchased by parent-teacher organizations or be contributed by the businesses that sell the uniforms. This is the *cost factor* issue.

5. Uniforms are common in life, among both children and adults. Service men and women wear uniforms. So do doctors and nurses. Teachers follow a dress code. Children wear uniforms in Scouts or the uniform of their soccer team. They also are expected to adhere to dress codes in public and in houses of worship. Childhood is a good time for children to learn that expectations differ from one setting to another. This is the *awareness of differing expectations* issue.

The Con Position

1. Requiring students to wear school uniforms tends to diminish children's individuality. That is, students are denied the opportunity to express themselves in the selection of their clothes and the ways they wear them. Instead, they are expected to dress like a group of identical manikins. The decision to wear school uniforms or not should be a parental and child choice, not a requirement foisted on the family. This is the *freedom of expression* issue.

2. Requiring students to wear school uniforms forces parents to buy clothes that children are unlikely to wear after school or on the weekends. Thus, they are likely to outgrow the uniforms before the clothes wear out. This is a *financial* issue.

3. Wearing school uniforms is developmentally inappropriate. While it is true that adults are sometimes required to wear uniforms, children should be allowed to be children. When they wear uniforms, it should be because they make the choice (as in Scout activities). This is the "children should be allowed to be children" or *developmentally appropriate* issue.

Conclusion

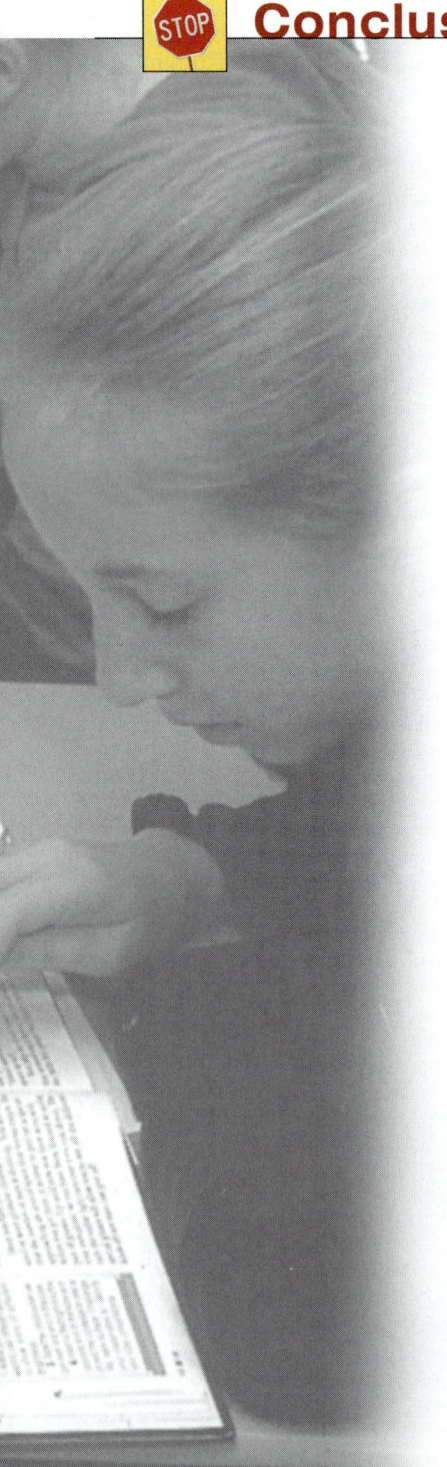

The contemporary curriculum that exists in the 21st century is in many ways similar to the curriculum that ushered in the 20th century. This is not surprising given that the influences on curriculum, particularly in the public schools, are the same today as they were 100 years ago. Only the names have changed. Still, parents, legislators, the structure and administration of the schools, special interest groups, and the use of textbooks printed for a national audience are the key aspects that determine what is taught in school. It is interesting to note that many of the special interest group agendas are little changed, if at all, after decades of curriculum "reform."

This chapter also provided you with a consideration of some prevalent issues in education. Keeping in mind that issues are problems for which there is no absolutely right or absolutely wrong position, these several presentations were intended to help you understand that there can be two sides, two passionate sides, to many of the problems that face formal education. Although there may not be a right or wrong answer, these are issues that need some sort of resolution. Those in education do not have the luxury of "abstaining" from taking a position or of postponing making a decision. No matter what arguments adults may get into, children still show up to school every day. It is the responsibility of those adults—and particularly of professional educators—to find *the most appropriate resolution* to these questions under the prevailing circumstances and with an eye toward the future. Now, here are some of the major points from the chapter:

1. Factors influencing curriculum design can range from the parents of the children attending a particular school to the desires of popular culture.

2. Particularly on the local level, parents can, and do, have a profound effect on what is taught in the school and often bring an impassioned perspective to the discussion.

3. Special interest groups, though by definition narrow in their focus, are valuable in that they enable the American people to speak out loudly about their wants and needs.

4. The legislative input can be seen in at least three ways: the allocation of funds for the education budget, laws passed by the state legislature, and the legislature's influence over the direction that the state's department of education takes.

5. A key difference between the school's influence and that of legislatures is that those who work directly with the school see children on a regular basis.

6. The curriculum in many states is a function of what is written in textbooks even though textbook content is largely derived from the requirements of Texas and California.

7. From its beginnings as a regional concern, curriculum has lacked a national cohesiveness even though it has developed a significant national "sameness."

8. The development of national educational standards has emerged from the work of national professional organizations even as states retain the responsibility for public education within their sovereign boundaries.

Key Terms

local education agency   standardized testing   adoption states
special interest groups   e-publishing   professional organization

Educational Engineering

Case Studies in Education

Enter the information from the table below into the Educational Record for the student you are studying.

	Degree of Parental Involvement	Child's Success with Standardized Tests	How Well the Child Tests
Davon	Davon's mother stays completely out of the picture. She ignores the daily communication folder and refuses to attend parent conferences.	Davon has no problem reaching state standards.	Davon is able to demonstrate his skills. Kindergarten assessment is child friendly and not set up as formal testing situations. He is assessed through collecting authentic work samples and observations noted in anecdotal records.
Andy	Andy's grandparents agree that he has difficulties in school but do not actively involve themselves on a consistent basis. His grandmother met with his teachers during the first nine weeks of this school year. She is aware of his diagnosis of ADHD but is very hesitant concerning medication. She asserted that they do homework together, but often his homework is not completed. Unfortunately, his grandparents do not seem to understand, regardless of notes sent home or phone calls made concerning his poor progress, that Andy is in danger of being retained this year due to the state's testing criteria.	As stated before, Andy is two years below level in reading. He has great difficulty decoding text. He also does not attend to what he reads, probably due to his low fluency ability, and therefore does not comprehend what he reads. He is not meeting state standards for reading. Additionally, Andy has great difficulty with written expression. Poor spelling skills aside, he does not write complete sentences. His written thoughts are fragmented and hard to comprehend. Conversely, he does perform within the average range in math.	Andy has great difficulty with testing. He has trouble attending to the time on task required of standardized testing and often does not complete the required number of questions within the allotted time period.
Judith	Little involvement of the parents. Vast majority of work that Judith brings home is beyond the academic level of her parents. They will sign papers and will respond to requests for conferences (though scheduling is often difficult).	Judith has difficulty with state standards in all subjects. She comes closest in reading but is nowhere near passing. She can read fairly well on a fourth-grade level.	Judith finds testing, particularly standardized testing, very frustrating. It is difficult for her to remain focused throughout a lengthy test.

(Continued on next page)

Tiffany	Tiffany's parents are very involved in her education. They always attend parent conferences and visitation days and keep in contact throughout the year with the teacher. They are available to help as needed and teach Tiffany to value education and respect teachers.	Tiffany does not have difficulty reaching any state standards.	Tiffany thrives on tests and assessments. She comes to school prepared with pencils and erasers. When results are distributed, she learns what they mean, asks questions, and analyzes her work.
Sam	Sam's mother is involved with his education though she usually does not take the initiative to contact the school. She attends all of his IEP (Individual Education Plan) meetings and is an active participant, asking questions and offering helpful insights. She responds immediately and positively to phone calls regarding any educational issues.	Sam has passed Functional Reading, Writing, and Math tests, which had previously been a state requirement for all students expecting to receive a high school diploma. With the implementation of the No Child Left Behind Act, these tests are being replaced with the High School Assessments. Because he will graduate soon, he will not be required to pass the HSA.	Sam has difficulty demonstrating achievement in testing situations. His significant processing deficits and marginal responses to questions impede his success. Testing accommodations/modifications as outlined in his IEP include taking tests in a small group or individually, having tests read orally, and being allowed extra time and the use of a calculator.
Bao	Mr. and Mrs. Nguyen don't feel confident with their English, so they avoid open houses, teacher conferences, and other forums, and are unable to help Bao with her homework. She does have an older brother who is able to help her when she asks.	Bao has met standards in every subject. She knows what is expected of her in school, and works very hard to meet those expectations. Whether or not that translates into deep understanding of subjects and topics is a different matter entirely.	Bao is a strong test-taker and does better on normed tests than she does with her grades. Again, this could be a function of her knowing the expectations and that standardized tests often focus on skills and information rather than on comprehension and understanding.

1. How involved are the parents in the education of this child? Do they help with homework? Attend parent-teacher conferences and open house events? Do they support the work of the school and classroom teacher? From the picture that the information provided to you presents, what challenges and collaborative opportunities do you see for your work with this student?

2. Would you say that your student is able to demonstrate his or her achievement on standardized tests? If the information indicates that a true picture of achievement is not being provided through standardized testing, how would you argue to your local principal or district officials that you are being successful in the teaching of that child?

 # Designing the School of the Future

In the previous chapter you had the opportunity to articulate the general curriculum of the school you are designing in terms of the four types of curriculum. At this point you need to start filling in the blanks with the courses and course work that will meet the demands of that curriculum.

1. Will your school have an arts program? If not, why not? If so, how extensive will it be?

2. Will your school have a vocational program? If not, why not? If so, what trades and skills will be taught?

3. Select any two of the content areas discussed in the section titled "Emerging Standards." Use the Internet to look up the full listing of standards from the sponsoring professional organizations. (Note: Do not look up your state's version of the standards. In that case, decisions have already been made about what to include and what not to include.) Rather than downloading the standards for all grades, select a level such as elementary, middle school, or high school. Within the standards, mark those that you feel the school should address. Cut and paste the standards so that you are left with a document representing the standards for the school you are designing. Provide a brief introduction to the separate content areas that explains the reasoning you used in selecting the particular standards.

4. Will students at your school wear uniforms? Why or why not? If so, design the uniform. How do uniforms relate to any or all of the four curriculum types?

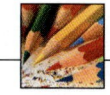

Praxis Practice

Many states will require that you successfully complete the Praxis Series of examinations to qualify for certification. One or more of those tests will be subject-area tests. Another, which has a more practical orientation, will be the Principles of Learning and Teaching (PLT) examination that is appropriate for your certification area.

Completing the Quick Check Quizzes for Chapter 6 in the Unit Workshop will give you practice with the multiple choice format of the PLT. The Case Studies in Education and Designing a School of the Future activities will help prepare you for exercises that require reading a scenario and providing short answers asking questions of what you might do in such a situation.

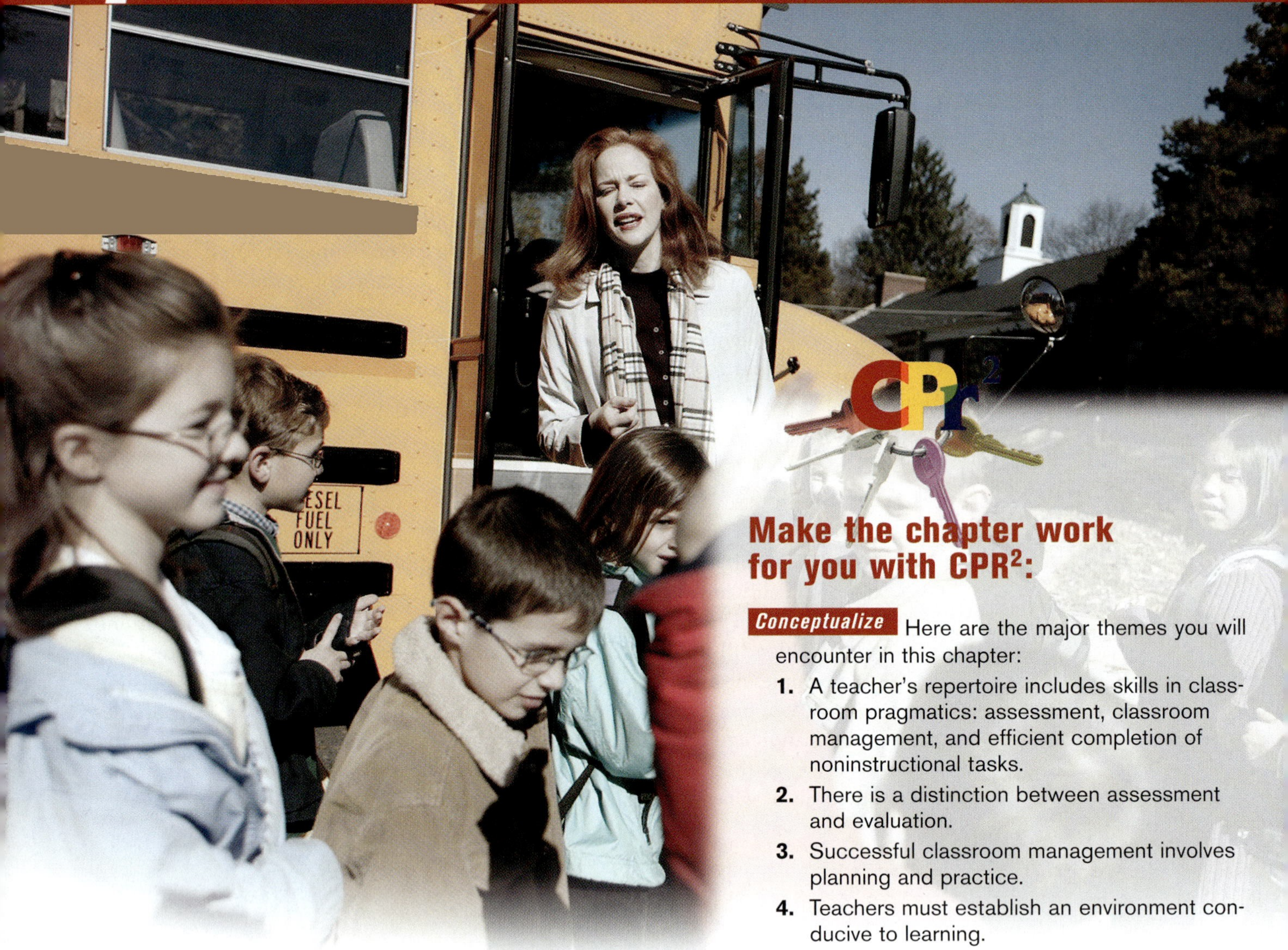

Classroom Pragmatics

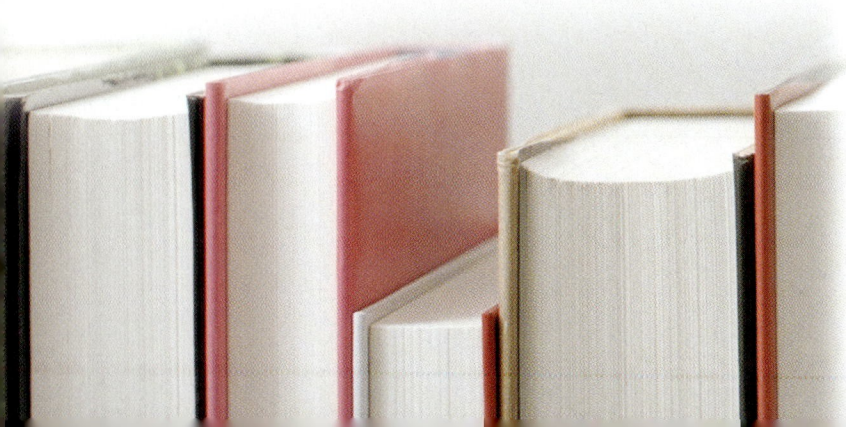

Make the chapter work for you with CPR²:

Conceptualize Here are the major themes you will encounter in this chapter:

1. A teacher's repertoire includes skills in classroom pragmatics: assessment, classroom management, and efficient completion of noninstructional tasks.
2. There is a distinction between assessment and evaluation.
3. Successful classroom management involves planning and practice.
4. Teachers must establish an environment conducive to learning.

Preview Read the chapter headings; look at any figures, tables, and activities; and read through the items in the conclusion.

Activity 7.1	Go Online! An "A" for Effort
Activity 7.2	Gain Scores or Mastery of Objectives?
Activity 7.3	Rules in the Classroom
Activity 7.4	Field Observation Activity—Identifying Classroom Procedures
Activity 7.5	What Teachers Will Say about Working with Parents

Read Now read through the chapter. Mark or highlight information that you consider to be especially important or about which you have a question.

Reflect Consider these questions as you read: Do you see classroom management as a challenge or as a worry? Who is best prepared to assess a student's progress?

Photo: © Comstock Images/Picture Quest

How Should You Be Graded?

How many grades do you suppose you've received through all of your school years? Counting quizzes, reports, tests, and grades for classes and courses, it has to number in the thousands! With all of that experience, this Ice Breaker should be a cinch.

Let's suppose that your professor has decided to let you determine how the grading should be done for this class. *How should you be graded*? What would be the most appropriate assessment methods from your perspective? We've provided a list of possibilities and considerations. Select those that you feel would provide the best picture of your achievement. Circle the number for each item you will use, and make any appropriate decisions within the item.

Assessment Opportunities

1. A. This course will have _____ examinations. Exams will / will not be cumulative.

    B. Exam formats (can be more than one):
    _____ Selected response (e.g., multiple choice, matching, true/false)
    _____ Essay
    _____ Performance (demonstrating a skill)
    _____ Personal communication (one-on-one discussion with the professor)

2. There will be _____ quizzes. Quizzes will / will not be regularly scheduled.

3. Students will write _____ report(s) / paper(s). Topic(s) will be selected by the student / assigned by the professor.

4. Students will receive points for participation in class discussions and assignments.

5. Attendance will count for part of the final grade.

6. There will be a graded project or assignment.

7. Students will be required to keep a journal.

8. Students will receive points (or consideration at the final evaluation) for "effort."

9. Extra-credit assignments will be allowed.

Assigning Grades

10. Final grade will be the average of all grades received during the course.

11. Different assignments/requirements will have different values toward the final grade (e.g., exams might be worth more than quizzes).

12. The grading scale will be based on a percentage of the points available as follows:

A = _____ to 100%
B = _____ to _____
C = _____ to _____
D = _____ to _____
F = Below _____

If you have included item 11 as part of your plan, it will be necessary to decide how much weight (or how many points) will be given to each of the items you selected. After thinking it over, write out your list of requirements and your rating scale (item 12) and see what your professor has to say about it! Be prepared to support the choices you have made.

Course Requirements

Item	Possible Points or Percentage of Final Grade
_____	_____
_____	_____
_____	_____
_____	_____
_____	_____
_____	_____
_____	_____
_____	_____

Grading Scale

A = _____ to 100%
B = _____ to _____
C = _____ to _____
D = _____ to _____
F = Below _____

What you do on the first days of school will determine your success or failure for the rest of the school year. You will either win or lose your class on the first days of school.

Harry K. Wong (1991)

■ Introduction

classroom pragmatics Tasks that a teacher routinely accomplishes apart from "instructional" activities. Examples include classroom management and the assessment of student performance.

Classroom pragmatics is a term we use for tasks that a teacher routinely accomplishes apart from "instructional" activities. As the name is intended to imply, these are practical concerns that are just as much a part of a teacher's day as is the teaching. *Assessment of student progress,* the first topic of this chapter, is something that a teacher does on a regular basis. In addition to providing an opportunity for students to demonstrate their progress and receive a grade for their work, assessment is the practical tool that a teacher uses to make instructional decisions. *Classroom management,* our second major topic in this chapter, is another area of expertise that a teacher must develop. It is not necessarily an instructional activity, but it does dramatically affect the educational environment within the classroom.

We have assembled these topics as a stand-alone chapter because we believe you need to know right up front that teaching is just one aspect of a teacher's professional responsibilities. You should not assume that the tasks described in this chapter "take care of themselves" or that they can be "worked in." It would be unfair to lead you to believe that such is the case. Assessment, management, and the other noninstructional tasks that we will present are each viable subject areas in their own right. We are sure that over the years you have noticed considerable differences among teachers with regard to each of these tasks. It is likely that some of your teachers wrote horrible tests, and you never felt as if your understanding of a topic had really been tapped. Without a doubt you have seen wide differences between teachers' styles when it came to managing a classroom. It is just as feasible that you have known teachers who were organized and ready for any contingency, and others who were working from bell to bell. This chapter should give you a broader understanding of what teachers do and a foundation for developing your own expertise. We will begin with the topic of assessment because it is something you should be planning for before your students ever enter the classroom.

■ Assessment

assessment The means by which a teacher gathers information to make a variety of decisions. It may include paper-and-pencil activities, demonstrations, reports, teacher observation, projects, and so on.

So much time is put into the planning and preparation of a lesson, followed by the actual presentation, that **assessment** is often thought of as something that just "happens" at the end. It is much more than that. Assessment is the means by which information is gathered to make a variety of decisions ranging from what and how to teach a topic to determining what your students have learned. Since it comes at the beginning *and* end of instruction, it is a major component of any effective educational strategy. In this section we will consider assessment from four perspectives: the aims of assessment, standardized and classroom assessment, assessment as part of instruction, and the assigning of grades.

The Aims of Assessment

Assessment devices on any level can serve either or both of two purposes. One purpose is to give an *individual* some indication of actual *achievement.* The other purpose is to identify trends among *groups.* In the context of administrative decision-making, assessments are used in several areas:

- Policymaking
- Selecting appropriate schoolwide curriculum materials
- Funding decisions
- Measuring school accountability

These decisions are most often based on the results of the standardized tests that are administered each spring. Clearly, the focus in this instance is on group trends. The information compiled from standardized tests tells districts how their students are doing compared with students in similar situations around the state or nation. From this information, districts can make decisions about the delivery of their educational program.

Standardized and Classroom Assessment

Standardized testing refers to a system of assessment that is administered to a wide population of students. A test could be used districtwide, statewide, nationally, or even internationally. Elementary and secondary schools may use a standardized test to measure student achievement in various subject areas. College-entrance exams might reflect verbal and mathematical abilities.

Standardized tests are typically administered to all test-takers under the same conditions and restrictions. The results of the test are reported in terms of the scores for a group of test-takers who were identified as being representative of the population that would be using the test. The scores for that group, the **norm group,** were used to set the *standard* for the test.

Standardized testing from first grade through high school has embraced a statistical model, the **normal curve** (sometimes called the bell curve), that anticipates a particular distribution of test scores (see Figure 7.1). According to the model, we can expect a distribution of students' scores to have a certain percentage of grades in the high range, a similar percentage in the low range, and the majority of scores (approximately two-thirds) to be distributed just above and below the average.

Across the broad spectrum, the concept of the normal curve seems to make sense. If the performances of enough people are measured on any characteristic, scores do seem to distribute themselves normally. If you watch the distribution of scores from your own teaching over the years, you will likely see a normal distribution. Keep in mind that even if the grades are consistently high, those high grades will distribute themselves into the few that are really high, those that are low high (so to speak), and a majority of grades in the mid-high range. This distribu-

standardized testing The use of norm-referenced tests to determine the performance of individual students, the grade and school achievement levels, and the progress of students from one year to the next (spring to spring or fall to spring administrations).

norm group A group of test-takers specifically identified as being representative of the population for whom the assessment was designed. Results from the norm group are used to set the standard for the test.

normal curve A statistical model in which 34 percent of the scores fall at or just below the middle score, and another 34 percent fall at or just above the middle. Another 13 percent of the scores fall farther above the middle while 13 percent more fall farther below the middle. About 3 percent of the scores fall at one extreme and another 3 percent at the other.

Figure 7.1

The Normal Curve

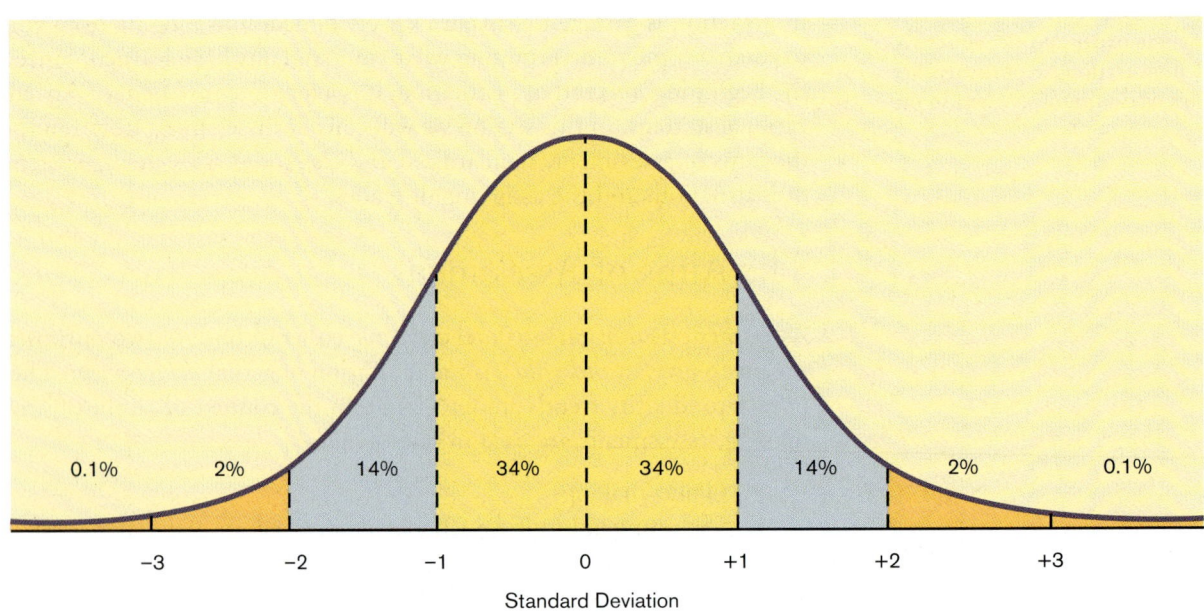

tion occurs if your assessment instruments are well designed. If not, you may have scores of 100 on a 100-point scale year in and year out. But in this case it is more likely that the assessment instrument was not as fine an indicator of the differences among students as it could have been. The concept of the normal curve is intriguing both in theory and in practice.

Classroom Assessment

classroom assessment Assessments that are typically designed by the classroom teacher to assess a very specific population with regard to material specifically presented in that class.

Of greater importance to you as a teacher is **classroom assessment** of the students with whom you will work. We refer now to the tests you will use as you assess the students on what has been specifically presented in your class. Even here it can be anticipated that the principal in your building will expect your grading to reflect the normal curve. You probably don't like this idea of being *expected* to assign low grades to some of your students. However, you can overcome such expectations and bring a greater number of your students to a level of excellence as long as your assessment program effectively documents that your students have achieved at a higher level. To accomplish this, you will have to understand the difference between *assessment* and *evaluation* and how each comes into play as part of an educational strategy.

Assessment versus Evaluation

"Assessment" is a term that tends to be used interchangeably with another similar term and consequently loses some of its meaning. In order to avoid such a situation, we want to make a clear distinction between *assessment* and *evaluation*. We cannot ensure that you won't see them used interchangeably elsewhere, but our hope is that you will have a broader perspective of this important instructional tool.

When information about the characteristics or qualities of something is gathered, that constitutes an *assessment*. For example, a house may be assessed in terms of size, building materials, location, and number of bathrooms. That's the assessment. Typically, another step is taken by which the assessment information is compared to some *value structure* that assigns a dollar amount to the house for tax or sale purposes. That second step represents **evaluation.** In your work as a teacher, there will be times when you need information for purposes of making instructional decisions and other times when you will need to place an academic value on the information gathered.

evaluation The process of placing a value (a grade) on a piece of student work.

For instance, your professor might assess a paper you've written by writing comments in the margin. She might even include a summary statement on the last page that indicates strengths and weaknesses. To that point, what you have is an assessment. You could use that information to rewrite the paper in a different way. If, on the other hand, your professor adds a *grade* to your paper, then she has placed a value on the assessment information and represented it as a score that has some meaning in terms of your academic achievement (at least in her opinion). So as you can see, *evaluations always include assessments, but assessments are not necessarily evaluations.*

Formative and Summative Assessments: Tools for Teachers

formative assessment An assessment in which information is gathered for instructional purposes. Usually the assessment is based on a relatively small body of information.

Rather than switching back and forth between *assessment* and *evaluation,* we can simplify our discussion by considering assessment in two categories. A **formative assessment** is an assessment in which information is gathered for *instructional purposes.* For instance, if your professor asks questions while teaching a class, she is likely conducting a formative assessment that will tell her whether or not the students are grasping the subject matter. If it seems they are not, she might rephrase something, recommend additional reading (or that students read what they were

Teachers use formative assessments before and during lessons, and summative assessments when a lesson is completed.

Courtesy of Guilherme Cunha

summative assessment An assessment given to assign a grade. Usually it is based on a relatively large amount of information and addresses content that will not be retaught.

supposed to have read already), or perhaps take an entirely different instructional approach. In any event, what has occurred is an assessment of student understanding *for the purposes of modifying instruction.* No grades are assigned, no bad marks are written in the grade book, no one is given a note to take home to a parent.

Summative assessment, which we might typically think of as evaluation, is intended specifically for the purpose of assigning a grade. The instructor does not plan to reteach the topic based upon the assessment results but instead considers the instruction for the particular topic to be complete; students are assessed for their mastery of the material, and the class will move on to the next topic. Both forms of assessment are indispensable aspects of effective instruction, but clearly the aims are different. The former is used to modify or plan instruction, the latter for recognizing the level of academic achievement a student has reached. Both are a vital part of mastery teaching and learning (Bloom, Hastings, & Madaus, 1971). Table 7.1 summarizes the distinctions between formative and summative assessment.

Assessment as Part of Instruction

The decisions regarding the selection and administration of standardized tests are usually made at district and state levels and thus are out of the hands of the classroom teacher. *Classroom assessments* are a different matter. Many writers, such as Stiggins (2001), suggest that it is classroom assessment that paints the true picture

Table 7.1 Formative and Summative Assessment	
Formative Assessment	**Summative Assessment**
Teacher might ask questions, use observations, or give a written test	Teacher might ask questions or use a written test
Responses tell the teacher whether students are ready to move on or if students need more instruction	Responses used to assign a grade; there will be no reteaching

of a student's academic achievement. After all, the assessments that are provided in the classroom are designed for those students in particular and are based on what has actually been done in class. This assumes that the assessment instruments used are of a high quality.

Ensuring quality is a responsibility of the classroom teacher. Curricular materials are often provided by the textbook publisher along with test banks, quizzes, and worksheets. The presumption that these materials are of high quality is dangerous on at least two counts. First, the prepackaged assessments draw from the entire text, though teachers may choose not to cover everything in each chapter. Second, the assessments, whether written by the textbook authors or (as is often the case) delegated to others, may not have been prepared using best assessment-design practice. On the other hand, a teacher with a solid background in test design is well equipped to construct and administer assessment instruments—and to evaluate the data they collect—for any topic she has taught.

A key aspect of the assessment component of an effective teacher's strategy will be consistent use of *formative assessments.* Rather than plowing through some unit of study and simply having a test (summative assessment) at the end, a teacher who uses formative assessments throughout instruction can monitor the progress of her students and *adjust instruction accordingly.* This is the purpose of formative assessments. Whether as structured as pencil-and-paper tests or as informal as asking questions during instruction, ongoing assessment can provide the teacher with valuable feedback about group and individual understanding of the lesson being taught.

It is important for you to understand that formative and summative assessment techniques are skills that a teacher must develop. Simply asking a class, "Does everybody understand?" will not suffice. Students who do understand will likely answer affirmatively while students who don't understand may prefer not to make that point known. No one likes to look foolish in front of one's peers; thus formative assessments must be conducted in a manner that protects the student's self-concept.

A teacher might conduct formative assessments by asking open-ended questions and watching to see who responds and who does not. She might direct questions at individual students, but ask for opinions or rephrasing. The teacher could also ask a question and, upon receiving no response, rephrase the question as if the difficulty had been in the original phrasing. Paper-and-pencil tests, quizzes, and other exercises that are *ungraded* protect the anonymity of a student among classmates but provide the teacher with assessment data that can clarify the instructional route she needs to pursue either with the group or with individuals in need of additional assistance.

When constructing *summative assessments,* Stiggins (2001) recommends that teachers keep the perspective that the real users of assessment data are the students themselves. Merely receiving a letter or numerical grade advises a student of the value placed on her work, but it does not do anything to clarify the learning that has—or has not—taken place. That is, what questions were answered correctly? Which were incorrect? Assuming that the information was taught because it bears some importance, what does the student still need to learn? Keeping the focus on students and learning as assessments are designed represents the first step toward high-quality assessments.

As Table 7.2 shows, Stiggins suggests that a high-quality assessment has a clear target, focused purpose, appropriate method, suitable sample size, and no distortion. The first three are concerned with the questions of *what, why,* and *how.* The implication is that if the test designer cannot answer these questions clearly, the assessment instrument is likely of poor quality. Think of it in terms of designing a building. If the architect does not know what the building will be used for, why the client wants it built, and how best to build given the circumstances, she will find it difficult to design an appropriate building.

Table 7.2	Keys to Sound Assessment
Clear Target	
What is the teacher trying to assess? This is a question of the specific content or skill.	
Focused Purpose	
Why is the assessment being conducted? For example, is this assessment formative or summative?	
Appropriate Method	
How should the student be assessed? Should the assessment be multiple choice? Essay? Performance? What is the best way to assess the target?	
Sample Size	
Of all the content taught, or all the skills taught, how much does the student have to demonstrate so that the teacher is confident of the student's achievement?	
Free from Distortion	
How can the teacher be certain that the test items are clear to the test taker?	
(Adapted from Stiggins, 2001)	

The teacher must now address the final two considerations: how best to sample the material that has been taught and how to ensure that the testing materials clearly present the academic challenge. With regard to the first of these two, a teacher typically can't ask about *everything* discussed in class and the accompanying materials, so she must decide how much to include on a test to safely infer a student's level of achievement. With regard to the final concern, the test designer must be sure that the test items do not impede assessment by having errors or obstacles within the questions themselves. For instance, questions written at a reading level that is higher than that of the test taker or in a language that the test taker does not understand fluently will affect performance for reasons other than the student's understanding of the material taught.

Test design is a skill that the teacher must develop. You can begin to develop these skills by paying close attention to the techniques your teachers use. Listen for questions that fall into the category of formative assessment during a lesson. And by all means, look closely at the summative assessment instruments that are presented to you. Ask yourself (and if you dare, your professor) whether you can find evidence of each of the five keys to quality assessment within the instrument.

Assigning Grades

All of this discussion of assessment leads to one of the professional facts of a teacher's life—the assigning of grades. When the grades are good, and everyone can smile, this is not a particularly difficult situation. However, for a wide variety of reasons there will be many times when the grades are not so good, and the teacher will agonize over what to do. Though this would seem to be a very clear-cut issue, education is nonetheless a human and personal experience. When you consider that grades are a communication not just between the teacher and the student but also between the teacher and the parent or caregiver, you can see that grading can involve more than counting up the correct responses on a test.

Meeting Objectives

In their most fundamental form, grades represent the degree to which a student has or has not met identified objectives. To facilitate grading in this manner, pre-service teachers typically receive instruction in the writing of objectives. As in-service teachers, they often write objectives that are keyed to the subject matter contained within the adopted curriculum materials, to district standards for what children are to learn, and perhaps even to statewide educational standards. While this degree of cross-referencing is of little consequence to the child sitting in a classroom, it does speak to the emphasis on clearly articulated educational objectives.

In many classrooms, teachers post the day's goals and objectives so that students know what to expect.

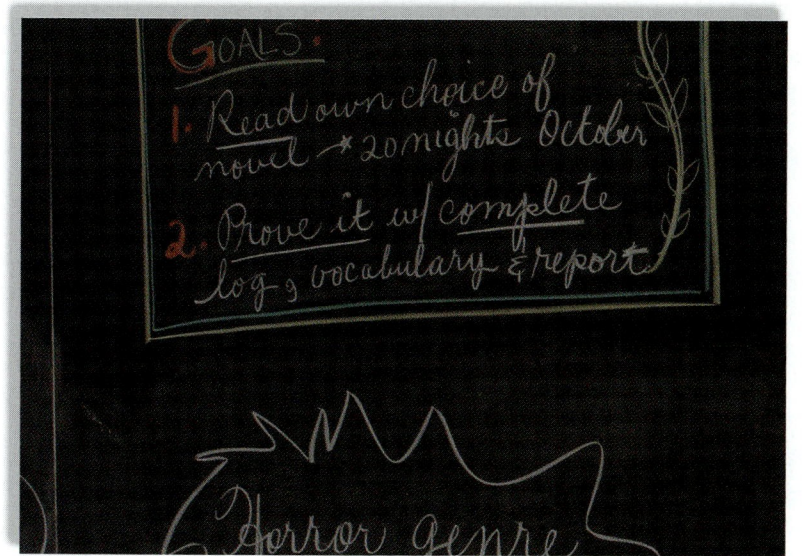

Courtesy of David Ottenstein Photography

In many districts, teachers are expected to post daily objectives in the classroom. The familiar "TSWBAT" ("the student will be able to . . .") format of a Mager objective (1975) states the skill, knowledge, or understanding that a student is to demonstrate, along with the conditions under which the demonstration will occur and the degree of mastery expected. For instance, as part of your observations in schools you may visit a classroom and notice the following written on the board: "The student will be able to complete 30 two-digit-number-by-two-digit-number multiplication problems within 10 minutes with a degree of accuracy of at least 80 percent." In this case, the expectations are very clear, and the grading is obviously based on a simple matter of whether or not the student succeeds.

An "A" for Effort?

Let's assume for a moment that one of the children attempting to meet the objective described above comes in for help after school each day for the week prior to the test. Let's also assume that she stays up late studying and practicing, and you have even heard from the parent that the student is working diligently to succeed. Now the big day comes, and try as she might, she only gets 70 percent of the questions correct. Would you say she has failed to meet the standard, or would you boost that score just a bit in view of the extraordinary effort and commitment the student has shown? After all, dedication to a task and working beyond what is asked are both characteristics of a strong work ethic, something that schools try to encourage.

Whether you would choose to report the grade as is or instead provide those few extra points, you would not be alone. The debate over awarding points for effort has raged for a long time and likely will continue to do so. It must be acknowledged that work ethic, character, citizenship, and cooperation are all virtues that schools very definitely attempt to foster in students. Yet it is also true that those same characteristics are not assessed on the yearly achievement tests or on tests such as the SAT or any of the standardized tests that you will take on your way to certification as a professional teacher. The establishment of clear objectives is supposed to clear up this dilemma, but the humanistic side of education is one that cannot be ignored. Activity 7.1, An "A" for Effort, will help you formulate your own position on this issue.

1. To begin, consider whether you think it is appropriate to award students credit for effort as part of their academic grade.

2. Survey any 10 of your friends or classmates and ask the same question. Avoid influencing their answers or making them justify the response; just ask.

3. If you are observing in a school as part of your teacher education program, ask five educators—including, if possible, a principal or other administrator—the same question as in item 1. Again, just ask rather than look for explanations.

4. Now that you know how some people feel about the topic, use the Internet to find an argument in favor of recognizing effort as part of one's grade and an argument in opposition. You might begin with a search for "grading students for effort."

5. What is your opinion now? Did you change your opinion from what you'd said in item 1? If so, why? If not, what evidence have you found that supports your opinion?

Gain Scores

gain score The difference between pre-test and post-test scores, thus the student progress in a specific body of information.

The argument over rewarding effort becomes even more difficult with the question of **gain scores.** Though often seen as a solution to the effort versus achievement debate, gain scores open up the discussion to an entirely different line of thinking in terms of how student achievement should be measured. As opposed to simply meeting or not meeting a predetermined standard, gain scores measure student *progress.* That is, a system based on gain scores will determine precisely where a child stands, academically speaking, prior to instruction, and then measure the progress made after instruction is complete.

Let's use reading as an example for this discussion. It is not at all uncommon that by third grade many students are reading below grade level. So let's assume one child enters third grade reading on a 2.2 level (that is, second grade, second month according to an achievement test). Another child in the same class begins the year on a 3.4 level. At the end of the year, our first child is reading at a 2.9 level while the second child in our example is reading at a 3.5 level. According to the test, our first child has gained seven months in terms of reading ability but nonetheless has failed to reach a third-grade level. Our second child has gained only one month over the course of an entire school year, yet *is* on the third-grade level. How should each of these students be graded? Notice that we are not asking about effort in this example. One student has gained seven times as much as the other. Do we consider that failure? Admittedly, there is a catch to this example. Schools are currently structured to grade students on the meeting of objectives rather than on how much they have gained during the year. So our question to you is really one of broader educational policy: Is our current structure the most appropriate perspective for the assessment of *learning*? And how does that structure vary from school to school? Activity 7.2 will help you articulate your own position on this issue.

Grade Inflation

Grades, like money, are only as valuable as the standards upon which they are based. Grade inflation is what happens when the questions that we have been raising for you in these last sections remain unanswered. You have probably found

ACTIVITY 7.2
Gain Scores or Mastery of Objectives?

Which approach would you prefer in your college courses: gain scores or mastery of objectives? Of course, not all of your classes are appropriate for a gain score approach because they involve new concepts or skills. But what about some of your general courses in English composition, literature (where reading comprehension is the focus), mathematics, or even foreign language?

1. For which courses might this be most appropriate?

2. Would you prefer to be graded on how much progress you make in a course rather than on whether or not you master some percentage of the objectives? Why or why not?

3. What differences do you see between your college education and your K–12 schooling in the context of gain scores and mastery of objectives?

already that students from other high schools seem to have received higher or lower grades than your own in the same subjects, yet you find yourself superior (or inferior as the case may be) and wonder how this could happen. How could an A at one school be only as good as a B at another? It seems as though something is amiss.

Grade inflation is also a function of the humanistic side of education. It would be easy enough to say that a student receives credit for correct answers, and the percentage correct will dictate the grade. But it is also true that education, or learning, occurs in a context. That is, rather than being something that can be separated from all other influences, human performance on any task is affected by real and extenuating circumstances. The problem is that we have yet to find a way to account for the humanistic side in a fair way. Should the child who overcomes a substantial obstacle (recent illness, the death of a close family member, etc.) be given "special" consideration when it comes time for grading? Sounds fair for that child, but is it fair for the child who doesn't have to overcome some peculiar obstacle but receives a higher score based purely on performance?

This is a real problem because grades are supposed to be reflective of a standard. You might think of it this way: Would you want to trust your life to a surgeon who made it through medical school with inflated grades? This may sound like a drastic example, but the example has credence when you consider that the precedent for grade inflation was established long ago in elementary school when that surgeon was "just a child." Also, keep in mind that this problem is national in scope, not confined to just the local or state levels (Wildavsky, 2000). Grades represent the "currency" by which students gauge their own academic achievement and by which the achievement of students is gauged against other students, schools, and even nations.

When assigning grades, you will find it difficult to completely separate the humanistic aspect of this situation from the established objectives. Students will always ask if they can do "extra credit" work, if they can have more time, if they can do things over. Yet the classroom teacher needs to be able to balance extenuating circumstances against whether or not a student has actually learned what it is necessary for the student to know. A focus on earning "points" has shifted the educational emphasis from *learning* to the *completion of requirements*. If all of those requirements add up to learning, so be it. If, however, those requirements add up to little more than completing a variety of activities, then the difficulties of assigning grades can be expected to persist.

Effort, character, citizenship, and so on can be a part of the grading ingredients. But they can't be haphazard or widely varying ingredients. As someone just beginning to join the educational profession, you should start thinking about how to combine the humanistic and academic aspects of education in a way that truly reflects the learning that is accomplished in school. Though we cannot resolve the questions of grade inflation for you within this text, we encourage you to consider how you will ensure that grades you assign will truly represent what you intended, expected, *and announced in advance* that your students should be able to do as a result of instruction in your class.

Assessment, much more than an instructional afterthought, is an integral component in the development of an educational strategy. Whether planning centers on a unit of study, on the study of a chapter from a novel, or on year-long goals for classroom instruction, a teacher can design and use assessments to improve her instruction and the overall achievement of her students.

Though you have been receiving grades for your work throughout the years you have spent in school, you may find the idea of assigning grades to others difficult to accept. This is not uncommon. However, a teacher's greatest ally when the time for grading arrives is a well-planned and well-executed strategy for high-quality assessment.

Classroom Management

"Effective classroom management," according to Darling-Hammond and Bransford (2005), "starts with the creation of curriculum that is meaningful to students and with teaching that is engaging and motivating" (p. 37). The vast majority of your teacher education program will focus on preparing you to do just that. However, that's the "start." Despite your best efforts to design the perfect lesson, it will not be perfect enough for the child who comes to school one morning just after her parents announced that they are getting a divorce, or who forgot to bring in a signed permission slip and so cannot take part in some special function, or who just got back a failing grade on a history paper. The behavior of your class involves many factors that you cannot anticipate. And that's where a classroom management plan becomes important.

classroom management Activities in which a teacher engages before, during, and after interacting with students. These activities, which focus on the prevention of misbehavior, allow instruction to take place.

Classroom management is included in our chapter about the pragmatics of teaching to demonstrate to you that it is not something to be considered *after* the students have arrived. It is not something that one can simply spend a few minutes thinking about when all of the other instructional concerns have been addressed. It is a complete topic in and of itself. As Weber (1990) suggests, teaching involves two major activities: instruction and management. Instruction is concerned with the presentation, demonstration, and assessment of a curriculum, and it is what most people think of when they consider what it is to be a teacher. Management involves those activities in which a teacher engages before, during, and after interacting with children to allow instruction to take place.

Long and Morse (1996) remind us that no other topic in education receives greater attention or causes more concerns for teachers and parents than that of classroom discipline. They add that it is the lack of effective classroom discipline or behavior management skills that is the major stumbling block to a successful career in teaching. Cangelosi (2004) notes the range of teacher effectiveness in classroom management:

Some teachers orchestrate smoothly operating classrooms where students cooperatively and efficiently go about the business of learning with minimal disruptions. Other teachers exhaust themselves struggling with student misbehaviors as they attempt to gain some semblance of classroom order. Those from the latter group who remain in the teaching profession eventually give up the struggle, deciding that today's students are so unmotivated and out of control that it is futile to attempt anything more than surviving the school day. (p. 4)

A survey of K–5 and 6–12 teachers (Shuler, et al., 1998) revealed the following:

1. 40 percent of K–5 students and 71 percent of students in grades 6–12 cheated "often" or "almost always."
2. 35 percent of K–5 and 34 percent of 6–12 students often or almost always made verbal wisecracks about the teacher.
3. 36 percent of K–5 and 73 percent of 6–12 students were tardy often or almost always.
4. 30 percent of K–5 and 31 percent of 6–12 students engaged in disruptive personal grooming activities.
5. 38 percent of K–5 and 42 percent of 6–12 students often or almost always tried to humiliate the teacher in class.
6. 28 percent of K–5 and 49 percent of 6–12 students often or always talked back to the teacher.
7. 40 percent of K–5 and 52 percent of 6–12 students often or almost always lied or made ridiculous excuses.

Yes, instruction and management are at the heart of the educator's profession, but no, they are by no means the same thing.

Some Perspectives on Classroom Management

A discussion of classroom management can take many different perspectives and theoretical approaches. For example, the *Assertive Discipline* program developed by Lee Canter and Marlene Canter (1976) puts the teacher squarely in control of the classroom environment. This is the teacher-centered approach. The assertive teacher they speak of is "one who clearly and firmly communicates her wants and needs to her students, and is prepared to reinforce her words with appropriate actions. She responds in a manner which maximizes her potential to get her needs met, but in no way violates the best interests of the students" (p. 9). In a sense this might be thought of as teachers "taking back" control of the classroom.

Others argue that the traditional notion of teacher as controller is not necessarily a good thing. Kohn writes, "Educators . . . may find themselves caught in an undertow, pulled back to traditional assumptions and practices that result in their doing things *to* students rather than working *with* them" (2003). In this approach the student is at the center of the educational enterprise, and we might well expect the student also to be at the center of an effective approach to classroom management. Such a perspective sees the student in a collaborative relationship with the teacher.

And then there is the broad expanse between the teacher-centered and student-centered perspectives. Some schools adopt a

A classroom management program that works for you will be the basis for establishing an environment where learning can take place.

Courtesy of Becky Stovall

particular classroom management/discipline program, or develop their own, and then expect all teachers to follow that plan. In many situations, however, teachers combine approaches. It is not at all uncommon to find as many variations on the classroom management theme as there are teachers on a given faculty.

As you progress through your teacher education program you will probably learn about classroom management from a theoretical perspective in much greater

Teacher Testimonial
Feature 7.1   On Classroom Management

My father used to ask me if I wanted a straight answer. I always said no because I knew that it simply meant the answer was "no." Do you want a straight answer to successful classroom management? The answer is not so simple but yet it really is . . .

I went into teaching to be the deliverer of content and to truly make a difference. I just knew the children would come to me ready to learn and engage in all of my planned activities. Well, I was in for a surprise!

Let's just say my lovely class of 30 fifth graders chose to chew me up and spit me out. After many tears (in private) and talking with my school mom and friends, I knew I would have to make a change if I couldn't figure this out. Then the answer was so close: a Saturday classroom management workshop. Finally, an answer to my prayers!

With my new legal pad, a fresh pen, and eager ears, I was ready for the instructor to tell me "how" to do it. Being a most conscientious student, I sat on the front row ready to take down each and every direction. I left disappointed. I realize that there is really no straight answer for questions of classroom management.

Classroom management is a mindset. It is a personality, a climate, or a perception. When I realized this I became a teacher watcher. I watched my colleagues and then began experimenting but putting my own personal twist on things. I began to analyze what worked and what motivated my students. I began to get to know my students and used interpersonal relationships to build classroom community. I saw a tremendous change when my attitude changed. At that point I viewed classroom management with excitement and became very motivated to learn what made students tick. It was amazing how the pieces started meshing together and teaching and learning was now falling into place.

Though the pieces never fit together perfectly, I have found that these components helped me learn to love the classroom management part of teaching:

1. *Recognize the differences in children.* Many children come from unstable environments. The teacher should be a constant in the child's everyday experiences. A warm, inviting teacher is reassuring to the child, and this climate sets the tone for the day's activities. Children can sense if people like what they are doing, and a friendly, happy teacher gives the child an opportunity to experience a good feeling. All children need many opportunities to feel successful.

2. *Teach discipline.* Teach discipline techniques throughout the day. Use a lot of positive reinforcement. For example:

    I like the way Antwon is walking down the hallway. Suzy is listening so well.
    Who will be a good citizen and lend Billy a pencil? Thank you, class, for sitting so nicely.

    When you set up your class rules, discuss together why we walk in a straight line. Explain to kids how if other classes are coming down the hallway, you will have enough space. We walk quietly down the hallway so we will not disturb other children's learning.

3. *Set high expectations for behavior.* Most kids today are asking for structure. Let kids know exactly what you expect and it will be done in that manner. If they aren't sure about how to do it, model the behavior. Show kids how to sit on the rug properly. Then let them practice and praise them for their practice. *Expect* your class to be the best!

4. *Be a role model for behavior.* You are going to hear arguments on both sides of the issue as to whether teachers are (or should be) role models for students. All I can tell you is that my experience as a teacher tells me that students—of any age—learn from watching their teachers in all sorts of situations. The older kids might not be as obvious about wanting to emulate their teacher, but they are internalizing what they see. So if I want my students to walk quietly in the hallway, I can't walk along with them and chat with another teacher all

detail. Our intention is to offer a pragmatic—practical—look at classroom management just to introduce you to the topic. As such, our discussion blends many perspectives. The challenge of classroom management can be reduced to workable terms with a good foundation in what classroom management is all about. We will approach the matter in terms of two areas of concern: *keys to successful classroom management* and *establishing a learning environment in the context of managing a classroom.*

along the way. If I want my students to learn preparedness and responsibility, I have to be prepared for class and I have to demonstrate that I take responsibility for my actions. And above all, if I want my students to have a positive and caring attitude, then that's what they have to see from me in all situations—at school and away from school as well.

5. *Model happiness and show humor.* I believe that you need to teach your kids how to laugh and enjoy. Sure, children know how to laugh, but it is in school that they learn the difference between appropriate and inappropriate situations in a social setting. Humor is wonderful and modeling happiness gives kids a real respect for your commands. Let loose a little bit—do the Hokey Pokey, the Teaberry Shuffle (if you remember that!), and a few basketball shots. My kids would focus an hour on math skills just to see me do the Teaberry Shuffle for 30 seconds.

   Another important skill to teach is how to cut it off and get back on task. This again has to be taught, not just expected. Let them know what your signals are for getting back on task.

6. *Be a motivator.* Get excited about what you are going to teach! Try to take the positive route because positive energy increases the odds for success. The bases are loaded with two outs, and your team is behind by one run. You are up to bat. You view this as a challenge, a chance to succeed! The burnouts view it as an opportunity to fail, and then the odds are greater that you will fail.

   Plan your lessons so they will enable you to share your excitement and enthusiasm for learning. This climate will draw the excitement for good behavior. "Speaking of exciting lessons, we are going to do one right now," I would say. "I need good listeners so you will know exactly what to do." This style of teaching will motivate the children to be good learners. They want to know what you are going to say and do next. Excitement prevails and children are tuned in.

7. *Provide hands-on materials for "doing" learning.* Hands-on materials provide many creative ways to teach a skill. The use of these manipulatives helps children to understand concepts and gives them concrete practice. Hands-on materials help to make the learning real. Many educators agree and research supports that *doing* is the best road to *learning.*

8. *Communicate nonverbally.* I discovered nonverbal communication accidentally. With trepidation I walked into a fifth-grade classroom one day with no speaking voice. Relying on my nonverbal communication skills proved to be one of my most successful measures of control. Thanks to this powerful tool, I had a great day.

   One of the most effective ways to change a behavior is eye contact. Along with eye contact, closeness with calmness will aid in changing behavior. This often avoids power struggles and allows you to emerge from the situation without breaking stride. For more blatant behavior, eye contact with wait time will sometimes solve the problem. Know your kids and know what will work best with each individual. With some children a comforting hand on one's shoulder will remind them to stay on task. While moving around the room monitoring activities, I walk toward children who need to feel my presence.

Beth Elliott is Principal at Pontiac Elementary School, a Presidential Blue Ribbon School. Consider carefully what she has presented to you here, as well as what has been said throughout this discussion of classroom management. It can make all the difference in your teaching! ■

Keys to Successful Classroom Management

Beginning teachers usually spend a lot of time going over the fresh new curriculum materials that the school principal has placed in their hands. In those weeks before school they cut out letters, prepare bulletin boards, and perhaps even practice a "good morning, class" or two. These are good things to do. But before teachers can realize the fruits of any of those instructionally oriented labors, they must have a solid system of classroom management in mind and in place. A well-founded program of classroom management requires understanding classroom management terms, planning, and practicing.

Classroom Management Terminology

Classroom management refers to the things a teacher does to organize students, space, and time to prevent or minimize behavior problems that would interfere with instructional time. Among the concerns that fall under this heading are the behaviors that the teacher expects of the students, the materials needed for various lessons along with the convenient storage and retrievability of those materials, the consequences for inappropriate behavior, and the means by which those consequences will be meted out. We also want you to understand that *classroom management* differs from *discipline,* which differs from *rules.* Understanding the difference between the terms, which unfortunately are often used interchangeably, will help you develop a clear picture of behavior management in the classroom.

We also advise you to expand your perspective on classroom management to include preventing inappropriate *teacher* behaviors as well as student misbehaviors. What teacher behaviors might one want to avoid? Having to leave the classroom, or send a student out, to retrieve papers or materials needed for a lesson just begun would be an inappropriate behavior. In this case instructional time is being lost because of something the teacher has failed to accomplish. Lowering a student's academic grade as punishment for misbehavior is an example of inappropriate teacher behavior because academic achievement and discipline are separate issues.

discipline Actions a teacher takes after misbehavior occurs.

Discipline Whereas classroom management focuses on the prevention of misbehavior, **discipline** refers to actions a teacher takes *after* misbehavior has occurred. Clearly, planning for how the class is to run is a different matter from planning for what to do if things run awry. Keeping the distinction between management and discipline in mind will help you plan for each with much greater clarity of purpose.

The efficacy of discipline in a teacher's classroom will be directly related to the rules established for the class, the consequences announced, and the enforcement, or nonenforcement, of the consequences. We will discuss rules in greater detail in the next section. For now, the pertinent notions to keep in mind are these: (1) Merely posting rules does not constitute planning for discipline, (2) rules are enforced by imposing consequences, and (3) whether or not rules are made to be broken, for one reason or another, at one time or another, they *will* be broken—so be sure the announced consequences are something you can comfortably impose.

rules Descriptors of required observable behaviors.

Rules **Rules** are another primary concern in the development of a management plan. During the course of your teacher education program you will spend time observing, assisting, and eventually practicing the things you learn in real classrooms with real students. Particularly during those observation opportunities, look around in each classroom you visit. Almost without exception you will find "the class rules" posted somewhere in the room (though you may have to search). Locate and read the rules for the classes you observe, then compare the rules with the behavior of the class and the teacher's enforcement of the rules. See Activity

© Dennis MacDonald/PhotoEdit

Clearly stated and conspicuously posted, classroom rules represent the code of behavior that a teacher expects from the students.

7.3, Rules in the Classroom, for an opportunity to begin observing and considering the various ways that teachers use rules in the classroom.

Class rules represent the code of behavior that a teacher expects the students to follow (Burden, 2003). As such, they are clearly a part of the overall classroom management plan. Of particular importance is that the students are aware of the rules, that the rules are considered fair and reasonable (that doesn't mean that everybody has to like them), and that abiding by the rules clearly serves the best interests of the students. Without doubt you have seen lists of "don't do this, don't do that" rules. In such a situation the only motivation to abide by the rules is to avoid some sort of punishment. So rather than focusing on "don't" rules, the teacher may emphasize "do" rules. For example, "Don't be late" could be written as "Be on time and ready to begin class." In this way, the teacher can continually emphasize the behavior that is desired rather than emphasizing the behavior that is considered inappropriate.

For rules to be effective in managing behavior and fostering positive social behavior, rule-following must be acknowledged by the teacher. In the early weeks of the school year, a teacher could bring successful rule-following behavior to the students' attention daily. As time goes by, acknowledgment of appropriate behavior may come less often, but nonetheless it must be made evident to the students if the teacher wishes to see that behavior continue.

consequences The results that inevitably follow when students fail to observe the rules.

Consequences   It is also important that failure to follow reasonable rules that serve the best interests of the student carries **consequences.** These consequences must be made as clear to the students as the rules themselves. As was the case with the rules, the consequences must be fair and reasonable even though they will necessarily be aversive from the students' perspective. The teacher's perspective is important here as well. If a teacher announces a consequence that she is uncomfortable administering (or perhaps could lead to problems—such as sending too many children to the office), then those consequences need to be reconsidered. We cannot overemphasize that if rules and consequences are part of the classroom management plan, *they must be consistently enforced.* The teacher who believes the rest of the class will not notice when she fails to enforce the class rules a time or two makes a serious mistake. Innocent though it may be, children always test the limits. Within a week they will know whether the teacher means what she says.

According to Borich (1996), "Consistency is a key reason why some rules are effective while others are not. Rules that are not enforced or that are not applied evenly and consistently over time result in a loss of prestige and respect for the person who has created the rules and has the responsibility for carrying them out" (p. 364). Note that Borich doesn't mention in this passage that instructional time is lost or that students fail to learn necessary lessons. Rather, he makes it clear that *the teacher loses prestige and respect* in the eyes of those for whom she bears the responsibility for teaching. This, in itself, is an important lesson for any prospective teacher to learn very early on. Classroom management is not only a matter of what the student may lose (in terms of educational opportunities), but very much a matter of what the teacher stands to lose.

procedures The ways in which particular activities (e.g., taking attendance, collecting money, moving from place to place) are conducted.

Procedures and Routines   **Procedures** are the manner in which particular activities are to be carried out. Of course, during the school day, many different procedures must be followed. At the elementary levels, they include the categories relating to different spaces within the room, throughout the school, whole class and small group activities, and miscellaneous procedures. At the secondary levels, procedures can be grouped as beginning class, instructional activities, ending the class,

Field Observation

ACTIVITY 7.4   **Identifying Classroom Procedures**

Classroom procedures differ from rules in that procedures tell the student *how* to do something. You will likely have many more procedures for your students than rules. For that reason, practicing the procedures will be very important.

1.   Select a grade level that you are interested in teaching, or use the classroom that you are observing if your course includes observations in the schools.

2.   List as many procedures as you can think of that would help your class run smoothly. We have mentioned some already (for example, taking attendance and walking in the hallway). What others can you think of? If you are stuck, think of your own Introduction to Education class. What procedures can you identify?

3.   From your list, consider how you would teach that procedure to your students and how you would let them know that they are carrying out the procedures well.

4.   If you are observing a classroom, ask the teacher about procedures that she has implemented in the classroom. Are there more or less than you had expected?

routines Behaviors that are learned or demonstrated so well that they become automatic.

and miscellaneous (Jones & Jones, 2001). There are also procedures for taking attendance, for collecting lunch money, for walking in the hallway as an individual or as a class. This is a short list; certainly you could think of many more examples. Those procedures that are used to the point of being "automatic" behaviors are referred to as **routines.** For example, a teacher's process of taking attendance may become a routine. For students, the manner in which they are expected to enter the class and begin work (procedure) should become something they can do on their own without the teacher having to instruct them to do so (a routine). Activity 7.4, Identifying Classroom Procedures, will allow you to observe the degree to which some teachers emphasize procedures while others do not. Watch for differences in student behavior.

Wong (1991) asserts that the number one problem in classrooms is not discipline but a lack of procedures and routines. The paradox is that procedures are a major part of any school day and a major part of any person's life. So rather than leaving the following of procedures and the development of routines that facilitate learning to chance, teachers must specifically teach procedures and routines. In fact, the teaching of procedures, which carries with it a clear description of behaviors expected of students, should occupy much of the first weeks of school each year. The learning of procedures not only makes classroom tasks easier to accomplish, but it also minimizes the opportunities for misbehavior.

Planning for Classroom Management

A most important key to successful classroom management is *planning* for classroom management. Much as we all would like to have this element of education take care of itself, the bottom line is that it will not. The teacher must be well ahead of the students long before any one of them sets foot in the classroom. Planning. Let us say that another way just so that you will understand how important it is: planning. OK, that was the same way, but that's because there is no getting around it. As Wong (1991) says, "Readiness is the primary determinant of teacher effectiveness" (p. 94). He's not talking about the teacher's knowledge of subject material in this instance. No, he's talking about readiness for managing the class.

Researchers at the Research and Development Center for Teacher Education at the University of Texas found that effective classroom managers are nearly always good planners (Evertson, Emmer, Clements, & Worsham, 2000). This is to be expected, when you think about it, for despite the fact that curriculum does not change much from year to year, the combination of students entering your classroom certainly does. In fact, if you are teaching above the elementary level, those combinations change several times a day with each new class period. Though planning for classroom management is definitely an exercise in preparing for an unknown quantity, there are some consistencies that can guide that planning and preparation. Understanding that planning is imperative is the first step. Understanding what must be planned comes next.

Table 7.3 lists some of the items that a teacher needs to address when conceptualizing a classroom management plan. The list is certainly not exhaustive, but we want you understand the broad range of concerns that fall under the heading of managing a classroom. Diverse as they may seem, however, the underlying theme throughout is organizing for maximum instructional effectiveness and limiting opportunities for behaviors that interfere with learning.

If all a teacher had to be concerned with was keeping a child in her seat, classroom management might not require quite the finesse that it does entail. In fact, a mark of a truly effective teacher is so much finesse that one doesn't even notice that a classroom management program is in place and running. Anybody can spot

Table 7.3	Classroom Management Concerns

Student Seating:
  Assigned?
  Group?
  Rows?
	Handling Student Birthdays and Holidays

	Class Rules

Traffic Flow in the Classroom	Routine Procedures:
	  Collecting Lunch Money
	  Beginning the Day
	  Attendance
	  Leaving (Bus, parent pickup, walking, driving)

Learning Centers (if any)	
Emergency Management	
Responding to Student Behavior	Bathroom Breaks

Storage:
  Teacher Materials
  Student Materials
	Practicing Procedures

	Grading
	Parent Contact
Preparation of Materials	Disciplinary Consequences

Assignments:
  Academic
  Student Responsibilities
	Decorating the Room:
	  What's Enough?
	  What's Overstimulating?

a poorly managed class, but leave a room that has a well-thought-out and well-implemented program and you are likely to think that you "didn't see" any evidence of classroom management techniques. They were there, and that's finesse! And, what is more, the planning and organization involve activities before school starts and on opening day (Flaxman, 2000).

Practice

The third and final key to successful classroom management is practice using the rules, following the procedures, and developing the routines that the teacher expects of her students. Think about this for just a moment. How often do people learn a new skill or behavior without practicing it for some period of time? Everything from handwriting to painting masterpieces requires practice. Yet how often is it the case that teachers present students with a list of rules and an explanation of procedures they want the students to follow but fail to allow time to practice? We all know that repetition facilitates developing a new skill, but it is also true that practice provides the opportunity for students to *experience the specific behavior* the teacher is requiring. Through practice they come to know what expectations the teacher has for them.

Particularly with elementary children, but not to exclude secondary students (or college students, for that matter), time spent at the very beginning of the school year (or new course of instruction) practicing procedures, developing routines, and demonstrating appropriate behavior will be time that more than pays for itself through the *prevention* of lost instructional time later in the year. This can be an enjoyable experience that brings the class together around a common goal.

As we mentioned with regard to classroom rules, it is also important to keep in mind that practice is not something done in a few weeks and never done again. Take a look at the medical and legal professions. Those folks refer to their entire careers as a practice! Similarly, be prepared to practice again when skills seem to be slipping. And by all means, be sure to acknowledge both the demonstration of appropriate behavior and procedures or routines carried out well *and* the positive results of having done so.

Establishing a Learning Environment

In the previous section, Keys to Successful Classroom Management, we looked at what a teacher needs to consider in preparing an organizational plan. Now we turn our attention to the *implementation* of that plan. Keep in mind that despite the fact that we are talking about managing student behavior, our emphasis is on *teacher* behaviors.

Communicating Expectations to the Students

The following three guidelines will help ensure that your students understand and accept your classroom management plan as something that is in their best interests:

1. Communicate expectations to the students.
2. Involve the students (and others) in the development of the rules and behavior management procedures.
3. Make sure the rules and procedures are positive behaviors that facilitate instruction and the development of positive self-esteem.

As long as the rules are reasonable and clearly communicated to the students, then many of the arguments about "not knowing I couldn't do that" are eliminated. But, of course, there's more to it.

The loss of instructional time due to misbehaviors has led to an increasing sense of the teacher as the boss and the students as the followers. However, in an enterprise such as education—one in which the students are not willingly trading their time for an agreed-upon compensation (as in an employer/employee relationship)—there exists a very special relationship motivating the behaviors that occur. William Glasser (1997) suggests that teachers "must give up bossing and turn to leading" (p. 600). He recommends that "quality" environments be established in classrooms in accordance with *choice theory*. The idea is that people make choices that help them satisfy four needs: (1) the need to belong, (2) the need for power, (3) the need for freedom, and (4) the need for fun. The misbehavior you see occurring in classrooms indicates that the classroom environment is preventing students from creating their own quality worlds.

Of course, it is not reasonable to say that one must set up the classroom in a manner that allows children to simply do whatever they please. Actually, the understanding of limitations within a society is part of the educational experience. In the section on classroom management terminology we discussed rules as being the behavioral guidelines for your classroom. Here we want to elaborate by suggesting that students can be involved in the formation of class rules under the teacher's guidance and thereby feel that they have a stake in how the class will operate.

Note that the recommendation being made is to help students follow the rules by allowing them to help make the rules. This is a far cry from the typical attempt at "buying" rule conformity by offering gifts, candy, and even the trade-off of instructional time for free time. If the rules are worth following, the following of them should be rewarding. Table 7.4 ties together this idea of rules as instructional tools for enhancing the learning environment and positive self-esteem.

Notice the degree to which the Principles of Effective Discipline swirl around *interpersonal relationships* much more so than adopting a tone of "my way or the highway." Perhaps you can see the three classroom management guidelines (communicating expectations, involving students in the development of rules and procedures, and seeing that the rules and procedures are positive parameters) as being very much evident in this list. How difficult do you think it would be to garner the support of parents and your school administrators for a program based on principles such as these?

Table 7.4	Principles of Effective Discipline

1. Students should be treated with dignity and respect.
2. Effective teaching reduces discipline problems.
3. Students need a limited say in what happens in the classroom.
4. It takes time to develop an effective classroom management plan and style.
5. Most discipline problems are created by how teachers teach and treat people.
6. Bored students become discipline problems.
7. Lack of self-esteem is a major reason why students act up.
8. No one wants to fail. A student would rather be bad than appear to be stupid.
9. Anything you can do to make people feel good about themselves will help to minimize discipline problems.
10. People who feel powerless will find ways of expressing their lack of power.
11. We deny most the students who need to learn responsibility, by denying them the experience to have responsibility.

(Adapted from Wong, 1991)

Table 7.5	Involving the Students in Making the Rules

1. Communicate your expectations to the students.
2. Involve students in establishing the rules that will guide their behavior.
3. Use rules that foster positive classroom participation
4. Keep the list of rules to about five so that they are easily remembered.

From what we see in the list, teachers could go about establishing class rules with the assistance of the class. When doing so, it is important to keep in mind that the task at hand is not to take on the legislative load of Congress. Rather, the teacher and students simply need a list of perhaps five rules to govern the class (fewer than five probably won't cover enough, many more than five are difficult to readily remember).

The rules should be drafted by the students themselves. This ensures that they are understandable by those who are expected to abide by them. In keeping with this, the rules should be simple. If extensive discussion is required to clarify a rule, the rule is too cumbersome. Break it into two rules or decide what is to be expressed and then rephrase the rule more succinctly. Try to keep the rules positive. Emphasize the appropriate behaviors that are expected rather than focusing on examples of inappropriate behavior. As teachers, we don't want to practice bad behavior just so we can then say, "And then I would tell you to stop doing that." And finally, academic issues should not be a part of the rules as prescriptions for behavior, and certainly not as consequences for misbehavior. Keep the two separate.

Communicating expectations to the students, involving them in establishing the rules that will guide their behavior, and utilizing rules that foster positive classroom participation are the themes that drive an effective management program. Relinquishing some of one's own sense of "power" is a requirement for empowering others. This is as true in the teacher/student relationship as it is in the administrator/teacher relationship. Interesting how that happens, isn't it? See Table 7.5 for guidelines in preparing class rules.

Consequences for Inappropriate Behavior

Inevitably, some student will violate the established rules of your classroom. It will happen for a wide variety of reasons, but the teacher must keep a particular perspective in mind. Part of that perspective is to remember that (1) the focus should be on the behavior, not the person, and (2) discipline and academics are two different entities. With any discipline problem at least one person will be operating from an unreasonable position. Whenever possible, that person should not be the teacher. Keep a clear head and clear focus and address the behavior.

Responding to Student Misbehavior Students will be very much attuned to a teacher's enforcement or nonenforcement of the class rules. If the students were involved in establishing those rules, they will be even more aware of whether or not violations occur and whether or not the teacher responds as she promised. In your own classes in college there are students (certainly not *you*) who will test the limits, and children are just the same. A teacher's response to violations of the rules tells the students whether or not the teacher means what she says. If the word is out that she doesn't follow through, then one can expect that many more transgressions will start occurring. The teacher will ultimately decide that she has a "bad" class, but in actuality it is her own behavior that led to the situation.

Consequences for Misbehavior We have indicated more than once, and in more than one way, that rules are effective only when there are consequences to enforce them and plausible benefits for following them. Since we are now discussing a teacher's response to misbehavior, our focus is on the aversive consequences of misbehavior. Whether your approach to classroom management tends toward full involvement of the students, toward full control by the teacher, or somewhere in the middle, it is imperative that the students know and understand that *whatever* the consequences are, the teacher *will* enforce them.

When students are allowed to help identify consequences, they are more likely to embrace the rules and perceive the consequences as fair and agreed upon. However, some schools have an established discipline code that must be followed; if such is the case, it must be explained to the students. In either situation, it is important that the consequences for infractions be perceived as logical (in light of the violation) and fair. The best consequences are those that will enable a student to choose between acceptable and unacceptable actions. It should be clear that unacceptable behavior is not worth the administration of the consequence. Even better, and this becomes the teacher's task to explain, the students should be able to clearly understand that *following* the rules is *beneficial* to them.

It is unlikely that a school's discipline code will impose *academic* penalties for misbehavior (for example, lowering a grade or failing the student in an academic subject). The same should be true for consequences established within the classroom. Lowering a student's grade in a subject area for arriving late or talking out of turn dilutes the efficacy of assessment. Keep behavior and academic achievement in proper perspective. When dealing with misbehavior, make every effort to address the behavior and not criticize the person. No student comes to school hoping to have his dignity, intellect, or decision-making ability insulted. Doing so will only exacerbate an already difficult situation. The effective teacher is one who can maintain a calm demeanor and enforce the rules quietly and without anger or accusations. The particular infraction and agreed-upon consequence can be pointed out to the student without further discussion. If the student persists, the teacher can quietly speak to the student and indicate that the rules and consequences were established by the class and that it was the student who chose to violate the rules. Additional discussion about the situation, if necessary, could be held at an appropriate time if the student so desires.

Enforcement of the Rules and Consequences It is obvious that having rules and consequences is not going to be enough when a child wishes to challenge all that has been presented. At this point the teacher is very much engaged in a decision-making process. With a solid classroom management and discipline plan in place, these decisions can be much easier to make. The teacher must remember that allowing infractions to go by without attending to them is a mistake. Reference to the rules and consequences, as well as indicating who "owns" this particular problem, takes only a few seconds. When a student protests ("I'm late because my last teacher let us all out late!"), a teacher can offer the chance to discuss the matter outside of class time but indicate that it is a separate issue. The issue that is obvious is that the class rule has been broken. Keep a clear head and clear focus and address the behavior. We've said that once already, and here it is again at no additional charge.

This issue of students protesting the consequence because of extenuating circumstances is a good argument for choosing consequences that are reasonable and justifiable. If such is the case, the consequence can be enforced immediately, as briefly as possible, and even be mildly severe, as Brophy (1983) recommends. Instruction need not be brought to a halt, and in fact should not be stopped. In a case like this a student is not ruined for life or shamed beyond redemption. But it is imperative that some action be taken so that the message is clear: The rules will be enforced, and the teacher will not acquiesce based on insufficient information. Next time around, a student who is detained by another teacher will ask for some sort of pass to present in class. There are multiple lessons to be learned.

Beyond the Rules: Recognizing Extenuating Circumstances   For the vast majority of situations, reference to the class rules and pointing out that a rule has been violated will be sufficient to defuse the situation and allow instruction to continue. There is no need for the teacher to enter into a power struggle if she can maintain a quiet demeanor and focus on the behavior. The teacher may even tell the student that she has no argument with the student; it's just that this particular behavior does not serve the best interests of the student or class. In fact, the teacher must avoid a power struggle with a student at all costs, for in such a struggle the student has nothing to lose and the teacher has everything to lose. If you find yourself in this sort of situation, ask yourself who is controlling the event. If you are losing your temper and saying things that will only make matters worse, then the child is controlling you. Think about that: A child is controlling you and your reactions. This seems like a good place to repeat again: Keep a clear head and clear focus and address the behavior. Factors may well be at play that will require you to think beyond the rules and consider a broader perspective. Let's consider what some of those factors might be.

A child's inappropriate behavior can result from troubles that have absolutely no relationship to school. Students can come to the classroom with problems, worries, and concerns that make a set of classroom rules inconsequential. Parents argue and sometimes separate or divorce. Family members, or pets for that matter, become sick and sometimes die. Lunch money is lost on the way to school. Some children pick on weaker children. Medications kick in, don't kick in, or wear off. There are more possibilities than we could mention, and children are not necessarily going to show up at school with a note pinned to their collars explaining the situation. What all of this is leading to is that sometimes a teacher will have to take a situation beyond the rules. It is too much to ask that a teacher solve the domestic problems for all children in the class, but an astute teacher needs to be aware that inappropriate behavior can have motivations that go far beyond what occurs in class.

problem-solving conference
A meeting involving the teacher and student (and perhaps the parents/guardians) to help a student assume responsibility for his or her actions and find a way to resolve the situation without losing the student's sense of dignity.

The Problem-Solving Conference   A **problem-solving conference** is one attempt to go beyond the rules with a student while still focusing on the behavior. As we've said, the teacher can't be expected to solve all of the student's problems, and the primary goal at this point is to defuse the situation, preserve instructional time, and, if necessary, direct the child to resources better equipped to work with the particular problem. With that said, the problem-solving conference helps a student take responsibility for his actions and find a way to resolve the situation without

A problem-solving conference helps a student take responsibility without losing dignity.

Courtesy of Bill Lisenby

losing his sense of dignity. Problem solving, sometimes called conflict resolution, has several general steps:

1. Have the student evaluate and take responsibility for her behavior.
2. Help the student make a plan for a more acceptable way of behaving. Come to an agreement on how the student will behave in the future and on the consequences for failure to follow through.
3. Require the student to make a commitment to follow the plan.
4. Avoid using punishment or reacting to a misbehaving student in a punitive manner. Instead, remind the student of the consequences for failing to follow the plan.
5. Stay with it! Reinforce good behavior, and ask for the student's perspective on how it's going.

These steps are not an alternative to consequences. Nor does this process release the student from being accountable for her behavior. It does, however, allow the student and teacher to come to terms with a situation that may have distinct outside influences involved. So while the teacher has "gone beyond the rules," the rules have not been forsaken. As a result, the integrity of the learning environment and the classroom management plan is not lost.

Implementing Procedures and Routines

There is a key word regarding the implementing of procedures and routines. The word is not "control." The word is not "authority." The word is *practice*. Practice is something to be done *with* the students. As the school year begins, the teacher will be well aware that there are many procedures and routines that will contribute to a smoothly running classroom. We are not suggesting at all that children become "automatons" or mindless followers. Such could not be farther from the truth. Instead, it is now that the teacher teaches and practices those activities (skills) that are performed for the very purpose of enhancing the overall learning experiences that the students will encounter.

The teaching of procedures follows the same process as the teaching of any other skill: explain, rehearse, and reinforce. If the school in which you teach requires that the class walk on the right side of the hallway, in line, silently, then you must explain this to the students. Do you have to justify every policy and procedure for your class? No, but you should be able to explain why the procedure is of value. Even if you don't particularly agree with the procedure but are expected to abide by it, find some understandable explanation for it and make that clear to the students. Then, go out and practice. If your students need to walk up and down the hallways for half an hour to learn this, then walk up and down the hallways for half an hour. All the while, find examples of appropriate "hall walking" behavior and reinforce it with well-directed praise. Students may need to practice each day for a week or two. If that is the case, then that is what needs to be done. This is a learning experience with goals, objectives, and observable outcomes.

Following procedures and accomplishing beneficial routines is a good thing. For that reason, the teacher needs to bring to the students' attention that their conscientiousness is worthwhile and appreciated. Such activities can actually become a source of pride. The teacher must also keep in mind that many factors affect performance, and so when those procedure and routine skills start to slide, there is nothing wrong with practicing again to bring the students back up to an acceptable level. The value of this lesson is often lost on pre-service and beginning teachers. But don't let it be lost on you—we want you to know now that many "overwhelming" days, frustrating sleepless nights, and hours of trying to figure out what's wrong can be avoided by spending real instructional time at the very beginning of the year teaching students how to behave as you want them to behave.

Teacher Behaviors

We have become increasingly specific as we work our way through this topic of classroom management. Now let's look at the issue in terms of what the teacher might be expected to do from Kounin's characteristics of effective teachers (1970) to Emmer's physical features of the classroom (Emmer et al., 2002), plus a few other notions along the way.

When Jacob Kounin studied what made a teacher effective, he found a common theme: Effective teachers were good classroom managers. Three key characteristics were "withitness"; the ability to supervise several situations at one time; and the adept handling of transitions from one task to another. Over three decades later, his findings are still illustrative of teacher behaviors that lead to well-managed classes. Though it's easy to say that we should still be doing what Kounin advises, it may be even more important to realize that teachers have been doing some very effective things for a very long time—and so let's emulate that.

"Withitness" Effective teachers, Kounin concluded, had a certain "withitness" that allowed them to know what was going on throughout the classroom. Have you ever had a teacher who seemed to have eyes in the back of her head? That's what Kounin means. These teachers stay in touch with what's happening in the class at all times. Perhaps they will make a comment to a student or quietly walk around the room to place a hand on a student's shoulder. It is not a mystery, really; it's paying attention—and effective teachers do this.

Supervising Multiple Situations Another characteristic of effective teachers is the ability to supervise several situations at one time. A key here is knowing what needs to be done and how to do it. From that point on it is a matter of being able to focus on what needs to be done and not be flustered by distractions. This by no means suggests a teacher should ignore situations, but rather have the confidence and expertise to take them in stride and deal with them effectively.

Effectively Handling Transitions Effective teachers are also adept at handling transitions smoothly. This refers to bringing one activity to an end and moving efficiently to the next. The transition could be from one subject to the next or it could be from completing a lesson to taking the children to lunch. These actions are not accomplished automatically. Though the lesson has ended, the teacher's work has not. Transitions may not be instructional periods, but they are very much management zones. Transitions are not student downtime. Effective teachers are very much attuned to this. Did you know that at the elementary level, 31 major transitions occupy 15 percent of the school day (Burns, 1984)? Well, now you do. Fifteen percent of the day is spent in transitions; that represents about one hour out of a six-hour day!

Arranging the Classroom for Effective Management Emmer and his associates (2002) make several recommendations for the physical arrangement of the classroom that can enhance a teacher's ability to function as Kounin suggests. When arranging the layout of the classroom, avoid congestion in what will be high-traffic areas such as near the doorway or teacher's desk, around the pencil sharpeners, and around storage areas (particularly if they must be accessed during teaching time). Be sure that you can see all students and then monitor their activities. Arrange teaching materials and supplies so that time is not lost during class. Be certain that whatever seating arrangement is used, it allows all students to comfortably see and participate in the activities of the day.

Proximity to Students Effective teachers will move around the room and attempt to maximize their proximity to the students. Often student teachers will plant themselves at the front of the room and seemingly attach themselves to the chalkboard. Granted, this is something done out of nervousness; nonetheless, a teacher's proximity to students is a major force in minimizing student misbehavior. Students need to know that a comic book hidden in their social studies textbook is eventually going to be discovered.

In summary, the teacher's behavior when establishing rules, acknowledging the value of abiding by those rules, and following through with consequences in a calm manner when violations occur will set the tone from the very beginning. As David Berliner (1985) has stated, "In short, from the opening bell to the end of the day, the better classroom managers are thinking ahead. While maintaining a pleasant classroom atmosphere, these teachers keep planning how to organize, manage, and control activities to facilitate instruction" (p. 15). There really are very few "bad" children, and children will typically allow the teacher to take charge of the classroom and lead them. Whether or not she does will determine the tone of the school year. So the real choice of what type of classroom to have rests with . . . *the teacher.*

Without a doubt, classroom management is a complex and challenging aspect of being a teacher. It is not something that new teachers should learn "on the job."

Table 7.6   Effective Teacher Behaviors and Classroom Arrangements
Teacher Behaviors
"Withitness"—knowing what's going on throughout the classroom and indicating, quietly, that you know
Supervising several situations at once
Handling transitions smoothly
Classroom Arrangements
Avoid congestion in "high-traffic" areas
Be sure that furniture, work centers, and desks are arranged so that you can see all students at all times
Organize your teaching materials so they are readily available
Arrange furniture so that you can move easily throughout the room and maintain proximity to students as necessary

Our discussion of classroom management and discipline has been organized around key aspects of the topic, and so you should be able to watch for those elements during visits that you make as part of observations in schools. You could look for examples of what has been discussed in your college classes as well. It is no insult to say that what has been presented here can be seen in class meetings of adult students, for, as is the case with so much of education, the fundamental aspect of teaching is that it is first and foremost an exercise in interpersonal relationships.

■ Noninstructional Tasks and Responsibilities

Our final topic in this chapter about the work of a teacher is addressing the reality of noninstructional tasks. Though these concerns typically do not involve the amount of time and consideration that goes into developing instructional strategies and classroom management plans, they do occupy some of a teacher's time and always come with a measure of responsibility. Some tasks are carried out as part of the classroom routine. Some tasks are within school but in addition to classroom responsibilities. And of course, there's that whole life outside of school!

Outside of the Classroom

The extent of responsibilities that teachers bear outside of the classroom varies from school to school. The school is, however, an organic whole, so teachers must expect to be involved in "the running of the school" beyond the walls of their own classrooms. Many schools require teachers to rotate through a bus-duty schedule in the mornings and afternoons. Elementary school teachers often eat lunch with their classes, and middle and high school teachers usually serve on a rotating schedule of lunch duty.

Teachers are also asked to sponsor clubs and activities that may be conducted during the day or after school. Chaperoning on trips and at social functions is another task. Granted, much of this can be an enjoyable experience (well, maybe not lunch duty), but it has to be remembered that these are still responsibilities. Students enjoy seeing their teachers outside of school, but like it or not, teachers must be aware that they are teachers 24/7/365 in the eyes of their students. This is an exceptional and deeply rewarding responsibility that teachers bear.

Then there are also parent conferences, open house, and PTA or PTO meetings. Parents are a very particular audience indeed. Some will see the teacher as a godsend. Others see the teacher as the source of all the child's difficulties. Yet the teacher must work with all of them in a manner that brings credit to the student, the school, and the profession. Veteran teachers can offer excellent advice about working with and even enlisting the aid of parents. As a pre-service teacher, you would be wise to use your practicum or internship time to seek out some words of wisdom from a number of teachers. Activity 7.5, What Teachers Will Say about Working with Parents, offers you the opportunity to ask several teachers about effective ways to collaborate with parents. Don't be surprised if there is a wide range of views about this among the teachers you interview!

Committee Work

Schools, like most organizations, function by committee. It may not seem that way when a principal lays down the law without discussion. But even so, teachers have many opportunities to work collaboratively with one another. Typically these

ACTIVITY 7.5
What Teachers Will Say about Working with Parents

Teachers vary in their opinions about the amount and type of help they would enjoy from parents. The best way to get a sense for parental collaboration in and out of the classroom is to ask classroom teachers.

1. If you are observing a classroom, ask your cooperating teacher the interview questions listed below. Ask for permission to speak with two other teachers as well. If you do not have access to a classroom, compile the interview questions as a questionnaire (perhaps as a class activity) and ask the principal at a local school to distribute it to 10 teachers.

2. When you have received the responses to your interview/questionnaire, analyze the results for (a) differing perspectives, (b) common trends or themes, and (c) recommendations for having effective collaboration with parents.

The interview questions:
  A. Does the school have a parent involvement program that brings parents into the classroom? If so, could you explain the program? If not, is there a particular reason that the school does not?
  B. In your own classroom, how do you involve parents in the education of your students?
  C. What would you say is (are) the best way(s) that parents can help you accomplish your job as a teacher?
  D. What advice about working with parents would you give to me as a preservice teacher?

opportunities also extend to the district level as well. True instructional leaders will find themselves engaged with committee work on the state level or as members of professional teacher organizations.

Also, many individual schools are moving toward a "site-based" management program. Though the school remains accountable to the local district, much of the day-to-day decision making is left to a council composed of building administrators, teachers, parents, and perhaps college or university educators. These site councils depend to a large degree on the principal's willingness to relinquish a substantial measure of traditional control. However, the empowerment that is afforded to teachers can send a wave of professionalism throughout the school.

Planning for a Substitute Teacher

We've discussed planning quite a bit already, but one aspect we have not discussed is that of preparing for someone else to do the teacher's job, temporarily of course. That is, when that day comes that a teacher is just too sick to come to school (and for teachers this is often a matter of being *really* sick), plans must be in place for someone else to take over. Teachers cannot just call all the parents and cancel school for the day. Plans need to be drawn up, in advance, and materials need to be ready to go. Though this sounds "instructional," it actually contributes to maintaining the flow of your classroom management system.

No doubt you have had a "substitute" or two during your K–12 experience. You know how students typically respond to a substitute. One cannot expect that a stranger can walk into a classroom on short notice and simply pick up where the teacher left off the day before. That's why it is very much a teacher's responsibility to have contingency plans in place when a day simply must be missed. Substitutes have gotten a bad reputation and have suffered a lot of grief because of a teacher's failure to take some time to prepare for being away. Even worse is that in a school year already packed to bursting with instructional objectives, the loss of an entire day or more can be difficult to overcome. All it takes to avoid this is some planning. You could even start right now to develop a dossier of educational activities that can be left ready to use when the time comes that you miss a day of school. Collect these activities over the years (good substitutes and veteran teachers you know will be an excellent source of this information). Organize the ideas and update them, and substitutes will love coming to your class—and of course will lament how rarely the opportunity arises!

It might seem that noninstructional tasks alone could occupy a full work day. The keys are planning and organizing. If you have not already developed the habit of writing down appointments and assignments, now would be a good time to start. Al Devito of Purdue University has said, "The dullest pencil records what the sharpest mind forgets." That's difficult to argue with. If you want to be high-tech about it, use an electronic organizer. In any event, start practicing your organizational skills. That way, everyone can go ahead and believe that you are indeed superhuman, and we'll just keep the secret to ourselves.

 Conclusion

This chapter was intended to give you an honest representation of the breadth of responsibilities that teachers bear. It was our feeling that to scatter the information across several chapters of this book would have obscured the picture and would have made it difficult to truly appreciate all that is expected of classroom teachers. So we presented it to you here, and with this picture in mind you can decide whether or not you feel up to the task and are ready to continue with all that we have yet to consider in this introduction to teaching. If you've been looking for a career that will challenge you each and every day (even when you're away from school), this is it. Your understanding of classroom pragmatics will improve your ability to keep the passion for learning alive and well in your classroom.

Here are some of the major points presented in the chapter:

1. Assessments are used to collect data.
2. Evaluations place value on the data collected.
3. Formative assessments are those inquiries that a teacher makes, either formally or informally, to design, monitor, and modify instruction.
4. Summative assessments are used for assigning grades.
5. Effective teachers develop skills in the design and use both of formative and summative assessments.
6. Classroom management does not just "happen"; a teacher must plan for it.
7. Classroom management is prevention-oriented; discipline focuses on responding to misbehavior.
8. Effective rules represent an agreed-upon code of conduct and are accompanied by consequences that are consistently enforced.
9. Procedures and routines are behaviors that accomplish specific tasks. Procedures typically involve teacher direction. Routines are tasks that students can be expected to accomplish without the teacher prompting the behavior.
10. For students to demonstrate appropriate behavior, they must know what appropriate behavior is from the teacher's perspective and be provided the opportunity to practice and receive feedback from the teacher.

11. Noninstructional tasks include work with children in the classroom, work at school-sponsored events, work away from the typical instructional setting, committee work, instructional planning, and planning for days when the teacher might not be able to come to school.

Key Terms

classroom pragmatics	evaluation	rules
assessment	formative assessment	consequences
standardized testing	summative assessment	procedures
norm group	gain score	routines
normal curve	classroom management	problem-solving
classroom assessment	discipline	conference

Educational Engineering

Case Studies in Education

Enter the information from the table below into the Educational Record for the student you are studying.

	Work Ethic and Emphasis on Grades	Ability to Follow Rules/Procedures	Child's Reaction to Substitute Teachers
Davon	Davon is not a perfectionist but he is very thorough. Has difficulty with fine-motor skills. Is becoming aware of this and is making a conscious effort to develop his writing skills. Spends extra time practicing and compares it to his peers' work.	Davon has difficulty keeping his hands and feet to himself. If he feels threatened or treated unfairly, he reacts with aggressive behavior. Has learned it's not OK to physically touch someone who has upset him. Now upsets peers verbally instead.	As long as he feels important and is given positive attention, Davon complies with new adults in charge.
Andy	Andy cares little about completing assignments on time. He often daydreams or finds other things to occupy him in order to avoid completion of classroom requirements. He does not seem to be concerned about the consequences of receiving poor grades.	Any problem Andy has with classroom rules concerns his off-task behavior. He is not defiant or violent. He simply does not see the value of completing assignments. Neither does he appreciate that he is keeping his classmates from completing theirs.	Andy does not like substitute teachers. While he does not always follow classroom rules, he feels very secure with his regular teachers. His off-task behaviors are magnified when a substitute is in his classroom. His regular classroom teachers are savvy to his behaviors and can help him avoid situations in which he will get in trouble. Substitutes assume his behavior is wanton rather than physiological.
Judith	Works hard but rarely gets "good" grades; neither does she respond negatively to poor grades. By no means a perfectionist, she expects low grades as the norm for her. As long as she remains focused, she does work hard on assigned tasks.	The only difficulty Judith has with class rules is that she wants to interact with other students and the teacher. So, she may speak out of turn. Class rules are part of going to school. A rule such as "Be prepared for class" could be problematic.	Judith does not give the substitute any difficulty on her own. Will innocently inform the teacher that the class is trying to do something inappropriate. When the class reacts negatively she is likely to follow their lead.

(Continued on next page)

Tiffany	Tiffany's parents are concerned that Tiffany is becoming too much of a perfectionist. They report that she is becoming more and more obsessive with assignments and grades and would like suggestions to help her. Tiffany's school experiences have always been positive with perfect grades and perfect attendance.	Tiffany respects the teacher and the classroom rules. She will often police other students when they are not meeting the classroom expectations. Tiffany would never do anything against rules or policies.	Tiffany makes sure substitutes are comfortable in class and helps them throughout the day. Her name is always mentioned in a substitute letter as being very helpful, supportive, and honest.
Sam	When receiving appropriate instruction and special education support, Sam can be successful. He wants to work independently, sometimes to a fault. Teacher monitoring of his work in all class settings is very important.	Sam has no difficulty complying with class rules. He understands what is expected and does not question authority. The fact that he has been relatively successful in school even though he is confronted with severe educational challenges can be partially attributed to his excellent conduct.	When a substitute has responsibility for class, Sam is cooperative and does not take advantage of the situation. He may talk with classmates more than usual but does not act out. Typically, he follows directions and does what is expected of him.
Bao	Bao has perfected the art of working "just hard enough"—she knows how to listen well, realizing that what is needed on assignments can be found in class lectures, discussions, and teacher comments. A strong reader, she has no problems comprehending texts. She struggles when an assignment calls for higher-order thinking skills and then utilizes the teacher or another student. Because of this coping mechanism, Bao has never received a grade below a C; most of her grades are Bs and she is proud of that.	Bao would never consciously choose to disobey a teacher, even if she didn't like the rule. Bao rarely gets reprimanded, but when she does, it is for visiting, or writing and passing notes. She understands the explicit and implicit rules of school very well, and is willing to abide by them to achieve the academic reward of good grades.	Bao follows the lead of the other students in class without ever actually being disobedient. It is doubtful that a guest teacher would even notice Bao's existence. If the class were behaving well, Bao would follow suit; if the class were misbehaving, so would Bao, but in invisible ways, such as writing letters instead of doing her assignments.

1. Is your student one who works hard but still fails or only achieves low grades? If so, what can you do to improve the child's self-esteem other than to raise the grade based on effort? What advice would you give to a parent who sees the child working very hard but not succeeding? What if the parent decides that the problem is your teaching?

2. Does this child have any difficulty following the class rules? If so, what possible causes for the difficulty do you see based on all you know of the child? Are the extenuating circumstances sufficient to allow this child to "bend" the rules? In your opinion, what would be the best way to handle this child's difficulty with the rules?

3. If your student is one who has no difficulty with class rules or procedures, how can you use this to your advantage with the rest of the class? Will you give a good "rule follower" special privileges? Why or why not?

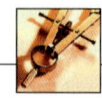 # Designing the School of the Future

The topics discussed in this chapter provide many interesting possibilities for your school of the future. From testing programs to parent involvement, it is all subject to your vision of what is and is not appropriate for a professional educational system. Consider the following sets of questions as part of your classroom pragmatics design efforts.

1. What role will parents have in the school of the future? As the designer, the choice is yours. Do you want parents to be regularly involved? Should some level of involvement be required of all parents? Is their responsibility to the educational process one of supporting the work of the school and assisting their children at home? Do you want them in the classrooms working with the teachers on a day-to-day basis? Will their involvement require special training?

2. Your school of the future is not bound to any testing program in existence today. Therefore, examine some of the issues that cause testing to be so controversial.
   a. Use search terms such as "standardized testing" or "school accountability" to find arguments for and against high-stakes testing programs.
   b. Decide what the testing program of the future should accomplish:
      i. What is the purpose of standardized testing in our school?
      ii. What will be the targets of our testing program (for example, academics, character education, citizenship)?
      iii. How often will students be tested?
      iv. What will the results be used for (for example, graduation, grade placement)?

3. Will your school of the future adopt a single classroom management program for the entire school? If so, where will teachers get their training in the specific program? If teachers have their own systems for classroom management, will they be required to explain that system before being hired in your school? To what degree will students be involved in making the rules in school? If the rules are violated, are there particular consequences that will or will not be allowed in your school? If so, what are they and why are they allowed or not allowed?

Praxis Practice

Many states will require that you successfully complete the Praxis Series of examinations to qualify for certification. One or more of those tests will be subject-area tests. Another, which has a more practical orientation, will be the Principles of Learning and Teaching (PLT) examination that is appropriate for your certification area.

Completing the Quick Check Quizzes for Chapter 7 in the Unit Workshop will give you practice with the multiple choice format of the PLT. The Case Studies in Education and Designing a School of the Future activities will help prepare you for exercises that require reading a scenario and providing short answers to questions asking what you might do in such a situation.

Educational Engineering

The chapters of Unit II discussed three aspects of education that are part of a teacher's everyday life but are not instructional responsibilities. Curriculum along with classroom management and assessment, which we refer to as *classroom pragmatics,* are practical issues with which a teacher needs considerable expertise.

Case Studies

Suppose that you are to have a meeting with the parent(s) of the child you have been studying. This is not a meeting that you have requested because the child has caused some difficulty, but instead is a conference to discuss the educational progress of the student. The information you have gathered thus far may give you some insight with regard to the cooperation you can expect from the parent.

1. Prepare an outline to guide the comments you would want to make. We suggest that you organize it as (a) an introduction during which you mention that it's your pleasure to have the child in class, (b) a discussion of the child's preferences as noted in Chapter 5, and your thoughts about those preferences, (c) the child's experience with standardized tests and classroom assessments, (d) how things are going in terms of classroom management, and (e) your recommendations for how the parent(s) can be involved to ensure a quality educational experience.

2. Either in class or with one of your friends, role-play this scenario (you be the teacher) using the notes you have assembled. Your professor may want to have several of these "meetings" in class, so pay attention to what happens as you watch the other conferences.

3. After your meeting, think about your strengths and weaknesses during the discussion. What will you do differently next time?

Designing the School of the Future

In Chapter 2 you were asked to write a vision statement for your school. That statement was to indicate what your school *aspires* to be or to accomplish. With that statement in mind, now write the *mission statement* for your school. The mission statement, in no more than a paragraph or two, states very clearly "this is what we will do." Eventually, the mission statement can be followed with a lengthy description of the plan for accomplishing that mission. For now, we need a concise statement of what this school will do.

Your mission statement should explain the type of curriculum (Chapter 5) that will be exemplified in this school, and why. It should also state the school's content standards. Your statement does not have to delineate specific instructional outcomes, but you should be able to state which subject areas will be the focus of this school and why. For example, will your school emphasize reading skills because reading is fundamental to all other subject areas? If so, say so. And finally, be sure that your mission statement includes a discussion of how assessment and classroom management will be integrated into this new approach.

It may take a number of drafts to craft a good mission statement. A mission statement should be strong and to the point. Elaboration can be provided in other formats, but the mission statement should clearly set the tone for what is going to be done. We recommend that whether you are working in groups or individually, the mission statement be presented to the class while a work in progress so that you can benefit from other people's reactions and interpretations. The mission statement helps you articulate your thinking so that it is clear to other people.

✔ Quick Check

Answer keys with page references are in Appendix E.

Chapter 5

1. Legislation in the 1950s that led to extensive curriculum changes was known as which of the following?
   a. The Elementary Science Improvement Act
   b. The Elementary and Secondary Education Act
   c. The National Public Education Act
   d. The National Defense Education Act

2. The ancient curriculum known as the quadrivium included which four subjects?
   a. geography, art, music, science
   b. arithmetic, geometry, music, astronomy
   c. reading, writing, arithmetic, science
   d. art, music, physical training, mathematics

3. The text suggests that you conceptualize "curriculum" as which of the following?
   a. an emphasis on outcomes rather than on providing certain experiences
   b. the means and materials with which students interact to achieve identified outcomes
   c. a collection of subjects deemed suitable for exposure to children
   d. an organized effort to pass on the values and beliefs of a given community

4. The authors suggest that it is important for teachers to understand the foundation and structure of curriculum for which of the following reasons?
   a. Understanding curriculum will facilitate effective lesson planning.
   b. Teachers are ultimately responsible for the design of curriculum.
   c. Actually, they just suggest that it's good "background" information to have.
   d. As a teacher you represent the curriculum in the eyes of the community.

5. A curriculum concerned with the subjects that will be taught, the identified mission of the school, and the knowledge and skills students are expected to require is referred to as which of the following?
   a. explicit curriculum
   b. extra-curriculum
   c. implicit curriculum
   d. null curriculum

6. Which of the following curriculum types refers to the lessons that arise from the culture of the school and the behaviors, attitudes, and expectations that characterize that culture?
   a. explicit curriculum
   b. extra-curriculum
   c. implicit curriculum
   d. null curriculum

7. Which of the following curriculum types refers to the options students do not get to choose, the ideas and perspectives that are not introduced, and the skills and concepts that are not presented to them?
   a. explicit curriculum
   b. extra-curriculum
   c. implicit curriculum
   d. null curriculum

8. Which of the following curricula represents a variation of the cognitive perspective that emphasizes the acquisition of a particular body of knowledge?
   a. core
   b. student-centered
   c. subject-centered
   d. explicit

9. The text suggests that which of the following is an obstacle to the mastery learning approach?
   a. Not all students can master a subject.
   b. Elementary teachers have broad-based knowledge rather than master-based knowledge.
   c. The subject-centered curriculum tends to keep all students moving at the same rate.
   d. Schools are not provided with sufficient materials to allow all children to learn to mastery.

Chapter 6

1. Though parents can have a profound effect on the curriculum of a school, one drawback to their influence is which of the following?
   a. They have a vested interest in the education of children.
   b. Parents can have first-hand knowledge of what is taught in the local schools.
   c. Their interests tend to center around just the years that their children are in school.
   d. Their taxes are what keep the schools going.

2. Which of the following represents a vital aspect of the work of Parent Teacher Associations (PTAs)?
   a. They provide the opportunity for great numbers of parents to speak with a unified voice.
   b. They regulate the hiring and firing of teachers.
   c. Referendums can be cleared through them before being presented to the public at large.
   d. By law they occupy one seat on all boards of education.

3. That political administrations serve "at the pleasure of the voters" results in which of the following?
   a. consistency of educational funding from one administration to the next
   b. that a child in kindergarten under one administration will most likely graduate from high school under a different administration
   c. that the school curriculum must be changed with each change of administrations
   d. school boards of education must have new elections with changes of administrations

4. The faculty of a particular school can affect the curriculum in which of the following ways?
   a. Characteristics that define the faculty of a school will also define the curriculum that is presented.
   b. It is the faculty's option to choose which portions of the curriculum to teach.

10. Character education is most closely related to which of the following curriculum perspectives?
   a. broad-fields curriculum
   b. cooperative learning
   c. activity curriculum
   d. humanistic education

   c. All curriculum is unaffected by faculty strengths and weaknesses because certification programs require that all teachers teach in the same way.
   d. The faculty members at each school are responsible for writing the curriculum.

5. Which of the following supports the argument that teacher-designed tests can offer the best picture of student achievement?
   a. Teacher-designed tests mirror standardized tests.
   b. The results of teacher-designed tests can be used to compare one class to another.
   c. They are less expensive to design and administer.
   d. Such tests are tailored to the actual students in the class and the actual learning experiences provided.

6. The text suggests that which of the following may be an effect of e-publishing?
   a. fewer publishers, more consistent textbooks
   b. greater "nationalization" of the curriculum because of the ease of publication
   c. states choosing their own curricula with little influence from other states
   d. drastic reduction in the cost of textbooks

7. States that review textbooks and select those from which school districts may choose are known as:
   a. review states
   b. curriculum assessment states
   c. adoption states
   d. selection states

8. The tension between forces that advocate state control of education and those that advocate a national orientation has resulted in which of the following?
   a. a lack of national cohesiveness accompanied by a significant degree of "sameness"
   b. the desire for states to band together to build regional "super curricula"
   c. efforts by the federal government to regulate curriculum
   d. the emergence of privately developed "canned" curricula

9. The development of national educational standards has been spearheaded by which of the following?
   a. state legislatures
   b. state education agencies
   c. learned and professional organizations
   d. the federal government

10. How many subjects are included as the basis for contemporary curriculum design?
    a. 10
    b. 8
    c. 6
    d. 4

Chapter 7

1. "Classroom pragmatics" refers to which of the following?
   a. design of lesson plans
   b. time spent in observations and student teaching to "practice" teaching
   c. practical concerns that are noninstructional responsibilities of the teacher
   d. hands-on activities that are designed to involve students in learning

2. How did the text define "assessment"?
   a. the means by which information is gathered to make a variety of decisions
   b. providing students with grades to reflect their performance
   c. review of instructional plans prior to implementation
   d. district-based systems for evaluating teacher performance

3. In standardized testing, what is the function of the "norm group"?
   a. to review the content of the test prior to administration to other students
   b. to set a standard for the test based on a representative population of test-takers
   c. to grade the test by following the "normal procedures" set for that test
   d. to see that the test is administered under consistent conditions and restrictions

4. A formative test differs from a summative test in which of the following ways?
   a. Formative tests determine whether a child advances to the next grade level.
   b. Formative tests are formal (such as written tests); summative tests are informal.
   c. Summative tests take longer to administer.
   d. The instructor does not intend to reteach based upon results of a summative test.

5. Which of the following represents a student's progress as opposed to the meeting of objectives?
   a. standardized scores
   b. gain scores
   c. summative assessment
   d. grade inflation

6. Those activities in which a teacher engages before, during, and after interacting with students to allow instruction to take place are known as:
   a. classroom management
   b. discipline
   c. assessment
   d. planning

7. According to the Research and Development Center for Teacher Education, effective classroom managers are nearly always good at which of the following?
   a. managing people
   b. enforcing rules
   c. planning
   d. evaluation

8. According to Borich (1996), failure to enforce classroom rules consistently can cause a teacher to lose which of the following?
   a. valuable instructional time
   b. sleep
   c. student achievement
   d. prestige and respect

9. Which of the following is *not* one of the underlying themes of classroom management discussed in the text?
   a. collaborating with other teachers to develop your own classroom rules
   b. communicating expectations to the students
   c. involving students in development of class rules and consequences
   d. ensuring that the rules represent positive behaviors leading to positive self-esteem

10. When responding to inappropriate behavior it is important for a teacher to do which of the following?
    a. establish who is the authority in the classroom
    b. focus on the behavior, not the person
    c. allow the student ample opportunity to explain his or her perspective immediately
    d. establish a consensus among the student's classmates

The Institution of Education

The chapters of Unit III are concerned with what is often referred to as the foundations of education. This section includes the history of education, philosophy, and governance and law.

Chapter 8, History of American Education, provides you with an overview of formal education from the ancient Greek civilizations to contemporary times. You may be surprised to find how little has changed even with the developments in education.

Chapter 9, Philosophy and Education, discusses the philosophical influences that have been brought to education throughout the centuries. In Chapter 1 we asked you to consider your personal philosophy of education. In Chapter 9 we take a much broader view as we consider how philosophy underlies the institution of education.

Chapter 10, Ethics in Education and Matters of Law, addresses your own code of ethics as an individual and as a teacher. From ethics we move to a discussion of teachers' and students' rights under the law. Finally, we examine legislative acts that have very definite implications for your work as a teacher.

Chapter 11, Education: Purpose, Organization, Governance, and Funding, discusses the many stakeholders who influence the institution of education and the sources of revenue that make it all possible. From the constitutional assignment of education as a state's responsibility to the impact of local citizens in the functioning of school, education is tightly woven into the fabric of our society.

8

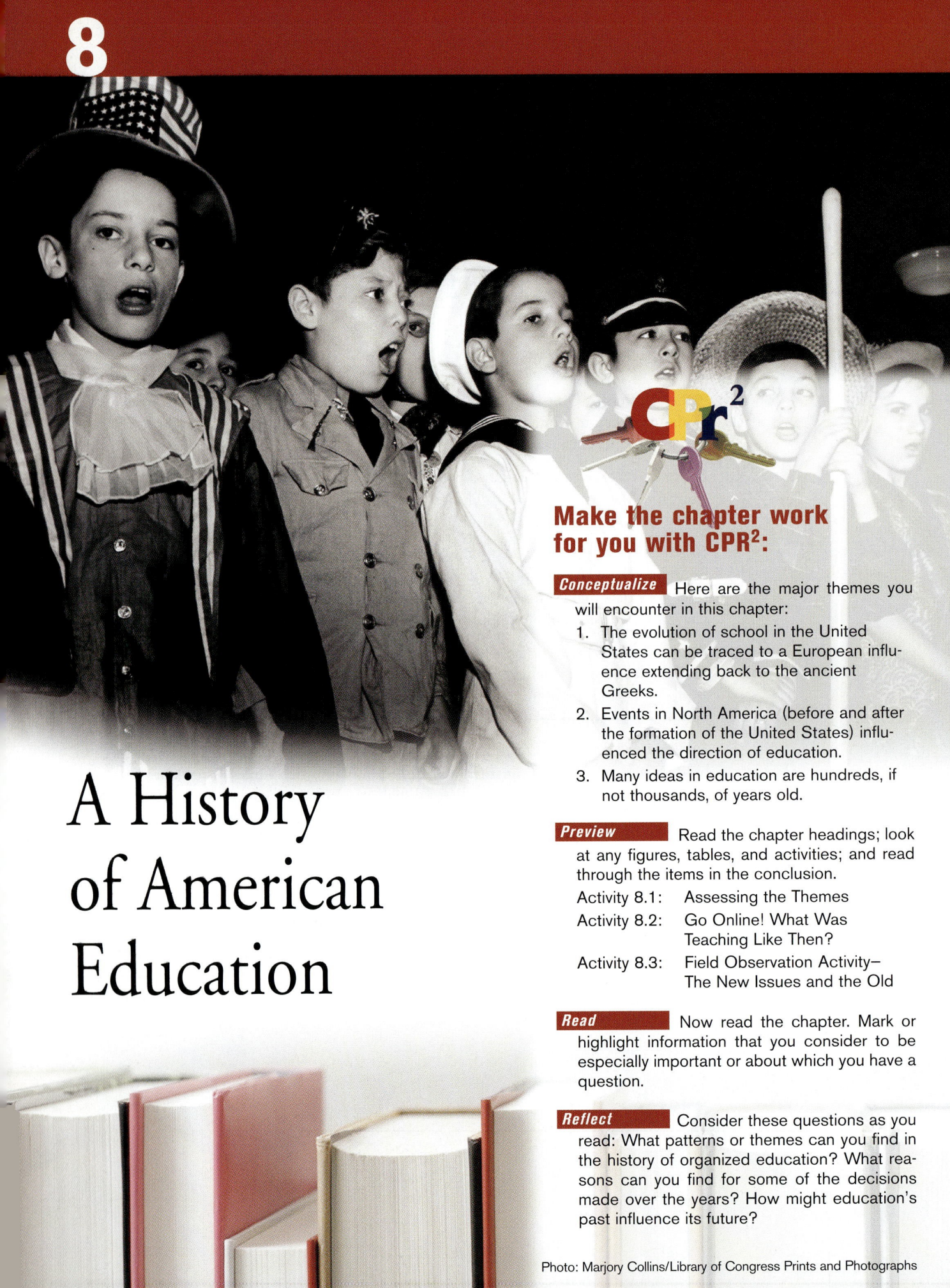

A History of American Education

Make the chapter work for you with CPR²:

Conceptualize Here are the major themes you will encounter in this chapter:

1. The evolution of school in the United States can be traced to a European influence extending back to the ancient Greeks.
2. Events in North America (before and after the formation of the United States) influenced the direction of education.
3. Many ideas in education are hundreds, if not thousands, of years old.

Preview Read the chapter headings; look at any figures, tables, and activities; and read through the items in the conclusion.

Activity 8.1: Assessing the Themes
Activity 8.2: Go Online! What Was Teaching Like Then?
Activity 8.3: Field Observation Activity– The New Issues and the Old

Read Now read the chapter. Mark or highlight information that you consider to be especially important or about which you have a question.

Reflect Consider these questions as you read: What patterns or themes can you find in the history of organized education? What reasons can you find for some of the decisions made over the years? How might education's past influence its future?

The following standards from the Interstate New Teacher Assessment and Support Consortium (INTASC) will be addressed in this chapter. As you read the chapter, consider how events in the history of American education are tied to these principles.

Principle 3 The teacher understands how students differ in their approaches to learning and creates instructional opportunities that are adapted to diverse learners.

Principle 5 The teacher uses an understanding of individual and group motivation and behavior to create a learning environment that encourages positive social interaction, active engagement in learning, and self-motivation.

ice breakers

Meet the Folks!

In this chapter you will be introduced to many of the people who have had a profound impact on education. Below is a "group photo" of some of them. Beneath the photo is a list of accomplishments attributed to these folks. Who do you suppose matches with each?

1. Famed for his questioning techniques and the admonishment, "Know thyself!"
2. Brought the idea of "a garden where children can learn" to the United States.
3. Championed the notion of public schools for all children and "normal schools" for the education of teachers.
4. A believer in the power of great literature to transcend time.
5. Operated a school for African American girls in the 1800s (and was persecuted for doing so).
6. A pragmatist philosopher whose work led to the Progressivist movement in education.
7. Campaigned for the education of the "Talented Tenth" of African Americans who would become business and political leaders.
8. Opened the first kindergarten in the United States.
9. Recognized that children's play is actually a sophisticated form of learning.
10. Among the first in the United States to suggest that education should be provided at public expense to all children.
11. Pioneering principal in an African American normal school, the Tuskegee Institute in Alabama.
12. Introduced the first American spelling book.

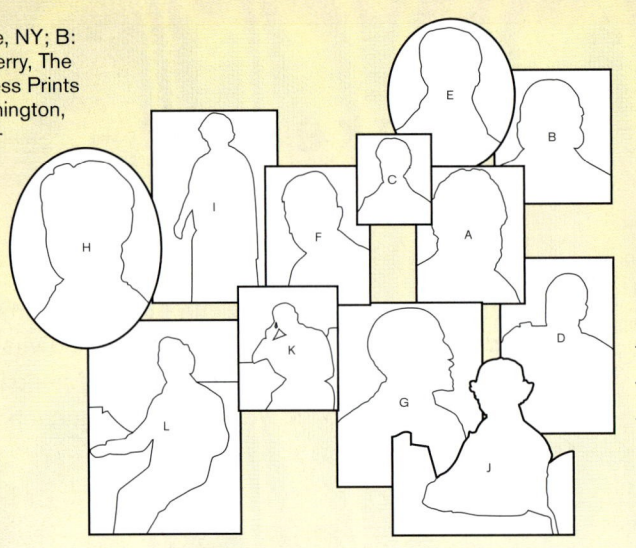

1. A: Socrates
2. B: Friedrich Froebel
3. C: Horace Mann
4. D: Robert Maynard Hutchins
5. E: Prudence Crandall
6. F: John Dewey
7. G: W. E. B. DuBois
8. H: Margarethe Schurz
9. I: Maria Montessori
10. J: Thomas Jefferson
11. K: Booker T. Washington
12. L: Noah Webster

> *And what is history but a fable agreed upon.*
>
> *Napoleon*

Introduction

Napoleon's observation is important because it exposes the fact that history is merely what we make of it. For instance, the history of any war is told differently from the perspective of the victor than from the perspective of the vanquished. Same war, two perspectives. We mention this because we want you to approach this chapter with a different perspective from the one you might typically bring to a history lesson. That is, rather than simply reading another recounting of selected events and the description of various key figures in the progress of education, we want you to see how dynamic events in their own time contribute to the dynamic nature of education today. So as you study the people and events that have molded contemporary education, ask yourself what lessons we have learned and what lessons we seem to have difficulty learning.

The Emerging Need for Education

Even with a history dating back nearly 400 years to Colonial America, the truth is that education has been a pretty hot topic for well over 2,000 years. It was of considerable importance even before that in ancient Egypt and China, but it was the influence from ancient Greece that laid the foundation for education as we know it today. Our look at the pre-Colonial development of education will focus on the ancient Greeks, then the Romans, and finally the several periods within the Middle Ages. Strange as it may seem, issues of curriculum and equal access to education that we know of today were evident thousands of years ago as well.

The Ancient Greeks

Organized educational efforts in ancient Greece were developed under the separate influences of each city-state. Chief among these were the cities of Sparta and Athens. Sparta emphasized an education that prepared young men to be warriors;

physical strength, obedience to authority, and an ability to endure hardship were key attributes. Athens centered educational efforts around intellectual concerns. The program, however, was specifically provided to Athenian boys and was not provided to girls, slaves, or noncitizens. If Athenian girls were to receive an education at all, they received it at home.

Athenian boys attended a series of schools in which they received education in grammar, reading, writing, basic computation, gymnastics, and music. Included with music were history, drama, poetry, science, and speaking. The Athenians believed that as grammar, reading, and writing laid the foundation for intellectual development, music laid the foundation for aesthetic appreciation (that is, the appreciation of beauty). From the ages of 16 to 20, young men received training for citizenship and military service. As you can see, the basic curriculum in ancient Greece was not much different from what may have been available in your own high school—right down to the military training (if your high school had a Junior ROTC program).

During the fifth century BC, as Athens grew and became more commercially oriented, a group of teachers known as the **Sophists** emerged. These individuals were not tied to any one school but instead wandered about teaching rhetoric and oratory to whoever had the funds to meet the tuition. That which we know of today as the *liberal arts* was founded in the Sophists' curriculum of grammar, logic, and rhetoric.

Perhaps the most accomplished of the Sophists was Protagoras (485–415 BC), who developed an instructional method that survives today. Protagoras employed a five-step approach to the teaching of his students: (1) as a model of good speaking, he would first deliver a speech; (2) the students would then study the great speeches of other speakers; (3) students would specifically study rhetoric, logic, and grammar; (4) they would then develop and deliver orations of their own that Protagoras would critique; and finally (5) they would present orations in public. Does this format sound familiar to you?

The Influence of Socrates, Plato, and Aristotle

The development of education from the middle of the fifth and down to the fourth century BC is peculiar in that three individuals—Socrates; Plato, who was Socrates' student; and Aristotle, who was Plato's student—were all from the same locale and contributed work that has influenced educational and philosophical thought for literally thousands of years. Some of the points on which they disagreed remain as points of debate today. For example, Plato favored schooling for all children (free children, that is) while Aristotle saw no need in educating girls.

Socrates (469–399 BC) did not agree with the Sophists' emphasis on education as an exercise in business-skills training. As an idealist, Socrates believed that people must question and examine their own knowledge in order to discover universal principles of truth and of beauty. He believed that universal ideas are not something to be learned or found somewhere else; they exist *within* us and must be drawn out. He sought to facilitate such understanding by carefully questioning his students that they might draw out the knowledge within. This form of questioning is what we refer to today as the Socratic method.

Plato (427–346 BC) chronicled Socrates' teachings and shared his idealist philosophy. A teacher, Plato founded a school known as the **Academy.** Plato wrote extensively, particularly in the form of dialogues in which Socrates was the primary character. Among his many works was *The Republic,* in which he outlined the design and function of a city-state based on the idea that the most intellectually accomplished should lead the society.

Sophists Ancient Greek teachers with a wide range of expertise in many fields who taught rhetoric and oratory.

Academy The Greek school established by Plato. The term is often used to refer to a liberal arts college.

© Scala/Art Resource, NY

Plato.

Lyceum The Greek school founded by Aristotle that emphasized rational thinking for good citizenship.

Plato's *Republic* had a number of visionary elements in an educational sense. For example, Plato believed each citizen within the republic should serve the society based on his or her particular abilities. A system of organized education would provide the means by which individuals sought and found their place in society. Those with an athletic prowess became the soldiers and guardians while others took jobs as laborers, with still others becoming clerks and administrators. Others progressed further and further, studying increasingly more philosophical and mathematical subjects until eventually one individual—presumably the most intellectually capable—rose to the top and, around the age of 50, became the "philosopher-king."

Under this system education was to be open to all free citizens, male or female. In fact, should a woman rise to the highest level and become the leader of the society, so be it. As you might expect, this was contrary to popular Athenian opinion, and the cause of education for women—as we will see—remained a struggle for thousands of years (and remains so today in many societies).

Aristotle (384–322 BC) was Plato's student. Aristotle wrote prolifically on a wide variety of topics from philosophy to ethics to science, and also was a teacher and founder of a school, the **Lyceum.** Adopting a realist philosophy that sought the same truth Plato did, though through a study of the real world, Aristotle suggested that the state was best served by citizens capable of rational thinking. He believed that women were intellectually inferior to men, and so the liberal education that he advocated was directed toward boys as they grew to become rational men. Women would get their education, of a domestic sort, at home.

The Ancient Romans

In the last century BC and the first two centuries AD, Greek views on philosophy and education spread to the western Mediterranean with the rise of the Roman empire. The Romans focused their system of education on the development of the practical intellectual skills that would benefit the empire in political, military, and administrative tasks. Again, education was for boys, but the Romans did succeed in the development of entire *systems* of education.

The most esteemed of the Roman educators at this time was Quintilian (AD 35–95). In his *Institutio Oratoria,* he described the theory and practice of education at the time and made recommendations for the development of Roman education. He suggested three components for an educational system: (1) the preparation to study rhetoric, (2) the study of rhetoric and educational theory, and (3) public speaking.

Quintilian suggested that birth to age seven was a time when children were concerned with their immediate needs and interests, and so he advised that parents be careful in selecting those individuals who would interact with the child. For example, the nurses who cared for the child and the **pedagogues** who escorted the child to school should be carefully chosen as their conversations with the child would affect the child's development of language.

pedagogue Literally, the Greek adult who led a child to school, discussing important issues (and thus tutoring) the child on the way. In colonial days the term was used to refer to a teacher.

From age seven to age 14, Quintilian said, the child should learn to write the language that he spoke. Writing would hone his mind to think clearly and improve his memory. He would gather information from his sensory experiences and would be influenced by the character and competence of his teachers at the ludus (school).

In Their Own Words

Feature 8.1   Aristotle

This passage from Aristotle's work Politics *describes the sort of curriculum that would be appropriate for the development of "correct thinking." You may find similarities not only to the curriculum we now know but also to the appropriate ages for formal education and the purposes of that education.*

There are two periods of life into which education has to be divided, from seven to the age of puberty, and onward to the age of one and twenty. [The Poets] who divide the ages by sevens are not always right: we should rather adhere to the divisions actually made by nature; for the deficiencies of nature are what art and education seek to fill up.

That education should be regulated by law and should be an affair of state is not to be denied, but what should be the character of this public education and how young persons should be educated are questions which remain to be considered. For mankind are by no means agreed about the things to be taught, whether we look to virtue or the best life. Neither is it clear whether education is more concerned with intellectual or with moral virtue. The existing practice is perplexing; no one knows on what principle we should proceed—should the useful in life, or should virtue, or should the higher knowledge, be the aim of our training; all three opinions have been entertained. Again, about the means there is no agreement; for different persons, starting with different ideas about the nature of virtue, naturally disagree about the practice of it. There can be no doubt that children should be taught those useful things which are really necessary, but not all things; for occupations are divided into liberal and illiberal; and to young children should be imparted only such kinds of knowledge as will be useful to them without vulgarizing them.

The customary branches of education are four in number: (1) reading and writing, (2) gymnastic exercises, (3) music, to which is sometimes added (4) drawing. Of these, reading and writing and drawing are regarded as useful for the purposes of life in a variety of ways, and gymnastic exercises are thought to infuse courage. Concerning music a doubt may be raised—in our own day most men cultivate it for the sake of pleasure, but originally it was included in education, because nature herself, as has been often said, requires that we should be able, not only to work well, but to use leisure well; for, as I must repeat once and again, the first principle of all action is leisure. Both are required, but leisure is better than occupation; and therefore the question must be asked in good earnest, what ought we to do when at leisure?

It would therefore be best that the state pay attention to education, and on right principles, and that it should have power to enforce it, but, if neglected as a public measure, it would seem to be the duty of every individual to contribute to the virtue of his children and friends, or at least to make this his deliberate purpose. ■

From age 14 to age 17, education would revolve around the liberal arts as the young man studied Greek and Latin grammar, literature, history, mythology, music, geometry, astronomy, and gymnastics. Education would be conducted in both languages, and an appreciation of both cultures would be included in the exercise. Rhetorical studies were taken on from age 17 to age 21. A system of education was emerging.

Of course, the Romans were not the only people emphasizing education in the first several centuries AD. The Talmud represents the collective thought and wisdom of the Hebrew people spanning the thousand years between 500 BC and AD 500. Written over the three centuries between AD 200 and 500, it contains numerous references to the education of children. Some passages refer to the consequences for failing to value education, such as "Jerusalem was destroyed only because scholars were despised therein" (Shabbath 119b, R. Hamnuna). Other passages provide suggestions for education. For example, "They therefore ordained that teachers should be appointed in each prefecture and that boys should enter school at the age of sixteen or seventeen . . . and they used to rebel and leave the school. . . . At length Joshua ben Gamala came and ordained that teachers of young children should be appointed in each district and each town, and that children should enter school at age six or seven" (Baba Bathra, 21a). As we shall see, this is only the beginning of the influence of religion in education.

The European Middle Ages

In the 10 centuries between the rise of the Greek influence on philosophy and intellect through to the fall of the Roman empire (AD 476), a system of education became entrenched in terms of both its value to a civilized society and the basic curriculum that was offered. Though formal education was for men, and "free" men at that, strides had nonetheless been made in the theory and practice of teaching and learning. With the fall of the Roman empire, a new influence began to control education, and that influence has had a strong impact on education ever since. The influence: religion in general, and the Roman Catholic Church of the Middle Ages in particular.

The medieval period, the Middle Ages, spanned from approximately AD 500 to 1400. During this time the Church exercised virtually complete control over government and education. In fact, the control was so great and the educational opportunities to the general public so restricted that during the period from approximately AD 400 through 1000—*six centuries*—education and intellectual development regressed to the point that this time has become known as the Dark Ages. During the Dark Ages free thought and intellectual inquiry itself, anything that could question the doctrine and dogma of the Church, was stifled. Education was reserved for young men who would enter some sort of religious vocation.

In the late eighth century AD, the Roman emperor Charlemagne sought someone to improve the condition of education. His selection was Alcuin (735–804), who became Charlemagne's educational advisor. It was during Alcuin's time that the liberal arts we have mentioned became codified as "the seven liberal arts." They could be divided into two groups: the *trivium,* consisting of grammar, rhetoric, and logic, and the *quadrivium,* consisting of arithmetic, geometry, music, and astronomy.

scholasticism The religious-philosophical study resulting from the rediscovery in the 11th century of Aristotle's works.

Fueled by the rediscovery of the works of Aristotle, a new form of religious-philosophical study, **scholasticism,** emerged in the 11th century. Scholasticism increased interest in education, and as a result the number of universities increased. Many of today's institutions of higher education are modeled after medieval universities such as the University of Bologna (founded in 1158), the University of Paris (1180), Oxford University (1214), and the University of Salerno (1224). In addition, craft schools began to emerge, providing training in specific trades. Education for the many was being reborn.

Saint Thomas Aquinas (1225–1274) reconciled scholasticism into a workable system that harmonized scriptural faith with rationalism as articulated by Aristotle. Aquinas's major work, *Summa Theologica,* provided the foundation for what is referred to as Thomism, a Christian religious sect endorsed by the Catholic church. As an educator, Aquinas believed that teachers must possess several characteristics in particular; they must be skillful in instruction, of course, but also be experts and scholars in their fields and possess a love for humanity. Would you say that this still holds true?

The Renaissance and Humanism

The Western world moved into a period known as the Renaissance during the fourteenth and fifteenth centuries. This transitional period between the Middle Ages and the modern age was marked by the evolution of classical **humanism,** with its literature-based emphasis on human virtue. Desiderius Erasmus (1466–1536) brought a humanist perspective to education in his works *The Right Method of Instruction* and *The Liberal Education of Boys.* Though the humanist movement was not sufficient to overthrow the authority of the church in society, it was sufficient to lay the foundation for the Reformation that was about to follow, led by individuals such as John Calvin and Martin Luther.

humanism A philosophy that emphasizes the value and meaning of education rather than the mere dissemination and acquisition of facts.

ACTIVITY 8.1
Assessing the Themes

Some of the major themes in education from the fifth century BC to the beginning of the 1600s are evident in the structure and curriculum that you have experienced. Consider each of the following questions:

1. What elements of the seven liberal arts can you find either in the high school curriculum you followed or in the program of study you intend to follow in college?

2. Have you ever felt that a formal education (that is, an organized system of education such as our K–12 and college levels of education) was being denied to some people and provided to others? What examples can you find from the pre-1600 history of education to explain that situation?

3. What would you consider to be the strengths and weaknesses of the educational foundation established prior to American education in the 1600s?

vernacular schools Schools established by Protestants. These schools used the common language rather than Latin for instruction.

As variations of the Christian faith developed, so did diverse perspectives on the purpose of education, the components of the curriculum, and even the language in which school would be conducted. Protestants established **vernacular schools,** in which Latin was no longer the language of instruction. Though the Catholic church did not turn away from conducting Mass in Latin, eventually they, too, began to teach school in the vernacular languages, thus making education available to more children.

We can see that a significant shift had occurred in education. Some of the issues were still the same (see Activity 8.1), such as education for girls and for the disenfranchised members of society, but it was the religious division between Catholic and Protestant that had tensions running high. Education had become a tool as much for submission (that is, by keeping most people uneducated) as it was of enlightenment. As the 17th century dawned, some groups looked for another place to be. That other place was across an ocean, in America.

■ Education in America

Each of the four centuries of education in America can be considered in light of the social struggles during that period. In the 1600s the struggle was between an emerging social order and a frontier territory. During the 1700s the newly established society sought to declare its autonomy from England and embrace its own sovereignty. The growing pains of a new nation were evident in the 1800s as countrymen fought countrymen in the Civil War. The 1900s saw a nation that had become so strong that it influenced world events both in peace and in war. Across the centuries the evolution of our formal educational system has been intimately tied to those themes. As you consider our educational history, you might ask yourself what theme will emerge from the 21st century.

The New World (1600s)

The Protestant settlers of New England, the Pilgrims, arrived 13 years after the first permanent English settlement in America was settled (Jamestown, Virginia, 1607) and a year *after* black slaves were first brought to the colonies (1619). The Pilgrims, too, were supposed to have settled at Jamestown. Bad weather and navigational errors during their voyage to the new world resulted in their landing in what is now Provincetown, Massachusetts, in November of 1620. The idea of establishing their own colony was not completely abhorrent to them (which, after two months at sea, doesn't seem surprising), and so after drafting and signing the Mayflower Compact—the first democratic constitution in America—41 men along with 60 women and children disembarked one month later across the bay at what became Plymouth, Massachusetts.

Religion and Education in the New World

When formal education in the "new world" began to take shape, the curriculum was pretty well set: Schooling taught children (especially boys) to read, and the textbook was the Bible. Proper conduct and religious devotion were the lessons to be learned. The Puritan view that people are inherently sinful made a religiously oriented education imperative so that the community might survive the hardships it faced. Yet this was also a time punctuated with "reforms" that were practical for the time and were visionary for the future of education. The public funding of school and the enactment of laws requiring the compulsory education of children provide two examples.

The notion that the Pilgrims simply wanted people to be free to worship without persecution is not completely accurate. Indeed, religious freedom was their aim, but it was freedom from the Church of England. The Puritans established their new religion in America with no intention of tolerating *other* spiritual views. It was the Puritan way or no way, and persecution at the hands of the Puritans was harsh. The result was the development of many school systems throughout the colonies—some more or less secular (that is, not connected with a church) and others that were markedly denominational.

The Beginning of Secular Education

dame schools Colonial schools typically run by educated widows or housewives in their own homes for a fee. They provided initial academic instruction for boys, particularly those from the middle and upper classes.

Latin Grammar Schools The forerunners to what we now consider "high school," they were patterned after schools in Europe and prepared students to enter divinity schools.

Providing a basic education for children was at first a parental task. However, as communities grew, schooling became more organized. **Dame schools,** typically run by educated widows or housewives in their own homes for a fee, provided initial academic instruction for boys, particularly those from the middle and upper classes. Girls who received some instruction typically learned household skills such as cooking and sewing. Children from poorer families were often apprenticed to tradesmen or indentured, in which case the masters were responsible for their education.

Academically capable children of the wealthy went on to attend **Latin Grammar Schools,** the first one in America being the Boston Latin Grammar School, founded in 1635. The forerunner to what we now consider "high school," Latin Grammar Schools were patterned after schools in Europe and prepared students to enter divinity school. In America, the first such school was Harvard College, established in 1636.

Education Becomes a Matter of Law

Some 2,000 years earlier Plato had suggested that parents are not necessarily the best teachers for their children, and the Puritans apparently had some concerns as well. In Massachusetts the first education law was passed as early as 1642. You might think of it as the first "accountability" initiative as it called for periodic checks to be certain that children were learning to read, write, and understand scriptural lessons. When the education of children was found to be deficient, the parents or masters of those children could be fined or lose custody of the children. The first accountability laws held the *parents* responsible!

compulsory education A requirement that parents enroll and send their children to school. In America it dates to the Massachusetts Act of 1642.

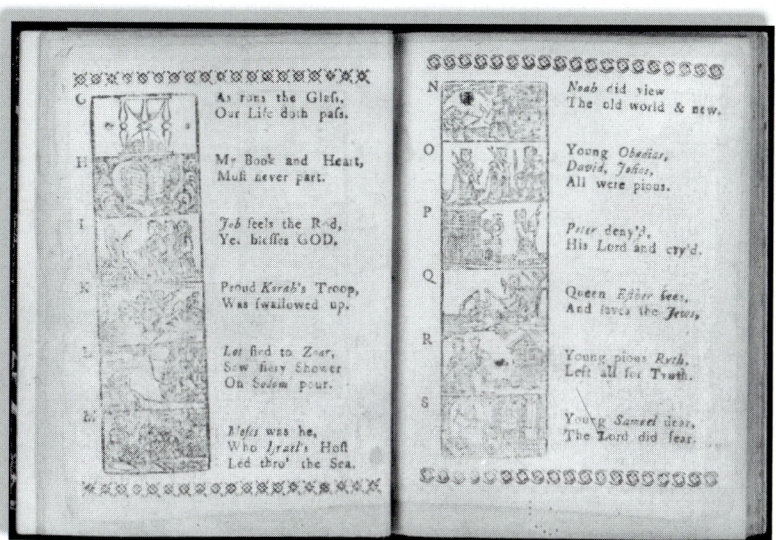

Library of Congress Prints and Photographs Division, Washington, DC

Pages from the *New England Primer.*

hornbook A copy of the alphabet laminated onto a paddle-shaped piece of wood using a thin transparent sheet made from a cow's horn.

New England Primer An illustrated textbook that offered religious readings. Originally published in 1690, the *New England Primer* was the mainstay of colonial education for more than 100 years.

parochial schools Schools affiliated with some religious group. They originally were established by churches such as Baptist, Catholic, Mennonite, and Quaker.

private venture schools Schools established with private rather than public funds. They include parochial schools as well as non-denominational private schools.

vocational training Training as preparation to enter the world of work in some trade (e.g., as a carpenter, electrician, mason, mechanic).

More than just a matter of accountability, the Massachusetts Act of 1642 led the way for what would become **compulsory education.** Prior to that time, parents had been able to choose whether to send their children to school or to educate them themselves. But now the need for an organized system of education was becoming evident. Five years later the Massachusetts Act of 1647—also known as The Old Deluder Satan Act—required every town of 50 or more households to establish a school and hire a teacher, so that children would be educated to resist the temptations of Satan. Towns of 100 or more households were also required to establish a Latin Grammar School to prepare students for university study. Education was beginning to come of age a mere 27 years after the establishment of the Massachusetts colony. The emphasis was clearly for religious purposes; to avoid the temptations of that Old Deluder Satan, it was imperative that children be able to read and write.

Boys (and some girls) entered this educational environment around the age of six or seven and learned the alphabet, numerals, and the Lord's prayer. Unfortunately, schools did not have the compassion and sensitivity toward the needs of children that had been suggested hundreds of years earlier in ancient Rome. Instead, schools tended to be grim and strictly disciplined places. Rather than emphasizing a broadening of the mind, organized education focused on memorization and obedience.

Other than the Bible, the textbook in early colonial elementary schools was the **hornbook.** This consisted of a copy of the alphabet laminated onto a paddle-shaped piece of wood using a thin transparent sheet made from a cow's horn. Having learned the basics, students progressed to the ***New England Primer,*** an illustrated textbook that offered religious readings. Originally published in 1690, the *New England Primer* was the mainstay of education for more than 100 years. For many children these three or four years of elementary education constituted their entire formal schooling.

Regional Differences in Education Begin to Emerge

Though we tend to think of 17th-century America as "the colonies," a unified group, significant regional differences began to emerge. The New England colonies were closely contained and under the strict influence of the Puritans. They understandably grew into communities that reflected a singular religious orientation both in its culture and within its schools.

The middle colonies (New York, New Jersey, Pennsylvania, and Delaware) were far more diverse in ethnicity and religious denominations, and their communities emphasized commerce and the skills needed to conduct business. Immigrants of Dutch, Irish, German, and Swedish descent wanted their children educated in keeping with their own beliefs. Quakers, Catholics, Baptists, Mennonites, and others established their own **parochial schools.** These church-affiliated schools were licensed by the government as **private venture schools,** but they did not receive public funding. The growing mercantile influence of the region further gave rise to private schools that specialized in **vocational training.**

In the relatively rural southern colonies (Virginia, Maryland, North Carolina, South Carolina, and Georgia), wealthy settlers established large plantations that

Figure 8.1

Significant People and Events
of the 1600s

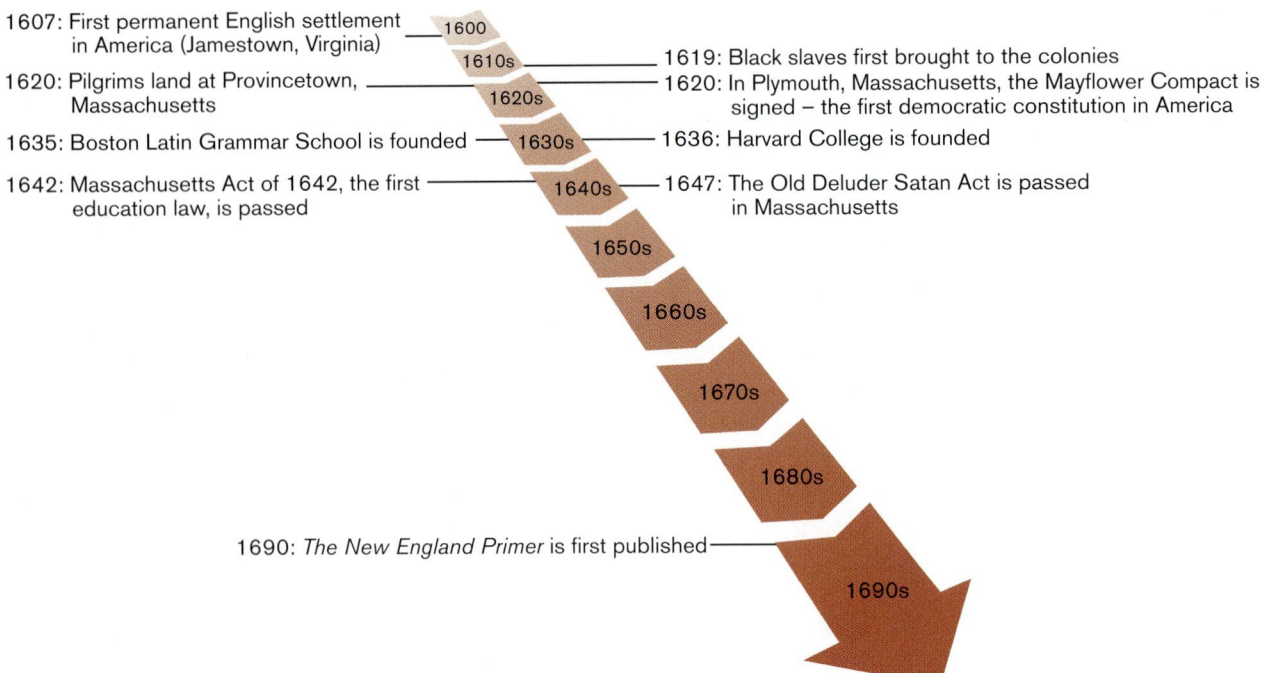

were a stark contrast to the close-knit communities of New England. Community schools were not favored over the practice of private tutors brought to the homes of the students. Though the emphasis on education in the South was to promote religion and also to prepare students to attend a university, the goal was typically to send sons to universities in Europe.

The educational fate of women remained essentially the same as we have seen all along. Girls in wealthy families might receive a basic education, but the focus was clearly on fostering their abilities to accomplish their social responsibilities. As for poor white children, their education was largely a matter of home instruction that addressed reading, writing, and basic computation. Native Americans and African Americans were specifically denied schooling. Black children in the South found themselves barred from education by law. Eventually, some schools were established for these populations by religious groups such as the Quakers. As we will see, educational opportunities for African Americans also came about in the 1700s under the sponsorship of none other than the Church of England. Figure 8.1 summarizes the significant people and events of the 1600s that we have discussed.

The New Nation (1700s)

By the 1700s, surviving in the American territory had given way to growing the colonial economy. The colonies were now a network of functioning towns, cities, and states. Though the influence of religion continued, the school curriculum began to feel the pressures for offering a more practical education. Particularly in the middle colonies, rapid growth in middle-class businesses built the need for a secondary education system that would provide young men with business-oriented skills. Job training and night schools offering everything from bookkeeping to foreign languages began to emerge.

Secondary Schools Evolve

English Grammar Schools As a response and alternative to the Latin Grammar School, these secondary schools emphasized a practical education with classes conducted in English rather than in Latin. Some English Grammar Schools admitted females.

A new sort of secondary school appeared, the **English Grammar School.** The Latin Grammar school was increasingly considered a "luxury" education rather than a practical one. The English grammar schools emphasized a practical education with classes conducted in English rather than Latin. Being more flexible, some English grammar schools even admitted females.

Not surprisingly, once there were two variations of secondary schooling, a third was bound to emerge combining qualities of both. That newer version was referred to as an academy. Still considered to be private venture schools, the academy concept sought to embody the best of both educational worlds. In 1749, Benjamin Franklin offered a proposal for the design of such a school. In his *Proposals Relating to the Education of Youth in Pennsylvania,* Franklin wrote, "the good education of youth has been esteemed by wise men in all ages, as the surest foundation of the happiness both of private families and of commonwealths" (1749). As a result, the Philadelphia Academy was established two years later in 1751. We know it today as the University of Pennsylvania.

The Philadelphia Academy offered a broader and more practical curriculum than the Latin grammar schools. In addition to teaching English grammar and literature, the academy also offered subjects such as mathematics, foreign languages, science, astronomy, athletics, dramatics, agriculture, and even navigation. The school was not bound by a religious influence and did include a distinctly democratic form of governance—which in itself was an innovation at the time. Girls as well as boys were admitted as long as they could afford the tuition.

In the years to come, and particularly following the American Revolution, private academies flourished in response to the increasing needs of business. By the late 1700s the Philadelphia Academy and the Boston Latin Grammar School were considered the premiere secondary institutions in the country. What is surprising, however, is that the academies gradually moved back toward a classical curriculum. The practical aspect of the academy was not lost, but for one reason or another the traditional curriculum that had been in existence for nearly 3,000 years was reasserting itself.

Post–Revolutionary War: Education for a New Nation

It became evident in the postrevolution years that a system of education that would bind the nation together was essential. A clear voice in that call was a familiar one: Thomas Jefferson (1743–1826). Jefferson wanted to see a program of educational opportunity that extended beyond the social elite. In 1779 he proposed to the Virginia legislature his Bill for the More General Diffusion of Knowledge, which outlined a plan for the education of children throughout Virginia. Students were to be examined at intervals along their educational careers, and those who proved themselves the most academically capable would continue their education at public expense. The proposal considered only academic progress and not wealth or social station. Students who were not selected to continue their education at public expense were free to continue at their own expense. Ultimately, according to the proposal, the examiners "shall chuse [*sic*] one among the said seniors, of the best learning and most hopeful genius and disposition, who shall be authorised by them to proceed to William and Mary College, there to be educated, boarded, and clothed, three years; the expence of which annually shall be paid by the Treasurer on warrant from the Auditors" (1779). The proposal was not well received.

Noah Webster (1758–1843) believed that a common American language was necessary to bind people together as countrymen and to create their own national identity apart from Great Britain. In 1783 he published the *American Spelling Book*. The small book is considered by many to be the most successful schoolbook ever written, selling over 100 million copies. The book included moral lessons, word lists, and pronunciation guides. In addition, it set the style for American spelling by changing the spelling of British words such as *colour* to *color* and substituting -er for -re in words such as *center* and *theater*.

Educational Opportunities for Ethnic Minorities

Education for African Americans, slave or free, and of Native Americans saw pockets of progress during the 1700s, but not as something embraced by the nation. The providing of education to these populations was largely accomplished by religious organizations. As early as 1704, Elias Neau had started a school in New York City for African Americans and Native Americans. The school was sponsored by the Church of England, to help convert people to Christianity. Similarly, the Reverend Cotton Mather established a school for slaves in New England in 1717.

The South, too, saw schools conducted along religious lines such as those established by the Society for the Propagation of the Gospel in Foreign Parts. Similarly, believing that slavery was immoral, Quaker leaders such as Anthony Benezet and William Penn established schools in the middle colonies. Benezet opened a school for slaves and free African Americans in 1773 in Philadelphia. A year later, the president of the Abolitionist Society, Benjamin Franklin, established another such school. In 1787 the African Free School was established in New York City with private funds. In the 1800s the city began providing public funds to the school and eventually took over operation of the facility in 1824.

It may seem as if schools were popping up everywhere and that thousands upon thousands of minority children were finally receiving an equal educational opportunity. But this was not the case. We have mentioned notable efforts at providing education to children, but these efforts did not represent the mainstream of education. Sadly, we see in the 1700s issues of segregation and unequal funding in

Go Online!

ACTIVITY 8.2   What Was Teaching Like Then?

1. Choose any one of the four centuries of education in America and compile two lists as follows. On one list, write down all of the similarities that you can think of between schools today and schools in the time period you have chosen. On the second list, write those things you can think of that we consider to be part of everyday school life, but would have amazed a teacher from the past. Based on your lists, what can you say about changes in teaching over the centuries?

2. Using the topics listed below, use the Internet to research what teaching was like in the century you have selected.

   Teacher Contracts   Teaching Conditions   School Curriculum

   Teacher Responsibilities   School Funding   School Discipline

   Here are a couple of URLs to help get you started:
   http://www.schenectadyhistory.org/education/neisuler/07.html
   http://wakingbear.com/history.htm

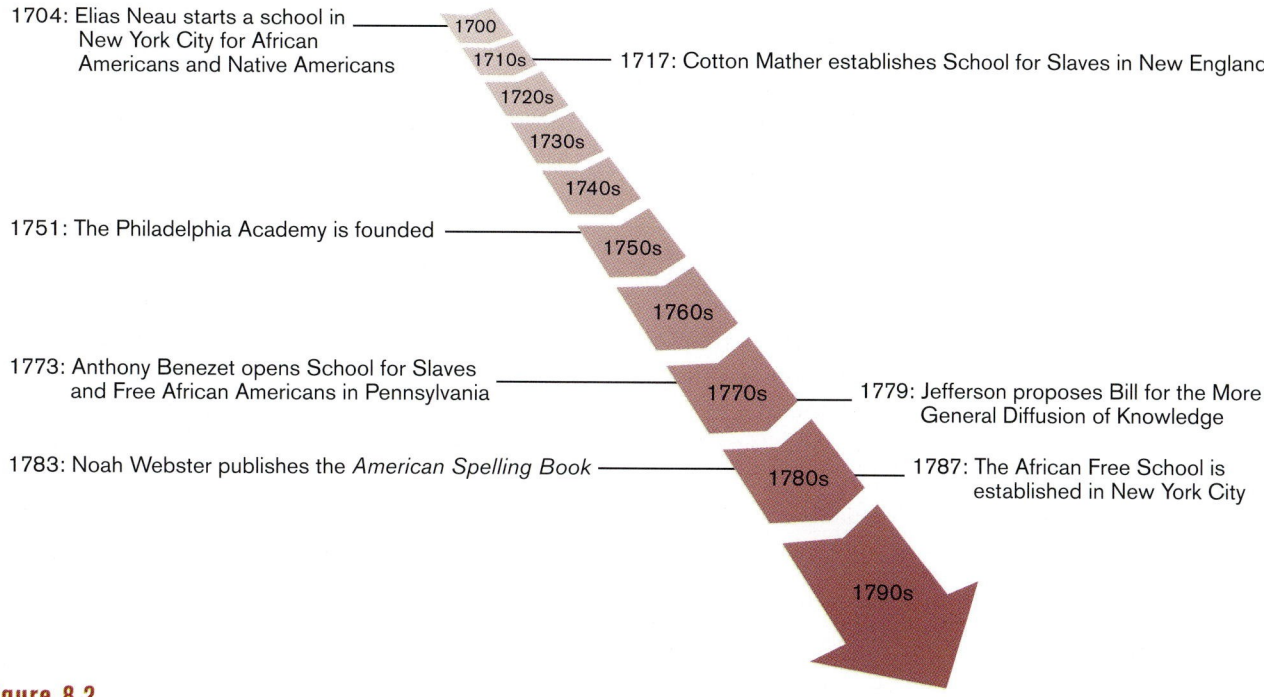

1704: Elias Neau starts a school in New York City for African Americans and Native Americans — 1700

1710s — 1717: Cotton Mather establishes School for Slaves in New England

1720s

1730s

1740s

1751: The Philadelphia Academy is founded — 1750s

1760s

1773: Anthony Benezet opens School for Slaves and Free African Americans in Pennsylvania — 1770s — 1779: Jefferson proposes Bill for the More General Diffusion of Knowledge

1783: Noah Webster publishes the *American Spelling Book* — 1780s — 1787: The African Free School is established in New York City

1790s

Figure 8.2

Significant People and Events of the 1700s

schools that persist to this day and evidence that important figures of the time recognized the inequities that existed.

The Federal Government Addresses Education

The Constitution and the Bill of Rights delegate the responsibility for education to the separate states. However, the federal government did enter the educational arena shortly after the conclusion of the Revolutionary War. In 1785 the Land Ordinance Act was passed, followed two years later by the Northwest Ordinance of 1787. These articles of legislation indicated that "Religion, morality, and knowledge being necessary to good government and the happiness of mankind, schools and the means of education shall forever be encouraged." To that end, the law stated that every township established in the Northwest Territories (what we now know of as the territory from Ohio to Minnesota) was to be divided into 36 sections, one of which was to be set aside for public schools. Education was now on both the federal agenda and the state agenda. Figure 8.2 provides a summary of the people and events of the 1700s that we have discussed.

Developing an Educational System for a New Nation (1800s)

A new social order had emerged and with it a new role for education. As an infant country, the United States needed people educated to assume the responsibilities of nurturing a social and political system that had never existed before. Literacy to support both commerce and democracy moved to the forefront of educational priorities. The United States had to start making some difficult choices about the evolving institution of American education. The 1800s brought a new tone for education, new schools, new voices, and greater governmental influence.

The Utilitarian Value of Education

The new tone of the 1800s reflected the fact that education had taken on a utilitarian value for the society. For a democratic government to survive, it was necessary that the populace be capable of making intelligent decisions. Though remnants of an aristocracy remained, the United States was without a noble class, and opportunity existed for those with the initiative, talent, and determination to pursue it. A common education would be to everybody's benefit.

The New England Primer was eventually replaced by the six-volume **McGuffey Readers.** Written by the Reverend William H. McGuffey and published in 1836, the Readers sold more than a million copies by 1906. Its message of moral virtue influenced generations of Americans. Poems and stories emphasized honesty, truth, obedience, and hard work. Indeed, education was becoming a socializing force that fostered a new and common identity: that of an American.

McGuffey Readers Six volumes written by the Reverend William H. McGuffey and published from 1836 to the early 20th century. Poems and stories emphasized honesty, truth, obedience, and hard work. Their message of moral virtue influenced generations of Americans.

New Ideas for Schooling Emerge

New ideas were also showing up in American education. Along with an influx of immigrants in the middle of the century, a new wave of pedagogical ideas arrived from Europe. Johann Pestalozzi, a Swiss educator, recommended an education that addressed the "whole child" rather than just the academic aspects of memorization and skill development. Horace Mann, the strongest advocate of education in America, would return from a visit to Pestalozzi's school overwhelmed by the caring and compassionate ways in which students were treated.

The German educator Friedrich Froebel had a profound impact on the structure of education at the time with his introduction of the kindergarten, a "garden where children grow." The kindergarten concept stressed developing the motor skills of children before they met the intellectual demands of academics in elementary school. The idea caught on, and in the United States the first kindergarten was established in 1855 by Margarethe Schurz of Watertown, Wisconsin. It was a small, neighborhood school with classes conducted in German. In Boston, Elizabeth Peabody opened the first private English-speaking kindergarten in 1860. And in 1873, Susan Blow in St. Louis opened what is considered to have been the first public kindergarten in the United States.

Changes in Curriculum and School Administration

At the same time, the school curriculum expanded with courses in geography, history, natural science, and government, because good citizenship required a broader and more well-rounded education. You might notice the return to the classical liberal arts curriculum that had fallen out of favor in the 1700s. In addition to curriculum changes, the business model of top-down management, derived from the work of Frederick Taylor, founder of *scientific management,* also found its way into the schools. This approach to school administration has remained in place ever since.

Educational Opportunities Were Not Equal for All

Unfortunately, the cause of education for African Americans did not proceed with the same enthusiasm. In Canterbury, Connecticut, in 1833, a white school teacher named Prudence Crandall began providing schooling to African American girls. The villagers poisoned her well, tried to burn down the house, and essentially stormed the school—forcing it to shut down. In a separate situation a precedent was set when the parents of Sarah Roberts sought to have her admitted to a white school in Boston in 1850. The Massachusetts Supreme Court ruled that "equal, but separate" schools were available for her to attend (*Roberts v. City of Boston,* 1850). In the South, the trend toward separation of blacks and whites was pushed

Francis Benjamin Johnston Collection/Library of Congress
Prints and Photographs Division, Washington, DC

Segregating children according to ethnicity has been a divisive issue throughout our history as a nation.

with the force of law. Though enrollment of African American children in school had steadily increased, after 1877 the passage of the "Jim Crow" laws effectively separated African Americans from mainstream opportunities in virtually all aspects of life. The doctrine of "separate but equal" withstood a Supreme Court challenge in 1896, and it was not until the mid-20th century that the high court ruled it unconstitutional.

By the middle of the 19th century, Hispanics represented a new cultural influence in the United States. Unfortunately, the road to equal educational opportunities for Hispanic children has been much like that of Native Americans and African Americans. Mission schools provided the earliest formal education. Yet even after public schools opened their doors to these children, the emphasis on spoken English—to the point of testing children in English when they spoke only Spanish—gave rise to substantial discrimination against them. Not until 1968, with the Title VII amendment to the Elementary and Secondary Education Act, were schools compelled to meet the needs of children from non-English-speaking families.

More Educational Opportunities and the Common Schools

Kindergarten was not the only new aspect of school to emerge in the 1800s. By 1855 there were more than 6,000 English academies throughout the country. The academies, however, were private schools that charged tuition to students. Thus, it was a system that excluded the children of the poorer working class. The movement toward **common schools** that would occupy the entire century sought to bridge the gap between elementary school and higher education opportunities. To that end, the first publicly supported high school was established in Boston in 1821. Once again, the school was for boys. Though five years later a similar school was opened for girls, it was not until 1852 that a high school for girls was able to sustain itself.

common schools Free schools for working-class students, both girls and boys.

Educational opportunities for young women did begin to appear more often in the early 1800s. Sarah Pierce's Litchfield Academy was started with two students, and classes were held in her home. The academy eventually enrolled more than 100 students. Poet Emma Hart Willard opened the first women's college in the country, Troy Seminary, in 1821.

Normal Schools for Preparing Teachers

Female seminaries prepared young women for further education and for work outside the home. In particular, education for women included normal courses. These courses taught the normal practices for the teaching of children. **Normal schools** existed in New England as early as 1823, and the first public normal school in the United States was opened in Lexington, Massachusetts, in 1869.

normal schools The forerunners of teacher-preparation colleges and universities. They taught their prospective teachers the normal practices for teaching children.

In 1881 Booker T. Washington (1856–1915) was called upon to become the principal for an African American normal school. Washington, who had been born a slave, found that the Tuskegee Institute in Alabama lacked a physical plant, was virtually without students, and had very little community support. Practicing a philosophy of raising the plight of African Americans through hard work and compromise, Washington and his students literally built the schools and farmed the land to raise cash crops. Washington is the acknowledged leader of a conciliatory movement that sought to find a place in American society for well-trained African American workers.

The Doctrine of "Separate but Equal" Education is Challenged

Even though it was based on a "separate but equal" premise, the establishment of the Tuskegee Institute represented the capstone in an educational infrastructure for African Americans that extended through higher education. However, not everybody was in agreement with Washington's conciliatory philosophy. Most notable was William Edward Burghardt DuBois (1868–1963).

W. E. B. DuBois, a graduate of Harvard University and the first African American to receive a Ph.D. in the United States, was one of the founders of the National Association for the Advancement of Colored People (NAACP). DuBois vigorously argued that if African Americans were to become full-fledged members

In Their Own Words

Feature 8.2 — W. E. B. DuBois

The abridged excerpt below is from DuBois's book The Souls of Black Folk. *Originally published in 1903, this passage focuses on the struggle to establish equal and effective educational opportunities for Negroes. Remember that DuBois disagreed with Booker T. Washington's "conciliatory" approach to the education of African Americans. Watch for DuBois's reference to the "Talented Tenth" who should aspire to be leaders in the society rather than followers. Consider, in particular, how the work of this one man through the late 19th and early 20th centuries influenced schooling for an entire segment of society historically denied access to education.*

Sadly did the Old South err in human education, despising the education of the masses, and niggardly in the support of colleges. Her ancient university foundations dwindled and withered under the foul breath of slavery; and even since the war they have fought a failing fight for life in the tainted air of social unrest and commercial selfishness, stunted by the death of criticism, and starving for lack of broadly cultured men. And if this is the white South's need and danger, how much heavier the danger and need of the freedmen's sons! how pressing here the need of broad ideals and true culture, the conservation of soul from sordid aims and petty passions! Let us build the Southern university—William and Mary, Trinity, Georgia, Texas, Tulane, Vanderbilt, and the others—fit to live; let us build, too, the Negro universities: Fisk, whose foundation was ever broad; Howard, at the heart of the Nation; Atlanta at Atlanta, whose ideal of scholarship has been held above the temptation of numbers. Why not here, and perhaps elsewhere, plant deeply and for all time centres of learning and living, colleges that yearly would send into the life of the South a few white men and a few black men of broad culture, catholic tolerance, and trained ability, joining their hands to other hands, and giving to this squabble of the Races a decent and dignified peace?

Teach workers to work,—wise saying; wise when applied to German boys and American girls; wiser when said of Negro boys, for they have less knowledge of working and none to teach them. Teach thinkers to think,—a needed knowledge in a day of loose and careless logic; and they whose lot is gravest must have the carefulest training to think aright. If these things are so, how foolish to ask what is the best education for one or seven or sixty million souls! shall we teach them trades, or train them in liberal arts? Neither and both: teach the workers to work and the thinkers to think; make carpenters of carpenters, and philosophers of philosophers, and fops of fools. Nor can we pause here. We are training not isolated men but a living group of men, nay, a group within a group. And the final product of our training must be neither a psychologist nor a brickmason, but a man. And to make men, we must have ideals, broad, pure, and inspiring ends of living, not sordid money-getting, not apples of gold. The worker must work for the glory of his handiwork, not simply for pay; the thinker must think for truth, not for fame. And all this is gained only by human strife and

Booker T. Washington and W. E. B. DuBois.

Library of Congress Prints and Photographs Division, Washington DC

Library of Congress Prints and Photographs Division, Washington DC

longing; by ceaseless training and education; by founding Right on righteousness and Truth on the unhampered search for Truth; by founding the common school on the university, and the industrial school on the common school; and weaving thus a system, not a distortion, and bringing a birth, not an abortion.

If it is true that there are an appreciable number of Negro youth in the land capable by character and talent to receive that higher training, the end of which is culture, and if the two and a half thousand who have had something of this training in the past have in the main proved themselves useful to their race and generation, the question then comes, What place in the future development of the South ought the Negro college and college-bred man to occupy? That the present social separation and acute race-sensitiveness must eventually yield to the influences of culture, as the South grows civilized, is clear. But such transformation calls for singular wisdom and patience. If, while the healing of this vast sore is progressing, the races are to live for many years side by side, united in economic effort, obeying a common government, sensitive to mutual thought and feeling, yet subtly and silently separate in many matters of deeper human intimacy,—if this unusual and dangerous development is to progress amid peace and order, mutual respect and growing intelligence, it will call for social surgery at once the delicatest and nicest in modern history. It will demand broad-minded, upright men, both white and black, and in its final accomplishment American civilization will triumph. So far as white men are concerned, this fact is to-day being recognized in the South, and a happy renaissance of university education seems imminent. But the very voices that cry hail to this good work are, strange to relate, largely silent or antagonistic to the higher education of the Negro.

Strange to relate! for this is certain, no secure civilization can be built in the South with the Negro as an ignorant, turbulent proletariat. Suppose we seek to remedy this by making them laborers and nothing more: they are not fools, they have tasted of the Tree of Life, and they will not cease to think, will not cease attempting to read the riddle of the world. By taking away their best equipped teachers and leaders, by slamming the door of opportunity in the faces of their bolder and brighter minds, will you make them satisfied with their lot? or will you not rather transfer their leading from the hands of men taught to think to the hands of untrained demagogues? We ought not to forget that despite the pressure of poverty, and despite the active discouragement and even ridicule of friends, the demand for higher training steadily increases among Negro youth: there were, in the years from 1875 to 1880, 22 Negro graduates from Northern colleges; from 1885 to 1890 there were 43, and from 1895 to 1900, nearly 100 graduates. From Southern Negro colleges there were, in the same three periods, 143, 413, and over 500 graduates. Here, then, is the plain thirst for training; by refusing to give this Talented Tenth the key to knowledge, can any sane man imagine that they will lightly lay aside their yearning and contentedly become hewers of wood and drawers of water? ∎

of the society, it would not be by accepting manual labor and inferior status. He campaigned for the education of the "Talented Tenth" among African Americans who would correspondingly become business and political leaders.

Between the end of the Civil War and the turn of the century, the idea of publicly supported common schools was no longer radical. By the end of the century, public and private schools existed from kindergarten through the university level. Elementary school enrollments alone exceeded 10 million students.

Library of Congress Prints and Photographs Division, Washington, DC

Horace Mann.

New Advocacy for Education

We have seen that many great thinkers over the centuries have been advocates of education. In the 1800s we see advocacy raised to a new level. We could characterize it as a level of *professionalism,* for now there were people who furthered the condition of education as their life's work, as their place in society.

Horace Mann There was likely no greater advocate for the schooling of all children during the 1800s than Horace Mann (1796–1859). Mann had been a lawyer and a Massachusetts senator. In 1837 he helped to form the first state board of education and subsequently became its secretary, a position equivalent to state superintendent of education. Mann's primary concern as he took over a rag-tag system of education was education for the common person. In Mann's view, all children should receive a quality education that prepared them for effective citizenship. The building blocks for such a common school were available, but it was a hard sell.

Mann insisted that a common education would yield significant benefits to business and industry and thereby to the economy as well. A well-schooled citizenship would also help to identify talents and abilities no matter what social class they were to be found in. In short, effective education for each individual was a mechanism to solve our social problems and to further our society. Business, however, lamented the potential loss of child labor, and taxpayers railed at the notion of supporting the education of all children.

Mann's particular talent was in tailoring his comments to fit whatever audience he was addressing. The themes of universal education, of the better treatment of children, and of preparing people specifically to teach remained consistent, though a business audience would hear them presented in ways that made the advantages for business clear while a political audience would hear them presented as social imperatives. In a series of twelve annual reports submitted during his tenure as secretary of the board of education and through the *Common School Journal* (which he founded), Mann brought the cause of education to the forefront. In the Fifth Annual Report (1841), he argued the benefit to business of the common-school movement. The Seventh Annual Report (1843) discussed his trip to Prussia to observe Pestalozzi's methods in education. The Tenth Annual Report (1846) detailed the imperative for public funding of schools and why all citizens should be taxed for such purposes.

Mann's advocacy of common schools brought with it a significant proposal that has had an effect on *your* situation today. Mann argued for schooling especially designed to teach people to be teachers. Patterned after the French *école normale,* normal schools were professional programs of teacher education that included instruction in pedagogy, new teaching methods, and even the management of children as opposed to the routine use of corporal punishment.

Mann's extraordinary efforts established Massachusetts as the leader in public education. By 1867 Massachusetts, Vermont, and the District of Columbia had not only

In Their Own Words

Feature 8.3   Horace Mann

Horace Mann had a particular talent for tailoring his remarks so that regardless of the audience, it would soon become evident how the common school movement was fantastically to their benefit. In this passage from the Tenth Annual Report (1846), Mann argues for the cause of the common school and that it is an endeavour that should be funded at public expense by all members of the public.

I believe in the existence of a great, immortal, immutable principle of natural law, or natural ethics,—a principle antecedent to all human institutions, and incapable of being abrogated by any ordinance of man,—a principle of divine origin clearly legible in the ways of Providence as those ways are manifested in the order of Nature and in the history of the race, which proves the absolute right to an education of every human being that comes into the world; and which, of course, proves the correlative duty of every government to see that the means of that education are provided for all.

In regard to the application of this principle of natural law,—that is, in regard to the extent of the education to be provided for all at the public expense,—some differences of opinion may fairly exist under different political organizations; but, under our republican government, it seems clear that the minimum of this education can never be less than such as is sufficient to qualify each citizen for the civil and social duties he will be called to discharge,—such an education as teaches the individual the great laws of bodily health, as qualifies for the fulfillment of parental duties, as is indispensable for the civil functions of a witness or juror, as is necessary for the voter in municipal and in national affairs, and, finally, as is requisite for the faithful and conscientious discharge of all those duties which devolve upon the inheritor of a portion of the sovereignty of this great Republic.

The will of God, as conspicuously manifested in the order of Nature, and in the relations which he has established among men, founds the right of every child that is born into the world, to such a degree of education as will enable him, and, as far as possible, will predispose him, to perform all domestic, social, civil, and moral duties, upon the same clear ground of natural law and equity as it founds a child's right, upon his first coming into the world, to distend his lungs with a portion of the common air, or to open his eyes to the common light, or to receive that shelter, protection, and nourishment, which are necessary to the continuance of bodily existence. And so far is it from being wrong or a hardship to demand of the possessors of property their respective shares for the prosecution of this divinely-ordained work, that they themselves are guilty of the most far-reaching injustice when they seek to resist or to evade the contribution. The complainers are the wrong-doers. The cry, "Stop thief!" comes from the thief himself. ∎

---

established systems of public education but had also passed compulsory attendance laws. By 1900, 32 states had passed such laws, and by 1930 all states had done so.

The National Education Association (NEA)   Another form of education advocacy arose in the 19th century. In 1857 the National Education Association (NEA) was founded. The NEA and another advocacy group, the American Federation of Teachers, founded in 1916, are still vibrant organizations that continue to work to professionalize teaching and improve education.

In the late 1800s the debate over the purpose of schooling was raging. Business, of course, wanted well-trained workers and thus advocated education with a vocational emphasis. Other educational factions argued that school was essentially a cultural experience and so favored more "traditional" subjects. The NEA appointed several committees to examine these issues.

In 1892, the Committee of Ten on Secondary Studies was convened. Chaired by Charles Eliot, president of Harvard University, the committee returned the following recommendations in 1893 regarding the high school curriculum: fewer electives should be offered, a series of traditional and classical courses should be offered in sequence, and classes meeting four or five times a week over the course

Carnegie Unit A course credit for the successful completion of a specified high school course (e.g., Spanish I, Algebra II). It includes satisfactory grades and may also include passing an end-of-course test developed by the state.

of a year would be awarded one **Carnegie Unit,** which would serve to monitor the student's educational progress.

Subsequently, in 1893, the NEA commissioned the Committee of Fifteen to study the elementary school curriculum and in 1895 commissioned the Committee of Thirteen on College Entrance Requirements. A committee studying the high school curriculum would convene in the early 20th century under the auspices of the NEA.

With regard to advocacy, the bridge to the 20th century was John Dewey (1859–1952), an American philosopher and educator who has had a profound impact upon education. In 1896 Dewey and his wife, Alice, established the Laboratory School at the University of Chicago. The school was a platform for testing the principles of progressive education that Dewey had derived from his pragmatist philosophical background (pragmatism will be discussed in Chapter 9). Originally enrolling 16 students, by 1902 the school had 140 students and 23 teachers. Schooling, and the way people learn, had become a topic of study in and of itself.

Governmental Influence in Education Broadens

Though American education was influenced both directly and indirectly by the state and federal governments through the 1800s, the state-federal relationship made educational opportunities for Native Americans virtually nonexistent. Education was a state rather than federal responsibility, but Native Americans were placed on reservations administered by the federal government, outside the jurisdiction of the state. It would be well into the 20th century before Native Americans were accorded U.S. citizenship, and even that did not mean immediate equal educational opportunity.

Meanwhile, the common-school movement at public expense was finally taking root. High school, however, was still considered somewhat of a luxury, and many questioned why the public should pay the bill. In 1874 the courts ruled in a Kalamazoo, Michigan, case that leaving a gap between publicly funded elementary schools and publicly funded universities made no sense. It was determined that high school be funded with tax dollars as well.

Land-Grant Colleges

The Morrill Act of 1862 provided a significant boost to institutions of higher education. Congressman Justin Morrill (1810–1898) of Vermont sponsored a bill that provided to each state 30,000 acres of federal land per representative and senator in its delegation. The states were allowed to sell or rent the land only if they used the proceeds to establish and fund colleges for the study of agricultural and mechanical arts. Over 17 million acres were provided under the legislation. Many of these **land-grant colleges,** some with "A&M" (agricultural and mechanical) in their names, became the large state universities that we know of today, such as Texas A&M, Purdue University, the University of California, Michigan State University, and the University of Nebraska.

land-grant colleges Colleges established and funded for the study of agriculture and the mechanical arts. Funds were secured from the rent or sale of public lands in each state. See the Morrill Act of 1862.

The difficulty that the United States was having with the issue of ethnicity, particularly that of white and black, was evident in a second Morrill Act, passed in 1890. In this act additional land was provided for the land-grant program, but money could not be given to a college with an admission policy that discriminated against nonwhites *unless* there was a separate—and presumably equal—facility nearby. It's difficult to deny that the "spirit" of the law represented an effort to address social inequities, though apart from the clearly divisive sentiment of the

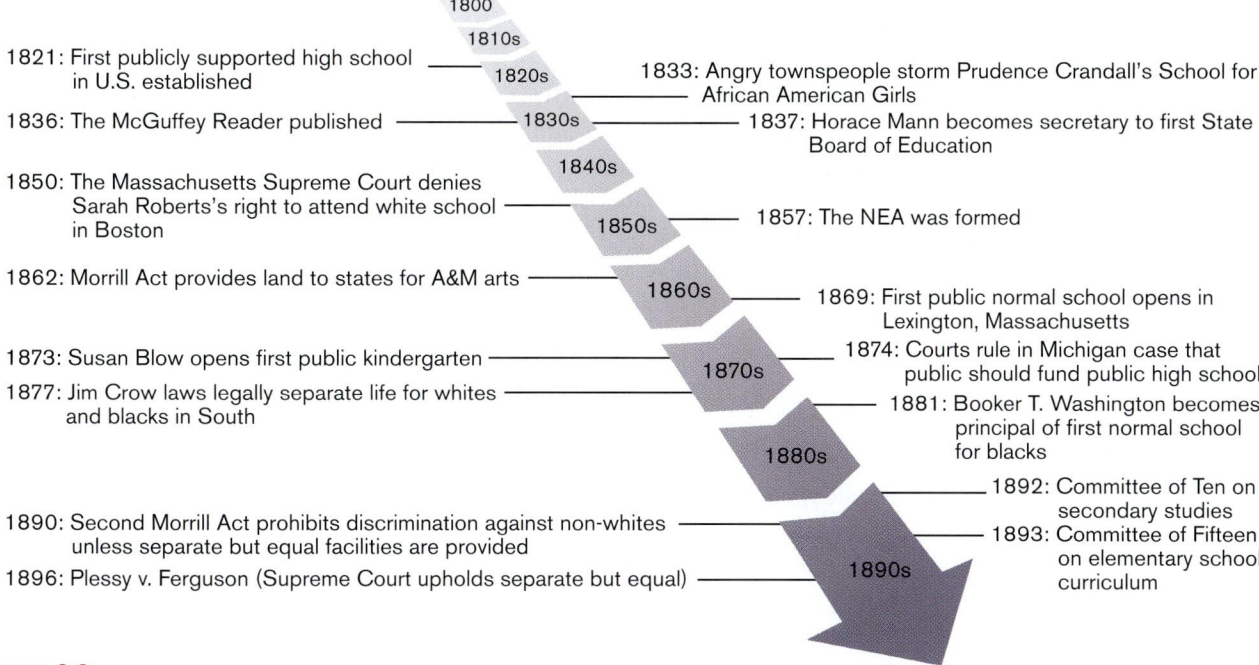

Figure 8.3

Significant People and Events of the 1800s

Timeline contents:

- 1800
- 1810s
- 1820s — 1821: First publicly supported high school in U.S. established
- 1830s — 1833: Angry townspeople storm Prudence Crandall's School for African American Girls; 1836: The McGuffey Reader published; 1837: Horace Mann becomes secretary to first State Board of Education
- 1840s
- 1850s — 1850: The Massachusetts Supreme Court denies Sarah Roberts's right to attend white school in Boston; 1857: The NEA was formed
- 1860s — 1862: Morrill Act provides land to states for A&M arts; 1869: First public normal school opens in Lexington, Massachusetts
- 1870s — 1873: Susan Blow opens first public kindergarten; 1874: Courts rule in Michigan case that public should fund public high school; 1877: Jim Crow laws legally separate life for whites and blacks in South
- 1880s — 1881: Booker T. Washington becomes principal of first normal school for blacks
- 1890s — 1890: Second Morrill Act prohibits discrimination against non-whites unless separate but equal facilities are provided; 1892: Committee of Ten on secondary studies; 1893: Committee of Fifteen on elementary school curriculum; 1896: Plessy v. Ferguson (Supreme Court upholds separate but equal)

times it was nonetheless the case that "separate" was accomplished with much greater success than "equal." Among the institutions that emerged from the 1890 legislation are Florida A&M University, Prairie View A&M (Texas), South Carolina State University, and Tuskegee University (Alabama).

Immigration Presents New Challenges for Education

The precedent set with the doctrine of "separate but equal" would only serve to make matters more difficult for the growing country. By the mid-1800s immigration had extended to the Atlantic and Pacific coasts. A wave of Chinese immigrants, typically poor and uneducated, readily entered the work force as unskilled laborers, intensifying discriminatory sentiments as they were perceived as taking jobs from white workers. The United States now had growing populations of Asian Americans, Native Americans, and African Americans in addition to the Western European majority. If ever the nation needed an Americanizing influence, this was the time to put it in place. Instead, in 1882 Congress passed an act halting Chinese immigration. Similar legislation followed in 1924, stemming the tide of Japanese immigration, and again in 1930 in response to Filipino immigration. The United States had not only established itself as a new and independent nation, it had also begun to recognize that such status brought with it many difficult issues. See Figure 8.3 for a summary of the people and events we have discussed in this section.

Education in 20th-Century America

In the 1900s the United States was not only a sovereign country, but within a decade or two it would assume "superpower" status among the nations of the world. The United States had become a political and economic force recognized worldwide. One momentous event, the launching of the Soviet satellite, Sputnik, is particularly important because it prompted a *national* call for change in our public schools in the name of *national defense.* We are not suggesting that all that has transpired in the last 50 years is tied to the space-race frenzy of the late 1950s and early 1960s. In fact, much of the momentum for educational reform stemmed from the 1954 United States Supreme Court decision in the case of *Brown v. Board of Education of Topeka,* which rejected the constitutionality of "separate but equal" schools and, in a separate ruling in 1955, required integration "with all deliberate speed." But it was the possibility of armed conflict with another nation, the other superpower, that drove a series of educational initiatives from the federal level, the likes of which had never been seen before.

The First 50 Years of the 20th Century

In 1857 just over half of the school-age population in the United States was enrolled, but by 1918 that had increased to 75 percent (Butts & Cremin, 1953). Immigrants were arriving on both coasts of the United States, and rural residents were migrating to the cities for jobs arising from the Industrial Revolution. Whereas increased enrollments had previously called for more schools and districts, the new trend was to consolidate smaller districts into larger, unified school districts to manage more effectively the numbers of students involved.

Regional Issues

Each region of the country had its particular issues, and in a way they were not so different. For example, schools in the North were not segregated by law, as in the South, but as people were either forced into "ethnic" neighborhoods or self-selected them to be with others of their own heritage, segregation was inevitable. The same questions of "separate but equal" would eventually surface in the North as well. In the South the disparity between whites and nonwhites widened rather than narrowed. In 1912 white teachers were paid roughly three times the salary of blacks. Meanwhile, though Native Americans were accorded citizenship in 1924, their education continued to be directed by the Bureau of Indian Affairs into the 1970s. Surprisingly, the first quarter of the century, with its vibrant nature, its automobiles and airplanes, and even the "melting pot" of enculturation, did not see schools as the means for forming a multiethnic bond among the people of the United States.

Categorical Funding from the Federal Government

categorical funding The funding by the federal government of special programs (e.g., free lunch program for economically disadvantaged students, school construction, work programs for high school students).

The federal government continued its involvement in education in terms of **categorical funding.** That is, without the power to impose a curriculum or standards for education, the federal government funded particular programs. Especially during the years of the Depression, money flowed to the states and then to the schools for free-lunch programs for poor children, for work programs for high school students, and for the construction of schools. But the constitutional line between the state and the federal government remained intact. Ultimately, school was the responsibility of the state.

The National Education Association (NEA) Convenes a Second Curriculum Committee

In 1918 the National Education Association (NEA) convened a second committee to review the high school curriculum and its role. Specifically, the committee was concerned with what the high school could do to improve the lives of citizens

Underwood & Underwood, NY/Library of Congress Prints and Photographs Division, Washington, DC

John Dewey.

in an industrial society. The committee's report, *Cardinal Principles of Secondary Education,* identified seven goals: (1) health, (2) worthy home membership, (3) command of fundamental academic skills, (4) vocation, (5) citizenship, (6) worthy use of leisure time, and (7) ethical character. As you can see, organized education, and the high school in particular, was to address many aspects of the individual's life in society. Perhaps of even greater importance is to understand that it would be the classroom teacher who would provide this broader educational experience.

The Progressivist Movement Begins

As the 20th century began, John Dewey's work in educational pragmatism became known as progressive education (progressivism is discussed in detail in Chapter 9). Following his work at the University of Chicago, Dewey was professor of philosophy at Columbia University from 1904 to 1930. He combined his knowledge of psychology with a pragmatic philosophy arguing that, for a

---

In Their Own Words

Feature 8.4   John Dewey

This passage offers a bit of a twist on all of the curriculum considerations that have been discussed thus far. As you'll recall, the emphasis has been on which subjects to teach. However, if you've ever tired of having to memorize names and dates just as an exercise in name and date memorization, John Dewey is here to help you out. This excerpt, from the chapter "Thinking in Education" in his renowned work Democracy and Education *(1916), argues that real thinking occurs when students have real problems to solve.*

No one doubts, theoretically, the importance of fostering in school good habits of thinking. But apart from the fact that the acknowledgement is not so great in practice as in theory, there is not adequate theoretical recognition that all which the school can or need do for pupils, so far as their minds are concerned (that is, leaving out certain specialized muscular abilities), is to develop their ability to think. The parceling out of instruction among various ends such as the acquisition of skill (in reading, spelling, writing, drawing, reciting); acquiring information (in history and geography), and training of thinking is a measure of the ineffective way in which we accomplish all three. Thinking which is not connected with increase of efficiency in action, and with learning more about ourselves and the world in which we live, has something the matter with it just as thought. And skill obtained apart from thinking is not connected with any sense of the purposes for which it is to be used. It consequently leaves a man at the mercy of his routine habits and of the authoritative control of others, who know what they are about and who are not especially scrupulous as to their means of achievement.

And information severed from thoughtful action is dead, a mind-crushing load. Since it simulates knowledge and thereby develops the poison of conceit, it is a most powerful obstacle to further growth in the grace of intelligence. The sole direct path to enduring improvement in the methods of instruction and learning consists in centering upon the conditions which exact, promote, and test thinking. Thinking is the method of intelligent learning, of learning that employs and rewards mind. We speak, legitimately enough, about the method of thinking, but the important thing to bear in mind about method is that thinking is method, the method of intelligent experience in the course which it takes.

Processes of instruction are unified in the degree in which they center in the production of good habits of thinking. While we may speak, without error, of the method of thought, the important thing to remember is that thinking is the method of an educative experience. The essentials of method are therefore identical with the essentials of reflection. They are first that the pupil have a genuine situation of experience—that there be a continuous activity in which he is interested for its own sake; secondly, that a genuine problem develop within this situation as a stimulus to thought; third, that he possess the information and make the observations needed to deal with it; fourth, that suggested solutions occur to him which he shall be responsible for developing in an orderly way; fifth, that he have opportunity and occasion to test his ideas by application, to make their meaning clear and to discover for himself their validity. ■

child, school is not a preparation for life but *is* life. Therefore, education ought to be relevant to the life of the child and participatory (as opposed to lecture-oriented) in nature. The emphasis should be on engaging the student in activities that paralleled life outside of school. It was through this impetus during the 1920s, 1930s, and 1940s that classes in home economics, citizenship, wood shop, and family living began to appear in the curriculum.

A shift was occurring away from the *cognitive* perspective (a focus on academics) to an *affective* perspective (a focus on values and worthy citizenship) in terms of what schools should accomplish. Though Dewey argued for more of a balance between the two, the progressive movement began to move in different directions. Ultimately, even Dewey would try to distance himself from the aberrations of his original work.

In 1919 the Progressive Education Association (PEA) was founded with the purpose of reforming education. In particular, the progressivists believed that (1) children should be free to develop naturally, (2) work that interests the child will be naturally motivating, (3) the teacher is a guide, (4) student development must be measured scientifically, (5) health and physical education must be addressed, (6) the school and the home must work together, and (7) progressive schools must take the lead in trying new ideas. Thus, progressive education focused on social development, individual growth, and, most practical of all, vocational education.

The work of Maria Montessori (1870–1952), an Italian physician, also had a considerable impact on schooling for young children in the child-centered atmosphere of progressive education. Montessori championed the notion of developmentally appropriate educational activities and argued that the "play" of young children was actually a sophisticated learning experience. Montessori materials and methods continue in wide use today as part of early childhood education.

To demonstrate the validity of their claims, the Progressive Education Association conducted a longitudinal study from 1932–1940 (the Eight-Year Study). Over the period of the study 30 public and private high schools were given an opportunity to develop curricula emphasizing problem solving, creativity, self-directed study, and more extensive counseling for students. Curriculums could be developed and delivered without regard for college and university entrance requirements because over 300 schools had agreed to accept the graduates of these innovative programs.

Ralph Tyler (1949) evaluated the study. He matched nearly 1,500 students who had graduated from these experimental schools and gone on to college with an equal number of students entering college from other high schools. The results showed that the students from the experimental group had slightly higher grade point averages in all subjects with the exception of foreign languages. He also found that students from the experimental group tended to score higher in areas such as problem solving, inventiveness, and motivation.

Library of Congress Prints and Photographs Division, Washington DC

Maria Montessori.

Progressivism Faces Challenges

Faced with all of this information, you might wonder why schools did not wholeheartedly embrace the format offered in the experimental schools. Indeed, there was another significant event occupying the collective conscience of the country at that time—and again it was a war.

World War II, with its emphasis at home on efficiency in all matters whether domestic, industrial, or educational (particularly with regard to training), effectively derailed progressivism as a movement. With the 1940s came considerable criticism of Dewey and of progressive education. Declining test scores in academics brought charges that the child-centered curriculum lacked rigor. In particular,

In Their Own Words

Feature 8.5   Maria Montessori

As you read this passage from Montessori's The Secret of Childhood *(1939), the influence of ancient Greek philosophy should become evident to you. Here's a hint: A later subheading in her book is: "Know Thyself!" The excerpt following is from a chapter titled "The Task of the Teacher." In particular, she will point out the challenge of "the new education."*

We must face the startling fact that the child has a psychic life of which the delicate manifestations pass unperceived, and of which the adult may inadvertently mar the pattern or hinder the development.

The adult's environment is not a life-giving environment for the child. Rather it is an accumulation of obstacles, leading him to a creation of defenses, to deforming efforts at adaptation, or else leaving him the victim of suggestion. It is the outward aspect he thus presents that has been considered in the study of child psychology; it is from this that his characteristics have been defined, as a basis for education. Child psychology is thus something that must be radically revised. As we have seen, behind every surprising response on the part of a child, lies an enigma to be deciphered; every form of naughtiness is the outward expression of some deep-seated cause, which cannot be interpreted as the superficial, defensive clash with an unsuitable environment, but as expressing a higher, essential characteristic seeking manifestation. It is as though a storm were hindering the child's soul from coming forth from its secret hiding-place to show itself in the outer world.

It is plain that all the incidents that mask the hidden soul in its continual endeavors to actualize its life, all the fits of temper, struggles, deviations, give no idea of a personality. They are merely a sum of characteristics. But there must be a personality behind them if the child, the spiritual embryo, is following a constructive pattern in his psychic development. There is a hidden man, a hidden child, a buried living being, who must be liberated. Here is the first urgent task of education: liberation in this sense means knowledge, or indeed a discovery of the unknown.

If there is an essential difference between what psycho-analysis has discovered and this psychology of the unknown child, it consists primarily in this: that what lies secret in the subconscious of the adult is something repressed by the individual himself. The individual himself must help to disentangle the tangled skein formed by complex and resisting adaptations, by the symbols and camouflage organized during a lifetime. Whereas the secret of the child is barely hidden by his environment. It is on the environment that we must set to work to enable the child to manifest himself freely; the child is at a period of creation and expansion, and it is enough to open the door. Indeed that which he is creating, which from not-being is passing into existence, and from potentiality to actuality, at the moment when it comes forth from nothing cannot be complicated, and where it is a question of an expansive energy there can be no difficulty in its manifestation. Thus by preparing a free environment, an environment suited to this moment of life, natural manifestation of the child's psyche and hence the revelation of his secret should come about spontaneously.

Without this principle the efforts at education can only go farther and farther into an inextricable maze.

Here is the aim of the new education: first of all to discover the child and effect his liberation. In this, we may say, lies the first problem of existence: simply to exist. . . . However, the environment is fundamental; it must facilitate the expansion of the being in process of development by a reduction of the obstacles to a minimum, and must allow free scope for a child's energies, by offering the necessary means for the activities to which they give rise. ■

the military was finding that the academic abilities of the thousands of young men being inducted were extremely poor. As the war drew to an end and the 1950s approached, criticism continued despite the postwar optimism of the time. Hyman Rickover, an admiral in the U.S. Navy and developer of the nuclear submarine program, was particularly acerbic in his denunciation of progressive education. His complaints about the "watered down" curriculum would become even more influential when Sputnik streaked across the sky in 1957.

Nonetheless, it must be admitted that the progressive education movement ushered in many aspects of education that we take for granted today. Ideas such as inquiry-based learning, flexible scheduling, student projects, and even field trips were among the "experiments" of the progressives.

The Second Half of the 20th Century

The post–World War II years were marked by a feeling of invincibility, an awareness of what a nation could accomplish with a solid work ethic, a virtual explosion of knowledge from wartime research and development, an industrial reliance on the "factory" model of production, and, of course, the "baby boom." Although peacetime was short-lived, each factor in its own way had an effect on the public school and its curriculum.

The early 1950s brought the anticommunist activities led by Senator Joseph McCarthy and the Korean conflict as well as a growing dissatisfaction with "schoolness." There arose questions not only about declining test scores but also of the role of school and especially the inequities associated with segregation. *Brown v. Board of Education of Topeka* (1954) signaled the need for change more than it signaled desegregation. A year later the court ordered integration to proceed with "all deliberate speed," but the road ahead would not be easy. Interestingly enough, in the early 21st century we now hear calls from a number of factions seeking single-sex and single-ethnic environments. Several large school districts are already working on plans for single-sex classes with the goal of entire single-sex schools being established.

Education Becomes a Matter of National Defense

The catalyst for a *unified* look at public education was, as we have mentioned, the launch of Sputnik by the Soviet Union. Backyard fallout shelters could not protect people from what many perceived as a new threat to the nation's security. Suddenly the world was no longer as safe as it had seemed, and for the first time *national defense* was addressed in terms of the public schools. Vocal critics of the progressive curriculum pointedly attacked the lack of academic rigor in the curriculum and called for a revolution in the nation's approach to education.

The federal government's response was the National Defense Education Act of 1958. Though the federal government did not mandate what would be done in school, nearly a billion dollars began to flow toward curriculum reform projects in science, mathematics, and the "new" subject of social studies. In addition, the National Defense Education Act provided for curriculum development in foreign languages and for student guidance. The programs were education-oriented, but the mandate was to improve "the security of the nation" and to develop "the mental resources and technical skills of its young men and women."

The National Defense Education Act began a period of unprecedented federal involvement with public and private education. In 1964 Congress extended the act for three years and also added funding for curriculum development in reading, English, geography, and civics. A year later the Elementary and Secondary Education Act of 1965 provided funding for programs aimed at disadvantaged children. Head Start, Upward Bound, and the Job Corps, all of which are ancillary to the traditional K–12 curriculum, were established to fight the War on Poverty. Millions of dollars also made their way to private and religious schools through programs that were part of the 1965 legislation.

There was another obstacle to equal education, however, and that was language. The 1965 Elementary and Secondary Education Act was amended in 1968 with Title VII. Hispanic, Native American, and eventually Asian children representing a wide variety of languages (restrictions on Asian immigration were lifted in 1965) were provided support for what has become **bilingual education** offered to children "of limited English speaking ability." In 1974 the Supreme Court ruled in *Lau v. Nichols* that schools must offer students special instruction as necessary to ensure an equal educational opportunity.

bilingual education Education provided to children with limited English-speaking ability.

The School Curriculum Comes under Scrutiny

At the same time, leading theorists offered perspectives that led to new ways of looking at curriculum offerings. For instance, Jerome Bruner (1966) contended that any subject could be taught in an intellectually appropriate way to very young children. When Bruner's assertion was considered with Benjamin Bloom's (1964) analysis that 50 percent of all cognitive development occurred by age 4 and 75 percent by age 8, the clear implication was that content should be introduced at lower levels than had previously been done and that schooling should focus on the early childhood years. Thus were planted the seeds of more difficult content and earlier emphasis on academics.

With the 1970s came the call for "back to basics." But now the call was coming from parents as well as business and politicians. A move toward **teacher accountability** began, though with precious little attention to acknowledging the responsibilities of parents in a child's education. Homeschooling, alternative schooling, a migration toward private schools for those who could afford it, and a wide range of curriculum reform efforts were the result. All of these, by the way, exist in today's educational picture as well.

The 1970s also brought a series of legislative actions that addressed a wide range of issues faced by the public schools. In 1972 the Title IX Education Amendment prohibited sex discrimination. Perhaps the most far-reaching for the work of the classroom teacher and for the provision of services to children with special needs was the Education for All Handicapped Children Act in 1975. The original legislation (Public Law 94-142) has since been amended and expanded and provides support for millions of children with the mandate of providing a "free and appropriate education."

teacher accountability The concept that the teacher is responsible for the achievement of students, regardless of their circumstances (e.g., cognitive, social, psychological, environmental, physical).

A Nation at Risk Raises Concerns about the Condition of American Education

As you might expect, all of the measures discussed thus far provided more services to more children, but they did not necessarily contribute to what many consider to be the academic bottom line: test scores. Even the academic gains of children who had been in Head Start tended to diminish over time. Throughout the 1970s, and as the 1980s began, many began to believe that the schools had tried to do too much. In 1983 the National Commission for Excellence in Education published a report that sounded the wake-up call for American education.

The Commission published *A Nation at Risk: The Imperative for Educational Reform* and formally ignited the debate that had informally occupied many in education for decades. The document startled the nation with its warnings of the implications for failing to reform the system of public education. Education in America was mediocre at best, it suggested, and rankings against the school systems of nations around the world could support the statement. Among its recommendations were (1) more academic course requirements for all high school students, (2) more rigorous college entrance requirements, (3) upgraded textbooks, (4) longer school days and longer school years, and (5) the "new" basics—four years of English, three years of mathematics, three years of science, three years of social studies, and one-half year of computer science.

A definite outcome of the 1983 report has been the increased emphasis (many would argue *over*emphasis) on standardized testing as an indicator of educational achievement and on "accountability" as the means toward improving test scores. To that end, through the 1990s learned societies representing the various academic disciplines have identified standards for educational achievement. The states have then designed their own versions of those standards to drive the curriculum for their schools. Subsequently, the states adopt or design assessment instruments to determine whether or not the standards are being met.

The story of education in the 20th century is largely one of wrestling with the institution that education has become. Some say that the framers of the Constitution omitted education because people feared what could happen if education were centralized with the federal government. Others say they were simply

Figure 8.4

Significant People and Events
of the 1900s

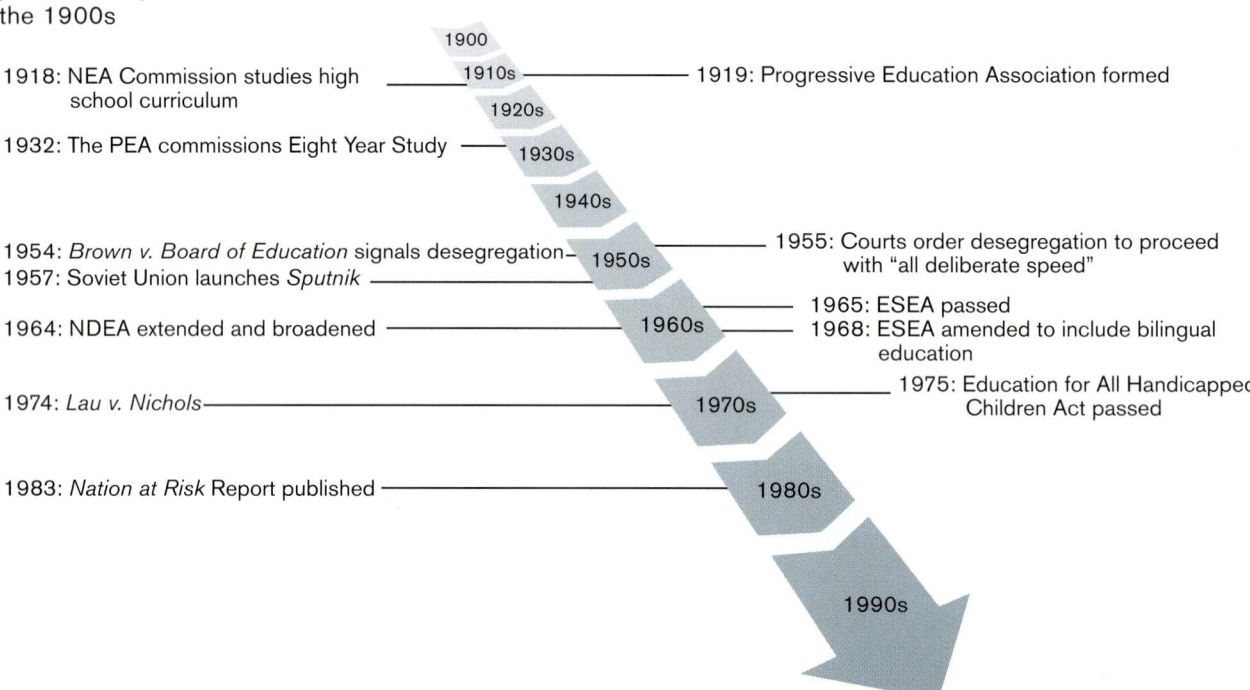

1918: NEA Commission studies high school curriculum

1919: Progressive Education Association formed

1932: The PEA commissions Eight Year Study

1954: *Brown v. Board of Education* signals desegregation

1955: Courts order desegregation to proceed with "all deliberate speed"

1957: Soviet Union launches *Sputnik*

1965: ESEA passed

1964: NDEA extended and broadened

1968: ESEA amended to include bilingual education

1975: Education for All Handicapped Children Act passed

1974: *Lau v. Nichols*

1983: *Nation at Risk* Report published

1900
1910s
1920s
1930s
1940s
1950s
1960s
1970s
1980s
1990s

Field Observation

ACTIVITY 8.3   The New Issues and the Old

Working either alone or in small groups, make two lists of issues based upon this chapter. On one list, Old Issues, list as many of the educational issues from this chapter that you can. For example, your list might include "access to education" and "vocational education" among many others. On your other list, New Issues, list those concerns that you know of in education today that are not on the Old Issues list. It may take some discussion to correctly place many items. For example, you can see from the chapter that public funding of education has been an issue for hundreds of years.

1. Do your two lists cite an equal number of issues? Why or why not?

2. Which issues from either list would you consider to be the most important issues facing education?

3. What solutions can you think of that would prevent the issues on your Old Issues list from showing up on a similar list 50 years from now?

In your field observation placement, or if you can simply chat with a classroom teacher:

1. Share your list of old issues. Ask whether the teacher feels that these old issues have been addressed, or are they still prevalent. Next, ask for any reasons that might have kept this issue from being resolved.

2. Without first sharing your list, ask the teacher what issues he or she thinks will be the new issues in education. Were any of them on your list as well? Share your list and ask for the teacher's perspective.

3. When back in class, discuss what you found from talking with the teacher.

too distracted at the time to think about it. In any event, we can see that many influences have made education what it is today. Still, there are many questions and issues—some of them ancient—that remain to be resolved. Figure 8.4 provides you with a summary of the people and events of the 20th century that were discussed in this section. Activity 8.3 offers you an opportunity to see how much has changed and how much bears a strong resemblance to the past.

STOP Conclusion

The history of education in the United States has roots in ancient Greece. It is marked by the work of some of the world's greatest thinkers, and is also marked by many issues that have not been resolved for hundreds, and sometimes thousands, of years. The good news is that the foundation of education has strength. The exciting news is that there is so much yet to build. Here are some highlights from the chapter:

1. In ancient Greece, education was provided to boys but not provided to girls, slaves, or noncitizens. Grammar, reading, and writing laid the foundation for intellectual development; music laid the foundation for aesthetic appreciation.

2. It was Socrates' belief that people should seek to discover universal principles of truth and of beauty and that to do so they must question and examine their own knowledge.

3. Adopting a realist philosophy that sought the truth through a study of the real world, Aristotle suggested that the state was best served by citizens capable of rational thinking.

4. As variations of the Christian faith developed, so did diverse perspectives on the purpose of education, curriculum, and the language in which school should be conducted.

5. Formal education in the "new world" consisted of teaching children (especially boys) to read, and the textbook was the Bible. Proper conduct and religious devotion were the primary lessons.

6. The Massachusetts Act of 1647—known as The Old Deluder Satan Act—required every town of 50 or more households to establish a school and hire a teacher. Towns of 100 or more households were also required to establish a Latin Grammar School to prepare students for university study.

7. The academy concept combined the best elements of Latin and English Grammar schools.

8. Passage of the "Jim Crow" laws after 1877 effectively separated African Americans from mainstream opportunities in virtually all aspects of life.

9. W.E.B. DuBois campaigned for the education of the "Talented Tenth" among African Americans who would correspondingly become business and political leaders.

10. In 1837 Horace Mann helped to form the first state board of education.

11. In 1857 the National Education Association (NEA) was founded, followed by the American Federation of Teachers in 1916.

12. In 1892, the Committee of Ten on Secondary Studies was convened. In 1893, the Committee of Fifteen studied the elementary school curriculum.

13. The Morrill Act of 1862 provided to each state 30,000 acres of federal land per representative and senator in its delegation. Proceeds were to be used for

establishing and funding land-grant colleges for the study of agricultural and mechanical arts. A second Morrill Act was passed in 1890.

14. John Dewey's work in educational pragmatism eventually became known as progressive education. In 1919 the Progressive Education Association (PEA) was founded with the purpose of reforming education.

15. In 1983 the National Commission for Excellence in Education published *A Nation at Risk: The Imperative for Educational Reform,* which startled the nation with its implications for failing to reform the system of public education.

Key Terms

Sophists
Academy
Lyceum
pedagogues
scholasticism
humanism
vernacular schools
dame schools

Latin Grammar Schools
compulsory education
hornbook
New England Primer
parochial schools
private venture schools
vocational training
English Grammar Schools

McGuffey Readers
common schools
normal schools
Carnegie Unit
land-grant colleges
categorical funding
bilingual education
teacher accountability

Educational Engineering

Case Studies in Education

Enter the information from the table below into the Educational Record for the student you are studying.

	Heritage	Aspirations	Cultural Identity
Davon	African American	Davon believes the sky's the limit right now. He is confident in his ability to learn and does so enthusiastically.	Davon feels neglected by his mother but is secure in his school. He made the following statement in a book he wrote: "I used to be sad, but I have been happy ever since I came to this school." He feels no cultural deprivation.
Andy	White Anglo-Saxon Protestant	Andy's grandfather is a former police chief of our community and is actively involved with his church. Andy feels confident that nothing bad will happen to him. He has his grandfather to protect him. When asked about what he would like to be when he grows up, Andy just shrugs. He did state that he would like to pass the third grade.	Andy is a likable child and is accepted by his peers. He has made friends in his homeroom class and also fits in well in his reading–instruction class. Any shortchanging he may feel is because he does not live with his mother and he knows that he doesn't read well. Considering that our school has many children living with grandparents and in foster care, he is not in a small percentage.

Judith	Judith's father is Caucasian and her mother is Hispanic. This is not uncommon in the population for our school.	Ethnic factors do not seem to enter into Judith's aspirations nearly as much as socio-economic status (SES) factors do at this time. She often indicates that she would like to become a teacher.	Judith does not seem to feel disenfranchised from the culture at large. She will sometimes confide that she has no friends or is unhappy. Yet she is as much a part of the mainstream life of children in school as she possibly can be.
Tiffany	Tiffany's father is Caucasian and her mother is Spanish. Her parents are Catholic.	Tiffany has never demonstrated any positive or negative aspirations concerning her future and its connection to her ethnic heritage.	There is a mild Spanish presence in Tiffany's environment, but otherwise her cultural identity would be characterized as "American."
Sam	African American	Sam's family background has influenced his aspirations. His family lacks formal education beyond 10th grade, and he has had very little exposure to experiences that would allow him to consider a variety of options. The IEP (Individual Education Plan) is required by law to link him with appropriate agencies to assist in transitioning to employment and obtaining appropriate employment training.	Sam's perception of his place in the culture at large is not very realistic or well developed at this time. With the appropriate education and support services necessary during and following high school, however, he should be able to take his place in mainstream society as a productive citizen.
Bao	Bao is a Vietnam-born U.S. citizen.	Sometimes Bao is frustrated because her family, friends, and society (both Vietnamese and mainstream American) expect her to be a doctor "just because she's Asian." Though Bao doesn't appreciate this pressure, she still wants to do well, and has chosen a respectable career aspiration. She plans on attending a four-year university and majoring in business.	Bao feels comfortable within both Vietnamese and American (white) cultures, and can move from one to the other with ease.

1. How has the history of education as presented helped or hindered educational opportunities for your student?
2. How could your perspective of the history of education influence the way you would interact with this student?
3. If your student were to ask you why people are treated differently (refer to the Heritage and Cultural Identity information as a guide to their concern), what would you say?
4. How will your career as a teacher affect the direction that education takes in the future?

 # Designing the School of the Future

It is very likely that the school you and your colleagues have designed thus far shares the foundation of education that has been described in this chapter. Under the heading of Historical Influences, address each of the following questions with regard to your evolving design.

1. Which issues in education presented in the chapter are present in your current design of the school of the future?
2. How can you use the lessons of history to improve your design?
3. For every issue there are at least two sides. How will the history of education serve to support your design against its critics?

 # Praxis Practice

Many states will require that you successfully complete the Praxis Series of examinations to qualify for certification. One or more of those tests will be subject-area tests. Another, which has a more practical orientation, will be the Principles of Learning and Teaching (PLT) examination that is appropriate for your certification area.

Completing the Quick Check Quizzes for Chapter 8 in the Unit Workshop will give you practice with the multiple choice format of the PLT. The Case Studies in Education and Designing a School of the Future activities will help prepare you for exercises that require reading a scenario and providing short answers to questions asking what you might do in such a situation.

Philosophy and Education

Make the chapter work for you with CPR²:

Conceptualize   Here are the major themes you will encounter in this chapter:

1. The conceptual clusters: metaphysics, axiology, epistemology, and logic
2. The schools of philosophy: idealism, realism, pragmatism, and existentialism
3. Philosophies in schools: perennialism, essentialism, progressivism, and social reconstructionism
4. Educational psychologies: behaviorism, humanism, and constructivism

Preview   Read the chapter headings; look at any figures, tables, and activities; and read through the items in the conclusion.

Activity 9.1: A Brief Look at Eastern Philosophy

Activity 9.2: Identifying Long-Lasting Consequences

Activity 9.3: Who Is Most Represented in a Perennialist Curriculum?

Activity 9.4: Field Observation Activity– Behaviorism in the Contemporary Classroom

Read   Now read through the chapter. Mark or highlight information that you consider to be especially important or about which you have a question.

Reflect   Consider this question as you read: How would you explain the impact of philosophy on education to someone else?

Photo: © Nancy Honey/Photonica/Getty Images Inc.

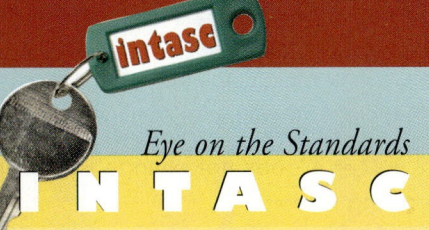

The following standards from the Interstate New Teacher Assessment and Support Consortium (INTASC) will be addressed in this chapter. As you read the chapter, consider how philosophy in general, and your philosophy in particular, are tied to these principles.

Principle 1 The teacher understands the central concepts, tools of inquiry, and structures of the discipline(s) he or she teaches and can create learning experiences that make these aspects of subject matter meaningful for students.

Principle 2 The teacher understands how children learn and develop, and can provide learning opportunities that support their intellectual, social, and personal development.

Principle 3 The teacher understands how students differ in their approaches to learning and creates instructional opportunities that are adapted to diverse learners.

Principle 5 The teacher uses an understanding of individual and group motivation and behavior to create a learning environment that encourages positive social interaction, active engagement in learning, and self-motivation.

Principle 9 The teacher is a reflective practitioner who continually evaluates the effects of his/her choices and actions on others (students, parents, and other professionals in the learning community) and who actively seeks out opportunities to grow professionally.

Principle 10 The teacher fosters relationships with school colleagues, parents, and agencies in the larger community to support students' learning and well-being.

ice breakers

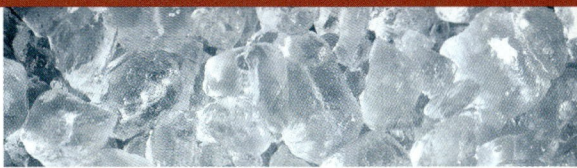

What Is Your Philosophical Disposition?

Read the statements below and mark the *four* statements that you consider most important with regard to education and teaching. You might find yourself struggling between two or three of them, but try to identify the four that you consider to be the most fundamental perspectives.

1. There are certain works of literature, such as *The Odyssey, Romeo and Juliet,* and *A Tale of Two Cities,* that everybody should read.

2. The job of the schools is to produce citizens who can improve our society and solve the problems it faces.

3. We use science even more than we think we do. For instance, we use it in cooking all the time, so it is necessary that people understand basic science principles such as forces, motion, and changes in states of matter.

4. We must understand math to survive in the world. For example, we use math when measuring things or when buying something. We need to know basic math because it is part of daily living.

5. Things change, fads come and go, but there are certain values that remain the same, like honesty, integrity, and personal responsibility. This is what students need to learn.

6. A child knows what his or her interests are, and that knowledge should guide the curriculum.

7. The problem with children today is poor parenting, and the best way to solve that problem is for the schools to teach adolescents how to become good parents.

8. Students should learn to appreciate beauty in the world because beauty is eternal. For instance, paintings that were considered beautiful hundreds of years ago are still considered beautiful today.

9. If the country is to survive, we must share the same values. All children should learn those basic values at school as well as at home.

10. If children are to function effectively in society, schools should provide them with experiences that reflect society such as exercises in democracy and good work habits.

11. Our public schools should "level the playing field" by providing equal opportunities for the social and intellectual development of all children.

12. We can begin solving the problems of the future by what we teach children today.

13. School is about more than just what's in books. It includes how one lives his or her life, worthy home membership, and wise use of leisure time.

14. Math is a constant; the idea of 2 + 2 = 4 does not change. Children need to learn these basic and enduring lessons.

15. The language of the United States is English, so everybody ought to learn to read, write, and speak proper English.

16. Schools educate individuals, not masses. The emphasis of school should be on the development of each individual.

Use the guide below to determine your philosophical disposition as you begin reading this chapter. If you have selected two or more items from a particular philosophy, it indicates that your thinking might match well with that perspective. If each of the items you chose is from a different category, your philosophy might be called *eclectic,* that is, a combination of philosophies. *Note:* This brief exercise is only intended to get a glimpse into your philosophical perspective. It is not an absolute measure of your philosophical perspective.

Perennialism	Essentialism	Progressivism	Social Reconstructionism
Items:			
1, 5, 8, 14	3, 4, 9, 15	6, 10, 13, 16	2, 7, 11, 12

This chapter will explain each of these philosophies. After completing the chapter you may find it interesting to read through this survey again to see whether your opinions have changed or remained the same.

In modern times there are opposing views about the practice of education. There is no general agreement about what the young should learn either in relation to virtue or in relation to the best life. . . . Men do not prize most highly the same virtue, so naturally they differ also about the proper training for it.

Aristotle

Introduction

Whether you have articulated it or not, philosophy is at the heart of your perspective of the world and of life. And it is, at least on this earth, the sole province of humankind—for no other life form that we know of is capable of considering philosophies. That we can do so is both a blessing and a curse. Philosophy is what has driven people to understand their world, to explore other worlds, to create works of art, and to invent the tools and machinery that extend our capabilities. Yet philosophy is also what has driven humans to war, destruction, and incredible cruelty to fellow human beings. There is perhaps no more powerful subject that you could entertain, nor another as intellectually challenging. It is also implicit in the work of teachers. Not surprisingly, the world's great philosophers were also teachers.

Teachers are frequently asked, Why do I have to learn this? What use will this have for me? Do not leave such questions for others to answer. You are becoming a professional with a *license* to facilitate the thinking of children as they develop into adulthood. The teacher, more so than most in our society, has an obligation to understand and articulate a clear philosophy. There is nothing mystical about this, and you are as capable as anyone to take part.

■ Developing Your Philosophical Perspective

In Chapter 1 we asked you to begin considering your own philosophy of teaching. We wanted you think about this important topic without a lot of "-ologies" and "-isms" getting in the way. Now you have had the opportunity to reflect on those first ideas and you have likely discussed a number of education issues on your way to this chapter. So let's get more specific about the philosophies that influence formal education, and look to see which (or perhaps a combination of several) would best help to articulate your own thinking. Keep in mind that a personal philosophy is, well, a personal matter. Nobody is trying to tell you what to think. Within this fascinating topic you must let your own thinking develop. It is entirely possible that a brand new philosophy might emerge.

Courtesy of Guilherme Cunha

Philosophy influences the messages we send to students formally and informally. Posting classroom rules or classroom student helper assignments are formal messages.

Though you should not be intimidated by philosophy, it is nonetheless a complex topic. The fact that questions entertained thousands of years ago are still under consideration is testament to that. However, applying some organizational structure to the topic will make it easier to handle, at least in the specific context of philosophy and education.

The word "philosophy" comes from the Greek words *philia,* "love," and *sophia,* "wisdom." The "love of wisdom" and the search for knowledge are broad concepts. We will narrow this vast topic by focusing on four *conceptual clusters* within the domain of philosophy: metaphysics, axiology, epistemology, and logic.

Our discussion will move from the conceptual clusters of philosophy to four of the major *schools of philosophy:* idealism, realism, pragmatism, and existentialism. These four schools of thought address the questions raised by the various branches of philosophy. In essence, each school of thought represents a perspective on the great questions facing humanity. These systems will lead us to "practical" applications of philosophies. In particular, our look at *philosophies in schools* will revolve around perennialism, essentialism, progressivism, and social reconstructionism. You have likely encountered versions of each of these philosophies in the schools you have attended.

Finally, our discussion will turn to several *psychological perspectives* that have been drawn from the philosophies we discuss. Behaviorism, humanism, and constructivism are all concerned with the way people learn things—or come to know things (epistemology)—but each focuses on psychological processes and interpersonal relationships more so than on philosophy. In essence, you might think of psychology as applied philosophy, that is, as philosophy made practical.

More Philosophical Perspectives

As we saw in Chapter 8, A History of Education, schooling in the United States has been most heavily influenced by western European philosophy. Elements of both philosophy and pedagogy dating back to the ancient Greeks and Romans can still be found in contemporary education. However, we do not want you to get the idea that western philosophical thought represents the only perspective on education. Indeed, just as we considered student diversity in terms of a multi-ethnic society (see Chapter 3), philosophy and its impact on education can be considered from various cultural perspectives. Let's look at a few examples.

Because all philosophies have "humanity" at their core, we can certainly expect to find overlapping ideas from one culture to another. However, as we saw in Chapter 3, the various ethnicities represented in our society bring different values to the classroom. For example, *community* is at the very heart of Native American philosophy. The emphasis that western philosophy (particularly the American version of it) places on the *individual* is completely contrary to the value system of Native American students and their families. The student-centered perspective that has developed in American public schools is in contrast to the very teacher-centered classrooms of Asian schools (e.g., those in PR China).

Education as an emancipating force within a society is a theme found in a number of educational philosophies. In *The Souls of Black Folk* (1903) W. E. B. DuBois argues with pointed conviction that education for the African American is more than just learning to read, write, and cultivate a vocation. Rather, it is the force for political and social change that will find a place for the black man in boardrooms and banks, in medicine and management. Similarly, Paulo Freire's landmark work, *Pedagogy of the Oppressed* (1968), used philosophic insight to develop an educational methodology that would empower people otherwise disenfranchised in an oppressive Latin American political climate.

In the years to come we may well anticipate that additional "non-western" influences will become part of the fabric of American education. Even now, if you look closely at the schools you will see how the examples we have discussed have influenced the course of education. We say "look closely" because much of the influence will be found on the level of the implicit curriculum rather than the explicit curriculum. For instance, although schools in the United States do emphasize individual effort and achievement, there are many implicit messages of community and teamwork. Did your high school have any athletic teams? Was there a band? How about school colors and perhaps a school song? All of these are implicit messages of working within a community. What other examples can you find? And perhaps even more provocatively, when you look at the world situation, what new influences can you anticipate? We have provided just a few brief examples because each of these philosophical perspectives could be a chapter of its own. All of this is what makes philosophy such a dynamic and complex intellectual endeavor.

■ Conceptual Clusters of Philosophical Questions

Our discussion of philosophies begins with the way in which trains of thought are conceptualized. We will discuss four conceptual clusters: metaphysics, axiology, epistemology, and logic.

Metaphysics

metaphysics The branch of philosophy that considers questions about the physical universe (e.g., the nature and origin of the physical world).

Metaphysics is the branch of philosophy that considers questions about the physical universe. The word physics refers to those things physical. The word "meta," however, implies a consideration that goes beyond mere physics, a consideration that *transcends* the physical world. What would constitute going beyond physics? In terms of philosophy, that would be a discussion of the nature and origin of the physical world itself. Questions such as What is real? or What is the origin of the world? would constitute metaphysical concerns. If you have ever wondered what exists

Figure 9.1

Philosophy Flow Chart

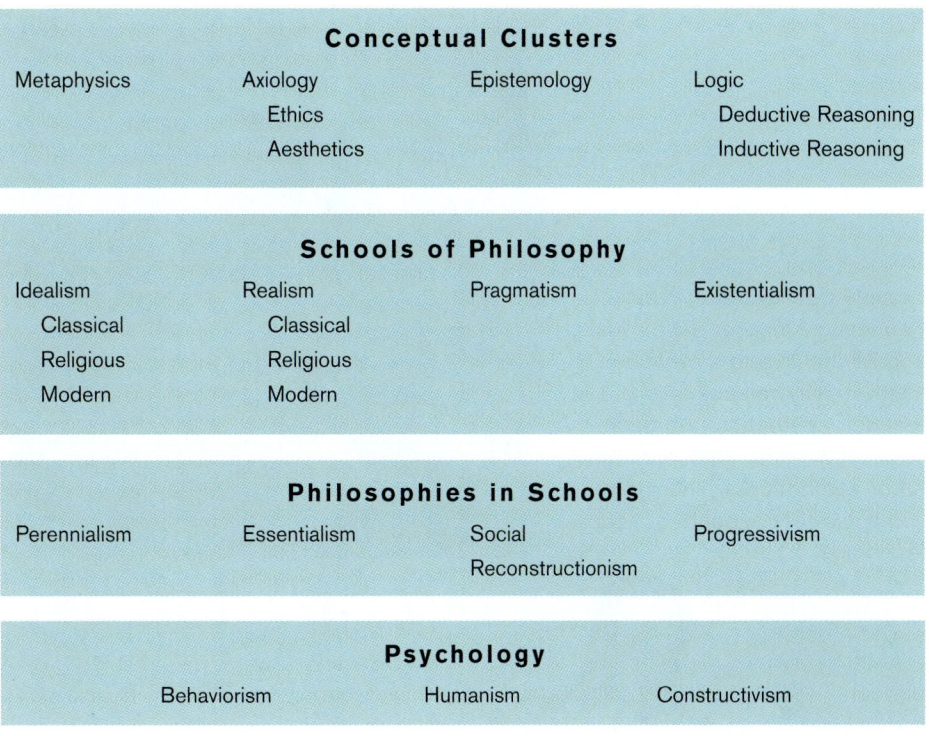

beyond the stars or have marveled at photographs taken by the Hubble space telescope, then you have entertained metaphysical thoughts. If you have ever considered the wonder of human development or asked yourself about your own abilities and potential, then you have also engaged in thought about metaphysical issues.

Axiology

axiology The branch of philosophy that considers the study of fundamental ideas or principles (i.e., the universally accepted truths of ethics and aesthetics).

Axiology is a term that may seem unfamiliar to you at first glance. However, if you think back to all of those "axioms" your high school math teacher spoke of, you will be right on track for understanding what this branch of philosophy is all about. No, the focus of axiology is not on mathematics but it is on those ideas or principles that are considered *fundamental;* those truths that are so universally accepted as to be considered self-evident. From the Greek word *axios,* meaning "worth," axiology is the study of values. In particular, axiology is concerned with two aspects of that which we value: ethics and aesthetics.

A study of *ethics* focuses on the ideas and beliefs that are valued by a society in a moral sense. You might think of it in terms of the moral underpinnings of a society. Morals represent a collective a view of what is right and wrong, whereas ethics represent the code of conduct for abiding by that view.

For instance, it is widely considered immoral—wrong—to take the life of another human being. You've been taught that idea since you were a child. So you probably believe at this point that it is wrong to end another's life; thus your code of ethics (and those laws adopted by our society) prevents you from doing so. Yet when a state executes a death sentence, the taking of another's life is considered ethically acceptable. The moral implication of that "self-evident truth" has remained unchanged, but ethically there is a justification for the act. Or is there? That debate continues today with no less fervor than in years gone by.

Aesthetics is the second arm of axiology. Here the concern is with the appreciation of beauty and the determination of what constitutes beauty for a given society.

Society deems both Wassily Kandinsky's *Improvisation XIV* and Michelangelo's *Pietà* as aesthetically valuable. As a teacher, aesthetics (a branch of axiology) and what is beautiful or aesthetically pleasing to you will affect aspects of your teaching.

© Giraudon/Art Resource, NY

© DesignPics Inc./Index Stock Imagery

What *does* constitute beauty? Is beauty as fundamental as those principles of ethics that seem to be self-evident? Though styles change, tastes change, and fads come and go, is there an "essence" to beauty that transcends all of these changes? These questions may sound like something that matters only to philosophers, but the fact is that the answers to these questions affect your life each day and certainly affect the work of teachers.

Societies place value on those things that they consider to be beautiful. Sometimes those things are superficial concerns such as one's weight or physical appearance. Sometimes beauty is valued in the structures that people design and build or in a painting or a song. These artifacts then become the symbols of the cultures from which they come. There is a considerable difference between the abstract expressionist beauty of Kandinsky's *Improvisation XIV* and the realism of Michelangelo's *Pietà*. Both, however, are considered to embody aesthetic value.

The artistic items of a primitive society might lack the "sophistication" of a more developed civilization but will not lack the sense of beauty that those artifacts represent. The question of what is and thus what should be valued for its beauty is always at issue within a society. A diverse society such as ours is challenged to resolve this question in the context of the many cultures we represent. You will see the "resolution" of the issue in the way that classrooms from kindergarten through high school are decorated.

Epistemology

epistemology The branch of philosophy that considers how people come to know what they know.

Epistemology has a considerable influence on formal education. Its root is the Greek word *episteme,* "knowledge" or "understanding." Thus, this is the study of how people come to know what they know. It is concerned with the nature and origin of truth and knowledge. Socrates was known for his notion that men were "pregnant with knowledge." By this he meant that knowledge exists within us and we merely need to bring that knowledge to the surface. Others, such as John Locke, would maintain that we come into this world with no knowledge at all, a *tabula rasa,* and we learn all we know from the world around us. Questions such

Table 9.1	Deductive/Inductive Reasoning
Deductive Reasoning	**Inductive Reasoning**
General statements are used to explain a particular example	Particular examples are gathered to make general statements

as whether truth and knowledge are absolute or relative, or whether knowledge is empirical (found from examining the "real world") or rational (all in the mind), fall into the domain of epistemology. "Think about this," a teacher might say, imploring students to rationalize the meaning of some lesson. "Let's compare this with what we found in our investigation yesterday," the teacher may say as students search for patterns in the physical world.

Logic

logic The branch of philosophy that seeks to bring order to the reasoning process. It includes inductive and deductive reasoning.

The fourth conceptual cluster of philosophy that we will consider is **logic**. You may feel better acquainted with this branch than any of the other three because it has informed much of your own education. Logic is the tool that seeks to bring order to your reasoning process. A logically defensible argument is one that rests on some intellectual structure rather than on unsubstantiated assumptions. Could teachers get through the day without the application of some logical framework to explain the behavior of their students? Perhaps, but it isn't likely.

Two important forms of logical reasoning are deductive reasoning and inductive reasoning (Table 9.1). *Deductive reasoning* characterized scientific inquiry for hundreds of years. This line of reasoning proceeds from general principles to explain specific events. Plato's use of the dialectic and Aristotle's use of the syllogism are good examples as they provide a major premise, a minor premise, and a subsequent conclusion. For example: All men are mortal (major premise). Socrates is a man (minor premise). Therefore, Socrates is mortal (conclusion). You can expect this sort of reasoning from young children. If you were to ask a child where a flower comes from, the response may well be that it came from God. Why? Because God made everything, something made this flower, and so it was made by God.

Though we won't argue theological issues in this book, we will point out the problem with deductive reasoning: If the major premise is incorrect, the conclusion is likely to be incorrect as well. Such was Galileo's dilemma when he questioned the current "wisdom" that Earth was the center of the universe.

Galileo also provides us with an example of the other form of logical reasoning, *inductive reasoning,* in which information from specific events is used to make generalized statements. Galileo's observations of the movement of heavenly bodies led him to conclude that the planets revolve around the sun. Induction, which largely from the work of Francis Bacon became the basis of scientific investigation as we know it today, demands items of evidence and a logical relationship among those items to draw broader conclusions.

■ Schools of Philosophy

As education in the United States was born of a European perspective, schools of Western philosophy are particularly relevant to our educational system. We look now at four such schools: idealism, realism, pragmatism, and existentialism.

Idealism

idealism The philosophy that the only true reality is that of ideas.

In a sense, all philosophies owe their existence to the philosophy of **idealism**. The reason is in the very term itself. Idealism is the philosophy of ideas. In fact, it might be more appropriate to refer to it as *ideaism*. Classical, modern, and religious idealism all rest on one theme: The only true reality is that of ideas. All else can be thought of as an elaborate illusion, a product of one's thinking. The "real world" from an idealist perspective is simply too changeable, too unstable to be taken as representing truth. Ideas, however, are universal and eternal. The concept of 2 + 2 = 4 (in a base 10 mathematical system) is unchanged by the weather, by war, by economics, or by religion. The truth of the idea is solid and enduring.

Classical Idealism

The "works" of Socrates were actually chronicled by Plato (427–347 BC), who used Socrates' conversations as the basis for the dialogues he wrote. Thus, reading Plato is like reading a play with Socrates a featured character.

The "Socratic method" refers to Socrates' habit of engaging people in conversation and, through careful questioning, pointing out both what they do know and what they do not know. The more proper term for the Socratic method is *maieutics,* which refers to midwifery. As you'll recall, we mentioned that Socrates believed men to be "pregnant with knowledge." His task, as he saw it, was to assist in the birth of that knowledge, just as a midwife assists in the birth of a child.

From an idealist perspective the truth, or knowledge, is something that exists. We do not create knowledge, we discover it. The search for the absolute truth, or what Plato referred to as the Good, is the quest of the philosopher. Our bridge to that truth is the mind. So, when Socrates admonishes "know thyself," he is indicating that the truth exists within us (by virtue of our minds) and that we have an obligation to bring that knowledge forth.

© Erich Lessing/Art Resource, NY

Socrates

Religious Idealism

You likely have been exposed to the notion of idealism through the various religions of the world. St. Augustine (AD 354–430) argued that there is a world of man and a world of God. As a result of original sin, man had been cast out of the world of God. It is our purpose to return to that world. The bridge between the two worlds is the soul. Because God has already created knowledge, we may discover it in our search for God. The truth, as established by God, is unchanging.

Idealism is also embodied in Far Eastern religions such as Buddhism and Hinduism. The primary distinctions between classical idealism and religious idealism are that the truth has a name (such as God or Buddha, for example), and that our bridge to finding the truth is the soul rather than the mind.

Modern Idealism

Rene Descartes (1596–1650) and George Berkeley (1685–1753) are among the leading thinkers of "modern" idealism. Descartes approached the issue of the material world versus the world of the mind with a system of methodical doubt. He asked himself what he really knew for certain. That is, of what could he truly say he had no doubt? The result was the Cartesian first principle: *cogito, ergo sum*— I think, therefore I am. Establishing the clear centrality of the mind, he concluded that the one thing of which he could be certain was that because he was thinking, he must exist. Yet the conclusion that he exists leads to another question; if he exists, where did he come from? Clearly there must be some other cause, some *first* cause. There must exist some Deity that enabled Descartes to exist.

George Berkeley, a theologian, tried to further clarify idealist philosophy by arguing for the existence of God as the cause of all things. Berkeley asserted that all existence depends upon some mind to "know" it. His conclusion, *esse est percipi*—to be is to be perceived—states that all any of us "know" is that which we perceive, and thus anything that is not perceived cannot be said to exist. The mind, he argued, was necessary to perceive those things. No doubt you have heard the classic example: If a tree falls in a forest, and there is no one there to hear it, does it make a sound? That is, does the "sound" depend upon somebody hearing it to exist? But the problem for Berkeley was, if *our* existence depends upon being perceived, who perceives us? Berkeley suggested that we can be said to exist because we are perceived by God.

What does a philosophy of idealism bring to the table with regard to school? A system of education that emphasizes idealism will focus on intellectual activity and develop morals and ethics. At a time when many are calling for character development experiences in the public schools, idealism offers the notion that there do exist ideals and truths that govern us all.

Realism

You probably noticed the realists in your classroom as soon as the discussion of idealism began. The ones who immediately asserted that the real world exists "because it does" are grounded in the philosophy that has governed much of our system of formal organized education. Of course, "because it does" does not constitute a strong philosophical argument. However, the arguments of the empiricists (those who seek evidence) as opposed to the rationalists (those who say it is all a function of mind) are compelling.

realism The philosophy that maintains that matter is real and that ideas underlie matter.

Aristotle

© Louvre, Paris, France, Giraudon/The Bridgeman Art Library

Classical Realism

The philosophy of **realism** can be traced to Aristotle (384–322 BC), Plato's neighbor in ancient Greece. Aristotle, once Plato's student, established his famous school, the Lyceum, adjacent to Plato's Academy. It is not uncommon for a student to extend or transform the work of a teacher, but it is extraordinary to think that these two philosophies have endured for thousands of years and yet were developed within a single community by two collegial contemporaries.

The philosophy of realism maintains that matter is real and exists independent of the mind. Though you may not perceive and study a particular object, the realist contends that the object nonetheless exists. Aristotle did not completely reject the notion of ideas as being the true reality. Instead, he suggested that Forms (ideas) can exist independent of matter, as in the case of mathematics, but that matter cannot exist independent of Form. That is, there is an underlying idea to all matter. This means that the study of matter will ultimately lead to an understanding of Form. So, in realist philosophy the emphasis is not on the question of whether only ideas exist, but instead is focused on what physical matter can tell us about ideas. From an Aristotelian perspective we should try to understand the reality of all things.

How do we go about studying this real world and uncovering the Form it contains? According to Aristotle we must ask the appropriate questions. At times those questions deal with physical things and at other times with philosophical ideas. Underlying all inquiry, however, is the question of *purpose:* What is an object's purpose? For people, he goes on to say, the purpose is to think—and to think intelligently. Through such thinking we will come to understand.

Clearly, though, many people fail to think to their potential. How can this be if thinking is our purpose? Aristotle asserted that part of our thinking ability is the capacity to exercise free will. Some people use that free will to make the determination not to think intelligently. No doubt you know many people who prefer not to think deeply or thoroughly about many things. Such a decision, from Aristotle's perspective, is at cross-purposes to the thinking abilities that people have.

The consequence of failing to think intelligently is that people fall victim to the extremes that can affect their lives. In all things one can find an extreme of excess and an extreme of restraint. Aristotle recommends that the proper course is one of moderation. We should seek what he calls the Golden Mean. Education develops one's reasoning capacity, and we should use that ability for the making of proper choices.

Religious Realism

There is also a religious perspective to realism. In the 13th century St. Thomas Aquinas (1225–1274) explained the real world versus the world of God in terms of reason. God, he maintained, is pure reason, and thus the universe is reason as well. By using reason we can understand the truth of all things. Our senses provide us with knowledge of the world. Since our purpose is to reunite the soul with God, it is the real world working with our spiritual existence that fulfills our purpose in life: a search that moves us from our imperfect world to the perfect world of God. As you can see, the religious perspective of realism follows very closely to Aristotle's perspective, and both seek to find the same ultimate Truth that Plato sought.

Modern Realism

Some problems with idealism and realism bothered thinkers through the ages. One of the greatest concerns was the emphasis on deductive reasoning, an issue we raised earlier in this chapter. Francis Bacon (1561–1626) sought to change the course of systematic reasoning from the deductive approach to the inductive approach. Bacon argued that one should begin with the particulars—the physical world around us—and avoid preconceived notions. He discussed the preconceived notions that cloud our thinking as the four Idols:

Idol of the Den—We believe what we believe because of our limited experiences. There may be more information available, but we stick with what we already know.

Idol of the Tribe—We believe what those around us believe. This is not hard to understand because typically we are taught the accepted belief or explanation. The problem is that we often fail to question the truth of the explanation, an action that could lead to ostracism.

Idol of the Marketplace—What we believe may be based on miscommunication. Language is often unclear and misleading.

Idol of the Theatre—We may unquestioningly accept religious and philosophical positions. (1889)

John Locke (1632–1704) offered a perspective that emphasized the influence of the physical world. There are no innate ideas, spiritual or otherwise, in Locke's view. The Socratic notion that men are "pregnant with knowledge" would be non-sense. Rather, at birth our minds are a blank slate, a *tabula rasa,* and all that we come to know will be written by the hand of experience. The ideas that we may one day have will be derived from *sensation* (detection of experiences in the real world) and *reflection* (thinking about those experiences). This may sound familiar to you if any of your professors require that you keep a reflective journal of your observations in schools. You are probably required to chronicle what occurs in the classrooms you visit and to reflect on those experiences. The result is knowledge that you previously did not possess.

As you reflect on your own educational experience, you may see that it has provided you with *particular* experiences. Those experiences represent the values and priorities of the culture in which you were raised. Your reflection upon those experiences has made you who you are.

As you study more about human development and educational psychology, you will encounter references to Pestalozzi, Froebel, Herbart, and Montessori. For each of these educators, the real world played an integral part in the education of children. Pestalozzi championed the cause of object study. Froebel introduced the idea of the kindergarten. Herbart believed that the purpose of school was moral development, and also saw the need for relating all subjects to each other. Montessori saw the value of play in learning. In all cases, the emphasis is on inter-action with "the real world."

A realist-based education would emphasize a strong moral character because there are enduring truths to be understood. With its focus on inquiry we could also expect educational efforts to be systematic, highly organized, and fairly rigid. Indeed, schools have long embraced a realist perspective toward understanding the world. A realist emphasis in education would call for teachers who are both experts in their particular subject and liberally educated so they might appreciate the place of their subject in relation to others.

Go Online!

ACTIVITY 9.1   A Brief Look at Eastern Philosophy

Eastern philosophy has influenced education in the United States less than Western philosophy has. However, as the Asian and Middle Eastern populations in the United States increase, we can expect to see an increasing Eastern influence in the schools. This activity is suggested so that you can consider a perspective that is possibly new to you.

Select one or more of the schools of thought listed below and use the Internet to find information to help you answer the questions that follow.

Buddhism	Hinduism	Confucianism
Zen Buddhism	Islam	Taoism

1. How does the school of thought you have chosen differ from Western thought as you know it?
2. How is it the same?
3. How could an Eastern philosophical influence become part of the culture of school as we know it? Would it be part of the entire culture? Would it be something recognized only during a selected month of the school year?
4. Which of the Western philosophies most closely parallels the Eastern philosophy you have selected?

Pragmatism

pragmatism The theme that ideas must serve a useful purpose.

The philosophy of **pragmatism** is much more contemporary than that of idealism or realism. Though its roots can be traced to the ancient Greeks, it has emerged as a school of thought largely during the past two centuries. That may sound like a pretty lengthy history, but remember that the philosophies of idealism and realism are in their third millennium.

Pragmatism, meaning "work," refers to a philosophical theme based on the notion that ideas must serve a useful purpose. Pragmatism focuses on seeking out processes that help people to reach desirable ends, and that includes a consideration of the *consequences* of those actions. Thus, it is a very practical approach to philosophy. Those who see philosophy as intellectual game-playing may see pragmatism as a philosophy that works for them in the real world. Not surprisingly, it has had a tremendous impact upon public education in the United States over the last century.

Establishing the Foundation for Pragmatism

The foundation for contemporary pragmatism refers us once again to the work of Francis Bacon (1561–1626). As you will recall, Bacon's work was instrumental in the shift from a deductive to an inductive approach to inquiry. That same emphasis on induction and "the scientific method" was also evident in the work of Charles Sanders Peirce (1839–1914). In "How to Make Our Ideas Clear" (1878), Peirce argued that reality exists independent of mind (as Aristotle argued), but that our understanding of objects in the real world is tied to our *individual* perception and thus our individual ideas about the objects. In essence, your understanding of some object or event may be quite different from that of any one of your classmates, and yet both explanations can be legitimate representations of the world. Because of this it is important that we be extremely careful and precise in the formation of those ideas.

Here's an example. Perhaps you have sent an e-mail that was misinterpreted by the recipient. Maybe something you meant as a joke was taken as a serious comment. For a time, the two of you operated with different ideas about the same situation. Your individual responses to those ideas, of course, were based on your perception of the original event. Neither one of you were actually wrong about the situation, but you had different perspectives, and your responses were based on the reality that you constructed.

John Dewey

© Corbis

William James (1842–1910) took this notion a step further when he suggested that truth itself must then be a relative term. James suggested that the universe itself is in process. That is, rather than "being," it is still "becoming." Thus, it is useless to assume that a single Truth or Absolute exists. This does not mean that *all* experiences are necessarily truthful just because we wish it so. Instead, James argued, all experiences can and should be examined for the truth they may contain. James referred to this examination as "radical empiricism."

Pragmatism Becomes Practical

Pragmatism comes in several varieties: romantic naturalism, experimentalism, and progressivism. One name that will appear prominently in a discussion of each is that of John Dewey (1859–1952). In realist philosophy Aristotle had suggested that the purpose of humans is to think. Dewey, as a pragmatist—or more properly, an experimentalist—took that notion a step further. He suggested that genuine thought begins with *a problematic situation*. That is, when people think, they do so for the purpose of solving some problem or question. Thus our purpose in a pragmatic sense is to solve problems.

Creative intelligence is fostered by solving real problems according to Dewey, and "the scientific method" can be used in solving a vast array of problems. He sees ideas as the instruments for solving problems and outlines a five-step process for accomplishing the task:

1. Recognize that a problem exists.
2. Clearly define the problem.
3. Suggest possible solutions.
4. Consider the potential consequences of the possible solutions.
5. Carry out further observation and experiment leading to a solution's acceptance or rejection. (Dewey, 1933)

Notice the prominent role of reflection in Dewey's work as he suggests that we consider possible solutions to a problem in terms of their consequences. As you study educational psychology, you will find steps much like these discussed in problem solving today.

For Dewey, the main purpose of all education was the "reconstruction or reorganization of experience which adds to the meaning of experience and which increases ability to direct the course of subsequent experiences" (1916, pp. 89–90). This, of course, is what scientists do, and Dewey saw no reason why it could not be applied in other situations. His approach considers "truth" in the same tentative manner as scientific knowledge. The examination of such truth is a problem-solving process that employs our ability to reflect upon experiences and consider the impact of our intentions. As Dewey says, "We always live at the time we live and not some other time, and only by extracting at each present time the full meaning of each present experience are we prepared for doing the same thing in the future" (1938, p. 51). In this constant interplay of individuals with their environment, experience is the key.

ACTIVITY 9.2
Identifying Long-Lasting Consequences

Pragmatism's relevance to daily life is not difficult to demonstrate. Unfortunately, it is often easier to identify examples in which people have failed to consider consequences. For example, you are likely taking notes during this course with a disposable pen rather than a fountain pen or even one that uses replaceable cartridges. Yet all of those throw-away pens have to go somewhere. What do you suppose are the consequences?

1. For each of the following categories, list some events or decisions that have had long-lasting consequences. Consider whether those consequences had been anticipated.

   Political   Educational   Environmental

2. Take a stand on each of the following education issues. If your stance were adopted, what would be the immediate consequences? What might the consequences be 20 years from now?

   Single Gender Schools   School Uniforms   Vouchers
   Comprehensive Testing   Lottery Funding   Year-Round Schools

So we must consider that students live in the present time and are not in school merely to be prepared for a future time. The experiences of school must facilitate problem-solving ability and reflection. If students are to become good citizens, they must have experiences that foster good citizenship and have practice solving problems as a good citizen would be expected to do. If they are to become democratic in their thinking, they must have democratic experiences to build upon.

In the first half of the 20th century, Dewey's experimentalism became an explosive philosophical movement in education known as *progressivism.* The progressivist movement sought to interpret curriculum development with an eye toward changing times. Rather than focusing on traditional subject matter, the idea was to focus on problem solving. Topics can change, as does the accumulated body of knowledge as time goes by, but the *skill* of problem solving remains. Such an approach in our information-rich world of the 21st century offers phenomenal opportunities to prepare generations that will solve problems in new and visionary ways. The classroom teacher in such a system must be a risk taker who is capable of understanding a bigger picture than is required in the typical subject-centered approach of school, but who is also able to entertain possibilities for an even bigger picture to come.

Existentialism

existentialism The philosophy that emphasizes thoughtful personal reflection about one's identity, beliefs, and choices.

Existentialism demonstrates the progression of thought from idealism to realism to pragmatism. The shift is from an emphasis on the mind to *understand* the universe to an emphasis on the mind to *create* the universe. In our discussion of idealism we mentioned the question of "if a tree falls in a forest. . ." and indicated that for an idealist, perception of the event was the key component in the riddle. An idealist, therefore, would say that if the event was not perceived, it cannot be said that it actually occurred. The realist would say that the trees in the forest do not require our perception in order to exist, so that which is part of "tree falling-ness" happens whether or not someone is there. The pragmatist says that if she wasn't there and it has exerted no influence on what she's doing, what difference does it make? We live life in the here and now, so let's concentrate on what we are doing. The existentialist simply says, "What tree?"

Existentialism is associated with individuals such as Jean-Paul Sartre (1905–1980), Soren Kierkegaard (1813–1854), and Friedrich Nietzsche (1844–1900). Fundamental to existentialism is the notion that for each person death is inevitable. The worldly existence that we enjoy is only temporary; that which lies beyond our existence is no more than pure speculation. Thus there is a sense of dread, of angst, about existentialism even though it offers hope as individuals take responsibility for their own lives. Existentialism emphasizes thoughtful personal reflection about identity, beliefs, and individual choices.

Existentialism places the *responsibilities* that come with being a thinking being squarely on the shoulders of each individual. For the existentialist, there is no divine plan, no predestination that one can rely upon. As George Knight explains, "The traditional philosophies surrender man's authority to a logical system, the Christian leans on God, the realist looks to nature for meaning, and the pragmatist relies on the community. All of the avenues are ways of removing man from the frightful reality of being responsible for his choices" (1982, p. 72). Indeed, the existentialist philosophy allows tremendous latitude to the individual but also holds that individual responsible for the choices she makes.

In essence, the primary choice made by an individual from an existentialist perspective is that of self-determination. The existentialist must choose whether to

© Hulton-Deutsch Collection/Corbis

A. S. Neill at the
Summerhill School

define herself and be the person she wants to be or to be defined by others. One of the two will happen—the choice is left to the individual.

Education can be very much influenced by an existentialist approach. This philosophy seems tailor-made for American public schools because we presumably champion individual freedom of choice and the development of individual potential. Yet the underlying message of school is often conformity, teamwork, and the greatest good for the greatest number even though that might infringe upon the freedoms of the individual. Existentialism's emphasis on individual self-fulfillment lacks the group orientation that is typical of schools today. And certainly, providing an individualized curriculum for each of the 50 million students enrolled in public schools would carry tremendous obstacles.

Smaller-scale private educational agencies might find it easier to advance an existentialist approach to education, allowing students to direct their own learning and pace their own progress. One example of a school based on an existentialist perspective is Summerhill, founded in 1924 by A. S. Neill (1883–1973) and still in operation today.

It should be noted that some of the best of teaching and learning is exemplified by existentialist philosophy. The emphasis on reflection, dialogue, and the determination of one's own point of view are worthwhile exercises. Teachers in such a system would put a premium on divergent thinking, open and honest discourse, and allowing students to formulate ideas—that could be further discussed—rather than imposing ideas on students.

■ ■ ■

Idealism offered us the notion of a universe that exists with its own indisputable truths and unchanging ideas. We could be a part of that universe by virtue of the mind. Perception of the "real world" was not to be trusted, and so rational thinking was the key. Realism went on to say that the real world provides the evidence from which we can come to know universal truths. Thinking is the key, and the stuff of reality is the lock into which that key fits to open the way to understanding. Pragmatism comes along and says all that's fine, but what have you done for me lately? That is, while an independent reality might exist apart from our mind, we nonetheless influence that reality with our decisions and our actions as we live each day. The pragmatist insists that though body and mind exist, their interaction is part of their mutual existence—the one affects the other—so let's put our minds to work to accomplish practical ends. Now along comes existentialism. Here the bottom line is that the world is what we make of it—no more, no less. Reality as you know it depends upon you. No universal truths, no immutable ideas, no independent universe to speak of, only that which you have come to believe. The Truth is your own.

Philosophies in Schools

Idealism, realism, pragmatism, and existentialism represent four major philosophical systems. They can influence individuals and societies in many ways. As we discuss *perennialism, essentialism, progressivism,* and *social reconstructionism,* look for the links they have to the four schools of philosophy that we have considered.

Perennialism

perennialism The perspective that certain ideas and truths transcend time and are prevalent in the great literature of the ages.

Perennialism maintains that there are ideas and truths that are, well, perennial. Influenced both by idealism and realism, the perennialist perspective asserts that such ideas have transcended time and remain as vital today as they ever were. These themes are prevalent in the great literature of the ages and provide an insight into the universe and the place of humanity within it. In this view, education should represent an organized effort to make these ideas accessible to students and to guide their consideration and understanding of those ideas.

Perennialism has been referred to as a *culturally conservative* perspective because it is based on classic works and reveres the foundation laid by tradition. Universal truth is unaffected by pop culture or the circumstances of a given time. As an idealist would say, seeking out and understanding that truth is our purpose in life. As the realist would suggest, the great works of civilization provide the tools for that search. There is stability and constancy in the perennialist approach. If you can accept the notion that the more things change, the more they stay the same, then the perennialist perspective is one that you may well embrace.

Perennialism as an Educational Philosophy

Perennialism as an educational philosophy poses some very interesting challenges for American public schools. Ours is a heritage still in process. Despite our Western roots, our national complexion is very diverse. For a perennialist perspective to survive in the 21st century and beyond, it may well be necessary to examine the truths of civilizations and societies that have not been "traditionally" included in the American portrait.

Nonetheless, perennialism offers guidelines for the conduct of schools and even for the students within those schools. Two of the leading proponents of the perennialist approach in the latter half of the 20th century were Robert Maynard

In Their Own Words

Feature 9.1   Robert Maynard Hutchins

The following passage is excerpted from The Great Conversation *(1952), in which Hutchins presents the case for a liberal arts education based upon what are considered the great works of literature from the ancient to modern era. Following the defense of the liberal arts, he and his colleagues laid out a ten-year reading list to accomplish their aims. This passage is from Chapter 4: The Disappearance of Liberal Education.*

The results of universal, free, compulsory education in America can be acceptable only on the theory that the object of the schools is something other than education, that is, for example, to keep the young from cluttering up homes and factories during a difficult period of their lives, or that it is to bring them together for social or recreational purposes.

These last purposes, those which are social and recreational, the American educational system, on a very low level, achieves. It throws young people together. Since this does not take any greater effort than is required to

pass compulsory school laws and build buildings, the accomplishment of this purpose would not at first blush seem to be a matter for boasting. Yet we often hear of it as something we should be proud of, and even as something that should suggest to us the main line of a sound educational policy. We often hear that bringing young people together, having them work and play together, and having them organize themselves "democratically" are the great contributions to democracy that the educational system can make. This is an expansion of the doctrine that was popular in my youth about the moral benefits conferred on everybody through intercollegiate athletics, which was, in turn, an adaptation of the remark dubiously imputed to the Duke of Wellington about the relationship between the battle of Waterloo and the playing fields of Eton.

No one can deny the value of getting together, of learning to get along with others, of coming to appreciate the methods of organization and the duties of member-

Hutchins and Mortimer Adler. Adler's *Paideia Proposal: An Educational Manifesto* (1982), which pays homage to Horace Mann (equal education for all children), John Dewey (education should promote reflective thinking and skills that will improve a student's life), and Robert Hutchins (education should draw out the "common humanity" of those being educated), is a fascinating treatment of how a perennialist approach could be implemented in the public schools.

Subject matter is at the heart of education for the perennialist: Schools must focus on the skills of reading, writing, speaking, and listening, particularly in the early grades so that students will be able to study the great works of literature, history, and philosophy in the later grades. Relentless drill-and-practice will prepare students for the intellectual challenges that await them. The use of textbooks and lectures would be severely curtailed as students are engaged in seminars and debate. Vocational training would be eliminated. The school is responsible for the cultivation of mental discipline that affords the ability to assume a lifelong quest for the truth. Job training, in the perennialist view, is the responsibility of an employer.

Essentialism

Have you ever heard someone say that education needs to get back to the basics? That was a call for an *essentialist* curriculum. Essentialism is the perspective that suggests there are core skills and knowledge that all students should acquire, skills that are essential for sustaining our social order. As was the case with perennialism, essentialism seeks to preserve a society's cultural heritage.

essentialism The perspective that there are core skills and knowledge that all students should acquire.

Essentialism emphasizes the training of the mind by virtue of a subject-centered curriculum. It is a philosophy that came into being during the first half of the 20th century when leading educators hotly debated the purpose and future course of organized education. Essentialism's most vocal proponent at the time was William C. Bagley (1847–1946). Bagley and his colleagues firmly believed that the purpose of school was not to change society, but rather to preserve it. School

---

ship in an organization any more than one can deny the importance of physical health and sportsmanship. It seems on the face of it a trifle absurd, however, to go to the trouble of training and engaging teachers, of erecting laboratories and libraries, and of laying out a program of instruction and learning if, in effect, the curriculum is extra and the extra-curriculum is the heart of the matter.

. . . There can be little argument about the proposition that the task of the future is the creation of a community. Community seems to depend on communication. This requirement is not met by improvements in transportation or in mail, telegraph, telephone, or radio services. These technological advances are frightening, rather than reassuring, and disruptive, rather than unifying, in such a world as we have today. They are the means of bringing an enemy's bombs or propaganda into our homes.

The effectiveness of modern methods of communication in promoting a community depends on whether there is something intelligible and human to communicate. This, in turn, depends on the common language, a common stock of ideas, and common human standards. These the Great Conversation affords. Reading these books should make a man feel himself a member of the species and tradition that these books come from. He should recognize the ties that bind him to his fellow members of the species and tradition. He should be able to communicate, in a real sense, with other men.

. . . Imagine the younger generation studying great books and learning the liberal arts. Imagine an adult population continuing to turn to the same sources of strength, inspiration, and communication. We could talk to one another then. We should be even better specialists than we are today because we could understand the history of our specialty and its relation to all the others. We would be better citizens and better men. We might turn out to be the nucleus of the world community. ■

should provide a student with the skills to study the culture and understand its traditions. In that regard essentialism is similar to perennialism as a culturally conservative philosophy of education.

But essentialism differs from perennialism in distinctive ways. The perennialist goal of understanding truths and universal principles takes a backseat to the essentialist goal of preserving the culture. Essentialism focuses on academic skills. Rather than seminar and dialogue, an essentialist education is focused on lecture, memorization, practice, and assessment. The early years of schooling should be devoted to the learning of skills in reading and computation. The later years will put those skills to work in studying the people and events that have fashioned our culture, our traditions, and the institutions that have arisen within our society. Vocational training, social promotion, and course offerings that fail to advance the rigorous culture-bound curriculum have no value within this philosophical perspective.

Essentialism was a contender in the educational debates of the early 20th century and is more than just a footnote in educational history. Throughout the past century and even now in the 21st century, the back-to-basics call has been repeated in very strong voices. The landmark 1983 report *A Nation at Risk* warned of the watering-down of the American public school curriculum. It recommended a core curriculum for high-school students that included English, mathematics, science, social studies, and computer science.

The movement toward essentialism did not end with *A Nation at Risk.* In 1987 E. D. Hirsch Jr., published *Cultural Literacy.* In this work Hirsch acknowledged the lament of essentialists from 50 years earlier: Schools are failing to provide instruction in the common culture that binds a nation together, there are skills and knowledge that all students should acquire, and the continued failure to provide a rigorous and culture-based education will be detrimental to the nation itself. "There is a pressing need," Hirsch wrote, "for clarity about our educational purposes" (1988, p. 25). The message that the essentialist curriculum is a curriculum for all students in a democratic society has been argued persuasively for nearly 100 years in our nation. As Hirsch suggests:

> Although nationalism may be regrettable in some of its world-wide political effects, a mastery of national culture is essential to mastery of the standard language in every modern nation. This point is important for educational policy, because educators often stress the virtues of multicultural education. Such study is indeed valuable in itself, it inculcates tolerance and provides a perspective on our own traditions and values. But however laudable it is, it should not be the primary focus of national edu-

Go Online!

ACTIVITY 9.3   Who Is Most Represented in a Perennialist Curriculum?

The view of perennialism as "culturally conservative" implies that a particular and identifiable culture exists that perennialists wish to conserve.

1. Working individually or in small groups, construct a definition of "American culture." That is, what does it mean to be an American? Your definition should describe you and all other Americans.
2. In 1952 perennialists Robert M. Hutchins and Mortimer Adler selected works to be published as the series *Great Books of the Western World.* Find a list of these books on the Internet. In what ways do the books on that list support your definition of what it is to be American? What sort of books, if any, are missing?

cation. It should not be allowed to supplant or interfere with our school's primary responsibility to ensure our children's mastery of American literate culture. The acculturative responsibility of the schools is primary and fundamental. (1988, p. 18)

To provide an effective essentialist curriculum, teachers need to be subject-area specialists. This is a contrast to the liberally educated teachers called for in the perennialist tradition, though very much in keeping with the No Child Left Behind Act of 2002 that mandates highly qualified and credentialed teachers in each subject area. The contemporary emphasis on achievement testing is central to the essentialist approach. Similarly, the move toward "accountability" of students, teachers, and schools falls within the "academic rigor" advocated by an essentialist philosophy.

Progressivism

progressivism The philosophical focus on positive change that individuals with various educational backgrounds can provide.

The educational philosophy of **progressivism,** more so than that of perennialism and essentialism, needs to be considered in a very particular cultural context. The 1800s represented the United States' first "full century" as a nation. During that time, the visionary tenets of democracy laid out in the late 1700s were tested in many ways, not the least of which was the divisive state-against-state struggle of the Civil War. The nation withstood these internal tests, accepted throngs of immigrants, made a dramatic shift to becoming an industrialized society, and entered the 1900s with an innovative vigor. That this same momentum might trickle down to the public schools is of no particular surprise.

The cultural conservatives had the perspective that the culture "had arrived" and that school was the experience that taught that culture to a new generation. The progressivists, however, felt that the time was ripe for change. In this philosophy the focus is on positive change that individuals with a particular educational background could provide. Change was based on "doing" more so than on "knowing," and on solving problems more so than on passing on the culture as it existed. Within the schools this would mean a shift from the subject-centered perspective of the traditional curriculum to a child-centered approach.

Courtesy of Becky Stovall

Progressivism is characterized by a child-centered curriculum in which the child determines his or her own course of study

The *romantic naturalism* vein of progressivism stemmed from the work of Jean-Jacques Rousseau (1712–1778). Believing that people are basically good and are corrupted by civilization, Rousseau advocated an education away from the influences of the city and in a venue that allowed nature to be the classroom. The interests of the child would guide the curriculum.

Following the teachings of John Dewey, the progressivists adopted the perspective that people learn best from experiences that are meaningful in their lives. Talk of disciplining the mind to pursue universal truths is replaced with talk of the relevance of life experience. Progressivism had a high regard for the individual and embraced the pragmatist ideas of a scientific method in the development of thinking and the solving of problems, scientific or otherwise. This, combined with the acceptance of change, made the progressivist philosophy in education an obvious fit for a changing, developing country with high aspirations. In 1938 Boyd Bode, a leading progressive proponent and watchdog in the fight to maintain a philosophic integrity within the movement, wrote: "The emphasis of progressive education on the individual, on the sinfulness of imposition, and on the necessity of securing free play for intelligence, is a reflection of the growing demand, outside of school, for recognition of the common man" (p. 11).

Progressivism was indeed having an impact on educational thought in the United States. It is difficult to say that it ever *replaced* the traditional education, but rather it inched its way into the curriculum as the years went by. As you know from your own educational experiences, there has been a core of subjects that students were responsible for studying. Yet your school likely offered a far wider array of educational opportunities than were standard in the early years of the 20th century. However, all was not well within the progressivist camp.

Many versions of progressivism arose, leading to divisions within the movement. Bode became a leading challenger to the progressivist policy of allowing children to determine their own curriculum. There were those who argued that progressivism was specifically preventing children from benefiting from the knowledge that adults possessed and the collective wisdom of the ages. Bode wrote: "[T]he purpose of sound education is precisely to emancipate the pupil from dependence on immediate interests. A person cannot remain a baby all his life" (1938, p. 63).

Ideally, in a progressive curriculum one would never hear students ask why they had to learn one thing or another; the value of the learning would be self-evident. Moreover, as Carlton Washburne, superintendent of the Winnetka schools in Illinois, wrote: "Childhood is a beautiful section of life, and children should be given a chance for free, full living. . . . We believe in colorfulness, coziness, hominess in our classrooms; in an opportunity for spontaneity. We want children to want to come to school" (1926, p. 349). Conceptualy, all this was good. Practically, however, any innovation has to answer to the results, and that seemed to be a problem for the progressivist movement, particularly in light of the inconsistencies that were developing within the movement.

The progressivists were never successful in fashioning a statement of philosophy that spoke for the entire movement. They did agree on aspects of the traditional school that they disliked, such as a textbook-based curriculum, teachers as disseminators of information rather than facilitators of thinking, and the school's relative "distance" from the real world. They even agreed on some of the things they favored, such as the child-centered curriculum, the teacher as a facilitator, and the stimulation of interest through direct experience. But there was no unanimity for carrying out the philosophy. In the late 1940s and the 1950s, exceedingly low literacy rates among young men entering the military and the Soviet launch of Sputnik both served notice that changes needed to be made. The 1990 report *Science for All Americans* suggested that the school curriculum had become "overstuffed and undernourished" (p. viii), indicating that education had lost precisely the academic rigor for which the perennialists and essentialists had argued.

Social Reconstructionism

social reconstructionism
The perspective that schools are the agency for solving societal problems.

Social reconstructionism is another product of the educational debates of the early 20th century. It is a perspective that specifically sees the schools as the agency for solving the problems of society. Schools provide the future leaders for the community, state, and nation, and therefore must present a curriculum that prepares students to meet the challenges that lie ahead. With this said, it might seem that the social reconstructionists take a *proactive* approach to education, that is, looking toward educating a generation of problem-solvers. The more accurate statement, however, is that proponents of social reconstructionism are *reacting* to the significant social problems that exist today (and "today" could have been 75 years ago or it could be as you read this text in the 21st century) and that threaten to unravel our culture and social system. This represents a very different approach from anything we have discussed thus far.

As a reaction to socioeconomic inequities, social reconstructionism is not really a philosophy. It would be difficult to assign it to any one of the conceptual clusters: metaphysics, axiology, epistemology, or logic. Instead, social reconstructionism seems to be more of an antidote to social problems and uses the schools as part of the prescription. However, it does have similarities to other philosophies we have discussed. Theodore Brameld (1904–1987), an eminent American philosopher of education, is credited with codifying the principles of reconstructionism. Though it has obvious similarities to the practical education advocated by the progressivists, Brameld suggested that social reconstructionism could also be compared with perennialism and essentialism.

Reconstructionist curriculums could be considered idealist in that they sought to improve the human condition with an emphasis on human dignity and the continuing need to restructure a changing society. It also sought to remedy social inequities *as they exist* in the specific context of a multiethnic culture. That sounds very much like pragmatism and its educational variants, experimentalism and progressivism. Social reconstructionism sought to preserve cultural heritage while recognizing that the culture is constantly in transition. Reconstructionists did not seek to "solidify" a particular cultural identity, as the perennialists and essentialists did, but instead sought to make the emerging culture more equitable for all.

From a social reconstructionist perspective, schools were building a caste system that favored the wealthy and subjugated the poor. The opportunities that our country was supposed to afford to all were being systematically denied to many. Social reconstructionists argued that schools fostered the knowledge and skills that empower the most privileged and very much established class distinctions. Such socioeconomic distinctions can be true of private schools almost by definition, and these schools can legitimately choose to cater to a particular clientele and their desires. However, within the public schools today we also find specialty schools (schools for science and math, schools for the arts, etc.), magnet schools, and, increasingly, charter schools that may or may not be required to meet state quotas for ethnic representation. The social reconstructionist perspective would oppose all of this.

It was the philosopher George Counts (1889–1974) who emerged as the leading advocate of social reconstructionism. The decade of the Great Depression made his comments even more poignant in the call to restructure. The schools, he argued, were being used as the vehicle for socioeconomic stagnation rather than for solving the evident problems of the nation. He implored that education "emancipate itself from the influence of the [ruling upper classes], face squarely and courageously every social issue, come to grips with life in all of its stark reality, establish an organic relation with the community, develop a realistic and comprehensive theory of welfare . . . and become less frightened than it is today at the bogeys of imposition and indoctrination" (1932, pp. 9–10).

From the social reconstructionist perspective, classroom teachers would have an affective emphasis and engage students in questions of moral dilemmas as a means to understanding the implications of one's actions. This echoes the ideas that were offered by the pragmatists. It is important, however, to remember that the reconstructionists maintain an agenda of social reform rather than simply fostering problem-solving ability.

Psychology: The Pragmatics of Philosophy

The practical expression of a philosophy is in terms of behavior. That is, since a person's thoughts can't be seen, their beliefs or philosophy become evident by the way they behave. Thus, we offer three educational perspectives from psychology that have roots in philosophy: behaviorism, humanism, and constructivism. Each has had, and in many regards still has, a significant impact upon education in the United States.

Behaviorism

John Watson (1878–1958), an influential American psychologist, suggested the following: "Give me a dozen healthy infants, well-formed, and my own specified world to bring them up in and I'll guarantee to take anyone at random and train him to become any type of specialist I might select—doctor, lawyer, artist, merchant-chief, and yes, even beggar-man and thief, regardless of his talents, penchants, tendencies, abilities, vocations, and race of his ancestors" (1924, p. 82). As far as we know, no one ever took him up on his offer, but nonetheless the claim was not one to be dismissed out of hand. There seemed to be something to the whole notion of behaviorism.

The Roots of Behaviorism

behaviorism The perspective that since behavior is caused, altering the surrounding circumstances alters the behavior.

The roots of **behaviorism** are in the work of Ivan Pavlov (1848–1936) in the early 1900s. Pavlov was conducting experiments involving the digestive system in dogs when he came upon an interesting turn of events. He found that he could cause the dogs to salivate (a reflex action) without actually providing them with any food. He did this by first repeatedly pairing the stimulus for salivation (that is, feeding the dogs) with the ringing of a bell. Eventually, he could simply ring the bell and the dogs would salivate. He had *conditioned* the dogs to respond to a stimulus that does not ordinarily cause the reflexive response. The procedure was therefore called *reflexive conditioning.*

B. F. Skinner

© Bettmann/Corbis

Of course, in schools we do not teach reflexive responses to students because they are, after all, reflexes. And so reflexive conditioning (also known as "classical conditioning") was not of much use in the educational setting. Despite Watson's claims of being able to utilize conditioning procedures, conditioning did not find a place in school until B. F. Skinner (1904–1990) provided a useful variation to classical conditioning that was useful in education. It did, however, find a very lucrative place in the world of advertising.

Skinner's version was known as *operant conditioning* because the individual's behavior "operated" on the environment. In this perspective, learning involves reinforcements. That is, an individual or an animal will perform a particular behavior depending upon the consequences of that behavior. If the behavior brings some sort of reinforcement—something the person wants—the probability of the behavior being repeated is increased. From a strict Skinnerian perspective, the only reason that people do things is to receive reinforcement. No reinforcement, no behavior (desired behavior, that is). The tricks are in (1) selecting the appropriate reinforcer for the particular individual, and (2) deciding whether you are going to manipulate the behavior in your environment or the environment is going to manipulate your behavior.

Behaviorism in the Classroom

Teachers using a behaviorist approach would avoid punishing children at all costs. Instead, children are reinforced for appropriate behavior and not reinforced for inappropriate behaviors. Those reinforcements may initially take the form of extrinsic rewards such as gold stars, praise, treats, or items selected from the "treasure box." The goal, however, is to gradually replace the *extrinsic* rewards for *intrinsic* rewards. Intrinsic rewards are feelings of accomplishment from a job well done or personally recognizing that one has learned or achieved to a high level.

Unfortunately, the extrinsic-reward aspect is one that teachers tend to lean upon. The result is a student who works only for the extrinsic reward. The teacher who begins the year with her elementary students making trips to the treasure chest is unsuccessful, from a true behaviorist perspective, if the treasure chest is still in use in May.

Humanism

humanism A philosophy that emphasizes the value and meaning of education rather than the mere dissemination and acquisition of facts.

Among the outside influences that contributed to the demise of behaviorism was the emergence of **humanism** as a psychological perspective. Whether the manipulative nature of behaviorism led to the rise of humanism or whether behaviorism simply succumbed to changing social attitudes is a debate that could go on for many years to come. What is interesting is that schools seem to be evolving a combination of the two. Computers have allowed many effective applications of *programmed instruction,* which are based on behaviorist principles. Simultaneously we see increased efforts toward "character education," which is clearly humanistic.

Humanism in the Classroom

Humanism as a psychological perspective is very much tied to the 20th century. The psychologist Carl Rogers (1902–1987) popularized the term "client-centered counseling," referring to a form of psychotherapy in which clients talk their way through the problems they face. That is, through skillful questioning and guidance by the psychotherapist, clients find their way to the source of their conflicts and then to a solution. Borrowing from this perspective, education adopted a "student-centered" approach to teaching and learning in which teachers necessarily see a classroom of *individuals,* each with their own needs and desires. Teachers seek to meet these needs by using traits described by Rogers (1961, 1962):

 Field Observation

ACTIVITY 9.4   **Behaviorism in the Contemporary Classroom**

Behaviorism is very much evident in contemporary classrooms. For many years a variation of behaviorism, *behavior modification,* has been used for classroom management purposes.

1. Observe a classroom in a local school (or use one of your own classes if you don't have access to a K–12 classroom) and watch for examples of behaviorist techniques. Does the teacher use reinforcements for good behavior or performance? What sort of reinforcements (e.g., praise, points, privileges, "free time") are used? Would you say the practice is effective? Why or why not?
2. What is your opinion of trading instructional time for desired behavior? That is, should teachers provide "free time" (or let classes out early) because the student(s) behaved well? What about the reverse—could teachers make additional instructional time a reinforcement? How?

Unconditional positive regard—The teacher accepts students for who they are without judgment or preconceived opinions.

Empathy—The teacher is able to see situations from the students' point of view.

Genuineness—The teacher treats students with sincerity and honesty.

The classic representation of humanism has been that of Abraham Maslow's Hierarchy of Needs (1954). Maslow asserts that human beings are motivated to meet a series of needs (Figure 9.2). Arranging those needs in a pyramid model, he suggested that our most basic needs are at the lower levels of the pyramid. These *deficiency needs* include such things as shelter, food, and clothing. The next level up is that of safety, and above that are the needs for a sense of belonging and self-esteem. Unless these needs are met, the individual is unable to move on to satisfy higher-level *growth needs*. In the context of the hierarchy, a child who is hungry or who feels unsafe is simply not concerned about learning lessons in school. For that reason, schools offer breakfast programs, free and reduced-price lunch programs, after-school programs, and so forth.

As a classroom teacher you may often be lulled into seeing a sea of faces rather than a collection of individual human beings, each with his or her own set of life influences. Certainly it is easier for a teacher to approach instruction on a "class" basis rather than addressing the needs of 20 or more individuals. From the humanist perspective, however, they are indeed each unique individuals.

Constructivism

constructivism The perspective that students "build" their knowledge as new experiences are related to previous experiences.

Constructivism emerged in the 20th century with potential for the way in which schools might *facilitate* learning. As a philosophy, it represents an epistemology, an explanation of how people come to know what they know. John Locke had suggested that people came into this world as a blank slate, and that experience was the source of the knowledge that would subsequently be written across that slate. Constructivism builds upon that idea.

However, unlike a blank slate onto which discrete bits of knowledge are added, the constructivist perspective suggests that people actively "build" their knowledge as new experiences are related to the *previous* experiences. Thus, new knowledge is a combination of one's previous knowledge and the current experience. For instance, your impression of the course in which you are enrolled will be influenced by your

Figure 9.2

Maslow's Hierarchy of Needs

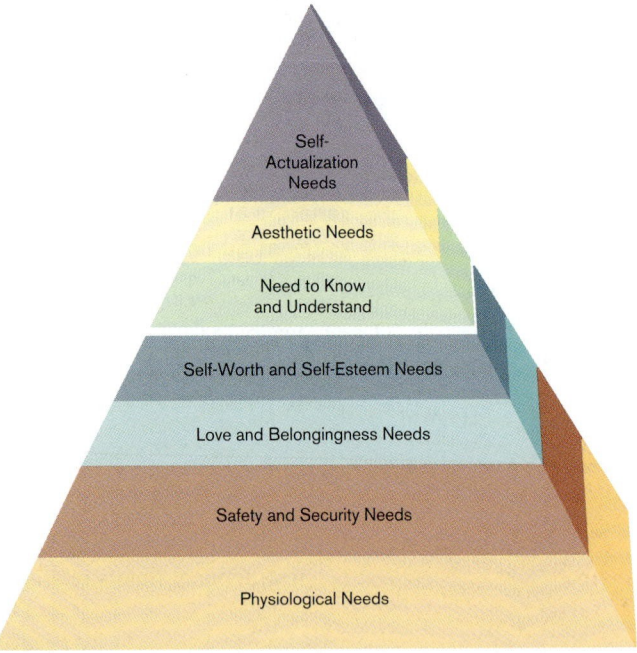

experiences in other courses. Is this one better, more challenging, more interesting? The answers will depend on your personal experiences. It would be difficult for you to consider this course completely without reference to other course work you have done. We use experience to *construct* our knowledge. It is obvious, then, that constructivism might work very well with a philosophy such as pragmatism that puts a premium on human experience.

From a psychological point of view, constructivism borrows heavily from the work of Jean Piaget and of Lev Vygotsky. From Piaget comes the idea of an ever-expanding and dynamic knowledge base as individuals learn more and more. For Piaget, this is accomplished by the processes of assimilation and accommodation. From Vygotsky we have the idea of learning as an exercise in *social interaction*. There is a give and take because information acquired from another individual has been "filtered" by that person's unique set of experiences and prior knowledge.

Courtesy of Becky Stovall

Constructivism emphasizes letting students interact with materials to construct knowledge through experience.

Constructivism in the Classroom

In practice this means that teachers must be aware that they are not just transferring information from one source (themselves) to a target (the students). Rather, whatever a teacher says can likely be interpreted in as many different ways as there are students in the class. It is therefore necessary that teachers take great care in the design and presentation of lessons to guide a student's progress toward a particular concept. It is just as important that teachers use frequent formative assessments to determine how the students have processed a given lesson. As Bentley, Ebert, and Ebert (2000) point out, "By acknowledging the personal nature of 'sense making,' a constructivist approach to education provides the teacher with considerable insight about what students know as they enter the classroom, what occurs during instruction, and how to account for the eventual outcomes of instruction" (p. 70). Teaching from this perspective can be a fascinating experience for you as it affords the opportunity to stimulate student thinking and then watch as students make meaningful connections between the lesson and their own experiences. You will, in a very real sense, be witnessing the construction of new knowledge.

 # Conclusion

We have considered more than a dozen philosophical perspectives and their variants that influence the work of professional educators. We wish to emphasize to you the importance of considering what *your* philosophical perspectives are on the role of schools and teachers in the development of young and impressionable minds.

1. Metaphysics is the branch of philosophy that considers questions about the physical universe.
2. Axiology is concerned with the study of values, and in particular with two aspects: ethics and aesthetics. Ethics focuses on the ideas and beliefs that are valued by a society in a moral sense. Aesthetics is concerned with the appreciation of beauty and the determination of what constitutes beauty for a given society.
3. Epistemology is the branch of philosophy that explores understanding or knowing. Thus, it is the study of the nature and origin of truth and knowledge.

Table 9.2	Outline of Philosophers and Their Philosophies

Idealism

Socrates (469–399 BC)	Rene Descartes (1596–1650)
Plato (427–347 BC)	George Berkeley (1685–1753)
Augustine (AD 354–430)	

Realism

Aristotle (384–322 BC)	Francis Bacon (1561–1626)
St. Thomas Aquinas (1225–1274)	John Locke (1632–1704)

Pragmatism

Charles Sanders Peirce (1839–1914)	John Dewey (1859–1952)
William James (1842–1910)	

Existentialism

Soren Kierkegaard (1813–1854)	Jean-Paul Sartre (1905–1980)
Friedrich Nietzsche (1844–1900)	

Perennialism

Robert Maynard Hutchins (1899–1979)	Mortimer Adler (1902–)

Essentialism

William C. Bagley (1847–1946)	E. D. Hirsch Jr. (1928–)

Progressivism

Jean-Jacques Rousseau (1712–1778)	John Dewey (1859–1952)

Social Reconstructionism

George Counts (1889–1974)	Theodore Brameld (1904–1987)

Behaviorism

Ivan Pavlov (1848–1936)	B. F. Skinner (1904–1990)
John Watson (1878–1958)	

Humanism

Carl Rogers (1902–1987)	Abraham Maslow (1908–1970)

Constructivism

Lev Vygotsky (1896–1934)	Jean Piaget (1896–1980)

4. Logic is concerned with the rules of reasoning.

5. Idealism is the philosophy of ideas. Its underlying theme is that the only true reality is that of ideas.

6. Realism is a philosophy that explores what physical matter can tell us about ideas rather than asserting that only ideas exist.

7. Pragmatism, meaning "work," is based on the notion that ideas must serve a useful purpose.

8. With an existentialist perspective we shift from an emphasis on the mind *understanding* the universe to an emphasis on the mind *creating* the universe. The existentialist notion refers to the existence of *a universe of your own making.*

9. The perennialist perspective asserts that certain ideas have transcended time and remain vital today. Education should represent an organized effort to make these ideas accessible to students.

10. Essentialism is a perspective that suggests there are core skills and knowledge that all students should acquire for sustaining our social order.

11. Progressivist philosophy focuses on positive change, a change for the better, that individuals with a particular educational background could provide. It is based on "doing" more than on "knowing," and on solving problems more than on preserving the culture as it exists.

12. Social reconstructionism is a perspective that specifically sees the schools as the agency for addressing the problems of society.

13. Behaviorism suggests that human beings respond to the reinforcements that they find, or do not find, in their environment. A behaviorist would characterize learning as a relatively permanent change in behavior.

14. Humanism is a perspective that focuses on the intrinsic worth and the individual dignity of all human beings.

15. The constructivist perspective suggests that people actively "build" their knowledge as experiences are processed relative to their previous experiences. New knowledge results from combining previous knowledge with the current experience.

Key Terms

metaphysics	realism	progressivism
axiology	pragmatism	social reconstructionism
epistemology	existentialism	behaviorism
logic	perennialism	humanism
idealism	essentialism	constructivism

Educational Engineering

Case Studies in Education

Enter the information from the table below into the Educational Record for the student you are studying.

	Religious Orientation	Parent's Expectations of Schools	Child's Appreciation of Art/Beauty
Davon	Davon does not attend church.	Davon's mother expects the school to be the teacher and the parent. She expects the school to provide him with a change of clothes when he is dirty and a bed when he is sick and needs to rest.	Davon seems to appreciate the artwork he views in picture books. He tries to imitate such works in his own illustrations.

(Continued on next page)

Andy	Andy attends a local Protestant church with his grandparents. He does not discuss his church life unless asked. There has been no conflict between his religious and school educations.	Andy's grandparents seem to expect only that he be happy in school. His progress reports have shown that he is struggling with reading and has behavior problems. Though his grandmother expressed concern about his being promoted to 4th grade, she has not made contact with his teachers on her own accord. While Andy's grandparents are actively involved in their church, their disassociation with Andy's day-to-day struggles and achievements in school suggest that they are indifferent to his success.	Since Andy needs kinesthetic opportunities during the day in order to think and learn, he might be expected to be attracted to the arts. Surprisingly, he shows little interest in drawing. When he does draw, he does not like to color. Many students use color to hide what they did not include in their drawings. He will give only cursory attention to illustrations when doing a picture walk through a story to help with prediction opportunities before reading.
Judith	Judith's mother was raised Catholic and her father Baptist. Judith does not make overtly religious comments at school other than referencing where "bad people go" or that it is sinful to lie or steal.	Her parents accept the school as the authority on what is to be taught and how. They do not have particularly high expectations of their daughter and so attribute her lack of progress to Judith rather than to the school.	Judith would say that any picture is "art." There has been no outward appreciation of artistic beauty. She mentioned that she liked the classical music played during one of her classes (not a music class). She thought it was "peaceful."
Tiffany	Although her parents practice Roman Catholicism, Tiffany has recently pronounced that she is an atheist. This has just occurred during her sixth-grade year. Tiffany is very outspoken about this belief and will tell anyone when and where she deems appropriate.	Tiffany's parents expect her to respect students, teachers, and the school in general. They have taught her that education is the number one priority and expect her to attend college and become a professional.	Tiffany will remark when an artwork appears to be pretty, colorful, or impressive. However, art is not a huge interest of hers and she will not focus on this topic for a long period.
Sam	Sam's religious orientation is not known. There is no evidence that religion has affected his perspective in school.	Sam's mother expects the school to educate her son and to help him reach his potential academically. She also expects the school to model the values that she has taught Sam—honesty, fairness, responsibility, pride in one's accomplishments, and good citizenship.	Sam has taken no art classes in high school nor has he had any exposure to art. He has, however, demonstrated an interest in and appreciation of music, as evidenced by his participation in concert choir for three years.
Bao	Bao's parents and family are Buddhist; Bao accompanies them to temple and follows Buddhist ceremonies. Though she would identify herself as a Buddhist if asked, her religion is more cultural than personal, and does not inform her decisions.	It would never occur to Bao's parents to question the school or the teachers. They assume that respect, diligence, and excellence are being taught, and Bao's excellent record gives them no reason to question this.	Like many of her peers, Bao respects (is, in fact, seduced by) mainstream portrayals of beauty, so her appreciation of art stems from the physical beauty of the subject, rather than the skill of the artist. She is disinterested in art that does not have people in it; the "artwork" on her walls at home are mostly pages from magazines.

1. How do you think the religious beliefs of the child in your case study would affect what you will do as a classroom teacher? Will you have to learn more about a particular religion? Or is it the case that you can conduct classes completely free of any religious influence over the curriculum or perspectives that you bring to class?
2. Given the parents' expectations of the school, will there be any conflict with the way you feel your students should be educated? Are there any subjects that would be better left unaddressed (e.g., evolution or the recognition of particular holidays)?
3. How will this child's appreciation of art/beauty be broadened in your class? How will your own appreciation of art/beauty become a part of the education that you provide to this child?

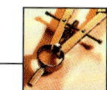

Designing the School of the Future

1. The school of the future that you design will have an underlying philosophy. You can either put it in place, or it can "evolve" based upon the curriculum you adopt, the people you employ, and the perspectives of the families you serve. In either case you have to make a decision. From a *philosophical perspective,* what should your school of the future seek to accomplish?
2. Having answered question 1, you can now determine which philosophy or collections of philosophies would provide the structure for accomplishing your goal. Will you focus on a study of the real world? Will your school be the mechanism for solving social problems? Does your school feel that our culture has "arrived," or is it still in progress? Construct a statement or explanation of your school's philosophical theme that you could present to a parent who asked about the philosophy of the school.
3. Finally, how will you establish the school to meet those goals? For example, will teachers of a similar philosophy be hired to work here? Will there be a program within the school that tries to develop the philosophy or culture of the school much as athletic teams try to build a common bond among teammates? How will your school's philosophy be able to adapt to changing times and to the people who are served by the school?

Praxis Practice

Many states will require that you successfully complete the Praxis Series of examinations to qualify for certification. One or more of those tests will be subject-area tests. Another, which has a more practical orientation, will be the Principles of Learning and Teaching (PLT) examination that is appropriate for your certification area.

Completing the Quick Check Quizzes for Chapter 9 in the Unit Workshop will give you practice with the multiple choice format of the PLT. The Case Studies in Education and Designing a School of the Future activities will help prepare you for exercises that require reading a scenario and answering questions about what you might do in such a situation.

10

Ethics in Education and Matters of Law

Make the chapter work for you with CPR²:

Conceptualize Here are the major themes you will encounter in this chapter:

1. The distinctions between morals, ethics, and laws, and how they apply to you as a teacher.
2. Education has been heavily influenced by legislative acts throughout our nation's history.
3. The courts attempt to balance the rights of the individual and the good of the society at large.

Preview Read the chapter headings; look at any figures, tables, and activities; and read through the items in the conclusion.

Activity 10.1: If Not Now, When?

Activity 10.2: Field Observation Activity– Should All Teachers Affirm an Oath of Ethical Conduct?

Activity 10.3: Go Online! Researching Federal Law

Activity 10.4: Go Online! Researching Court Rulings Concerning Education

Read Now read through the chapter. Mark or highlight information that you consider to be especially important or about which you have a question.

Reflect Consider this question as you read: What are the different roles of federal, state, and local governments with regard to education?

Photo: © FogStock LLC/Index Stock Imagery

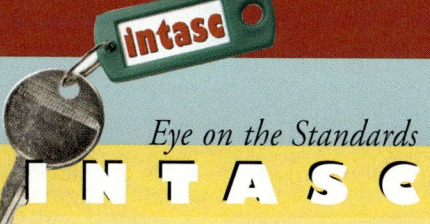

Eye on the Standards
INTASC

ice breakers

The following standards from the Interstate New Teacher Assessment and Support Consortium (INTASC) will be addressed in this chapter. As you read the chapter, consider how school law and educator ethics are tied to these principles.

Principle 3 The teacher understands how students differ in their approaches to learning and creates instructional opportunities that are adapted to diverse learners.

Principle 5 The teacher uses an understanding of individual and group motivation and behavior to create a learning environment that encourages positive social interaction, active engagement in learning, and self-motivation.

Principle 7 The teacher plans instruction based upon knowledge of subject matter, students, the community, and curriculum goals.

Principle 9 The teacher is a reflective practitioner who continually evaluates the effects of his/her choices and actions on others (students, parents, and other professionals in the learning community) and who actively seeks out opportunities to grow professionally.

Are You Legal?

Your life as a student has been, and your career as a teacher will be, affected by many legislative acts and legal decisions. Here are a few examples of what you will find in this chapter. Try matching the act or the Supreme Court decision with its explanation.

_____ Public Law 78-346– The Servicemen's Readjustment Act

_____ *Lau v. Nichols*

_____ The Buckley Amendment

_____ Public Law 94-142 (renamed IDEA in 1990)

_____ *Brown v. Board of Education*

_____ Title IX of Public Law 92-318–The Education Amendments of the Indian Education Act

_____ *Ingraham v. Wright*

A. Provided for a free and appropriate education for all children ages 3–18 with handicaps

B. Overturned the ruling that "separate but equal" schools for minorities were constitutional.

C. Decided that the use of corporal punishment in the schools was *not* a violation of the Eighth Amendment (the injunction against cruel and unusual punishment).

D. Greatly increased college and university enrollment, particularly among minorities.

E. Prohibited sex bias in public elementary and secondary schools (this had a profound effect on athletics).

F. Required that non-English-speaking students be provided special instruction to ensure a good education.

G. Protects students (like you) from having their grades or records disclosed except when there is a "need to know."

Check your answers with the scoring key below to see how you did. These decisions represent some of the major legislative acts and decisions which should be part of your background knowledge of the profession. You will read about many more—along with other influences on the curriculum—in this chapter.

__D__	Public Law 78-346– The Servicemen's Readjustment Act	Greatly increased college and university enrollment, particularly among minorities.
__F__	*Lau v. Nichols*	Required that non-English-speaking students be provided special instruction to ensure a good education.
__G__	The Buckley Amendment	Protects students (like you) from having their grades or records disclosed except when there is a "need to know."
__A__	Public Law 94-142 (renamed IDEA in 1990)	Provided for a free and appropriate education for all children ages 3–18 with handicaps
__B__	*Brown v. Board of Education*	Overturned the ruling that "separate but equal" schools for minorities were constitutional.
__E__	Title IX of Public Law 92-318–The Education Amendments of the Indian Education Act	Prohibited sex bias in public elementary and secondary schools (this had a profound effect on athletics).
__C__	*Ingraham v. Wright*	Decided that the use of corporal punishment in the schools was *not* a violation of the Eighth Amendment (the injunction against cruel and unusual punishment).

> *Education, then, beyond all other devices of human origin, is a great equalizer of the conditions of men—the balance wheel of social machinery.*
>
> *Horace Mann, 1848*

■ Introduction

If you want a chapter about the big ideas that have engaged human thinking for centuries, then this is the chapter for you. Despite the emphasis that schools place on reading, writing, and arithmetic (the *explicit curriculum* that we discussed in Chapter 5), schools reflect and perpetuate the values of the communities in which they operate. The schools teach implicit messages of order and cooperation, and have the goal of educating law-abiding citizens. In this chapter we will look at how moral beliefs lead to a sense of ethics, which become codified for the society as laws, and which then empower citizens both with rights and responsibilities. In addition we will spend time discussing the tenuous balance between church and state as it applies to education.

This chapter will also provide you with something not often found in Introduction to Education textbooks. Rather than just presenting case law as examples in our discussions of how the law affects teachers and students, we provide you with an annotated listing of major federal legislation that concerns education. Many of these laws have affected your schooling, though you may never have known it. We follow the section on legislation with an annotated discussion of challenges to the law. It is the responsibility of the U.S. Supreme Court to be the final arbiter and interpreter when people or institutions question what the law intends. As with legislation, the decisions of the Court also affect the work of teachers across many dimensions of the educational enterprise. We don't expect that you will be required to memorize all of these laws and cases (maybe some of them). However, we do believe that you will form a stronger foundation as a professional teacher if you are aware of these significant influences on the work of teachers. We hope that you will find these sections fascinating and illuminating.

■ Ethics

Morals, Ethics, and Laws

In Chapter 9 we spoke of a branch of philosophy known as axiology, which is the study of values. Ethics, as you will recall, was one aspect of axiology (aesthetics was the other). In particular, we indicated that a study of ethics focuses on the ideas and beliefs that are valued by a society in a moral sense. *Morals,* for a society, represent a collective view of what is right and wrong, whereas *ethics* represent the code of conduct for abiding by that view. You may have your own morals and ethics but they are likely influenced greatly by those of the society in which you live. Because of that variation from one individual to the next, societies typically write *laws* that clearly specify behaviors that are and are not acceptable. In essence, laws seek to iron out the ethical differences that might exist between people. Law does not mandate that you accept the social version of appropriate behavior, but you are expected to abide by that version if you are to live in that environment. For all people, some sort of ethical standard, some code of ethics, guides their behavior—particularly in this social sense. For teachers, this is an even more important matter because morals, ethics, and laws are a prominent part of their work—and their lives away from work—every day.

You as an Ethical Person

As a college student you are not expected to have adopted or defined a professional code of ethics. So a discussion of professional ethics right now would be premature. You are, however, *you,* and you have ethical beliefs that characterize the person you are. Let's take a moment to consider some of those beliefs. Please keep in mind that we are not trying to convince you to adopt a particular ethical perspective—that's for you to decide—but we simply want to provide you with an opportunity to examine your own ethical standards more closely.

Articulating Your Beliefs

Do you have a code of ethics? Could you articulate it if asked to do so? When interviewing students for admission to our Teacher Education Program, we often ask these questions. Not surprisingly, students frequently have difficulty answering. That's not because they are unethical people, but simply because they have not taken the time to examine the principles that guide their lives. And for most people, and for most of the time, it can be left that way. They have a "sense" for their ethical standards but typically don't need to explain it to others. For teachers, however, morals and ethics are not only a personal concern but a community concern as well.

While there are many moral issues that could be discussed, let's look at three that can have an impact on your personal life as well as your life as a teacher. Consider your ethical viewpoint for each of these moral matters: honesty, the humane treatment of others, and loyalty.

Honesty If you value honesty, you are not one of those students who downloads term papers and turns them in as your own, or who pays someone to write them. The morality of the question is clear: It would not be right to do so. The "law" of the issue is clear as well—no doubt your institution does not condone plagiarism. But it's the ethics of the matter that gets sticky. Suppose a friend of yours *did* download a term paper and submit it as his own. What does your code of ethics tell you to do? Should you say nothing? Attempt to prevent him from submitting the paper? Turn him in? Your personal code of ethics will direct the action—or nonaction—that you take.

Humane Treatment of Others Questions of how you treat others have an ethical component. In your circle of friends and acquaintances, perhaps even within your Introduction to Education class, do you respond to different people in different ways? Sure you do. But if the humane treatment of all people is important to you, you likely do not make fun of people who seem to be different from you, and you do not use language that denigrates groups of people or individuals. And though you certainly like some people more than others, you do not allow your preferences to be translated into favoritism on one hand and discrimination on the other.

As with our example of honesty, the moral issue is fairly clear, and, even without reading the rest of this chapter, you know that there are laws that apply to this concern as well. But how about *your* ethical approach? Have you ever made a disparaging comment to a friend about someone with whom you'd had a disagreement? Have you ever not helped someone because he was not your "type" of person? We are mentioning this not to admonish you for any possible misdeeds in your past, but because as a teacher you are going to face a diverse group of students in your classes. It will be the strength of your ethical principles that ensures all of them will get the best you have to offer.

Loyalty Would you include loyalty as something of importance to you? If so, you are not a person who is known as a "fair-weather friend" and so abandons a friend in need. Rather, you are one who can be counted upon "through thick and thin." Families, churches, and schools attempt to teach the lessons of loyalty. But what if you know that what is happening is a bad course of action? Does loyalty have an ethical limit? For instance, suppose a group of your friends conspire to play a trick on someone with whom you, but not the rest of the group, are friends. In this simple example, where do your loyalties lie, and how do you justify your disloyalty to the other person or group? You would make a decision one way or the other if you were in this situation, and it would be your code of ethics that influenced which way that decision went. Understanding your own ethics is sounding more and more important, isn't it?

We have provided just three brief examples of ethics in action. What other characteristics comprise your code of ethics? Do you see anything in your perspective that differs substantially from your friends and others with whom you interact? As you consider this, remember that we are talking about the principles that guide your actions in moral situations, not about simple differences of opinion on an issue (e.g., in politics or other current events). Activity 10.1 will give you an opportunity to think about this in some greater depth.

ACTIVITY 10.1
If Not Now, When?

When is the best time to think deliberately about your own code of ethics? How about now? If not now, when? A topic like this (seemingly simple but really very serious) is so easy to set aside. Do yourself a favor and think about it for a few minutes. You need not solve the problems of the world, but at least give yourself five or ten minutes to consider where you stand on moral questions.

We have provided three topics to get you started: honesty, humane treatment of others, and loyalty. Add just two more to the list for this exercise. Perhaps your class can decide what the two other topics should be. Without discussions with others, write down a statement after each topic that summarizes your perspective on the topic. No clichés allowed (e.g., "honesty is the best policy")—if that's the best you can do, you're not ready for this exercise. What you should try for is a statement that explains who you are as a person so that someone else would know what to expect from you in a challenging situation. For example, you might write, "Loyalty is more important to me than right or wrong because being true to a friend is always right."

If you put enough thought into this, perhaps you will be willing to let your statements begin a class discussion leading to a code of ethics.

1. Honesty

    _____

    _____

    _____

2. Humane treatment of others

    _____

    _____

    _____

3. Loyalty

    _____

    _____

    _____

4. _____

    _____

    _____

5. _____

    _____

    _____

Ethical teachers are caring, humane, honest, and loyal.

Courtesy of Bill Lisenby

You as an Ethical Teacher

We mentioned that we had chosen honesty, the humane treatment of others, and loyalty for our examples because they play so heavily both in one's personal life and in the life of a teacher. You can likely understand how these three could be important in the educational setting. You will find yourself modeling these traits as part of what you teach to your students (do you recall our discussion of the "hidden curriculum" in Chapter 5?). You will also find that these three moral concerns will characterize your interactions with colleagues, administrators, and others with whom you interact in your professional capacity (e.g., parents).

Teachers Occupy a Position of Influence

One of the reasons that strong moral and ethical character is important for teachers is that teachers occupy positions of tremendous influence (Halverson, 2004). No matter what grade level you choose to teach, what you say and do will have a definite impression on the students with whom you work. The young children will think that you simply know everything—because, after all, you are the teacher. Among the older children, some will consider you to be the source of wisdom in their world. Being in a position of authority in the classroom, being the person who evaluates the work and behavior of students and who assigns grades that determine a student's future, brings with it not only a responsibility but the need to understand how pervasive your influence and impact can be. Whether or not you've gotten around to articulating your personal and professional ethics, they will be on display for a wide audience each and every day.

On Being an Ethical Teacher

We cannot provide you with a checklist to follow that will make you an ethical teacher. And that's not such a bad thing because if we could, we would really just be handing you a list of rules—laws—that would essentially tell you who to be rather than allowing you to be the individual that you are. Your school will have rules, there's no doubt about that, but an ethical teacher is one who understands what rules accomplish for people and how to apply those rules in situations that come with their own unique circumstances. Joyce Garrett (2006) prefers to conceptualize it in terms of four characteristics of an honorable teacher:

- *Teachers of honor care about humanity.* They are good listeners and communicators who embrace the needs of others before their own.
- *Teachers of honor live by the credo "Who dares to teach must never cease to learn."* They continuously engage in the scholarship of their discipline and bring their own sense of curiosity to the classroom, thus establishing safe environments for student inquiry.
- *Teachers of honor give back to their professional and civic communities.* They mentor, take leadership roles, continue their professional development, and take the spirit of giving into their classrooms and community-based projects.
- *Teachers of honor work hard.* They work diligently to guarantee that all students have equal access and equal opportunity, and they devise ways to engage all learners in meaningful endeavors. (Adapted from Garrett, J., 2006)

As you can see, this certainly is not a list of rules. Rather, it is a description of the behaviors that we might expect from a teacher whose ethical code of conduct stems from a moral conviction about the responsibilities inherent in being a professional educator.

A Code of Ethics for the Teaching Profession

Now that we have discussed ethics from a personal perspective and from the perspective of being a teacher, the next logical step is to consider the topic from the perspective of the profession at large. That is, we come to the topic of a code of ethics for teachers. This would not be unlike the Hippocratic Oath that physicians affirm in the practice of medicine or the oath that attorneys affirm to the bar association of their state. Teachers, however, are not expected to affirm an oath of ethical conduct as part of becoming a professional. Keep in mind that we are not referring to an oath of loyalty to state laws or to the Constitution, but rather to something that specifically addresses the ethics of teaching.

It must be said in all fairness that physicians and attorneys typically (though not always) engage in the private practice of their professions whereas the vast majority of teachers become state employees. For the state government to impose a code of ethics specifically on the teachers in that state may be an unwieldy task in many respects. Ultimately, it would be necessary to write and enforce codes of ethics for every facet of state employment. But on a more philosophical level the question remains as to whether there should or could be an oath that teachers affirm as the guiding principle behind their work.

Codes of Ethics from Professional Organizations

As we saw in the curriculum discussions of Chapter 6, which indicated that professional organizations had taken the lead in the development of curriculum standards, such activities have also occurred with regard to ethics. One broad-based organization, the National Education Association (NEA), has published a Code of Ethics for teachers (see Figure 10.1). Specialty organizations have also authored codes. The National Association for the Education of Young Children (NAEYC), for example, publishes and periodically updates its Code of Ethical Conduct and Statement of Commitment (Pizzolongo, 2005). Some institutions with teacher education programs have an educator's code of ethics for their students. Still, it could become problematic if teachers are affirming oaths to national codes, specialty codes, and perhaps local codes. It becomes difficult to maintain a true sense

Figure 10.1

NEA Code of Ethics

Source: Code of Ethics of the Education Profession, adopted by the NEA Representative Assembly, 1975. The National Education Association, Washington, DC.

of substance of meaning when there are so many variations of the theme. What are your thoughts? Should teachers be expected to affirm an oath of ethics to the profession? What would you identify as the core ethical principles that could guide the work of teachers? Activity 10.2 offers you the opportunity to conduct a survey of people's thinking about an oath for professional educators.

Preamble

The educator, believing in the worth and dignity of each human being, recognizes the supreme importance of the pursuit of truth, devotion to excellence, and the nurture of democratic principles. Essential to these goals is the protection of freedom to learn and to teach and the guarantee of equal educational opportunity for all. The educator accepts the responsibility to adhere to the highest ethical standards.

The educator recognizes the magnitude of the responsibility inherent in the teaching process. The desire for the respect and confidence of one's colleagues, of students, of parents, and of the members of the community provides the incentive to attain and maintain the highest possible degree of ethical conduct. The Code of Ethics of the Education Profession indicates the aspiration of all educators and provides standards by which to judge conduct.

The remedies specified by the NEA and/or its affiliates for the violation of any provision of this code shall be exclusive and no such provision shall be enforceable in any form other than one specifically designated by the NEA or its affiliates.

Principle I

Commitment to the Student The educator strives to help each student realize his or her potential as a worthy and effective member of society. The educator therefore works to stimulate the spirit of inquiry, the acquisition of knowledge and understanding, and the thoughtful formulation of worthy goals.

In fulfillment of the obligation to the student, the educator:

1. Shall not unreasonably restrain the student from independent action in the pursuit of learning,
2. Shall not unreasonably deny the student access to varying points of view,
3. Shall not deliberately suppress or distort subject matter relevant to the student's progress,
4. Shall make reasonable effort to protect the student from conditions harmful to learning or to health and safety,
5. Shall not intentionally expose the student to embarrassment or disparagement,
6. Shall not on the basis of race, color, creed, sex, national origin, marital status, political or religious beliefs, family, social or cultural background, or sexual orientation unfairly:
   a. Exclude any student from participation in any program,
   b. Deny benefits to any student,
   c. Grant any advantage to any student,
7. Shall not use professional relationships with students for private advantage,
8. Shall not disclose information about students obtained in the course of professional service, unless disclosure serves a compelling professional purpose or is required by law.

Principle II

Commitment to the Profession The education profession is vested by the public with a trust and responsibility requiring the highest ideals of professional service. In the belief that the quality of the services of the education profession directly influences the nation and its citizens, the educator shall exert every effort to raise professional standards, to promote a climate that encourages the exercise of professional judgment, to achieve conditions that attract persons worthy of the trust to careers in education, and to assist in preventing the practice of the profession by unqualified persons.

In fulfillment of the obligation to the profession, the educator:

1. Shall not in an application for a professional position deliberately make a false statement or fail to disclose a material fact related to competency and qualifications,
2. Shall not misrepresent his/her professional qualifications,
3. Shall not assist any entry into the profession of a person known to be unqualified in respect to character, education, or other relevant attribute,
4. Shall not knowingly make a false statement concerning the qualifications of a candidate for a professional position,
5. Shall not assist a noneducator in the unauthorized practice of teaching,
6. Shall not disclose information about colleagues obtained in the course of professional service unless disclosure serves a compelling professional purpose or is required by law,
7. Shall not knowingly make false or malicious statements about a colleague,
8. Shall not accept any gratuity, gift, or favor that might impair or appear to influence professional decisions or actions.

Source: Code of Ethics of the Education Profession, adopted by the NEA Representative Assembly, 1975. The National Education Association, Washington, DC.

Field Observation

ACTIVITY 10.2   Should All Teachers Affirm an Oath of Ethical Conduct?

Within your class and among as many teachers as you can, conduct a survey of opinions regarding an Oath of Ethical Conduct for teachers. Ask the following questions:

1. Should all teachers publicly (that is, in some sort of ceremony) affirm an oath of ethical conduct either upon graduation from a teacher education program (as a function of the college or university) or upon licensure/certification by the state (as a function of the certification process)?

2. If so, what key elements should be contained in the oath?

3. If not, why not?

Prepare a survey card such as the one below. You could put two copies of this on a single page, make copies, and then cut the page in half to double the survey cards.

An Oath of Ethical Conduct for Teachers

This survey is conducted as part of Introduction to Education at   *(name of institution)* . We would appreciate your opinion about the following questions:

1. Should all teachers publicly affirm an oath of ethical conduct either upon graduation from a teacher education program or upon licensure/certification by the state? Yes _____   No _____

2. If "yes," please list elements that you believe must be included in such a statement: _____
   _____
   _____

3. If "no," briefly explain why you would not support this idea: _____
   _____
   _____

Thank you for your participation.

After collecting your data, analyze the responses. What is your perspective about what people had to say? Draw your conclusions and share your results with the class as a discussion starter.

■ Teachers and the Law

It may have seemed to you as a young child in school that teachers were all-powerful. They ruled the classroom with the word of final authority. They told you what to do and when, and then they told you whether you'd done it correctly or not. We hope that your experiences weren't quite as stark as this, but your teachers likely did "run the show" from the time you arrived at school in the morning until you departed in the afternoon. Indeed, the history of schooling recognizes that the schools were expected to operate **in loco parentis,** that is, "in the place of parents." Your welfare, educationally and otherwise, was placed in the hands of the school. To a considerable degree that is the case today.

Times have changed somewhat, however. In contemporary society the obligations of the school, the teacher's rights, and the student's rights as well are very much a matter of law. Though not every circumstance can be anticipated by law, it is important for you to understand that there are legal implications for much of

in loco parentis "In the place of parents."

what takes place at school. This is not meant to intimidate you. Rather, it is to make you aware that as a *professional educator,* an awareness of law should be a part of your professional knowledge base. For a comprehensive and excellent review of law as it applies to teachers, see *Teachers and the Law* (Fischer, Schimmel, & Kelly, 1999).

The Teacher and the Protection of Due Process

due process Procedures intended to ensure fairness and accountability of both parents/guardians and educators. They include the rights of parents to have evaluations conducted by personnel outside the school system and to request a hearing when they disagree with the school's proposed plans.

Among the most fundamental rights granted to each of us under the Constitution of the United States is that of **due process.** The principle of due process has been established to ensure that an aggrieved party (e.g., a teacher accused of mistreating a student) is provided a fair process in the consideration of the circumstances of the event. So important is due process that it is mentioned in not one, but two amendments to the Constitution. The Fifth Amendment states that "no person shall . . . be deprived of life, liberty, or property without due process of law." Though education is the responsibility of the states, the Constitution extends each person's privilege of due process protection to state matters in the Fourteenth Amendment, which states "nor shall any State deprive any person of life, liberty, or property without due process of law."

Due process comes in two varieties: *substantive due process* and *procedural due process.* Substantive due process refers to the actual incident and whether or not it constitutes an actionable offense. For instance, whether or not a teacher could be terminated over an issue of personal grooming would be considered a matter of substantive due process. Procedural due process, as it sounds, refers to whether or not a fair or appropriate procedure was employed in making a decision. In such instances due process would include at the minimum:

- A hearing before an impartial body,
- Timely and specific notice of charges,
- The opportunity for both sides to present evidence and to confront adverse witnesses. (Fischer, Schimmel, & Kelly, 1999, p. 42)

Due process is a principle that protects teachers (or any accused party) from arbitrary or capricious decisions in actions against them. In particular, you may find questions of substantive and procedural due process arising in the performance of your teaching responsibilities as well as in your employment with a school district.

Employment: Contracts, Tenure, and Dismissal

It is the responsibility of the state to ensure teacher competence. This is accomplished through state statutes and certification requirements that govern both the accreditation of teacher education programs and the credentials that prospective teachers must ultimately submit to the state for licensure. Once licensed, teachers are employed by the school boards of local districts.

Contracts

contract A binding agreement between two parties.

A **contract** is a binding agreement between two parties (of which you would be one) that states the rights and responsibilities of each party. Contracts issued by local school boards can vary widely not only from state to state but also from district to district. In some districts, teachers are hired by the principal, with the approval of the school board, for a particular school. In other situations, it is the district that hires the teacher and assigns him to a school according to district needs. Though the formality and specificity of contracts can also vary widely, the document will typically establish salary level, insurance provisions, sick leave policies, grievance procedures, and expectations of the teacher's performance. For a contract to be legally binding, it must do the following :

- Represent the mutual assent to the terms
- Indicate the exchange of something of value (for example, your teaching in exchange for a salary)
- Represent legal subject matter
- Be entered into by parties who are competent to do so and are of legal age
- Be written in definite terms understandable to both parties

Note that the contract does *not* have to be in writing, unless state law requires such, as long as all of the required legal elements are included.

breach of contract The failure of either party in a contract to meet obligations.

If either party in a contract fails to meet the stated obligations, a **breach of contract** results. In such a case, the party that violated the terms of the contract can be sued for damages. The court may order that the contract be fulfilled, that monetary damages be paid, or perhaps both. There are two important points for you to remember. First, contracts are binding on *both* parties. Both you and the school district, in the case of a teacher's contract, have rights and responsibilities. Second, you alone are responsible for understanding a contract before signing it. If something is unclear, ask for clarification. A contract represents a professional commitment.

Induction and Tenure

During your first years of teaching with a district, you will be offered some form of a probationary contract. This probationary period, typically from one to three years, is sometimes referred to as an **induction period** because the school is not only evaluating your work but is trying to bring you along within the system. The goal, after all, is to identify and develop quality teachers rather than just "trying out" anyone who comes along.

induction period A probationary period, typically from one to three years, during which a newly hired teacher is mentored and evaluated.

tenure An ongoing contract to teach (sometimes referred to as a *continuing contract*).

Following the probationary period, many schools offer **tenure,** which is an ongoing contract to teach (sometimes referred to as a *continuing contract*) acknowledging the teacher's demonstration of competency in teaching. Each state determines the eligibility requirements for tenure.

Tenure provides teachers with a level of job security in a people-oriented profession where personalities and perspectives can be expected to differ. In the 1957 case of *Smith v. School District of the Township of Darby,* the Pennsylvania Supreme Court determined that

Your first years of teaching will be times of mentoring and evaluations.

> Time and again our courts have stated that the purpose of the tenure provisions of the School Code is the main tenance of an adequate and competent teaching staff, free from political or arbitrary interference, whereby capable and competent teachers might feel secure, and more efficiently perform their duty of instruction. (Fischer, Schimmel, & Kelly, 1999, p. 31)

Though tenure reflects job security as a teacher, it does not mean that you will have the same grade level or teaching assignment but simply that you will continue to have a teaching position with the district.

Courtesy of Guilherme Cunha

Dismissal

A variety of reasons can lead to the dismissal of a teacher: It could become apparent that despite the teacher's best intentions, he just doesn't have the ability to teach; a teacher could make a serious mistake and mistreat a child physically or verbally; philosophical differences might arise between a teacher and his colleagues or the school administration. These are just some examples. Not a pleasant topic, but one that needs to be addressed.

State laws can determine the grounds for the dismissal of a teacher, and local school board policies may add their own. Generally, the grounds most typically considered for dismissal include insubordination, incompetence as a teacher, immorality, and unprofessional conduct. Obviously these concerns cover a lot of territory and leave a lot of room for interpretation. A teacher's right to due process, as we have already discussed, ensures that any cause for dismissal is considered fairly.

For a teacher on probationary status, the dismissal process is not as complex as it is for a tenured teacher. If a district wanted to remove a probationary teacher from the classroom during the school year, the teacher can expect to be fully advised of the reasons for the action and to engage in a full hearing of the matter. At the end of the year, however, a district can refuse to extend a probationary teacher's contract for another year without having to justify its reasons. That's what "probationary" is all about.

Dismissal of a tenured faculty member can be more difficult—assuming the issue is not a clear violation of the safety and welfare of the students—because tenure implies that the district has already determined the individual to be a competent teacher. Tenure itself becomes a "property" of the teacher and is thus protected under the 14th Amendment which, as you will recall, mandates that the individual be afforded full due process of law. Many states have laws that include "good and just cause" as grounds for dismissal, though even with a catchall phrase such as this the state will have the burden of demonstrating to the court that dismissal is justified. Some states also have laws stating that tenured teachers must be given the opportunity to remediate deficiencies before being dismissed. It is typically left to the courts to determine what is "remediable." For example, if a teacher's grading practices were shown to be inconsistent and not reflective of student achievement, that situation might be considered remediable. A criminal conviction or improper contact between a teacher and student could be considered irremediable.

There is one circumstance in which a tenured teacher might be dismissed even though he is competent and has not exhibited any sort of inappropriate behavior. When a district is compelled for economic reasons to have a reduction in force, teachers tenured and otherwise may lose their positions. Typically, teachers would be laid off on the basis of seniority.

Tort Law and Teacher Liability

liability Legal responsibility for an incident.

tort law A civil or private wrong other than a breach of contract.

What does **liability** mean? In short, it means "blame." That is, if you are liable for some action, you may be taking the blame. Questions of liability fall under what is known as **tort law.** Tort refers to a civil or private wrong other than a breach of contract. With regard to school-related matters, there are four main types of tort cases: corporal punishment, search and seizure, defamation of character, and negligence. Cases of negligence against schools and teachers far outnumber the other three types.

Intentional and Unintentional Torts

Intentional torts are those that are, well, committed intentionally. Calling a student by a derogatory or mocking name would be considered an intentional tort. In such a case the student would have to prove that some damage was suffered due to the name-calling (*Phillips v. Lincoln County School District,* 1999). Negligence cases involve *unintentional torts.* This could be a situation in which a child is injured in class and it is argued that the injury was due to the teacher's negligence. For the court to decide that negligence is the cause, four elements must be present:

- The person charged with negligence must have had a duty of care in the situation.
- There must have been a violation of duty. For instance, could the educator have foreseen the injury occurring, and would the educator's presence have made any difference?
- The violation of duty must be the proximate cause of the injury.
- Injury must have been sustained. If there is no injury, there is no case of negligence. (Dougherty, 2004)

Accidents and every possible source of an accident simply cannot be anticipated. Further, it is a fact of life that teachers typically must supervise many students at once. It is virtually impossible to monitor all students all the time. Even the best precautions against an issue of liability still cannot prevent students or their parents from bringing a charge against a teacher if they choose to do so. However, habitually acting with "reasonable prudence" would be, in a word, prudent. As part of your instructional planning, and particularly for special events (e.g., field trips) or potentially hazardous situations (e.g., a chemistry lab), try to anticipate dangerous situations:

- Be certain that proper supervision will be maintained (this could be as simple as the arrangement of the classroom or securing additional teachers to help supervise events as needed).
- Take adequate precautions.
- Establish in advance the rules of behavior during the event.
- Warn the students of potential dangers and how to minimize them.

When you accept a teaching position with a school district, ask about district policies regarding teacher liability and about liability insurance coverage for teachers. Liability insurance does not protect the teacher from facing a charge, but provides legal assistance in the event of such a situation. Many professional organizations, state teachers' organizations, and national teachers' organizations make liability insurance coverage available to their members.

Reporting Child Abuse

In 1974 Congress enacted the Child Abuse Prevention and Treatment Act, which defined child abuse and neglect as the physical or mental injury, sexual abuse, negligent treatment, or maltreatment of a child under the age of 18 by a person who is responsible for the child's welfare under circumstances that indicate that the child's health or welfare is harmed or threatened thereby. Teachers have specific responsibilities when they suspect that a child may be suffering abuse. Failure to meet those responsibilities, despite the delicacy of such circumstances, can be cause for a teacher to be held liable on the grounds of negligence. Every state requires that teachers report suspected cases of child abuse.

Watching for signs of possible abuse and reporting it are among a teacher's responsibilities.

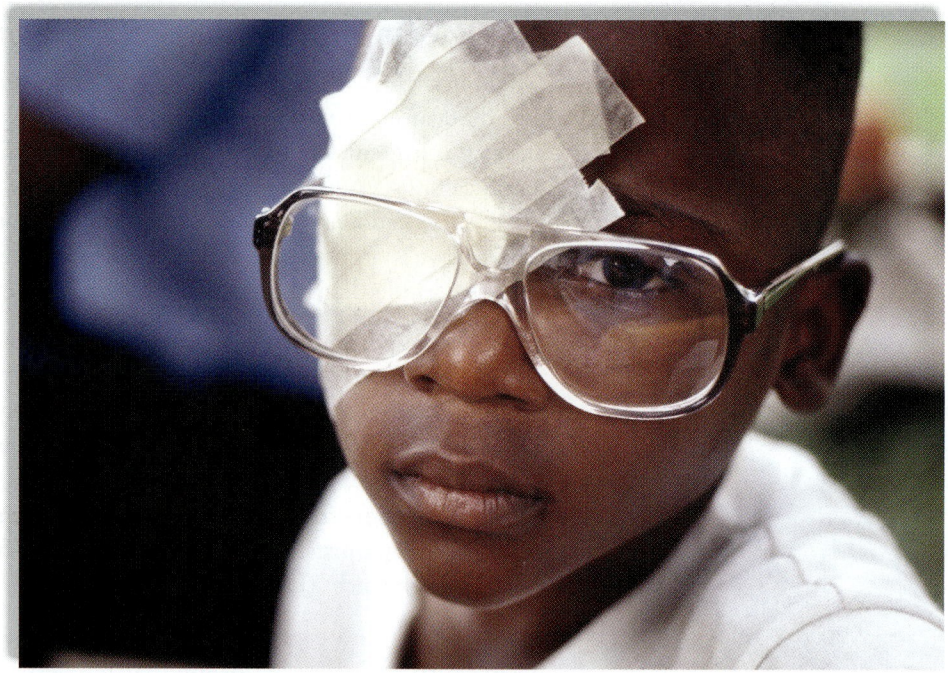

© Robert Ginn/Index Stock Imagery

Since poor school performance and poor behavior in school are common problems associated with child abuse, you as a classroom teacher may need to report possible cases of maltreatment. You may notice that a child becomes withdrawn or demonstrates very low self-esteem. You may notice a significant change in the student's academic performance or social behavior. You may even observe bruises, burns, or cuts on a child. You will have to check with your school district for the proper reporting procedures. In some instances reports may go to school personnel. In other situations, it could be your responsibility to report the concern directly to your state's agency for social services.

This is a slippery slope. No one wants to report a case of child abuse only to find out that the child fell at home and injured himself. It might seem that the requirement exposes a teacher to the possibility of being sued. However, in some states teachers are considered to be **mandated reporters,** which means that they are required to report any suspicion of child abuse and cannot be sued or prosecuted for doing so.

In Chapter 12, Social Issues Affecting Students and Schools, you will find a detailed discussion of child abuse and neglect, including some of the warning signs.

mandated reporter A person, such as a teacher, who is required by law to report suspected child abuse or neglect, and thus is immune from prosecution or lawsuit for doing so.

Reasonable Force

"Reasonable force" is not really a topic that springs to mind when thinking about school and teaching, but it is in fact something that you need to know about. Schools are, of course, places where we find large numbers of people for whom cognitive, social, emotional, and physical development are the name of the game. The chances for altercations between students of varying levels of maturity are great. Chances for altercations between a student and a teacher are significant as well.

With regard to students fighting students, teachers are in a unique position. Allowing a fight to proceed without trying to intervene could leave the teacher liable if one of the students is injured in the scuffle. On the other hand, stepping into the middle of a schoolyard fracas can put not only the teacher at risk, but the students as well. In breaking up a fight, a teacher is allowed to use *reasonable force.* What is "reasonable" will depend on the circumstances, for instance the age of the students and the number of students involved. Even if a student is injured by a teacher who is intervening, the courts have not held the teacher liable for injuries where it could be shown that the teacher did not use undue force. This is not a license for a teacher to attack a student, but an acknowledgement that in the process of separating students, injuries can occur. The difficult part is maintaining a clear head in the midst of a physical confrontation.

A teacher who is assaulted by a student does have the right to self-defense. Again, however, the principle of reasonable force comes into play. Whatever the student's motivation—and goal—in the assault might be, the teacher will be expected to respond appropriately for the situation. As in the case of intervening in a student-student fight, teachers need to remain clear-headed and to defend themselves appropriately without entering into full-scale retaliation.

Copyright Laws

Despite having a contemporary sound to it, not only is copyright protection established in the United States Constitution, but it is among the clauses of Article I. (You will recall that such things as free speech [First Amendment] and federal guarantee of due process of law [Fifth Amendment] were among the first 10 *amendments,* known as the Bill of Rights, and that state guarantee of due process of law was not granted until the 14th Amendment was approved.) In Article I, Section 8, Congress is given the power to "promote the progress of science and the useful arts, by securing for limited times to authors and inventors the exclusive right to their respective writings and discoveries." The first federal copyright law was passed by Congress in 1790. With a precedent like that, you might want to think twice before plunking someone else's work on the photocopier and cranking out thousands of copies.

All humor aside, copyright protection and copyright infringement are serious concerns. In the Copyright Act of 1976 (that's more contemporary), Congress established guidelines for the duplication of copyrighted works. In particular, Section 107 of the Act establishes the "fair use" doctrine. Though fair use is not specifically defined, the general principle is "not to impair the value of the owner's copyright by diminishing the demand for that work, thereby reducing potential income for the owner" (McDaniel, 1979, p. 707). The courts turn to four criteria when considering cases of copyright infringement, though for education there are special exceptions to the fair use doctrine. Classroom guidelines (Wagner, 1992) allow duplication of copyrighted material without obtaining the owner's permission under the following conditions:

Teachers may make a *single* copy of:

- A chapter from a book
- An article from a periodical or newspaper
- A short story, short essay, or short poem
- A chart, graph, diagram, drawing, cartoon, or picture from a book, newspaper, or periodical

Teachers may also make *multiple* copies of copyrighted work for use in the classroom providing they meet the tests of brevity, spontaneity, and cumulative effect as follows:

Brevity:
- A complete poem, if it is less than 250 words and printed on not more than two pages
- An excerpt from a longer poem, if the excerpt is not more than 250 words
- A complete article, story, or essay if it is less than 1,000 words or 10 percent of the work, whichever is less
- One chart, diagram, cartoon, or picture per book or periodical

Spontaneity:
- The copying is at the insistence and inspiration of the individual teacher, *and*
- The inspiration and decision to use the work and the moment of its use for maximum teaching effectiveness are so close in time that it would be unreasonable to expect a timely reply to a request for permission.

Cumulative effect:
- The copying of the material is for only one course in the school in which copies are made.
- Not more than one short poem, article, story, essay, or two excerpts are copied from the same author, or more than three from the same collective work or periodical volume during one class term.
- There are not more than nine instances of such multiple copying for one course during one class term.

Electronic Media

Other than making a backup of a program, the copying of computer software is a copyright violation. Copying a program for distribution to your students would be a violation.

With regard to videotapes, nonprofit educational institutions (typically the librarian/media specialists) are permitted to make a copy of a program broadcast to the general public in accordance with the following guidelines: The tape must be shown for instructional purposes within 10 days of the taping, and may be reshown only once for instructional reinforcement. After that the tape can be played again only for the purpose of evaluating its educational usefulness, and it must be erased after no more than 45 days.

When it comes to the Internet, the laws are still evolving. Much of what is available, especially if it is from a public agency such as government or schools, can be printed and copied for classroom use. However, some sites may stipulate that their information is copyrighted as intellectual property. If so, copying would be a violation. Keep in touch with the librarian/media specialist in your school to stay current with the revisions in copyright law as it affects all types of media, electronic or otherwise.

Freedom of Expression

The preceding section considered copyright as it applies to what others have expressed. How about your own freedom of expression? Certainly you know that under the First Amendment to the Constitution, you have a right to free speech, but let's take a look at how that applies to your work as a teacher. There are several types of expression that we need to consider: your own freedom of speech, symbolic expression, and academic freedom.

Free Speech

There are several aspects to the issue of free speech that you should understand. First is that your right to free speech as established in the United States Constitution refers to matters of *government actions*. The First Amendment (federal level) and the Fourteenth Amendment (state level) provide that governmental action cannot be taken against you that would violate your right to free speech. That is, if the public school district (a state agency) dislikes some comments you have made about the administration, you cannot be fired simply for having made those comments. You may not be so lucky if, rather than working for a public school, you are working for a private school. The case of *Pickering v. Board of Education* (1968) provides an example of the law as it relates to public schools.

Marvin Pickering had written a long, sarcasm-laced letter to his local newspaper roundly criticizing the actions of the school district where he worked. Much of what he said turned out to be inaccurate, but nonetheless he was summarily fired. Pickering contested the firing, but the lower courts, including the Illinois Supreme Court, decided in favor of the school district, stating that he "is no more entitled to harm the schools by speech than by incompetency." The U.S. Supreme Court, however, ruled that Pickering had the same right as any other citizen to express his opinion. Justice Thurgood Marshall wrote that it is necessary "to arrive at a balance between the interests of the teacher, as a citizen, in commenting upon matters of public concern, and the interests of the state, as an employer, in promoting the efficiency of the public services it performs through its employees." Pickering had not divulged any information that was not of public record, nor had his claims interfered with his ability to teach. He was subsequently reinstated.

You should also understand that the right to free speech does not entitle you to make abusive, disruptive, or vulgar comments to or about people. Clearly, there exists a difference between the professional and the unprofessional expression of an idea. The courts may be expected to uphold the right to free speech, but they will rarely support a teacher who becomes a disruptive force in the school or who makes irresponsible statements. The right to free speech is better thought of as the *privilege* of free speech. We would encourage you to develop the ability to make cogent and constructive statements about issues rather than verbally lashing out at a situation.

Symbolic Expression

The spoken word is not the only way that ideas are expressed. The way you dress and the symbols (whether armbands, lettering, jewelry) or buttons (with statements or logos) that you might include also express your opinions. Courts will usually support these symbolic expressions unless they prove to cause "substantial disruption" within the school. Thus, a campaign button for a legitimate candidate in a public election would probably not be cause for concern. A button showing support for the genocide that took place in Nazi Germany during World War II could easily be construed as disruptive. *If the efficiency or safety of the school is compromised,* the offending use of particular symbolic expressions could be curtailed, and the decision to do so would likely be upheld in the courts.

Academic Freedom

academic freedom Extends to teachers the right to speak freely about the subjects they teach and to introduce varied—and competing—viewpoints on an issue to encourage inquiry, experimentation with new ideas, and critical consideration of topics.

Academic freedom extends to teachers the right to speak freely about the subjects they teach and to introduce varied—and competing—viewpoints on an issue to encourage inquiry, experimentation with new ideas, and critical consideration of topics. It is not absolute, however, and does not mean that teachers can say or do just about anything and have it protected as part of their freedom of expression. Instead, the exercise of academic freedom brings with it responsibility.

A discussion of academic freedom almost by default implies introducing alternative perspectives (when discussing topics and issues) or new or different teaching methods (when discussing the presentation of a lesson). The courts typically view the school as the expert on these matters and the teacher as the professional charged with making decisions in the classroom. As a result, the courts do not have a history of condoning the idea that education—or teaching—should be "scripted." Even so, when it comes to issues, everyone has an opinion; thus, it is not uncommon for the various constituencies involved in education (e.g., parents, business, local politics) to have differences of opinion about what should or should not be presented to children in school. Because of this, when cases of academic freedom do reach the courts, the following four guidelines are often considered:

- The teacher's purpose in the use of the material or method
- Relevance of the material or method to the curriculum
- The age of the students involved in the exercise
- The quality of the teaching materials and its effect on the students (Fischer, Schimmel, & Kelly, 1999)

Courtesy of Bill Lisenby

Academic freedom permits teachers to use methods and materials in the way they deem most appropriate for effective instruction and student learning.

We cannot emphasize enough the degree to which the concept of academic freedom represents the protection of what education is all about, and how fragile that privilege can be when handled irresponsibly by professionals in education. As a licensed teacher, you will enjoy the benefit of being able to express well-considered and diverse perspectives that invite children and adults to consider a wide variety of issues. *You* will be expected to find the best sources of information and most appropriate methods for developing your students as knowledgeable, creative, and critical thinkers. Academic freedom does not mean you have a pulpit for preaching your own views, but instead means that you are expected to bring the world to your students.

Lifestyle

The matter of a teacher's appearance at work and his behavior away from work is, as you might expect by now, unique. On the one hand the teacher is a role model for the students in his care. On the other hand, the teacher is an individual with rights of his own. Is it fair to hold teachers to a different standard in their personal deportment? Well, it's impossible to know which way the courts would rule in such cases, but in every case it must be admitted that the individual chose to be a teacher—a position second only to parents in terms of having an influence on the development of young children. With every choice there are consequences, and in the case of teachers it can have an effect on their lifestyle.

Personal Appearance

You might recall from the 1915 teacher contract shown in Chapter 2 that there was a time when the expectations for a teacher's appearance and behavior both at work and away from work were very specific. The courts at the time considered the school systems to be the experts in such matters and tended not to dispute the requirements that schools imposed on their teachers. By the middle of the 20th century, and particularly during the decades of the 1960s and 1970s, the courts were more inclined to decide such matters in favor of the teacher as a citizen with the same rights as anyone else. More recently, however, "style of plumage" (hair styles) and "sartorial choice" (how one dresses) have been seen by the courts as matters that *do not* carry constitutional rights of choice. It is doubtful that we will again see contracts such as those of 100 years ago, but it is quite likely that your school or district may set personal grooming expectations.

Private Sexual Behavior

Interestingly enough, while the courts tend to side with the school districts in terms of personal grooming, the inclination with regard to private sexual behavior is in favor of the individual. Homosexuality, pregnancy out of wedlock, or unmarried cohabitation, for example, are seen as private matters separate from a teacher's public life *provided that* the situation is never part of the teacher's relationship with students, does not affect the teacher's relationship with colleagues, and does not intrude into the classroom or have any effect on the individual's work as a teacher.

A teacher's public behavior away from school is expected to serve as a model for the students and the community. Instances of public drunkenness or lewd behavior—even away from the community—could be considered sufficiently damaging to the dignity of the individual and to the profession that it may not be accepted. How the courts would rule in such cases would depend on the particular circumstances. What you need to understand at this point in the journey toward becoming a teacher is that whether the force of law is behind you or not, you can operate effectively as a teacher only if you hold the respect of the community that you serve. It is a higher standard than is expected of everyone else, and that's a choice you make.

Conduct with Students

Earlier in this chapter we used the phrase *in loco parentis,* which means "in the place of parents." Because schools and the teachers within the schools work *in loco parentis,* the relationship between teacher and student differs from that of colleagues working in an office, for example. In view of, or perhaps because of, this situation the courts are firm with regard to socially inappropriate behavior that finds its way to the classroom or to individual students. A sexual advance to a student, or even the ill-advised turn of a phrase that could be construed as a sexual advance, could lead to the end of a teacher's career—not to mention punitive measures as well. Taking drugs, drinking alcoholic beverages, using inappropriate language, or engaging in socially unacceptable behaviors with or around students would be all but indefensible in court. As we have said repeatedly, a teacher is a role model, and while a district cannot tell you what sort of person to be, it can tell you whether or not you are the sort of person that it wants to serve as a role model for the students in its schools.

The situations mentioned in the previous paragraph do seem a little extreme (though by no means beyond the realm of possibility). However, it is possible to establish relationships with students that are "innocent" in fact but questionable in perception. Lavishing too much attention on a particular student during or away from school could lead to the misperception of one's motives. Even with high school students, with whom a teacher might enjoy a stimulating intellectual relationship, it will always be the case that one person is the teacher and the other is a student—this particular dynamic precludes the possibility of being "friends" in the traditional sense. Many readers might not like to hear this, but the simple fact is that when we talk about teachers and the law, virtually all of the students that could be involved in such a discussion are minors. We are not suggesting that you maintain a cold distance between yourself and your students, but we are encouraging you to realize that as a teacher you will hold a position of influence—in the eyes of your students and those of the community—so don't ever believe that if challenged about a situation you could claim that it was just a bunch of friends getting together. Be professional.

■ Students and the Law

Though we ended the previous section by pointing out that most classroom students are minors, that doesn't mean that they are without rights. The rights accorded under the United States Constitution are provided to all citizens of the nation. As you know, the Constitution is a powerful document.

The Student and Due Process

Schools in our contemporary society are policy-driven institutions. What does that mean? Well, it means that there is an established policy for just about every function that takes place, from riding on a school bus to the marching order at graduation. And if there is something that is not addressed by a policy, there is likely a committee being formed to draft one. The impetus behind this has been the changing, though vague, expectations of the role that schools should play. Though teachers are still expected to be caring and compassionate in their work with students, published policies and procedures represent a step toward ensuring that students are provided their right to due process—particularly in disciplinary situations (LaRoche, 2005) that can be as extreme as exemption from compulsory attendance at school. We are a litigious society, and the balance between compassion and constraints of law can be difficult to achieve at times.

Suspension and Expulsion

As a student's behavior becomes increasingly disruptive, to the point of requiring that he be removed from a classroom, several options are typically available: in-school suspension, short- or long-term suspension (which prohibits a student from attending the school for a specified period), and expulsion (which forbids a student to attend the school in question). For minor disciplinary actions, schools are still afforded a considerable amount of discretion in resolving the situation. Minor infractions and those that are resolved with in-school or short-term suspension require at a minimum that the student be given some kind of notice and afforded some kind of hearing. Notice may be oral or written, and if a student denies the charges the school must explain the evidence it holds and the student must have an opportunity to present his side of the incident.

Long-term suspension and expulsion involve the separation of the student from the school for extended periods of time. Given that attendance at school is compulsory, it is obvious that steps this extreme must be handled with the full provision of a student's right to due process. The guidelines for educators in such instances are that students be provided

- Written notice of the charges against them
- Notification (time and place) of the hearing
- A description of the procedures to be followed at the hearing

Students are entitled to know what evidence will be presented, the names of witnesses that will be called, and the substance of the testimony that the witnesses will provide. They have the right to cross-examine the witnesses and provide witnesses of their own. They also are entitled to appeal the decision.

Pregnancy/Parenthood/Marriage

We mentioned in the section on teachers and the law that court interpretations of the law tend to reflect the thinking of the society at large (you will see this demonstrated clearly in Feature 10.1: Chief Justice Earl Warren Writes the Court's Opinion in *Brown v. Board of Education*). This is readily seen in cases of teen pregnancy, students as parents, and pregnant or married students. There was a time when young women who were pregnant or who had given birth were considered to be morally corrupting influences in the schools and were dismissed. Today, although teen pregnancy and motherhood may be considered inappropriate, a student's right to educational opportunities is not abridged. Title IX of the Education Amendments of 1972 has a lot to do with this, though in an unanticipated way (Title IX is discussed in this chapter under Civil Rights). The law was intended to prevent discrimination based on sex, and one profound effect was in essentially determining that athletics programs for girls should be as comprehensive as those for boys. In the situation of teen pregnancy, depriving a female of educational opportunities because of pregnancy, for example, would constitute sexual discrimination and thus be illegal.

Corporal Punishment

The use of corporal—that is, physical—punishment in the schools can be traced back for hundreds of years and continues in American schools even today. Given all we have discussed thus far about protection under the law and the eroding of the principle of in loco parentis, it almost seems incongruous that teachers and administrators would still be allowed to paddle children in the public schools. We are sorry (yes, we are biased) to say that as of 2006, 23 states still allow corporal punishment.

Though the U.S. Supreme Court has never issued a decision regarding corporal punishment in the public schools, lower courts have ruled that it is permissible under certain conditions: Corporal punishment can be used only as a disciplinary measure and must be "moderate" and "reasonable." Some states require that a second teacher or administrator be present as a witness when corporal punishment is administered. Commonly, the building principal or assistant principal will be the only one authorized to discipline a student in this manner.

As a classroom teacher, you must be aware of the laws regarding corporal punishment in your state and of the policies within your district. Even if corporal punishment is sanctioned where you teach, courts are not likely to uphold a legal

In Their Own Words

The passage below is an abridged version of the Opinion of the Court as written by Chief Justice Earl Warren, and found in the text of the 1954 Supreme Court Decision in Brown v. Board of Education *(Topeka, Kansas). For the sake of brevity, we have excluded those portions of the opinion that recounted the presentation of the case before the Court. Of particular note in this landmark opinion is that it involves reversing a previous Supreme Court decision* (Plessy v. Ferguson, 1896) *with the acknowledgment that the law must be interpreted in light of the times.*

The plaintiffs contend that segregated public schools are not "equal" and cannot be made "equal," and that hence they are deprived of the equal protection of the laws. Because of the obvious importance of the question presented, the Court took jurisdiction. Argument was heard in the 1952 Term, and reargument was heard this Term on certain questions propounded by the Court.

Reargument was largely devoted to the circumstances surrounding the adoption of the Fourteenth Amendment in 1868. It covered exhaustively consideration of the Amendment in Congress, ratification by the states, then existing practices in racial segregation, and the views of proponents and opponents of the Amendment. This discussion and our own investigation convince us that, although these sources cast some light, it is not enough to resolve the problem with which we are faced. At best, they are inconclusive. The most avid proponents of the post-War Amendments undoubtedly intended them to remove all legal distinctions among "all persons born or naturalized in the United States." Their opponents, just as certainly, were antagonistic to both the letter and the spirit of the Amendments and wished them to have the most limited effect. What others in Congress and the state legislatures had in mind cannot be determined with any degree of certainty.

An additional reason for the inconclusive nature of the Amendment's history, with respect to segregated schools, is the status of public education at that time. In the South, the movement toward free common schools, supported by general taxation, had not yet taken hold. Education of white children was largely in the hands of private groups. Education of Negroes was almost nonexistent, and practically all of the race were illiterate. In fact, any education of Negroes was forbidden by law in some states. Today, in contrast, many Negroes have achieved outstanding success in the arts and sciences as well as in the business and professional world. It is true that public school education at the time of the Amendment had advanced further in the North, but the effect of the Amendment on Northern States was generally ignored in the congressional debates. Even in the North, the conditions of public education did not approximate those existing today. The curriculum was usually rudimentary; ungraded schools were common in rural areas; the school term was but three months a year in many states; and compulsory school attendance was virtually unknown. As a consequence, it is not surprising that there should be so little in the history of the Fourteenth Amendment relating to its intended effect on public education.

challenge if it can be shown that the teacher used excessive force or punished the child out of spite, revenge, or anger. As is obvious by the fact that nearly half the states still allow corporal punishment, corporal punishment is a multidimensional issue with proponents on both sides of the argument. If your administration does not allow it, the decision is made for you. If your state or district does permit it, you will have to address this issue as part of your personal philosophy of teaching.

Search and Seizure

The Fourth Amendment to the U.S. Constitution provides protection from *unreasonable* search and seizure of person or property by government or law enforcement agencies. But what about students at schools? For one thing, students are in the custodial care of the schools they attend, which puts a level of supervisory responsibility (the administration) between the student and the agency. For another, the lockers in which students keep their possessions are the property of the school, not

Supreme Court in *Brown v. Board of Education*

In approaching this problem, we cannot turn the clock back to 1868 when the Amendment was adopted, or even to 1896 when *Plessy v. Ferguson* was written. We must consider public education in the light of its full development and its present place in American life throughout the Nation. Only in this way can it be determined if segregation in public schools deprives these plaintiffs of the equal protection of the laws.

Today, education is perhaps the most important function of state and local governments. Compulsory school attendance laws and the great expenditures for education both demonstrate our recognition of the importance of education to our democratic society. It is required in the performance of our most basic public responsibilities, even service in the armed forces. It is the very foundation of good citizenship. Today it is a principal instrument in awakening the child to cultural values, in preparing him for later professional training, and in helping him to adjust normally to his environment. In these days, it is doubtful that any child may reasonably be expected to succeed in life if he is denied the opportunity of an education. Such an opportunity, where the state has undertaken to provide it, is a right which must be made available to all on equal terms.

We come then to the question presented: Does segregation of children in public schools solely on the basis of race, even though the physical facilities and other "tangible" factors may be equal, deprive the children of the minority group of equal educational opportunities? We believe that it does.

We conclude that in the field of public education the doctrine of "separate but equal" has no place. Separate educational facilities are inherently unequal. Therefore, we hold that the plaintiffs and others similarly situated for whom the actions have been brought are, by reason of the segregation complained of, deprived of the equal protection of the laws guaranteed by the Fourteenth Amendment. This disposition makes unnecessary any discussion whether such segregation also violates the Due Process Clause of the Fourteenth Amendment.

Because these are class actions, because of the wide applicability of this decision, and because of the great variety of local conditions, the formulation of decrees in these cases presents problems of considerable complexity. On reargument, the consideration of appropriate relief was necessarily subordinated to the primary question—the constitutionality of segregation in public education. We have now announced that such segregation is a denial of the equal protection of the laws. In order that we may have the full assistance of the parties in formulating decrees, the cases will be restored to the docket, and the parties are requested to present further argument on Questions 4 and 5 previously propounded by the Court for the reargument this Term. The Attorney General of the United States is again invited to participate. The Attorneys General of the states requiring or permitting segregation in public education will also be permitted to appear as amici curiae upon request to do so by September 15, 1954, and submission of briefs by October 1, 1954.

It is so ordered. ■

the property of the student. Should the school therefore be allowed to search those lockers at any time? Once again, constitutional protection extends to students, though in a specialized way.

Probable Cause and Reasonable Suspicion

For government or law enforcement agents to perform a search and seizure against a private citizen, they must first demonstrate *probable cause*. That is, they must demonstrate beforehand that they are likely to find what they are seeking. Search warrants must specify what is being sought and where the search will be conducted. Indiscriminate searches and seizures are illegal.

School personnel are empowered to conduct searches of student lockers and property (such as purses or book bags) if they have *reasonable suspicion* that illegal or dangerous items may be in the student's possession. Reasonable suspicion is a less rigorous version of probable cause. Courts have ruled in favor of school districts that have demonstrated that a reasonable suspicion warranted the search. Random searches, on the other hand, constitute a violation of students' Fourth Amendment rights.

Searches of lockers and other personal property are not considered to be "invasive" searches. Searches of students' clothing and strip searches, however, are considered invasive and require a greater attention to the rights of the student in question. Due to the invasive and potentially humiliating nature of strip searches, schools must be very careful in making a decision to conduct such a search.

Lower courts have been divided on the issue of strip searches. It is therefore incumbent upon the school administration to demonstrate that they have substantial evidence from reliable sources that a student may be concealing illegal or dangerous items. Though there has not been a ruling from the Supreme Court concerning strip searches, the U.S. Court of Appeals for the Sixth Circuit has ruled class strip searches unconstitutional (Hendrie, 2005).

Drug Tests as Searches

Generally speaking, schools are not permitted to use urine tests to detect or prevent drug abuse. However, courts have upheld the use of urine tests for students involved in interscholastic athletics. In the late 1980s an Oregon school district observed a marked increase in drug use among its students. Noting that a disproportionate number of students involved were on athletic teams, it instituted a policy of random urine-testing as a condition of participation. When one student and his parents refused to consent to the program, the case went to court and eventually was heard by the U.S. Supreme Court (*Vernonia School District v. Acton,* 1995). The Court ruled for the school district; Justice Scalia, writing for the majority, indicated that the compelling interest of the state in having a drug-free environment in the schools outweighed the limited invasion of the student's privacy. The Court further stated that while the school's policy was upheld because of the circumstances of the case, random searches must be justified by virtue of a compelling interest of the state. Writing for the dissenting opinion, Justices O'Conner, Stevens, and Souter argued that individualized suspicion should be the impetus for testing by procedures such as urinalysis, and that random testing was not reasonable in light of our Constitution.

Freedom of Speech

Students do enjoy the privilege of free speech as set forth in the First Amendment. As is the case with adults, the right is not absolute, and in the particular case of students in the public schools the right is not limitless. The landmark case of *Tinker v. Des Moines Independent School District* (1969) is frequently cited as the precedent for acknowledging the free speech—or perhaps more correctly, free expression—rights of students. In this incident several students had been suspended for wearing black armbands to school in protest of the Vietnam war. Lower courts upheld the position of the school district, but the U.S. Supreme Court ruled that prohibiting the armbands violated the students' right to free expression. Of key importance was that the wearing of the armbands could not be shown to have caused any disruption within the school. The Court said that unless the expression would "materially and substantially" interfere with either the operation of the school or the rights of others, the policy of banning such expression would be unconstitutional.

However, as we mentioned, the privilege of free speech is neither absolute nor limitless. The courts have ruled that schools are entitled to establish limits of decorum in spoken, written, and symbolic expression. Thus, if, for instance, a student wants to complain about the way the administration operates within a school or the decision of the president of the United States to commit troops to a war, such expression is within one's rights. If the student chooses to phrase those opinions in terms that are derogatory, insulting, vulgar, obscene, or defamatory, the school is empowered to ban such expression.

From the perspective of the courts, the schools are charged with upholding the rights of citizenship granted by the constitution and with providing an environment in which students learn to exercise those rights in a responsible and mature manner. Courts have repeatedly indicated that it is not the charge of the public schools to teach students what to think. You would do well to spend at least a few moments reflecting on the extraordinary freedoms that you—and your students—enjoy.

Sexual Harassment

sexual harassment Unwanted and unwelcome sexual behavior that interferes with the victim's life.

The majority of reports concerning **sexual harassment** in the schools involve student-to-student interactions. However, a study commissioned by the American Association of University Women (AAUW) (2001) found that 25 percent of the reports from females and 10 percent of those from males involved school employees. The AAUW defines sexual harassment as "*unwanted* and *unwelcome* sexual behavior that interferes with your life" (p. 2). Such matters may once have been thought of as being confined to the high school population, or at least to the behavior of adolescents. But now, with the broad range of behaviors that can be construed as harassment and the legitimate sensitivity of parents, cases of sexual harassment are found even in the primary grades. What becomes of critical importance in terms of liability is that, as the definition states, the behavior is unwanted and unwelcome and it has been brought to the attention of the teachers or administration (see Figure 10.2).

The legal basis of claims against the school is Title IX of the Education Amendments of 1972, which prohibits discrimination on the basis of sex. In the pivotal case of *Davis v. Monroe County Board of Education* (1999), the U.S. Supreme Court decided by a vote of 5 to 4 that schools could be sued for failing to deal appropriately with matters of harassment. Writing the majority opinion,

Figure 10.2

Percentages of Student Reports of Sexual Harassment That Involve School Employees

Source: American Association of University Women, 2001

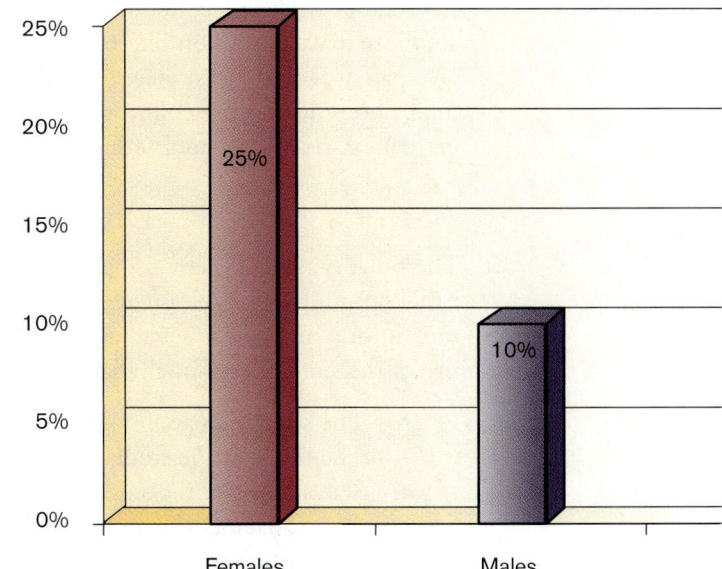

Table 10.1	Guidelines for Addressing Sexual Harassment Issues in Schools

- Adopt legally defensible policies and procedures for dealing with harassment.
- Swiftly investigate harassment complaints filed by students.
- Be certain that policies reflect zero-tolerance toward student-on-student harassment.
- Design comprehensive staff development programs for faculty and staff.
- Provide education and awareness programs for students.
- Encourage students to freely report alleged harassment.
- Create and maintain a respectful and considerate school environment.
- Maintain maximum confidentiality for students.
- Hold liability workshops or seminars for school personnel.
- Maintain confidential records of harassment allegations.

(From Essex, 2000)

Justice O'Connor indicated that "lawsuits against schools are only valid when the harassing student's behavior is so severe, pervasive, and objectively offensive that it denies the victim equal access to an education guaranteed by federal law . . . and that harassment claims are valid only when school administrators are clearly unreasonable and deliberately indifferent toward the alleged harassing conduct" (Essex, 2000). Students are entitled to an education environment that is neither threatening nor uncomfortable. Thus, matters of harassment must be taken seriously and dealt with effectively. Table 10.1 provides guidelines for addressing sexual harassment issues in the schools.

Records and Students' Right to Privacy

The information age offers an interesting dichotomy: an overwhelming access to information combined with an unprecedented need to keep information secure. For our discussion of the public schools, the information that must be secure is students' academic and disciplinary records.

The Buckley Amendment

In 1974 Congress passed the Family Educational Rights and Privacy Act (FERPA), also known as the Buckley Amendment. FERPA allowed parents to have access to the official educational records of their children, and to be provided with explanations about what was contained in those records when requested. Official records are those that are kept on file (or in databases). The Buckley Amendment does not give parents the right to view *unofficial* education records such as those a teacher might keep during the course of instruction. The result is that when it comes to permanent records, school officials tend to be very careful about what is written.

Disciplinary Records

The Buckley Amendment also protects student records. Without parental consent, FERPA prohibits the release of education records or *personally identifiable information,* information from which another party would be able to determine the identity of the student. Personally identifiable information includes

- The student's name
- The name of the student's parent or other family member
- The address of the student or the student's family
- A personal identifier such as the student's social security number or student number

- A list of personal characteristics that would make the student's identity easily traceable
- Other information that would make the student's identity easily traceable (Anderson, 2003)

The various states can determine what constitutes an official "education record." However, federal law supersedes state law. In the interesting case of *The United States v. The Miami University* (2000/2002), the university had released some student disciplinary records to the student newspaper under order from the Ohio Supreme Court to do so. In federal district court it was determined that the provisions against releasing identifiable information as established by FERPA took precedence, and so the records should *not* have been released!

Schools and Religion

Part of the First Amendment to the United States Constitution (the Establishment Clause) declares that "Congress shall make no law respecting an establishment of religion, or prohibiting the free exercise thereof." The role of religion as it relates to public education is determined primarily by the judicial branch of the government. Sometimes a final decision is rendered by the Supreme Court; more often a decision is handed down by a federal district court (and therefore applies only to the states in its jurisdiction) or by the supreme court of a state. Especially when a court at a still lower level rules, the decision is appealed to the next higher level, eventually reaching the high court, which might decide to hear the case or to let the decision of the lower court stand.

Recent years have witnessed a plethora of court decisions with regard to religion and the schools. Almost 40 years ago, the Supreme Court established a three-part test intended to assure that three unacceptable factors did not prevail in matters of religion and the public schools: sponsorship, source of financial support, and active involvement of school authorities. In *Lemon v. Kurtzman* (1971), the Court ruled that to be constitutional, a state law must meet three conditions: (1) The purpose of aid must be clearly secular, not religious; (2) its primary effect must neither advance nor inhibit religion; and (3) it must avoid an "excessive entanglement of government with religion." So what has the Supreme Court ruled?

Some teachers and administrators still begin the school day and school programs with an invocation that could be of questionable legality.

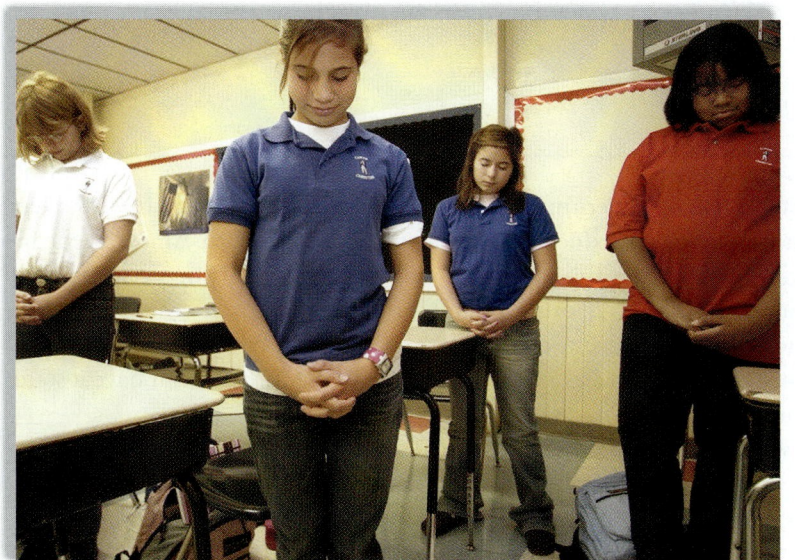

© John McCusker/Newhouse News Service/Landov

Prayer in the Public Schools

Prayer in the public schools is not permitted when it is composed by some governing body. This applies to the school's intercommunication system, classroom teachers, and special events such as graduation exercises (*Engel v. Vitale,* 1962, and later cases, including *Lee v. Weisman,* 1992). (In an interesting event, a class valedictorian at graduation walked to the podium and paused. Suddenly the entire senior class "sneezed." "God bless each and every one of you," she responded, and returned to her seat.) Student-led prayers at football games are also unconstitutional (*Santa Fe Independent*

School District v. Doe, 2000). "Silent prayer" (also called "moment of meditation") has been ruled to be a violation of the Establishment Clause (*Wallace v. Jaffree,* 1985). And reading from the Bible and requiring students to say the Lord's Prayer not permissible (*Abington School District v. Schempp,* 1963, and others).

Religious Instruction in Public Schools

Public funds may not be used to support instruction in religion. It is generally recognized that public schools may teach content from the Bible from an historical or literary perspective but not from a religious viewpoint. Thus, an English teacher might teach several of the Psalms to analyze their structure, and a history teacher might discuss the fall of Jerusalem as part of the actions of the Roman Empire. However, a local group (e.g., a ministerial association) may fund textbooks (usually a Bible) and a "religion teacher" who provides instruction in a nearby off-campus site (*Zorach v. Clawson,* 1952). Students who wish to receive such instruction may schedule the class.

Public Funds for Parochial Schools

Under the child-benefit theory, parochial schools may receive public funds for purchasing textbooks that are not religion related, such as reading and math books (*Board of Education v. Allen,* 1965). Likewise, public funds may be used by parochial schools to secure, administer, and grade standardized achievement tests (*Committee for Public Education v. Regan,* 1980).

Religious Clubs/Prayer Groups

Schools that provide opportunities for organizations to meet on campus during or after school hours are required to permit Christian clubs, for example, to do the same. However, the sponsors cannot be paid (*Westside School District v. Mergens,* 1990). This ruling used the Lemon Test (*Lemon v. Kurtzman*) to rule that the Equal Access Act was constitutional.

As in other aspects of teaching, if you are unsure of a practice, check with someone who should know. Typically that is a veteran mentor teacher, but an administrator is even better, and a policy handbook is best.

■ Federal Law

The United States federal government does not assume full responsibility (or even major responsibility) for the education of its citizens. The Tenth Amendment to the Constitution, part of the Bill of Rights, states, "The powers not delegated to the United States by the Constitution, nor prohibited by it to the States, are reserved to the States respectively, or to the people." Thus, education is a responsibility of each state. There is also a clear indication that education can have a state and a local component.

Then how has the federal government managed to become so deeply involved in education? For the constitutional answer, we need to refer to Article 1, Section 8, which states in part that "Congress shall have power to lay and collect taxes [and] provide for the common defense and general welfare of the United States." Federal involvement in education is a function of the "general welfare" clause. And what of providing for the common defense? Well, as we will see, the government's involvement in education stems from that as well.

During the past two centuries, Congress has become increasingly involved in education, enacting a series of laws that affect everyone enrolled at every level of any educational institution. A few of these laws are outlined here to give you a sense of the scope of the federal government's involvement and ways in which the laws have directly or indirectly influenced your life.

For purposes of discussion, we have assigned the laws we have selected for review to the following categories: higher education, elementary and secondary schools, civil rights, exceptional education, compensatory education, school subjects and topics, and information and research. You will find them summarized in Table 10.2 on page 352.

Laws are both named and numbered. The numbering system is based on the session of Congress and the order in which the bill approved by the House and the Senate was approved by the President. Thus Public Law (PL) 94-142 refers to the 94th Congress (the 94th two-year session beginning with the first Congress) and the 142nd law passed by that Congress during its two-year term of office. Since our government has existed for over 200 years, we have had over 100 Congressional terms. Much of the following information is derived from two sources: *American Educators' Encyclopedia* (Dejnozka & Kapel, 1982) and *The Condition of Education* (2002).

Higher Education

The Morrill Act (1862) authorized land grants that the states were to use to establish and maintain agricultural and mechanical colleges. These A&M colleges exist in all states today and produce large numbers of graduates in specialized fields. In 1890, a second Morrill Act allocated funds to support instruction in the land grant colleges. All states and Puerto Rico currently receive federal funds for land-grant institutions (Griffin, 1982).

In 1944, **PL 78-346, The Servicemen's Readjustment Act** (also known as the GI Bill), was passed to enable returning veterans to pay for higher education. The result was greatly increased college and university enrollment, particularly among minorities. The GI Bill was eventually extended to veterans of the Korean and Vietnam wars.

The Economic Opportunity Act (PL 88-452) of 1964 provided funds for college work-study programs for students with family incomes below specified levels. It also funded Head Start, Follow Through, and Volunteers in Service to America (VISTA).

PL 89-329, The Higher Education Act of 1965, provided funds for college libraries, instructional equipment, and teacher education programs. It also funded the National Teachers Corps, insured student loans, and provided graduate fellowships in teacher education.

Elementary and Secondary Schools

The Northwest Ordinances (the earliest federal land grants) of 1785 and 1787, which originally applied to the land north of the Ohio River and east of the Mississippi River, set aside section 16 of each township for public schools (Dejnozka and Kapel, 1982). The ordinances eventually granted public lands to 39 states. The grants, to be used for educational purposes, were the first instances of federal aid to education.

Courtesy of Bill Lisenby

Many of these children may be receiving free or reduced-price lunches as a result of federal legislation.

The 1950 Amendments to the Lanham Act (PL 76-849, 1941) provided funds for constructing, operating, and maintaining schools in areas with large numbers of federal employees (as in the case of a military base). The intent was to help local areas avoid financial problems caused by unusually large enrollments of the children of adults in federal service.

The National School Lunch Act (PL 79-396, 1946) provided funds for public school use in establishing, operating, and maintaining school cafeterias and lunch programs. Funding was also provided for distribution of food to school lunch programs. Eight years later, through **PL 83-597 (The School Milk Program Act),** funds were allocated for the purchase of milk for school lunch programs.

Head Start, which was part of **The Economic Opportunity Act (PL 88-452)** of 1964, originally enrolled only four- and five-year-old children from low-income families, but that rule was later relaxed. The major objective of Head Start is to prepare young children for entry into school. In 1972, a requirement was added that at least 10 percent of the slots for Head Start were to go to handicapped children.

As its title suggests, Follow Through was intended to maintain the academic gains of children in Head Start and to increase their achievement in the primary grades. Despite some notable exceptions (e.g., the Perry Preschool Project in Ypsilanti, Michigan), long-term results of early childhood compensatory education programs have been disappointing (Besharov, 1992). Not only is the body of available research "insufficient for use in drawing conclusions about the impact of national programs" (Joyner, 1998), the Third Progress Report (Zill, et al., 2001) found that at the end of Head Start, the children were "substantially behind national norms." Nevertheless, the programs are extremely popular politically.

VISTA is a program intended to provide volunteers to community agencies that are developing long-term solutions to problems caused by rural and urban poverty.

Civil Rights

PL 88-352, The Civil Rights Act of 1964, allocated funds for public school districts (and institutions of higher education) to provide in-service programs intended to help educators deal with issues related to desegregation. The act prohibited discrimination based on color, race, religion, or national origin. **Title VII** specifically forbade discrimination in hiring.

PL 92-318, The Education Amendments of the Indian Education Act of 1972, covered a variety of topics. **Title IV** established an Office of Indian Education (which supported culturally relevant education and parent involvement) and attempted to improve educational opportunities for Native Americans and reduce the unacceptably high levels of illiteracy. **Title IX** prohibited sex bias (against both males and females) in public elementary and secondary schools as well as in admission to post-secondary education institutions for any program receiving federal financial assistance.

The Family Educational Rights and Privacy Act (FERPA) of 1973 is also called the **Buckley Amendment.** It protects students from having their grades or records disclosed except when there is a "need to know," as would be true for a teacher, guidance counselor, and, for students under age 18, parents (Zirkel, 2001, 2003). As a teacher, you will be interested in knowing that the United States Supreme Court has ruled unanimously that the checking of papers by students' peers is an acceptable practice (Zirkel, 2003). This amendment also advises teachers not to place defamatory comments in a student's file. Thus, you will want to focus on facts rather than opinions when you document behavior. To avoid possible violations of FERPA, read Essex's (2000) article on confidentiality.

In 1974, **The Child Abuse Prevention and Treatment Act (PL 93-247)** created a national center that collects data on child abuse and neglect, conducts research, and publishes training materials (Dejnozka & Kapel, 1982).

In 1990, **PL 101-542, The Student Right-to-Know and Campus Security Act,** was passed, requiring postsecondary institutions that receive financial aid to provide the federal government with information about the graduation rates of student athletes. Schools were also required to provide security services and file annual crime reports with the FBI.

The Safe Schools Act (PL 103-227, 1994) allocated money to fund grant proposals to schools with serious crime problems. The proposals were required to focus on strategies such as conflict resolution and peer mediation.

Exceptional Education

The Education of Mentally Retarded Children Act (PL 85-926, 1958) provided funds for training teachers of the handicapped. It can be considered the forerunner of all subsequent laws related to exceptional education.

PL 90-247, The Elementary and Secondary Education Amendments of 1968, provided regional centers for the education of handicapped children, services for deaf or blind children, information resources for the handicapped, and support for bilingual education programs and dropout-prevention programs.

The Handicapped Children's Early Education Assistance Act (PL 90-538, 1968) allocated funds for programs for preschool and other early childhood education programs for the handicapped from birth through age six.

Section 504 of the Rehabilitation Act (PL 93-112, 1973) is a civil rights law relating to exceptional education. It provides for children who have or have had a physical or mental impairment that substantially limits a major life activity (e.g., walking, seeing, hearing, speaking, breathing, learning, working, caring for oneself, and performing manual tasks) or is regarded by others as disabled. This law also forbade discrimination against students because of handicaps and also required that architectural barriers be replaced.

In 1975, the landmark **Education for All Handicapped Children Act (PL 94-142)** provided for a free and appropriate public education (FAPE) for all handicapped children between ages 3 and 18. Renamed IDEA in 1990, it consisted of six major concepts:

1. *Zero reject.* No school system could refuse to serve any eligible child.
2. *Nondiscriminatory evaluation.* A comprehensive and individual evaluation must be appropriate for the child's cultural and language background and must precede placement in an exceptional education program. A reevaluation must occur no later than three years.
3. **Individualized education program** (IEP). This written plan, specific for each child, must describe the child's current performance, the goals for the year, the services to be rendered, and the means by which the results will be measured.

individualized education program (IEP) A written plan, specific for each child, that consists of a description of the child's current performance, the goals for the year, the services to be rendered, and the means by which the results will be measured.

least restrictive environment (LRE) The requirement that, to the extent possible, a handicapped child must be educated with nonhandicapped children, that is, in a mainstreamed environment.

4. **Least restrictive environment** (LRE). To the extent possible, a handicapped child must be educated with nonhandicapped children, that is, in a mainstreamed environment. However, the term "mainstream" does not appear in the law.

5. *Due process.* Procedures intended to ensure fairness and accountability of both parents/guardians and educators include the rights of parents to have evaluations conducted by personnel outside the school system and to request a hearing when they disagree with the school's proposed plans.

6. *Parent/guardian participation.* Parents are entitled to see their children's records and to participate fully in the development of the IEP.

The Education of the Handicapped Act Amendments of 1983 (PL 98-199) required that architectural barriers to access be eliminated. Have you ever wondered why schools are often one story tall and have access ramps? Multiple floors make access difficult and the solutions (such as elevators) are an expensive way to meet the mandates of the law.

The 1986 Education of the Handicapped Act Amendments (PL 99-457) included services for developmentally delayed children from birth to age two. The act encouraged states to assess each eligible child, develop an individualized family services plan, and provide family counseling, speech or language therapy, occupational or vocational therapy, and special education services as needed. The availability of free and appropriate public education (FAPE) was expanded to include children ages 3–5.

The Technology-Related Assistance for Individuals with Disabilities Act (PL 100-407, 1988) funds statewide programs to provide appropriate technology for handicapped people of all ages.

PL 101-336, the Americans with Disabilities Act (ADA) of 1990, prohibits discrimination against people with disabilities. This is another landmark case. In this law, a "child with a disability" refers to a child:

"**1.** With mental retardation, hearing impairments (including deafness), speech or language impairments, visual impairments (including blindness), serious emotional disturbance (hereinafter referred to as 'emotional disturbance'), orthopedic impairments, autism, traumatic brain injury, other health impairments, or specific learning disabilities; and

2. Who, by reason thereof, needs special education and related services."

The Amendments to the Individuals with Disabilities Education Act (IDEA) (PL 105-17, 1997) extended IDEA through fiscal year 2002. This law frequently is referred to as IDEA '97. Although the Congress agreed to fund 40 percent of the cost, in fact it allocated moneys for only 15 percent to 17 percent, making the law an underfunded mandate (Opportunity to Excel, February, 2001; The Politics of IDEA Revisited, 2003).

IDEA was reauthorized by Congress in November 2004. The reauthorization decreases the paperwork, requires the Department of Education to develop a model IEP form, allows states to spend 15 percent of the IDEA funds to help students who have not yet been approved for assistance, allows a school to suspend a seriously disruptive student for up to 45 days while the IEP team determines how to deal with the situation, and requires that a parent prove that the misbehavior was caused by the student's disability rather than the school prove it was not (Lewis, 2005; What Will the New IDEA Do?, 2005; White, 2005). Importantly, it established a "glide path" to funding at the 40 percent level by 2011, which was first promised in the 1970s (Lewis, 2005).

Compensatory Education

In 1965, the **Elementary and Secondary Education Act (ESEA), PL 89-10,** provided funds to elementary and secondary schools that served large numbers of students from low-income families. The funds could be used for remedial teachers and materials for libraries and instruction. This act was a watershed in federal programs for economically disadvantaged populations and, as reauthorized and renamed, it continues today, as popular as ever, despite some negative long-term research studies. **The Bilingual Education Act (PL 90-247, 1968)** was a series of amendments to ESEA. Known as **Title VII,** it provided aid to students with "limited English-speaking ability." This act and its successors is increasingly important: 11 percent of the United States population is foreign born (Drucker, 2003), 41 percent of the 3,000,000 teachers surveyed by the National Center for Education Statistics teach limited English proficient students (NCELA, 2002), and it takes up to seven years for these students to perform academically as well as their peers (Collier & Thomas, 1999). Indeed, Collier and Thomas write, "Native English speakers are not sitting around waiting for ESL students to catch up. They are continuing to make one year's progress in one year's time in the English language development and in every school subject" (p. 1).

block grants Grants that allow state education agencies the flexibility to use the funds to meet their specific needs within the framework of the federal law. In essence, a number of special programs are folded into a block grant.

categorical grants Grants that allow state education agencies maximum flexibility to apportion the funds according to their specific needs.

  PL 97-35 (1981), the **Education Consolidation and Improvement Act (ECIA),** combined 42 programs into seven **block grants.** From a political point of view it was an attempt to remove decision-making ability from the federal government and to provide the states with the flexibility to use the funds to meet their particular needs within the broad framework of the law. Thus began the effort to use **categorical grants,** which left to the states the responsibility to apportion the money according to their needs.

  The Elementary and Secondary School Improvement Amendments (PL 100-297, 1988) reauthorized through fiscal year 1993 such programs as remedial education teachers, bilingual education, math-science education, Indian education, and adult education.

  PL 103-382, the Improving America's Schools Act (1994), reauthorized ESEA, continuing to provide remedial teachers for children from low-income homes. It also provided funds for professional development programs for teachers, safe and drug-free schools, and community support.

Go Online!

ACTIVITY 10.3 Researching Federal Law

Laws are far more complex than the brief descriptions we can provide. You may be surprised to find how involved a law can be. Though many laws are much too lengthy to download, the Internet makes it practical for you to see how laws are formatted and what sorts of provisions are included in the legislation.

  Select one of the laws in the text to research. You can begin your search with the Government Printing Office's Web site, www.gpoaccess.gov/plaws/index.html, which provides access to laws enacted from the 104th to the 108th Congress. A search with the term "public laws" will help you find other sites.

1. What did you find within a law that you had not expected?

2. What, if any, other legislation was included with the law you researched?

PL 105-285, the Educational Excellence for All Children Act (1999), was the next five-year reauthorization of ESEA. Its major focus was on accountability of the states and the school districts. It advocated higher standards for teachers, opposed *social promotion* while insisting that additional support be provided so students could acquire the information being presented, and required that **Title I** (low-income) schools be treated the same as non-Title I schools in terms of quality of faculty, physical condition of the school, and the curriculum. It also required that each school issue to parents an annual report card detailing the progress of the students in the school.

Research on the effectiveness of Title I (remedial education) of ESEA and its periodic reauthorization bills has sometimes been disappointing, particularly in long-term studies. In general, the finding is that interventions don't increase student achievement after grade 3 and have a limited impact in the primary grades (Dyer & Binkney, 1995). Others (Puma, et al., 1997) have found Title I to have limited impact on increasing children's reading achievement. A more positive report prepared by the Center on Education Policy indicates that over the past 30 years, additional funding has had a greater impact on the achievement of minority and disadvantaged students than on their more advantaged classmates. The gains made by African Americans, Hispanics, and white disadvantaged students have closed one-third to one-half of the achievement gap (Jennings, 2000).

PL 107-110, the No Child Left Behind (NCLB) Act of 2001, is a massive education omnibus. In its goal to have all children as proficient readers by the school year 2013–2014, it mandates testing in reading and math for students in grades 3–8 and once in the three-year period of grades 10–12, and requires each state to develop standards and objectives for all elementary and secondary grades and then administer **high-stakes tests** (so called because they have serious negative implications for students and schools that do not meet predetermined criteria) aligned to the standards. Furthermore, it mandates that all test data be analyzed by race or ethnic group and economic status and reported for students with disabilities and limited English proficiency. The proficiency standards, which are different for each state, gradually increase until 2014, at which time 95 percent of students are supposed to perform at or above grade level in reading and math. This expectation holds for each subgroup (e.g., Hispanics, African Americans, students with learning disabilities, English language learners). A school that misses the goal for any subgroup "fails to meet standards" and is subjected to a series of consequences that increase each year. In the spring of 2002, 8,632 schools were classified as failing to meet state standards according to NCLB (Million, 2002). As the standards rise, the number of "failing" schools will also rise, even if the schools continue to make progress! The law also authorizes two new programs: Reading First (to raise achievement of at-risk children in kindergarten through grade 3 and students with exceptionalities K–12) and Early Reading First (for at-risk preschoolers). Reading First grants are awarded for three years; then there is a progress check to determine whether a second (and final) three-year grant should be awarded (Barone, Hardman, & Taylor, 2006).

Although Reading First and its parent program, NCLB, were passed with strong bipartisan support, it is quite controversial. Complaints include misuse and overuse of standardized tests (Allington, 2002; Guisbond & Neill, 2004), serious discrepancies between the research and the purported findings (Garan, 2002; Krashen, 2002; Yatvin, Weaver, & Garan, 2003), expectations of one year of progress annually for subgroups such as English language learners (Abedi & Dietel, 2004), expectations that 95 percent of the students in all subgroups will achieve the standards by 2014 (Mathis, 2003; Guisbond & Neill, 2004; Schroeder, 2004), and the huge costs, most of which must be borne by state and local governments (Lewis, 2005; Mathis, 2003).

high-stakes tests Standardized achievement tests that are used for promotion, graduation, or assignment of school grades and that carry penalties for poor schoolwide performance (as well as rewards for good performance). Thus, they have serious negative implications for students and schools that do not meet predetermined criteria.

School Subjects and Topics

In 1958, **PL 85-864, the National Defense Education Act (NDEA),** was passed as a reaction to the launching of Russia's Sputnik and federal fears that the United States would be outdistanced in science and technology. The NDEA provided funds for strengthening math, science, and foreign language courses in public schools, foreign language offerings in post-secondary institutions, and dissemination of the effective use of the technology of the time (television and movies, primarily). Many programs for retraining teachers were conducted across the country.

PL 91-516, the Environmental Education Act (1970), established an Office of Environmental Education, disseminated environmental education information, and promoted the development of environmental programs at the elementary and secondary levels.

PL 95-561, the Education Amendments (1978), replaced the National Reading Improvement Program with a basic skills program and promoted the use of the schools for community purposes.

In 1984, the **Education for Economic Security Act (PL 98-377)** funded science and math programs at all levels of education. Notice that this act, as was the case with NDEA in 1958, is an education act driven by a social exigency.

PL 101-239, the Childhood Education and Development Act (1989), expanded Head Start and included childcare services.

In 1990, **PL 101-600, the School Dropout Prevention and Basic Skills Improvement Act,** authorized efforts to diminish "dropoutism" by enhancing students' basic skills.

The School-to-Work Opportunities Act (PL 103-239, 1994) was funded to prepare students for the world of work and for subsequent education. Schools were directed to include career-related academics, career development activities, and work experiences connected to the schools. Unfortunately, a study in eight states that received early funding found that only 3 percent of the high school seniors had participated in all three components (Hershey, Silverberg, & Haimson, 1999).

PL 105-277, the Omnibus Consolidated and Emergency Supplemental Appropriations Act (1998), established the Reading Excellence Act, which expected all students to be able to read independently by the third grade. It also provided funds to reduce class size in the primary grades. Eventually the act was folded into PL 107-110 (No Child Left Behind Act).

PL 108-265, the Child Nutrition and WIC (Women, Infants, and Children) Reauthorization Act, required that wellness policies be established in schools receiving federal aid.

Information and Research

In 1954, **PL 83-531, the Educational Research Act,** was designed to promote close working relationships among state education agencies and post-secondary institutions in conducting and disseminating education research.

PL 93-380, the Education Amendments of 1974, established the National Center for Education Statistics, which today publishes summaries of information related to education at all levels. One sample is the *Digest of Education Statistics.*

In 1993, **PL 103-33, the National Assessment of Educational Progress (NAEP) Assessment Authorization,** permitted the use of the NAEP for comparisons by state. The NAEP samples student achievement nationwide on a regular schedule for each area of the curriculum. The ages sampled are 9, 13, and 17 (approximately the end of elementary, middle school, and secondary school). Statistical data on student performance as well as responses to questions about school and nonschool

Table 10.2 Selected Federal Education Legislation

Higher Education

Morrill Land-Grant Act of 1862
Morrill Land-Grant Act of 1890
PL 78-346, Serviceman's Readjustment Act
PL 88-452, Economic Opportunity Act
PL 89-329, The Higher Education Act

Elementary and Secondary Schools

Northwest Ordinances of 1785 and 1787
PL 76-849, Amendments to Lanham Act
PL 79-396, National School Lunch Act
PL 83-597, School Milk Program Act

Civil Rights

PL 88-352, Civil Rights Act
PL 92-318, Education Amendments of the Indian Education Act
PL 93-247, Child Abuse Prevention and Treatment Act
Family Educational Rights and Privacy Act
PL 101-542, Student Right-to-Know and Campus Security Act
PL 103-227, Safe Schools Act

Exceptional Education

PL 85-926, Education of Mentally Retarded Children Act
PL 90-247, Elementary and Secondary Education Amendments
PL 90-538, Handicapped Children's Early Education Assistance Act
PL 93-112, Rehabilitation Act
PL 94-142, Education for All Handicapped Children Act
PL 98-199, Education of the Handicapped Act Amendments
PL 99-457, Education of the Handicapped Act Amendments
PL 100-407, Technology-Related Assistance for Individuals with Disabilities Act
PL 101-336, American with Disabilities Act
PL 105-17, Amendments to the Individuals with Disabilities Education Act

Compensatory Education

PL 89-10, Elementary and Secondary Education Act
PL 90-247, Bilingual Education Act
PL 97-35, Education Consolidation and Improvement Act
PL 100-297, Elementary and Secondary School Improvement Amendments
PL 103-382, Improving America's Schools Act
PL 105-285, Educational Excellence for All Children Act
PL 107-110, No Child Left Behind Act

School Subjects and Topics

PL 85-864, National Defense Education Act
PL 91-516, Environmental Education Act
PL 95-561, Education Amendments
PL 98-377, Education for Economic Security Act
PL 101-239, Childhood Education and Development Act
PL 101-600, School Dropout Prevention and Basic Skills Improvement Act
PL 103-239, School-to-Work Opportunities Act
PL 105-277, Omnibus Consolidated and Emergency Supplemental Appropriations Act
PL 108-265, Child Nutrition and WIC (Women, Infants, and Children) Reauthorization Act

Information and Research

PL 83-531, Educational Research Act
PL 93-380, Education Amendments
PL 103-33, National Assessment of Educational Progress

activities are compared with information obtained from the previous cycle on a given subject area and then summarized in reports that receive widespread attention. For instance, data collected on reading achievement in nine urban areas in 2003 revealed that over 50 percent of urban fourth graders scored in the "Below Basic" category. For the nation as a whole, the figure was 38 percent (Flynt & Cooter, 2005).

Challenges to the Law

From time to time the United States Supreme Court is called upon to adjudicate a disagreement over the constitutionality of an education law or part of a law. In that case, the nine justices serve as the final arbiters; there is no recourse to their decision. As a major example, in 1954 the Supreme Court ruled 9–0 in the case of *Brown v. Board of Education* that school segregation was unconstitutional. "Separate and equal" as upheld in the 1896 case of *Plessy v. Ferguson* was neither possible nor permissible. A year after *Brown,* the Court ruled that integration was to occur with "all deliberate speed."

During the past half century, the Supreme Court has become the final arbiter in a large number of cases that affect both public and private education. Like the federal laws, there are a number of significant cases with which you should be familiar. Table 10.3 summarizes the annotated listing below. Activity 10.4 provides an opportunity to look at Supreme Court cases in greater detail. You can use the Internet to research one of the cases we have discussed in this chapter.

Integration

Sweatt v. Painter (1951) The University of Texas Law School was required to admit African Americans. Note that this decision preceded and foreshadowed *Brown v. Board of Education* by four years.

Swann v. Charlotte-Mecklenburg (North Carolina) Board of Education (1971) Busing was ordered to achieve desegregation. Consequently, many parents of minorities sent their children to schools outside their neighborhoods, marking a decrease in parental involvement in the schools.

 Go Online!

ACTIVITY 10.4   Researching Court Rulings Concerning Education

The outcome of any court case is just part of the story. The cases discussed in this chapter have shaped education as we know it, and continue to influence the course of education in the United States. Yet, just as one example, what was the case of *Plessy v. Ferguson* actually about? You might be surprised.

Select one of the cases from the text to research. The URLs below will begin to open the world of Supreme Court rulings to you:

www.supremecourtus.gov (Official web page of the U.S. Supreme Court.)
www.law.cornell.edu/supct/search/search.html (Good site for older cases.)

1.   Who were the principal litigants in the case?

2.   What was the complaint?

3.   What was the vote on the final decision?

4.   On what rule of law was the majority opinion based?

Church and State

Engel v. Vitale (1962) The state-written prayer "Almighty God, we acknowledge our dependence upon thee, and we beg thy blessings upon us, our parents, our teachers and our Country" was an unconstitutional violation of the First Amendment regarding the separation of church and state.

Zelman v. Simmons-Harris, Hannah Perkins School v. Simmons-Harris, and Taylor v. Simmons-Harris (2002) Using vouchers for parochial schools is not a violation of the separation between church and state if students have a variety of options in addition to specific public schools (e.g., nonsectarian schools and other public schools as well as church-related schools).

Exceptional Children

Mills v. Board of Education of the District of Columbia (1972) The school district was required to provide public education for the seven handicapped children for whom the case was argued and for other handicapped children as well. This case foreshadowed the passage of PL 94-142, Education of the Handicapped Act.

Pennsylvania Association for Retarded Citizens (PARC) v. Pennsylvania (1972) Along with the Mills case, this is a major case granting educational rights to the handicapped. The Court required that the state *provide a free and appropriate public education to all of its handicapped children,* educate them in the least restrictive environment, pay for private school education if the state could not meet children's needs in public schools, and attempt to locate other handicapped children (Reynolds, 2000).

Honig v. Doe (1988) Official hearings must be held before disruptive students with disabilities can be removed from their placement as indicated on an IEP. For instance, they cannot be placed on homebound instruction, suspended, or expelled prior to the hearing.

Student Diversity

Lau v. Nichols (1974) The San Francisco Board of Education was found to have violated the civil rights of Chinese children by not providing them with English-language instruction and was required to offer special instruction to enable the Chinese-speaking students to receive a good education. In practice, the major ethnic group that benefited from this ruling was Hispanics.

Civil Rights

Goss v. Lopez (1975) Contending that the right to an education is a "property right," the Supreme Court ruled that a school or school district could not suspend a student in an arbitrary manner or without due process.

Ingraham v. Wright (1977) The use of corporal punishment (paddling) was not a violation of the Eighth Amendment (the injunction against cruel and unusual punishment, which applies to people found guilty of crimes) and parents did not need to be notified before the administration of the punishment. Nevertheless, schools could be held liable for damages and for malice.

Regents of the University of California v. Bakke (1978) The quota system in college admissions was prohibited, but the constitutionality of granting advantages to minorities was upheld.

Hazelwood School District v. Kuhlmeier (1988) School officials are permitted to regulate school newspapers.

Table 10.3	Selected U.S. Supreme Court Rulings

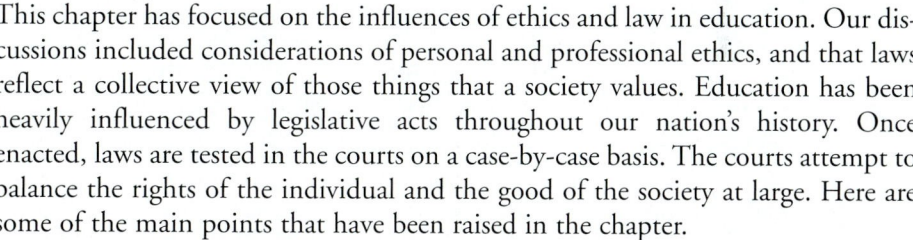

Integration

1896–*Plessy v. Ferguson*
1950–*Sweat v. Painter*
1954–*Brown v. Board of Education*
1971–*Swan v. Charlotte-Mecklenburg Board of Education*

Church and State

1962–*Engle v. Vitale*
2002–*Zelman v. Simmons-Harris, Hannah Perkins School v. Simmons-Harris,* and *Taylor v. Simmons-Harris*

Exceptional Children

1972–*Mills v. Board of Education of the District of Columbia*
1972–*Pennsylvania Association for Retarded Citizens (PARC) v. Pennsylvania*
1988–*Honig v. Doe*

Student Diversity

1974–*Lau v. Nichols*

Civil Rights

1975–*Goss v. Lopez*
1977–*Ingraham v. Wright*
1978–*Regents of the University of California v. Bakke*
1988–*Hazelwood School District v. Kuhlmeier*

Conclusion

This chapter has focused on the influences of ethics and law in education. Our discussions included considerations of personal and professional ethics, and that laws reflect a collective view of those things that a society values. Education has been heavily influenced by legislative acts throughout our nation's history. Once enacted, laws are tested in the courts on a case-by-case basis. The courts attempt to balance the rights of the individual and the good of the society at large. Here are some of the main points that have been raised in the chapter.

1. Ethics are the guidelines we use to stay true to our moral beliefs. Laws are a formalized version of ethics that speak for a society's values.
2. Because teachers occupy positions of influence, their ethical character must be beyond reproach.
3. Teachers and students are entitled to due process of law in legal matters.
4. Issues of teacher liability are considered under tort law.
5. The United States federal government does not assume full responsibility for the education of its citizens. That right is reserved to the states.
6. Religion in the public schools continues to be a volatile issue. The U.S. Constitution mandates a separation of religion from state and federal functions.
7. Congress has become increasingly involved in education, enacting a series of laws which affect everyone enrolled in any level of any educational institution.
8. During the past half century, the U.S. Supreme Court has become the final arbiter in a large number of cases that affect both public and private education.

Key Terms

in loco parentis	liability	least restrictive
due process	tort law	environment (LRE)
contract	mandated reporter	block grants
breach of contract	academic freedom	categorical grants
induction period	sexual harassment	high-stakes tests
tenure	individualized education program (IEP)	

Educational Engineering

Case Studies in Education

Enter the information from the table below into the Educational Record for the student you are studying.

	Ethics and Students' Rights	Laws That Would Apply to This Child
Davon	Perhaps seeking acceptance, Davon readily follows the directions of any authority figure. His unkempt appearance, however, often leaves him isolated or the target of teasing.	Davon receives free lunch.
Andy	As a result of his challenges with hyperactivity and attention deficit, contact with caregivers is frequent. Custody issues have made it difficult for teachers to know to whom to release information.	Andy's school is a Title I school, and so he is able to benefit from before-school tutoring, paid for by Title I funds. He does not receive free or reduced lunch.
Judith	It is apparent that Judith would benefit from attention outside of school. Her family situation precludes participation in anything that would involve an expense. The school is meeting its legal obligations, but teachers feel that an ethical obligation is being overlooked.	Judith receives free breakfast and lunch at the school. Her teachers feel that she would benefit from special educational services, but there has been no evidence of specific learning disabilities or of physical or emotional impairments.
Tiffany	Because of her breadth of knowledge concerning world current events, Tiffany has opinions on topics that many children have no knowledge of. On occasion, other parents have asked that Tiffany's expression of perspectives be curtailed around their children.	Tiffany does not receive any special programs for disadvantaged students. Tiffany is involved only in the seminar group where she works with other Gifted and Talented students to work on projects and increase their divergent thinking skills.
Sam	Sam's teachers are troubled by Sam's situation from an ethical standpoint. With students such as Sam the typical perspective is to prepare them for some sort of unskilled labor. Sam has language difficulties, but in an electronic age there are probably computer-based opportunities that would work for him.	Sam's education is directly affected by public law. Every step of the educational process since he became eligible to receive special education services has been guided by the Individuals with Disabilities Education Act (IDEA) and Free and Appropriate Public Education (FAPE). His IEP is a legal document.
Bao	Bao has lived in the United States since she was three, and has full citizenship. Yet during a discussion in class that touched on the internment of Japanese Americans during World War II and the treatment of POWs during the Vietnam War, Bao's opinions were taken as those of a "foreigner" by her classmates.	Bao receives no special services. She may have received ESL services in elementary school, but at this point she is fluent in English.

1. What ethical issues or issues of students' rights has your student faced in school? As a teacher, what impact could you have on the situation? What line can you define as to how far a teacher can or should go in attending to a student's needs from an ethical perspective?

2. As you review the laws that would apply to the student you are studying, what effects can you identify that the law has had on that child's education? How might the laws affect your own work as a classroom teacher and your own perspective of the society? (For instance, if "One nation, under God" were to be removed by law from the Pledge of Allegiance, or if it remains, how would you personally interpret that situation?)

Designing the School of the Future

The school of the future, just as the school of today, must operate within the law. However, there are some considerations to be made. For instance, schools that accept federal money are subject to the requirements of the federal government. States can't afford to turn down money, and thus public schools are typically subject to the federal mandates. It is also true that the school of the future may need legislation that is not on the books at this time. Is new legislation needed? Are there old laws that need to be removed from the books?

1. What changes do you recommend in federal or state law that would allow your school to operate more effectively? This question can involve new legislation as well as the revision or removal of old legislation. Be visionary, but not reckless, as you consider how laws both promote and restrain education.

2. Will a code of ethics be required in the school of the future that you design? If so, what will that code state? Write either an oath for teachers in the school of the future or a brief code of ethical conduct that would be expected of your teachers. Remember, not only would you expect your teachers to abide by this oath or code, but it would essentially be a public document that the school makes available to the community at large. That means that the oath or code will have to be something that the community is willing to embrace as well.

Praxis Practice

Many states will require that you successfully complete the Praxis Series of examinations to qualify for certification. One or more of those tests will be subject-area tests. Another, which has a more practical orientation, will be the Principles of Learning and Teaching (PLT) examination that is appropriate for your certification area.

Completing the Quick Check Quizzes for Chapter 10 in the Unit Workshop will give you practice with the multiple choice format of the PLT. The Case Studies in Education and Designing a School of the Future activities will help prepare you for exercises that require reading a scenario and providing short answers to questions asking what you might do in such a situation.

11

Education: Purpose, Organization, Governance, and Funding

Make the chapter work for you with CPR²:

Conceptualize Here are the major themes you will encounter in this chapter:

1. The federal, state, and local governments all have responsibilities regarding education.
2. Each level has a role in the funding of education.
3. Primary responsibility for a public system of education rests with each state.

Preview Read the chapter headings; look at any figures, tables, and activities; and read through the items in the conclusion.

Activity 11.1 Field Observation Activity– The Purpose of School

Activity 11.2 Go Online! Who's Who? Education Officials in Your State

Activity 11.3 Go Online! Who's Who on the Local Level?

Activity 11.4 State and Local Education Expenditures in Your Hometown

Read Now read through the chapter. Mark or highlight information that you consider to be especially important or about which you have a question.

Reflect Consider this question as you read: What are the different roles of federal, state, and local governments with regard to education?

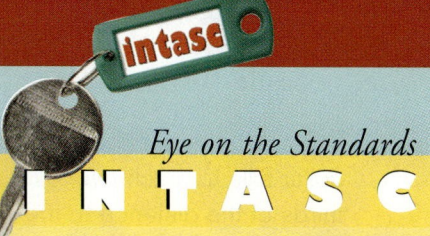

intasc

Eye on the Standards

INTASC

The following standards from the Interstate New Teacher Assessment and Support Consortium (INTASC) will be addressed in this chapter. As you read the chapter, consider how school governance and school finance are tied to these principles.

Principle 7 The teacher plans instruction based upon knowledge of subject matter, students, the community, and curriculum goals.

Principle 9 The teacher is a reflective practitioner who continually evaluates the effects of his/her choices and actions on others (students, parents, and other professionals in the learning community) and who actively seeks out opportunities to grow professionally.

Principle 10 The teacher fosters relationships with school colleagues, parents, and agencies in the larger community to support students' learning and well-being.

ice breakers

It Costs *How* Much?

Education always seems to need more money. And when we talk about financing public education, we are talking about a lot of money. Not just a bunch of money, *a lot* of money. As you will find in this chapter, funding for education is the greatest single expense in every state's budget. Even the federal government, which does not bear the burden of providing public education, sends billions of dollars toward the schools every year. What would all of that amount to? Well . . . see if you can match them up.

What It Does

A. Total nationwide expenditures for education in 2000–2001

B. In 2001, the amount of money the federal government spent on education

C. Approximate total expenditures of the states for elementary and secondary education in one year

D. Approximate Agriculture Department subsidies to reduce the price of school lunches

E. Approximate yearly expenditures for all state and local governments for education

What It Could Do

_____ Laid end to end, it's enough dollar bills to reach two-thirds of the distance to the Sun

_____ Buy a Caffè Latte at Starbucks each day for every man, woman, and child in the country for a year

_____ Pay for downloads of every song that has ever been or ever will be written, plus an iPod to play them on (or provide a new iPod to every public school student in the country on the first day of school for the next 22 years)

_____ Buy 38 brand new Boeing 747 jets, with a little left over for fuel

_____ Buy a fleet of 20 Nimitz-class aircraft carriers (aircraft are extra)

What It Does		**What It Could Do**	
A.	Total nationwide expenditures for education in 2000–2001 **$700 Billion**	A	Laid end to end, it's enough dollar bills to reach two-thirds of the distance to the Sun
B.	In 2001, the amount of money the federal government spent on education **$92.8 Billion**	C	Buy a Caffè Latte at Starbucks each day for every man, woman, and child in the country for a year
C.	Approximate total expenditures of the states for elementary and secondary education in one year **$318 Billion**	E	Pay for downloads of every song that has ever been or ever will be written, plus an iPod to play them on (or provide a new iPod to every public school student in the country on the first day of school for the next 22 years)
D.	Approximate Agriculture Department subsidies to reduce the price of school lunches **$9.5 Billion**	D	Buy 38 brand new Boeing 747 jets, plus have a little left over for fuel
E.	Approximate yearly expenditures for all state and local governments for education **$450 Billion**	B	Buy a fleet of 20 Nimitz-class aircraft carriers (aircraft are extra)

> *Thus it is true that the tax is voted by the legislature, but it is the township that apportions and collects it; the existence of a school is imposed, but the township builds it, pays for it, and directs it.*
>
> *Alexis de Tocqueville*

■ Introduction

In this chapter we look at the organization, governance, and funding of this tremendous enterprise known as school. We will begin with an overview of the purpose of school, its grade-level structure, and the increasing number of options available outside of the traditional structure. We will follow that with a look at the governmental influences on schools. In the quotation that begins this chapter, de Tocqueville (writing in *Democracy in America,* published in 1835) marveled at the interplay of government influence combined with the local public administration of a system of education. To illuminate that interaction, we will look at the roles played by the federal, state, and local government in the context of public education. Finally, all of this has to be financed somehow. We will take some time to consider where the funding for school comes from and how it is dispersed. Along the way there will be several opportunities for you to become more familiar with the governance and funding of your own local school districts.

■ An Overview of Schools: Purpose, Grade Levels, and Options

Purpose of Schools

What is the purpose of school? You've spent quite a lot of time there, so you should be an expert on this topic. Yet don't be surprised if you ask three people about the purpose of schools and get three very different answers. In 1988 Robert Fulghum published a popular book of essays under the title *All I Really Need to Know I Learned in Kindergarten.* He wrote: "All I really need to know about how to live and what to do and how to be I learned in kindergarten. Wisdom was not at the top of the graduate-school mountain, but there in the sandpile at Sunday School" (p. 6). At least he credits kindergarten with contributing to his education. But what does his comment say about the bulk of schooling? Where is, what is, the purpose? Mark Twain is credited with the comment, "Don't ever let schooling interfere with your education." Satire notwithstanding, don't be surprised if somewhere along your journey as an educator you find yourself having to defend what you do at school. So now might be a good time to consider how you will respond to the question of the purpose of schooling.

Parental Perspectives

The purpose of schools depends on the people to whom you speak. Some parents consider schools as a babysitting service that also provides free or inexpensive meals. You will recognize these parents when they are concerned about what to do on days that children are dismissed early or are not expected to attend (as during teacher work days). On the other hand, some parents expect the school to assume total responsibility for the academic, physical, emotional, and social development of their children. You may have difficulty contacting some (but not all) of these parents except when their children receive low grades on their report cards or are designated to repeat a grade. Fortunately, there are also parents who see themselves as part of a team to produce the best possible results and who see the schools (and you) as the enablers of their children's futures. So, different parents have different expectations, both of the school and of you.

Business Perspectives

And, of course, there are other influential adults. Businesspeople, including for example the Chamber of Commerce, may feel strongly that one of the major purposes of the school is to prepare students for the world of work. They may insist on accelerated curricula, advanced courses, vocational training, and high school internships in various businesses. To a large measure, business leaders have been prime movers in the education reform movement, partly because they have found that too many of their new employees are unprepared (either in terms of academic achievement or in such world-of-work behaviors as promptness, dependability, good work ethic, ability to work independently, intent to perform in a highly qualified manner, and willingness to take and follow directions) for further specific job-related training.

Education Administration Perspectives

School board members and the district and local school administrative and supervisory staff also bring to their positions certain purposes that they believe should be emphasized. Some will stress the importance of maintaining high achievement test scores (now that high-stakes tests are almost the only game in town). Others may advocate policies that reflect a particular community interest (e.g., fine arts, athletics, safety, zero tolerance for certain behaviors).

Teacher Perspectives

And what about teachers? What purposes do they espouse? Once again, it depends on which educators you ask. Some will suggest that the major purpose is to teach children to read, write, and do math (the traditional three Rs). Primary-grade teachers often give such answers. Other teachers contend that a major purpose of the schools is to teach students to be good citizens. At some levels this may consist of exhorting students to sit up straight, stay in your seat, be quiet, do your work, don't interrupt, don't bother other people or their belongings, use good manners, clean up the messes you make, and so on. At other grade levels, it may also take the form of understanding democracy and its institutions, following the rules, and practicing fair play and humane behavior with their classmates and the adult staff.

Yet other educators will insist that the major purpose is to give all students a good classical education or to transmit the key elements of the common culture or to see that the school society is properly integrated in terms of activities, opportunities, and awareness of the diversity of the world.

Of course, you will also get vague responses such as "to see that everyone gets a good education" and "to teach students to get along with each other." Left undefined are the real meanings and the implications of these purposes (and, of course, there are others).

So what are the purposes of the schools? As you can tell, they are multiple in nature and depend on the people involved. That means you must consider a plethora of possibilities as you prepare for your entrance into the profession. Unfortunately, there are no simple answers. How would you answer the question? How would your classmates? Use Activity 11.1 to conduct a survey of the purpose of schools. What do your results tell you?

School Levels

As you know, schools are organized by grade levels. You probably also know that the clustering of grades in a particular school varies from community to community and sometimes changes within a community. It is not unusual for those grade clusters to change based either on population within a specific attendance area or the prevailing recommendation by education theorists. Thus, the comments we make here may be somewhat different from your specific situation.

Probably the most common grade clusters begin with preschool (prekindergarten or even lower) and include grades through 4 or 5 in an arrangement called *elementary*. Grades 6–8 is then called *middle school,* though in some instances 7–9 might be called *junior high.* Grades 9–12 or 10–12 are typically referred to as *high school,* or secondary school. As we noted above, there are variations. *Primary* school may contain prekindergarten through grade 3 with elementary school covering grades 4–8. Or, an elementary (or grammar) school may encompass the prekindergarten

 **Field Observation**

ACTIVITY 11.1   **The Purpose of School**

Being a teacher requires you to appreciate (though not necessarily agree with) many different perspectives on just about any topic. A good way to get a sense for that is to ask people what they consider to be the purpose of school.

1. Select a sample:
    Two teachers:
    A. _____
    B. _____

    Principal or assistant principal:
    C. _____

    Two parents (you might be able to find one or two at your field observation school):
    D. _____
    E. _____

    Two students:
    F. _____
    G. _____

    One adult who is not affiliated with a school and does not have a child in school:
    H. _____

2. Prepare a survey form to give to each person. Rather than asking for their names on the form, you can use the letters we provided beside each name to code the forms. Include at least the following two questions on the form, and provide enough space for a response. (If you are in a primary or elementary setting, you may need to interview the students and fill out the form for them.)

    - In your opinion, what is the purpose of school?
    - Do you believe that the school is accomplishing its purpose?

      In addition, include the following categories on your form and ask that the respondent check all that apply:

    - Schools are responsible for student's development:

      ❑ Socially   ❑ Emotionally   ❑ Cognitively

      ❑ For Citizenship   ❑ For Job Training   ❑ Other: _____

3. After receiving your response forms, analyze the data and draw your conclusions. Was there a consensus about school purpose or a divergence of opinion? What questions about school does this survey bring to mind?

4. Compare your results with those of others in your class. Can you identify trends in the larger sample when your results are combined with those of your classmates?

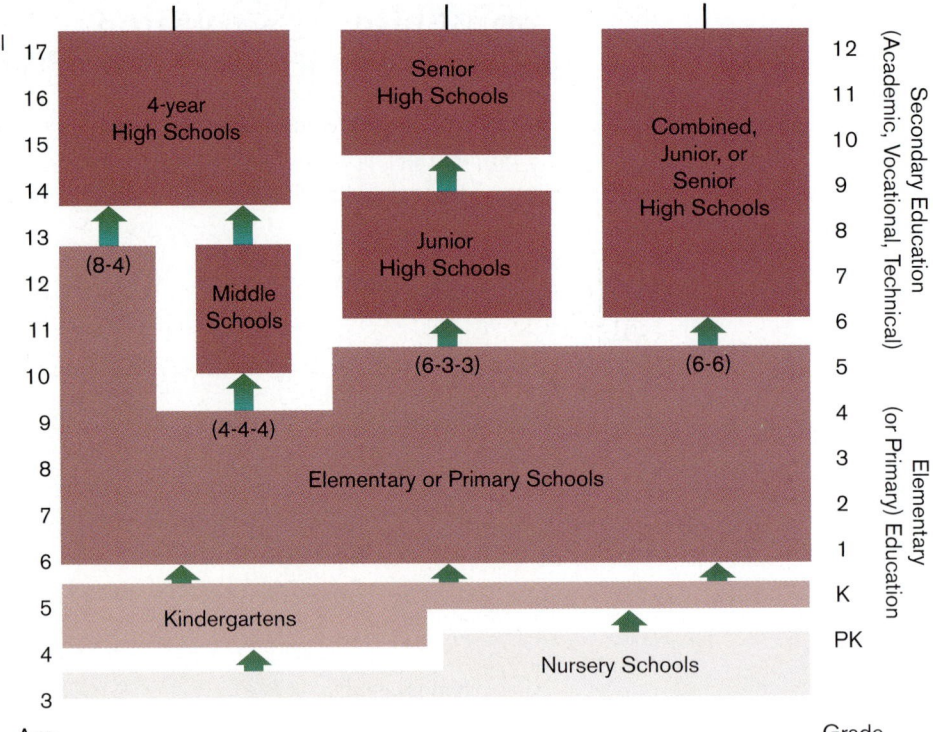

Figure 11.1

Structure of K–12 Education in the United States

Source: U.S. Department of Education, Intitute of Education Sciences, National Center for Education Statistics.

through grade 8. The historic community or union school running from prekindergarten through high school rarely exists except in rural, lightly populated areas (although one can often find such an arrangement in parochial and other private schools). It is also true that some high schools (also called secondary schools) have arrangements with local higher education institutions to cover years 13–14 (if we don't count kindergarten and prekindergarten in our numbering system).

Of course, there are the unusual combinations. For instance, there may be a kindergarten or prekindergarten or perhaps a sixth-grade or ninth-grade center in which all of the students in a larger attendance area are assigned to one school operating at that level. There also are schools with very narrow grade-level bands, e.g., prekindergarten and kindergarten in one school, grades 1 and 2 in another, grades 3–5 in still another, and so on. You might be surprised to know there are even schools with grades that are not adjacent, for example, one school with prekindergarten, kindergarten, and fifth and sixth grades. And there are centers that focus on special needs of children by busing them to a particular school with advantageous facilities and professional personnel. In these cases, the grade levels are less important than the services that can be provided, especially to students with low-incidence (uncommon) disabilities.

Available and appropriate space often dictates the distributions of grade levels. For instance, the opening of a new high school might mean that junior high or middle school students acquire the old building. How many students it can house will often determine how many grade levels it can accommodate. Especially for very young children, the length of the students' bus ride often affects how many grades will be in a particular school.

On a related topic, you may also be aware that schools are not limited to the traditional 180-day schedule (nor does every state require that exact number of student contact days). Some schools prefer a 45–15 arrangement, which means that students attend class for nine weeks and then have a three-week break. Thus, there are the typical 36 school weeks and 12 "vacation" weeks during the year. The

Table 11.1	Typical Clustering of Grade Levels
Prekindergarten–Grade 3	Primary
Grades 4–5	Elementary
Grades 6–8	Middle School
Grades 9–12	High School

60–15 plan does the same thing but has 12 weeks of classes followed by three weeks of "vacation." Often the purpose of such arrangements is to eliminate the long summer vacation and thus decrease the amount of summer regression (loss of achievement). Table 11.1 lists the typical clustering of grade levels that you will find.

As a future teacher you should be willing to teach in a variety of settings and be flexible enough to adapt to any changes that are made from time to time.

Purpose of Each Level

As noted elsewhere, there is considerable difference in grade-level clusters; for our discussion, let us consider prekindergarten through grade 3, grades 4–6, grades 7–8, and high school (grades 9 through 12).

Prekindergarten through Grade 3 (Primary School)

Often called the primary grades, the prekindergarten through grade 3 years are actually widely divergent in purpose. A school-based or school-oriented nursery or day care or Head Start may see itself as preparing students for entrance into school. That once was perceived as a function of kindergarten. However, in recent decades, kindergarten has changed from "play school" to the introduction of academics such as beginning reading (emergent literacy) and math as well as some science, social studies, and health. In that sense, it has been the doorkeeper to more formal instruction. Socialization (e.g., teaching students to listen, follow directions, take turns, treat other people and property with respect) is an important part of the primary school's efforts up through kindergarten. We contend that prekindergarten and kindergarten are the most important years for the development of language, which forms a basis for further learning. No Child Left Behind (NCLB) stresses the development of phonemic awareness and phonics at this point.

Many teachers consider teaching citizenship and good manners to be an important purpose of school and are responsible for conveying these skills to students.

In grade 1, students are introduced to more formal reading and math instruction, making that the key year for reading achievement, since students who do poorly in reading in first grade tend to fall farther and farther behind each year. Grades 2 and 3 continue the reading and math and, in the 21st century, expect students to meet expectations that formerly were delayed until the elementary school years. For instance, many vocabulary terms and concepts are unfamiliar to a large number of students in some schools. Thus, they are expected to pronounce words for which they have no language base. No Child Left Behind stresses oral fluency, phonemic

Courtesy of Becky Stovall

awareness, phonics, and (some) vocabulary and comprehension at these grade levels. Handwriting and spelling instruction are often deemphasized or presented in conjunction with reading. Science and social studies typically are not emphasized (because they are not tested) and are conducted orally because many children are unable to read the texts. Composition is introduced but often not stressed until it is part of the achievement-test structure.

Grades 4 through 6 (Elementary School)

In the elementary grades, increasing emphasis is given to composition, which is tested, and, in states that test science and social studies, to those subjects as well. Grade 4 is often considered the point at which students complete their emphasis on learning to read and begin to focus on reading to learn.

However, if you aspire to teach this particular level, you should know that this transition of reading emphasis is dubious for several reasons. First, many students enter grade 4 or above still reading at a primary level. They are thus unprepared to engage in in-depth content-area reading. Second, though the assumption is that reading skills (e.g., primarily as fluency, phonemic awareness, and phonics) *should* be mastered in the early grades, many important general reading skills (e.g., vocabulary meanings and word identification skills such as syllabication and accenting) are not appropriate until the elementary grades and above.

A third reason that learning to read and reading to learn cannot be easily compartmentalized into grade levels is that students should be reading to learn even in first grade. While some teachers, especially those in first grade, give short shrift to the development of vocabulary and comprehension, they do so at the peril of their students' comprehensive reading development. For instance, Biemiller (2006) notes that "at present there is evidence that vocabulary is not influenced by schooling in the primary years, and that children whose vocabulary and language development is below average by fourth grade continue to lag behind others, even if they have adequate reading skills."

Finally, content-area reading involves a different structure than fiction reading does. If students entering grade 4 and above have had very little experience reading content passages and hearing content texts read to them for oral vocabulary and comprehension, they tend to have considerable difficulty in reading to learn. Thus, we should not be surprised when Ivey (2002) points out that teachers complain the content texts are either too difficult or too boring or both. Fortunately, there are strategies that primary teachers can use, including:

Courtesy of Guilherme Cunha

At grade 4, many students complete their emphasis on learning to read and begin to focus on reading to learn.

- Increase students' access to informational text
- Increase the time students spend working with informational text in instructional activities
- Explicitly teach comprehension strategies
- Create opportunities for students to use informational text for authentic purposes (Duke, 2004)

Of course, reading is not the only subject taught in grades 4–6. However, if you consider that reading facilitates study in all of the other subjects, then you can see how important it will be that you are prepared to teach reading at an appropriate level no matter what "grade" your students might be in.

Grades 7 through 8 (Middle School)

In middle or junior high school, which is usually either on a block or departmentalized schedule, students often have their first opportunity to choose an elective course (e.g., music, shop, art). Students with a history of low achievement frequently take a second reading or language arts course. Some students take advanced classes that once were not introduced in middle school (e.g., pre-algebra, foreign language) and participate in a number of clubs and teams (e.g., Math Counts, junior varsity sports).

You may have noticed that the comments included under the category of grades 4–6 also apply here (and, for that matter, to the high school levels). One major difference is the increased emphasis the curriculum and standardized achievement tests place on the use of various *types* of material. These include, but certainly are not limited to, reference sources, magazines, newspapers and news magazines, the Internet, poetry, manuals, cartoons, scripts, and plays (Worthy, 2001). The wide variety naturally means that each teacher is expected to be conversant with a plethora of types of material and possess a wide-ranging general knowledge of at least some of the content. In recent years, increasing attention has been given to preparing students in grades 7 and 8 for high school courses. Thus, we often see pre-algebra and even algebra courses in the middle school years.

Grades 9 through 12 (High School)

In high school, courses typically carry Carnegie unit credit, which is prescribed by state and local boards of education, and have end-of-course or end-of-year examinations. Also commonplace in high school are advanced placement classes, International Baccalaureate programs, cooperative arrangements for taking college courses during the senior year, classes preparing students to pass the high school exit examination, and business and public school internships. The range of extracurricular and student organizations based on interests is broad (e.g., agriculture, ROTC, chess club, journalism and the school yearbook, and Odyssey of the Mind). Students entering high school in Florida, for example, are now required by state law to declare a major, the intent being to help them focus on their future.

State departments of education produce curriculum guides identifying subject matter to be addressed each year and specific competencies that are expected at each grade level. Your principal or department chairperson can provide you with those documents. You should read them carefully before the school year starts so you can engage in long-term planning.

Regardless of the subject or level you teach, you should be aware that the National Center for Education Statistics (2002) finds that two-thirds of adolescents have difficulty reading proficiently. Fortunately, a fairly recent report (Biancarosa & Snow, 2004) identifies nine research-based instructional strategies that teachers can use to address this situation. They include the following:

- Direct, explicit instruction in comprehension
- Effective instructional principles embedded in the texts being used
- Motivation and self-directed learning
- Collaborative (cooperative) learning based on textual material
- Supportive structural elements such as a coordinated literacy program, extended time for literacy, professional development for teachers, and teacher teams
- Effective tutoring
- A wide variety of texts to meet different student interests

- Intensive writing experiences
- The use of technology
- Ongoing formative (frequent) assessments

These strategies extend to the range of courses that students take, not just to English or language arts or exceptional education. Your role as a teacher will be to relate these strategies to your classroom and subject matter.

School Options

Though public education is the responsibility of each state individually, it is nonetheless true that school systems are very much alike and structured in essentially the same way across the United States. There are regional differences in the tone of schools and some of the course offerings within and across states, but a third grader in Connecticut, for example, could be moved across the country and readily assimilate into a third-grade classroom in California. That represents a remarkable amount of institutional consistency and cooperation.

Yet even with all of this structure, the public schools offer a considerable amount of flexibility. Combined with increasing privatization of schools and with homeschooling, educational options range from specialized courses of study to relief from underperforming schools. Gates and Stuht (2006) suggest that educational options, once considered matters of "alternative education," have now become "an integral part of a comprehensive school district's array of school choices" (24).

School choice is an issue on the contemporary educational landscape that generates strong opinions pro and con. Interestingly, it can be considered from a number of distinct perspectives, not all of which are academic concerns. For instance, the discussion could center around the poor quality of a child's neighborhood school, or that a child has a particular talent that is not served locally, or that the family has moved to another district but wants their children to remain in the school they've been attending, or that a parent whose child attends a private school should not have to pay school taxes (or at least get some sort of credit for it), or that a parent just doesn't really like anything about the public schools and thinks he or she could do a better job teaching them at home (though many believe that their children should still be entitled to engage in extracurricular activities at the local school). It is a broad issue indeed.

school choice An array of options beyond the child's neighborhood, traditional school placement.

Vouchers

Vouchers represent a means by which parents can send their children to a public school other than the one in their home district. It is an allocation equal to the average per-pupil cost for a child's education in a specific area's public school. When the child is taken to another public or private school, that school can redeem the voucher to the government in the amount of the allocation. The No Child Left Behind Act (NCLB) (see Chapter 10) provides parents the right to move their children to another school if the school they presently attend fails to show Adequate Yearly Progress (AYP) toward reaching the goals of NCLB as demonstrated by yearly achievement testing. Another version of vouchers provides tax credit to parents who send their children to private schools.

voucher An allocation equal to the average per-pupil cost for a child's education in a specific area's public school.

Magnet Schools

Magnet schools are public schools that focus on a particular academic, vocational, or specialty study. For example, many districts have magnet schools for math and science and for the fine arts. As a public school, the enrollment is open to all, though based on the number of spaces available for students. These schools are

magnet schools Public schools that focus on a particular academic, vocational, or specialty study.

typically required to enroll a mix of students that mirrors the ethnic demographics of the district. Some schools use a lottery system for selecting students. Specialized schools such as those for the performing arts may require auditions. In any case, the magnet school is intended to *attract* students based on its specialty. Not surprisingly, when students attend a school that fosters a special interest, achievement scores tend to reflect their increased motivation for study.

Charter Schools

charter schools Public schools organized under a charter established by parents, teachers, or other individuals to provide a particular educational experience.

Charter schools are public schools that have been organized by groups of teachers, parents, or other individuals to provide a particular educational experience for their children. Such schools are free from many of the state statutes that govern public schools, but are bound by the details of the charter regarding matters such as the curriculum to be presented, achievement expectations, and enrollment, among others. Though students are still accountable for subject-area study, the school may specialize in providing a particular experience. This could be in terms of course offerings, for instance in fine arts, or in the style of teaching, for instance an inquiry-based model. Charter schools are sometimes organized in response to the closing of a school due to district restructuring. For example, if for economic reasons a district decides to consolidate several schools into one, parents in one area may petition for a charter school to maintain the "small school" environment that had existed before the consolidation.

School Privatization

privatization The management of public schools by private enterprises, often referred to as education management organizations.

Throughout your teaching career it is likely that you will be exposed to the controversy surrounding the **privatization** of public schools. Unlike a traditional private school, privatization refers to the management of public schools by private enterprises, often referred to as education management organizations (EMO). One example, the Edison Project, spearheaded by Christopher Whittle (Whittle Communications was the creator of Channel One, still a controversial business incursion into the public school classroom), set out to establish a chain of for-profit schools across the country. That venture was not particularly successful. Now the emphasis has shifted to the private management of established public schools. That is, with an agreement between the state and the EMO, management of the school is assumed by a private corporation.

Up to this point the privatization effort has been an inexact science. As some argue that a business model represents the salvation of the public schools, others argue that imposing an economic bottom-line perspective on a school will certainly result in school closings and loss of service to children. After all, unlike businesses, schools do not have the "luxury" of shutting down for a bankruptcy reorganization, or of simply laying off workers and dramatically increasing class sizes to preserve profits. According to Ayers and Klonsky (2006), Chicago's Renaissance 2010 project, an effort to bring EMOs into the management of some of its most difficult schools, "which was originally promoted as a new-school initiative, is now being pushed primarily as a school-closing strategy" (p. 454). However, increased pressures toward providing parents with school choice may serve to motivate refinement of the models for public school privatization.

Homeschooling

homeschooling Education provided to children in the home by the parent or caregiver.

Yet another educational option is that of **homeschooling.** This is not to say that the approach is sanctioned by or in collaboration with the public schools (though some districts make curriculum materials and support available to parents who are homeschooling their children), but the states will recognize a parent's desire to

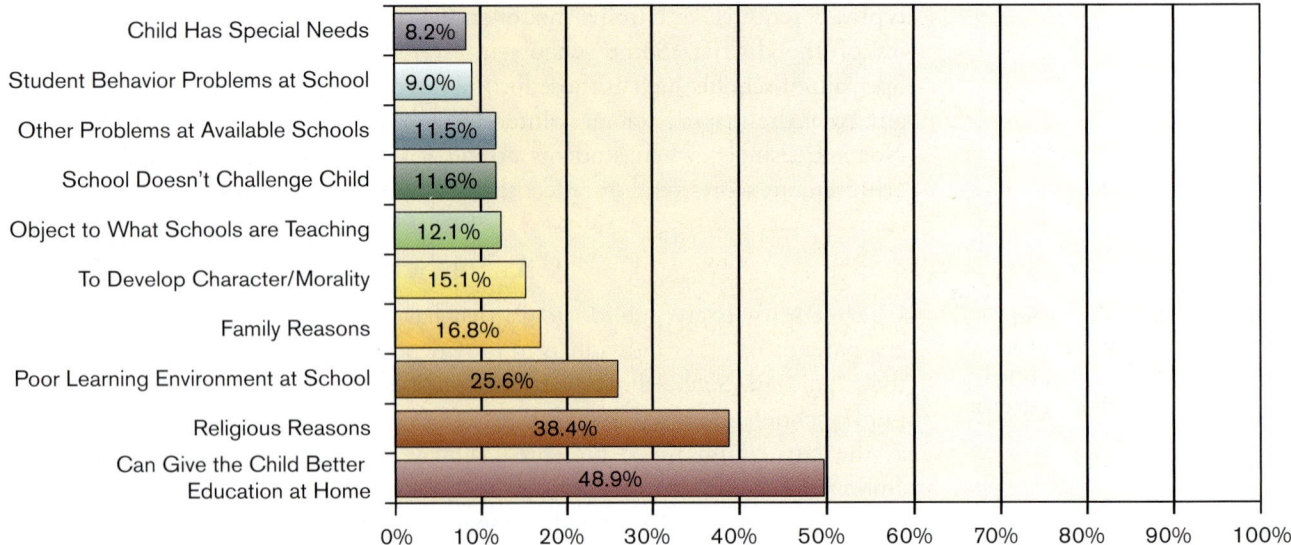

Figure 11.2

Parents' Reasons for Homeschooling

Source: U.S. Department of Education, National Center for Education Statistics, Parent Survey of the National Household Education Surveys Program, 1999.

homeschool their children. The state still maintains expectations for course of study and demonstrated progress.

According to figures from the National Center for Education Statistics (Bielick & Chandler, 2001), in 1999 there were 850,000 students nationwide being homeschooled. Of that number, a greater percentage of homeschoolers compared to non-homeschoolers were white and non-Hispanic, and of those, most parents were college-educated and the children were living in a two-parent family.

Parents give a variety of reasons for homeschooling their children (see Figure 11.2). Bielick and Chandler (2001) report that of the parents surveyed, 48.9 percent said that they homeschooled their children to give them a better education. Parents also cited religious reasons, poor learning environment at school, lack of challenge for their child, special needs or disability of the child, and developing

Table 11.2	Alternatives to the Traditional Neighborhood School
Vouchers	
Allows parents to send their children to a different public or private school and have local per-pupil expenses transferred to that school.	
Magnet Schools	
Public schools that emphasize an academic, vocational, or artistic theme. Enrollment based on availability.	
Charter Schools	
A public school designed by teachers, parents, or other individuals who establish a "charter" with the state delineating the functions and expectations of the school.	
Privatization	
Administration of a public school is assumed by an education management organization as a for-profit enterprise.	
Homeschooling	
Responsibility for educating the child is assumed by the parent or primary caregiver. Some districts provide support in the form of textbooks and materials.	

character or morality in the child. Table 11.2 provides a summary of the school options that we have discussed.

In the years to come we can expect to see more options for schooling. Electronic technology has made distance education and "the virtual classroom" readily accessible to thousands of students. Whether these innovations will blur the distinctions of urban, suburban, and rural school systems—making essentially all education a global enterprise—remains to be seen. Perhaps most exciting is that you will be part of these new and emerging approaches. When your authors began teaching, the notion of hand-held electronic calculators or of computers in nearly every home was pure science fiction. And cell phones, well, never in a million years! What innovations do you suppose you will see? If you have been working on Designing a School of the Future, educational options may well be part of your plan.

■ The Federal Role in Education

As you know, at the federal level of educational governance the president appoints members of the cabinet, an advisory and administrative group that is not referred to in the United States Constitution. President George Washington established the first cabinet of advisors, and all of his successors have done the same. The secretary of education serves at the pleasure of the president and administers a large federal department and many billions of dollars in funds for education at all levels.

Congress does not assume a subservient role. Each house has a committee on education, composed, like other committees, with the same percentage of each party as their membership in the House or Senate. The chairperson is a member of the predominant party, and the vice-chairperson comes from the other party. Membership on education committees comes from seniority as well as interest in education issues. Thus, members of education committees typically possess more background information and expertise than most members of the executive branch. Legislators and executive officers employ aides who typically have considerable expertise in education and usually numerous contacts with important groups such as professional education associations.

It is important to remember that the president, like members of Congress and the administration, must keep in mind several important factors. First, having a good idea is not the same as having a good law. The idea must have sufficient support to be passed and signed. Obtaining support for an idea often requires political compromise (e.g., agreeing to support someone else's bill or adding an amendment to the favored bill—even a proposal a member doesn't like—in return for someone else's support).

A second factor that members of Congress must keep in mind is that they are members of a political party and are thus subject in some form to the discipline of their elected party leaders. Thus, if one party takes a strong stand on some aspect of an education bill, the rank and file members are strongly encouraged to support that public stance.

There is also a factor three: Job security requires that legislators not abandon their constituents, either the individuals or the political action committees that provide campaign funds or the special interest groups with access to the press. Members of the House must stand for election every other year. There is no such thing as tenure, even if they do a superb job. Accordingly, they must not take positions, even those their leaders advocate, if public sentiment in their district or state is strongly in opposition or if the election is expected to be very close. Thus, the writing and the passing of education laws are matters of give and take.

The State Role in Education

The 10th Amendment to the United States Constitution forms the legal basis for a state to organize and operate a public school system. Although there are many similarities in the roles of the federal and the state governments as they relate to education, there are also a number of differences, some of which are based on state constitutions and some based on legislation. One major difference is that states determine the minimum conditions that students must fulfill to graduate. According to the Center on Education Policy, 24 states have exit exams and 19 withhold diplomas from students who fail them (Ashford, 2003). Despite the concerns, the tests are rated as not particularly demanding, that is, covering only seventh- and eighth-grade material (Lewis, November 2004) or eighth- and ninth-grade material (Lewis, April 2004).

Characteristics of State Control

Most state constitutions specifically address education. Thus, the state's role is rather clearly spelled out and not particularly subject to disagreement. States also pay the greatest share of the cost of education. So, they are responsible for raising and allocating large amounts of funds for the various programs in the schools. Increasingly states are being challenged in court to provide educational equity. In a recent major example, the Supreme Court of Kentucky ruled in 1989 that the education system of that state was ineffective and unconstitutional. It directed the governor and legislature to develop a proposal for a new state system. In 1990, the legislation was enacted into law as the Kentucky Education Reform Act. More cases are working their way through the court system. Stay tuned.

State-level educators are directly responsible to the people. While many federal positions are appointed either by the president or the secretary of education, practices at the state level are considerably different. Typically the superintendent of education (or some similarly titled official) is elected by the people after having run on a platform and (usually) in a Democrat or Republican primary.

The laws that govern education in each state are debated and voted upon in the state's legislature.

© Tony Kurdzuk/Star Ledger/Corbis

The Governor

How does the state government operate in terms of education? As noted above, the chief state executive officer for education is the superintendent of education. However, in recent years education has received so much attention that while the superintendent of education is the de jure head, the governor is the real director.

Every governor has one or more senior advisors on education. These people, often former educators though increasingly people from the business community, conduct many of the public information and input meetings that are held throughout a state. These advisors also serve as liaisons with the state legislature (two branches in all states but Nebraska, which has a unicameral legislature) and help draft education legislation. That is, they help take a governor's broad framework of ideas and translate them into rules and regulations.

State Superintendent and the Board of Education

Usually the state superintendent is a member of the governor's cabinet and has influence depending on the extent to which superintendent and governor are in agreement and the amount of political influence each possesses. A superintendent who is elected is less subject to a governor's influence than one who is appointed. In any case, they typically attempt to work together.

The state superintendent sometimes serves as chairman of the state board of education, a group whose members may be appointed by the governor, elected by the people, or hold membership by virtue of their executive or legislative office. Since the state board of education derives its authority from the state legislature, it often follows the political lead of the legislative branch while considering and sometimes attempting to reconcile different recommendations from the state superintendent. The state board usually focuses on the approval or disapproval of policy while the superintendent's office assumes responsibility for proposing policies and carrying out those that are approved. Teachers should know who's who in education. Activity 11.2 gives you a chance to find out who the folks are that are making key decisions about education in your state.

Go Online!

ACTIVITY 11.2 Who's Who? Education Officials in Your State

It would be worthwhile for you to know who in your state directs educational matters and what their opinions are. You can use the state department of education URLs in Appendix D as a start, but you may also wish to locate a URL for your state government.

1. Who is the chief education officer? Is this position elected or appointed?

2. Is there an education advisor to the governor other than the chief education officer? If so, who? Is this position filled by appointment or by election?

3. Who are the chairpersons of the education committees in the state legislature? What views do they hold about public education?

4. Who are the members of your state board of education? Are they elected or appointed? What credentials and experience do they bring to the position?

It is possible in your state that the board of education determined the exit exams you had to pass to graduate from high school, the achievement tests you took during your school years, the number of years you must serve in a probationary status until you receive tenure as a teacher, and the requirements you must meet to become a teacher.

"Grading" the Schools

Your state assigns grades or achievement descriptions to each of its public schools. Although the designations differ from state to state, the meaning is rather clear. A school typically is either given a letter grade (A, B, C, D, F) or a descriptor grade (e.g., excellent, above average, average, below average, unacceptable). These grades must be published in the local and state newspapers, and parents, other educators, the community at large, and, of course, the **state education agency** members view the results. In some states, there are provisions for the department of education to "take over" the schools, even the school board, if there is a recurring pattern of unacceptable performance. Administrators and even teachers can be removed or shifted to other schools.

state education agency A state department of education responsible for directing and overseeing the local education agencies within its jurisdiction.

The state tests cover a range of grade levels, usually at least 3 through 8 and one of the three grades from 10 to 12 (as federal law requires). Some states also mandate tests in the primary grades. As a minimum, the tests cover math and reading. Beginning in the 2007–2008 school year, states must also administer tests based on their science standards, but the tests do not need to be a part of the No Child Left Behind measure of adequate yearly progress (AYP) used in the school grading system (Lewis, September, 2005). Some also include writing (composition), and there is an increasing tendency to add social studies and science to the list. Physical education is not on the list, an omission that is blamed for the decrease in physical education teachers and the increase in overweight and obese children (Cook, 2005). While the procedures for determining school grades vary from state to state, they always include some measure of reading and math achievement based on required percentages of students scoring at certain performance levels. Recently, states are adding another dimension: the performance of historically low performing students. This **disaggregate analysis** identifies the performance of students by ethnic group, by economic status of the family (through eligibility for free or reduced school lunches), and by gender. The performance of students for whom English is a second language is also being increasingly factored into the equation, as is the performance of students with varying exceptionalities. Much of this has come to pass at the state level as a result of the No Child Left Behind Act of 2002.

disaggregate analysis An analysis of test data that identifies the performance of students by ethnic group, by economic status of the family (through eligibility for free or reduced school lunches), and by gender.

One other element increasingly being included in the procedure for determining school grades relates to the progress of the lowest-performing students in the school. Thus, the students performing at the lowest quartile (bottom one-fourth) may be identified so their improvement in reading and math can be tracked to ensure that they are making progress "at their level."

Education and the State Legislature

Each branch of the state legislature has an education committee whose members oversee education matters from a legislative viewpoint (that is, funding and the politics of funding) and propose the adoption or elimination of various education regulations. Like the governor's office, the legislative committees have education advisors (aides) to assist them in gathering information (e.g., statistics, material on programs adopted in other states, federal regulations). The aides are, of course, appointed, and they serve at the pleasure of the committees they serve. However, the members of the legislature are elected, usually every other year, and thus they are expected to be very responsive to the people, specifically the ones in their electoral district. State legislative politicians' views on various education issues often reflect the voting power "back home." A legislator representing an inner-city district may have distinctly different points of view from a legislator serving an affluent suburban district or one elected by a rural district.

Judicial Influence

As we saw in Chapter 10, Ethics in Education and Matters of Law, the judicial system also exerts an influence on what happens in local schools. The state supreme court or district or regional courts rule on a variety of issues that never reach the United States Supreme Court. Some of these courts operate under the state judicial system and some are branches of the federal system. In any case, they may issue rulings that affect what you can do and what you are enjoined from doing in your class. For instance, lower courts have ruled that students may not check each others' papers (on the grounds that it violated the privacy of their educational records). In that case, the court ruling applied to half a dozen states until it was overturned by the United States Supreme Court.

Thus, a variety of perspectives combine to make your life as a teacher most interesting. You are expected to become familiar with and follow the mandates of the state board of education, the declarations of the governor, the laws of the state, the court decisions, and the policies of the state department of education. And don't forget our previous discussion of the role of the federal government!

■ The Local Role in Education

Just when you thought we might have completed our discussion of external forces that affect your everyday life as a teacher, we reach the local level, the point at which influences become immediately apparent.

The Local School Board

You should become very familiar with local policies and procedures, for they affect your professional life on a daily basis. At the top of the ladder, so to speak, is the *local* school board. Regardless of its official name, the local board is the policy-setting organization and makes the final decisions in hiring and firing. You will not have a job until the school board acts.

The business of the local school district is directed by its board of education, whose membership is drawn from the local community.

Proceedings of school boards are public information (except when personnel matters are considered in executive session). It would be a good idea for you to attend these meetings to understand the perspectives of "those people." They rarely are fortunate enough to make decisions that keep everyone happy.

Local school board members are elected, sometimes by attendance area within the district and sometimes at-large (running throughout the district). Their terms of office are usually four years, and they typically receive reimbursement for their services. Usually any adult can serve. Notice, there is no requirement for educational background. Thus, it is theoretically possible for a high school dropout to serve on a school board. If that thought is disquieting, remember that a highly educated person who is quite vocal and actively opposed to many issues that educators support is also eligible for election.

© Alex Brandon/Newhouse News Service/Landov

Superintendent of Schools

Operating in conjunction with the school board but usually under its authority is the superintendent of schools. This person is typically appointed or hired by the school board and so is dependent on it for continued employment. In some cases, the superintendent is elected by the people. In those situations, the superintendent cannot be fired by the board and thus is "free" to disagree strongly with the board, remembering at the same time that the board still is responsible for approving policy.

Superintendents often serve for four-year terms. In fact, the typical superintendent stays in one position an average of only three years. Thus, there frequently is not a great deal of stability in the position. On average, you may serve under 10 superintendents during your professional career. You will like some and dislike some. You may not know any of them unless you live in a small school district.

A superintendent works with the other administrative and supervisory members of the district office to run the schools on a daily basis. Usually the superintendent is a manager or a public relations person or a proponent of some specific program to improve the schools. Thus, she sets the tone, assigns responsibilities, and makes decisions after receiving recommendations from the district staff, school-based personnel, community activists, the attorney for the school district, and perhaps outside specialists. All of the decisions go to the school board for approval. Typically there may be some modifications of the recommendations, but an astute superintendent will already have "done her homework" to secure board support before the proposals are ever submitted.

It is the school superintendent who will recommend dress codes, zero-tolerance policies for certain types of behavior, promotion standards, and numbers of Carnegie units (course credits) for graduation (although that state will have established a minimum number of credits and specific courses that must be included in that number). The superintendent will also recommend that certain courses be included or eliminated from the curriculum. For instance, music (orchestra or band) or a foreign language or technology instruction may be offered in elementary or middle school. Vocational skills (e.g., masonry, carpentry, electricity, plumbing, automotive mechanics) may be offered in the high school, or they may be included in separate vocational schools or community colleges. International Baccalaureate (IB) and an extensive range of advanced placement (AP) courses may be offered, or the offerings may be much more constricted.

District Personnel

The district office consists of less than a dozen educators in a small system to hundreds in a large system. The office may be organized by categories such as curriculum and instruction, planning and assessment, transportation, communications, facilities, finance, and personnel. Each of these areas has specific responsibilities and a host of federal and state laws with which it must comply, and every district organizes itself in a different way. Thus, you should consider the categories in the discussion that follows as one means of providing some information with which you should become familiar.

Curriculum Specialists

Curriculum specialists are often called supervisors, except at the very top level when they may be executive directors or assistant or associate superintendents. They are responsible for the overall direction of the curriculum and instruction activities of the district. They arrange guest speakers for the beginning of school and for selected "staff development" days scheduled periodically throughout the year. They may arrange for short-term or long-term consultants to serve in a variety of capacities, usually to "get test scores up" or to address classroom management, discipline, motivation, and so on. In small districts, they may provide many of these services themselves.

Curriculum specialists organize and direct much of the committee work within the school district. When there is a new basal adoption (for almost every area of the elementary and secondary curriculum), a curriculum supervisor organizes a committee to evaluate the materials, possibly share that information with the schools, and then help select the series. Curriculum specialists also oversee the production of district guides for each aspect of the curriculum from kindergarten through the secondary levels. These guides usually include objectives for each subject area, indications of the content to be covered, sample means of assessment, and so forth. Since the guides are intended to match state objectives as identified on the high-stakes tests, they do not typically have a significant relationship to the textbooks being used. For instance, one study (Brophy, 1982) of same-level math texts and tests found that only about one-half of the test content was covered by the math textbooks, and only one-half of the textbook materials were covered on the tests.

Planning and Assessment

Personnel at the district level are responsible for developing, implementing, and coordinating the planning and the assessment strategies for the entire school system. They are also responsible for gathering statistical data about the effectiveness of the schools. Some of this information is required by federal agencies, some by state agencies, and some by the local education agency. When districts receive special funding grants, the planning and assessment personnel are expected to handle the accountability of those projects as well. In some districts, these people also assist schools in writing grant proposals.

Finance

The people in the finance section write your paycheck each month, among many other checks to keep the school operating. On the downside, they also deduct from your salary a host of taxes sufficient to decrease the amount by perhaps one-third. Don't blame those employees. They are doing exactly what the law requires. However, you should feel free to call and ask for explanations of certain deductions. And, of course, you will already have filled in certain financial forms when you accepted employment. Keep all of the correspondence together. You're going to need it eventually, and spending five minutes setting up a file will save you several hours of looking for copies of various forms.

Personnel

We end this discussion of district personnel with one group that you will meet at the beginning of your employment. After you have been accepted, the personnel office (which you probably contacted at the beginning of your search) will ask you to complete a number of forms.

The personnel director keeps your employment file as well as any letters of reprimand, official evaluations, honors and awards, and information related to your application for employment. This includes letters of recommendation you receive from college and university faculty and other personnel. Those letters carry the most weight when you waive your rights to see the evaluations, the assumption being that a person who knows you are going to look at the comments is less likely to be completely candid. Your case for employment is enhanced by signing the waiver and performing so well that those who write recommendations will have many positive comments to make.

Building-Level Administration

To get even closer to home with regard to your work as a classroom teacher, let's look at the principal and her role in the school. By law the principal is charged with ultimate responsibility for all of the activities of the particular school. That includes the cafeteria workers, the school bus employees, the aides (e.g., teacher assistants, paraprofessionals) and volunteers, the custodial staff, the secretary, and the professional staff.

The School Principal

Operating within the framework of federal, state, and district requirements, the principal establishes school policy (sometimes with the advice and consent of the faculty, sometimes with the advice but not consent, and sometimes without either advice or consent).

Likewise, the principal determines which students can be retained (within policies established by the federal, state, or local school board). You can recom-

Teacher Testimonial

Feature 11.1   The Care and Feeding of the Principal

Principals are unusual beings. They are empowered with keys, radios, and authority. They have a myriad of responsibilities, not the least of which is recommending the continuing employment of effective teachers. He or she is the school's advocate in the community. Typically, they have had classroom experience, yet teaching (in the sense of a classroom full of students) is not what they do all day. So how does a teacher properly attend to the "care and feeding of the principal"? While chocolate-chip cookies have their place, the best way to enjoy good relations with the principal is by being effective in the classroom. In fact, you will find that just as the principal contributes to the effectiveness of teachers, things work the other way around as well. But there's more. As you expect the principal to understand your situation, it would be wise for you to step back and try to understand the principal's situation.

Everybody Wants to Be Effective

As a prospective teacher, you should exhibit the knowledge and skills associated with teaching effectiveness when you meet with a principal. He or she is always looking for teachers who can address the needs of the students. A positive attitude and good interpersonal skills are excellent traits to develop as well. Principals value teachers who are unselfish in their efforts to meet the individual needs of students.

You will also find in your conversations that an effective principal is one who has the interest of teachers among her highest priorities. Education is a people business, and it takes a strong collaboration between teachers and administrators to make a school really work. So talk to these folks while you are in your teacher education program. Try to get a sense for how the principal tries to make the teachers effective in their classrooms.

Look for the Forest and the Trees

Teachers and principals make multiple decisions during the course of a school day. And although they both have basically the same goals (providing a quality educational experience to each student), their perspectives necessarily differ. As a teacher, you will be responsible for a limited number of students, in a restricted space for a specific time period. No doubt the issues and emergencies that arise within your class will take top priority from your perspective. And that's understandable. The principal, however, has responsibility for *all* of the students, faculty, staff, and facilities. So when you must approach the principal with some problem, don't expect that he or she will minimize it, but do anticipate that it will be seen in a broader perspective than yours. That's not necessar-

Courtesy of David Ottenstein Photography

By law the principal is charged with ultimate responsibility for all of the activities of the particular school.

mend, and you can state your best case, but you cannot make the ultimate decision. The principal must decide and then take the heat from irate parents, angry students, or even an upset school board member. The issue of social promotion is becoming a little less vocal now that higher standards and graduation expectations are being phased in and now that many politicians have strongly supported retention in grade.

Did you know that the principal can establish a policy (with the approval of the school board) that determines the grades you give to students? She can. Some middle and high schools have a policy that no student can receive a grade lower than 60 for the first grading period (there being four grading periods in most schools). The rationale is that if a student's first-grading-period average is so low that she cannot possibly pass the semester, she may make no effort for the remainder of the term. While you may disagree with that policy (we do) on the grounds that it actually encourages early-in-the-term poor academic behavior that makes it

ily a bad thing, and the effectiveness of both you and the principal in resolving the problem will be increased if you can each appreciate the other's perspective.

Problems: Some Are Yours and Some Are the Principal's

Simply stated, the principal makes decisions and solves problems. And it goes on all day. Since so much of the principal's day involves some sort of "conflict resolution," you will want to be in the business of problem aversion. Your relationship with the principal can be greatly improved through solving the majority of your own challenges as opposed to transferring problems to the administrative staff. This is not to say by any means that the principal should be shielded from problems. Rather, it simply means that you should accept the responsibility for solving problems that are part of your work in the classroom. If the problem persists or is beyond your expertise, then it should be taken to the principal—it is her job from that point on. Your effectiveness and success in the classroom enhances the success of the building principal, the other teachers, and the school.

Time

Principals and teachers have busy days. You can enhance your relationship with your principal by being consider-

ate of his or her time. Therefore, you will want to schedule your time with the principal as opposed to just dropping in without notice. Most administrators have an open-door policy. However, as a thoughtful teacher, you will want to present your principal with only the most urgent matters in a timely way.

As you can see, the care and feeding of the principal is a two-way relationship. Both the teacher and the principal are professionals and both have specific responsibilities—otherwise, one or the other wouldn't be there. You should be able to anticipate administrative support in the form of your principal backing up your decisions as well as by providing the necessary resources for your classroom. Conversely, the principal should be able to count on your support both in words and deeds, especially in the faculty lounge. Keeping a collaborative perspective in mind with regard to problem-solving, time management, and appreciation of each other's responsibilities will go a long way toward making both you and the principal effective in the school. With that said, it's up to you to decide whether the chocolate-chip cookies might be a good idea!

Dr. David W. Blackmon served as a principal in elementary, middle, and high schools for 13 of his 30 years in public education. He is now a Professor of Education and Chair of the Education Department at Coker College. ∎

impossible for students to understand the following and more complex learning, you are required to adhere to the policy. If you wish to work for the elimination of the policy, more power to you. But, in the meantime, follow the rules.

Your principal may require the faculty or, in middle or high school, the department, to post at least 10 grades spaced throughout a nine-week term for each subject. While this requirement may seem unnecessary to you (especially if you have an abundance of grades), it may really be directed to one or two faculty members who either have a very small number of grades (say two unit or chapter tests) or have many tests during the last several weeks of the term.

Your principal (and sometimes a grade-level or departmental chair) will conduct faculty meetings, usually on a regularly scheduled basis. These meetings are often held to communicate important information and to solicit input about decisions that must be made. Even if you find the sessions as boring as some of your college lectures, you are expected to attend. What is more, you should take careful notes and file them along with any handouts either in a manila folder or a loose-leaf notebook. Don't assume you will remember all of the strategies or details (times, dates, places, purposes, people involved) a month later. You do not want to spend your time trying to locate that information or apologizing for missing an important meeting or failing to turn in some paperwork on schedule. If you have learned to take and save good notes in high school, you will be ahead of the game as a teacher. If you need to become organized, now is a good time to start.

Your principal may appoint you to one or more committees, even during your first year. While some people like committee work far more than others, the responsibility will fall to almost everyone. You are most likely to be happy if you get an assignment that suits your interest. Find out what committees are available, what responsibilities are involved (and how time-consuming they are), and when during the year the major responsibilities occur. Then match them with your interests and volunteer immediately.

The principal will expect to be kept fully informed about any conditions in your class that are out of the ordinary or that might become problematic. This is not nosiness but good leadership and, in the case of parent involvement, good public relations, both for you and the principal. Imagine, for example, that you are teaching high school and decide to take your math classes outside to apply what they have been learning by determining the heights of several trees using trigonometry concepts. If you notify the principal of the purpose of the activity and the time frames, you can avoid problems when parents drive by the school and see students milling around but fail to see the teacher. If they conclude that the school is remiss in its responsibility; an informed principal can quickly make a beautiful case for the application of curriculum to real life.

As you would expect, the principal will stress the importance of your students' doing well on the achievement tests, whether they are state-mandated end-of-course or end-of-grade tests or standardized achievement tests (developed either by or for the state or selected from those that may be used in a variety of states). You will be strongly encouraged to be sure all of your students do well, and you may be encouraged to use test preparation booklets and stacks of worksheets with multiple-choice responses. In the months immediately preceding the administration of these tests, your colleagues may spend less time teaching and more time cramming. You must decide what you think is educationally sound. If you weigh in on the side of teaching, then your instruction must be sufficiently strong to avoid the temptation to assign massive amounts of bubble-in sheets. Reconciling what is best for students with what is required on the test will be one of your challenges and one that will reflect your best professional judgment. Activity 11.3 is the local level version of Activity 11.2.

Go Online!

ACTIVITY 11.3   Who's Who on the Local Level?

The most immediate influence on the administration of a school comes from the local level. Who are the people that make decisions for the district? Contact your local school district (or the district from your hometown or the district where you would like to teach) and obtain the names of the superintendent and the members of the school board. Many school districts now have Web sites that provide this information.

1. Who is the superintendent? Was this person hired by the board of education? What credentials and experience does he or she bring to the job?

2. Who are the school board members? How is the school district divided for purposes of electing board members? What sort of expertise do each of the members bring to the board?

3. Can a teacher who lives in the district in which she teaches, and perhaps has a child attending school in that district, run for and hold a seat on the school board while continuing to be a teacher in the district? Do you think this should be allowed? (Note: Some states prohibit this, though the prohibition could be challenged on constitutional grounds.)

Financing Education

In the year 2000–2001, the total amount of money expended for all educational activities was estimated to be approximately *$700 billion.* Of that total, just over 60 percent ($423 billion) went to elementary and secondary institutions and nearly 40 percent ($277 billion) went to post-secondary institutions (Digest of Education Statistics 2001, 2002). With these facts in mind, let us consider the means by which public education is financed, once again from the three perspectives: federal, state, and local.

The Federal Role

A number of federal departments contribute funds or products or services to the public schools. These include the Departments of Education, Health and Human Services, Agriculture, Labor, Defense, and Energy. In fiscal year 2001, the federal government spent an estimated $92.8 billion on education. Approximately 40 percent, $36.8 billion, was spent by the Department of Education. Another $19.5 billion was disbursed by Health and Human Services, and $11 billion from Agriculture.

Of the $92.8 billion total, $48.7 billion was allocated for elementary and secondary education institutions, $15.3 billion for post-secondary institutions (e.g., colleges, universities, technical institutes, community colleges), $22.8 billion for research (mainly at educational institutions), and $6 billion for other programs (see Figure 11.3).

Of the $36.8 billion distributed by the Department of Education, $17.6 billion (about one-half) went to school districts, $6.2 billion to college students, $6.1 billion to institutions of higher learning, $4.9 billion to state education agencies (SEA), and small amounts to subsidize student loans (see Figure 11.4).

Figure 11.3

Federal Expenditures for Education (in billions of dollars)

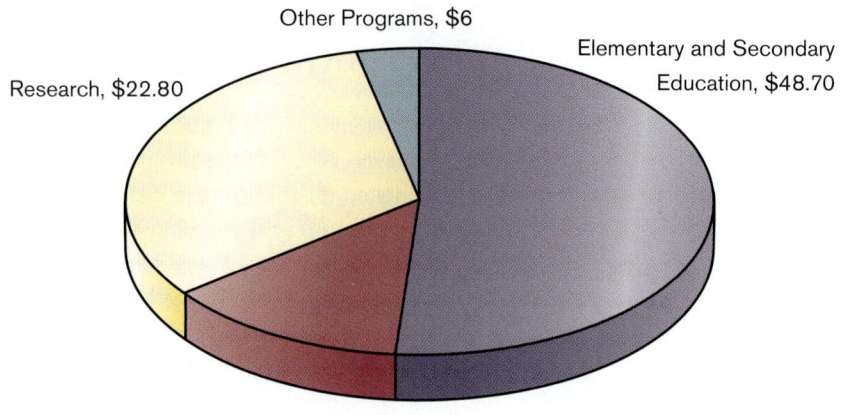

Figure 11.4

Federal Funds Dispersed through the U.S. Department of Education (in billions of dollars)

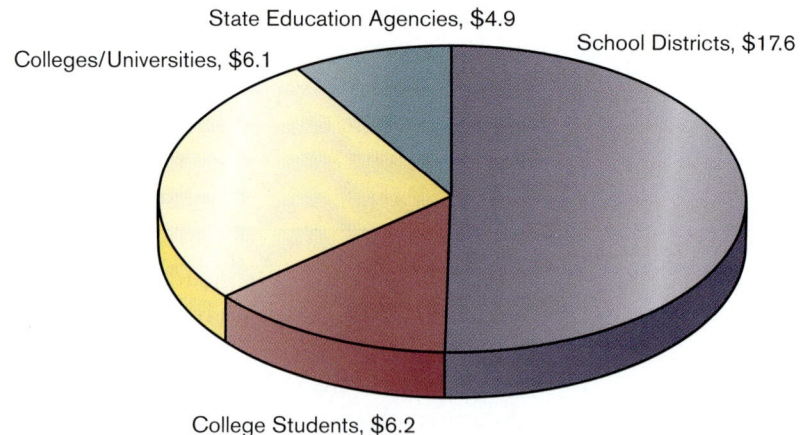

As you can see, we're talking about a lot of money. After being adjusted for inflation, the amount of federal funding for education increased 56 percent from 1985 to 2001 (Digest of Education Statistics 2001, 2002). Many of the federal laws related to education that we discussed in Chapter 10 carried funding (although it is true that there are a number of underfunded mandates).

In 1993–1994, 33 percent of public school students (38 percent of elementary students, 22 percent of secondary students) received free or reduced lunch (Digest of Education Statistics 2001, 2002). If you were not one of those students, you might not think you got anything free in your lunch—but could you buy the same lunch in town for the price you paid at school? Of course not. The federal government subsidizes school lunches for *everyone* by providing surplus farm products to the lunchroom program. That's a $9.5 billion contribution by the Agriculture Department.

Approximately 13 percent of elementary and secondary education students received Title I services in 1993–1994 (Digest of Education Statistics 2001, 2002). These services (about $8.5 billion worth) were provided by the Department of Education to students with low levels of achievement (according to standardized tests) in schools with high concentrations of families with low incomes.

The second-largest amount of money from the Department of Education ($5.8 billion) was allocated for special education services. You will remember that a number of the laws identified in Chapter 10 related to exceptional education. In 1999–2000, those funds helped to serve over 6 million people between the ages of birth and 21. (Notice those ages include people before the age of school entry and after their departure.)

A third allocation of funds was $3.3 billion for school improvement efforts. If your school was engaged in such an effort, you might have been aware of it. However, it is altogether possible that you were not aware that faculty were being (re)trained or that special programs were being implemented.

Another $1.7 billion was provided for vocational and adult education. Some of your classmates, for example, may have dropped out of school and later obtained a GED (general equivalency degree) instead of a high school diploma. Some of those people attend college and do very well when their circumstances are altered.

The Department of Health and Human Services provides $6.2 billion dollars for the Head Start program, one of the most popular education endeavors of the federal government.

The Department of Labor administers a number of training programs involving education. These programs, funded for $4.2 billion in fiscal year 2001, include training under the School-to-Work Opportunities Act. This act is intended to help bridge the gap between education and the workplace and has strong support among businesspeople, who have long complained about the lack of preparedness of many of the new members of their workforces.

Smaller amounts are expended for a myriad of other federal programs. They range in scope from Native American education to bilingual education to the construction of educational facilities to ROTC.

With the funding of programs comes the set of regulations under which they operate. Politicians are spending your money (or will be once you start making some), and they want assurances that the expenditures yield results. So there are regulations and still more regulations. If schools want the money (and they actually can decline it, as private schools often do), they must accept stewardship of the money, must develop plans for using it in a way the law intended it to be used and then document expenditures and uses of the funds and the resulting benefits.

The State Role

In 1997–1998, one-third of all expenditures of state and local governments were for education. Thus, $450 billion of $1.3 trillion dollars went to the public schools. Elementary and secondary schools received $318 billion while colleges and universities received $112 billion. As you can tell by comparing these data with those from the federal budget, the greatest share of the education budget for public schools comes from the state coffers. However, the proportion of the budget that comes from a state varies considerably, with some states providing almost all of the non-federal funding while other states rely on individual school districts to fund their schools.

Likewise, the amount expended by local and state agencies varies considerably (see Table 11.3). For instance, in 1997–1998, some states (Indiana, Iowa, Michigan, Texas, Utah, and Wisconsin) allocated approximately 40 percent of their funds to education. The District of Columbia allocated about 17 percent and Hawaii and Alaska slightly less than 25 percent. Three states—Connecticut, New Jersey, and New York—and the District of Columbia spent more than $10,000 per student in average daily attendance in 2000–2001. At the other end of the spectrum, Utah spent less than $5,000 per student in average daily attendance (Digest of Education Statistics 2002, 2003). It is important to remember that with increased public focus on education, the numbers (although not necessarily the ranks) may change.

Obviously, there are gross financial disparities between some schools and others. It is easy to recognize, for instance, that a state that leaves education financing to its local education agencies will see significant differences in the amounts of money provided the "rich" districts (those with a strong tax base because of industry, technology, tourism, etc.) and "poor" districts (predominantly inner city or rural). Thus, the case can be made for a state's funding all of its schools, at least at a basic level. In fact, the United States Supreme Court has ruled that the absence of significant state funding in general may unconstitutionally deprive students of equal educational opportunities. The relevant case is *San Antonio v. Rodriguez,* which has resulted in a number of lawsuits in which the courts required that the financial resources of the state be distributed more equitably among its school districts (Henkoff, 1991).

From a broader perspective, the same situation of uneven funding applies across the country. Some states are far wealthier than others, and thus the students in some states have far greater access to financial support than do their cohorts in other states.

Table 11.3	Total Per-Pupil Expenditures by State or Jurisdiction: 2000–2001		
State	**Expenditure**	**State**	**Expenditure**
U.S. Average	**$ 7,376**		
Alabama	5,885	Montana	$ 6,726
Alaska	9,216	Nebraska	7,223
Arizona	5,278	Nevada	5,807
Arkansas	5,568	New Hampshire	7,286
California	6,987	New Jersey	11,248
Colorado	6,567	New Mexico	6,313
Connecticut	10,127	New York	10,716
Delaware	8,958	North Carolina	6,346
District of Columbia	12,046	North Dakota	6,125
Florida	6,170	Ohio	7,571
Georgia	6,929	Oklahoma	6,019
Hawaii	6,596	Oregon	7,528
Idaho	5,725	Pennsylvania	8,210
Illinois	7,643	Rhode Island	9,315
Indiana	7,630	South Carolina	6,631
Iowa	6,930	South Dakota	6,191
Kansas	6,925	Tennessee	5,687
Kentucky	6,079	Texas	6,539
Louisiana	6,037	Utah	4,674
Maine	8,232	Vermont	9,153
Maryland	8,256	Virginia	7,281
Massachusetts	9,509	Washington	6,750
Michigan	8,278	West Virginia	7,534
Minnesota	7,645	Wisconsin	8,243
Mississippi	5,175	Wyoming	7,835
Missouri	6,657		

Source: Digest of Education Statistics 2002, 2003

Of course, this argument also applies at the micro level, the individual school district. Within any school system there are schools with many affluent parents, involved business partners, and active parent volunteers eager to engage in fund-raising activities. Just a few miles away are schools with little or no family involvement in school activities and no discernible tax base. The case can just as easily be made that these latter schools are unable to provide equal educational opportunities.

While our purpose here is not to debate the relative merits of various funding formulas, you may still wish to raise some issues related to this topic and consider them from time to time as you engage in your school field service or internships during the next few years. You will find that there are no easy answers. You might wish to read Kozol's *Savage Inequalities: Children in America's Schools* (1991). It will fuel your thinking.

How do the states get their funds for education? Once again, it depends on the individual state. In general, however, there are two major sources, both accounting for almost exactly one-third of the state budget for education. One source is the sales tax you pay every time you go to a grocery store or fast-food establishment or car dealership. Almost all states have sales taxes, but the percentages vary. Since everyone buys goods, everyone pays sales taxes. Another source that provides a similar amount of income for schools is the state income tax, which you will soon be paying unless you live in one of the very few states that do not have such a tax.

The remaining one-third of state sources of education funding consists of smaller amounts (percentage-wise) drawn from taxes on gas, alcohol, tobacco, estates, and gifts, and taxes paid by corporations. Just in case you are wondering about the contributions from a lottery, you may be surprised to learn that in the states that have a lottery (a majority of them, by the way), only 2 percent of the education budget is derived from that source (Significant Features of Fiscal Federalism, 1995).

The Local Role

What about the local contribution to education? Just as the states vary in how they raise money for education and how much money they raise, so do local districts. By far the largest source (76 percent) of local money for education comes from property taxes. You may hear property owners complaining about them from time to time, especially when property is reassessed to bring the tax roles up-to-date or when the millage (property tax rate) is increased. Oftentimes a rate increase requires a vote of the citizenry, but not always. In any case, as a teacher you will be in an interesting situation: The property taxes you pay are used partly for your salary and accompanying benefits.

In eleven states, at least 98 percent of the local tax revenue comes from property taxes (Significant Features of Fiscal Federalism, 1995), which means that people who don't own property don't have to pay. Thus, school supporters (financially speaking) are property owners. At the time of a bond issue or a tax reassessment, they may be quite vocal.

Channeling Funds to the Schools

Now, how do we get the funds in the first place? Well, that depends on which funds we are considering. Some funds come from federal grants. Frequently these are funneled through the state education agency, which solicits proposals for grants from schools and school districts. An example is the Title I money provided for remedial assistance to students in low-income schools. Someone at the district office writes a proposal detailing goals, objectives, strategies, roles and responsibilities of various people, time frames, budget, and so on. The proposal is forwarded to the state education agency for approval, disapproval, or request for clarification or change. If the proposal is approved, funds are channeled to the local district, which hires personnel, purchases materials, oversees the project, evaluates the effort, and reports its results.

Sometimes the federal funds are provided without a complex project proposal. An example is the Title VI grant, which provides one additional teacher for a school's primary grades. The main restriction may be that only someone not already employed as a teacher in the district can be offered the job. The intent is not to shuffle teachers around but to locate "new" teachers (because of the serious shortage in some parts of the country). Thus a principal needs to determine which primary grade is most eligible for class-size reduction and then find a new teacher who can handle the job.

Other funds arrive without formal projects. Many times these moneys (usually from the state) come as a result of regulations providing specific amounts of money for each student in the school. The funds may be allocated for specific purposes: textbooks, library books, supplies, and so on. They can be spent only for the category to which they apply. Thus, library book money cannot be used to give teachers a raise or to purchase teacher supplies. Some funds can be carried over from one school year to another; most cannot. If not expended, they revert to the agency that originally provided them. Thus, there is often a flurry of activity at the beginning of school (when funds are newly available) and at the end of the year (just before the June 30 deadline).

In some cases the board of education allocates local funds for specific purposes. They may be for teacher supplements (increasing the rate of pay established by the state) or for additional teachers (e.g., coaches, music, art, classroom teachers to decrease the teacher-student ratio). In a financial crunch, the teacher supplements may be decreased or teachers may lose their jobs. The latter is usually the final recourse, but it sometimes happens. You can understand why if you recognize that

The needs of school libraries and media centers, for example, are met through categorical funding.

Courtesy of Guilherme Cunha

> **ACTIVITY 11.4**
> ## State and Local Education Expenditures in Your Hometown
>
> It will not be difficult for you to find out how much money your state spends on K–12 education per year or how much that represents per child per year. The Digest of Education Statistics, published by the Government Printing Office, can help you. The Digest is likely available in your school or local library, and much of it is available online at http://nces.ed.gov. The numbers for closer to home might be a bit more of a challenge. Nonetheless, this is public information, so you should be able to access it.
>
> 1. How much money was provided to your hometown district last year?
>
> 2. How much money did the district contribute above the state base (e.g., from property tax and business taxes)?
>
> 3. How much does the district pay (from all sources) per student per year? How does this compare to the national average?

about 65 percent of the education budget is spent on employee salaries and another 17 percent on employee benefits. Thus, there is not a large portion of the budget that can be cut when hard times come. For instance, schools still must pay for materials for facility repairs, gas for school buses, electricity, and telephone service. Those items can hardly be cut, but the supply budget can be. Thus, you could discover that there is a limit to the amount of material you can photocopy or that certain "really important" supplies are not readily available. When the economy falters, someone has to make some difficult decisions about how to conserve money. The decision may be made to freeze many sources of funds and, if they are local in nature, to divert them to other uses. Activity 11.4 will give you an opportunity to research school funding at the local level.

Fortunately, other funds are often available, especially to people who exercise a high degree of initiative. A number of foundations and companies provide money for specific projects. The grants may range from several hundred dollars so teachers can purchase specific supplies to conduct a project, to hundreds of thousands of dollars for a school to engage in reforming its curriculum and instruction. These projects often are funded for one year with the option of continued funding for two more years if the efforts seem to be proceeding appropriately. It is likely that you as a teacher will be responsible for writing small grant proposals. For a larger project (say, obtaining computers, software, and other technology), you may be part of a committee that drafts a proposal.

You should consult the state department to find out what is available. How about a computer-building workshop at which teachers who participate for two days receive free computers? How about a grant to secure school computers or computers and other technology for your school? The state department may have the money or know what group does. An Internet contact or a telephone call can open many doors.

Even more immediate are people and businesses in your area. What do you need? What do they have that can be contributed? You may be reluctant to ask businesses for various goods or services, but be aware that they expect to be asked. Fast-food services are particularly interested in providing support, and so are companies that do business with the schools. For instance, one large-scale study (reported in Hopkins & Wendel, 1997) found that 78 percent of the businesses surveyed contributed money and 64 percent contributed equipment or supplies, or both.

So, decide what you need and ask to see the manager. Be prepared to explain how the item will help. You can use the paint or the potted plant to make your room more attractive. You can use straws for math projects. You need boards for a bookshelf that you are willing to build (or have someone build). You need incentives to reward students for good academic or social behavior. Then, when you return home, write a thank-you note on school letterhead to the manager or owner and send a copy to the principal. You won't regret it, and the contributor won't forget it.

Conclusion

This chapter focused on the organization, governance, and funding of education. In both the governance and funding of education, there are influences at the federal, state, and local levels. Some of the participants are elected, some appointed, and some hired. There are financial factors at play as well as judicial and sociological concerns. This chapter demonstrated that school is intimately connected to the society at large and that tremendous amounts of financial resources are directed to the education of children. Listed below are some of the key points that were raised throughout the chapter.

1. The grade-level structure of K–12 education can generally be clustered as: prekindergarten through grade 3 (primary), grades 4–6 (elementary), grades 7–8 (middle school), and 9–12 (high school). There are variations of this general arrangement.

2. School choice options include voucher systems, magnet schools, charter schools, private schools, school privatization, and homeschooling.

3. The secretary of education is appointed and administers a large federal department and many billions of dollars in funds for education at all levels.

4. Each house of Congress has a committee on education, composed, like other committees, with the same percentage of each party as their membership in the House or Senate.

5. Usually the state superintendent is a member of the governor's cabinet and has influence depending on the extent to which the superintendent and governor are in agreement and the amount of political influence each possesses.

6. The state superintendent sometimes serves as chairman of the state board of education, a group whose members may be appointed by the governor, elected by the people, or hold membership by virtue of their executive or legislative office.

7. The state supreme court or other district or regional courts may rule on a variety of issues that never reach the United States Supreme Court.

8. The local school board is the policy-setting organization for individual school districts and makes the final decisions in hiring and firing.

9. Operating in conjunction with the school board but usually under its authority, the superintendent of a school district works with the other administrative and supervisory members of the district office to "run" the schools on a daily basis.

10. By law the principal is charged with ultimate responsibility for all of the activities of the particular school.

11. A number of federal departments contribute funds or products or services to the public schools.

Key Terms

school choice   charter schools   state education agency
voucher   privatization   disaggregate analysis
magnet schools   homeschooling

Educational Engineering

Case Studies in Education

Enter the information from the table below into the Educational Record for the student you are studying.

	Adequacy of Local Services	Adequacy of Funding
Davon	The local educational services are adequate to meet Davon's needs. The school has a full time counselor, child psychologist, parent educator, social worker, and resource officer on site.	The school is funded through Title 1 and Act 135, which help to provide for the basic and special needs of the children.
Andy	At this time, the school provides what is necessary for Andy to receive a good education. Since his achievement is not adequate, he has been referred to the child study team to determine if he should be tested by the school psychologist for a learning disability. If he has a disability, the school will provide both resource and consultative models to meet his special needs.	Since this is a Title I school, it does not feel the pinch of poor funding like many other schools. While there are many things on the school's wish list, it is adequately funded for basic educational needs.
Judith	The local educational services are adequate to meet Judith's needs. However, her teachers believe that socioeconomic factors are primary contributors to her lack of progress.	The school is adequately funded. Heavy industry in the district provides a substantial tax base above the state funding and federal funding for compensatory programs.
Tiffany	The local educational services are adequate to meet Tiffany's needs. There is growing concern that Tiffany's emotional and social needs are not being met as she prepares to begin secondary school.	The school is adequately funded to meet its program and operational needs. However, the source of the funding is far from fair with the majority of the resources being provided by local taxpayers instead of the state government.
Sam	Local educational services are adequate to meet Sam's needs. He has been receiving special education services since kindergarten, and the extent of his services has varied based on his needs. For example, he has received speech and language services in the past when it was determined as part of his IEP that these measures were indicated.	Funding has usually been adequate for provision of basic educational services and special services. At no time has Sam been denied an appropriate education because of lack of funding.
Bao	The local services available to Bao meet all of her academic and extracurricular needs in the context of school services.	Though any school would say it needs additional funds, Bao's high school is well supported and considered to be an excellent school.

1. Does the structure of the school system adequately serve the needs of your student? Which, if any, of the educational options discussed as "School Choice" might serve your student better?
2. Based on what you know of your student and his or her family history, how would your student's parents characterize the purpose of school? How might knowing the parents' expectations help you to understand your student?
3. Many laws are based on good intentions but have not been adequately funded. As you consider the child you are studying, do you feel it is the teacher's responsibility to provide instructional materials and supplies (within reason) on her own when the district is unable to make the purchases?

Designing the School of the Future

The school of the future will have to address issues of funding just as schools always have. Where will the money come from, and where will it go? But that does not mean that funding sources and formulas of today will have to be the rule in the future. In what ways could schools become revenue producing? As you now know, funding is just one issue. Will your school of the future use the same organizational structure? Will it answer to the same governance structure of state and local control that we discussed in this chapter? How will you empower teachers to take a greater role in the issues of organization, governance, and funding?

1. Will your school (and let's think in terms of its being a public school) accept federal funds for programs? What sort of "compromise program" can you design for a school of the future that avoids funding dilemmas that schools usually face?
2. What sort of building-level administrative policy will you use? Will teachers be empowered as part of the decision-making process? Will teachers serve as administrators on a rotating basis (e.g., each teacher serves a two-year duty as teacher/assistant principal followed by a two-year duty as principal)?
3. What credentials and experience will be required for service as a member of the board of education?

Praxis Practice

Many states will require that you successfully complete the Praxis Series of examinations to qualify for certification. One or more of those tests will be subject-area tests. Another, which has a more practical orientation, will be the Principles of Learning and Teaching (PLT) examination that is appropriate for your certification area.

Completing the Quick Check Quizzes for Chapter 11 in the Unit Workshop will give you practice with the multiple choice format of the PLT. The Case Studies in Education and Designing a School of the Future activities will help prepare you for exercises that require reading a scenario and providing short answers to questions asking what you might do in such a situation.

Educational Engineering

The chapters of Unit III have been concerned with what is often referred to as the foundations of education. You might think of it in terms of the world of the classroom running into the real world. Though Dewey maintained that school *was* the real world for children, it is still the case that politics, social values and beliefs, and philosophies and religion have an effect on what happens within the four walls of the classroom. What you have seen of the history of education should give you a greater appreciation of what it means to provide an equal educational opportunity to all. Our look at philosophy points out there are many different but legitimate ways of considering any issue. And law is the attempt to reconcile all of it into a system that does the greatest good for the greatest number. These influences on school can have a profound effect on your case study and on the design of a school of the future.

Case Studies

Having followed your student through 11 chapters, you have probably become protective of his or her interests. At the very least, you have likely become the student's advocate. This is your opportunity as a pre-professional to take a step back and look at the needs of the student, the goals of the greater institution of education, as well as how your own perspectives relate to the two. Complete these activities as journal reflections rather than as something that would be written as a report for others to read.

1. How have the history of education and the government's role in education combined to meet the needs of your student? What battles, if any, do you see your student facing today that seem similar to the struggles of children in the past as they sought an education?

2. What philosophy of education can you find reflected in the laws that pertain to education and in the role that various governmental levels play in the delivery of education? How do these philosophies and influences match with your own philosophy of what education should accomplish?

3. With regard to your student, have the schools been asked to do too much? Are they doing enough? Do you see your student's needs being met in the context of what you know of our educational history, philosophy, and law? If so, how so? If not, what needs to be done differently so that your student can be provided the best educational opportunity?

 Designing the School of the Future

You have a rare opportunity in this exercise. Laws typically represent the nexus of a need based upon what has happened in the past combined with a philosophical perspective of where we want to be in the future. That is, they are not only intended as the solution to an existing problem but also as the vehicle for a preferred condition in the future. In this case, you do have the history of education as a foundation but you are *anticipating* a need and asking whether the philosophy you have adopted can meet that need. The next step, legislation, becomes *proactive* rather than *reactive*.

In a sense, you are being doubly visionary because you are taking the fanciful exercise of designing a school of the future (since it's in the future, you really aren't responsible for whether or not it would work) and trying to make it practical (if your ideas have merit, someone will ultimately have to find ways to make it work). You are pioneering two territories: the school of the future and the social order to support it. Pretty exciting!

1. Begin by considering what you wrote in the exercises following Chapter 8. What issues and lessons from our educational history stand out as particularly important as you look to the future? Equity? Academics? Civic responsibility? List whatever you consider to be the elements that simply must be kept in mind.

2. Is there a philosophy, or combinations of philosophies, from Chapter 9 that should underlie our society's perspective toward education? Should the emphasis be on preserving our heritage? Should it be on individual empowerment? Should it be on solving social problems? What, philosophically, should the school of the future be instituted to accomplish?

3. And now, what laws—that is, the practical example of a society's decision to adopt a course of action—need to be in place to see that the school can accomplish the aims you have identified in item 2? Perhaps those laws are in place. If so, what are they? Or is it the case that as a nation we must adopt particular legislative agreements with regard to the funding of school, establishment of the curriculum, or even for the expectations of student achievement? Should these be federal laws or state laws?

4. This is a tall order because it requires you to put a conscience behind the plans you have been developing. You may well need to discuss these issues with your classmates. The final product should be a Bill for the Educational Welfare of the Nation. Lest you think this is too esoteric an exercise, consider that Chapter 8 introduced you to two prominent figures in American history who independently introduced just such political initiatives. Can you remember who they were? What lessons from their efforts can you bring to this exercise?

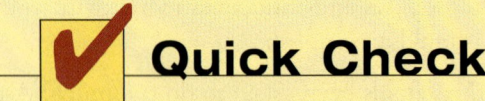 # Quick Check

Answer keys with page references are in Appendix E.

Chapter 8

1. A group of traveling teachers in ancient Greece were known as which of the following?
   a. philosophers
   b. sophists
   c. peripatetics
   d. tutors

2. One of the earliest Roman educators to recognize the special needs of young children and who warned parents to be careful in the selection of those who would interact with their children was which of the following?
   a. Caesar
   b. Eberticus
   c. Aquinas
   d. Quintilian

3. A period during the Middle Ages during which free thought and intellectual inquiry itself, anything that could question the doctrine and dogma of the Church, was stifled, was known as which of the following?
   a. The Age of Repression
   b. The Pre-Enlightenment Era
   c. The Dark Ages
   d. The Age of Religious Jurisdiction

4. For whom were dame schools intended?
   a. boys
   b. girls and boys
   c. all free children
   d. girls

5. Which of the following legislative acts led the way for compulsory education?
   a. Massachusetts Act of 1642
   b. Old Deluder Satan Act of 1647
   c. National Defense Education Act
   d. No Child Left Behind Act

6. Which of the following textbooks included moral lessons, word lists, and pronunciation guides that began to generate a national identity apart from Great Britain?
   a. The Hornbook
   b. The New England Primer
   c. The American Spelling Book
   d. The McGuffey Reader

7. In the late 1800s, "Jim Crow" laws effectively served which of the following purposes?

   a. initial integration of public schools
   b. separation of African Americans from mainstream opportunities within the society
   c. segregation of public schools
   d. integration of African Americans into mainstream opportunities within the society

8. Which of the following was a staunch advocate for the provision of a high-quality education to all children in the 19th century?
   a. Noah Webster
   b. Thomas Jefferson
   c. Horace Mann
   d. John Dewey

9. The Progressive Education movement is most closely aligned with the pragmatist philosophy of which of the following thinkers?
   a. Plato
   b. St. Thomas Aquinas
   c. Alfred North Whitehead
   d. John Dewey

10. The report of the National Commission for Excellence in Education that served as a "wake-up call" for American education was known as which of the following?
    a. The First Whitehouse Report on American Education
    b. *A Nation at Risk*
    c. Project 2061
    d. The Bilateral Report on *Brown v. Board of Education*

Chapter 9

1. Axiology is characterized by an emphasis on which of the following?
   a. questions about the physical universe and its origin
   b. truths that are so universally accepted as to be considered self-evident
   c. the nature and origin of truth and knowledge
   d. the attempt to bring order to the process of reasoning

2. Which of the following represents the branch of philosophy concerned with the way in which people come to know things?
   a. metaphysics
   b. axiology
   c. logic
   d. epistemology

3. Rene Descartes' maxim, *cogito ergo sum,* is most closely linked with which philosophy?
   a. Idealism
   b. Realism
   c. Pragmatism
   d. Existentialism

4. Which philosophy would hold the expectation that teachers should be experts in their subject matter and liberally educated so they might appreciate the place of their subject in relation to others?
   a. Idealism
   b. Realism
   c. Pragmatism
   d. Existentialism

5. Which philosophy places the responsibilities that come with being a thinking being on the shoulders of each individual?
   a. Idealism
   b. Realism
   c. Pragmatism
   d. Existentialism

6. "Back to Basics" and the idea that there are core skills and knowledge that all students should acquire for sustaining our social order is characteristic of which philosophy?
   a. Perennialism
   b. Essentialism
   c. Progressivism
   d. Social Reconstructionism

7. John Dewey is most closely associated with which of the following philosophical movements?
   a. Perennialism
   b. Essentialism
   c. Progressivism
   d. Social Reconstructionism

8. Which of the following philosophies suggested that teachers should have an affective emphasis and should engage students in questions of moral dilemmas as a means to understanding the implications of one's actions?
   a. Perennialism
   b. Essentialism
   c. Progressivism
   d. Social Reconstructionism

9. The text suggests that the growing use of computer-based programmed instruction along with an emphasis on character education represents a combining of Behaviorism and which other psychological perspective?
   a. Pragmatism
   b. Constructivism
   c. Humanism
   d. Socialism

10. Which of the following borrows from Piaget's idea of an ever-expanding and dynamic knowledge base and from Vygotsky's notion of learning as an exercise in social interaction?
   a. Behaviorism
   b. Constructivism
   c. Humanism
   d. Socialism

Chapter 10

1. Ethics relate to morals in which of the following ways?
   a. Ethics represent underlying values and morals represent a code of behavior.
   b. Ethics refer to law, morals refer to religious belief.
   c. Ethics represent a code of behavior for preserving one's moral beliefs.
   d. Ethics are the basis on which morals are developed.

2. The text suggests that a code of ethics is important for a teacher for which of the following reasons?
   a. Teachers are licensed professionals.
   b. Teachers hold a position of influence.
   c. The text does not suggest that a code of ethics is important for a teacher.
   d. A teacher's code of ethics determines what moral values will be taught.

3. A Code of Ethics for Teachers has been published by which organization?
   a. The National Education Association (NEA)
   b. The Association of Educators International (AEI)
   c. The Organization for the Ethical Conduct of Teachers (OECT)
   d. Classroom Teachers of America (CTA)

4. What is meant by the phrase *in loco parentis*?
   a. parental dysfunction
   b. acting in partnership with parents
   c. parents in need of transportation
   d. acting in the place of parents

5. Some say the federal government's responsibility with regard to education is included in the U.S. Constitution while others say it is not. Which side is correct?
   a. The federal government's responsibility is clearly established in Article 1, Section 8.
   b. Education is a matter of state's rights according to the 10th Amendment to the Constitution.
   c. Both sides are correct; it is the federal government's responsibility.
   d. Neither side is absolutely correct because education is not specifically mentioned in the U.S. Constitution.

6. The earliest of the federal land grants providing land for public schools were which of the following?
   a. The Morrill Acts
   b. The Northwest Ordinances
   c. The Louisiana Purchase
   d. Amendments to the Lanham Act

7. Your rights to privacy as a college student are part of what federal legislation?

   a. The Buckley Amendment
   b. The Student Right-to-Know and Campus Security Act
   c. The Safe Schools Act
   d. The Elementary and Secondary Education Amendments of 1968

8. In 1975, Public Law 94-142 required schools to provide a free and appropriate public education to which of the following groups?
   a. all children of U.S. citizenship regardless of the citizenship of their parents
   b. handicapped children between the ages of 3 and 18
   c. children suffering from socioeconomic disadvantage
   d. Native American children

9. Which of the following Supreme Court decisions deemed the policy of "separate but equal" educational opportunities as unconstitutional?
   a. *Plessy v. Ferguson* (1896)
   b. *Lau v. Nichols* (1974)
   c. *Brown v. Board of Education* (1954)
   d. *Engle v. Vitale* (1962)

10. Which of the following Supreme Court rulings handed down the decision that a state-written prayer for use in schools was an unconstitutional violation of the First Amendment?
    a. *Plessy v. Ferguson* (1896)
    b. *Lau v. Nichols* (1974)
    c. *Brown v. Board of Education* (1954)
    d. *Engle v. Vitale* (1962)

Chapter 11

1. It has been difficult to articulate the purpose of schools because:
   a. The purpose cannot be defined.
   b. Different groups (parents, business, educators, politicians) have different expectations.
   c. Laws keep changing.
   d. School demographics change.

2. The grade-level cluster of prekindergarten through grade 3 is referred to as:
   a. primary
   b. grammar
   c. elementary
   d. induction

3. The school grade range at which there is a shift in emphasis from learning to read to reading to learn is:
   a. primary
   b. elementary
   c. middle (or junior high school)
   d. grammar

4. *School choice* refers to which of the following?
   a. the school's responsibility to choose curricular materials for its student population
   b. the school's responsibility to choose appropriate disciplinary actions
   c. available educational options apart from the neighborhood school
   d. the parent's right to send a child with disabilities to a private facility

5. Which of the following would be an example of *privatization*?
   a. A group of parents opens a charter school when the district consolidates their local school.
   b. A private academy opens in a community and draws students from the public schools.
   c. A school does not allow visitors on campus during the school day.
   d. An education management organization assumes administration of a public school.

6. Which of the following is the reason most often given by parents for homeschooling their children?
   a. religious beliefs
   b. discipline problems at the school
   c. the child can get a better education at home
   d. the school does not challenge the child intellectually

7. The greatest share of education funding and the responsibility for securing and disbursing that funding is best described by which of the following?
   a. It is a collaborative effort between the federal government and each state.
   b. Each state bears the responsibility for public education within its borders.
   c. The federal government provides funding to regional consortiums of states.
   d. Funding of schools is accomplished independently by each school district.

8. Which of the following is charged with setting policy and hiring and firing in individual public school districts?
   a. local board of education
   b. state board of education
   c. state superintendent of education (or other similarly titled position)
   d. superintendent of schools for each local school district

9. By law, which of the following individuals would be charged with responsibility for overseeing all activities of a particular school building?
   a. superintendent
   b. assistant superintendent for facilities and grounds
   c. principal
   d. board of education

10. Recent figures indicate that of all expenditures of state and local governments nationally (approximately 1.3 trillion dollars), what percentage went to the public schools?
    a. 10
    b. 35
    c. 45
    d. 65

Keys to Learning

Challenges for Today and Tomorrow

A message throughout this textbook is that the professional educators of tomorrow must be more than just teachers. That is not to say anything bad about teaching. After all, we are teachers too. However, for teaching to truly be a *profession,* its practitioners must become key players in the progress of the profession itself. We offer a chapter on changes in education—often referred to as *reform,* and a chapter of what education might become. We won't try to tell you what it will be. Instead, we invite you to help design the future. We begin, however, with a chapter about the social influences that affect students and the schools they attend.

Chapter 12, Social Issues Affecting Students and Schools, is included in this unit as the starting point. To a degree we will discuss student diversity once again, though this time it is a diversity that is imposed upon students. Socioeconomic status and social issues affect children and schools in a number of ways. This chapter is the preamble to considering how schools should respond to the effects of social issues so that students might receive the most appropriate educational opportunities.

Chapter 13, Reform Efforts and the Professional Educator, is a chapter that is unique to this textbook in terms of the scope of its consideration of educational reform. As you speak with in-service teachers you will quickly find that there is a constant stream of reform efforts in the schools. Everything from scheduling to the menu in the cafeteria is up for grabs. We, however, don't want you to be someone to whom reform is "done." Instead, this chapter is intended to help you become one of those who makes reform effective.

Chapter 14, Innovations and the Future, offers some possibilities for you to consider for education in the future. The chapter addresses technological, logistical, instructional, and fiscal possibilities along with a consideration of the global nature of education made possible with modern-day telecommunications. Everything presented here is intended as a discussion starter, not as prescriptions for what will be. Take this as your opportunity to ask "what if?" questions that will contribute to your chosen profession.

Social Issues Affecting Students and Schools

Make the chapter work for you with CPR²:

Conceptualize Here are the major themes you will encounter in this chapter:

1. There are social issues that are imposed upon children and others that children and youth can make choices about.
2. Socioeconomic issues include family structure, at-risk students, poverty, homelessness, and child abuse and neglect.
3. Issues that children and adolescents face as decision makers include substance abuse, violence and vandalism, sexual activity, and adolescent suicide.

Preview Read the chapter headings; look at any figures, tables, and activities; and read through the items in the conclusion.

Activity 12.1 Field Observation Activity–Talk with School Officials

Activity 12.2 Go Online! Possible Interventions

Read Now read through the chapter. Mark or highlight information that you consider to be especially important or about which you have a question.

Reflect Consider these questions as you read: Are social problems the responsibility of the teacher or school? How could you help students overcome some of the obstacles they face?

Photo: Courtesy of Becky Stovall

ice breakers

A Short (and Fictional) Family History

Jocelyn is a bright and personable teen in her junior year of high school. In one of her English classes, students were given the assignment to research and then write about their own family history. Most of the students were excited about the task, but Jocelyn sensed that this might be a bit of a challenge.

About 20 years ago Jocelyn's mother, a college professor, decided that she was not interested in the whole "marriage thing," but that she did want to have a child. After doing the sort of research that college professors are prone to do, she decided upon an artificial insemination procedure that left the identity of the donor father anonymous. The pregnancy was without incident, Jocelyn was born healthy, and the two began a happy life together.

After just a few years Jocelyn's mother found that her time was being increasingly taken up with academic duties. To ease the strain, the two of them moved in with her parents. Jocelyn's grandparents were never particularly thrilled about the whole child-without-a-father idea, but they were happy to have her in their lives.

Tragically, while on a summer semester excursion to Greenland, Jocelyn's mother slid off the edge of a glacier and was never heard from again. Unable to care for Jocelyn on their own, the grandparents allowed the Department of Social Services to place her with a family. She stayed with that new family until she was 10 years old.

On her 10th birthday, Jocelyn's Uncle Bob decided to make Jocelyn a part of his little family, which already consisted of his two children from a previous marriage. When Jocelyn was 13, her Uncle Bob married a woman who brought a child of her own from a previous marriage to the group. Bob and his wife adopted all of the children as one family. The children get along well as brothers and sisters, and the family remains intact.

In this chapter we will be discussing, among other things, family structures. In the space below, list the different family structures that you can find in the Ice Breaker story. If you know the term for a type of structure, fill it in. Otherwise, come back to this page after reading the chapter and fill in the terms for the structures you identified.

Family Members   *Family Structure*

_____   _____

_____   _____

_____   _____

_____   _____

_____   _____

_____   _____

_____   _____

_____   _____

_____   _____

As you look at these structures, consider whether any one was superior or inferior to any other. Did Jocelyn have an advantage or disadvantage in her social or emotional development in one structure compared with the others? What does this say about family structures? Read the chapter and see what the research has to say.

> *What [children] obviously do need is even more face-to-face connection—to people who care about them, and to healthy activities in the real world that excite them and that will help them develop a broad range of skills.*
>
> *T. Oppenheimer (2004, p. 423)*

■ Introduction

In Unit I we discussed student diversity in the context of the *profession* of teaching. The reasoning was that issues of culture, ethnicity, differences in learning ability, and even differences arising from physical impairments must be addressed by the institution of education because they represent circumstances over which no one has control. Certainly, a child does not *choose* to have a learning disability or giftedness any more than he chooses his ethnicity. In this chapter, however, we will look at a different aspect of student diversity, one which does involve the choices that people make.

Our concern here is with social issues and socializing influences that are either imposed upon children (e.g., child neglect or homelessness) or are choices made by children (e.g., drug or alcohol abuse, or violence). Do you recall our discussion of *social reconstructionism* in Chapter 9? These are some of the issues in our society that the reconstructionists believed an appropriate education would resolve.

In particular, this chapter shows up in our unit on challenges for today and tomorrow because it discusses problems in contemporary society. It may well be the case in years to come that a different list of issues would occupy a chapter such as this. For now, these are some of the situations you may face as a classroom teacher in the years ahead. Above all, use this chapter to understand that children come to the classroom with a unique set of circumstances. Understanding those circumstances can help you to more appropriately work with what is, or is not, occurring in the classroom.

■ Socioeconomic Issues

One of the difficult aspects of this topic is the incredible amount of overlap and exceptions. That is, though we present discrete topics such as child abuse and neglect, homelessness, and alternative family structures, *combinations* of these conditions can all be influencing the life of a particular child. They do not typically stand in isolation from one another. It is also true that statistics tell us about *trends* in populations, which means that specific aspects will be true for some people but not for others. For instance, a child from a single-parent home is not necessarily at risk for failure in school, but statistically the chances are greater than for a child from a "traditional" two-parent home. Keep these points in mind as you read. Teaching is a complex task because children, people, are very complex.

What *social* forces contribute to the development of young people and eventuate in diversity among students? In his well-known ecological model, Uri Bronfenbrenner (1996) suggests five levels of environmental influence proceeding from the home and expanding throughout society. This greatly simplified description of his levels begins with the closest to home:

1. Parents, siblings, caregivers, classmates, and teachers
2. Relationships between the child and one or more of these contributors
3. Relationships between two or more of the contributors but not directly connecting with the child
4. Influences of culture, government, religion, education, and the economy
5. Changes in any of the aspects (e.g., parental divorce and remarriage, parental loss of job)

To further simplify the ecological model for this portion of the chapter, let's consider societal influences in the following categories: family structure, "at-risk" students, poverty, homelessness, and child abuse and neglect.

Family Structure

nuclear family A family structure that consists of one or more parents or guardians or foster parents and may include one or more children.

Families can be classified in several ways. One common way is to divide them into nuclear and extended groups. A **nuclear family** consists of one or more parents or guardians or foster parents and may include one or more children. Although it is tempting to say that the nuclear family is the traditional model in the United States, that is not necessarily the case. Historically, families representing more than

© Comstock/PictureQuest

Students come from a variety of family structures.

extended family A family structure that includes the presence of several generations, which can include aunts and uncles or other relatives as well as grandparents.

latchkey children Students who carry a house or apartment key, return to an empty home for the hours immediately after school, and often have little or no supervision between the time they leave school and the time their parent(s) get home from work.

two generations have often lived in the same household. Sometimes the reason was financial; on the frontier, it was often for safety or convenience. In any case, the presence of several generations is referred to as an **extended family,** which can include aunts and uncles or other relatives as well as grandparents. In some situations, one or more grandparents may be raising the child.

Single-Parent Families

With a divorce rate approximating one-third of all marriages, the number of children living in households headed by a single parent or in a home with a stepparent has increased dramatically in the past 50 years. One-half of all students live in a one-parent household at some point in their lives (Rubin & Borgers, 1991). At any one time, 49 percent of black children live with their mothers only (see Figure 12.1). The percentage for Hispanic children is 25 percent; for white children it is 17 percent (Barton, 2003). When the mother (usually but not always the parent with primary custody of the child) is the wage earner, children often return from school to an empty house. These **latchkey children** (so called because they carry a house or apartment key, sometimes on a belt or around their necks) have little or no supervision and are subject to dangers imposed by others and by poor choices they may make. The absence of supervision and direct positive guidance can have far-reaching consequences, especially for boys, who may have no immediate positive male role models for academic and social growth.

Some latchkey children come from affluent homes whose parents are busy with their jobs, community activities, and social lives. These children are, at best, provided day care (even a nanny!); at worst they are often left to their own devices. Thus, they have financial security but not family stability. In school they sport the

Figure 12.1

Percentage of Children Living with Mothers Only by Ethnicity (Barton, 2003)

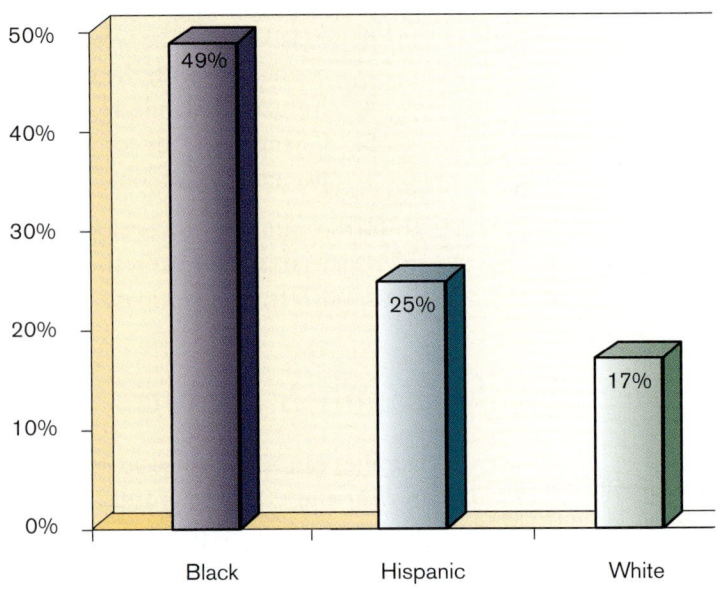

latest styles and talk about where they have been and the games, toys, and amusements they have. Research has indicated they may have little discipline (external or self-imposed), may be overindulged by parents who are willing to spend money but not time with their family, and may have difficulty coping with emotional stress, particularly as adolescents (Bobo, Gilchrist, Elmer, Snow, & Schinke, 1986; Fenzel, 1989; Eitzen, 1995).

Current research indicates that there is more to this story in our changing society. Latchkey children are not *necessarily* at risk. In fact, a shift in the wage-earning paradigm throughout the United States has led researchers studying the latchkey child situation to look in new directions. In the 1950s and 1960s the traditional and prevalent family circumstance was that of a stay-at-home mother and a wage-earning father. Research at that time focused heavily on the perceived negative effects of mothers in the workplace. In particular, children were found to suffer from role strain and coping anxieties (Bird & Kemerait, 1990). Today two-wage-earner families are the norm and researchers look to other adaptive influences to explain the difficulties *and successes* in these families. For instance, Gottfried, Gottfried, and Bathurst (1997) considered the following factors: the proximal environment, father involvement, parent's job satisfaction and satisfaction with parenting, work-related issues, and socioeconomic status and culture. When these issues are appropriately addressed, the researchers conclude, behaviors that have been previously associated with latchkey children are not necessarily a problem.

Divorce often results in lowering the economic status of children due to changes in family income, and causes other problems as well. Among them are believing that the divorce was caused by something the children did, negotiating the tension between two angry separated parents, or losing contact with a parent (and sometimes both parents when for economic or other reasons a child or children must go to live with other relatives). In fact, research indicates that in single-parent households resulting from divorce, children are more negatively affected by the family conflict preceding the divorce than by living with one parent (Amato, 2001; Amato & Keith, 1991).

The single-parent family dynamic has several other variations. For example, children in single-parent homes due to loss (the death of a father or mother), as opposed to divorce, may not experience the psychological stress of interparental conflict but they may suffer the economic difficulties that such a loss might impose. Their emotional needs may tend toward overcoming the loss rather than overcoming any imagined guilt.

Another single-parent possibility is the situation in which there never were two parents in the home, whether because the mother and father did not marry or live together or because the mother became a parent without a partner via artificial insemination or adoption. Children in the first subcategory (generally known as "born out of wedlock") have experienced a greater disadvantage academically than children of divorced or separated mothers (Korenman, Kaestner, & Joyce, 2001). There is little information thus far, however, with regard to children in the second subcategory, which is a small but growing segment.

Alternative Family Structures

blended family A family in which both partners (whether married or not) bring children from previous relationships to the new relationship.

Sometimes there is a second "father" or "mother." When both partners (whether married or not) bring children to the relationship, we have what is called a **blended family.** Thus, the children may be his, hers, and theirs. This family structure causes unique social relationships that must be addressed. According to work done by Beller and Chung (1992), the chances of dropping out of school or pursuing opportunities to attend college are much the same for children from blended families as for those from single-parent families.

Once again, this is not an indictment of single-parent families or of blended families. We simply want you to know, as a future teacher, that *statistically* children in these situations are at greater risk. Pong, Dronkers, and Hampden-Thompson (2003) conclude their analysis of children's school achievement in single-parent versus two-parent families by saying:

> What seems apparent from our investigation is that the detriment of single parenthood on children's education, so widely noted in the United States and elsewhere, is not a necessary consequence of single parenthood. Economic assistance to the children in single-parent homes, in the form of family or child allowances or parental leave, can partially offset these detrimental consequences. (p. 696)

foster care A family placement for children who are separated from their parents (for example, if the parents are deceased or the children are removed from the home for child welfare reasons).

Some of the children you work with may be placed in **foster care,** for instance when both parents are deceased or are unable to care for the children. About 440,000 children are in foster homes, and 100,000 are waiting to be adopted (Thomas, 1996). While these situations often involve loving families, such is not always the case, for the academic and social expectations of foster parents sometimes differ considerably from the habits, attitudes, and values of the receiving children.

Another alternative family structure is that of children in households with gay or lesbian parents. Without doubt, your exposure to this emerging family structure will be affected by the region in which you teach, because support for same-sex partnerships varies widely across the country. Typically, couples in such relationships do not receive the same sort of social support as couples in heterosexual marriages (Oswald, 2002). As a result, key words in an analysis of families in same-sex relationships are *resiliency,* the processes that facilitate family survival under difficult social conditions (McCubbin, Thompson, Thompson, & Futrell, 1999), and *intentionality,* which refers to actions taken by partners to validate themselves as family members and to strengthen their network of support (Oswald, 2002). For example, Tasker and Golombok (1997) found that children of lesbian mothers were most positive about their family situation when they felt that they had some control over who knew about their mother(s) being lesbian. There are few data at this time to indicate whether children in these families are at a disadvantage academically. Gay or lesbian households do, however, present an interesting version of the alternative family structure. From one perspective we can expect that such families may encounter significant obstacles in terms of achieving social legitimacy and support under the law (Oswald, 2002). On the other hand, support networks with members from all sexual orientations can provide children in these families with a broad range of influences.

"At-Risk" Students

at-risk students Students who are achieving sufficiently below their potential and/or grade level so as to be likely to drop out of school or to be unable to acquire the competence needed to function in the larger society.

At-risk students are those who, for a variety of reasons, statistically have a high probability for dropping out of school or failing to acquire the competence needed to function in the larger society. Which students are at risk? And under what circumstances are they at risk? Based on a Census Bureau survey of 50,000 U.S. households, the following risk factors were identified for students ages 5–17: (1) lack of English proficiency, (2) the presence of a personal disability, (3) school retention, (4) absence of either or both parents in the home, (5) at least one foreign-born parent of recent immigration, (6) unemployed parent or guardian, and (7) low family income (Kominski, Jamieson & Martinez, 2001). With regard to the last item, the 2000 census found that 17 percent of children lived in poverty (Statistical Abstract, 2001).

Students with low achievement test scores are also at risk, especially in school districts that tie promotion or graduation to student performance on high-stakes tests. Since achievement tests are constructed in such a way that one-half of the students score at or above grade level (i.e., passing) and the other one-half score below grade level (i.e., below passing), a typical school will always have large numbers of students who are unable to keep up with their peers. A mother once lamented, "I knew my child was not in the top half of the class, but I had no idea he was in the bottom half." The bottom half is constantly at risk, year after year.

Some groups of minority students are frequently—although not necessarily—at risk, often because of the factors described above. Black children have a much higher likelihood of being at risk, particularly if the school that serves them has a high proportion of low-income families. Studies consistently show large achievement gaps between whites and blacks. For instance, according to the National Center for Education Statistics, the average eighth-grade minority student performs at about the level of the average fourth-grade white student (Barton, 2004). Studies also show large gaps involving Hispanic students, many of whom are non-English-speaking when they enter school. Limited-English speakers as a group comprise 33 percent of the students between ages five and 17 (Futrell, Gomez, & Bedden, 2003). One study (in Gilroy, 2001) found that the typical non-English-speaker needed three to five years to acquire oral English proficiency. Moreover, we have already noted that these students need five to seven years to catch up to their peers for whom English is the first language (Collier & Thomas, 1999).

The high dropout rates for Hispanic girls (26 percent) are a sharp contrast to black girls (13 percent) and white girls (7 percent) (Canedy, 2001). For Hispanics born outside of the United States, the dropout rate is 44 percent, according to the National Center for Education Statistics (in Allen, 2002), as shown in Figure 12.2. Boys are also at risk. A summary of studies (Hunsader, 2002) indicates that (1) boys receive 70 percent of Ds and Fs on report cards, (2) they are 50 percent more likely than girls to be retained, (3) they are three to five times more likely than girls to be labeled as learning disabled, and (4) they represent 70 percent of school suspensions. Nationally, about two-thirds of all entering high school freshmen graduate in four years. For blacks and Latinos, the rate is about one-half (Orfield, 2004).

Here's a surprise for you: Some students are at risk even though they make good grades. This phenomenon occurs when students compile a fine grade point average for the wrong reasons: they may do better than most of their classmates and therefore get the "good" grades; they may be well behaved, have a pleasing personality, and have nice manners; they may have a parent or guardian who is actively involved, either as a supportive adult or as one who is quick to assume a confrontational role in parent-teacher contacts; they (or their parents or guardians) may do extra credit projects to "pull up" low grades; they may depend on open-book tests, multiple-choice exams, cooperative group grades, and take-home tests; and they may engage in cheating, which is also a common practice, even among high achievers. In one study, 80 percent of students listed in *Who's Who Among American High School Students* admitted cheating on an exam (Bushweller, 1999). Indeed, studies indicate that most high school graduates have cheated but have not been caught (Cizek, 2002/2003). Recently Internet plagiarism has become a serious problem (Gardiner, 2001; Bugeja, 2004). In a Harris interactive poll of 1,100 students, 91 percent knew that digital media files were copyrighted but still downloaded the files ("Majority of Youth Understand Copyright But Continue to

Figure 12.2

Dropout Rates for Girls by
Ethnicity (Canedy, 2001)

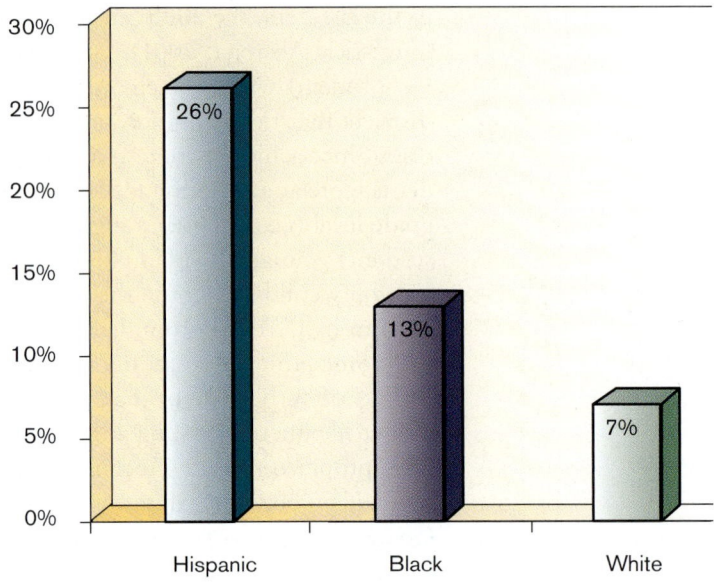

Download Illegally," 2004). As a result, students receive grades for which no corresponding amount of learning has been acquired. Regardless of the situation, studies show that grade inflation is rampant, from kindergarten through graduate school. The net result is to place students at risk of frustration and failure at subsequent levels when their skills prove insufficient to meet expectations.

Poverty

As we noted earlier, there is overlap among the broad categories we have chosen to use in discussing social considerations that result in differences among students. Poverty has a pervasive influence with clear ramifications for social development. Surely you have noticed that some people in your schools wore designer clothes while others had very few outfits, which were definitely out of style.

In her important book *A Framework for Understanding Poverty,* Ruby Payne (1998, pp. 11–13) quotes some important statistics and sources:

- In 1996 one-fourth of people under age 18 lived in poverty (Center for the Study of Poverty, Columbia University).
- In 1989 one-third of Latino children lived in poverty (Miranda, 1991).
- "Poor children are much more likely than non-poor children to suffer developmental delay and damage, to drop out of high school, and to give birth during the teen years" (Miranda, 1991).
- "Poor inner-city youths are seven times more likely to be the victims of child abuse or neglect than are children of high social and economic status" (Renchler, 1993).
- "Poverty is caused by interrelated factors: parental employment status and earnings, family structure, and parental education" (Five Million Children, 1992).
- The largest poverty group was white children; the largest percentage of children in poverty was minority groups. (There are far more white children, so even with a lower percentage, there are greater numbers of them living in poverty.)

Poverty is more likely to be at the heart of a school's challenge than race or ethnicity is. Thus you will see its effects every day in many ways. Poor students may move often, and the effect of frequent mobility on student achievement is clear. One study indicates that a student who moves more than three times in six years can lose a full year of academic growth (Vail, 2003). Although there is no stereotypical situation, students living in poverty may be subjected to more violence and more family instability. They may have less access to books and computers and watch television more than their more affluent peers. They often live in substandard housing and have less space at home, encountering more noise and more secondhand smoke (Evans, 2004). In terms of school, poor students feel left out because of the condition of their clothing; they cannot come to school because their one pair of shoes no longer have soles or an only dress has holes. Poor students cannot bring you a present or pay for a field trip; cannot see the latest movies or have transportation to the town or city library; cannot participate in the band because they don't have the money for an instrument; have parents who cannot afford to hire a needed tutor; have parents who hold several jobs and thus cannot attend parent-teacher conferences. If these thoughts are new to you, give thanks for the special privileges that you have enjoyed. At the same time, you must remember the debilitating influence of poverty and be sure your classroom does not become an added dimension of an impoverished environment to the children of poverty.

Homelessness

When you look at the children in a classroom, yours or one in which you observe while preparing to become a teacher, you might be surprised to find that some of those children are among the homeless. They may live on the street, in an abandoned house, in a shelter, in a motel, or perhaps in a car. They may live with their parents or guardians or, less frequently, wander from place to place for protection and the fulfillment of basic human needs like food and clothing. As with poverty, homelessness is a condition that befalls families and can turn concerns such as education into a luxury item.

Some estimates suggest that up to 2 million adults and 1 million children are homeless. Others say the figure is considerably higher. As you can imagine, it is virtually impossible to make an accurate count because these families often move from place to place. The 2000 U.S. Census identified 170,706 people who were living in emergency and transitional shelters. Children under the age of 18 accounted for 43,887 of these people (Smith & Smith, 2001). The National Coalition for the Homeless (1999) reports that children represent the fastest growing segment of the homeless population. Families with children constitute about 40 percent of people who become homeless. And this is not a problem confined to urban areas; approximately one-quarter of those living in shelters for the homeless are in rural areas.

What does it mean to be homeless? Juanita Fagan (2001), principal at a small rural school in Oregon, says her school follows the criteria as established in Title I of the

Family poverty and homelessness often negatively affect children's educational outcomes.

© Allen Russell/Index Stock Imagery

Teacher Testimonial

Feature 12.1   Unique Challenges and Opportunities

Working with students from low socioeconomic backgrounds offers unique challenges and opportunities for teachers. For novice teachers, knowledge of some of the differences between low socioeconomic and middle class is critical to having a successful year. Students from disadvantaged backgrounds bring an assortment of issues with them into the classroom. As school is often the only stable environment for many children, teachers need to learn as much as possible about their students.

Students from low socioeconomic backgrounds face several issues that affect their performance, including acting as the parent, lack of background experience, home environment, hunger, and lack of parental involvement and education.

Acting as the Parent

It is not unusual for these students, even young elementary, to be responsible for duties normally reserved by parents. One year, I had a third-grade student who missed a great deal of school. When I asked her why she was so often absent, she replied that she had to stay home to babysit her little brother. Her mother verified that this was indeed true. This mother was not consciously neglecting her child; she simply had no other resources available to her.

Lack of Background Experiences

Teachers also need to realize that students from poverty also lack many of the experiences that are taken for granted in middle-class settings. Because of this, educators need to provide students with a variety of experiences. To build students' vocabulary, teachers must talk, read, and write about these experiences with their students. As a beginning teacher, when teaching a third-grade class about reptiles and amphibians, I used the phrase "frogs and toads." One student, an above-average student, asked what a toad was. I was flabbergasted! I had assumed that the students were familiar with the term *toad*. This eye-opening experience showed me that I needed to provide my students with as many language-building experiences as possible.

Home Environment

Most of the behaviors exhibited in the classroom are a manifestation of the home environment. My second year of teaching, I had a young male student who, on Mondays, slept most of the day. At the beginning of the year, I spent many futile hours trying to wake him and then get him to stay awake. Like all "good" teachers I tried calling his mother and sending notes home. I tried to punish him into staying awake. I reviewed his cumulative folder to see if there was any medical reason for his sleepiness. Finding nothing to explain his behavior, one day at lunch I voiced my frustration to a second-grade teacher. She informed me that his sleeping was not new, that he had slept through a good part of second grade. I then asked her if she knew the reason for his sleepiness, and she told me that his home life left a great deal to be desired. This student had four other brothers (both older and younger). His mother often entertained until late in the night, and because the house only had two bedrooms, he had to sleep on the couch. Most weekend nights he was not going to bed until after midnight. I then realized that his inability to stay awake was beyond his control. He was usually awake for the first hour of school and for about an hour after P.E. I decided to take advantage of this and restructured my day so that I was teaching reading and math while he was usually awake.

Another way that the home environment affects the student is through physical behaviors such as hitting, pushing, and pinching. In many low socioeconomic households, this is considered acceptable behavior. When students from low socioeconomic backgrounds misbe-

Elementary and Secondary Education Act, which includes children who

- Live in substandard housing with cold or no running water, no electricity, and no heat
- Live in multifamily housing
- Have moved more than three times in the last year
- Have chronic head lice

As you might expect, homeless students can have much in common with at-risk children. They often have difficulty in making friends or communicating with

have, it is often a result of not knowing what is expected. To help students learn what type of behavior is appropriate and expected at school, procedures must be modeled and practiced numerous times. An old rule of thumb is that to have a productive year, teachers should spend the first two weeks of school teaching, modeling, and practicing procedures and expectations.

Hunger

Hunger may be another factor a child faces, with school-provided breakfast and lunch being the only nutritious meals of the day. Weekends and holidays can be trying times for lack of food. To combat growling stomachs, many teachers find it advantageous to have a class snack time. This is a common occurrence in primary classrooms, but it is often beneficial in the intermediate grades. I used to keep large bags of generic animal crackers and boxes of cereal in the cabinet so that all students would enjoy a snack. Many of the students brought their own nutritious snacks; I just ensured that everyone would have something. If you have students who are tardy, see if the cafeteria will serve them breakfast, as even eating a doughnut is better than eating nothing at all.

Lack of Parent Involvement

The lack of parental support and involvement is often a source of frustration for teachers. Many times parents of students from low socioeconomic backgrounds had a negative school experience. As a result, they are hesitant to become involved because they are afraid of having a repeat experience. As teachers, it is critical that we refrain from using educational jargon. We can inadvertently make parents feel "dumb" when we use the many different acronyms that exist in education today. If parents perceive the teacher as having an air of superiority, then establishing lines of communication is almost impossible. Parents do want what is best for their chil-

dren. They want them to have a successful school career and eventually, as adults, have a better life. We need to do whatever it takes to ensure that the parents know that we value all children equally. Starting with the first week of school, teachers should make positive phone calls home. More often than not, parents of disadvantaged children are used to receiving phone calls only when there is a problem. An alternative to calling home (remember, many of these students do not have working phones) is to mail a friendly postcard.

Lack of Parent Education

Parents are sometimes so defensive about their own lack of education that they belittle education to their children. In some households, speaking correct English is considered "uppity" and kids are sometimes punished for it. You almost have to teach English as a second language in the regular classroom. You will also find that you have to do double work on Mondays, as over the weekends students revert to their home language. One Monday morning, a young man in a teacher's class was telling about his weekend and was using vocabulary and grammar that was not acceptable to her. After she corrected him, he explained to her that when he "talked proper" at home, his mother thought he was being disrespectful and he would get in trouble.

An excellent reference for all teachers of low socioeconomic students is *A Framework for Understanding Poverty* by Ruby K. Payne, Ph.D. In this book, Payne explains the characteristics of families living in poverty, the differences in language used in home settings and school settings, ways to help establish support systems, and instructional practices. This book should be on every educator's professional bookshelf.

Julie Allen is an assistant principal in the Polk County School District in Florida. ■

adults. Many feel insecure and often demonstrate low self-esteem. They may find cooperative activities with other students somewhat challenging. Fagan (2001) notes that they are often shy, keep to themselves, and feel stressed or overwhelmed when asked to participate in front of the class. Koblinsky, Gordon, and Anderson (2000) found that homeless students had significantly more behavioral problems in school than did their housed peers.

In 1987, Congress established The McKinney Education of Homeless Children and Youth Act (EHCY) in response to estimates that as many as 50 percent of homeless children were not attending school. Funds were made available to state

Make an appointment with a principal or district administrator to discuss the issues listed below in terms of their incidence in the local schools. If you are attending school away from home but plan to return when you become a teacher, you may wish to contact your old school district. Keep in mind that the schools will be reluctant in some cases to be very specific, and prevented by law in others, but you should certainly be able to get a new appreciation of the many challenges faced by children and school districts.

Family Structure
- Is there a range of family structures represented in the district?
- Do teachers or the district personnel have special issues to address in working with children from alternative family structures? Or does it go essentially unnoticed?

At-Risk Students
- Are at-risk students specifically identified? (You are not asking for identification, just whether students are identified.)
- What must the district do to address the needs of at-risk students?

Poverty and Homelessness
- What percentage of children in the district fall into either of these categories?

Child Abuse and Neglect
- Is this a problem in the district?
- Is there any estimate of the percentage of students in the district who may be subject to abuse or neglect?

and local educational agencies to provide access to schooling to homeless children. Though attendance increased, budget cuts over the years have stifled the progress of the initiative.

If you have homeless children in your classroom, you can be sure that they will look to you for understanding, support, and acceptance. Unlike situations of child abuse or neglect, families experiencing poverty and homelessness are more often characterized by desperation, a focus on basic survival, and issues of poor self-esteem that can make working with schools difficult. Children may be physically dirty because they have no regular access to shower or tub facilities, and poorly clothed. They may be teased by other children. Your compassion must come into play as you foster their intellectual, emotional, and social growth.

Keep in mind that maintaining communication with these families is a challenge you may face. Communicating with the parents by phone could be problematic. It may be the case that the only time a parent can call is on the weekend or in the evening. This aspect of your work as a teacher is something to which you should give considerable thought and development. A teacher needs to be able to communicate with students and parents in a way that affirms the inherent dignity of all human beings. Activity 12.1 provides an opportunity for you to use your field observation placement to discuss the issues presented here with a school official. We admonish you to appreciate that these are serious issues that people face. If you do address Activity 12.1, do so with a commitment to professionalism that reflects the reality of a world outside of a textbook or a comfortable classroom.

Child Abuse and Neglect

child abuse and neglect At a minimum, any recent act or failure to act on the part of a parent or caretaker that results in death, serious physical or emotional harm, sexual abuse, or exploitation, or an act or failure to act that presents an imminent risk of serious harm.

Child abuse and neglect, as well as its variations, are likely far more prevalent than you suspect. Even more tragic, it is often the case that children suffering abuse or neglect see their environment as "normal," as if all children live in the same situation. Golden (2000) reports that more than 2.8 million cases of maltreatment were investigated in 1998, with approximately 903,000 cases yielding evidence of maltreatment. The data indicated that 80 percent of the perpetrators of these acts were parents. The U.S. Department of Health and Human Services (2000) estimated that 1,118 children died as a result of maltreatment. Children younger than four years of age accounted for more than 75 percent of those fatalities.

As long ago as 1974 Congress enacted a Child Abuse Prevention and Treatment Act, which defined child abuse and neglect as the physical or mental injury, sexual abuse, negligent treatment, or maltreatment of a child under the age of 18 by a person who is responsible for the child's welfare under circumstances that indicate that the child's health or welfare is harmed or threatened thereby. Today, child maltreatment is classified into four categories: (1) physical abuse, (2) neglect, (3) sexual abuse, and (4) emotional maltreatment. The 1996 version of the Child Abuse Prevention and Treatment Act provides this definition for child abuse and neglect: The term "child abuse and neglect" means, at a minimum, any recent act or failure to act on the part of a parent or caretaker that results in death, serious physical or emotional harm, sexual abuse, or exploitation, or an act or failure to act which presents an imminent risk of serious harm (Section 111[2]).

The reasons that parents or other caregivers might abuse a child are many, but of equal concern is the trend indicating that patterns of abuse are passed on from one generation to the next. English and Papalia (1988) reported that 90 percent of all violent criminals and 97 percent of hard-core juvenile offenders had been abused as children. But it is also true that abuse is not always violent in nature (e.g., emotional abuse) nor does it necessarily indicate an ongoing pattern of behavior (review the definition of abuse and neglect in the previous paragraph). Parents under psychological stress or extreme financial pressure or whose expectations of the child are unrealistic may also become abusers. In such cases the abuse a child suffers may be the result of a moment of rage. Far from excusing the behavior, you can see that a single action—or failure to act—constitutes maltreatment. Even the teacher who loses his temper and refers to a student as "stupid" or who demeans a child can be accused of emotional abuse.

Since poor school performance or poor behavior in school are common problems associated with child abuse, it may fall to you as a classroom teacher to report possible cases of maltreatment. You may notice that a child becomes withdrawn or demonstrates very low self-esteem. You may notice a significant change in the student's academic performance or social behavior. You may even observe bruises, burns, or cuts on a child. Most states require that you report your concerns. You will have to check with your school district for the proper reporting procedures. In some instances reports may go to school personnel. In other situations, you may be required to report the concern to your state's agency for social services.

This is a slippery slope. No one wants to report a case of child abuse only to find out that the child fell down at home and injured himself. It seems like this just sets a teacher up for being sued. However, in states that require the reporting of suspicion of child abuse, teachers are considered to be mandated reporters (we discussed this in Chapter 10), which means that they are held immune from prosecution because the information at hand warranted a report in "good faith and without malice." A teacher *can* find himself held liable when a case of child abuse

Table 12.1   Signs of Child Abuse and Neglect

General Signs of Abuse or Neglect

The child
- Shows sudden changes in behavior or school performance
- Has not received help for physical or medical problems brought to the parents' attention
- Has learning problems (or difficulty concentrating) that cannot be attributed to specific physical or psychological causes
- Is always watchful, as though preparing for something bad to happen
- Lacks adult supervision
- Is overly compliant, passive, or withdrawn
- Comes to school or other activities early, stays late, and does not want to go home

The parent
- Shows little concern for the child
- Denies the existence of–or blames the child for–the child's problems in school or at home
- Asks teachers or other caretakers to use harsh physical discipline if the child misbehaves
- Sees the child as entirely bad, worthless, or burdensome
- Demands a level of physical or academic performance the child cannot achieve
- Looks primarily to the child for care, attention, and satisfaction of emotional needs

Signs of Physical Abuse

The child
- Has unexplained burns, bites, bruises, broken bones, or black eyes
- Has fading bruises or other marks noticeable after an absence from school

- Seems frightened of the parents and protests or cries when it is time to go home
- Shrinks at the approach of adults
- Reports injury by a parent or another adult caregiver

Signs of Neglect

The child
- Is frequently absent from school
- Begs or steals food or money
- Lacks needed medical or dental care, immunizations, or glasses

- Is consistently dirty and has severe body odor
- Lacks sufficient clothing for the weather
- Abuses alcohol or other drugs
- States that there is no one at home to provide care

Signs of Sexual Abuse

The child
- Has difficulty sitting or walking
- Suddenly refuses to change for gym or to participate in physical activities
- Reports nightmares or bedwetting
- Experiences a sudden change in appetite
- Demonstrates bizarre, sophisticated, or unusual sexual knowledge or behavior

- Becomes pregnant or contracts a venereal disease, particularly if under age 14
- Runs away
- Reports sexual abuse by a parent or another adult caregiver

Signs of Emotional Maltreatment

The child
- Shows extremes in behavior, such as overly compliant or demanding behavior, extreme passivity, or aggression
- Is either inappropriately adult (parenting other children, for example) or inappropriately infantile (frequently rocking or head-banging, for example)

- Is delayed in physical or emotional development
- Has attempted suicide
- Reports a lack of attachment to the parent

Source: U.S. Department of Health and Human Services (2004), Administration for Children and Families, http://www.childwelfare.gov/pubs/factsheets/signs.cfm.

indicates that he failed to make an appropriate report despite being confronted with signs suggesting the possibility of abuse. Table 12.1 provides some warning signs in terms of both the child's behavior and the behavior of parents and caregivers in their interactions with you.

The Society in Which We Live

Our society itself, ever changing, ever resisting change, presents challenges to children that are not of the child's making. "Adult issues" and the solutions that adults bring to those issues are entirely out of the hands of the children. Even so, the decisions have definite implications for children in school and in the greater community as well. We could not attempt to provide you with a detailed discussion of the many issues based on the diversity of perspectives facing the public schools, though you may have noticed that we have touched on some of them throughout this book. Our discussions of the explicit, implicit, and null curricula are good examples of issues that reflect the differing opinions that can exist in any social system.

Another example that will likely remain an issue for some time to come is what writers such as Jonathan Kozol (2005) refer to as the resegregation of the public schools. Kozol takes the issue even further by providing compelling evidence to suggest that schools never actually desegregated in the first place. He writes, "Schools that were already deeply segregated twenty-five or thirty years ago are no less segregated now, while thousands of other schools around the country that had been integrated either voluntarily or by the force of law have since been rapidly resegregating" (p. 41). You will recall that the decision in the landmark 1954 case of *Brown v. Board of Education* concluded that "separate but equal" educational systems were unconstitutional and that schools (after a period of slow compliance) were ordered to desegregate "with all deliberate speed." More than 50 years later we find that the issue is by no means resolved. And, as Kozol concludes, "equal" is nowhere in the equation.

Though one typically thinks of segregation issues as referring to ethnic distinctions, you may also find in your discussions of education that there is an increasing movement toward segregation of the sexes as more communities experiment with single-gender public schools. You will also find that charter schools, magnet schools, and specialized schools (such as schools for the arts or for science and mathematics) represent a form of segregation as different educational opportunities are offered to different constituencies. Should this be the case in public education? What is your opinion?

■ Issues Facing Children and Adolescents

In the previous section we discussed issues that children face through no fault of their own. A child does not choose to be homeless or to live in one family circumstance or another. Services must be provided to overcome these disadvantages, and teachers need to bring their compassion to the task of working with such children. Though services and compassion are necessary in this next set of challenges, the context has changed to a discussion of inappropriate or detrimental behaviors in which children and youth *choose* to engage. We wish we could offer you sweeping solutions to these issues, but the most we can do here is to make you aware of some of them.

Substance Abuse

The interaction among peers in school encourages the exchange of ideas and the development of behaviors. As children become older, issues involving negative peer influences become paramount. Of course, children are aware of drug use (including alcohol) by adults, even if only in its social context. By middle school, however, students may be experimenting with drugs and alcohol or have friends who are, and the desire to be a part of the group often overcomes common sense and consideration of consequences. **Substance abuse** most commonly involves alcohol, tobacco, and marijuana. The accessibility and use of more potent drugs is also an ongoing concern.

You could likely spend quite a bit of time debating the cause of alcohol and tobacco abuse in our society. Though in recent years alcohol and tobacco have been targets of widespread campaigns encouraging "appropriate" use, these particular drugs have nonetheless had a long history as socially acceptable substances. Children from one generation to the next have been exposed to mixed messages about alcohol and tobacco use through advertising, the media, and adult social behavior. The National Household Survey on Drug Abuse (May 2001) found that of students 12–19 years of age, 18.6 percent had used alcohol in the previous 30 days. Some evidence suggests that current smoking rates among youth are declining (Kann et al., 2000). More recently, the 2002 National Youth Tobacco Survey of over 26,000 students (Study: High School Student Smoking Rate Drops, 2003) found that the high school smoking rate had decreased from 28 percent in 2000 to 23 percent in 2002 while the use of any tobacco product decreased from 34.5 percent to 28.4 percent. But whether there will be a long-term change in the trend of juvenile smoking remains to be seen, for there were no significant changes among middle school students. The American Lung Association (2004) estimates that, unfortunately, 6.4 million children will die prematurely from a smoking-related disease.

The National Household Survey on Drug Abuse (2001) also found that in 1999, almost 8 percent of students 12–19 years of age had used marijuana during the previous 30 days. As you might suspect, the prevalence of marijuana smoking is far greater than parents suspect, or at least greater than they care to admit. Aside from whether or not parents recognize the problem, as a teacher you will find that individuals under the influence of marijuana can experience impaired cognitive functioning including deficits in short-term memory. Studies have shown four out of five school dropouts were regular marijuana users.

Though the context of our discussion is substance abuse by students, there is another aspect of such abuse that you may encounter at some point in your teaching career. In a course on human growth and development you will likely study the effects of *fetal alcohol syndrome,* which affects the unborn babies of mothers ingesting alcohol during pregnancy, and of a newer phenomenon, *crack babies,* children whose mothers used crack cocaine during pregnancy. For these children, the effects of substance abuse can be pronounced and lifelong.

© FogStock LLC/Index Stock Imagery

Substance abuse among adolescents most commonly involves alcohol, tobacco, and marijuana. Schools must fight the mixed messages about substance use and abuse that students get from society at large.

School Violence and Vandalism

School violence refers to aggressive acts against people. School vandalism refers to aggressive or destructive acts toward school property. Hopefully you will not be confronted with either of these situations, but chances are that to some degree you will. Violence and lack of discipline consistently rank among the general public's most frequently cited problems with public education. Not surprisingly, classroom management is a major concern cited by teachers with regard to problems in the schools. One major study (Violence in the United States Public Schools: 2000 School Survey on Crime and Safety, 2003) found five factors that affect the likelihood that a serious violent incident would occur. These characteristics were school enrollment size, school setting, percentage of males, the number of serious discipline problems, and the number of schoolwide disruptions. Schools with more than 15 percent of their students scoring below the 15th percentile on an achievement test were more likely to have at least one violent or serious incident than were schools with less than 5 percent of the students scoring below the 15th percentile.

During the 1996–97 school year, over 800,000 incidents of school violence were reported (Digest of Education Statistics 2002, 2003). Vandalism alone accounted for nearly 100,000 of those incidents, and the National Parent-Teacher Association has estimated that the resulting cost exceeds $600 million, a figure greater than the national budget for textbooks. Some estimates suggest that *reported* incidents represent just a small percentage of the actual total. Indeed, "Violence affects one in every five teenagers. Every day 160,000 students miss school because they fear attack, intimidation, or bullying" (Druck & Kaplowitz, 2005).

The prevalence of school violence is difficult to pin down because (1) not all incidents are reported, and (2) there is no consensus as to what constitutes "violence." For instance, Willert and Lenhardt (2003) suggest, "To define violence simply by its aftereffects—a theft, a fight, a murder—rather than by the behaviors that expose its roots—such as teasing, verbal taunting, and exclusion—is to ignore the sources of violence that can be effectively addressed through joint school and community action" (p. 111). You are probably familiar with the bullying that goes on in different ways in school, but have not considered it as violence. Yet these various degrees—teasing, verbal put-downs, shoving, and so forth—are not only the precursors to violent behavior but can also be the impetus to violent behavior from victims who otherwise would not have been violent. As you know from well-publicized reports, these incidents can escalate to tragic proportions; the ones you read about are just the tip of the iceberg. Many potentially serious incidents are either prevented when peers share concerns with adults or when perceptive and compassionate teachers prevent peer problems because they established a community of learners.

You never know until it is too late whether the hazing or "just teasing" or shunning of students results in intolerable social conditions, not only for the victims but also for the perpetrators. But here's one wakeup call: 71 percent of the elementary teachers in one survey admitted they avoided becoming involved when students engaged in teasing or bullying behavior (Schroeder, 1999). Stemming the tide of violence and vandalism is not solely the responsibility of the teacher. Teachers are, however, stakeholders in the community that shares the task of prevention and intervention. Prevention is the appropriate first step. Druck and Kaplowitz (2005) offer the following advice:

- Do not tolerate bullying.
- Set classroom behavior rules.
- Learn and teach conflict resolution and anger management skills.
- Learn the warning signs.
- Enforce school policies.
- Help implement a safe school plan.
- Report safety threats.

- Encourage and sponsor student-led antiviolence activities.
- Talk to parents.
- Cultivate a supportive classroom atmosphere.

However, when serious problems do arise, Quinlan (2004) proposes six steps for mediating conflicts:

1. Separate the students, have them each write their version of the conflict, and then ask for clarification if necessary.
2. Meet jointly with the students, explaining that mediation is not to produce a winner or loser but to resolve the issue.
3. Establish the mediation rules (take turns talking, talk only to the principal, stay seated, don't interrupt, keep information confidential).
4. Have each student explain the conflict, filling in the blanks: "I feel _____ when you _____ and I need you to _____."
5. Help students brainstorm to list possible solutions.
6. Draw up a contract that lists the agreement, have each student sign it, and give a copy to all parties.

Teen Pregnancy

You have probably noticed that none of the issues discussed in this chapter are clear-cut concerns that could be solved by one particular course of action or another. The matter of teen pregnancy is just the same. Over the last several decades the birthrate among teenage girls has declined. This is good, for babies born to teenage mothers are typically less likely to receive proper prenatal and postnatal care, and are more likely to have low birth weights and problems such as cerebral palsy, chronic respiratory problems, retardation and mental illness, blindness and deafness, and learning problems (Black, 1998). Even with the decline in birth rates, the incidence of children born to, well, children, is far greater in United States than in other industrialized nations. It is also true that the decline in births does not correlate to a decline in sexual activity among young people. Rather, with the availability of contraceptive devices, the percentage of teenagers engaging in sexual activity has actually increased.

We mentioned previously that children receive mixed messages about alcohol and tobacco use. This is certainly the case with regard to sexual activity. Though schools have provided sex education programs for decades, the society at large—particularly through media such as TV and movies—bombard children with sexually charged messages. Combined with the fact that adolescents turn to their peer groups for information and direction more than to parents or other adult authority figures, it is not surprising that inappropriate sexual activity and the unwanted consequences of teen pregnancy and sexually transmitted diseases are major concerns in our world today.

Sex Education

Though parents cannot be absolved of their responsibilities for sex education, the issue has nonetheless fallen to the schools for remediation. There have been three typical approaches: sex education, encouraging sexual abstinence, and increasing the availability of contraceptives (Out & Lafreniere, 2001). Unfortunately, none of these approaches has yielded significant results. More promising are role-playing approaches that bring the responsibilities of parenthood into the student's life. One such approach is the *Baby Think It Over* program (Jurmaine, 1994) in which the

Programs such as this one in Nebraska help teenage parents to learn to care for their children and stay in high school.

© Karen Kasmauski/Corbis

student becomes the caregiver for a newborn "infant." The infant is actually a sophisticated doll that, among other things, demands and maintains the student's attention.

Other successful approaches have emphasized a shift away from accentuating the negative aspect of a teen pregnancy to an emphasis on strengthening the family and support structure of the teen and her baby. In such initiatives prenatal and postnatal care are made available to the mother and child as well as child development education and vocational skills training. The purpose of all of this is to avoid the downward spiral typical of the adolescent who drops out of school following the birth of a child (Thomson & Caulfield, 1998).

Lest we end this section acting as if these teenage girls somehow had a baby by themselves, we should report that figures from 1994 indicated that 51 percent of births in that year to girls 17 and under were fathered by men 20 and older (Kids Count Data Book, 1997). With regard to teenage fathers, or potential fathers, programs such as *Baby Think It Over* are provided to the boys as well.

Adolescent Suicide

Suicide is one of the most common teenage problems. After accidents, it is the most frequent cause of death of white males 15–24 years of age and the third leading cause of death for all people in that age bracket (Health United States and Prevention Profile, 1992). According to the Centers for Disease Control, 17 percent of students in high school have considered suicide, and 9 percent have attempted it. Each year 1,700 students between 15 and 19 commit suicide. To decrease those numbers, a free screening is often available for teens (Ashford, 2005). Sometimes suicide results from long-term social issues; sometimes it comes from more immediate traumatic situations. In any case, such a loss of hope, particularly among children and youth, is a circumstance that teachers need to be able to recognize.

A complicating factor in detecting signs of suicidal thoughts is that people can react so differently to situations. Something that might not bother you at all could be the source of great emotional pain to someone else, perhaps even to one of your

Table 12.2	Warning Signs for Suicidal Tendency

- Suicidal talk such as "I won't be a problem much longer," or "It's no use"
- Preoccupation with death and dying (in conversation or written assignments)
- Marked decline in school performance and achievement
- Unusually disruptive or rebellious behavior
- Inability to tolerate praise or rewards
- Giving away special possessions
- Taking excessive risks
- Increased drug use
- Loss of interest in usual activities, friends, and family
- Unusual neglect of personal appearance

Go Online!

ACTIVITY 12.2   Possible Interventions

Choose one of the topics from the list below. Use the Internet to research current approaches to addressing the problem. Which interventions are having significant success rates? What is the outlook for the future? What recommendations can you find for teachers working with these students?

- Substance abuse
- School violence and vandalism
- Teen pregnancy
- Adolescent suicide

best friends. Unfortunately, you find out the truth only after a failed, or successful, attempt at suicide.

We do not want to suggest that as a classroom teacher you will be able to recognize all of the nuances of your students' behavior and thus be able to prevent something as tragic as a suicide. However, there are some signs that might give you reason to take a closer look. If you see these signs, report them to the appropriate personnel in accordance with the policy of your school district. In your interactions with the student, try to be positive and bolster the child's self-esteem.

There are many factors that could lead a child or adolescent to take such desperate action. Depression is typically a precursor to suicidal thoughts. Particularly at risk are girls who have been physically or sexually abused. Also, adolescents who seem to be struggling with their sexual orientation may be at greater risk for slipping into a depression that would result in thoughts of suicide. Table 12.2 lists other warning signs. Activity 12.2 is provided so that you can research current intervention techniques for some of the issues facing adolescents.

Other Societal Influences on Social Development

Extracurricular Activities

Another aspect related to social development and thus diversity among students is the influence of extracurricular activities. Some of these, such as band, athletics, special interest clubs, service organizations, honor societies, and even before- and after-school programs are part of the broader curriculum of the school; others, such as Brownies, Cub Scouts, Girl Scouts, Boy Scouts, religious youth groups, and various levels of youth sports, are sponsored by the community or religious organizations; and still others, such as music lessons, tutoring, and dance instruction, are the responsibility of the home. By participating in these activities, students can pursue and enjoy a variety of interests while simultaneously developing teamwork, persistence, and independence. Students involved in extracurricular activities also tend to complete more years in school and have higher educational aspirations (Otto, 1982). Of course, poverty may again become a factor influencing the range of choices for extracurricular programs because of economic considerations and transportation or the need of the student to take care of younger siblings or hold a job after school to augment the family income.

Parental Pressure

In his classic work *The Hurried Child,* Elkind (1981) expresses considerable concern about parents who push their children into a veritable merry-go-round of activities: sports, dancing, music, baton lessons, cheerleading, and so on. In school these hurried children are pushed to excel. Thus, they may have tutors—not because of remediation needs but to accelerate progress with good grades, high school honors, and college scholarships as the goal—and they may have parents who do their assignments for them. You will have these students in your classes too.

The Influence of the Media

The media (television, DVDs, computers, computer games, youth magazines, and, to a lesser extent, newspapers) exert considerable influence on the social development of students. Studies show that 50 percent of American children have their own televisions, and they spend five more hours daily watching TV than their peers without private TVs do (Johnson, 2003). All told, the average amount of TV viewing for children is 32 hours a week (National Institute on Media and the Family, in *Principal,* November 2001). The amount of TV viewing varies by ethnic membership (see Figure 12.3). In 2000, 8 percent of Asian/Pacific Islanders watched six or more hours per day. For whites the figure was 13 percent. For Hispanics and American Indians the figures were 22 percent and 23 percent, respectively. For blacks, it was 42 percent with another 8 percent watching five hours a day (Digest of Education Statistics 2001, 2002).

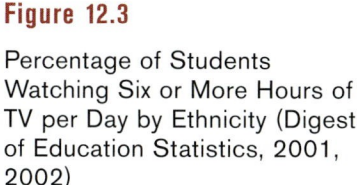

Figure 12.3

Percentage of Students Watching Six or More Hours of TV per Day by Ethnicity (Digest of Education Statistics, 2001, 2002)

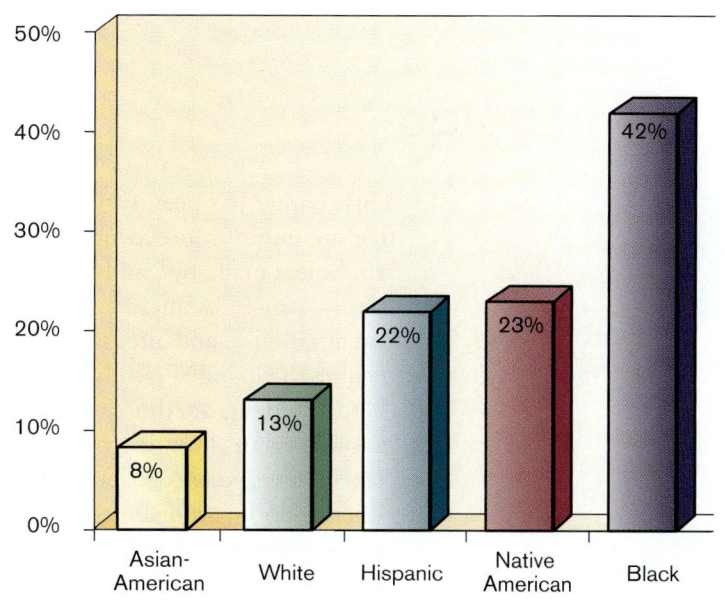

Critics of television programming options (Winn, 2002) note that exposure to excessive violence increases the tendency to deal with problems in negative ways and, along with movies, violent television shows frighten children and even older students (Cantor, 1998). The American Psychological Association (Bickerstaff, 2001) found that by grade 7 the average American has witnessed 8,000 murders and 100,000 violent acts on television. Other criticisms frequently leveled against TV producers are sexually explicit scenes and sexual innuendoes and street language. There is a general recognition that scheduling "adult" programs for late-night viewing does not prevent students from accessing them. Similar comments have been made about the Internet, movies, and DVDs. On the other hand, there is evidence (Collins, 1997) that educational television can increase preschoolers' chances for success in school. This is especially true for *Sesame Street,* which enhances both the academic and social skills of many lower- and middle-class students (Wright & Huston, 1995).

Computer Games

Computer games are often touted as enhancing motor skills while also being criticized as emphasizing destruction of property and annihilation of "the enemy." At their best, computer games are learning devices, but, like so many other aspects of life, the value of the computer games depends upon their careful selection and use. Unfortunately, parents typically do not monitor the media, leaving the ultimate decisions to students who may not be capable of exercising mature judgment about their use.

Social Observances

A brief but fairly intensive set of social influences occurs during the celebration of special events and holidays. Schools often provide useful information at all grade levels about these cultural events, and television does as well. Examples include holidays such as Christmas, Hanukkah, and Kwaanza, and month-long references to the contributions of various groups in society (e.g., Black History Month, Women's History Month, Native American Month, Hispanic American Month). Heroes male and female are often publicized during the associated time period, and students have opportunities to learn about heroes reflecting their culture and the culture of others. One problem is that the consideration of the contributions of people from diverse cultures is too often limited to the month set aside for that discussion.

Conclusion

1. This chapter has been concerned with social issues and socializing influences that are either imposed upon children (e.g., child neglect, homelessness) or are choices made by children (e.g., drug or alcohol abuse, violence).
2. Family structures include the nuclear family, the extended family, single-parent families, and alternative family structures. Alternative structures might include the blended family or families of gay or lesbian parents.
3. At-risk students are those who, for a variety of reasons, statistically have a high probability for dropping out of school. Factors include lack of English proficiency; the presence of a personal disability; school retention; absence of either or both parents in the home; at least one foreign-born parent of recent immigration; the absence of any employed parent or guardian in the household; and low family income.

4. Children living in poverty are much more likely than non-poor children to suffer developmental delay and damage, to drop out of high school, and to give birth during the teen years.

5. Homeless students can have much in common with at-risk children. They often have difficulty in making friends or communicating with adults, feel insecure, often demonstrate low self-esteem, and may find cooperative activities with other students somewhat challenging.

6. The term "child abuse and neglect" means, at a minimum, any recent act or failure to act on the part of a parent or caretaker that results in death, serious physical or emotional harm, sexual abuse, or exploitation, or an act or failure to act that presents an imminent risk of serious harm.

7. Substance abuse most commonly involves alcohol, tobacco, and marijuana. These particular drugs have had a long history as socially acceptable substances and thus children are exposed to a social model that sends mixed messages.

8. School violence refers to aggressive acts against people. School vandalism refers to aggressive or destructive acts toward school property. The cost of school vandalism has been estimated to exceed $600 million.

9. Even with the decline in birth rates among teenage mothers, the incidence of children born to teens is far greater in United States than in other industrialized nations.

10. Suicide is one of the most common teenage problems. After accidents, it is the most frequent cause of death of white males 15–24 years of age and the third leading cause of death for all people in that age bracket.

Key Terms

nuclear family

extended family

latchkey children

blended family

foster care

at-risk students

child abuse and neglect

substance abuse

Educational Engineering

Case Studies in Education

Enter the information from the table below into the Educational Record for the student you are studying.

	Family Life	Socioeconomic Status
Davon	Davon is an affectionate student. He loves hugs and gives compliments frequently. His family life is not secure. He often frets over moving. When he is sick it is difficult to get him picked up from the health room. He is one of five children under the age of seven in his single-parent home.	Davon qualifies for free lunch, which indicates a very low socioeconomic status. His mother does not have a family support system. The grandparents (who are listed on the emergency card) refuse to help with the children due to a problem between Davon's mother and themselves.

Andy	Andy's grandparents are white, middle class, and in their 60s. He attends church once a week and loves spending time with his grandfather. His brother lives with his mother and stepfather. Andy has no memory of his biological father.	Andy is supported entirely by his grandparents. They are considered to be strong and stable members of the community. However, both are retired and they live on a fixed income. Support for a child of Andy's age puts a strain on their resources.
Judith	Judith's family life is stable in that she lives with both parents. Their living conditions would be described as substandard. Her parents are not abusive to Judith or to each other. Yet there is an air of hopelessness and desperation in the family, something Judith struggles with daily.	Judith receives free breakfast and lunch at the school. Both parents are employed at this time, though their employment history is erratic and always characterized by minimum-wage positions.
Tiffany	Tiffany is an only child and has interacted and socialized primarily with adults most of her life. It is important that the teachers do not talk down to Tiffany because she expects to be talked to and treated like an adult. Her emotional maturity level is many years ahead of her peers and she expects to be treated and taught in a respectful, adult way. She rarely understands sarcasm and humor, which leads teachers to be very direct and unfeeling to her. However, Tiffany does not see this action in a negative way and is motivated by this method of conversing.	Tiffany is Caucasian/Hispanic and from an upper-middle-class family of professionals. She is exposed to many cultural events and meets people from prestigious positions in business and government. She receives immediate and appropriate medical care for any circumstance and wants for very little.
Sam	Sam appears to have a supportive family life where there has been nurturing and concern for his well-being as an individual and as a student.	Sam is an African American male who has been reared predominantly by his mother in a low socioeconomic environment. He lacks a background of knowledge and exposure to a variety of experiences that could have served to enrich his educational experiences.
Bao	Bao is the youngest of four children. Her parents are in their 60s, and would be considered detached by American standards. However, most of Bao's emotional needs are met by her older sister (who lives at home while attending college).	Bao's parents are upper-middle class and are able to provide Bao with what she needs for school and activities, and are approachable, kind, and supportive.

1. The issues raised in this chapter are all very delicate. Though matters of family structure and substance abuse do not readily fall under the heading of "education," the schools have become very much involved addressing these concerns. Based on what you have read in the chapter and the information provided about your student, what challenges might you encounter in involving the child's parents in the educational process? In what ways might the child's family life and family structure affect what happens in your classroom? Do you feel that teachers should be expected to accommodate these special needs of students?

2. Socioeconomic status does not dictate how children will behave in class or what their levels of achievement will be. In general, however, it has been shown to be a good predictor of behavior and achievement levels and may help you to tailor the most appropriate educational experience for each child. As soon as you begin observing classrooms as part of your teacher education program you will be able to spot differences in the students' socioeconomic

status. Notice how students interact with each other. How might you establish a classroom as a "socioeconomic-status free" zone that places all students on an equal footing? In particular, how would you address the needs of the student you are following?

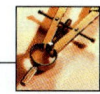

Designing a School of the Future

1. The Case Studies in Education section above mentioned the idea of classrooms as "socioeconomic-status free" zones that level the playing field, so to speak, for all children. The first question that you might address is whether or not this is a good situation. Consider that private schools have a long history of enrollments that are homogeneous in this regard. Many consider that to be elitist. The public schools, of course, must accept all students and thus have a heterogeneous mix of students with regard to socioeconomic status. So, how will your school seek to minimize socioeconomic distinctions (school uniforms are one of the typical approaches to this) or will the emphasis perhaps be on the acceptance of differences and a culture of academic success for all? There are many variations of this that you might consider; it is not a yes-no question.

2. A truly innovative plan for a school of the future will include the explicit involvement of parents and families in the education of each child. There is a tremendous amount of territory between the opposites of *no parent involvement* and *extensive parental control* in education. You might wish to begin your deliberations on this aspect of the school you design by considering the issues presented in this chapter. You will then have to decide which, if any or if all, of the issues should become a responsibility of your school. From there, consider carefully the expectations your school will have of parents, how you could attract parents to participate, what you will do with families that refuse to participate ("Education is your job, not mine; I'm the parent"), and what the outcomes of your new approach might be.

Praxis Practice

Many states will require that you successfully complete the Praxis Series of examinations to qualify for certification. One or more of those tests will be subject-area tests. Another, which has a more practical orientation, will be the Principles of Learning and Teaching (PLT) examination that is appropriate for your certification area.

Completing the Quick Check Quizzes for Chapter 12 in the Unit Workshop will give you practice with the multiple choice format of the PLT. The Case Studies in Education and Designing a School of the Future activities will help prepare you for exercises that require reading a scenario and providing short answers to questions asking what you might do in such a situation.

13

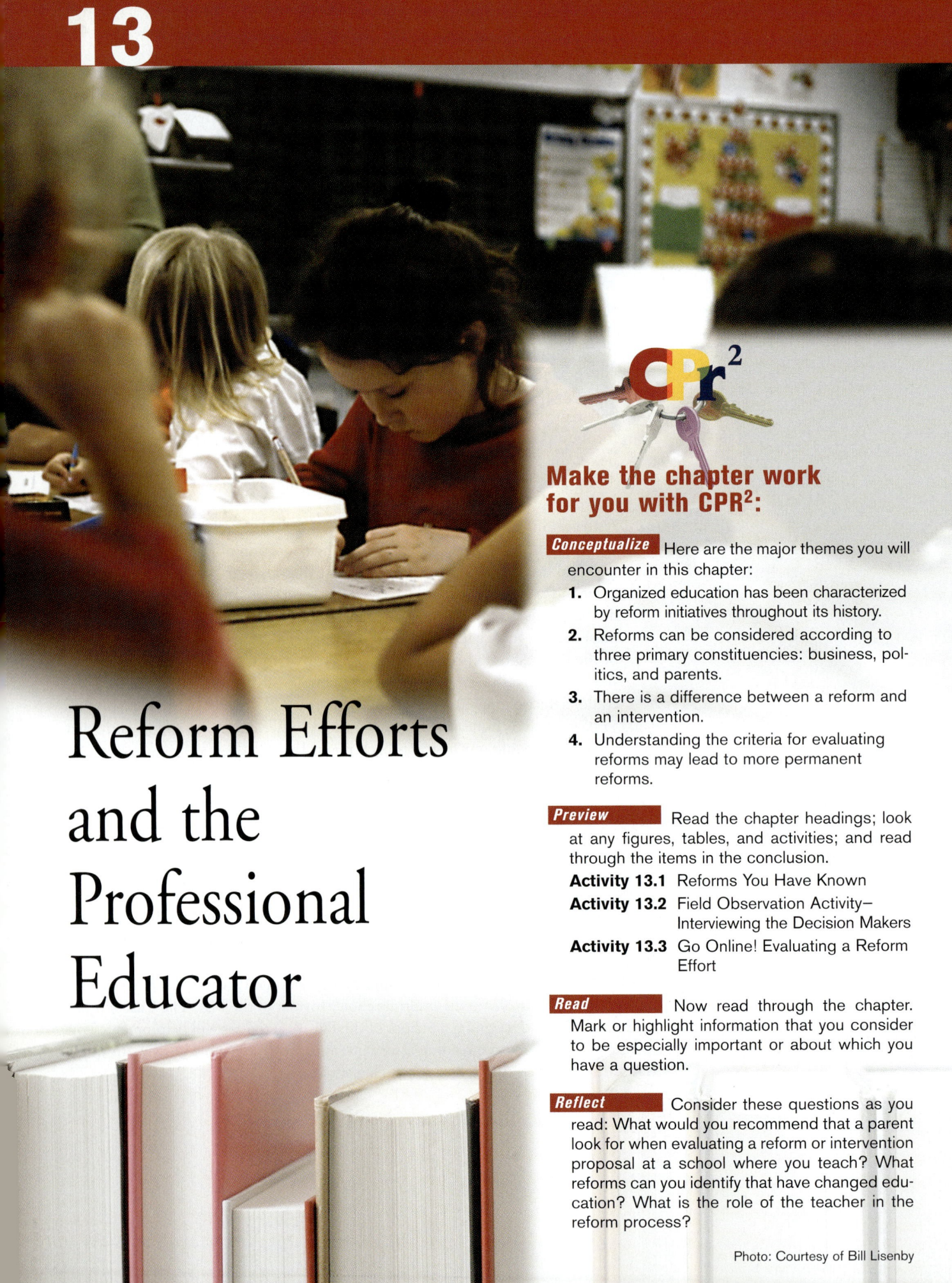

Reform Efforts and the Professional Educator

CPr²

Make the chapter work for you with CPR²:

Conceptualize Here are the major themes you will encounter in this chapter:

1. Organized education has been characterized by reform initiatives throughout its history.
2. Reforms can be considered according to three primary constituencies: business, politics, and parents.
3. There is a difference between a reform and an intervention.
4. Understanding the criteria for evaluating reforms may lead to more permanent reforms.

Preview Read the chapter headings; look at any figures, tables, and activities; and read through the items in the conclusion.

Activity 13.1 Reforms You Have Known
Activity 13.2 Field Observation Activity– Interviewing the Decision Makers
Activity 13.3 Go Online! Evaluating a Reform Effort

Read Now read through the chapter. Mark or highlight information that you consider to be especially important or about which you have a question.

Reflect Consider these questions as you read: What would you recommend that a parent look for when evaluating a reform or intervention proposal at a school where you teach? What reforms can you identify that have changed education? What is the role of the teacher in the reform process?

Photo: Courtesy of Bill Lisenby

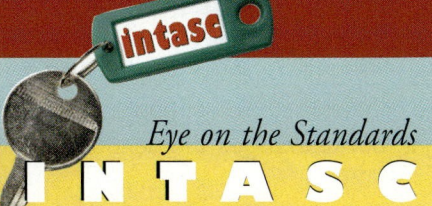

Eye on the Standards
INTASC

ice breakers

Have You Been Reformed?

If you've attended any portion of K–12 education in the United States, it's pretty safe to say that you've been part of one reform initiative or another. This chapter is provided to help you become a participant in "informed reform" rather than being the "target" of reforms without your input.

Below is a double-matching exercise. First, match the reform initiatives on the left with the decade in which they first made it into the school system. Then match each initiative with its type of reform: whether the reform was intended to change *what* is taught (curricular), *how* things are taught (instructional), or how school is *organized or administered* (administrative). You will not use all the time periods, but you will use the reform types more than once.

Initiative	Time Period	Type of Reform	Time Periods	Types of Reform
Block Scheduling	_____	_____	A. 1890s	1. Curricular
Addition of Social Studies	_____	_____	B. 1920s	2. Instructional
Whole Language	_____	_____	C. 1940s	3. Administrative
Open Concept Schools	_____	_____	D. 1950s	
Vocational Education	_____	_____	E. 1960s	
"New Math" and Hands-On Science	_____	_____	F. 1970s	
			G. 1980s	
			H. 1990s	

Block Scheduling	**H. 1990s**	**3. Administrative**

This form of scheduling, particularly in middle schools and high schools, does not change what or how the subjects are taught, but rearranges the school day to provide extended time with each subject.

Addition of Social Studies	**B. 1920s**	**1. Curricular**

The combining of subjects such as geography, history, and political science was first discussed in the late 19th century as a way of making education a "socializing" process. It debuted in the schools in the 1920s.

Whole Language	**G. 1980s**	**2. Instructional**

This effort did not change language or what is taught, but it did change the manner in which language was taught. It has since been modified and has lost some of its momentum as a movement in its own right.

Open Concept Schools	**F. 1970s**	**3. Administrative**

The 1970s saw the construction of many schools adopting the "Open Concept" approach. While content and teaching methods remained essentially the same, the schools themselves were built as large, open rooms—classrooms without walls—that ideally would have led to greater integration of subject areas.

Vocational Education	**A. 1890s**	**1. Curricular**

Following the report of the Committee of Ten in the 1890s, schools ceased to have a purely academic orientation and instead were also charged with providing vocational or manual training particularly to non-college-bound students.

"New Math" and Hands-On Science	**E. 1960s**	**2. Instructional**

The organization of school did not change, nor did the subject area, but the manner in which math and science were taught underwent dramatic changes following the events of the 1950s.

> *If there is a lesson to be learned from the river of ink that was spilled in the education disputes of the twentieth century, it is that anything in education that is labeled a "movement" should be avoided like the plague.*
> *Diane Ravitch (2000, p. 453)*

■ Introduction

Four themes have been woven throughout the narrative in this textbook: establishing a foundation of knowledge about education; development of your critical thinking; development of your creative thinking; and empowering you as a professional educator. This unique chapter on educational reform brings all four of those themes together. In essence, the entire chapter is an activity.

The typical presentation of education reform is another listing of this and that effort or initiative. But as the quotation that begins this chapter indicates, the history of "reform" in education is not one of unqualified successes. We believe that one of the reasons for the poor track record of reforms is that educators—classroom teachers in particular—are often among the targets of reform rather than being among the primary players in the conceptualization, evaluation, and implementation of effective initiatives. This chapter is intended to help make you a qualified and indispensable participant in education improvement efforts.

educational reform The process of improving one or more aspects of education on the local, state, or federal level, either piecemeal or as a total package. It may focus on curriculum or instruction and is usually based on some philosophical perspective.

If you attended a public school in the United States you did so during a period of **educational reform.** That's because, for a variety of reasons, reform in education is an ongoing activity. During the past several decades we have seen the emergence or reemergence of "the new math," phonics, Whole Language, the alphabet programs of science (ESS, S-APA, SCIS), Success for All, Back-to-Basics, change in the role of kindergarten, Progressivism, Behaviorism, Humanism, the Great Books, and vocational education, to name just a few. Carolyn Orange (2002) lists 125 programs that she and her colleagues reviewed as representative of contemporary education. These 125 are the ones they *selected* to review; the list was too long to take on all of them. We want you to understand that reform is not something that happens to you and your work, but instead is an aspect of organized education in which you should be a key participant. Such participation is what would make teaching, and education, a true profession. Throughout your career in education, reform will likely be a part of your professional life.

■ Change and Reform

In virtually all things from academics to Zen, from business to biology, from weather to work, the common denominator is *change.* But when it comes to education the call is not for change, but for reform. The difference between change and reform is that change can be fortuitous, serendipitous, purely accidental, by force of nature, and sometimes by force of will. It can seem good or it can seem bad, can be a consequence of our actions or a goal toward which our actions are directed. People don't always embrace change, but it is something we can live with and in fact is something we occasionally look forward to. It's actually the one thing we can count on. As Heraclitus taught, the only constant is change.

Reform, however, is always initiated out of dissatisfaction. Rarely, if ever, do folks sit around and think of ways to reform things that are paying handsome dividends and going really well. On the contrary, reform is something done because people don't like what is happening. It is difficult to find any period in the history of education in our country during which time someone did not have some complaint about "school." Dissatisfaction has historically been the impetus for change, and reform has been the mechanism of choice.

Dissatisfaction still exists despite all sorts of reform efforts, and current dissatisfaction is voiced over the *reforms themselves.* There are many poignant questions in need of answers when reforms fail to live up to their claims. Who made these apparently ill-informed decisions? Where was everybody when education became secular rather than a matter of religious indoctrination? Where were the mothers and fathers when the common school shifted parental responsibility from *educating* their children to seeing that their children *received* an education? Where were the legions of educators when the "progressivists" accomplished their coup d'état over the "traditionalists" in the early 20th century? Who stood in the schoolhouse doorway when the innovators and interventionists came along and challenged the curriculum? How can "Dick and Jane" be icons of American education *and* be the poster children of what many consider to be all that is wrong with reading education (that is, the replacement of phonics with the "look-say" method, a precursor to "Whole Language")? Where were the accomplished teachers, at any point in our history, who backed up their work by demonstrating that all children *were* learning under their tutelage? And where was business throughout all of this?

What happened in the 20th century was that "reform" came of age as the "reform model." That is, reform itself became part of the institution of education. The people who did show up for and otherwise influenced school board meetings and conferences made reforming the school into a business. As parents and other citizens backed away and let the institution run itself, "reform" became a vague term that could mean virtually anything from "back-to-basics" to the new frontier. The model provided sponsorship opportunities for business with no particular regard for outcomes, and a bottomless well of "research" opportunities for higher education, again without any particular need to dwell on the outcomes—for if this reform doesn't work, something else can always be tried. As Tyack and Cuban (1995) note, reforms often are add-ons to current programs rather than changes that transform.

The questions that needed answers in the past are the same questions that need answering today. Issues such as whether nonnative speakers of English should be taught to read and write in English *before* doing other coursework (which would be conducted in English) are still unresolved. Do *any* non-college-bound children need an academic education? Should everybody have a liberal arts education? These questions were and still are at the heart of what constitutes the American culture and where that culture wants to go. Unfortunately for the progressivists, and the traditionalists before them, the function of school in our unique democratic society has never been defined. That lack of definition, along with all of the other factors at work over the years (any time) has resulted in what Ravitch (2001) refers to as 100 years of failure in educational reform.

The accessibility to educational policy making that people in our society enjoy brings with it responsibility. We all have an appropriate part to play in determining the goals and objectives of formal schooling. But people need to take part in an *informed* capacity. We all need to be at the meeting if education is going to continue to function with considerable local control. Let's not confine ourselves to the reform model as we become change agents, but for now let's take a look at the reform model itself, reform and intervention efforts, and how to evaluate reforms and interventions that are being used in, or considered for, your local school. You could begin this process by using Activity 13.1 to find out what some professionals in education can tell you about the reform efforts they have witnessed.

ACTIVITY 13.1
Reforms You Have Known

For this activity consider the schools you have attended, or work with a local school. If your teacher education program includes spending time observing in a local school, that would be ideal for this exercise. Make an appointment to speak with a teacher or the principal and ask the following questions:

1. What have been the most effective reform efforts in the school in the past five years? Examples might include site-based management, outcome-based education (OBE), single-gender classes, coed PE, reading programs, and inquiry-based science. There are many possibilities.

2. Which of those that the teacher/principal lists does she still expect to see in place five years from now?

3. What makes some reforms succeed and others fail?

■ The Reform Model

The educational leaders of the early 20th century often made the claim that theirs was a *scientific* approach to social progress through the schools. But the emphasis on schools as the solution to social problems resulted in losing sight of the fact that the "science" of education was in the *pedagogy of learning,* not in schools as the instrument of social progress.

Nonetheless, a reading of the history of education in our country can leave one with the idea that educational reform was the headline in every newspaper across the country from 1900 to the late 1930s. The sense is given that heated and intellectually stimulating debate was provided every Saturday evening so that the townsfolk could consider the latest commentary of Dewey, Bode, or Bagley. The impression is made that children across the country were throwing their old textbooks out of the classroom windows and settling into discussion circles to consider what "worthy home-membership" meant. But this was not the case. These were essentially discussions among academicians, educational administrators, business leaders, and politicians. School today is largely the same as school was hundreds of years ago with two major exceptions: Reform is now part of the institution of education (a big and powerful academic, economic, and political part), and somewhere along the way a cohesive American culture was lost. Let's consider four aspects of the **reform model** that have an effect on education: higher education, business, politics, and parents.

reform model A model developed and instituted to implement a philosophical and educational perspective about how best to achieve the goals of the school and community.

higher education Any postsecondary education (e.g., community college, junior college, four-year college or university, graduate school).

Higher Education: The Reform Model Finds a Home

Higher education, as the gatekeeper of knowledge, has been associated with organized education from its inception. Scholars had long been the disseminators of knowledge and acted as curriculum consultants, but as primary and secondary education became an institution of society, the new academic discipline of *pedagogy,* the study of the teaching of children, emerged within the context of higher education. Departments of education were opened in colleges and universities for the preparation of teachers and the study of teaching and learning. Today, as part of their professional responsibilities, college and university professors are involved in everything from the academic content of instruction and the pedagogical "science" of teaching to the preparation of teachers and administrators to the writing of textbooks. Though steadfastly maintaining their autonomy from the K–12 organization, departments and schools of education are nonetheless components of the overall institution of education.

Despite this close relationship, an atmosphere of animosity often exists (at least in the larger institutional sense) between the schools and the scholars. Certainly healthy and productive relationships do exist as well, but one need not look very hard to find those who argue that higher education's "ivory tower" perspective does not understand the work of classroom educators. Many teachers would say that colleges and universities preparing new teachers are far removed from the realities of the classroom. Elaine McEwan (1998) suggests that professors "are protecting their own self-interests: tenure, opportunities to publish, and the golden-carrots of government-funded research" (68). To her credit, McEwan does not place *all* of the blame for failing schools on higher education, but she does suggest that the tertiary influence is just as harmful as it is helpful. To a degree she is correct, though at the same time professors complain that despite all of their efforts to teach new instructional techniques, student teachers and first-year teachers wind up teaching in the same traditional manner as their supervisors and induction-year mentors.

Because school reform is inevitable, teachers should strive to be active participants in educational change.

Courtesy of Bill Lisenby

It is true that professors seek tenure and that government-funded research is one of the avenues for publications. Tenure does protect an atmosphere conducive to the free exchange of ideas, a condition that is essential if one is to question the status quo. Further, government funding of research does facilitate investigation in academics and pedagogy that otherwise would not be possible. In fact, the "publish or perish" pressure that untenured professors face can even be said to force the development of new ideas and new understanding. So these are not necessarily bad things. The problem arises because the reform model that has evolved operates in the absence of what Senge (1990) refers to as a *shared vision.* The various groups within education are not necessarily at cross purposes but simply have never come together to define a *common* purpose.

What has resulted is a system that trades on reform. Professors and graduate students do research and develop programs based upon their research because that's what higher education folks do. Some of that work shows up as new programs to be tried in the schools while other work serves to clear a bit more of the path along the way to new insights and new instructional techniques. Government agencies fund research and facilitate work that otherwise could not be done, but at the same time they are hesitant to continue funding the *same* research. They want to see new and different ideas developed. Therefore, it is not at all surprising to find a lack of continuity, but it is easy to see the emergence of the reform model. Since there is no real definition of what the schools are supposed to accomplish (academic education? character education? democratic education? individualized education?), there is no need to *focus* all of these efforts, and dollars, toward a common goal. Thus all research is viable, all reform efforts are legitimate (if the current climate is accepting), and, despite the fact that nothing really changes, it always *looks* like something is happening. That perception is enough to satisfy the current generation of reformers. The model perpetuates reform for reform's sake.

Business: Who Will Blink First?

Another force that has a reform-based impact on education can be categorized generically as *business.* Given its prominence in a capitalist economy, business has never failed to make its interests known nor to miss an opportunity to direct the course of events. In matters such as primary and secondary education, business quietly influences change. Business is very much a part of what is right *and* wrong with the institution of education because it influences education in three ways: tax funding, involvement, and demands. Our intent is not to indict business. However, it is important to realize how business affects education with regard to the reform model.

Tax Funding

Perhaps most apparent in the consideration of business and education is that business can significantly affect a school district through the tax base that it provides. A community with no business presence (that is, something of the corporate variety that employs many people) will not receive significant local tax revenue to supplement the base funding supplied by the state. This effect trickles down to the salaries that can be paid for teachers and other personnel, the sophistication of instructional equipment that can be purchased, and the amount of supplies that can be kept on hand. One cannot fault business, per se, for this situation. However, this built-in disparity between school districts virtually breeds reform initiatives.

Involvement

Involvement in the educational enterprise—apart from taxes—is a second significant business activity. What we refer to here is sponsorship, grant funding, and scholarships. Let's begin with sponsorship. It is not uncommon, at an athletic event at a local school, to find that the scoreboard has been donated by business concerns. Logos representing everything from shoes to soft drinks are prominently displayed. It can be argued that without such "sponsorship" (it's really advertising space rather than sponsorship) those scoreboards would not be there at all. But if business was truly *supporting* the school rather than simply using it as an advertising venue, there would have been no need to include the corporate crest on the board. For as important a concern as public education, it may be worth questioning the motives of those funding sources and watching to see who blinks first: Will parents and schools refuse the money if it represents selling advertising space, or will business decide that philanthropy is not in their best interests? One thing we can tell you is that the existence of Chris Whittle's Channel One, which brings video advertising to millions of students at the beginning of each school day, suggests that the parents and schools blinked first.

Just one-third of this sign is devoted to the community and the achievement of its football team. Would businesses sponsor their communities and schools without the advertising opportunity? What do you think about that?

© Kari Goodnough/Bloomberg News/Landov

Involvement also takes the form of grant funding. Many large corporations contribute millions of dollars to education in the form of research grants to colleges and universities. To their credit, these foundations support a wide range of studies—though each, legitimately enough, may impose various restrictions and requirements. Also worthy of mention is that not a lot of fanfare is made with regard to these grants. Of course they are of great importance in the academic world, but companies rarely seem to trumpet their grant-funding activities to the general public. Then again, it is also not surprising that the range of projects that get funded—given the millions upon millions of dollars made available—lack a common focus. We don't mean to imply that all researchers should be studying the same thing, but one would expect that given all of the money spent on educational research through corporate grant funding alone, greater strides in pedagogy would have been made by now. Yet Horace Mann's call in the mid-19th century for the need to disseminate a common culture is repeated in the 21st century, and John Dewey's emphasis on solving real problems as part of education, suggested in the early years of the 20th century, still rings true. What progress, one might ask, has reform made?

Demands

Finally, there are the demands of business. That business sees the schools as the source of its future labor force is good. That business sees the *purpose* of school as preparing people for work is philosophically troubling. That the reform model has turned schools into the training programs for business is less than good. The return that business wants for its philanthropic and tax dollars is a competent, capable, and *trained* workforce. The reform model not only provides this training but allows schools to shift gears with the changing demands of the work environment.

What is especially interesting about the entire notion of school as a training ground for workers is that organized education originally took children away from job training and apprenticeships. Yet the paradigm shift that introduced "practical studies" to organized education goes back as far as the introduction of English grammar schools in the 1700s to counterbalance the academic orientation of the Latin grammar schools. Throughout the 1800s the debate continued over whether vocational training had a place in the public schools until the city of Baltimore opened the first public manual training high school in 1884. Since that time vocational education has soared. A contemporary high school is likely to have a sprawling vocational education program, wing, or building providing job training in everything from woodshop to fast-food-restaurant worker.

Today one will *not* hear a cry from business that schools should produce liberally educated young men and women that it can then train to do the work it needs done. Instead you will hear business demand that vocational education shift its focus to a greater degree on computer technology training. Years ago the emphasis was on manual and clerical skills. Years from now it will likely shift to biotechnology, and perhaps eventually to something such as laser-based teleportation devices that facilitate global or galactic business enterprise. What is lost along the way? Lost along the way is Aristotle's contention that our purpose as *human beings* is to think and through that thinking to understand our world. In its place is the idea that our purpose is to facilitate business.

Politics: The Assumption of Expertise

Business is all about profit, but politicians control the purse strings when it comes to education. There's good and bad news that goes along with that. The bad news is that there never seems to be enough money. The good news is that *money is not necessarily education's biggest problem.* That statement may seem counter to what you typically hear about education. This is not to say that education has all the money it needs, and certainly is not meant to encourage legislators to cut education budgets even further, but simply suggests that more money will not necessarily solve the problems of public education.

Consider that across the country during the 2000–2001 school year the combined spending of all states for elementary and secondary education was over *$400 billion* (Digest of Education Statistics, 2003, 2004). Education is typically the most expensive line item in a state budget. South Carolina, a relatively small state, spent in excess of $5.5 billion in school year 2000–2001 for elementary and secondary education (Digest of Education Statistics, 2003, 2004). California spent more than $50 billion dollars (Digest of Education Statistics, 2003, 2004). Again, this is just for elementary and secondary education; when public higher education is included, expenditures in these two states is on the order of $7 billion and $63 billion a year respectively.

In 2003, the federal government's on-budget funds for education (which is distributed across many agencies) topped *$124 billion* (Digest of Education Statistics, 2003, 2004), which comes in fourth after defense, welfare, and interest paid on the national debt. The national average for current expenditures per student per year based on these figures is approximately $8,000. A teacher with a second-grade class of 25 students is staring at approximately $200,000 worth of funding. This is a simplification to be sure, but we all must be aware that there *is* money going to education. The question is, *where* is it going and *why*? In the final analysis the money must be going either to maintain the program that exists or to reform it. This paradox of reforming what we also support is characteristic of the reform model.

With all of the money going to education, one would think educators would get to decide how to spend it. But "politics" is a term that describes the nebulous give-and-take of the legislative process. It is a process carried out by people who try to resolve a mind-boggling array of issues. It would not be uncommon for a legislator to encounter, in a single day, issues regarding grain subsidies, environmental impact debates, nuclear fuel and weapons concerns, the ethical ramifications of cloning, and . . . whether or not to approve funds for all-day kindergarten. The scope of the task, let alone the details, can be overwhelming.

The ideological umbrella of "politics" somehow makes this system of policy development and decision making acceptable even though no other social concern would ever operate in such a manner. Does the medical community come to elementary school teachers for advice on how to provide health services? Did Enron? Does Boeing ask a wheat farmer for decisions on the design of new aircraft? Does the wheat farmer ask Boeing for agricultural advice? Has the fire department come to you and asked which equipment would be best to purchase for the station house? Certainly not—because these decisions require expertise that only experts are legitimately expected to have. That's what makes them experts. But in politics there is the *assumption* of expertise.

Given the range of issues with which politicians are involved, it is virtually impossible for them to devote time toward understanding what Bruner (1960) referred to as the "structure" of education. Certainly these men and women can come to grips with the surface issues swirling around some school topic, but it is patently unreasonable to expect that they could, *or should,* have a conceptual grasp of the deeper structure of education (which includes its mission, objectives, pedagogy, techniques, facilities, ancillary responsibilities, credentialing, funding needs, support services, and cultural impact). The political perspective of education is typically a superficial perspective simply due to the nature of politics.

One might expect that political leaders would turn specifically to those who do have an understanding of the structure of education for advice. But that's not how the model works. Have you ever heard someone in politics include the phrase "When I was in school . . ." when talking about what to do with education? Sure, many people say this, but when it's mentioned by someone in politics there is particular reason to be concerned. That's because "when I was in school" is offered as some sort of indicator of valid experience for teaching or administering school when in fact it is only representative of what it was like for that person to be a student. It makes no more sense than to walk down to the local hospital and offer your advice about how the facility should function: "Well, when *I* was sick . . ."

In 1887 John Dalberg wrote, "Power tends to corrupt, and absolute power corrupts absolutely." Fortunately, our discussion is not going to take on the topic of possible corruption in politics, business, or higher education. But we suggest that the nature of politics is such that the power to make and enact decisions breeds an assumption of expertise on the part of the decision maker. Particularly with regard to education, an experience that virtually all adult members of the society share, the result is that decisions are often made by people with a minimal understanding of the *structure* of education, with little thought toward an articulated purpose of the institution, and even less consideration for the long-term effects of those decisions. Yet the reform model is able to accommodate this situation because politicians control the funding.

Parents

It can certainly be argued that parents find a comfortable fit with the reform model because most are committed to educational reform only while their children are in school. It would also be fairly safe to say that many parents are concerned with *their* child in school rather than with *all* children in school across the state and nation. Further, simply by virtue of having attended school, many parents are guilty of the same assumption of expertise that we spoke of before. The reform model fits.

There has been ample opportunity for parents to form a collaborative relationship with the schools. Parents have historically been afforded access to the rhyme and reason of schooling but they have consistently remained at arm's length. The tendency is to complain about what bothers them. Yet at the same time parents are willing to turn as much parental responsibility over to the school as possible. For instance, one study shows that high school parents tend to be as disconnected from the school as their sons and daughters are (Newman, 1997–1998). Another study indicates that 50 percent of all parents have no rules about what television programs their children can watch (Hymowitz, 2001), which has the potential for exposing students to a host of negative influences that show up as inappropriate behavior while at school. The schools are specifically charged with protecting the safety and health of students while in attendance, a condition referred to as *in loco parentis*—in the place of parents. Even organizations such as the PTO/PTA (Parent Teacher Organization/Association) have failed to live up to their potential. McEwan (1998) does not spare them from her disdain for professional organizations when she writes, "In many local districts, the PTA is merely a giant group of cheerleaders and fundraisers for the administration" (71). Parent involvement in the success of organized education is a key to our social and cultural future. But at the same time the reform model supports the short-range, "while my child is in school" perspective typical of parents.

The reform model does, as we have seen, manage to keep all constituencies occupied in such a way as to make them think that substantive changes are occurring. The interesting conclusion, after looking over the history of education in our country, is that very little has changed. A clear example is the current trend toward single-gender schools. As we saw in Chapter 8, it took hundreds of years to win equal educational opportunities for females and to overcome the doctrine of "separate but equal." Yet in the early 21st century we find a movement toward separate but equal and various forms of segregation. That is why we believe it is very important for teachers to understand more about reforms, to be proactive rather than reactive to them, and to know how to evaluate them with an educator's perspective. Activity 13.2 is included to provide you with an opportunity to interview some of the decision makers in education reform.

■ A Brief Look at Some Reforms and Interventions

There are hundreds, and likely thousands, of educational reform or improvement programs in the schools across the country today. If school has closed down for the summer, administrators, teachers, professors, graduate students, parents, and business leaders are now sorting through the results of last year's programs and planning what will be done next year. Grants are being written and the logistics of implementation are being laid out. Reform can sometimes appear to be as big an undertaking as the whole of the educational institution.

Any outline of the various programs affecting the nation's schools would have to be highly selective. Further, naming the "top 10" reform efforts would be virtually impossible, because any program is a function of the particular needs of the particular school. Perhaps the reading curriculum in your local school is simply fantastic but science is in need of attention. In another school the situation could be the reverse. Therefore, what we want to do is offer some distinctions between reform efforts and provide an example of each. When you start to visit schools or

 Field Observation

ACTIVITY 13.2   Interviewing the Decision Makers

This activity is included to help you broaden your perspective of education beyond children and teachers in the school. If you do this activity as a group, each member of the group could be responsible for interviewing one person.

Identify one individual to interview about education for each of these five categories: (1) Higher education (a professor or dean would be a good choice, and she does not have to be in the college/department of education), (2) classroom teacher, (3) someone from the business community, (4) a politician on the local, state, or federal level (don't be afraid to write a letter to your state senators and representatives), and (5) parents. Ask each of these people the following questions:

1.   What do you expect from the schools? What should the schools accomplish?

2.   If you could change one thing about education, what would it be?

3.   How much of today's issues in education is related to money?

Consider their responses:
- What common themes, if any, did you find?
- How do the opinions differ?
- What are the implications for the work of a classroom teacher?

talk with educators, board members, and perhaps politicians in your community, you will be able to start organizing what you hear to better understand just what is going on.

We will look at two versions of educational initiatives in particular: *reform* and *intervention*. A reform is a program that seeks to replace some aspect of the current educational operation. It could be a matter of philosophy, administrative style, curriculum, instruction, or conceptualization. In any case, what has been done up until the point of the reform effort will be eliminated and something new will take its place. For example, the look-say method (Dick and Jane) replaced the phonics approach in many schools. Individual schools did not provide phonics to some children and look-say to others; instead, they reformed their reading instruction program by replacing one approach with the other.

intervention An education effort that supplements normal procedure either by providing remediation or enrichment or by extending or reducing a teacher's responsibility or authority (as in a pull-out program).

An **intervention** is some effort that supplements normal procedure either by providing remediation or enrichment or by extending or reducing responsibility or authority. Interventions typically are in response to some specific need, and though they can be a permanent change they often do not have the intended longevity of a reform. Programs that pull specified children out for remedial reading instruction exemplify an intervention. The regular reading program has not been replaced, and the child's remediation can be discontinued if she improves her reading ability. The same is true of enrichment programs.

Reforms

If you read in the newspaper that the test scores in your district were very low and so the superintendent has recommended changing to a new reading instruction program, then the message is that the curriculum is in need of reform. If you hear terms such as "state systemic initiative" you know that reform is on somebody's mind. If your local newscast mentions that the school is going to adopt an "open concept" approach to teaching, you know that one instructional approach is going to be replaced by another. Here are some more examples across several categories.

Curricular Reform

curricular reform An education reform based on the development or adoption of the content to be taught at various points in a student's educational experience. The content is organized in grade-level standards.

You have very likely heard that your state has adopted curriculum benchmarks, frameworks, or standards for each of the subject areas taught in the school. This represents a **curriculum reform** because it involves determining what students will learn. Even more to the point, these efforts revolve around establishing standards—that is, the minimum learning expectations for all children. Benchmarks typically spell out the hierarchy of knowledge and skills for which students are responsible at each grade level. See Appendix D, State Departments of Education, for addresses and URLs to help you find the standards for your state.

Instructional Reform

instructional reform An educational reform based on a set of coordinated and differentiated strategies (both diagnostic and instructional) by which teachers and students address the curriculum.

Instructional reform programs seek to find better ways of teaching information, particularly in view of student diversity. An example is the Whole Language approach to reading instruction. Some might argue that this represents a curriculum issue rather than instructional reform. We consider it instructional reform because in terms of what is happening to the student, it is simply a matter of how she eventually gets to the point of reading. Another approach to reading instruction (if we look at reading instruction in very broad terms) is phonics. A third approach is comprehension-based; that is, the content is taught from a reasoning and thinking perspective.

Our discussion of educational history noted that the "look-say" method of reading instruction replaced the phonics approach in many public schools. Whole Language is an approach to reading that extends the "look-say" method. The idea is that rather than breaking reading down into component skills and discrete sounds (phonemes) that are then reassembled to make up words, language is left intact—whole—and learned in a context of authentic literacy events. Proponents argue that people learn language in this way and so should learn to read this way as well. Opponents believe that this leads to guessing at the meaning of words and problems with spelling. The division between phonics folks and Whole Language folks is often a sharp one, so tread carefully but deliberately when investigating these orientations. And remember that the purpose of reading (a reading book or a social studies text or a newspaper) is to construct meaning, not just memorize words or produce sounds.

Class size is another example of an instructional reform effort. In this case, the content of what students are taught is not changed, but the number of students in the class at one time is decreased. The long-held idea is that smaller class sizes would yield greater academic achievement. Unfortunately, some efforts have failed to find the right combination of several factors. Achilles et al. (2002) suggests that the key is not just in the number of students. He and his colleagues indicate that three conditions must be met for effectively using smaller class sizes:

1. *Early intervention.* Students start schooling in small classes in kindergarten or prekindergarten.
2. *Duration.* Students are in small classes for at least three, and preferably four, years.
3. *Intensity.* Students are in small classes all day, every day. (p. 25)

Even more unfortunate is that when tough economic times show up, small class size is considered a luxury that the district cannot afford. In this case, the concept of the reform may be legitimate pedagogically, but the difficulty was in the effective implementation.

Class size is an example of instructional reform because there is no effect on what is taught, only how it is taught. The long-held idea is that smaller class sizes would yield greater academic achievement.

Administrative and Conceptual Reform

Rather than focusing on what is taught (curricular reform) or how it is taught (instructional reform), administrative and conceptual reforms address the organization and operation of schools. For example, these could include the governance structure within a school or the manner in which students are grouped for instruction.

One of the most pressing reform issues is likely that of multiculturalism. You will find that virtually all subjects can now be taught from a "multicultural" perspective (e.g., Robertta Barba's *Science in the Multicultural Classroom: A Guide to Teaching and Learning,* 1995). Proponents suggest that multicultural education provides children with a respect and appreciation of the world's cultural diversity. Though as with any issue, there are other perspectives. For example, one could certainly ask at what age children are prepared to understand and appreciate cultural differences and global community membership. The answer is not so much a matter of a given age, but rather

Courtesy of Guilherme Cunha

Teacher Testimonial

Feature 13.1   Education Reform and the Teacher

It was 1957 when the Soviet Union beat the USA into space with Sputnik. Those were some scary times in the world. At noon, every Saturday, the wail of a siren would pierce the quiet, reminding everyone that nuclear missiles were pointed in our direction. Education suddenly became a matter not of reading, writing, and arithmetic but of national defense. What was wrong with the United States? Why were our children so backward that the Soviets could beat us into space with the first satellite?

The response to Sputnik obviously was not the start of school reform in the United States (John Dewey's ideas predate that period by nearly five decades) but it is my first recollection of the "reform movement." However, the emphasis on national defense in the reform movement lasted for quite some time, providing National Defense Student Loans (NDSL) for many first-generation American college students. I took advantage of that opportunity, and it took me a lot of years to pay my NDSL loan back after graduation.

It is pretty safe to observe that the concept of reforming our American education system is not a new idea. You may not know it, but during your years in K–12 education there were many new programs, changes in teaching techniques and materials, scheduling experiments, and curriculum adjustments going on. Some things worked and some did not. But when it comes to an institution that is so important not only to our national defense but to our national character, it is probably good that we are continually viewing a variety of ideas. I knew a corporate CEO who constantly admonished the employees in his worldwide company to continue improving. His mantra was, "When you stop getting better, you stop being good." The continuing push for education reform, or school reform, or classroom reform, should be viewed as a major benefit to those whose goal it is to be the best possible classroom teacher, because it can help them to keep getting better.

From John Dewey to Maria Montessori, from phonics to Whole Language, from Open Education to State

a function of the manner in which multiculturalism becomes a part of the greater educational fabric.

Today, multiculturalism *as a reform movement* is well-intentioned though still in its formative stages and lacking in cohesive goals. While educators such as McEwan (1998) may question just how much the movement contributes to academic learning in the schools, you might be able to see a parallel with another reform movement. The Progressivism that we described in Chapter 9, elements of which remain evident today, stalled as a movement because even its staunchest proponents were divided as to what progressivism represented and sought to accomplish. James A. Banks, who may be to multiculturalism what John Dewey was to Progressivism at its beginnings, recognizes multicultural education as "an idea, an educational reform movement, and a process" (1997b). It takes time, of course, for an ideology to develop and coalesce, and this is the task that multiculturalism faces early in the 21st century. Which brings us back to the question of what the schools are supposed to accomplish. Do you see how important these questions have become?

Interventions

The previous examples were classified as reforms because they sought to replace one perspective, approach, or curriculum with another. Interventions seek to, well, intervene. Though an intervention can be intended as a short-term remedy for a specific problem (e.g., supplementing a child's regular mathematics instruction), it can also be a program added to the curriculum with a long-term perspective.

Standards, there are nuggets of educational gold; in some cases, golden hills. As the leader in your classroom you will continually look for ways to help better engage, enliven, and educate your students. Reading the literature accompanying the current reform movements will help you uncover tactics that may work for you. Involving yourself in the staff development that is steering you into the newest solution to the continuing educational crisis will help you maintain your understanding of those with whom you are building your daily learning community.

As an educator you will also continue to be assaulted by those who can identify the problems with our schools and those who fervently believe they carry the solutions. Be grateful for their presence. Their caring, their concern, their calls for change are all a reaffirmation that you, as an educator, are at the center of the community; working daily to shape the lives of those who will eventually shape our world.

I would like to encourage you to also look at education reform in a broader picture. That is, rather than thinking of it as "Reform" with a capital R—something that overtakes an entire school or district—think of it also as the continual reforming of your own skills and techniques. When it comes to educational reform not everyone needs to be a trailblazer. Read, reason, and respond in the way that makes the most sense for the learning community that is your classroom. It is your own professional development and openness to new ideas that will have the most immediate effect on the way your students learn.

Richard Puffer is currently a professor of communications and the director of the Byerly Foundation, a nonprofit organization that funds educational improvement initiatives. He has served as the public relations director of a major international corporation and was a school board president during the difficult years following the end of segregation in our public schools. ■

Enrichment programs under the heading of *gifted and talented* are an example. In this case the regular school program remains intact, but special opportunities are available to students who qualify for the experiences. Interventions typically *supplement* rather than *supplant*.

Curricular Intervention

The multicultural movement falls under the heading of administrative and conceptual reforms because it seeks to change the tone of the entire curriculum. By contrast, *character education*, as an example, is an intervention designed to supplement the curriculum with experiences not addressed in the explicit curriculum. The curriculum remains intact, and experiences, such as character education terms posted on a classroom wall each day, are presented to the students.

Though the topic of character education is as current as they come, it is a debate that can be traced back at least 100 years in American education. In the tumultuous 1920s and 1930s, John Dewey was a strong advocate for character education. His suggestions were negated by educational research at the time that indicated that character education did not significantly affect children's behavior. The years since have caused considerable pause for reflection.

Chief among the problems facing character education efforts today, whether formal packaged programs or locally fashioned efforts, is the difficulty in defining just what sort of character should be educated. Concerned about the lack of civility in much of society, Burns (2003) suggests that teachers begin with manners and describes how he developed them in his classes. Thomas Lickona (2000) suggests a program directed toward core ethical values. The various constituencies disagree as to what character traits would constitute such values, and there is an ongoing fervent debate as to whether the school should be responsible for teaching them. It is not at all plausible to argue *against* character education, and many would argue that providing a value-free educational system would be impossible. Personal interaction necessarily involves the communication of value statements. What are our common core values? Are they honesty, telling the truth, respecting others regardless of racial or ethnic backgrounds—the values considered appropriate or highly appropriate by 95 percent of the general public in one research study (Schaeffer, 1997–1998)? Are there others? If so, what are they?

Instructional Intervention

An example of instructional intervention that is widely used and may well be in place in your local school (either as the formal package or as a variation of it) is Reading Recovery. This program was developed in New Zealand and introduced to the United States in 1974 through the National Reading Recovery Center at Ohio State University. The program provides one-on-one reading remediation with a whole-language orientation to the bottom 10–20 percent of first graders. It is a pull-out program that requires a contractual agreement with the parents of children enrolled to provide support for the activities.

Reviews of the program (Northwest Regional Educational Laboratory, 1998; McEwan, 1998; Orange, 2002) acknowledge both the effectiveness of the program and its staggering costs. Orange and McEwan add that questions have been raised about the reporting of the results; neither author discounts that the program can be successful, but both suggest that credibility could be an issue. Finally, though not the fault of the program developers or those who implement it, one must wonder if there is not another question to be addressed if significant numbers of children who have just started school are candidates for a "recovery" program.

Administrative and Conceptual Intervention

Another intervention that has become quite popular in recent years is that of "mentoring." We have included it under the heading of Administrative and Conceptual Intervention because teacher-to-teacher mentoring is administrative and student mentoring is conceptual—that is, the focus is on socioemotional development rather than academic instruction.

Sweeney (1990) identifies five forms of mentorship with regard to induction-year teachers: orientation, collaboration, sharing, jointly solving a problem, and encouragement. Similarly, a mentor teacher may assist a beginning teacher through the stages that Wong (1991) identifies: fantasy, survival, mastery, and impact. In any case, mentoring programs are designed to intervene at this critical time for the express purpose of improving the transition to the classroom so that the student's educational opportunity is not compromised by the teacher's instructional inexperience.

Mentoring programs can also be established for students. A mentor relationship is not the same as the relationship between student and teacher. There is less formality to the mentorship than in the traditional instructional setting. For this reason, mentorship programs can be an effective utilization of parental and community involvement. The typical stumbling blocks to a sound mentorship program in this regard are the failure of schools to provide adequate training for the volunteers and that ever-present nemesis in education: the failure to clearly articulate the goals and objectives of the program. This becomes particularly problematic with the use of volunteers because "mentoring" becomes synonymous with "buddy," and that is not what a mentoring program is about.

What Makes a Reform Effort Exemplary?

In the previous section of this chapter we discussed reforms and interventions that have already occurred. As you can see, such initiatives are everywhere out there. Even more important is that there are scores of "unofficial" interventions as well. By unofficial we mean those that may have been established in a local school (these are typically confined to a single school rather than being a district-wide program) between teachers and community members, such as parents of children attending that school. Though these are not always without merit, it is unlikely that such efforts will have a sound research base, a proven record of success, a plan for accurately assessing educational impact, and a team of credentialed individuals. These efforts are high on good intentions—and may even produce some positive results—but they are not sound elements of pedagogy, and yet other people's children are involved. When you examine such programs with the guidelines we provide next, you will be able to determine which, if any, deserve your support.

Now we take the bold step of addressing the question, "What can I do about influencing reform?" In particular, we want to take the perspective of you as a teacher, a credentialed professional in the classroom. In addition, being an informed participant in the process will be an important contribution that you can make as an adult who pays taxes, and perhaps as a parent with a child in the public schools. So, we present it here as a challenge to you: as a teacher, a citizen, a parent, an administrator—use the information that follows to empower your informed participation in the progress of school.

The review approach that we offer here has three major categories:

1. The Need for the Program
2. The Nature of the Program
3. Implementation

This is not intended as a simple-to-use five-minute checklist of educational reform. What follows will require you to develop your critical thinking skills. You may be using this format for considering a program that will cost your district millions of dollars over some number of years or a program that the teacher of your first-grade child would like to offer, so it needs to be both comprehensive and practical in the context of providing *informed collaboration*. You merely need to ask some simple questions; the answers will provide a clearer picture of what is being done.

These two classroom styles do not change the explicit curriculum. But do the implicit messages change (e.g., valuing cooperative work or individual work)? What would your position be on organizing students into small groups as an instructional reform?

Courtesy of Bill Lisenby

Courtesy of Bill Lisenby

Category I: The Need for the Program

As you begin to evaluate a proposed reform or intervention, the first category of questions concerns the need for the program. Education dollars are already expected to go a very long way, so it is important that they be spent wisely. As in any other industry, something new is always coming down the line and is always an updated and improved version of the older products. The question remains as to whether a particular school needs a particular product and whether or not the product is a good fit for that school and its circumstances.

Why Is This Program under Consideration?

It is reasonable for you to ask why the program is being considered at all. If there is a need for this program, there should be indicators pointing to the need for this particular change, addition, or deletion to the established curriculum. If the program is one of professional development of the teachers, there should similarly be identifiable reasons for doing what is going to be done.

What Evidence Is Available to Support the Need for the Program?

"Evidence" and "documentation" are not terms that are foreign to school personnel. You should understand that evidence and documentation can come in many forms. It is also true that some forms are more appropriate than others. With regard to student performance, appropriate evidence may be supplied in the form of standardized test scores. Do not be intimidated by responses that speak of percentiles, z-scores, and standard deviations. Those numbers are intended to quantify some aspect of achievement, aptitude, or potential. Standardized tests, however, are only as good as the norm group that was used to set the standards. Be sure that the norm group for the test matches the characteristics of your school district.

Teacher-made tests are good indicators of student performance if the program under consideration is intended to provide services to one or a small group of students. Those tests, however, should be available for review, and the designers of those tests should be able to explain their rationale plainly and logically.

Teacher observations are another good source of information. If this is the situation, those observations should be documented. The date, time, and circumstances surrounding the observations are data that should not be dismissed out of hand. The use of anecdotal records is not inappropriate, but as Stiggins (2001) indicates, relying on nothing more than one's memory of an event is rarely, if ever, a sound foundation for evaluating a situation.

What Purpose Will the Program Serve?

What will be different as a result of this program? If this is a reading program, will students be better readers? Better at comprehension? Better at word recognition? Better at sounding out unfamiliar words? If this is a math program, will the students be better at calculations? Better at word problems? Better at problem framing? There are many dimensions to virtually any undertaking in the school curriculum. Even more to the point, there should be some indication of the degree of significance of that change. Will students improve an entire grade level (watch out if this is the claim)? Will they be able to speak a foreign language fluently? Will they lower their cholesterol to a number below the national average? The proposal for an educational program should be able to indicate what difference will be made by making a change to this new, or at least different, method.

Table 13.1 Category I: The Need for the Program
Why is the program under consideration?
What evidence is available to support the need for the program?
What purpose will the program serve?
Are there any other programs like this available?

Are There Any Other Programs Like This Available?

People do comparison shopping on a regular basis and with reference to a host of criteria. It is not improbable that those who identified the program under consideration also considered other versions of the same thing. The education market is very big and very competitive. There are many products out there. If the program you are considering comes in several varieties, ask why this particular program is being considered. It is also possible that the program *is* the only one of its kind available, especially if it involves a grant-funded project with a university or it is a classroom-level program that will utilize the talents of local parents or community members.

None of the questions in this category are inappropriate to ask, and as you can see, all relate very specifically to the work you will do as a teacher. As professionals, teachers should feel comfortable asking these questions and finding the answers. You are not challenging people by asking questions such as these; rather, as is the case in all that teachers do, you are finding information to illuminate a situation and lead to greater understanding of the situation.

Category II: The Nature of the Program

What is the program all about? Begin with finding out who developed the program. This may be a collaboration between school personnel and faculty from a college or university, or perhaps with local business people or parents. Or the program could be a sophisticated product marketed by some educational enterprise. It is also possible that the program has been developed "in-house" at either the state, district, or school level.

Program Characteristics

After you have learned who developed the program, determine whether the program is intended as a *reform* or as an *intervention*. Essentially, a reform will make the claim of changing the way things are done on a fairly broad scale. For instance, a new mathematics curriculum for the entire school or district would fall into the category of reform. Efforts that change the requirements for teacher certification would also constitute reform. Interventions, on the other hand, generally leave the daily operations intact but affect some small, problematic segment of what is happening. For example, a pull-out program that provides individual assistance to one child would be an intervention. In the same vein, an enrichment program would also constitute an intervention.

The importance of the distinction is in the scope of the efforts. Reforms can be expected to be expensive and expansive, require changes in pedagogical philosophies, and almost always necessitate training of personnel. Interventions of an instructional nature can often be put in place with little if any additional funding and, depending upon the sophistication of services being offered, with little bureaucratic attention.

What is the specific target of the program: curriculum change, instructional change, enrichment, administrative change, or something to do with credentialing? With regard to *credentialing,* the credentials involved could be administrative, teacher, or staff. But that's not all. Substitute teachers, teacher's aides, parent volunteers, and student teachers (along with their college/university supervisors) are expected to have some sort of credentials.

If the program seeks to change the *curriculum* (either in terms of the "standard" curriculum or the provision of remedial services) or to provide *enrichment* activities (which can include academic or extracurricular activities), then the program description should note how broad the effect should be. Some programs, as we have discussed, are provided for just one child at a time while others may address the entire district. Determine whether the program you are assessing is targeted toward individuals, a classroom, an entire grade level, a school, or the entire district. This will give you not only a clearer idea of the human resources necessary to implement the program but also a sense of how many children are being served in relation to the amount of financial resources being expended.

Program Development

Programs that are offered through a college or university and published programs should certainly be based on research that supports their claims. Do not assume that the research basis is there just because higher education folks are involved or because the proposal comes in a nice box with three-color graphics on the front. Ask whether such a basis exists. If the answer is yes, take notes. If the answer is no, proceed with open-minded caution.

Next, ask whether the program has been tested in other schools. The fourth dimension of the Northwest Regional Educational Laboratory (NWREL) screening of programs asked for evidence of replicability. That is, can the program be replicated in other schools? A program that has had success somewhere else has a greater chance of being successful in your school. At this point the question is "fit" rather than viability of the program. If the program has been tested in other schools, the follow-up question is whether or not those schools are similar to your school. A program that enjoyed great success in a well-to-do suburban setting is not necessarily a good match for an underfunded urban setting.

Claims made for programs should be both verifiable and indicative of having a positive impact on student learning.

Courtesy of Bill Lisenby

The Claims

Now is the time to find out the specific claims of the program. If you have waited until now to ask this question you will be able to listen to the claims from a more informed perspective. You should know at this point whether the program has a solid research foundation, whether it has a record of success, and precisely what the targets are in terms of program characteristics. All of this casts a very different light on what you will be told the program can accomplish. In addition, having come just this far you should feel good about the quantity and quality of information you have collected. You may notice that you are beginning to feel more like a professional educator. As you take notes about the claims, keep in mind that no

Table 13.2	Category II: Issues Related to the Nature of the Program
Program characteristics	
Program development	
The claims	

program can be all things to all people. If the list seems to be going on and on, then there is reason to pay particular attention to the nature of the claims. For instance, goals and objectives are often considered to be synonymous when in fact they are not. The goal of a particular program may be to increase reading comprehension of fourth graders by one grade level. Objectives might include determining the reading level of each child who will participate in the program and designing appropriate experiences to allow that child to gain one year's reading improvement. Under these conditions it is possible that at the end of the program no child will be reading on a fourth grade level and yet the program could be a tremendous success. How? If all of the fourth graders were reading on a second grade level to begin with (not a far-fetched possibility) then one year's improvement could still have them one year behind. Whether this is a good thing or a bad thing is another question. As you listen to the claims, try to separate the goals from the objectives and ask for clarification whenever the two seem to be getting confused and particularly whenever goals seem to be giving way to desires.

It should be apparent that comprehensive planning requires the active involvement of the personnel who will be involved in implementing and supporting the program. This typically includes administrators, faculty and staff, parents, and the community. Their understanding and ability and willingness to support the effort are important to successful implementation. Because this process requires time, a full year of planning is a reasonable timetable (Culyer & Culyer, 1987).

Category III: Implementation

The trail of reform efforts in the country is littered with good programs that were poorly implemented. By empowering you as a highly educated professional who understands teaching and learning, we hope to see that trail become a superhighway of innovation. And so we now turn to the question of how this program will become a reality in the schools. It is important to identify who will actually do the work of implementing a new program. Is it really feasible to ask teachers to do yet another task? Are there funds for hiring specialized personnel? Chief among the sins of implementation is inadequate preparation of those who will deliver the program. That's why we recommend asking about the training of those who will conduct the program as well as asking about the costs involved.

Who Will Do the Work?

Good ideas are wonderful things, but without the people to implement them they cannot become any more than that: good ideas. This could be a rather complex issue. For instance, perhaps the work will be done by community volunteers but the scheduling of the program and making students available will have to be coordinated by the teacher. This also means that the teacher must account for working with a different class size for her own work and still be sure that the students participating in the program are not losing ground in other areas. If administrators will be responsible for implementation, that will usually avoid any loss of instructional time.

Table 13.3	Category III: Implementation
Who will do the work?	
What materials will be needed?	
What training will be required?	
What costs are involved?	

What Materials Will Be Needed?

Will additional books or other printed materials be needed for the program? Will there be a need for additional computer hardware, software, or other "technologies"? How about specialty work areas? Will the participants require access to special materials for their work or for their safety? Will there be a need for consumables? Consumables are supplies that get used up during a lesson or activity and must be replaced for the next time around. For instance, using batteries in a science class will require that those batteries get replaced at some point. We are sure that this sounds obvious to you and probably like not much of a problem. However, if you chat with a teacher or two you will find that many programs languish in storage closets and bins because after the first time through there was no budget for replacing the materials that were used.

What Training Will Be Required?

To implement this program, will it be necessary to conduct training sessions for those who will eventually deliver the program to the participants? You can probably recall some point(s) in your own educational experience when a brave new program was put in place. The materials were there, renovations to the classroom area were complete, and all was ready to go. The only problem was that no one ever got around to teaching the teachers how to do this neat new thing. Perhaps it was the shift to "open classrooms" in the mid-1970s. Or it could have been the new math of the mid-1960s. It takes time and planning to prepare people to do something different from what they've been doing. That aspect of implementation needs to be just as well conceived and arranged as any other element.

This extends to nonprofessional personnel as well. If community members are recruited into working with the school, they must be made aware of the many restrictions under which the school operates. What can and cannot be said to a child is an important issue. Whether or not it is permissible to put a hand on a child's shoulder is part of some school policies today. Even the way people dress to come and work with children is an important concern. If the program you are considering falls into this category, ask whether these people will receive any sort of indoctrination, professional oversight, and evaluation.

What Costs Are Involved?

At this stage of your involvement with school programs, it is not necessary to access detailed budgets of anticipated programs. In fact, if the program does involve salaries of specific individuals, it may be virtually impossible for you to review a detailed budget. However, you can certainly get an idea for the scope of the project. If the principal tells you that this program will cost the district about $100,000, you should already have a good idea of whether that seems reasonable. If a teacher tells you that the program she is going to run for her students won't cost anything, you probably have a pretty good idea of how reasonable that is as well.

That wasn't so bad, was it? It certainly is not a process that is beyond your capabilities. We are not trying to launch you on a career as an investigative journalist nor brand you as the local educational gadfly. But there are two things to keep in mind. One is that whenever you hear about dollars being spent on one program or another, as a taxpayer some of those are your dollars, and you are entitled to know if they are well spent. The other point is that when it is all said and done, by virtue of the involvement you have had through this inquiry, you can share in the "ownership" of this project and should be prepared to offer your assistance in any manner that is suitable. This sort of inquiry is but one aspect of being a **change agent,** that is, helping to determine whether this is the right change to make. The potential for reform in education is one of the most exciting aspects of the institution because it admits of an openness to change and improvement. We believe that teachers, as professional educators, should be key players in that exciting and dynamic aspect of the institution of education. It can happen if teachers *empower themselves first* by becoming informed collaborators in the process. We hope that *you* will accept the challenge presented here. Activity 13.3 is an opportunity to put the guidelines presented here into use as you research a reform effort of your choice.

change agent One who participates in curriculum or instructional dialogue with the purpose of making positive changes in the school program. A change agent is also one who institutes curriculum or instructional reform in the classroom or at the school level.

Go Online!

ACTIVITY 13.3   Evaluating a Reform Effort

Reform efforts are all around us in education. Even on your campus there may be institutional efforts such as strategic plan development, quality enhancement plans, curriculum reform reviews, and program assessment development. The local schools may be involved in implementing a new reading, math, or science program. The district could be investigating site-based teacher empowerment programs or considering year-round schooling. There are many possibilities for you to research.

1. Select the level you wish to research (early childhood, elementary, middle, high school, college/university). Identify an appropriate contact person (for example, teacher, principal, curriculum coordinator, professor, dean). Ask that person about the reform and intervention activities at her institution and select one to research.

2. Use the Internet to do some background research on your topic. For instance, you might type "teacher empowerment" into a search engine to get you started on that topic.

3. Use the information from the Internet to answer the questions in Category II: The Nature of the Program. Note: we recommend that you begin with Category II so that when you speak with the contact person she can *inform* you about the topic rather than *educate* you about it.

4. Now that you have researched the initiative, arrange to speak with your contact person about the questions from Category I: The Need for the Program and Category III: Implementation (see Tables 13.1 and 13.3).

5. Draw your own conclusions about the situation. Is the reform prudent? Is it being implemented appropriately? What do you predict for the short- and long-term results of the effort? Explain your findings in a report to your class, if possible.

Conclusion

Our intention has been to extend the notion of an informed consumer from one who knows *about* something to one who also knows *how to find out about* something so to make effective decisions. It is important that you understand that the perception people have of you may well change from this point forward. That's not necessarily a bad thing but something of which you should be aware.

It is also important, however, that you keep the fundamental problem in mind. That is, even with a more informed perspective on the reforms and interventions that take place in your local school, reforms—as we have discussed them thus far—are no more than minor adjustments that the educational institution will tolerate for the time being. Don't be lulled into thinking that a well-researched and well-implemented intervention will necessarily turn the schools around. Perhaps it will. Let's hope so. In her epilogue to *The Quick Reference Guide to Educational Innovations,* Carolyn Orange (2002) relates the story of an innovations graveyard in the district where she worked:

> Schools from around the city sent materials [here] from their abandoned programs: whole kits; used but mostly unused products; lots of manipulatives, workbooks, and books. Everything was delivered to the doorstep of the facility. I was told that on one delivery day, the products were left at the front door in the breezeway and most of the delivery was destroyed by rain. Brand-new, beautiful materials were literally thrown into rooms that were already stacked to the ceiling. The materials lay there untouched for over a year, dead in the sense that children were not using them. They had been sent to the graveyard of abandoned programs to rest in peace. Appalled at such blatant waste, I questioned the reasoning behind it. Why would schools that claim to have little money waste it on programs that they apparently did not want to keep? Perhaps the glamour of a program wears off as soon as a new program appears on the scene. Perhaps schools have a genuine lack of knowledge about the programs or practices appropriate for their educational setting. Unfortunately, they adopt a trial-and-error approach—and the error inevitably generates a lot of waste. (p. 120)

Here are some of the highlights of our review of educational reform and our look at evaluating reform proposals:

1. Education reform will likely be a part of your professional life throughout your career.
2. Unlike change, which is inevitable, reform is always a reaction to some dissatisfaction with the educational system.
3. Higher education, business, politics, and parents all play key roles in the relative success or failure of reform efforts.
4. A reform is a program that seeks to replace some aspect of the current educational operation.
5. An intervention is an effort that supplements normal procedure either by providing remediation or enrichment or by extending or reducing responsibility or authority.
6. The questions in Category I for reform assessment are designed to identify the need for a reform or intervention initiative.

7. Category II questions for reform assessment examine the characteristics of the proposed program including the claims being made.
8. Category III for reform assessment investigates the plans for implementation of an initiative. This can involve a consideration of costs, materials, and training.
9. Teachers can play a significant part in the evaluation of reform and intervention proposals.

Key Terms

educational reform   intervention   change agent
reform model   curriculum reform
higher education   instructional reform

Educational Engineering

Case Studies in Education

Enter the information from the table below into the Educational Record for the student you are studying.

	Child's "Fit" with Traditional Education	Parents' View about Classroom Research	Parents' View about Need for Change
Davon	Kindergarten classes have little traditional-style teaching. However, Davon attends well during lecture times, retains information, and responds to what he hears. He should do well with traditional teaching styles.	Davon's mother is totally disconnected from school involvement. She does not want to be contacted and probably wouldn't mind new teaching techniques being tested at the school as long as it didn't require anything from her.	Davon's mother does not communicate with the school. From all indications she would not see any need for education reform as long as the school provided total care for her child throughout the day.
Andy	Andy can learn under a traditional teaching approach. That being said, his hyperactivity demands that he be allowed to move often. He also requires concrete experiences that will meet his kinesthetic needs.	Andy's grandparents are not particularly involved in what goes on at school. They did grant permission for Andy to take part in a study required for a class in a doctoral program concerning oral and written language development. They did not ask to speak with the researcher before or after the study was completed.	As long as their grandchildren are happy at school, the grandparents are not involved and see no need for change in the schools. They are more concerned with how well Andy likes his teacher than how well the teacher teaches.
Judith	Judith will "fall through the cracks" if the current trend of passing her along with marginal skills and little subject-matter understanding continues.	Judith's parents see the school as responsible for the education of their child. They have never questioned the school's curriculum or teaching practices.	Judith's parents have never indicated any interest or opinion with regard to issues of school reform. They do attend open-house functions but have never attended meetings on school planning issues.

(Continued on next page)

Tiffany	Tiffany exceeds every expectation given to her. In that sense, she does not fit the traditional approach to education. Most students lack motivation with homework and projects, yet Tiffany rarely needs any help, understands concepts the first time, asks for additional homework and projects, and is never a behavior problem or lacking motivation.	Tiffany's parents have been supportive of any new innovations the school or classroom teacher has wished to pursue for the sake of improving education.	Tiffany's parents have been very pleased with the school program for their child. They consider themselves partners with their daughter's teachers and work together to form solutions.
Sam	Sam would have great difficulty being successful in the "traditional" approach to education if he did not receive special education services. Throughout the educational process, he has been provided an appropriate environment and accommodations and modifications in an attempt to meet his unique needs.	Sam's mother would be supportive of the school being used to "test" new teaching techniques if a particular method was explained to her, giving her the opportunity to raise questions and concerns.	His mother appears to be satisfied with what the school is doing to educate her child.
Bao	Bao is, in most respects, a model student. She is well-behaved and attentive, and rarely calls on the teacher for assistance. She is a strong test-taker and completes her homework. As long as she is not challenged to synthesize and construct her own meaning, she does quite well in school, and traditional teachers enjoy having her in class.	Bao's parents are unaware of classroom research, but were they aware, they would implicitly trust educational professionals to know how to best teach their child.	Bao's parents do not question the school. Because all of their children have done well in school, they have seen no need to question the system.

1. Based on the parents' attitude about research in the classroom, how could you assure them that a new approach your school has adopted is better and will not interfere with the child's education?

2. Do the parents of the child you are studying favor reforms (changes) in the school? Do you? How could you make both perspectives work for this child?

3. What does this child's "fit" with a traditional education program tell you about his or her potential for success? Should there be one program for all students? Should education be individualized? Is there another option that you can offer? Explain your answers.

Designing the School of the Future

If you have been designing a school through the previous chapters (a, below), this is your chance for a reality check. If you haven't done the Designing the School of the Future activities in the other chapters, this is an opportunity to turn your thinking wide open (b, below).

1. a. Look at the plan you have developed thus far. What problems that reforms try to address has your plan eliminated? What problems still show up in your plan?

    b. What are the major issues in education that you want to be sure your design for the future will address? How will your plan resolve those issues and improve schools in the year ahead?

2. What specific aspects of school as you know it should be continued in the school of the future?

3. Write a press release or design a brochure that explains to parents how your school of the future eliminates today's problems in education and offers students a better educational experience.

Praxis Practice

Most states will require that you successfully complete the Praxis Series of examinations to qualify for certification. One or more of those tests will be subject-area tests. Another, which has a more practical orientation, will be the Principles of Learning and Teaching (PLT) examination that is appropriate for your certification area.

Completing the Quick Check Quizzes for Chapter 13 in the Unit Workshop will give you practice with the multiple choice format of the PLT. The Case Studies in Education and Designing a School of the Future activities will help prepare you for exercises that require reading a scenario and providing short answers to questions asking what you might do in such a situation.

HORIZON LINE

Innovations
and the Future

CPR²

Make the chapter work for you with CPR²:

Conceptualize Here are the major themes you will encounter in this chapter:
1. Shaping the future of a profession is a responsibility of those who practice that profession.
2. Logistical innovations can involve the design and use of school facilities.
3. Instructional innovations can involve instructional delivery systems, experiential education, and instructional materials.
4. Schools have a responsibility to address the global nature of contemporary societies.

Preview Read the chapter headings; look at any figures, tables, and activities; and read through the items in the conclusion.

Activity 14.1 Field Observation Activity—Computers in the Schools and in Your Class

Activity 14.2 Identifying Common Characteristics of Schools and Their Campuses

Activity 14.3 Go Online! Around the Curriculum in 180 Days

Activity 14.4 Janus in the Classroom: Considering the Past and the Future

Activity 14.5 What Are the Experiences of Life That Should Be Experiences of School?

Activity 14.6 From a Node to Nations: The Global Creative Problem-Solving Consortium

Read Now read through the chapter. Mark or highlight information that you consider to be especially important or about which you have a question.

Reflect Consider these questions as you read: Will education be significantly different five, 10, or 20 years from now? Should we expect it to be? What part will you play in the progress of the education profession?

Artwork by Jim Boden

Eye on the Standards
INTASC

The following standards from the Interstate New Teacher Assessment and Support Consortium (INTASC) will be addressed in this chapter. As you read the chapter, consider how instructional techniques and future advances in educational practice and resources are tied to these principles.

Principle 1 The teacher understands the central concepts, tools of inquiry, and structures of the discipline(s) he or she teaches and can create learning experiences that make these aspects of subject matter meaningful for students.

Principle 4 The teacher understands and uses a variety of instructional strategies to encourage students' development of critical thinking, problem solving, and performance skills.

Principle 5 The teacher uses an understanding of individual and group motivation and behavior to create a learning environment that encourages positive social interaction, active engagement in learning, and self-motivation.

Principle 6 The teacher uses knowledge of effective verbal, nonverbal, and media communication techniques to foster active inquiry, collaboration, and supportive interaction in the classroom.

Principle 7 The teacher plans instruction based upon knowledge of subject matter, students, the community, and curriculum goals.

Principle 9 The teacher is a reflective practitioner who continually evaluates the effects of his/her choices and actions on others (students, parents, and other professionals in the learning community) and who actively seeks out opportunities to grow professionally.

Principle 10 The teacher fosters relationships with school colleagues, parents, and agencies in the larger community to support students' learning and well-being.

ice breakers

Let's Get Creative!

This chapter is all about seeing things in new ways and thinking about things from different perspectives. Throughout this chapter, we will offer ideas rather than solutions. So you need to bring your creative abilities along as you read about and consider the future of education. *Creative thinking* refers to a search for relationships, patterns, and perspectives (Ebert, 1994), and *creative problem solving* involves going beyond "the rules" of the problem to find new possibilities (Ebert & Ebert, 1998; Bentley, Ebert, & Ebert, 2000). Here are some puzzles and questions to get that creative process going.

Relationships

1. Each of the puzzles below represents a common phrase. Can you identify them?

A.	B.	C.
Knee Lights	ANOTHERONE	iirightii

2. Here are some puzzles. You'll know them when you solve them! Here's an example, 26 L. in the A. = 26 letters in the alphabet.

   A. 101 D.

   B. 29 D. in F. in a L.Y

   C. 5 D. in a Z. C.

   D. 3 B. M., S. H. T. R.

   E. 32 D. F., the T. at which W. F.

Patterns

Look at the two rows of candies. What would be the next color of candy in each row?

3. Y R B G O _____   Y R B G O Y R _____

4. Fill in the next number in each sequence and indicate the pattern you followed:

   a. 1　2　3　4　5　6　7　8　9　_____

   b. 1　2　4　8　_____

   c. 1　2　4　5　7　_____

Perspectives

5. Look at the series of Roman numerals below:

   IV　V　VI　VII　VIII　IX　X

   Adding only one line, change the 9 to 6. _____

6. Look at the Droodles (doodles that are also riddles) below. List three possibilities for what each drawing might represent. For example, drawing (A) could be looking down on two diving boards over a pool filled with beach balls.

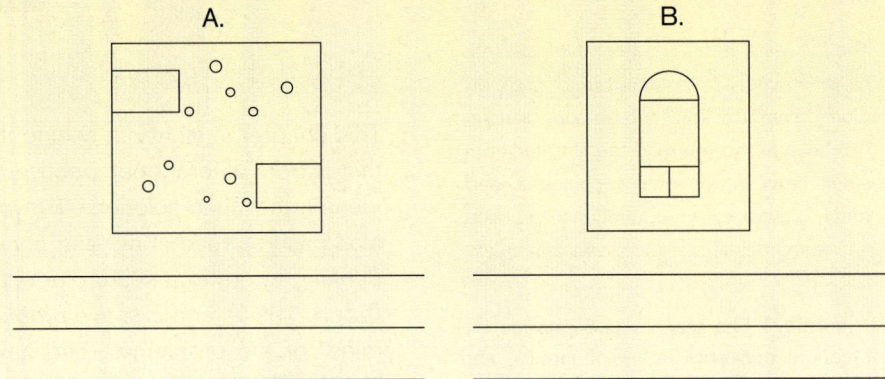

A.   B.

_____   _____

_____   _____

_____   _____

The problems may have been a bit frustrating along the way, but you probably smiled when you found the answer. Solving problems is what the brain does, and it is a rewarding experience. Here are the answers we were thinking of, though they are not necessarily the *only* answers!

Relationships: Relationships represent the most basic interaction between objects or events.

1. A. neon lights   B. one after another   C. right between the eyes

2. A. 101 Dalmatians
   B. 29 days in February in a Leap Year
   C. 5 Digits in a Zip Code
   D. 3 Blind Mice, See How They Run
   E. 32 Degrees Fahrenheit, the Temperature at which Water Freezes

Patterns: When a relationship repeats, a pattern is formed.

3. A. This one was tricky. If you said that another M&M would follow, then that is a pattern. If your focus was on the colors, however, there is no pattern until there is a repetition.
   B. There has been repetition here. One might expect the next M&M to be blue.

4. A. If you identify the pattern as each number increasing by one over the previous number, then we might expect 10 to be the next one to show up.
   B. Using the logic as in 4A, we might expect the next number to be 16 if each number is doubling the number preceding it. However, there's another pattern here that might even require a change of perspective. What might it be?
   C. Perhaps it showed up more clearly in this one. We suggest that the next number is 8. Why? Because the first number was a straight-line number. Then next was a curved number. The next was the next highest straight-lines number, and so on. What does this tell you about the possibilities for the sequence in 4B?

Perspectives: Switching perspectives means considering something from a decidedly different vantage point. People often need to tell themselves to consider a different perspective because we tend to be comfortable with the perspectives that have worked for us in the past.

5. You had to drop the perspective that the line had to be a straight line to be able to solve this one. With that simple perspective shift, adding an "S" to IX forms SIX.

6. Well, this one was just wide open! How did your descriptions of the drawings match up with those of your classmates? Every switch of perspective offers the possibility for another explanation for what the drawing represents!

> *Imagination is more important than knowledge.*
>
> *Albert Einstein*

■ Introduction

Although this is the final chapter in the textbook, it is by no means the end of the story. In fact, this particular chapter focuses on many things that have yet to be done in education. One of the great ironies of organized education is that while it prepares people to bring about change, such as through the development of new ideas, processes, products, and inventions, the system itself really doesn't seem to change a whole lot, nor does it foster the idea of its students being change agents. Progress and true innovation are slow to come to education. Education is a conservative enterprise. So, since we have been trying to expand and empower your thinking throughout this book, let's have a chapter of "what if. . . ." We will supply some ideas to start the discussion, and then you and your classmates (maybe just you if that's your style) can begin to formulate your own ideas of what education could be in the future.

■ Understanding "Technology"

technology The combining of information to make new products or processes that extend our capabilities.

Without a doubt, **technology** is going to be a prominent component of education in the immediate and distant future. But what is technology? These days it typically means computers, though to broaden the scope of the concept while at the same time narrowing down its meaning, some might say "electronics" (for example, an e-book is electronic but it is not a computer). Let's try to clarify it a bit more because neither "computers" nor "electronics" does justice to this incredible field.

Unlike the work of scientists, which brings to people a new understanding of the world around us, the work of technologists *combines* information to make new products or processes that extend our capabilities (Ebert & Ebert, 1998). The reading glasses that many people wear represent technology applied to the need of improving vision. Microscopes, whether optical or electronic, extend our capabilities for studying very small specimens. In this sense, anything that extends our capabilities can be considered as a product of technology. Thus, technology in the classroom can be the overhead projector that allows an entire class to see what the teacher is writing, just as it can be the LCD projectors that can project digital images across a large screen with marvelous detail. In a sense, technology is science made practical. Our emphasis is on finding products of technology that can improve instruction and learning.

■ Technology Past and Present

How prevalent has computer usage become in the United States? According to the *Digest of Education Statistics 2003* (2004), over 2,500,000 children *ages three to six years old* are using the Internet. Of that number, 6.2 percent are using the Internet at school (approximately 65 percent of them are using it to play games). Obviously, teachers in the future—the immediate future—must be proficient with using computer technology.

Computers, of course, have been around for a long time. It was the advent of the "affordable" personal computer (PC) that began making computers in public school classrooms a real possibility. In the early 1980s, many schools began offering computer science classes to small numbers of students with a handful of PCs. At the time, how computers work and the mysterious language of binary codes were part and parcel of instruction. Today, few users of computer technology have any understanding of the binary system and even less an awareness of what makes a computer "tick." At this point, software applications are what are important. Knowing how to use a word processor, access the Internet, or use e-mail are the skills that people are expected to have rather than being able to count to 100 using nothing but 0s and 1s. As a result, computers in classrooms and in computer labs are increasingly used as an instructional tool rather than as an instructional topic.

Technology in the Schools

Technology in the classroom consists of electronic tools that improve teaching and learning, including computer centers and listening stations that are part of well-planned lessons.

The current literature on technology in the schools offers both sides of the issue: the potential for good and for the not so good. But a common theme from many authors and school technology specialists is the goal of "seamless integration" of technology in the schools (Veronikas & Shaughnessy, 2006; Pitler, 2006). They are

Courtesy of Bill Lisenby

Courtesy of Bill Lisenby

looking for the day when electronic technologies such as computers and their peripheral devices are simply part of what goes on in school. In essence, the big deal will not be that students work with computers at their local school but the fabulous things students do with the computer as one of their tools. At present, however, issues of teacher professional development, student use of computers and access to the Internet, distance education (virtual schools), assistive technology (AT), and finance are matters of concern.

Technology for Teachers

For quite some time after computer technology ushered in the information age, hardware was simply too expensive to allow schools to enjoy the widespread use of computers for instructional purposes. The equipment schools did procure was often secondhand and on its way to obsolescence. This combined with teachers' limited knowledge of computers meant that machines often sat idle in a corner of the classroom. It was technology "in" the classroom all right, but it was not effective.

As software became more user-friendly, computer labs with remedial programs began to emerge. The computer made the programmed instruction ideas of B. F. Skinner workable. Programs would address students by name, give them immediate feedback, praise them for each correct answer, and direct them to more exercises on an appropriate level. But it was arguably the virtual explosion of the Internet into contemporary life that has moved computer technology from a record-keeping tool to an educational tool. With so much information available, the challenge to teachers is to make the shift from learning "from" computers to learning "with" computers (Ringstaff & Kelley, 2002).

Professional Development   "If schools add technology without providing adequate professional development, the only thing that will increase is their electric bill," says Howard Pitler (2006, p. 39) of Mid-continent Research for Education and Learning. The point that he is making is well known in the education community. That is, reforms that look great as somebody's plan will not succeed unless teachers are educated or trained to implement the plan. Failure to address this one point has been the fatal flaw in many a reform initiative. Professional development for in-service teachers and the true integration of electronic technology in the education of pre-service teachers are the keys to changing the traditional paradigm in teaching, in which the teacher lectures, he puts notes on a board for students to copy, and the students memorize the information. As Pitler (2006) suggests, the goal should not be to have "technology in the classroom" but to see technology as an instructional tool for accomplishing an articulated educational goal. The difference is that teachers would require the technology to do their work rather than trying to find ways to work technology into their lessons. At this point in your own efforts to become a teacher, you have a prime opportunity to make technology one of the tools you use to teach lessons. It will take practice, but that's what your program is all about.

Technology for Students

Without question, enabling students to use computer technology requires making the technology available to them. To that end, millions of dollars have been spent through tax-supported and grant-funded initiatives to purchase computer hardware and software for the schools. In addition, funding has gone toward wiring schools for Internet access. While this indicates that computer technology has found its way into the classroom, it does not mean that technology has truly found its way into the mainstream of education. A study by the Maryland Business Roundtable for Education found that despite multimillion-dollar investments in computers and other technology for the Maryland schools, teachers and students continue to use computers primarily for e-mail and word processing (Ishizuka, 2005). A mere 13 percent of schools reported that students used technology to "display data" every day, and less than 10 percent reported that students used the technology for the manipulation, analysis, and interpretation of information. Clearly, there is distance yet to go to find the seamless integration of technology that we mentioned earlier.

Now the good news. Most students reading this book will have lived all of their lives in the computerized world. Those readers who are studying to become teachers after following other life pursuits have lived their adult lives in a world that relies on computer technology. And *all* of the children, of whatever grade level, who will eventually come to your classroom will have lived their lives in a world in which computers and associated electronics are as common as record players were for us older folks. The seamless integration of computer technology will be a part of your career in education. You and your students will be able to use electronic information sources to research virtually any topic. And rather than spending time being fascinated by what computers can do, you and your students will fascinate others with what you are able to accomplish with the technology. You should be able to open your students' eyes to experiences that go far beyond the walls of your classroom. You should be able to have your students routinely communicating with students in other countries around the world. Given your willingness to integrate electronic technologies into your planning, presentation, and student-oriented activities, you are entering the education profession in one of the most exciting times that schools have ever seen!

Distance Education

Perhaps one of the most intriguing possibilities for the reconceptualization of school is **distance education** in the world of electronic technologies. Distance education, or the delivery of instructional programs to people in sites remote from the "school," originally began as correspondence courses by mail. Eventually, the advent of television and home videotape machines allowed distance education to become a multimedia— though still not "interactive"—experience.

Remarkable advances in computers and telecommunications have enabled distance education not only to reach students almost instantaneously but also to be interactive between teacher and student. Schools can now offer course work to students who are homebound or in remote sites, or even just as an alternative to being in a school building. This new version of education is often referred to as a **virtual school.**

Greenway and Vanourek (2006) report that during the 2002–2003 school year, 36 percent of U.S. school districts enrolled students in distance education courses. Further, they indicate that as of 2005 the North American Council for Online Learning listed 157 unique distance learning programs in 42 states. These programs included 32 virtual charter schools, three online home schooling programs, and 53 public, noncharter virtual schools (Greenway & Vanourek, 2006). No longer just a possibility, virtual schools are offering a new educational delivery system across the country.

"Typing" used to be a class many students took in high school. "Keyboarding" is a skill that many of even the youngest students will bring to class.

Courtesy of Bill Lisenby

distance education Delivery of instructional programs to people in sites remote from the school setting.

virtual school An electronic, telecommunications-based presentation of course work to students who are homebound or in remote sites, or even just as an alternative to being in a traditional school setting.

Assistive technology is an application of computer technology that can transform education for students with special needs.

Courtesy of Bill Lisenby

While virtual schools do have the potential to reach more students, there are concerns. One is the loss of social interaction that schools provide not only between teacher and student but among students themselves. In an era when multicultural awareness is a key concern in the traditional school, the virtual school—by virtue of its "cyber anonymity"—threatens to reduce that awareness to electronic images without the human interface. Another concern is that teaching in a virtual school involves a distinctly different pedagogical approach. Authors such as De Simone warn that adequate training or professional development of teachers is still piecemeal at best (2006). As we mentioned previously, the failure to adequately prepare teachers for new approaches has been the undoing of many programs.

Technology and Special Needs

assistive technology Applications of technology that improve the educational experience for students with special needs.

Assistive technology refers to those applications that improve the educational experience for students with special needs. Advances in technology have provided greater mobility to children (and adults) who use wheelchairs, have increased interaction between student and teachers through touch-sensitive computer screens, and have improved the ability of challenged students to be interactive communicators. Electronic technologies have led to computer-based word processing for communications, speech synthesizers, voice-recognition computers, and even something that many people see every day, closed captioning of television broadcasts. The Internet has provided not only access to materials and resources for students with disabilities but also discussion forums for teachers and students as well. The applications of computer and other electronic technologies to the special needs of students may be limited only by the imaginations of innovators and inventors who recognize a need to be filled. As a classroom teacher, *you* may be the one who identifies the need that technology can fill.

Technology Issues

Because electronic technology will likely be a prevalent part of your teaching career, we will consider some of the issues raised about the proliferation of computer technology in general and the use of computers in schools. Concerns range

Table 14.1   Issues with the Use of Technology in the Classroom

- What happens when the power goes off in a school that is dependent upon electronic technology? Can schools close for "inclement technology" days?
- What happens when the power is on? How can schools effectively monitor the appropriate use of electronic resources, in particular the accessing of inappropriate Internet sites?
- Funding of technology can be expected to remain an issue due to the rapid pace of technological development. How will school budgets be adjusted?
- Technology for the general population and for those who can benefit from assistive technology is not always culturally sensitive. For example, Goode (2005) points out that not all cultures value the independence that assistive technologies may afford. What should be the school's position in such cases?
- Computers are just the latest example of the ebb and "crash" of technology in education. Is this history repeating itself?

- Electronic technologies are so prevalent that children are increasingly educated *and* entertained by electronic entities (which accounts for the vast majority of a child's waking hours). Children are losing an appreciation of nature.
- Students tend to "use" information from the Internet as the answer to a question rather than "using" the information to form an answer. Is critical thinking being lost?
- The Internet is evolving from an information source into a commercial entity. Should students in schools be seen as an advertising market?
- Electronic communications remove the "human element" from interpersonal communication. Will this lead to a lack of socialization skills?
- E-mail and text messaging have given rise to a new version of English that we might call e-English. What are the implications of this for teaching "standard" English to a generation of students who use e-English when communicating with one another?

Field Observation

ACTIVITY 14.1   Computers in the Schools and in Your Class

There are two parts to this activity. In Part I, you will survey the computer use in the school where you do your field observation. In Part II, you will prepare your own technology-based presentation.

Part I: Survey of Technology in the Schools

1. Look around the classroom to which you are assigned. Is there a computer in the classroom? More than one? What tasks are accomplished with the computer? What tasks are accomplished *during class time*? Does the computer in the classroom have Internet access?

2. Observe your school's computer lab, if it has one. Are the computers up to date? Are they used for research, remediation, word processing, and/or other functions? What can the teacher in the computer lab tell you about using the programs available in the school?

3. Visit the library/media center. What use of electronic technology do you find? How accessible are the computer workstations (if any) to the students—during school, before school, after school? Is computer usage restricted or monitored?

4. What conclusions can you draw about the use of computers *as an instructional tool*?

Part II: Preparing Your Own Presentation

1. Either for your Introduction to Education class or some other, prepare a class presentation using electronic technology. The use of technology should not be the focus of the presentation. Rather, consider what you can do to utilize electronic technology to provide a more effective presentation.

2. Request feedback from your audience about the presentation. Do *not* specifically ask for an evaluation of the technology aspects of the presentation.

3. Considering that your goal is to put technology to use rather than demonstrating that you can use technology, did the feedback you receive focus on the use of technology in your presentation or on the effectiveness of your presentation?

4. What challenges do you see to accomplishing the seamless integration of technology as discussed in the text?

from funding of hardware and software to depriving youngsters of the opportunity to interact with nature, a condition that Richard Louv (2005) refers to as *nature-deficit disorder*. Table 14.1 lists some of the topics currently under debate (for more detail on a number of these issues see, for example, Oppenheimer, 2004; Cetron & Cetron, 2004; Ishizuka, 2005; Goode, 2006). Debate on these issues, and others, is not meant to remove technology from education (that would indeed be a step backward) but instead to find the most appropriate way to adapt the technology to the unique environment that schools represent. How would you address some of these issues? You could use Activity 14.1 as an opportunity to look at the use of computers in the schools and to develop an electronic presentation of your findings.

Technology and Tomorrow

Now that we've established a basis for considering the use of technology in the schools, let's consider some possibilities for education throughout your career in this 21st century. Not all of our ideas have to focus on electronics, though such technology can be brought into the planning phase of schools along with the instructional aspects. In fact, some of our work when looking at what schools could be will require some basic rethinking, a reconceptualization, of what school is all about. The potential power of electronic technology and its capacity for expanding education to a global enterprise may well influence that reconceptualization.

Logistical Innovations

logistical innovations Innovative changes that affect the physical aspect of school: the building, the interior and exterior facilities, the movement of people, and so on.

By **logistical innovations** we mean ideas for improving the physical aspect of school: the building, the facilities within, movement of people, and so on. Among these are a number of features of "schoolness" that we seem to take for granted. What if we changed our thinking just a bit? What do you suppose schools of the future might look like?

Design of School Facilities

If you look around at the design of school buildings, you will find that they fall roughly into two categories. We might call them prefederal and postfederal periods in education. You will recall from our discussions of the history of education (Chapter 8) and legal aspects of education (Chapter 10) that the National Defense Education Act of the late 1950s brought a sharp national focus to education. That's what we mean by prefederal and postfederal periods. This is by no means the only way of categorizing the styles, just one possibility. We invite you to bring your own perspective to the discussion. In fact, Activity 14.2 provides an opportunity for you and your classmates to consider how schools are the same and how they differ.

Prefederal School Design The prefederal building is an old building typically involving a lot of masonry work, wooden floors, tall windows, and an overall "massive" sort of demeanor. These buildings were not inexpensive, and so it is no surprise that they have been occupied in their various states of repair for decades on end. Such buildings were often multilevel, and access to upper or lower floors, perhaps even to the front doors, was by staircase. Today it is not uncommon to find one or more modern buildings attached to the older structure by a hallway or breezeway. Take a look at the cornerstone, and you will find dates that go back to the early 20th century. The photograph of School No. 2 (where one of your authors attended grades 2–4) has a cornerstone that reads 1908! Buildings such as these tend to become icons in and of themselves. These are the buildings we think of when imagining the footsteps of the great people who once roamed the hallways of public schools. As such, they are rarely demolished to make way for newer buildings. Yet the buildings are not necessarily maintained in a manner that preserves their glory. As of 1999, a full 50 percent of the approximately 78,000 public schools in our country had one or more building features rated as less than adequate (Digest of Education Statistics, 2003, 2004).

Postfederal School Design In the 1950s and 1960s education was seen as a national defense response to several world trends and events. Along with the development of new curricula, there was a building boom of American schools. In fact, some might argue that the real reform in education was in terms of construction techniques.

School No. 2, on the left, illustrates the pre-1950s architecture typical of schools. The school on the right, built in the 1950s, illustrates the one-level style still seen today.

Courtesy of E. S. Ebert

Courtesy of E. S. Ebert

equal access The federal requirement that buildings and facilities be structured in such a way that people with physical handicaps have access to the same information and opportunities as do people without handicaps.

Rather than building the large, labor-intensive structures that we know of from the prefederal days, the new buildings followed the general plan of cinderblock walls, metal-framed window units, welded steel roof trusses, and flat roofs. By and large, schools had less height and more sprawl. As the 1970s legislation affecting **equal access** and special services took hold, new construction often adopted a single-story design that eliminated, or at least minimized, the need for elevators for students with physical disabilities. Even the newest schools of the postfederal period often have a small city of temporary buildings, or "portables," out back to provide more classroom space to keep up with unanticipated increases in enrollment. In 1999, 39 percent of all public schools were using temporary buildings (Digest of Education Statistics, 2003, 2004). Of schools of 600 students or more (that's approximately 28,000 schools), one-half use temporary buildings.

For buildings of either period we can identify at least a few common threads. First, whether single story or multistory, schools take up a lot of space. If we consider the property that surrounds the school as well as the property it occupies, public schools account for billions of dollars' worth of real estate across the country. Second, the space that schools and their surrounding properties occupy are typically open areas. The truly urban inner-city school may be an exception, but even in such a case the facility occupies an open area to one degree or another. Third, the basic design of a school emphasizes the movement of people, lots of people, and often at the same time. Thus, schools are typically an arrangement of classrooms along a large hallway. Finally, it seems that schools are never big enough. A brand new school that opens during the semester that you read this book may well have a contingent of portable buildings blossoming in its backyard within a year.

The Physical Plant Let's start to design a new school! It would not be feasible to wipe the slate clean of all the schools that exist, so let's try to think in terms of what we can do with the old schools along with ideas that should be incorporated into the design of new schools.

Considering that schools take up a lot of open space, it would seem that one idea that can apply to old as well as new is that they should generate their own power. By this we mean that school rooftops, out in the open sun, are obvious candidates for arrays of **solar collectors.** Actually, by using passive collectors for heating water and photovoltaic collectors for generating electricity, schools could generate more power than they need and sell the excess back to the utility company. So rather than utilities being a major drain on the school budget, generating power could actually become a source of revenue. Wind-driven generators may also be particularly appropriate in some regions of the country. A little more cost in the building of the school may result in a school that is less costly to operate.

There is another major source of energy to be tapped within a school—the students. As you know from your own experience, the current trend that moves students from room to room throughout the day means that in many schools literally thousands of students walk through the hallways at peak times throughout the day. Suppose we could design a floor system that made use of the energy that a floor usually absorbs as people walk across it. The plan might be to sandwich a thin channel of water between two layers of waterproof material. With each step on the top layer, water is forced through the channel until it eventually passes through a turbine that generates electricity. Multiply the action of one person walking across the floor by the hundreds or thousands of students that walk through the hallway each day and the possibility exists for schools to capture "student power."

Such a technology might easily be adapted to other high-traffic areas such as airports or stadiums. Perhaps *you* could design such a system and insist that the

solar collectors Panels that capture heat from the sun and use it to heat water or heat the facilities.

Artwork by Jim Boden

There is a lot of energy in and around a school. How could that be harnessed for use in the school of the future?

manufacturer provide "power floors" free of charge to public schools in exchange for the right to market it for nonschool use. Could your classmates take on this challenge?

The sheer size of schools and their various buildings has come to be of concern for a number of reasons. Though there are many factors that influence the design of schools, most of those factors are not *pedagogical* concerns. Rather, they may involve questions such as the moving of students, controlling who gets into the building, how quickly large numbers of students can be moved through or out of the building, and the concerns of equal access for all students. However, it is also true that school "sprawl" leads to the necessity of moving students greater distances even within the building. What impact might there be if we conceptualized school buildings not as classrooms emanating from a central hallway but as hallways surrounding the classrooms? Certainly such an arrangement would make it easier to provide electronic capabilities for clusters of classrooms (not to mention electricity and plumbing), because such utilities could be more centralized.

While we are considering the size of the building, let us also consider the size of the classrooms. We have mentioned in this book, and you have no doubt heard the argument before, that class size has a long-term correlation with academic achievement (Benefits of Small Classes Found to Last Years, 1999) and benefits are retained even after students return to regular-size classes (Finn, 2002). Because of this, many schools—and even states—have mandated that class sizes be reduced. There are at least two factors, however, that have undermined the success of such initiatives: class size must be reduced to about 15 students (Small Class Sizes, 1999) to realize increases in achievement (thus far, class size reduction efforts have only brought class limits to around 20–22 students), and current classrooms *and classrooms in newly designed schools* are sized to accommodate several dozen stu-

Artwork by Jim Boden

Must school architecture use "big box" classrooms and long hallways? What changes in design for the school of the future could better accommodate students both for instruction and when moving from place to place?

dents. In the latter case it is a matter of "if you build it, they will come." That is, as long as schools provide space for larger numbers of students per class, eventually larger numbers will be placed there. So, what if a school were designed specifically for smaller class sizes? How might this work out in terms of the overall school design? Could breaking this conceptual block pave the way for more innovation in education?

Expandability of schools is another area that holds great potential for the creative thinkers concerned with education. Schools are typically designed for a finite number of students even though they just as typically have changing enrollments. It will never be practical for communities to build structures that far exceed present needs based only on speculation about the future. However, if expansion were part of school design, then meeting future demands would not have to occur in such a haphazard manner.

The future may well see an entire industry arise in the design and manufacture of "modular schools." In this case a district or community could purchase a set of modules for their particular needs. There could be administrative modules, instructional modules, special needs modules, energy modules, and so on. These units could be manufactured to allow schools to seamlessly add new modules as the need arose. Moreover, as needs change, modules could be removed and replaced with different modules that serve different purposes. Old modules could be refurbished, updated, and reused in other settings. It might even be the case that modules no longer needed by the school could be moved and used for other community activities such as community centers, youth centers, or senior centers. The questions to you and your classmates include, What types of modules should be developed and how should they be equipped? What should be included in a "classroom module" or in a "physical education module"? More importantly, how could the module concept be employed so that schools never become the antiquated buildings that are found throughout our country? How could such a system be established so that schools were always on the cutting edge, and so that others stood to benefit from that fact? Don't limit your thinking to cookie-cutter school designs. Designing expansion and change into a building system does not eliminate the "art" from architecture, it challenges it!

The Layout

The ideas mentioned in the previous section bring us to a discussion of the school layout. If you were about to put pen to paper to design a new school, what *does* that school need to have? Don't be constrained by the model for schools with which we are all so familiar. Instead, let's consider some of the things that go on at school and work from there. Perhaps the old design will prove to be the best—but let's see.

Necessary Facilities We have already mentioned that the traditional school layout is that of a backbone hallway flanked by large open rooms. You can easily embellish this model by adding a reception office, principal's office, cafeteria, library/media center, perhaps an office for a school nurse and a couple more for a guidance counselor or two, and certainly a gymnasium or some sort of physical activity room. Beyond this, schools also have parking areas for teachers and staff, and increasingly high schools provide large parking areas for students. What more can you think of? Compile a list, and having done so, underline each of the items that are *necessities*.

What constitutes a necessity? That's a question that you and your classmates may need to decide. For example, has the library given way to the more contemporary "media center"? And if so, does a media center really need to occupy as much space as a library once claimed? Is it necessary to have a band hall that is separate from an auditorium? Does parking, at a new school, have to be outside of the building? Perhaps parking garages could be built into the basements of new buildings. Is it necessary to provide parking for students? Maybe the design could call for a limited number of parking spaces that would be assigned as rewards for academic excellence or for social or civic contributions.

When you examine the necessities of schools you may find duplication and, yes, extravagance. Though education does deserves the best that can be provided, many schools have less than the best as it is, others have fine facilities but no money left to replenish **consumables** (paper, supplies, etc.), and still others use store rooms and closet space to accommodate academic activities. Think outside the school as you know it. How can new schools benefit from a new perspective?

A Look at PE Physical education is space- and equipment-intensive. It also is a conduit for extracurricular activities. As we consider the school of the future, PE is a logical place to begin changing our perspectives. To a considerable degree this is a curriculum issue, but we mention it here because PE affects the school in terms of physical facilities within the building as well as the space and facilities required for activities outside of the building.

The purpose of physical education is to teach an awareness of the needs of the human body, how to maintain its musculature and other systems to provide for a healthy life, and how to "fuel" the body. Notice that playing dodgeball or walking around a playing field is not among the purposes of PE. In fact, sports and exercise in general—the teaching of or the playing of—represent physical *activity*, not physical *education*.

There are at least two major problems with the sports-for-sports-sake orientation of contemporary physical education. The first is that not all students have an

consumables Materials and supplies that must be discarded after use. Examples are handwriting paper, workbooks, and photocopier paper.

Two important reasons for physical education programs are developing physical well-being and maintaining a healthy weight.

© Image Source/PictureQuest

interest in playing sports—and they should not be made to feel that such disinterest is antisocial or anti-physical-fitness. Second, few students successfully transfer their "learning" from physical education into lifelong activities that promote physical well-being. For instance, you may have been the star of your gym class when it came to leaping over the vaulting horse, swinging on the parallel bars, or walking across the balance beam (if your school had gymnastics equipment), but when was the last time you did any of these things once you left school?

Yet physical education is clearly as important as any other education in terms of the "whole student." As a society we take our physical condition for granted at the same time that we spend literally billions of dollars a year on health care. It is estimated that 61 percent of the adult population in the U.S. is overweight or obese (National Health and Nutrition Examination Survey, 1999). Over 10 percent of preschoolers are overweight (Vail, 2004). Moreover, 15 percent of American students age six to 11 may be severely overweight (Buchanan, 2005), which is defined as having a body-mass index exceeding 95 percent of their peers (Tanner, 2003). Approximately 16 percent of students age 12 to 19 are overweight; 25 years ago, the figure was 5 percent (Buchanan, 2005). The American Dietetic Association (Amschler, 2002) contends that 11 percent of American children are "clinically overweight" and another 14 percent are at risk of becoming overweight. The Centers for Disease Control and Prevention estimate that 25 percent of children are, or are at risk of becoming, obese. That message should directly affect the presentation of physical education in our schools. Children are not too young to learn about the care and feeding of their bodies, and they are not too young to learn habits of fitness and conditioning that could indeed last a lifetime. These habits have a major impact because overweight children are more likely to develop high blood pressure, asthma (Vail, 2004), and diabetes (Amschler, 2002; Vail, 2004). Because obesity is so widespread, federal law requires school districts to establish wellness policies including "goals for nutrition, physical education, and other school-based activities" (Buchanan, 2005). An excellent article with much practical information is "Rebuilding the Food Pyramid" (Miller, 2004).

What are the implications for physical education in our school of the future? For one thing, it means that we need to rethink just what PE is all about. This exercise can easily be carried over to other subject areas, but a consideration of PE provides a good starting point for practice in switching perspectives. Consider the possible implications of the suggestions in the following list. Add more items to the list as you think of them. In all cases, however, open up your thinking rather than being bound by what you've "always known."

1. The focus of PE is understanding the needs of the human body.
2. PE should guide students in fulfilling the needs of the body to maintain optimal health.
3. Sports can be used sparingly as a technique for exercising the body. Competitive sports, however, should only be extracurricular.
4. The topics of teamwork, competition, and striving to achieve a goal can be objectives of a physical education program. If so, they should be explicit objectives. Better yet, they should be explicit objectives of the overall curriculum for the school. Exercises to foster these traits should be evident across all subject areas.
5. Age-appropriate exercise equipment and the teaching of exercises that require no equipment should characterize all physical education programs.
6. High school (and perhaps middle school) physical education facilities should (a) tend toward physical fitness machines rather than sports equipment, (b) be of higher quality than home exercise equipment, and (c) be made available to the community (more on this later).
7. Physical education programs should be held accountable for identifying fitness models and routines for each child. This is so important that it may be reasonable to require some sort of physical fitness IEP (Individualized Educational Plan) for each student. This plan could be started in kindergarten and expanded, revised, and improved as children grow up.

By the way, as of 2005, only five states had comprehensive standards for physical and motor development (Scott-Little, Kagan, & Frelow, 2005).

Again, our look at PE is not intended as an attack. As we mentioned previously, PE as a subject area offers a good start in reconceptualizing what school is all about. Consider the other subject areas as well. The academics, the arts, and vocational education each have specific purposes, specific needs to be effectively presented, and specific outcomes. Examine each with regard to the purpose of school and its place in serving that purpose. In particular, how do those subject areas affect your design for the school of the future?

Flow No matter what we do with the school of the future, it will likely require the movement of large numbers of people from one place to another. This might involve getting students to and from school as well as getting them from one place within the building (or its surrounding facilities) to another within scheduling constraints. Even if school becomes an "at home" activity by virtue of electronic technology, the activities of many people will still need to be coordinated. We refer to all of this as the "flow" of the school.

For the foreseeable future, school will likely continue as a model that requires many students to come to a designated site for their educational experiences. As you consider the future of education, you may wish to emphasize this more immediate possibility. However, don't negate the possibility of school being a very different enterprise than anything you've experienced. When we were in high school, the notion of home computers, e-mail, and of course the Internet were not even considered. And as for calculators, well, we were taught to use slide rules! So go ahead, consider those ideas that no one else has considered. Ideas, after all, are the seeds of progress.

But let's get back to the flow of schools. As we see schools today, elementary students tend to be assigned to one classroom and one teacher and to stay there throughout the day. Middle school and high school students have a homeroom, but move throughout the building to many different classes and many different teachers. Is this the best model?

While teaching at a university in China for a semester, one of your authors had the opportunity to observe a different model. When students arrived at the university in their first year, they were assigned to a particular classroom. This became "their" room for the duration of the collegiate experience. Each student had a key to the room and together the students were responsible for keeping the room clean and orderly. Throughout the day professors came to that room to teach the different subjects. The classroom also became the meeting place for the students after classes. Students would come there to study and to talk, and occasionally they would have a class party. The model was that students stayed in one place while professors, of whom there were few, moved from room to room.

Could we apply a variation of this same model to American middle schools and high schools? Rather than putting several hundred students in motion every hour or so, a model such as this would do away with much of the lost time between classes, the delays in starting classes when students arrive late, and—as you will recall—the lost time at the end of a class as students prepare to depart before the period ends.

What effect would such a change have on the design of your new school? Would hallways need to be as big? If hallways were not as big, could that space (as square footage in the overall building) be better utilized or perhaps eliminated, thus decreasing the cost of the building? Perhaps the hallways could surround a pod of classrooms rather than dividing the rooms. In this way the rooms might be better organized to provide several different specialties such as a general classroom that opens into a science room, which opens into an arts room, all without leaving the central area.

As you consider the new school, consider the entire idea of moving people from one place to another. Time spent moving about is lost instructional time. According to Burns (1984), at the elementary level there are 31 major transitions occupying 15 percent of the instructional time available for the day. That's nearly an hour a day, and elementary students don't move from room to room for each subject!

Use of School Facilities

Schools were once thought of as the heart of a community. That's not difficult to understand since they were the places where the children were sent to learn. School was a socializing experience and it was funded in large part by the local community. Contemporary schools have a more distanced relationship to the community. That is, they are provided for a particular purpose, they are funded by a community that is often concerned with the high rate of taxes and fees that they must pay, and it is not uncommon that the only time people (other than students and school personnel) show up to the school are for various extracurricular activities. This issue certainly has two sides: (1) the school is established and funded for the purpose of educating students, but (2) the school is a public building that sits idle in the evenings, on the weekends, and for several months each year. So it might be worth our time to consider how the schools can be more fully utilized.

Year-Round School   The debate regarding keeping schools open all year long has raged for many years. Arguments for keeping schools open range from better utilization of the facilities to increased retention of prior learning. After all, a three-month hiatus from what one has just learned hardly contributes to improved achievement. Arguments opposed to keeping schools open often revolve around parents' and teachers' summer vacation plans as well as the increased costs of keeping the facility up and running for three additional months—particularly in a time when schools around the country are forced to close early because funding has run out. In any case, when we consider that literally hundreds of millions of dollars' worth of real estate is left idle for a quarter of every year, it is easy to understand that this is an area in need of attention.

As you may know, year-round school proposals do not usually involve extending the 180-day "school year" model. Instead, the days are simply distributed differently. For instance, students might have a week-long vacation after each six weeks of school with a four-week break after the third and sixth six-week period. The 45–15 and 60–15 days on/days off models are the most common. Another possibility is to stagger the starting date of different grade levels. At any rate, the number of days doesn't change, just the distribution of them.

Most any of these plans have legitimate pedagogical purposes, but all wreak havoc with working parents who depend on school to provide day care for their children. Of course, a school system using the six-week plan mentioned above also provides the opportunity for entrepreneurs to develop a day-care program that specifically works with the school's schedule—after all, that's what they do now.

The first question that you might want to investigate in terms of making better use of school facilities is that of innovative scheduling possibilities. Activity 14.3 provides you that opportunity, but notice that there are two parts to the activity: (1) use the Internet to research the various alternative scheduling proposals that have been made, and (2) spend time considering how to make the proposals work. As you redefine what school is, watch for these opportunities for new businesses to arise.

Community Activities The principal of your local public school may not like to hear this, but the truth is the truth: public schools are public facilities. There could be some debate as to whether they are owned by the community, the county (parish), or the state; nonetheless, they are bought, built, and operated with tax dollars. With that in mind, it is not unreasonable to suggest that schools be used for civic purposes to a much greater degree. Public schools are often used as polling places during election time. They should also provide a resource for the community at other times.

Go Online!

ACTIVITY 14.3   Around the Curriculum in 180 Days

1. Using search terms such as "year-round school" or "alternative school schedules" to get you started, research various models available for alternatives to the "traditional" school year schedule. (Note: You may find that as schools eliminate summer school because of *economic* reasons, year-round sessions may actually become more desirable for *pedagogical* reasons.)

2. For every alternative there is some counterargument. Select one of the alternatives you have identified and adapt both the model and the circumstances in which it would be used to make it workable in your school of the future. That is, try to find the reasonable, though pedagogically sound, compromise that would make the idea work.

3. From all you have found, is the "traditional" approach still the best? Do you think there might be a more effective way to schedule school (even if you haven't found it yet)? Why or why not?

There are probably few teachers or principals who welcome the idea of the community-at-large traipsing through the building when school is not in session (this could be in the evenings, on the weekends, or during vacation periods). We share their concern—after all, we are teachers too. Yet a community that takes responsibility for its activities at the school sets an example for the students who attend that school (and it is up to the community to determine what example it will provide) and also allows for the possibility of taking more pride by virtue of "ownership" in the school itself.

If we take this notion further, there are at least two categories of community use to be considered: nonprofit and revenue producing. You might allow such non-profit activities as community government (town meetings), civic organization meetings, and summer (vacation) programs for the children in the community. For revenue, you could charge admission for concerts or lecture series in the school auditorium, if you've included one. Continuing-education programs could use the facility in the evenings, and a portion of the participants' tuition would go toward renting the space. Opening that newly designed physical fitness center might also be an opportunity for producing revenue. Individuals who use the exercise equipment during the evenings could reasonably be expected to pay a membership fee of some sort because they are, after all, using equipment that must be maintained and eventually replaced. Or private businesses could lease the space during off hours and provide fitness classes to community members. Thus, funds for the continued maintenance of the facility would be provided without taxing the school's academic budget.

Possibilities such as these are not ones to be entertained lightly. It is a sad fact of our society that there are those who would abuse the access that is being granted. It is also true that there can be organizations that the community, for noble or less than noble reasons, does not want to allow access. This topic would be a good one for you to debate in your Introduction to Education class. The first question might be whether or not the community at large has a right to use the facility. Your next questions could be whether the community has a right to allow some activities and not others and how to define any limits. But keep in mind that the underlying issue that we are addressing is how the school facilities in their generic and specialized senses can be better utilized. As you've seen, one approach is to have more educational experiences, and another option is to allow non-educationally based activities. What is your opinion on this?

Ancillary Businesses

ancillary businesses Businesses with services that directly relate to the successful functioning of the school. Examples include transportation and food services and medical and psychological personnel.

Modern schools involve many **ancillary businesses.** Throughout this textbook we have been discussing education as an isolated entity. We have discussed teaching, teachers, students, history, and philosophy, all in the context of the school itself. However, long gone are the days when school was just a building in town where children met with a teacher. The administration of schools today includes transportation services, food services, supplies, medical attention, and diagnostic testing by professionals in a wide range of physical and psychological disciplines, to name just a few of the nonteaching aspects of school. To a degree this is the result of the school's being more than just an institution of education; to a considerable extent it has become a holistic child-care institution. This may sound familiar if you remember our previous discussion of social reconstructionism. That is, the school is sometimes seen as the mechanism for solving society's problems. Thus, schools provide breakfast to children who receive none at home. They provide lunch. They provide after-school programs for children who have nowhere to go until their parents can leave work for the day. You and your classmates should debate whether the school of the future should be responsible for such activities and services. What services should the school provide, and what services should be provided to the school by businesses? For instance, should schools and school districts that are responsible for educating children also be in the transportation business? Could this be better served by a private school bus service of some sort? Similarly, should schools provide food service with district personnel, or should this be contracted out as well?

At first blush it might seem that such things have to be done by the school because there is no business that provides the service, and the cost would be increased if private companies provided the services. Well, both of those concerns might be correct. However, we suggest that schools might be better off if their focus could be on education alone rather than also being responsible for repairing buses, providing after-school programs for monitoring children in loco parentis, or assuming the task of feeding hundreds of children. Further, encouraging ancillary businesses to take on many noneducational tasks would stimulate new business growth as well as healthy competition for the best product at the best price. What would be the effect if schools emphasized schooling rather than an overall package of child welfare? Could we legitimately expect parents to take a greater responsibility?

Keep in mind that if free and reduced lunch programs, breakfast programs, and so forth are what the community wants, they can remain as state and federally subsidized programs. The *providing* of the service, however, could be done by an ancillary independent business. Use this challenge as an opportunity to examine what schools do and what they provide, and discuss with your classmates those things that could be more efficiently handled by others.

Instructional Innovations

We move now to the question of what *teaching* might be like in the years ahead. It is curious that after hundreds of years, organized education is presented in much the same way that it always has been. A school built today will have roughly the same layout as the schools you may have attended as a youngster. The format of one teacher with a large group of students will continue, and even some of the educational tools will be the same.

For instance, a new school will likely have a chalkboard in each classroom. Chalk? How many years do you suppose teachers have been using chalk? Educational innovation in that area is represented by white boards and dry-erase markers. Of course, markers are much more expensive than chalk, and in a budget crunch replacing those markers becomes problematic. What other innovations can you identify that have truly changed instruction? Let's consider some possibilities for change in the way an education is delivered. Activity 14.4 offers an opportunity to consider school in terms of the past and the future.

Instructional Delivery Systems

When we think of instructional delivery systems for the future of education, there is no escaping the impact of computers and electronics. But when the power goes off for one reason or another, school must able to continue. You have likely had an experience at a store or in dealing with a company over the phone that was unable to take care of you because "the system" was down. In many of these instances, the fact that the system is down has no effect on your immediate need or situation, yet it has become an excuse for shutting down all sorts of business operations. The peculiar nature of education is that we do not enjoy the luxury of just shutting things down and sending everybody home. It sounds as though we are singing the

> ### ACTIVITY 14.4
> ## Janus in the Classroom: Considering the Past and the Future
>
> Janus was a Roman god with two faces, thus allowing him to see the past and the future at one time. Use this activity to take a look at the past and use that as your springboard to the future.
>
> Think about what teaching was like when you were in your K–12 school years. Chapter 8, A History of Education, will provide you with some insight about teaching over the past 2,000 years or so.
>
> 1. How would you describe what teachers did when you were in school? Keep in mind that this book has tried to show you that teachers do many things in addition to actually presenting a lesson.
>
> 2. When you think about yourself as a teacher, in what ways does it parallel your response to question 1?
>
> 3. With all you know of technology and global events, how would you expect the tasks of teachers to be different (if at all) in five, 10, and 20 years from now?

praises of chalk, doesn't it? You might be correct, but the real challenge for you in this section of the chapter is to create ideas within ideas, that is, ideas that have backup systems built in.

The Electronic Wall How about replacing the chalkboards (or dry-erase boards) in your school of the future with electronic walls? Suppose we arrange two classrooms with a narrow electronics service hallway between them. The wall of each room that backs up to either side of the hallway will be the electronic wall for that room. The classroom will face the electronic wall, much the same as a typical classroom faces a chalkboard on the front wall. In this case however, virtually the entire wall will be a display area. Let's say the display comes to within two feet of the floor so that even in the earliest grades the students should be able to write on the surface. Vertically, the display area goes to the ceiling, and horizontally from one end of the wall to the other.

Our Multimedia Academic Graphic Interface Computer Wall (a.k.a. the MAGIC Wall) could have many uses. In one upper corner, or wherever the teacher wishes it to display, could be the clock. Of course, MAGIC Wall that it is, with a few keystrokes on a wireless keyboard the teacher could bring up clocks with the time displayed for several countries around the world as well. Another portion of the screen could display the day's academic objectives. Another could provide class rules and, in the event of emergency, instructions for exiting the building. Our sophisticated wall could scan students as they enter the room to take attendance for the main office and pop up a picture of each student at his or her desk as part of a seating-chart display. The display would highlight empty desks so the teacher would be able to see at a glance whether all of the students were in class and ready to begin.

Certainly the most important use of the wall would be for instructional purposes. The wall would connect directly to the teacher's computer, probably an easily carried "task slate" (that has a schoollike sound to it, doesn't it?) with a touch-sensitive keypad or a writing pad. Whatever the teacher writes on the pad or whatever program is called up through the computer could be displayed on the front wall as well as on individual student consoles. As the teacher moves about the room and finds a student with a particularly good solution to a problem, that student's work could be displayed on the front board.

Artwork by Jim Boden

An entire wall that can accomplish instructional, management, and administrative needs and be useful even when shut down? It's not as much a stretch of technology as it is a matter of considering how technology really can be put to use in the schools. How would you say the MAGIC Wall could be put to use?

Our wall could also display individual or group responses to questions. As a problem is presented, the students would enter in their responses. The results could be displayed numerically or graphically on the front board, allowing all to see how the class had responded. Video programs from disks (Disks? What will replace disks in the future?) or television could also be displayed on our electronic wall.

Perhaps most useful would be that you as the teacher, or your students, could come up and write on the board just as if it were a dry-erase or chalkboard. Perhaps we would opt to use a stylus or just use a finger to write across the board. Whatever is written on the board could be saved, revised, or deleted just as with any other computer-generated information. Best of all, when the MAGIC Wall is shut down, or if the power goes off, the wall has a white appearance and dry-erase markers can be used on the surface. If we could think of a way to make that surface chalk-friendly, we'd really have it made! You probably know that all of the technology for a wall such as this is available today. What would it take to make it a reality? What other uses can you think of for the electronic wall that might require new steps in technology?

Holographic Displays Several years ago when the novelty of holography was stirring imaginations, the instructional implications of holographic technology seemed enormous. Since that time, medicine has made great use of this imaging technique, but very little impact has been felt within the schools. Yet holography could make some forms of instruction obsolete (perhaps that's why it hasn't flourished) and could greatly enhance others. Let's consider a couple of ideas.

High school biology courses would be among the most immediate beneficiaries of holographic materials, that is, as long as the purpose of dissecting frogs was for seeing organs in situ rather from the flat plane of two-dimensional photogra-

In Their Own Words

Feature 14.1   Bill Gates Discusses Education and Technology

Regardless of his or her ability or disability, each learner will work at an individual pace—inside or outside the classroom. Workers will be able to keep up-to-date on techniques in their fields. People anywhere will be able to take the best courses taught by the greatest teachers. The net will spread the availability of adult education, including job training and retraining and career-enhancement courses, all over the world. Computers with social interfaces will figure out how to present information so that it's customized for the particular user.

Many educational software programs will have distinct personalities, and the student and the program will get to know each other. A student will ask, maybe out loud, "What caused the American Civil War?" The computer will reply, describing the conflicting theories: that it was primarily a battle over economics or primarily a battle over human rights. The length and the approach of the answer will vary depending on the student and the circumstances. The student will be able to interrupt at any time to ask the computer for more or less detail or to ask for a different approach altogether. The computer will know what the student has already read or seen and will point out connections or correlations and offer links to related subjects. If the computer knows that the student likes historical fiction, war stories, folk music, or sports, it will use that knowledge to make the reply more interesting. It will exploit the child's predilections in order to teach a broader curriculum.

With a few notable exceptions, this kind of educational software and content isn't available yet. There isn't much good curriculum software, and there's only a modest amount of good supplemental software. Huge quantities of information have gone up on the Internet, but not much of it is aimed specifically at students. There really isn't much of a market for educational software yet because schools haven't demanded it.

What it means to "teach well" will change in some regards, but certainly not in others. Teachers will be pivotal in the future role of educational technology, doing much more than showing kids where to find information on the net. Teachers will still have to build kids' skills in written and oral communication. But they'll use technology as a starting point or an aid.

Educators, like so many in today's economy, have to adapt and readapt to changing conditions. First they must make a transition in which some teaching styles and skills will be perceived as more valuable and others less valuable than before. Class sizes may rise by a couple of students in some schools to help pay for the technology and possibly for better teacher compensation. Interacting groups will be smaller, however, and the learning environment more effective, so many teachers may see teaching as a more rewarding profession.

Bill Gates is the chairman and chief executive officer of Microsoft Corporation, the company he cofounded in 1975. These passages are excerpted from Chapter 9, Education: The Best Investment (pp. 218–231) of his book The Road Ahead *(1996).* ∎

---

phy. Holography would allow that three-dimensional view. And it could allow a three-dimensional view of far more than the few science specimens that are sanctioned for dissection in high school biology classes.

Biology would not be the lone benefactor: Physics, astronomy, and chemistry are overflowing with models that could be better understood if studied in three dimensions. The humanities would also be able to use the technology for the presentation of famous speeches (reenactments, that is, unless someone starts recording speeches in a holographic medium right away).

We could expect that a broader use of holographic displays, particularly across subject areas and in younger grades, could improve skills in mental modeling and in spatial reasoning. These are elements of Piaget's fourth stage of cognitive development; formal operational thinking. It is widely believed that this stage, generally occurring in late adolescence and through adulthood, is never reached by vast numbers of people. What sorts of applications can you think of that would allow students to develop their abilities for abstract thinking?

Experiential Education

experiential education An approach that seeks to make what is taught as part of school as realistic as possible. Field trips are an example.

Early in this textbook we spoke of instruction as a means for bringing the world to the students. For example, field trips actually take students to the world they are studying whereas lectures consider an aspect of the world that is not easily visited or easily brought to the classroom. **Experiential education** seeks to make what is taught as part of school as realistic as possible. Though we are trying to peer into the future, you know that this is not a new notion. As we've already discussed, the idea of experience-based education can be traced at least to the beginning of the 20th century. The pragmatist philosophy and the progressivist movement strongly advocated such an educational structure. What we know today as *constructivism* is based on providing students with experiences upon which to build—from which to learn. The problem that you face is how to integrate such an approach with classroom instruction.

We can learn some lessons from the one aspect of experiential education that did win broad acceptance in the public schools: vocational education. Whether or not vocational education has a place in your school of the future is another matter, a matter of your philosophy of education. However, vocational programs do represent the very practical application of learning. It is easy enough to see how a student who studies auto mechanics will apply that knowledge after leaving school. What is a little more difficult is determining how the student studying English or algebra will apply that knowledge outside of school. Yes, we have once again come up against the question of just what education is supposed to accomplish. Perhaps you can see how all of the chapters of this textbook are interrelated. After all, in this chapter regarding the future of education we have already referred to previous chapters on curriculum, teaching, philosophy, and history!

To determine what experiences from the real world can be applied to instruction in the world of school, you will have to decide what education in the future is supposed to accomplish. Do we learn algebra to do algebraic manipulations? To an extent that's true. But what of calculus or the dissections we mentioned earlier from biology? You must ask yourself at this point, What are the experiences students will face in the real world? Secondly, you can ask how best to prepare them for those experiences. There's little doubt that providing experiences rather than abstractions is the best way to go—after all, *experience, expertise,* and *expert* all seem to have some common thread, don't they? Activity 14.5 is an important exercise for you to complete. What are the experiences that schools should provide to students?

The Internet   The Internet has changed dramatically since its inception in the late 20th century. At first, it was a research tool that served to exchange information from mainframe computer to mainframe computer. The interconnected computer networks of the Internet provided the foundation for the *information age.* Now, as personal computers in all of their various forms from desktops to cell phones have proliferated, the World Wide Web, which is a collection of documents and other resources accessible via the Internet, has become largely a marketing tool. True, there is much information to be found via the Web, but it is also true that the ease with which information can be posted has led to a lot of information of dubious quality. This is not meant to disparage the Web, but rather to make three educationally important points: (1) the Internet is just as much a part of everyday life for vast numbers of people as is television, (2) information from the Web must be accepted with the same guarded skepticism as that which is provided through other media sources (just because something is posted on the Web doesn't mean it must be true), and (3) it is changing. With regard to that last item, we can expect it to change at least as drastically in the next 20 years as it has over the past 20 years, and probably at a much more rapid pace. What we might look toward is a "split-

ACTIVITY 14.5
What Are the Experiences of Life That Should Be Experiences of School?

Completing this activity will require that you (or your group if this is done with your classmates) decide what your school of the future is to accomplish. For example, should schools provide society with good citizens? Good workers? Independent thinkers? Certainly, there may be a collection of goals that you need to identify.

1. Identify one to five goals that you believe the school should accomplish for each child.

2. For each of the goals you have listed, identify the life experiences that schools should provide to students so they may reach that goal. For instance, good citizenship might be helped along by engaging students in community service projects as part of the regular curriculum.

3. Describe an activity that you would want to include as part of your school of the future. For example, what community service project could you design into the curriculum that would span multiple grade levels?

ting" of the Web. That is, the highly commercial aspect will continue in its own development while research and educational functions, for example, will develop in their own directions.

Each chapter of this book has provided you with opportunities to use the Internet to find information to help you answer questions and solve problems. We hope that you have noticed that none of the activities simply asked that you access and then repeat information. Rather, we have used the Web as a source of information that would facilitate your own solving of problems. But let's take a moment to shift that perspective somewhat. That is, rather than taking the Internet for what it is and trying to adapt our lessons to it, let's ask what we want the Internet to be so that it will better meet our needs. After all, that's the approach that established the Internet in the first place.

As you begin to think about the possibilities, focus on the idea that education fosters the development of an individual's abilities. It also develops the skills for putting those abilities to use in solving problems. In essence, we are recommending that you reconceptualize the Internet so that the next generation moves from the information age to the *age of problem solving*. In what ways can an electronic network of information sharing contribute to that mission?

Local Issues One of the most interesting by-products of the Internet has been its global nature. The phrase "World Wide Web" itself conjures up the notion of people from distant countries being in communication with one another. However, the Web is already serving to let people take the global aspect of the Internet for granted. In fact, the Internet is more "computer" than it is "global." That's unfortunate, for rather than breaking down the distance between people it has opened up a new territory, "cyberspace," that fosters a high-tech anonymity.

One way of getting around this issue, beginning particularly with younger students, could be to put the Internet to work on local issues. Children have enough of a challenge understanding the concept of a local community without trying to conceptualize a global version. So, what problem-solving scenarios could you develop that either address particular subject areas or integrate subject areas that would put students to work on locally relevant concerns? What are the current characteristics of the Internet that would facilitate such activities? What necessary characteristics does the Internet lack at this time that would contribute to meaningful problem solving for students in K–12? Could you design a curriculum strand for elementary school children using a local issue? Perhaps the middle school curriculum could contain a strand (or theme) that addresses a state-level issue. High school students could focus on national issues.

We hasten to add that we don't want to abandon the global capabilities that the Internet of today or tomorrow offers. Rather, we want children to build their appreciation of community, of society, through several levels much as Bruner (1960) advocated with his spiral curriculum approach that increased in sophistication as students learned more and more.

The Global Community A natural extension of what we have been saying could be the establishment of a Global Creative Problem-Solving Consortium as part of the curriculum. Such a project would allow schools in the United States to form problem-solving partnerships with schools in other countries. In this way, students could be involved in multiple subject areas and multiple cultural perspectives with genuine problems to solve. Ebert and Ebert (1998) refer to one such model as Topic Integration for Macro-Learning Experiences (TIME). In this particular model, students work in collaboration with their partner schools to consider the problem from three perspectives: (1) the cause of the problem, (2) the effect the problem has on people, and (3) the possible effect of the problem on the future. From that foundation the students work to find a solution that would be acceptable from all cultural perspectives involved. Could you make such an activity a component of your explicit curriculum in the school of the future? What would you need from a new educational Internet to make such a global problem solving consortium work? Activity 14.6 helps you to lay the foundation for a global problem-solving consortium. You don't have to wait until you are hired to begin an ini-

---

ACTIVITY 14.6
From a Node to Nations: The Global Creative Problem-Solving Consortium

Many schools across the country and around the world now have access to the World Wide Web and telecommunications. Far from the pen-pal days of years gone by, there is potential here to combine many academic subjects and elements of John Dewey's pragmatist philosophy (that is, giving students real problems to solve) while allowing children (elementary through high school) to communicate with children from many cultures. Schools today and schools in the future could make genuine communication among nations part of the standard curriculum.

Working as a group, identify a topic that elementary, middle school, or high school students in your area could study. From that topic, phrase a question that could be presented to the students. As part of your instructional planning, address the questions below.

1. How could you use the Internet as a source for studying the problem?

2. What subjects areas could be involved in studying the problem?

3. Does your local school have a "sister school" in another country? If so, can the problem be shared with those students as well? If not, how could you put students in your local school in contact with students in another country via the Internet?

Note: See Ebert, C., & Ebert, E. (1998). *The inventive mind in science.* Englewood, CO: Teacher Ideas Press, for a complete plan for establishing a Global Creative Problem Solving Consortium.

tiative such as this. Could your local school or your college's education department take on such a project? The prospects are exciting!

Instructional Materials

We've been using books for a long time, and books have changed the world. But has the preeminence of the printed page passed? If you visit a public school as part of your clinical internship, you'll no doubt notice that students carry virtually all of their books in bookbags. This raises physical development concerns, particularly for young children, as students must lean far forward to counterbalance the weight of the book bag. In addition to the question of health and safety, there are at least two dimensions of this issue that you might want to consider as you conceptualize the school of the future: print media versus electronic media, and textbooks (print or electronic) in general.

electronic books Books in a format that is electronically (computer) based.

Electronic Books Do **electronic books** (e-books) have a place in the school of the future? There are viable arguments for and against the use of such technology. Not surprisingly, we may find that many of the arguments on either side are not based on pedagogical concerns but instead are business concerns. Does this mean that the future of education is destined to be constrained by the same influences that constrain it today? That could be the case, but remember that "education" does not have a mind of its own—it is an institution guided by the minds of people. Here are some points to consider as you begin to think about the pros and cons of e-books for school.

Points in Favor of Electronic Books

1. All of the books that students now carry could be reduced to a single memory stick that is played on a lightweight and portable monitor. No more overloaded bookbags.
2. Use of memory sticks means no moving parts. Thus, electronic books would have minimal power-supply needs. In fact, they could utilize "wind-up" power technologies such as that used in radios.
3. Type size can be changed at will by the user. No straining one's eyes to read the text.
4. An electronic book may occasionally be damaged, but textbooks must be routinely replaced due to wear and tear.
5. It is easier to search an electronic text than a paper text.
6. Highlighting or bookmarking electronic text does not damage the page (for the next user).
7. Memory sticks (or whatever technology you envision) can be easily reprogrammed and updated. An entire textbook series could be updated rather quickly.
8. The costs of equipment could potentially be no more than the costs of stocking and restocking sets of books for each student and each subject area.
9. Electronic book publishers could key all state academic standards to the materials that they publish. As standards change, updating would be relatively easy.

That list is enough to get us started. What other benefits can you identify for switching from paper media to electronic media for student textbooks?

Points against Electronic Books

1. An electronic book is only as good as the power available to run it.
2. Equipment is too valuable to entrust to students.

Courtesy of David Ottenstein Photography

Would you prefer to use e-books rather than traditional print media? What other possibilities might there be?

3. Textbook publishers are set up for print. (Actually, many publishers of print material already make their listings available electronically.)
4. An electronic book can display only one page at a time. It would be difficult to switch back and forth between pages or to view pages from different "books" at the same time.
5. Paper producers would suffer drastic losses in business.
6. Equipment is more susceptible to damage than is a traditional book.
7. An increasing reliance on the storage of information in electronic form imperils the archiving of cultural history. That is, a simple electronic virus can do a lot of damage.
8. Students would have to find something else to throw at each other. (Is that a pro or a con?)

Whether or not to use electronic books may seem like a simple sort of question to you—perhaps even a nonquestion. Yet it is concerned with how we will handle the written word, both in presentation and degree, in the years to come. What sort of changes should there be? Might publishers of electronic textbooks come to see that their profits are in the "intellectual property" of the written word and make the equipment available to schools at little or no charge? After all, only those who have the machinery to run the books would be inclined to buy the books. Therefore, much like the photography industry, which depended upon the sale of film, the textbook industry might go out of its way to see that there's an electronic book on every desk the first day of school.

Textbooks We've spent some time now considering the way in which textbooks might be presented, but the larger question of content remains to be considered as well. In an earlier chapter we discussed the degree to which several large states influence what is found in textbooks. That influence is purely a matter of economics. The electronic book idea could change all of that. Perhaps publishers could make their materials available to the state education agency, and a textbook-content committee could then pick and choose what they want to appear in the electronic versions for their state. This technology, of course, is not years away. As you read these words, electronic publishing can easily accomplish such a task. What are the implications, good and bad, if every state can simply tailor a text for its students?

Perhaps more so than our previous "what if . . ." scenarios, this one may indeed have ramifications that could empower education on the one hand and sow the seeds of civil conflict on the other. As you are well aware, at this point states can choose the topics they want to include in the curriculum and which ones they wish to exclude. As education remains a matter of state's rights and technology allows more customization of teaching materials, we can expect that education across the nation could become more dissimilar than similar. Under our current system, such differentiation is held in check by the encumbrances of print media. Remove those encumbrances, however, and the situation could change dramatically.

As you plan for the school of the future, you should consider such issues. For example, do we want education to become more nationally influenced or more regionally influenced? Are there expectations that all states should be required to meet (essentialism)? Are there things about our culture that all students should know (perennialism)? Is our political and social allegiance to the state first and the nation second, or the other way around? Consider these issues carefully in discussion with your classmates and in discussion with other education professionals. We provided two curriculum-oriented chapters in this textbook because the issues were too complex for one chapter. The curriculum has never remained "static" for any appreciable length of time—and so there is no reason to expect that it will begin to do so now. Who will plan for the future?

■ Fiscal Education

A discussion of education in the future, whether tomorrow or a decade or so away, is not complete without a consideration of the fiscal nature of the enterprise. At this time, only three items in the federal budget are more expensive than education: defense, welfare, and interest on the national debt. In any state the most expensive item by far is education. According to the Digest of Education Statistics 2002 (2003), in 1998–1999 a full 35 percent of all state and local government spending, a whopping $490 billion, was spent on education and libraries. That's a lot of tax dollars. The question of funding education, therefore, is one that will always be on the political agenda.

Funding Education

Who *should* pay for school? If you pay income taxes, then you contribute funds toward education whether or not you have children attending school. Similarly, if you pay county property taxes, then you likely provide funding for your local school—again, whether or not you have children in school. As you know, one of the hotly debated funding issues for contemporary schools is whether parents who send their children to private schools should also have to pay local school taxes. In many states (and some local communities) a portion of the sales tax is directed toward the schools. In essence, virtually anyone with an income and anyone who spends that money is paying for school. Is that the most equitable system?

As we've mentioned, some people believe that if their children do not attend a public school, they should not have to pay school taxes. In that same vein, it is not uncommon to hear the argument that people who have no children, or whose children are not in school, should not be required to pay school taxes. It is easy enough to say that as Americans we should all support our military through tax dollars, for that's a matter of national defense. Education, however, is not recognized as a national responsibility. In the absence of a constitutional amendment, education will remain the responsibility of the various states (perhaps you see such an amendment in education's future). So, is there a precedent for arguing that not everybody should be responsible for contributing to education?

Another version of the funding argument says that those with children in school *should* bear the brunt of funding education. Much like the "use tax" charged to truckers, it might seem plausible that indeed the parents should take this responsibility. The good news would be that parents pay taxes only during those years that their children are in school. The bad news would be that the more children one has, the greater the burden. You may well ask whether such a system would actually constitute "public" education, but that may be the least of the problems.

What do you suppose would be the outcome when a family simply could not afford to send their child, or perhaps one or more of their children, to school? Is this an unreasonable scenario? Certainly it is not when you think of the number of students who receive free or subsidized meals at school. In 1990, nearly 20 percent of children in the United States between the ages of six and 11 were living in homes below the poverty level (Digest of Education Statistics 1999, 2000). No, this is a very real possibility. So how shall we fund education in the future? How do we insulate education from economic slumps that threaten to cut education budgets? In your school of the future, will we all pay a set "school tax" and then parents will pay a surcharge? Many parents believe that they pay a surcharge as it is in terms of fees to be paid and supplies to be furnished at the beginning of each school year.

Economic Education

economic pragmatics Skills in managing money.

While we are on the topic of funding, perhaps we could entertain another curriculum topic for the school of the future: economic education. You may have had some sort of high school civics course that included a unit on economics. Or perhaps you had an economics course that you took to fill out your schedule. Yet earning, using, and managing money is a major concern in adult life and it would seem reasonable that people should specifically learn about it in school. Some might say that money and finance is a personal matter, but then again, so is health. The school of the future could play an instrumental role in the teaching of **economic pragmatics,** skills for managing money. There's also that item known as "retirement." You might not be particularly concerned about that right now, but the economy can change very quickly, and if you are part of a district or state retirement system, those changes might come at an inopportune time for you. You could, however, be investing just a small amount of money each month in a retirement account (such as an IRA) right now as part of your overall plan. You see, going to work is often the center of attention for students nearing the end of their high school years, but few include practical considerations of their "golden years" as part of those deliberations.

How might you incorporate economic pragmatics into the curriculum of the school of the future? And how do you suppose that sort of education might pay off for school funding as those students become taxpayers? Do you think that if people in general knew more about economics in general, they might generally understand the economic needs of the school system and thus make better decisions?

Economic pragmatics could be a course of study that begins with the same introduction to money that curricula already incorporate. You might want to consider this issue in terms of the spiral curriculum proposed by Bruner. We have mentioned Bruner's approach before (and you will likely hear more about it in your educational psychology course), and the topic of money management in our free enterprise society would seem to be a prime candidate. Bruner has suggested that "any subject can be taught effectively in some intellectually honest form to any child at any stage of development" (1960, p.33). Through the spiral curriculum students are introduced to elements of the subject that are developmentally appropriate for them. From year to year the curriculum "spirals," adding increasingly sophisticated topics to the foundation being developed. So we certainly could weave a spiral curriculum into the curriculum at large that begins with the rudiments of money as a system of exchange (identifying coins and their value) and subsequently guides students through an understanding of the American economy, investing for the future, understanding taxes—to the point that they can ultimately take part in the establishing and levying of taxes, as well as balance a checkbook or use credit appropriately.

Be prepared, for you will undoubtedly find parents who believe that investing in anything but a savings account constitutes gambling, and they don't want you teaching their children to gamble. Perhaps a form of this same spiral curriculum could be constructed for adults as well. What do you think?

■ The Global Community

Finally, as you consider the school of the future you may well want to think in global terms. Though we hear it said all the time that the world is getting smaller, the fact is that it's the same size that it's been for thousands of years. It is true, however, that we see into many more lives and are keenly aware of events happening farther away than was the case a mere generation or two ago. We are "fellow Earthlings," and as such at the very least have a responsibility to peacefully coexist with each other. We would like to believe that as human beings our responsibility is still greater, that we have an obligation to contribute to humanity, but that borders on the political, and we will confine ourselves to the pedagogical.

The technology of electronics has radically altered communication on a local scale as well as on a global scale. We suggest that education should embrace such technology and raise mere communication to *genuine communication*. By genuine communication we mean people actually interacting with other people to solve real problems, to exchange personal opinions about everything from cultural custom to pop culture, and to celebrate that which we have in common as we understand those ways in which we differ.

Schools can lead the way in bringing people together. Actually, this takes us back again to our discussion of educational techniques as they attempt to bring the world to the students. Telecommunications as they exist, and as you might speculate that they could become, hold tremendous potential for making that world much more real, more accessible, and, well, bigger, for your students. So how will you incorporate technologies such as these in the school of the future? In your new design, what will be meant by "the global classroom"?

In his work *The Fifth Discipline,* Peter Senge (1990) describes the necessity for building a "shared vision" within any organization. Education, of course, is an organization that has grown into an institution. He explains it this way:

> A shared vision is not an idea. It is not even an important idea such as freedom. It is, rather, a force in people's hearts, a force of impressive power. It may be inspired by an idea, but once it goes further—if it is compelling enough to acquire the support of more than one person—then it is no longer an abstraction. It is palpable. People begin to see it as if it exists. Few, if any, forces in human affairs are as powerful as shared vision. At its simplest level, a shared vision is the answer to the question, "What do we want to create?" (p. 206).

This chapter has been about generating new ideas and finding new perspectives. It's fun and exciting. We can offer suggestions and some ideas of our own in the conceptualization of education's future, but the ultimate design and building of such a school will require a shared vision that you will have to take the lead in building. Indeed, we hope to see—to be a part of—that school of the future. We also understand that you, as a new member of the education profession, are the most important player in terms of seeing that it happens. Imagine!

Conclusion

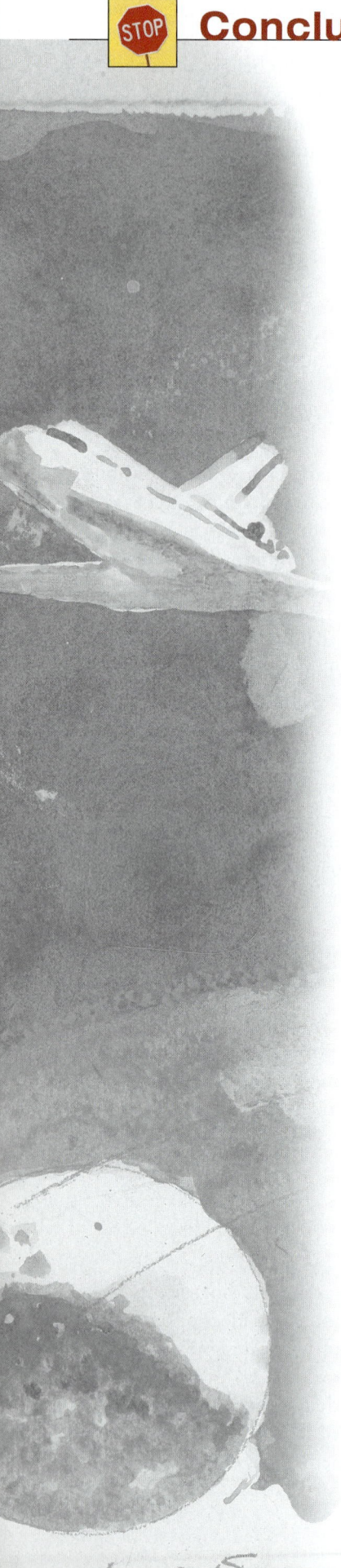

As you consider the school of the future, try to break yourself of the habit of thinking that makes the future so distant and chimerical. In 1903 the first powered airplane flew through the air for 12 glorious seconds. In 1947, less than 50 years later, the sound barrier had been broken, air travel was becoming commonplace, and sights were set on outer space. We are not talking about 1,000 years from now when we ask you to consider the future of education. We are asking you to consider the changes that could occur in education within a lifetime. We are asking you to be among the pioneers who will one day have people saying, "I can remember when schools didn't have _____ ." And the folks they say it to will wonder how schools ever got along.

Here are some highlights from the chapter:

1. The work of technologists is to combine information in new ways to make products or processes that extend our capabilities.
2. There are already over 2,500,000 children ages three to six years old using the Internet.
3. A common theme of many authors and school technology specialists is the "seamless integration" of technology into the work that teachers do.
4. A key to making technology-based reforms in education work will be appropriate professional development opportunities for teachers.
5. Among the most intriguing possibilities for technology in the schools are distance education and virtual schools.
6. Assistive technology focuses on applications of technology for students with special needs.
7. Along with the perceived benefits of technology in the schools, there are a range of issues regarding its presence and implementation.
8. As of 1999, a full 50 percent of the approximately 78,000 public schools in our country had one or more building features rated as less than adequate.
9. Enrollment trends that are difficult to forecast have resulted in the widespread use of "portables," buildings intended for temporary use. Often, temporary becomes semipermanent.
10. Considering that schools take up a lot of open space, they are good candidates for the use of alternative energy sources such as solar and wind power.
11. To address changes in enrollment and changes in instructional needs, school design in the future may turn to the design and manufacture of "modular schools."
12. The school of the future will likely require the movement of large numbers of people from one place to another in terms of getting students to and from school as well as getting them from one place to another within the building.
13. Arguments for keeping schools open all year range from better utilization of the facilities to better retention of prior learning. Arguments opposed often revolve around summer vacation plans, the increased costs of keeping the facility up and running for three additional months, and day care issues.
14. The administration of schools includes transportation services, food services, supplies, medical attention, and diagnostic testing by professionals in a wide range of physical and psychological disciplines, as part of a holistic child-care institution.
15. Instructional delivery systems for the future of education will likely focus on the use of computers and electronics. But schools must be designed to be able to continue even if the power goes off.
16. To determine what experiences from the real world can be applied to instruction in the world of school, we must decide what education in the future is supposed to accomplish.

17. Three educationally important points relate to the Internet: (a) the Internet is a part of everyday life for many people, (b) information from the Web must be accepted with the same guarded skepticism as that provided through other media sources, and (c) the Web is changing.

18. Electronic books have the potential of lightening students' loads, but as education remains a matter of state's rights and technology allows more customization of teaching materials, we can anticipate that education across the nation could become more dissimilar than similar.

19. Approximately 35 percent of all state and local government spending, $490 billion, is spent on education and libraries.

20. The schools of the future could play an instrumental role in the teaching of *economic pragmatics,* skills for managing money.

21. Education should embrace the fact that the technology of electronics has radically altered communication both on a local and on a global scale, and take it upon itself to use that technology to raise mere communication to *genuine* communication.

Key Terms

technology	logistical innovations	ancillary businesses
distance education	equal access	experiential education
virtual school	solar collectors	electronic books
assistive technology	consumables	economic pragmatics

Educational Engineering

Case Studies in Education

Enter the information from the table below into the Educational Record for the student you are studying.

	The Student's Needs and Technology	The Student's Computer Literacy	Year-Round Schooling Option
Davon	Technology is a fact of life, and kindergarteners are not afraid to learn about and use it. Davon responds to working on school computers and does so regularly both by free choice and in the computer lab during global arts.	Davon enjoys using the computer and is on grade level in his ability to use it appropriately. He engages in math and language arts activities on a regular basis.	Davon would benefit greatly from year-round school. It would provide a safe and secure environment. His stories center around moving from one place to another and being dropped off at places and not being picked up on time.
Andy	As Andy gets older, he will probably benefit from using a word processor rather than writing by hand. As far as using computer-assisted instruction, great care would need to be used in choosing the kinds of programs that would benefit Andy. His off-task behaviors are evident when he is in the computer lab. If he is not engaged, he will not perform well.	Andy navigates well on the computer. He also uses the Internet at his aunt's house.	A balanced calendar approach would probably benefit Andy. The long summer gap is harmful to his retention of learning.

(Continued on next page)

Judith	Computer-assisted instruction could help Judith practice basic skills in reading and math and offer positive reinforcement. She would not likely use the Internet critically enough, but keyboarding skills would be useful.	Judith has rudimentary keyboarding skills and knows how to turn on the computer and open a desired program. She has no access to computer technology outside of school, which has put her behind many other students on her grade level.	Judith would benefit from year-round schooling. Any gains made during the school year are typically lost over the summer months since it appears that there are no educational opportunities for her during the summer.
Tiffany	At this time, there are no particular technological innovations that would better serve Tiffany's needs.	Tiffany is very technologically literate. She can create charts, graphs, etc. for reports that her teachers would not easily be able to create. She is aware of the potential of most computer programs and uses many of the options. She has her own computer at home and her own Web site.	Tiffany would appreciate and welcome year-round school for the academic challenges. She has routinely commented that she is bored during the summer. However, year-round school would not meet Tiffany's immediate needs. She needs serious exposure to outside activities and nonacademic situations to increase her emotional and social well-being.
Sam	Sam uses computer technology to help meet his educational needs. He uses the computer to complete writing assignments and to do some limited research required by specific classes. At the end of the school year a computer reading program was made available to him, allowing him to scan assigned pages so that they can be read to him by the computer as he follows the text. This is a multisensory approach that allows him to compensate for his areas of disability.	Sam is not as technologically literate as most students at his age or grade level. He does not have access to a computer at home and has taken no computer classes in high school. For the upcoming year, however, he is enrolled in a computer class.	The consistency of year-round school would probably be of benefit to Sam since predictability and structure assist him in being more successful.
Bao	Though Bao's education would certainly be enhanced by more independent computer time, digital projectors, classroom Web pages and the like, she is a skilled learner and is more affected by classroom climate than the use of technology.	Like most of her peers, Bao is an adept instant-messenger, and is in charge of downloading the family's digital pictures to the computer. She even purchased all her holiday gifts online this year.	Whether year-round schooling would benefit Bao would depend entirely on the teachers she received. A strong teacher with whom Bao felt an affinity could definitely affect her, but a stressful class setting could create a dislike for school or a subject area. The issue is Bao's affective feelings for education more than the pedagogical issues of year-round school.

1. Based on this child's cognitive and physical abilities, how could technology improve his or her educational experience? What *new* technological innovations could you suggest?
2. If the child you are studying is not computer literate, is it the school's responsibility to address that deficiency? What skills should a student possess when he or she graduates from high school? What recommendations can you make for the use of technology (instructional, telecommunications, or assistive technology) to improve the educational experience of your student?

3. Based on the case study information about this child, what recommendations would you make for either keeping or changing the scheduling of school? Would you favor year-round schooling? Staggered schedules? The traditional schedule? Something new? How would you as a teacher be able to meet this child's needs under a traditional schedule?

Designing the School of the Future

This is your opportunity to do some visionary thinking. We have discussed just a few aspects of school that might see changes in the future. You can consider the same areas or identify additional aspects of particular interest to you.

Near Vision

Suppose that you were asked to consult with the architects of a school to be built next year. The designers want to know what issues you see as most important to the design and what recommendations you would make so that this would be a model that other school districts would want to copy. What recommendations would you make about instructional needs, the movement of people throughout the building throughout the day, and more effective use of the facility?

Distant Vision

One of the young architects on the project wants to make school design her specialty and, in particular, wants to be a leader in innovative school design. The architect feels that designing schools of the future will require much more collaboration between those who know architecture and those who know pedagogy. She was very impressed with your recommendations and asks whether you would contribute to the design of a futuristic school.

Having read this book and completed or discussed many of the activities, you are in good position to contribute a pedagogical perspective. Don't confine yourself to traditional perspectives for this conversation. Think beyond what school has been to consider what school could be. Where would you begin? What would be the first concerns you would bring to the architect's attention? What would you say about class size? About new technologies in the school? About the future of instruction?

What would the school of the future look like? Draw a plan for the school that you could provide to the architect. Don't be afraid to "think outside the school" for this exercise. The ideas you express now become the possibilities for the future.

Praxis Practice

Most states will require that you successfully complete the Praxis Series of examinations to qualify for certification. One or more of those tests will be subject-area tests. Another, which has a more practical orientation, will be the Principles of Learning and Teaching (PLT) examination that is appropriate for your certification area.

Completing the Quick Check Quizzes in each Unit Workshop will give you practice with the multiple choice format of the PLT. The Case Studies in Education and Designing a School of the Future activities will help prepare you for exercises that require reading a scenario and providing short answers to questions asking what you might do in such a situation.

Educational Engineering

A message throughout this textbook is that the professional educators of tomorrow must be teachers who take part in the character of society beyond the school, who contribute to the ongoing efforts at improving the quality of educational opportunities, and who do indeed look to the future prospects and potential of their profession. The three chapters of Unit IV have sought to demonstrate that your students reflect the society in which they live and make choices for themselves, and that you can be an active participant—in the near term, the long term, or both—in shaping that society. Few professions offer the opportunity to leave such an impression upon one's world. We encourage you to avail yourself of the intrinsic rewards that are being offered to you through such participation.

Case Studies

You have now considered the student you have been following in the context of the teacher, the teacher's role, the diversity characterized by your student in numerous regards, the qualifications of teachers, the history of education and the philosophies that underlie it, and even in terms of the future of education. It's time to put this all together in a form that you can share with your classmates.

Using presentation software such as PowerPoint (you can compile your project in a notebook if electronic technology is not accessible), prepare a presentation that summarizes what you have found and draws conclusions about providing educational opportunities for your student and about your own preparation as a professional educator.

You may wish to organize your presentation in accordance with the 14 chapters of the textbook, or perhaps in terms of the four units. Whatever organizational strategy you use, your presentation should include a description of the student, your perspective on the various educational issues that you have encountered along the way, and your conclusions about meeting the needs of this student. Finally, be sure to include a section that reflects upon your place in providing educational opportunities to this and other students. Your professor may have additional criteria that should be included in the presentation.

Be creative in your presentation! Try to avoid simply listing slide after slide of text. You may wish to include photographs of schools and perhaps a photograph of a friend or sibling to act as your "student." The composites contained in the book do not refer to one specific student, so it will be acceptable for you to "assign" an identity for the purposes of this project. We hope that your professor will allow you the opportunity to offer this presentation to your class.

Designing a School of the Future

By now, your design for a school of the future has probably taken on more of an identity than simply being an idea. You have formulated vision statements, mission statements, brochures, and presentations for different audiences throughout the course of this exercise. It is now time to compile it all into a compelling presentation that brings your design to life for other people.

Using presentation software such as PowerPoint (you can assemble your presentation in notebook form if electronic technologies are not accessible) compile a presentation that will educate others about your design and persuade them to share in the plans you have developed. You may wish to organize your presentation along the lines of the 14 chapters in the textbook, moving from one stage to the next, or perhaps in terms of the four units—the choice is yours. Your professor may have additional criteria for inclusion to correspond with your particular course.

Avoid making this a simple report of what you have done! Be dynamic and convincing! You have assembled a vision for a new school that either strengthens what we now have in place or offers something completely new. Inspire people with your presentation! Include floor plans and representative photographs as appropriate. If you have discussed your project with school personnel, legislators, and of course, your professor, include comments from these individuals—and perhaps a photograph of those people that you quote. Display the slogan you developed prominently throughout the presentation so that people remember your message.

We hope that your professor allows you the opportunity to make your presentation to the class. Whether or not others wholly embrace your ideas, putting those ideas out there gets other people thinking about possibilities as well. You may even want to revisit your presentation as you continue with your teacher education program. By the time you are facing student teaching, your continued look at the institution of education may become the foundation of an honors project. Whether or not it goes to that length, we would certainly like to hear about the design you have fashioned as you worked your way through this textbook. And by all means, throughout your career in education, keep looking to the future and to your ability as a professional to have an impact on the direction of organized education!

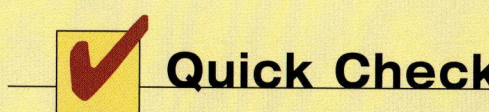 **Quick Check**

Answer keys with page references are in Appendix E.

Chapter 12

1. A family structure consisting of two parents and one or more children in the household is known as which of the following?
   a. nuclear family
   b. extended family
   c. functional family
   d. blended family

2. Research has shown that children of never-married mothers have been subject to which of the following?
   a. greater home stability
   b. an advantage in academic development over children of divorced parents
   c. greater disadvantage academically than children of divorced parents
   d. no academic advantage or disadvantage as compared to children in nuclear families

3. A family structure in which the children may be his from a prior marriage, hers from a prior marriage, and theirs is known by which of the following terms?
   a. nuclear family
   b. extended family
   c. functional family
   d. blended family

4. The terms *resiliency* and *intentionality* are of particular importance for which type of family structure?
   a. children of divorced parents
   b. same-sex relationships
   c. dysfunctional families
   d. multiethnic marriages

5. Which of the following was *not* among the factors identified by the Census Bureau as putting children at risk?
 a. ethnicity
 b. presence of a personal disability
 c. absence of either or both parents in the home
 d. lack of English proficiency

6. As recently as 1996, what percentage of people under 18 years of age lived in poverty?
 a. 15 percent
 b. 25 percent
 c. 33 percent
 d. 40 percent

7. Families with children constitute about what percentage of people who become homeless?
 a. 15 percent
 b. 25 percent
 c. 33 percent
 d. 40 percent

8. In states requiring the reporting of suspicion of child abuse, teachers are held immune from prosecution arising from making such a report because they are considered as which of the following?
 a. state employees
 b. agents of the child welfare agency
 c. mandated reporters
 d. "Need to know" personnel

9. Of the approaches taken by the schools to prevent teen pregnancy, the most promising have been programs emphasizing which of the following?
 a. abstinence
 b. sex education
 c. education for "safe sex"
 d. role-playing parental responsibilities

10. The average hours per week television viewing time of American children is:
 a. 22
 b. 32
 c. 42
 d. 52

Chapter 13

1. The text suggests that the impetus for reform in education has historically been due to which of the following?
 a. competition with other nations
 b. parents' desire for the best possible educational opportunities
 c. appreciation of change as necessary for progress
 d. dissatisfaction with the prevailing condition of education

2. Peter Senge argues that reforms fail because they fail to include which of the following?
 a. community support
 b. shared vision
 c. adequate funding
 d. research-based development

3. Which of the following does the text *not* mention as a way business is involved in education policy?
 a. tax funding
 b. financial involvement such as sponsorship, grant funding, scholarships
 c. business leaders as guest lecturers in high school classes
 d. demands of education such as preparing trained workers

4. Approximately how much money did the federal government contribute to education in the year 2003?
 a. $100 million
 b. $30 billion
 c. $90 billion
 d. $124 billion

5. With regard to protecting the health and safety of children while in attendance, the schools act in loco parentis, which means which of the following?
   a. in place of the parents
   b. with parental consent
   c. in conjunction with the parent
   d. as the legal parent

6. A program that seeks to replace some aspect of the current educational operation is referred to as which of the following?
   a. intervention
   b. systemic initiative
   c. revision
   d reform

7. Some effort that supplements normal procedure, either by providing remediation or enrichment or by extending or reducing responsibility or authority, is known as which of the following?
   a. intervention
   b. systemic initiative
   c. revision
   d reform

8. Enrichment programs under the heading of gifted and talented fall under which of the following categories?
   a. intervention
   b. systemic initiative
   c. revision
   d reform

9. Which of the following is *not* one of the primary categories that the text suggests for the evaluation of a reform initiative?
   a. Implementation
   b. Nature of the Program
   c. Duration of the Program
   d. Need for the Program

10. The reform evaluation model indicates that the question of costs involved for a program should be considered in which stage of considering a proposal?
    a. Implementation
    b. Nature of the Program
    c. Duration of the Program
    d. Need for the Program

Chapter 14

1. For design considerations, the text refers to possibilities that would affect the physical aspect of school, such as the building, the facilities within, and the movement of people, as which of the following?
   a. ergonomics
   b. logistical innovations
   c. people planning
   d. physical plant determinants

2. As recently as 1999 nearly 40 percent of all public schools were using what type of classroom facility?
   a. mixed-use buildings
   b. Internet-wired classrooms
   c. temporary buildings
   d. closed-circuit television

3. Which of the following represents one conceptual block that the text suggests serves to keep school design essentially the same as it has always been?
   a. Large buildings are cost effective.
   b. Large rooms will always be filled with large classes.
   c. It is impossible to keep pace with technology.
   d. Small buildings are cost effective.

4. The idea of schools being available for community use could raise which issue mentioned in the text?
   a. whether community use takes precedence over school use
   b. whether the state or the community has primary ownership of the facility
   c. whether community organizations can be relied upon to treat the facilities appropriately
   d. whether the community can grant access to some organizations but not to others

5. When designing the school of the future, it is important to remember that schools, unlike businesses, cannot do which of the following?
   a. make changes in midyear
   b. evaluate their "product" regularly
   c. shut down while changes are made
   d. hire additional personnel as needs arise

6. According to the text, which of the following areas of technology could have implications for classes such as biology and chemistry?
   a. holography
   b. DVDs
   c. Internet access
   d. lasers

7. An approach to education that seeks ways to make what is taught as part of school as realistic as possible is known as which of the following?
   a. vocational education
   b. progressive education
   c. experiential education
   d. technical education

8. The text suggests that we might see a significant change in Internet activity within a decade or two. Which of the following changes is discussed?
   a. "splitting" the web into commercial and academic versions
   b. provision of free access to the Internet
   c. business and education Internet-based collaborations
   d. faster download speeds

9. One suggestion discussed in the text for addressing the notion of the "global community" is to involve students in a school-based version of which of the following?
   a. Internet pen pals
   b. a global creative problem-solving consortium
   c. Web-based study of different cultures
   d. model United Nations

10. Which of the following reflects one concern raised in the text with regard to the increased use of electronic publishing of textbook materials?
    a. Content may be published before it is verified.
    b. Schools could not afford the equipment necessary to utilize electronic publications.
    c. Educational materials would become increasingly homogenized for a national audience.
    d. Education across the nation could become more dissimilar than similar.

Appendix A

Case Studies in Education

Below are descriptions of six students: two elementary school students, two middle school students, and two high school students. Each description (and the information that appears at the end of each chapter) has been written by a classroom teacher, and each represents a *composite* of students they have known: It would be an extremely inappropriate invasion of privacy to provide such personal information about an actual student. However, keep in mind that while the "student" may be fictitious, what the teachers are describing to you comes from experience in the classroom each day.

Read each of the descriptions and then choose one to be the case study you follow. You might select a student in the grade range you wish to teach, or one whose situation is of interest to you. The choice is yours. Following the last of the descriptions you will find directions for working with the case study. Before getting into all of that, take some time to be introduced to these students.

■ Brief Biographies

Elementary School

Student's name: Davon   **Age:** 5

Grade: Kindergarten   **Ethnicity:** African American   **Gender:** Male

General Description: Davon lives with his mother and four siblings, two older and two younger. Davon is tall and has a sturdy build for his age. He comes to school dirty and wearing tattered clothing that is often not appropriate for the weather. He frequently wets his pants and even comes to school wearing dried soiled clothing. Davon regularly shares worries of moving. He talks about how he loves his school and wants to stay. Davon's eyes and smile will light up your heart. Each morning he greets his teacher with a smile and a hug. Davon is quick to defend himself and points out anyone who is treating him unfairly or disrespectfully. He is a sponge for knowledge and loves learning. Davon loves to be a helper and puts forth his best effort in all that he does.

Student's name: Andy   **Age:** 9

Grade: 3   **Ethnicity:** Caucasian   **Gender:** Male

General Description: Andy has big brown eyes and strawberry blonde hair. He is personable and respectful of adults. He laughs easily and has a good sense of humor. Andy responds well to the special attention he receives from the teacher in his resource room and in his reading classroom. He lives with his grandparents, who received custody of him last year. His brother continues to live with his mother and stepfather. Andy has been diagnosed with Attention Deficit Disorder with Hyperactivity (ADHD). He has a history of struggling in reading and was almost retained in second grade. He is currently on a first-grade reading level.

Middle School

Student's name: Judith   **Age:** 13

Grade: 7   **Ethnicity:** Caucasian   **Gender:** Female

General Description: Not a strong student, Judith enjoys reading (fourth-grade level) much more than math or science. Neither parent completed school. The gross household income is barely above the poverty level. Judith's clothes are well worn and often in need of washing; opportunities for bathing and personal hygiene are apparently infrequent. This is becoming more problematic as she becomes an adolescent. Judith seeks a sense of belonging and desperately wants to have and be a friend, despite the teasing she takes from other children. For her 13th birthday she invited her "friends" to a party, and on the invitations had written "Please bring a present." No one showed up. Never a problem to her teachers, she seeks out their acceptance with a smile and conversation. This youngster wants to give to others, but needs a teacher willing to help her along in matters beyond the curriculum.

Student's name: Tiffany   **Age:** 11

Grade: 6   **Ethnicity:** Caucasian/Hispanic **Gender:** Female

General Description: Tiffany is from an upper-middle-class family. Both of her parents are professionals who have traveled extensively. Her father is from the northeastern United States. Her mother, the daughter of a Spanish diplomat, was born in Barcelona, Spain, and has lived around the world as the result of her father's assignments. Tiffany is a polite and pleasant child who has an enormous oral vocabulary. She loves to read and enjoys mind puzzles as a recreational activity. During her third-grade year, Tiffany's teachers recommended her for the Gifted and Talented program. She was placed there beginning her fourth-grade year.

Socially, Tiffany has no close friends. Most of her classmates consider her obnoxious and egotistical, and ignore her during nonstructured times. She enjoys talking and interacting with the adults and usually has a fair knowledge of current world events or local concerns to participate in the conversation.

During a parent-teacher conference, her parents and teachers expressed concerns that Tiffany is becoming too much of a perfectionist. They are also worried about her lack of social skills and close friends. Her parents have tried to get her involved in many activities, but she has no interest in any extracurricular sports or hobbies. They have tried taking her for counseling through her church and privately but to no avail. In fact, Tiffany has now proclaimed herself an atheist and verbalizes her belief whenever given the chance. She spends evenings reading in her bedroom. She does not enjoy talking on the telephone and finds television to be, as she says, "immature."

High School

Student's name: Sam   **Age:** 16

Grade: 11   **Ethnicity:** African American   **Gender:** Male

General Description: Sam is a handsome, polite, and reserved young man. He has a medical diagnosis of Attention Deficit Disorder (ADD), confirmed in middle school, for which he is prescribed medication. Sam is also a special needs student; his eligibility for special education services was first determined in kindergarten. Results of psychological and educational assessments place him in the Low Average range of intellectual ability with significant learning disabilities, which appear to be primarily language-based, in the areas of reading, math, and written language. Specific areas of concern included receptive and expressive vocabulary, auditory processing, and thinking and reasoning skills. In order to address these deficits, Sam received language therapy through sixth grade, at which time assessment results indicated that language performance and cognitive ability were commensurate, and speech/language services were discontinued. However, Sam's speech is still difficult to understand; he has a very soft voice and mumbles, often making it necessary to ask him to repeat what he says.

Sam lives with his mother and his younger sister. Extracurricular activities include participation in the school cross country/track program and, interestingly, concert choir.

Student's name: Bao   **Age:** 16

Grade: 11   **Ethnicity:** Asian American   **Gender:** Female

General Description: Meet Bao. She moved here from Vietnam when she was three and is fully adjusted to American life. In some ways, she is proud of her ethnicity: She goes to temple with her family, brings Vietnamese food to school for class parties, and enjoys family trips to Vietnam. In other ways, however, Bao is uncomfortable with her background. At school, her classmates and teachers call her Katy; at home, she responds to her parents in English.

Being Asian hasn't been an issue at school. A junior, Bao is a cheerleader and member of Future Business Leaders of America. Her grades, Bs and Cs, are just barely good enough to satisfy her parents. Bao gets along well with her teachers, and is well liked by most of her peers. She is cheerful to the extreme and shies away from conflict, so you'll never see her confronting her teachers or sharing an unpopular opinion during class discussion. All in all, she is known for being a good student, friendly and involved without really standing out in the crowd.

■ Setting Up a Case Study Folder

Though case studies can be used on a chapter-by-chapter basis as you consider the topics discussed in the text, this activity is designed so that you can compile a reflective dossier concerning one child as a semester-long project. If you take that approach, you will complete your introduction to education course with a product that documents *your* thinking about many issues and aspects related to teaching. Even the teachers who wrote these composites have commented that the experience allowed them to appreciate their own students to a greater degree.

You could make copies of a standard page (see Figure A-1) and then fill out the record by hand, but it is likely that you will compile your Educational Record using a word processor. Whether or not it must be printed and placed in a notebook or folder will depend upon the requirements in your course. We will describe the process assuming that you will use your word processor and then assemble the pages into a folder.

1. Prepare a cover page for the document. You might want to follow this example:

[Course Title]
Case Studies in Education
Educational Record

[Your Name]   **[Semester, Year]**

We recommend a cover page to help keep your student's information confidential. Of course, these student profiles are composites, not identifiable individuals, but you can begin the practice of maintaining confidentiality right now.

2. The next page after the cover page should list the student's name and basic information as given in the Brief Biographies. Include the general description of the student as well. You may wish to elaborate on the information provided by describing the community in which the child might live and attend school. You may decide to use a photograph of a local school as the context for your case study. Do not, however, include a picture of a child. Even though we all know that the case study does not describe the child in the photo, other people who see the folder may assume it does.

3. Now format a page to serve as a template for your educational records. The master page might look like the example in Figure A-1. Fill in your student's name, age, grade, gender, and ethnicity.

Figure A-1

Educational Record Information Sheet

Educational Record

Chapter (No. and Title): _____ Date: _____
Student: _____
Age: _____ Grade: _____ Gender: _____ Ethnicity: _____

Category: _____
Information: _____
_____
_____

Category: _____
Information: _____
_____
_____

Category: _____
Information: _____
_____
_____

Question: _____
_____

Question: _____
_____

Question: _____
_____

As you complete each chapter in the book, use your master page to create a new page for that chapter. At the top of the new page, enter the chapter number and title so that your record will have a context among all the topics discussed in the book. Under "Category" fill in the topic areas from the table at the end of each chapter. For example, Chapter 1 has three categories of information: (1) Type of Person the Student Responds To, (2) The Student's Academic Demeanor, and (3) Parents' Perspective of the School. No chapter has more than three categories.

Now fill in the information provided for the student you are studying. The entries are brief.

Finally, fill in the questions that are asked for that particular chapter.

4. A complete folder will have 14 of these pages, one for each chapter. Following each chapter page should be the all-important pages that you add as you answer the questions. A brief heading such as the one that follows will help keep the pages in order:

Educational Record—Personal Perspectives

Chapter No. _____   Date: _____

Question No.: _____

Appendix B
Designing a School of the Future

Designing a school of the future is an open-ended activity that allows you to go in any direction you wish. This activity is very different from the Case Studies in Education that we described in Appendix A. Though the case studies allow you to express your own thinking about issues, they are nonetheless very "structured" activities. As you will find over the years, assessing and providing for student needs *is* a very structured activity. Yet teachers can be "visionary" as well, and so we have provided this opportunity to design a school of the future.

The format for presenting your future-school design will be determined by you and by the requirements of your course. You may wish to present a folder that documents your work or that of your group or class, or you may want to prepare an electronic presentation using programs such as PowerPoint. The activity provides you with specific tasks and issues from chapter to chapter so that the project is not overwhelming, but you have in this activity the opportunity to provide brochures, requirements for certification, curriculum guides, and drawings for facilities or instructional tools. If you are really ambitious, you can build models of what you develop.

We recommend that you begin by establishing some parameters for the project. For instance, how far into the future do you want to go: five, 10, 20, or 50 years? Obviously, this decision will affect everything else you do. Likewise, *where* will you go in the future? That is, are you designing a school for the area in which you live now? Or a school system for the entire state or country? Or perhaps you want to consider school in new environments such as deep-sea communities or on permanent space stations. Though these seem fanciful at first, the ideas you develop for these challenging situations could, in fact, have implications for more traditional approaches to school.

Give your school system a name. Invest ownership in it as early on in the project as you can. Most importantly, see no constraints in the design of your school, only problems to be solved. Your instructor may wish to impose particular parameters that represent experiences he or she wants you to have. For instance, some professors emphasize traditional schools, some emphasize the possibilities offered by charter schools, and some emphasize the student rather than the "school" at large. All of these can help you to focus your work without confining your thinking.

Finally, when you come up with something for education that really excites you, that really seems to stimulate thinking about what education could be, let us know! We would very much like to hear about it: eebert@coker.edu.

Appendix C

State Departments of Education

States

Alabama

Alabama Department of Education
Gordon Persons Office Building
50 N. Ripley St.
P.O. Box 302101
Montgomery, AL 36104-3833
Phone: (334) 242-9700
Fax: (334) 242-9708
Web site: http://www.alsde.edu/html/home.asp

Alaska

Alaska Department of Education and Early
    Development
801 W. 10th St., Ste. 200
Juneau, AK 99801-1894
Phone: (907) 465-2800
Fax: (907) 465-4156
Web site: http://www.eed.state.ak.us/

Arizona

Arizona Department of Education
1535 W. Jefferson
Phoenix, AZ 85007
Phone: (602) 542-4361
Toll-Free: (800) 352-4558
Fax: (602) 542-5440
Web site: http://www.ade.state.az.us/

Arkansas

Arkansas Department of Education
General Education Division Room 304 A
Four State Capitol Mall
Little Rock, AR 72201-1071
Phone: (501) 682-4204
Fax: (501) 682-1079
Web site: http://arkedu.state.ar.us/

California

California Department of Education
P.O. Box 944272
1430 N St.
Sacramento, CA 95814
Phone: (916) 319-0791
Fax: (916) 319-0100
Web site: http://www.cde.ca.gov/

Colorado

Colorado Department of Education
201 E. Colfax Ave.
Denver, CO 80203-1704
Phone: (303) 866-6600
Fax: (303) 830-0793
Web site: http://www.cde.state.co.us/

Connecticut

Connecticut State Department of Education
State Office Building
165 Capitol Ave.
Hartford, CT 06106-1630
Phone: (860) 713-6548
Toll-Free: (800) 465-4014
Fax: (860) 713-7017
Web site: http://www.state.ct.us/sde/

Delaware

Delaware Department of Education
John G. Townsend Building
P.O. Box 1402
Federal and Lockerman Sts.
Dover, DE 19903-1402
Phone: (302) 739-4601
Fax: (302) 739-4654
Web site: http://www.doe.state.de.us/

District of Columbia

District of Columbia Public Schools
Union Square
825 N. Capitol St. NE
Washington, DC 20002
Phone: (202) 724-4222
Fax: (202) 442-5026
Web site: http://www.k12.dc.us/dcps/home.html

Florida

Florida Department of Education
Turlington Building, Ste. 1514
325 W. Gaines St.
Tallahassee, FL 32399-0400
Phone: (850) 245-0505
Fax: (850) 245-9667
Web site: http://www.fldoe.org/

Georgia

Georgia Department of Education
2054 Twin Towers East
205 Jesse Hill Jr. Dr. SE
Atlanta, GA 30334-5001
Phone: (404) 656-2800
Toll-Free: (800) 311-3627
Fax: (404) 651-6867
Web site: http://www.doe.k12.ga.us/index.asp

Hawaii

Hawaii Department of Education
Room 309
1390 Miller St.
Honolulu, HI 96813
Phone: (808) 586-3310
Fax: (808) 586-3320
Web site: http://doe.k12.hi.us/

Idaho

Idaho Department of Education
Len B. Jordan Office Building
650 W. State St.
P.O. Box 83720
Boise, ID 83720-0027
Phone: (208) 332-6800
Toll-Free: (800) 432-4601
Fax: (208) 334-2228
Web site: http://www.sde.state.id.us/Dept/

Illinois

Illinois State Board of Education
100 N. First St.
Springfield, IL 62777
Phone: (217) 782-4321
Toll-Free: (866) 262-6663
Fax: (217) 524-4928
Web site: http://www.isbe.net/

Indiana

Indiana Department of Education
State House, Room 229
Indianapolis, IN 46204-2795
Phone: (317) 232-6610
Fax: (317) 233-6326
Web site: http://www.doe.state.in.us/

Iowa

Iowa Department of Education
Grimes State Office Building
E. 14th and Grand Sts.
Des Moines, IA 50319-0146
Phone: (515) 281-3436
Fax: (515) 281-4122
Web site: http://www.state.ia.us/educate/

Kansas

Kansas State Department of Education
120 South E. 10th Ave.
Topeka, KS 66612-1182
Phone: (785) 296-3201
Fax: (785) 296-7933
Web site: http://www.ksde.org

Kentucky

Kentucky Department of Education
500 Mero St., 19th Floor
Frankfort, KY 40601
Phone: (502) 564-3421
Toll-Free: (800) 533-5372
Fax: (502) 564-6470
Web site: http://www.kentuckyschools.org/

Louisiana

Louisiana Department of Education
1201 N. Third
P.O. Box 94064
Baton Rouge, LA 70804-9064
Phone: (225) 342-4411
Toll-Free: (877) 453-2721
Fax: (225) 342-7316
Web site: http://www.louisianaschools
.net/lde/index.html

Maine

Maine Department of Education
23 State House Station
Augusta, ME 04333-0023
Phone: (207) 624-6600
Fax: (207) 624-6601
Web site: http://www.maine.gov/education/

Maryland

Maryland State Department of Education
200 W. Baltimore St.
Baltimore, MD 21201
Phone: (410) 767-0100
Fax: (410) 333-6033
Web site: http://www.msde.state.md.us/

Massachusetts

Massachusetts Department of Education
350 Main St.
Malden, MA 02148
Phone: (781) 338-3000
Fax: (781) 338-3395
Web site: http://www.doe.mass.edu/

Michigan

Michigan Department of Education
Hannah Building
608 W. Allegan St., 4th Floor
Lansing, MI 48933
Phone: (517) 373-3324
Fax: (517) 335-4565
Web site: http://www.michigan.gov/mde/

Minnesota

Minnesota Department of Education
1500 Hwy. 36 W.
Roseville, MN 55113-4266
Phone: (651) 582-8200
Fax: (651) 582-8727
Web site: http://education.state.mn.us

Mississippi

Mississippi Department of Education
359 North West St., Ste. 365
Jackson, MS 39201
Phone: (601) 359-3513
Fax: (601) 359-3242
Web site: http://www.mde.k12.ms.us/

Missouri

Missouri Department of Elementary
and Secondary Education
P.O. Box 480
Jefferson City, MO 65102-0480
Phone: (573) 751-4212
Fax: (573) 751-8613
Web site: http://dese.mo.gov/

Montana

Montana Office of Public Instruction
P.O. Box 202501
Helena, MT 59620-2501
Phone: (406) 444-2082
Toll-Free: (888) 231-9393
Web site: http://www.opi.state.mt.us/

Nebraska

Nebraska Department of Education
301 Centennial Mall South
P.O. Box 94987
Lincoln, NE 68509-4987
Phone: (402) 471-2295
Fax: (402) 471-0117
Web site: http://www.nde.state.ne.us/

Nevada

Nevada Department of Education
700 E. Fifth St.
Carson City, NV 89701
Phone: (775) 687-9141
Fax: (775) 687-9111
Web site: http://www.nde.state.nv.us/

New Hampshire

New Hampshire Department of Education
101 Pleasant St.
State Office Park South
Concord, NH 03301
Phone: (603) 271-3495
Fax: (603) 271-1953
Web site: http://www.ed.state.nh.us/

New Jersey

New Jersey Department of Education
P.O. Box 500
100 Riverview Plaza
Trenton, NJ 08625-0500
Phone: (609) 292-4469
Fax: (609) 777-4099
Web site: http://www.state.nj.us/education/

New Mexico

New Mexico Public Education Department
Education Building
300 Don Gaspar
Santa Fe, NM 87501-2786
Phone: (505) 827-6516
Fax: (505) 827-6588
Web site: http://www.sde.state.nm.us/

New York

New York State Education Department
Education Building
Room 111
89 Washington Ave.
Albany, NY 12234
Phone: (518) 474-5844
Fax: (518) 473-4909
Web site: http://www.nysed.gov/

North Carolina

North Carolina Department of Public Instruction
Education Building
6301 Mail Service Center
Raleigh, NC 27699-6301
Phone: (919) 807-3300
Fax: (919) 807-3445
Web site: http://www.ncpublicschools.org/

North Dakota

North Dakota Department of Public Instruction
Department 201
600 E. Boulevard Ave., 11th Floor
Bismarck, ND 58505-0440
Phone: (701) 328-2260
Fax: (701) 328-2461
Web site: http://www.dpi.state.nd.us/

Ohio

Ohio Department of Education
25 South Front St.
Columbus, OH 43215-4183
Toll-Free: (877) 644-6338
Fax: (614) 752-3956
Web site: http://www.ode.state.oh.us/

Oklahoma

Oklahoma State Department of Education
2500 N. Lincoln Blvd.
Oklahoma City, OK 73105-4599
Phone: (405) 521-3301
Fax: (405) 521-6205
Web site: http://sde.state.ok.us/

Oregon

Oregon Department of Education
255 Capitol St. NE
Salem, OR 97310-0203
Phone: (503) 378-3600
Fax: (503) 378-5156
Web site: http://www.ode.state.or.us/

Pennsylvania

Pennsylvania Department of Education
333 Market St.
Harrisburg, PA 17126-0333
Phone: (717) 787-5820
Fax: (717) 787-7222
Web site: http://www.pde.state.pa.us/

Rhode Island

Rhode Island Department of Elementary and
    Secondary Education
255 Westminster St.
Providence, RI 02903-3400
Phone: (401) 222-4600
Fax: (401) 222-2537
Web site: http://www.ridoe.net/

South Carolina

South Carolina Department of Education
1006 Rutledge Building
1429 Senate St.
Columbia, SC 29201
Phone: (803) 734-8492
Fax: (803) 734-3389
Web site: http://myscschools.com/

South Dakota

South Dakota Department of Education
700 Governors Dr.
Pierre, SD 57501-2291
Phone: (605) 773-3553
Fax: (605) 773-6139
Web site: http://doe.sd.gov/

Tennessee

Tennessee Department of Education
Andrew Johnson Tower, 6th Floor
710 James Robertson Parkway
Nashville, TN 37243-0375
Phone: (615) 741-2731
Fax: (615) 532-4791
Web site: http://www.state.tn.us/education/

Texas

Texas Education Agency
William B. Travis Building
1701 N. Congress Ave.
Austin, TX 78701-1494
Phone: (512) 463-9050
Fax: (512) 475-3447
Web site: http://www.tea.state.tx.us/

Utah

Utah State Office of Education
250 East 500 South
P.O. Box 144200
Salt Lake City, UT 84114-4200
Phone: (801) 538-7500
Fax: (801) 538-7521
Web site: http://www.usoe.k12.ut.us/

Vermont

Vermont Department of Education
120 State St.
Montpelier, VT 05620-2501
Phone: (802) 828-3135
Fax: (802) 828-3140
Web site: http://www.state.vt.us/educ/

Virginia

Virginia Department of Education
P.O. Box 2120
101 N. 14th St.
Richmond, VA 23218-2120
Phone: (804) 225-2020
Toll-Free: (800) 292-3820
Fax: (804) 371-2455
Web site: http://www.pen.k12.va.us/go/VDOE/

Washington

Office of Superintendent of Public Instruction
Old Capitol Building
600 South Washington
P.O. Box 47200
Olympia, WA 98504-7200
Phone: (360) 725-6000
Fax: (360) 753-6712
Web site: http://www.k12.wa.us/

West Virginia

West Virginia Department of Education
Building 6, Room 346
1900 Kanawha Blvd. E.
Charleston, WV 25305-0330
Phone: (304) 558-0304
Fax: (304) 558-2584
Web site: http://wvde.state.wv.us/

Wisconsin

Wisconsin Department of Public Instruction
125 South Webster St.
P.O. Box 7841
Madison, WI 53702
Phone: (608) 266-3390
Toll-Free: (800) 441-4563
Fax: (608) 267-1052
Web site: http://www.dpi.state.wi.us/

Wyoming

Wyoming Department of Education
Hathaway Building
Second Floor
2300 Capitol Ave.
Cheyenne, WY 82002-0050
Phone: (307) 777-7675
Fax: (307) 777-6234
Web site: http://www.k12.wy.us/

Territories

American Samoa

American Samoa Department of Education
Pago Pago, AS 96799
Phone: (684) 633-5237
Fax: (684) 633-4240

Commonwealth of the Northern Mariana Islands

Commonwealth of the Northern Mariana
    Islands Public School System
P.O. Box 501370
Saipan, MP 96950
Phone: (670) 664-3721
Fax: (670) 664-3796
Web site: http://www.pss.cnmi.mp/

Guam

Guam Department of Education
P.O. Box DE
Agana, GM 96932
Phone: (671) 475-0462
Fax: (671) 472-5003

Puerto Rico

Puerto Rico Department of Education
P.O. Box 190759
San Juan, PR 00919-0759
Phone: (787) 763-2171
Fax: (787) 250-0275

Virgin Islands

Virgin Islands Department of Education
44-46 Kongens Gade
St Thomas, VI 00802
Phone: (340) 774-2810
Fax: (340) 779-7153

Appendix D

The Praxis Series

Presently, nearly 80 percent of the states that include tests as part of their teacher licensure and certification process use the **Praxis series** of assessments. In addition, many colleges and universities use the Praxis series as a qualifying exam for entry into their teacher education programs.

The Praxis series of assessments are standardized tests that include multiple choice and essay exercises. The tests are administered at designated sites around the country under controlled conditions. Praxis I: Pre-Professional Skills Test can also be taken online. Candidates schedule appointments with designated computer testing centers.

The Praxis series consists of three categories. Students applying for admission to a teacher education program will complete **Praxis I.** This series of tests includes reading, writing, and mathematics components.

Praxis II: Subject Assessments will be completed by candidates who are applying for teacher licensure/certification following a program of teacher education. The number of tests and the specific tests are determined by the state licensing agency with regard to the candidate's major. The Praxis Series Registration Bulletin (likely available at your Education Department's office on campus) details the requirements by state.

The first year of teaching is assessed with the **Praxis III: Classroom Performance Assessments.** You will receive more information about the Praxis series (if your state requires it) as you reach various milestones in your teacher education program. You can obtain detailed information by logging on to the Educational Testing Service (ETS) Web site at http://ets.org/praxis.

Appendix E

Answer Key for Unit Workshop Quizzes

■ Unit I: The Profession

Chapter 1

1. b (p. 5)	4. a (p. 11)	7. b (p. 16)	10. d (p. 22)
2. b (p. 6)	5. a (p. 12)	8. a (p. 17)	
3. c (p. 10)	6. d (p. 15)	9. c (p. 22)	

Chapter 2

1. a (p. 33)	4. b (p. 37)	7. a (p. 47)	10. d (p. 50)
2. c (p. 33)	5. b (p. 47)	8. a (p. 48)	
3. b (p. 34)	6. d (p. 44)	9. c (p. 49)	

Chapter 3

1. c (p. 59)	4. a (p. 61)	7. d (p. 65)	10. c (p. 82)
2. b (p. 59)	5. d (p. 61)	8. d (p. 70)	
3. a (p. 60)	6. c (p. 63)	9. a (p. 79)	

Chapter 4

1. b (p. 105)	4. a (p. 109)	7. c (p. 107)	10. a (p. 133)
2. c (p. 106)	5. b (p. 119)	8. b (p. 108)	
3. d (p. 107)	6. d (p. 118)	9. d (p. 131)	

■ Unit II: Curriculum, Management, and Assessment

Chapter 5

1. d (p. 153)	4. d (p. 153)	7. d (p. 159)	10. d (p. 170)
2. b (p. 154)	5. a (p. 158)	8. a (p. 165)	
3. b (p. 153)	6. c (p. 158)	9. c (p. 166)	

Chapter 6

1. c (p. 183)	4. a (p. 186)	7. c (p. 189)	10. b (p. 193)
2. a (p. 183)	5. d (p. 187)	8. a (p. 190)	
3. b (p. 186)	6. c (p. 189)	9. c (p. 191)	

Chapter 7

1. c (p. 215)	4. d (p. 218)	7. c (p. 231)	10. b (p. 236)
2. a (p. 215)	5. b (p. 222)	8. d (p. 230)	
3. b (p. 216)	6. a (p. 224)	9. a (p. 233)	

■ Unit III: The Institution of Education

Chapter 8

1. b (p. 255)	4. a (p. 260)	7. b (p. 267)	10. b (p. 279)
2. d (p. 256)	5. a (p. 261)	8. c (p. 270)	
3. c (p. 258)	6. c (p. 264)	9. d (p. 272)	

Chapter 9

1. b (p. 291)	4. b (p. 297)	7. c (p. 305)	10. b (p. 311)
2. d (p. 292)	5. d (p. 300)	8. d (p. 307)	
3. a (p. 294)	6. b (p. 303)	9. c (p. 309)	

Chapter 10

1. c (p. 319)	4. d (p. 325)	7. a (p. 347)	10. d (p. 354)
2. b (p. 335)	5. d (p. 344)	8. b (p. 347)	
3. a (p. 323)	6. b (p. 345)	9. c (p. 353)	

Chapter 11

1. b (p. 362)	4. c (p. 368)	7. b (p. 383)	10. b (p. 383)
2. a (p. 365)	5. d (p. 369)	8. a (p. 375)	
3. b (p. 366)	6. c (p. 370)	9. c (p. 378)	

■ Unit IV: Challenges for Today and Tomorrow

Chapter 12

1. a (p. 401)	4. b (p. 404)	7. d (p. 407)	10. b (p. 419)
2. c (p. 403)	5. a (p. 404)	8. c (p. 411)	
3. d (p. 403)	6. b (p. 406)	9. d (p. 416)	

Chapter 13

1. d (p. 427)	4. d (p. 433)	7. a (p. 436)	10. a (p. 446)
2. b (p. 430)	5. a (p. 434)	8. a (p. 439)	
3. c (p. 430)	6. d (p. 436)	9. c (p. 441)	

Chapter 14

1. b (p. 461)	4. d (p. 471)	7. c (p. 476)	10. d (p. 480)
2. c (p. 463)	5. c (p. 472)	8. a (p. 477)	
3. b (p. 464)	6. a (p. 474)	9. b (p. 478)	

Glossary

academic freedom: Extends to teachers the right to speak freely about the subjects they teach and to introduce varied—and competing—viewpoints on an issue to encourage inquiry, experimentation with new ideas, and critical consideration of topics.

academy: The Greek school established by Plato. The term is often used to refer to a liberal arts college.

accreditation agency: An organization, most notably the National Council for Accreditation of Teacher Education, that certifies that an institution's teacher preparation program has met a series of rigorous standards.

activity curriculum: The designing of educational experiences based on the interests of particular students at a particular time.

add-on certification: The addition of one or more areas of additional certification. It requires the successful completion of additional coursework and a passing score on the corresponding standardized achievement test such as Praxis.

adoption states: Those states that narrow the list of eligible textbooks to a small number (usually five or fewer) and require school districts to select materials from that list. Texts usually must meet state criteria related to grade-level standards and be certified as based on scientifically based research. In nonadoption states, each school district makes its own determination.

affective perspective: The aspect of the curriculum that emphasizes feeling and valuing.

alternative certification: Certification that does not include study in a teacher preparation program. It may involve on-the-job coursework or, at a minimum, passing a test in the subject area to be taught, with the person having a college or university degree in any field.

American Federation of Teachers (AFT): A teacher's union formed in 1916. It is part of the American Federation of Labor/Congress of Industrial Organizations (AFL/CIO) umbrella. Its membership, while nationwide, is more concentrated in large population centers in the North.

ancillary businesses: Businesses with services that directly relate to the successful functioning of the school. Examples include transportation and food services and medical and psychological personnel.

assessment: The means by which a teacher gathers information to make a variety of decisions. It may include paper-and-pencil activities, demonstrations, reports, teacher observation, projects, and so on.

assistive technology: Applications of technology that improve the educational experience for students with special needs.

at-risk students: Students who are achieving sufficiently below their potential and/or grade level so as to be likely to drop out of school or to be unable to acquire the competence needed to function in the larger society.

Attention Deficit/Hyperactivity Disorder (ADHD): A persistent pattern of inattention and/or hyperactivity-impulsivity that is more frequently displayed and severe than is typically observed in individuals at a comparable level of development (American Psychiatric Association).

autism: A developmental disability that significantly affects a child's verbal and nonverbal communication, social interaction, and educational performance (Individuals with Disabilities Education Act).

axiology: The branch of philosophy that considers the study of fundamental ideas or principles (i.e., the universally accepted truths of ethics and aesthetics).

base salary: The minimum amount of money that is paid to an educator based on his or her certification(s), job description, and years of experience.

behaviorism: The perspective that since behavior is caused, altering the surrounding circumstances alters the behavior. Examples of behaviorism include classical conditioning and operant conditioning.

bilingual education: Education provided to children with limited English-speaking ability.

blended family: A family in which both partners (whether married or not) bring children from previous relationships to the new relationship.

block grants: Grants that allow state education agencies the flexibility to use the funds to meet their specific needs within the framework of the federal law. In essence, a number of special programs are folded into a block grant.

breach of contract: The failure of either party in a contract to meet obligations.

broad fields curriculum: Also known as integrated, or fused curriculum, it attempts to make logical connections among various subject areas and encourage the application of the information to real-life situations.

Carnegie Unit: A course credit for the successful completion of a specified high school course (e.g., Spanish I, Algebra II). It includes satisfactory grades and may also include passing an end-of-course test developed by the state.

categorical funding: The funding by the federal government of special programs (e.g., free lunch program for economically disadvantaged students, school construction, work programs for high school students).

categorical grants: Grants that allow state education agencies maximum flexibility to apportion the funds according to their specific needs.

certification: The process one undergoes (e.g., in an elementary or secondary education program) to obtain a teaching license.

certification examination: A standardized achievement test, frequently from the Praxis series, that prospective teachers must pass prior to their receiving certification.

change agent: One who participates in curriculum or instructional dialogue with the purpose of making positive changes in the school program. A change agent is also one who institutes curriculum or instructional reform in the classroom or at the school level.

character education: The introduction of moral and ethical issues into the curriculum along with the traditional subject matter.

charter school: A public school formed or reconstituted to deal either with special concerns of a community (e.g., providing a back-to-basics, technology, or fine arts emphasis) or with a particular group (e.g., at risk of dropping out, exceptional education) or to secure a greater degree of school and local control.

child abuse and neglect: At a minimum, any recent act or failure to act on the part of a parent or caretaker that results in death, serious physical or emotional harm, sexual abuse, or exploitation, or an act or failure to act that presents an imminent risk of serious harm.

classroom assessment: Assessments that are typically designed by the classroom teacher to assess a very specific population with regard to material specifically presented in that class.

classroom management: Activities in which a teacher engages before, during, and after interacting with students. These activities, which focus on the prevention of misbehavior, allow instruction to take place.

classroom pragmatics: Tasks that a teacher routinely accomplishes apart from "instructional" activities. Examples include classroom management and the assessment of student performance.

clinical experience: Experience during which a prospective teacher engages in classroom activities by observing, assisting a teacher and students, participating in other educational activities. Sometimes called *field service* or *internships*.

cognitive perspective: The aspect of the curriculum that focuses on the acquisition of knowledge.

common schools: Free schools for working-class students, both girls and boys.

compulsory education: A requirement that parents enroll and send their children to school. In America it dates to the Massachusetts Act of 1642.

computer-assisted instruction (CAI): The use of computers to deliver pre-programmed instructional tasks.

computer-managed instruction (CMI): The use of software that helps track grades and manage other clerical aspects of the teacher's role.

consequences: The results that inevitably follow when students fail to observe the rules.

constituencies: Those groups of people to whom educators are responsible. They include students, parents, the community in general, the school administration, and their colleagues.

constructivism: The perspective that students "build" their knowledge as new experiences are related to previous experiences.

consumables: Materials and supplies that must be discarded after use. Examples are handwriting paper, workbooks, and photocopier paper.

contract: A binding agreement between two parties.

convergent thinking: The process of taking one or more sources of information and drawing conclusions about their characteristics (perhaps similarities or differences) or implications.

cooperative learning: A philosophy and set of practices in which heterogeneous groups of students work together on clearly defined and meaningful goals.

core curriculum: A curriculum that emphasizes a particular body of knowledge within the subject areas that all students should learn.

critical needs area: (1) A professional area (e.g., mathematics, exceptional education) in which there is a shortage of teachers. (2) A geographical area (e.g., rural, inner city) in which it is difficult to secure sufficient numbers of certified and qualified teachers.

cultural pluralism: Acceptance of and interaction between multiple cultures in one society.

culture: The values, attitudes, and beliefs that influence the behavior and the traditions of a people. They are social, not biological, dimensions.

curricular reform: An education reform based on the development or adoption of the content to be taught at various points in a student's educational experience. The content is organized in grade-level standards.

curriculum: The program by which a school meets its educational goals. It includes planned as well as unplanned experiences and involves the means and materials with which students interact.

dame schools: Colonial schools typically run by educated widows or housewives in their own homes for a fee. They provided initial academic instruction for boys, particularly those from the middle and upper classes.

direct instruction: A means of delivering instruction by specifically explaining or demonstrating a skill and having the students attempt to replicate it.

disaggregate analysis: An analysis of test data that identifies the performance of students by ethnic group, by economic status of the family (through eligibility for free or reduced school lunches), and by gender. The performance of students for whom English is a second language is also being increasingly factored into the equation, as is the performance of students with varying exceptionalities.

discipline: Actions a teacher takes after misbehavior occurs.

discovery learning: An approach to instruction that focuses on students' personal experiences as the foundation for conceptual development. Students are expected and assisted to use their prior knowledge as a basis for making inferences and drawing conclusions.

discussion: Involves the interchange of ideas. With this approach a teacher hopes to develop greater depth of ideas and to foster the manipulation of information for solving problems rather than just the acquisition of knowledge.

distance education: Delivery of instructional programs to people in sites remote from the school setting.

divergent thinking: The process of taking information and creating new ideas or adapting it in original (to the thinker) ways.

diversity: The ways in which individuals and groups differ from each other.

drill and practice: An instructional technique that emphasizes the repetition of previously learned information or skills to hone the skill or provide a strong cog-

nitive link to the information to improve remembering it.

due process: Procedures intended to ensure fairness and accountability of both parents/guardians and educators. They include the rights of parents to have evaluations conducted by personnel outside the school system and to request a hearing when they disagree with the school's proposed plans.

dynamic content: The knowledge and skills that a teacher uses to do the teaching. This can change at any time based on what is happening in the immediate environment.

economic pragmatics: Skills in managing money.

educational reform: The process of improving one or more aspects of education on the local, state, or federal level, either piecemeal or as a total package. It may focus on curriculum and/or instruction and is usually based on some philosophical perspective.

electronic books: Books in a format that is electronically (computer) based.

emotional/behavioral disorder: A condition exhibiting one or more of the specific characteristics over a long time and to a marked degree that adversely affect a student's educational performance: (1) An inability to learn that cannot be explained by intellectual, sensory, or other health factors, (2) an inability to build or maintain satisfactory interpersonal relationships with peers and teachers, (3) inappropriate types of behavior or feelings under normal circumstances, (4) a general pervasive mood of unhappiness or depression, (5) a tendency to develop physical symptoms or fears associated with personal or school problems (Individuals

emotional/behavioral disorder, continued
with Disabilities Education Act).

English as a Second Language (ESL): Any program designed to teach English to nonspeakers of English while providing instruction in the various areas of the curriculum.

English Grammar Schools: As a response and alternative to the Latin Grammar School, these secondary schools emphasized a practical education with classes conducted in English rather than in Latin. Some English Grammar Schools admitted females.

epistemology: The branch of philosophy that considers how people come to know what they know. It is concerned with the nature and origin of truth and knowledge.

e-publishing: Electronic publishing that enables each state to custom-tailor the text materials to its specific interests.

equal access: The federal requirement that buildings and facilities be structured in such a way that physically handicapped people have access to the same information and opportunities as do people without handicaps.

essentialism: The perspective that there are core skills and knowledge that all students should acquire. Doing so ensures the maintenance of our cultural heritage and the sustaining of our society.

ethnicity: Sense of common identity based upon common ancestral background and the sharing of common values and beliefs.

evaluation: The process of placing a value (a grade) on a piece of student work.

existentialism: The philosophy that emphasizes thoughtful personal reflection about one's identity, beliefs, and choices. It places the responsibilities that come with being a human on the shoulders of each individual.

experiential education: An approach that seeks to make what is taught as part of school as realistic as possible. Field trips are an example.

explicit curriculum: The subjects that will be taught, the identified "mission" of the school, and the knowledge and skills that the school expects successful students to acquire. *See* **implicit curriculum.**

extended family: A family structure that includes the presence of several generations, which can include aunts and uncles or other relatives as well as grandparents.

extra-curriculum: All of the school-sponsored programs (e.g., athletics, band) that are intended to supplement the academic aspect of the school experience.

field experience or field service: *See* **clinical experience.**

flexibility: The ability to make adaptations or major changes in diagnostic, instructional, or evaluative procedures based on an awareness of student behavior. It depends on careful monitoring.

formative assessment: An assessment in which information is gathered for instructional purposes. Usually the assessment is based on a relatively small body of information.

foster care: A family placement for children who are separated from their parents (for example, if the parents are deceased or the children are removed from the home for child welfare reasons).

gain score: The difference between pretest and posttest scores, thus the student progress in a specific body of information.

gender: The social aspect of sexuality: behaviors that are considered masculine or feminine.

gender bias/sexism: Preferential treatment toward or discrimination against individuals or groups based on their gender or sex.

general education: A program of courses that almost every college and university student is required to take (except for those who enter with International Baccalaureate or advanced placement credits earned in high school or who exempt courses by passing placement tests).

gifted and talented: Students who show evidence of high performance capability in areas such as intellectual, creative, artistic, or leadership capacity, or in specific academic fields, and who require services or activities not ordinarily provided by the school in order to fully develop such capabilities (United States Congress). The gifted student has superior intelligence while the talented student shows unusually high ability in some special field of knowledge (Feldhusen).

higher education: Any postsecondary education (e.g., community college, junior college, four-year college or university, graduate school).

high-stakes tests: Standardized achievement tests that are used for promotion, graduation, or assignment of school grades and that carry penalties for poor schoolwide performance (as well as rewards for good performance). Thus, they have serious negative implications for students and schools that do not meet predetermined criteria.

homeschooling: Education provided to children in the home by the parent or caregiver.

hornbook A copy of the alphabet laminated onto a paddle-shaped piece of wood using a thin transparent sheet made from a cow's horn.

humanism: A philosophy that emphasizes the value and meaning of education rather than the mere dissemination and acquisition of facts. Students are viewed as individuals with unique desires and needs. Erasmus applied humanism to education, which formed the foundation of the Reformation.

idealism: The philosophy that the only true reality is that of ideas. It includes classical, modern, and religious aspects.

implicit curriculum: The lessons that arise from the culture of the school and the behaviors, attitudes, and expectations that characterize that culture. *See* **explicit curriculum.**

in loco parentis: "In the place of parents."

inclusion: A model in which an exceptional-education teacher provides assistance in a regular classroom to a student who has been identified as having a disability identified by one of the related laws.

individualized education program (IEP): A written plan, specific for each child, that consists of a description of the child's current performance, the goals for the year, the services to be rendered, and the means by which the results will be measured.

induction period: A probationary period, typically from one to three years, during which a newly hired teacher is mentored and evaluated.

inquiry: A sophisticated technique that attempts to engage students in generating relevant and meaningful questions about the topic under consideration.

instructional reform: An educational reform based on a set of coordinated and differentiated strategies (both diagnostic and instructional) by which teachers and students address the curriculum.

intelligence: An individual's capacity to learn from experience and to adapt to the environment (Sternberg & Powell). It differs from academic achievement, knowledge, and skillful ability in one domain or another.

intelligence quotient (IQ): The relationship between a person's mental age and his or her chronological age. A score of 100 (or a range from 85 to 115) is considered "average."

internships: *See* **clinical experience.**

intervention: An education effort that supplements normal procedure either by providing remediation or enrichment or by extending or reducing a teacher's responsibility or authority (as in a pull-out program).

land-grant colleges: Colleges established and funded for the study of agriculture and the mechanical arts. Funds were secured from the rent or sale of public lands in each state.

latchkey children: Students who carry a house or apartment key, return to an empty home in the hours immediately after school, and often have little or no supervision between the time they leave school and the time their parent(s) get home from work.

Latin Grammar Schools: The forerunners to what we now consider "high school," they were patterned after schools in Europe and prepared students to enter divinity schools.

learning disability: A disorder in one or more of the basic psychological processes involved in understanding or in using language, either spoken or written, which manifests itself in imperfect ability to listen, think, speak, read, write, spell, or do mathematical calculations (Individuals with Disabilities Education Act).

learning styles: The means by which individuals learn best (e.g., auditory, visual, kinesthetic, vocalic). Other aspects of learning styles include group size (e.g., individual or pair or group work) as well as environmental influences (e.g., heat, light, noise).

least restrictive environment (LRE): The requirement that, to the extent possible, a handicapped child must be educated with nonhandicapped children, that is, in a mainstreamed environment.

lecture: An instructional technique in which the teacher takes the active role of providing information while students take a more passive role by listening. Characterized by limited dialogue between teacher and student.

liability: Legal responsibility for an incident.

license: A document that certifies that the holder has successfully completed an education program in one or more areas of education.

local education agency: A separate school district responsible for administering the education program for a county, city, or other local education unit.

logic: The branch of philosophy that seeks to bring order to the reasoning process. It includes inductive and deductive reasoning.

logistical innovations: Innovative changes that affect the physical aspect of school: the building,

logistical innovations, continued the interior and exterior facilities, the movement of people, and so on.

Lyceum: The Greek school founded by Aristotle. He considered philosophy, ethics, and science and emphasized rational thinking for good citizenship.

magnet schools: Public schools that focus on a particular academic, vocational, or specialty study.

mainstream: An approach to integrating students with special needs into the general education population.

mandated reporter: A person, such as a teacher, who is required by law to report suspected child abuse or neglect, and thus is immune from prosecution or lawsuit for doing so.

mastery learning: A series of educational practices based on the belief that given appropriate instruction and sufficient study time, almost all students can meet the specified learning standards.

McGuffey Readers: Six volumes written by the Reverend William H. McGuffey and published from 1836 to the early 20th century. Poems and stories emphasized honesty, truth, obedience, and hard work. Their message of moral virtue influenced generations of Americans.

mental modeling: A technique used to foster students' ability to direct their own learning. It involves careful modeling of the cognitive processes required to solve problems.

mentoring: The process by which an experienced educator helps a less experienced educator in some aspect of teaching or professional development in a one-on-one setting.

metaphysics: The branch of philosophy that considers questions about the physical universe (e.g., the nature and origin of the physical world).

methods courses: Courses that address diagnostic, instructional, and evaluation strategies as they relate to specific subjects (e.g., reading, math, science).

monitoring: Observing student academic and social behavior, both individually and collectively, during a variety of activities.

multiculturalism: The social psychology perspective of how various cultural groups interface with each other.

National Board for Professional Teaching Standards (NBPTS): A national organization that establishes rigorous standards by which teachers can be certified by demonstrating exemplary classroom performance and reflecting critically on the effectiveness of their curriculum and instruction strategies and the needs of diverse learners.

National Education Association (NEA): The largest (with over 2,000,000 members) professional association for teachers, administrators, and other school personnel.

New England Primer: An illustrated textbook that offered religious readings. Originally published in 1690, the *New England Primer* was the mainstay of colonial education for more than 100 years.

norm group: A group of test-takers specifically identified as being representative of the population for whom the assessment was designed. Results from the norm group are used to set the standard for the test.

normal curve: A statistical model in which 34 percent of the scores fall at or just below the middle score, and another 34 percent fall at or just above the middle. Another 13 percent of the scores fall farther above the middle while 13 percent more fall farther below the middle. About 3 percent of the scores fall at one extreme and another 3 percent at the other. (Sometimes called the *bell curve.*)

normal schools: The forerunners of teacher-preparation colleges and universities. They taught their prospective teachers the normal practices for teaching children.

nuclear family: A family structure that consists of one or more parents or guardians or foster parents and may include one or more children.

null curriculum: The options students are not afforded; the perspectives they may never know about, much less be able to use; the concepts and skills that are not a part of their intellectual repertoire (Eisner).

outcome-based education (OBE): The practice of establishing the specific expected outcomes of education.

parent–teacher organization (PTO): A school-based organization that attempts to strengthen the relationship between parents and the school by promoting open communication and activities involving the joint participation of parents and teachers.

parochial schools: Schools affiliated with some religious group. They originally were established by churches such as Baptist, Catholic, Mennonite, and Quaker.

pedagogue: Literally, the Greek adult who led a child to school, discussing important issues (and thus tutoring) the child on the way. In colonial days the term was used to refer to a teacher.

pedagogy: The art and science of teaching children.

perennialism: The perspective that certain ideas and truths transcend time and are prevalent in the great literature of the ages. An organized study of these themes, which provide an insight into the universe and the role of individuals in the society, should be provided to students.

portfolio: A visual and physical record of achievement.

practicum: *See* **clinical experience.**

pragmatism: The theme that ideas must serve a useful purpose. It focuses on identifying processes that help people reach their goals.

Praxis series: A series of three tests developed by Educational Testing Service (ETS). Prospective teachers take these tests at various points in their professional preparation program.

private venture schools: Schools established with private rather than public funds. They include parochial schools as well as non-denominational private schools.

privatization: The management of public schools by private enterprises, often referred to as *education management organizations.*

problem-solving conference (sometimes called conflict-resolution conference): A meeting involving the teacher and student (and perhaps the parents/guardians) to help a student assume responsibility for his or her actions and find a way to resolve the situation without losing the student's sense of dignity.

procedures: The ways in which particular activities (e.g., taking attendance, collecting money, moving from place to place) are conducted.

professional development: Activities in which educators engage to expand their knowledge, skills, and general competence or contribute to the profession (e.g., engaging in research, mentoring, reading professionally, taking courses, attending conferences).

professional development schools: Public schools that function in close cooperation with a college or university's teacher education program. Many prospective teachers do their field service/practicum/internship and student teaching in the professional development school.

professional education: A program of education courses that provide overviews of topics important for prospective teachers.

professional organization: A group of educators organized to promote a particular interest. It may be general (as a group advocating on behalf of teachers, supervisors, and/or administrators, such as the National Education Association and the American Federation of Teachers) or specific (as a curriculum-related organization, such as the National Council of Teachers of Mathematics and the International Reading Association).

progressivism: The philosophical focus on positive change that individuals with various educational backgrounds can provide. Problem solving is emphasized over passing on the culture, and learning by doing is preferred over knowing a specific body of knowledge. The education application is a child-centered approach.

quadrivium: The study of four subjects—arithmetic, geometry, music, and astronomy—in the medieval university. *See* **trivium.**

question and answer: Instructional technique in which the teacher poses questions soliciting content-specific responses from the student.

realism: The philosophy that maintains that matter is real and that ideas underlie matter. Therefore, the study of matter leads to an understanding of ideas. Realism includes classical, modern, and religious aspects.

reciprocity: The act of accepting in one state the credentials issued in another state.

reflection: The process of thinking critically about experiences or observations and making connections with other ideas and/or drawing inferences for further consideration.

reform model: A model developed and instituted to implement a philosophical and educational perspective about how best to achieve the goals of the school and community.

role models: Those who engage in personal and professional behavior that provides an opportunity for students to observe desirable characteristics in practice.

routines: Behaviors that are learned or demonstrated so well that they become automatic.

rules: Descriptors of required observable behaviors.

scholasticism: The religious-philosophical study resulting from the rediscovery in the 11th century of Aristotle's works.

school choice: An array of options beyond the child's neighborhood, traditional school placement.

sex: A biological distinction between male and female.

sexual harassment: Unwanted and unwelcome sexual behavior that interferes with the victim's life.

sexual stereotyping: The expectation that males should fill particular roles while females fill other roles.

site-based management: The legal ability of a school to conduct its own governance, subject to specific local, state, and federal requirements. Charter schools are an example of site-based management.

social reconstructionism: The perspective that schools are the agency for solving societal problems.

solar collectors: Panels that capture heat from the sun and use it to heat water or heat the facilities.

Sophists: Ancient Greek teachers with a wide range of expertise in many fields who taught rhetoric and oratory. Today's concept of the liberal arts was founded in the Sophists' curriculum of grammar, logic, and rhetoric.

special interest groups: Groups that advocate and lobby for a particular direction, focus, or policy. A group may represent the interests of a particular culture, ethnicity, or religious group and may address issues from a liberal or conservative perspective.

specialization courses: Courses that focus on the teaching of particular subjects or other topics related to curriculum and instruction.

standardized testing: The use of norm-referenced tests to determine the performance of individual students, the grade and school achievement levels, and the progress of students from one year to the next (spring to spring or fall to spring administrations).

state education agency: A state department of education responsible for directing and overseeing the local education agencies within its jurisdiction.

static content: The curriculum that teachers are responsible for teaching. It is static because it doesn't change.

strategy: A means of coordinating the implementation of a set of procedures. A strategy combines subject matter, techniques, and the skills for implementing instruction.

student-centered curriculum: A curriculum that emphasizes the natural interests and curiosity of the child.

student teaching: A culminating experience in a teacher education program that provides an extended opportunity for the prospective teacher to assume fuller responsibility, under the guidance of the supervising teacher, for providing instruction to an entire class.

subject-centered curriculum: A curriculum that emphasizes the subjects that all students should learn.

substance abuse: Most commonly this refers to minors' inappropriate use of alcohol, tobacco, marijuana, or another controlled substance.

summative assessment: An assessment given to assign a grade. Usually it is based on a relatively large amount of information and addresses content that will not be retaught.

teacher accountability: The concept that the teacher is responsible for the achievement of students, regardless of their circumstances (e.g., cognitive, social, psychological, environmental, physical).

technology: The combining of information to make new products or processes that extend our capabilities.

tenure: An ongoing contract to teach (sometimes referred to as a *continuing contract*).

tort law: A civil or private wrong other than a breach of contract.

trivium: In medieval Europe, an educational curriculum based upon the study of grammar, rhetoric, and logic. See **quadrivium.**

vernacular schools: Schools established by Protestants. These schools used the common language rather than Latin for instruction.

virtual school: An electronic, telecommunications-based presentation of course work to students who are homebound or in remote sites, or even just as an alternative to being in a traditional school setting.

vocational training: Training as preparation to enter the world of work in some trade (e.g., as a carpenter, electrician, mason, mechanic).

voucher: An allocation equal to the average per-pupil cost for a child's education in a specific area's public school.

References

Abedi, J., & Dietel, R. (June 2004). Challenges in the No Child Left Behind Act for English language learners. *Phi Delta Kappan, 85* (10), 782–785.

Accomplished teaching validation study. (2000). Greensboro: University of North Carolina at Greensboro.

Achilles, C. M., Finn, J. D., & Pate-Bain, H. (February 2002). Measuring class size: Let me count the ways. *Educational Leadership, LIX* (5), 24–26.

Adler, M. J. (1982). *Paideia proposal: An educational manifesto.* New York: Macmillan.

Adler, M. J. (1983). *Paideia problems and possibilities.* New York: Macmillan.

Alba, R. (1990). *Ethnic identity: The transformation of White America.* New Haven, CT: Yale University Press.

All talk, no action: Putting an end to out-of-field teaching. (2002). N.P.: Education Trust.

Allen, R. (December 2002). Keeping kids in school. *ASCD Education Update, 44* (8), 4–5.

Allington, R. L. (1975). Improving content instruction in the middle school. *Journal of Reading, 18* (6), 455–461.

Allington, R. L. (2002). Accelerating in the wrong direction: Why thirty years of federal testing and accountability hasn't worked yet and what we might do instead. In R. L. Allington (Ed.), *Big brother and the national reading curriculum: How ideology trumped evidence,* pp. 235–263. Portsmouth, NH: Heinemann.

Altwerger, B., Edelsky, C., & Flores, B. M. (November 1987). Whole language: What's new? *Reading Teacher,* 144–154.

Amato, P. R. (2001). Children of divorce in the 1990s: An update of the Amato and Keith (1991) meta-analysis. *Journal of Family Psychology, 15,* 355–370.

Amato, P. R., & Keith, B. (1991). Parental divorce and adult well-being: A meta-analysis. *Journal of Marriage and the Family, 53,* 43–58.

American Academy of Pediatrics. (2000). Clinical practice guidelines; Diagnosis and evaluation of the child with attention-deficit/hyperactivity disorder. *Pediatrics, 105* (5), 1158–1170.

American Association of University Women. (2001). *Hostile hallways: Bullying, teasing, and sexual harassment in school.* Washington, DC: American Association of University Women Educational Foundation.

American Foundation for Vision Awareness, Vision and Learning (June 1, 2002). At www.pave-eye.com/vision/visionandlearning.htm.

American Lung Association. (November 2004). Smoking and Teens Fact Sheet. www.lungusa.org/site.

American Psychiatric Association. (2000). *Diagnostic and statistical manual of mental disorders* (4th ed., rev.). Washington, DC: Author.

Amschler, D. H. (January 2002). *Journal of School Health, 72,* 39–41.

Anderson, J. (2003). What schools can say about Johnny. *Principal Leadership (High School Edition), 4* (4), 67–70.

Anderson, L. W., & Krathwohl, O. R. (2001). *A taxonomy for learning, teaching, and assessing.* New York: Longman.

Anderson, P. J. (1995). Language variation in the United States: Untangling the issues. *Multicultural Education, 3* (4), 8–11.

Are you highly qualified under NCLB? (May 2003). *NEA Today, 21* (8), 28–29.

Aristotle, *Politics,* trans. and intro. by T. A. Sinclair. (1978). Middlesex, England: Penguin.

Asakawa, K., & Csikszentmihalyi, M. (2000). Feelings of connectedness and internalization of values in Asian American adolescents. *Journal of Youth and Adolescence, 29* (2), 121–145.

Ashford, E. (July 22, 2003). Re-thinking high school exit exams. *National School Boards Journal News, 23,* 1, 4.

Ashford, E. (June 28, 2005). The fight over screening students to prevent suicide. *School Board News, 25,* 1, 8.

Atkins, J., & Karplus, R. (September 1962). Discovery or invention? *Science Teacher, 29* (5), 45–51.

August, D., & Hakuta, K. (Eds.), (1997). *Improving schooling for language-minority children: A research agenda.* Washington, DC: National Academy for the National Research Council and Institute of Medicine.

Ayers, W., & Klonsky, M. (February, 2006). Chicago's Renaissance 2010: The small schools movement meets the ownership society. *Phi Delta Kappan, 87* (6), 453–57.

Bacon, F. (1889). *Advancement of learning and novum organum.* New York: Colonial.

Bandura, A. (1986). *Social foundations of thought and action: A social cognitive theory.* Englewood Cliffs, NJ: Prentice-Hall.

Banks, J. (1994). *An introduction to multicultural education.* Boston: Allyn & Bacon.

Banks, J. (1997). *Teaching strategies for ethnic studies* (6th ed.). Boston: Allyn & Bacon.

Barbe, W., & Swassing, R. (1988). *Teaching through modality strengths: Concepts and practices.* Columbus, OH: Zaner-Bloser.

Baren, M. (1994). *Hyperactivity and attention disorders in children.* San Ramon, CA: Health Information Network.

Barkley, R. (1998). *Attention-deficit hyperactivity disorder: A handbook for diagnosis and treatment.* New York: Guilford.

Barkley, R. (2000). *Taking charge of ADHD: The complete, authoritative guide for parents (rev. ed.).* New York: Guilford.

Barone, D., Hardman, D., & Taylor, J. (2006). *Reading First in the classroom.* Boston: Pearson.

Barton, P. (2003). *Parsing the achievement gap; baselines for tracking progress.* Princeton, NJ: Educational Testing Service.

Barton, P. (November 2004). Why does the achievement gap persist? *Educational Leadership,* 9–13.

Beller, A., & Chung, S. (1992). Family structure and educational attainment of children: Effects of remarriage. *Journal of Population Economics, 5,* 309–320.

Benefits of small class sizes found to last years. (April 30, 1999). *Charlotte (NC) Observer.* (From Cox News Service).

Bentley, M., Ebert, C., & Ebert, E. (2000). *The natural investigator: A Constructivist approach to teaching elementary and middle school science.* Belmont, CA: Wadsworth.

Berliner, D. (1985). Effective classroom teaching: A necessary but not sufficient condition for developing exemplary schools. In G. R. Austin & H. Garver (Eds.). *Research on Exemplary Schools.* Orlando, FL: Academic.

Berliner, D. (2006). Our impoverished view of educational research. *Teachers College Record, 108* (6), 949–995.

Besharov, D. (September 1992). New directions for Head Start. *Education Digest, 58* (1), 7–11.

Biancarosa, G., & Snow, C. (2004). Reading next: A vision for action and research in middle and high school literacy. A report to the Carnegie Corporation of New York. Washington, DC: Alliance for Excellent Education.

Biancarosa, G. (October 2005). After third grade. *Educational Leadership, 63* (2), 16–22.

Bickerstaff, L. (March 2001). Violence. *Odyssey: Adventures in Science, 10* (3), 24–27.

Bielick, S., & Chandler, K. (July 2001). *Homeschooling in the United States: 1999.* National Household Education Surveys Program. Washington, DC: National Center for Education Statistics.

Biemiller, A. (August 12, 2006). Downloaded from http://www.oise.utoronto.ca/ICS/site_LaidlawCentre/ResearcherProfiles/Profile_AndrewBiemiller.shtml.

Bird, G., & Kemerait, L. (1990). Stress among early adolescents in two-earner families. *Journal of Early Adolescence, 3,* 344–365.

Black, S. (August 1998). Facts of life. *The American School Board Journal, 185* (8), 33–36.

Black, S. (May 2003). If they can't hear it, they can't learn it. *American School Board Journal, 190,* 40–42.

Black, S. (May 2005). Easing ESL students into learning English well. *American School Board Journal, 192,* 36–38.

Blair, J. (May 7, 2003). Blacks apply but unlikely to win certification, *Education Week,* 5.

Block, J. (1971). *Mastery learning: Theory and practice.* New York: Holt, Rinehart & Winston.

Bloom, B. (1964). *Stability and change in human characteristics.* New York: Wiley.

Bloom, B. (1976). *Human characteristics and school learning.* New York: McGraw-Hill.

Bloom, B., Hastings, J. T., & Madaus, G. F. (1971). *Handbook on formative and summative evaluation of student learning.* New York: McGraw-Hill.

Bloom, B., Englehart, M., Furst, E., Hill, W., & Krathwohl, O. (Eds.) (1956). *Taxonomy of educational objectives: The classification of educational goals, Handbook I: The cognitive domain.* New York: Longman.

Bobo, J., Gilchrist, L., Elmer, J., Snow, W., & Schinke, S. (1986). Hassles, role strain, and peer relations in young adolescents. *Journal of Early Adolescence, 6,* 339–352.

Bobok, B. L. (March/April 2002). Teacher resiliency: A key to career longevity. *The Clearinghouse, LXXV,* (4), 202–205.

Bode, B. H. (1938). Progressive education at the crossroads. New York: Newson.

Boers, D. (January 2002). What teachers need of parents. *Principal, 81,* 52–53.

Borich, G. D. (1996). *Effective teaching methods* (3rd ed.). Englewood Cliffs, NJ: Merrill.

Boston's mentor program operating model. (October 2001). *Mentoring Leadership and Resource Network.*

Boyer, E. (1995). *The basic school: A community of learning.* Princeton: Carnegie Foundation.

Bracey, G. (March 2005). Checking up on charters. *Phi Delta Kappan, 86* (7), 554–555.

Brackett, A. C. (Ed.). (1893). *Woman and the higher education,* New York: n.p., 1–46.

Brendtro, L. K., Long, N. J., & Brown, W. K. (2000). Searching for strengths. *Reclaiming Children and Youth, 9* (2), 66–69.

Bronfenbrenner, U. (1994). Ecological models of human development. In T. Husen & T. N. Postlethwaite (Eds.), *International Encyclopedia of Education, Vol. III* (2nd ed.). Oxford, UK: Pergamon/Elsevier Science.

Brophy, J. E. (September 1982). How teachers influence what is taught and learned in classrooms. *Elementary School Journal, 83* (1), 1–13.

Brophy, J. E. (March 1983). Classroom organization and management. *Elementary School Journal, 83* (4), 265–285.

Browder, D., & Snell, M. (2000). Teaching functional academics. In M. Snell & F. Brown (Eds.), *Instruction of students with severe disabilities* (5th ed.), pp. 493–542. Upper Saddle River, NJ: Prentice Hall.

Brown, B. (1988). The vital agenda for research on extracurricular influences: A reply to Holland and Andre. *Review of Educational Research, 58* (1), 107–111.

Bruner, J. (1960). *The process of education.* Cambridge, MA: Harvard University Press.

Bruner, J. (1966). *Toward a theory of instruction.* Cambridge, MA: Harvard University Press.

Buchanan, B. (October 2005). Getting to wellness. Supplement to *American School Board Journal, 192,* 4–7.

Bugeja, M. (October 2004). Don't let students "overlook" Internet plagiarism. *Education Digest, 70* (2), 37–43.

Burden, P. R. (2003). Classroom management: Creating a successful learning community. Hoboken, NJ: Wiley.

Burgess, J., & Lorain, P. Preparing for your first teaching interview. Downloaded on July 20, 2006, from www.nmsa.org/portals/0/pdf/member/job_connection/first_teaching_interview.pdf

Burmeister, L. E. (1978). *Reading strategies for middle and secondary school teachers.* Reading, MA: Addison-Wesley.

Burns, R. (1984). How time is used in elementary schools: The activity structure of classrooms. In L. W. Anderson (Ed.). *Time and school learning: Theory, research, practice.* London: Croom Helm.

Burns, M. (March 2003). The battle for civilized behavior; Let's begin with manners. *Phi Delta Kappan, 84* (7), 546–549.

Bushweller, K. (April 1999). Student cheating: A morality moratorium? *American School Board Journal, 186,* 24–32.

Butterfield, R. A. (1983). The development and use of culturally appropriate curriculum for American Indian students. *Peabody Journal of Education, 61* (1), 49–66.

Butts, R., and Cremin, L. (1953). *A history of education in American Culture.* New York: Holt, Rinehart and Winston.

Cambourne, B. (May 2001). Why do some students fail to learn to read? Ockham's razor and the conditions of learning. *Reading Teacher, 54* (8), 784–786.

Canedy, D. (March 21, 2001). Often conflicted, Hispanic girls are dropping out at high rate. *New York Times,* 1, 20.

Cangelosi, J. S. (2004). *Classroom management strategies: Gaining and maintaining students' cooperation* (5th ed.). Hoboken, NJ: Wiley.

Canter, L., & Canter, M. (1976). *Assertive discipline: A take charge approach for today's educator.* Santa Monica, CA: Canter and Associates.

Cantor, J. (1998). "Mommy I'm scared": How TV and movies frighten children and what we can do to protect them. San Diego: Harcourt Brace.

Carbo, M. (February 1996). Reading styles: High gains for the bottom third. *Educational Leadership, 53* (5), 8–13.

Carnoy, M., Jacobsen, R., Mishel, L., & Rothstein, R. (2005). *The charter school dust-up: examining the evidence on enrollment and achievement.* Washington, DC: Economic Policy Institute and Teachers College Press.

Carrasquillo, A. L. (1991). *Hispanic children and youth in the United States.* New York: Garland.

Carroll, J. (May 1963). A model of school learning. *Teachers College Record,* 723–733.

Carter, R., & Parks, E. (1992). White ethnic group members and culture value preferences. *Journal of College Student Development, 33* (6), 499–506.

Cash, R. E. (October 2003). When depression brings teens down. *Principal Leadership, 4,* 11–15.

Cetron, M., & Cetron, K. (December 2003/January 2004). A forecast for schools. *Educational Leadership, 61* (4), 22–29.

Chao, C. M. (1992). The inner heart: Therapy with Southeast Asian families. In L. A. Vargas & J. D. Koss-Cioino (Eds.), *Working with culture: Psychotherapeutic interventions with ethnic minority children and adolescents,* pp. 157–181. San Francisco: Jossey-Bass.

Characteristics of private schools in the United States: Recovered from the 2001–2001 private school university survey. (2004). Washington, DC: National Center for Education Statistics.

Charter experience. (Summer 2003). *NRTA Live and Learn, 7.*

Charters fall short. (Fall 2002). *Scholastic Administrator, I* (4), 9.

Chavers, D. (2000). *Deconstructing the myths: A research agenda for American Indian education.* (ERIC Document Reproduction Service No. ED 447 985).

Cheng, L. L. (1987). *Assessing Asian language performance.* Rockville, MD: Aspen.

Child Abuse Prevention and Treatment Act, P.L. No. 104–235, 111, 42 U.S.C. 5105g (1996).

Cizek, G. J. (Winter 2002/2003). When teachers cheat. *Streamlined Seminar, 21,* 1–2.

Collier, V., & Thomas, W. (1999). Making U.S. schools effective for English language learners, Part 1. *TESOL Matters, 9* (4), 1–6.

Collins, P. A., et al. (April 1997). Effects of early childhood media use on academic achievement. Paper presented at the Society for Research in Child Development Convention, Washington, DC.

Committee for Economic Development. (1985). College Board, Academic preparation for the world of work; Investing in our children: Business and the public schools.

Condition of Education, 2001. (2002).Washington, DC: United States Department of Education, National Center for Education Statistics.

Conley, D. T. (September, 2005). Align high school with college for greater student success. *Principal Leadership, 6,* 16–21.

Cook, G. (August, 2005). Killing PE is killing our kids the slow way. *American School Board Journal, 192,* 16–19.

Counts, G. S. (1932). *Dare the schools build a new social order?* New York: John Day.

Coutinho, M. J., Oswald, D. P., & Best, A. M. (2002). The influence of socio-demographics and gender on the disproportionate identification of minority students as having learning disabilities. *Remedial and Special Education, 231* (1), 49–60.

Crawford, J. (2002). Making sense of census 2000. Arizona State University: Language Policy Research Unit.

Culyer, R. (April 1984). Interpreting achievement test data: Some areas of concern. *Clearing House, 55* (8), p. 374–380.

Culyer, R. (1987). *Suggestions for improving comprehension: Recommendations based on classroom observations.* Mt. Gilead, NC: Vineyard Press.

Culyer, R. (1989). Handbook 1 for *Making inferences: Identifying passages* (Practice exercises in reading comprehension). Mt. Gilead, NC: Vineyard Press.

Culyer, R. (2002). Comprehensive reading program using Culyer strategies in reading. In J. Killion (Ed.), *What works in the elementary school: Results-based staff development,* pp. 52–55. Washington, DC: National Staff Development Council and National Education Association.

Culyer, R., & Culyer, G. (1987). *Preventing reading failure: a practical approach.* Washington, DC: University Press of America, 1987.

Darling, S., & Westberg, S. (May 2004). Parent involvement in children's acquisition of reading. *Reading Teacher, 57* (8), 774–76.

Darling-Hammond, L. (1996). *What matters most: Teaching for America's future.* Woodbridge, VA: National Commission on Teaching and America's Future.

Darling-Hammond, L. (March, 1996). The quiet revolution. *Educational Leadership,* 4–10.

Darling-Hammond, L., & Bransford, J. (Eds.) (2005). *Preparing teachers for a changing world: What teachers should learn and be able to do.* San Francisco, CA: Jossey-Bass.

Dearman, C., & Alber, S. (April 2005). The changing face of education: Teachers cope with challenges through collaboration and reflective study. *Reading Teacher, 58* (7), 634–40.

Dejnozka, E., & Kapel, D. (1982). *American educators' encyclopedia.* Westport, CT: Greenwood.

Denmark, V., & Podsen, I. (Fall 2000). The mettle of a mentor: What it takes to make this relationship work for all. *Journal of Staff Development, 21* (4).

Deshler, D. (1998). Grounding interventions for students with learning disabilities in "powerful ideas." *Learning Disabilities, 13,* 29–34.

Deshler, D., Ellis, E., & Lenz, B. (1996). *Teaching adolescents with learning disabilities: Strategies and methods.* Denver, CO: Love Publishing.

De Simone, C. (2006). Preparing our teachers for distance education. *College Teaching, 54* (1), 183–84.

Dewey, J. (1897). My pedagogic creed. *The School Journal, 54* (3), 77–80.

Dewey, J. (1916). *Democracy and education.* New York: Free Press.

Dewey, J. (1933). *How we think.* Boston: D.C. Heath.

Dewey, J. (1938/1965). *Experience and education* (2nd ed.). New York: Macmillan.

Deyhle, D. (1995). Navajo youth and Anglo racism: Cultural integrity and resistance. *Harvard Educational Review, 65* (3), 403–444.

Digest of Education Statistics, 1999. (2000). Washington, DC: United States Department of Education, National Center for Education Statistics.

Digest of Education Statistics, 2001. (2002). Washington, DC: United States Department of Education, National Center for Education Statistics.

Digest of Education Statistics, 2002. (2003). Washington, DC: United States Department of Education, National Center for Education Statistics.

Digest of Education Statistics, 2003. (2004). Washington, DC: United States Department of Education, National Center for Education Statistics.

Digest of Education Statistics, 2004. (2005). Washington, DC: United States Department of Education, National Center for Education Statistics.

Directing direct instruction. (May/June 1997). *American Teacher, 81,* 10–12.

Diversity Data. (n.d.). *Children of 2010, Child Trends.* Washington, DC: United States Department of Education.

Dougherty, J. (2004). Torts and liability: An educator's short guide. *Phi Delta Kappa Fastbacks, 527,* 7–45.

Druck, K., & Kaplowitz, M. (April 2005). Preventing classroom violence. *New Jersey Education Association Review, 78,* 10–11.

Drucker, M. J. (September 2003). What reading teachers should know about ESL learners. *Reading Teacher, 57* (1), 22–29.

Duarte, A. (September 22, 2000). Wanted—2 million teachers, especially minorities. *Hispanic Outlook in Higher Education, 10,* 25–27.

DuBois, W. E. B. (1903). *The souls of black folk* (Bantam Classic Edition, 1989). New York: Bantam.

Duke, N. (March 2004). The case for informational text. *Educational Leadership, 61* (6), 40–44.

Dunn, R. (1995). *Strategies for educating diverse learners.* Bloomington, IN: Phi Delta Kappa Educational Foundation.

Dunn, R. (2001). Learning style differences of nonconforming middle-school students. *NASSP Bulletin, 85* (626), 68–74.

Dunn, R., et al. (1995). A meta-analytic validation of the Dunn and Dunn learning styles model. *Journal of Educational Research, 88* (6), 353–361.

Dyer, P. C., & Binkney, R. (1995). Estimating cost-effectiveness and educational outcomes: Retention, remediation, special education, and early intervention. In R. L. Allington & S. A. Walmsley (Eds.) *No quick fix: Rethinking literacy programs in America's elementary schools.* New York: Teachers College Press.

Ebert, E. (1994). The cognitive spiral: Creative thinking and cognitive processing. *The Journal of Creative Behavior, 28* (4), 275–290.

Ebert, C., & Ebert, E. (1998). *The inventive mind in science.* Englewood, CO: Teacher Ideas Press.

Education resume. (2006). Downloaded July 19, 2006, from http://purdue .placementmanual.com/education/education-03.html.

Einstein, A. (1919). Letter to *The Times* (London), 1919, quoted in Hoffman, *Albert Einstein: Creator and Rebel,* 139.

Eisner (1994). The educational imagination: On the design and evaluation of school programs (3rd ed.). New York: Macmillan.

Eitzen, D. F. (April, 1995). Problem students: New figures show wider gap between rich and poor. *Christian Science Monitor, 21,* 1, 8.

Elkind, D. (1981). *The hurried child: Growing up too fast.* New York: Addison-Wesley.

Emmer, E., Evertson, C., & Worsham, E. (2002). *Classroom management for secondary teachers* (6th ed.). Boston: Allyn & Bacon.

Engelmann, S. (1991). Making connections in mathematics. *Journal of Learning Disabilities, 24,* 292–303.

English, J., & Papalia, A. (January 1988). The responsibility of educators in cases of child abuse and neglect. *Chronicle Guidance,* 88–89.

Epstein, J., & Jansorn, N. R. (January/February 2004). School, family, and community partnerships link the plan. *Principal, 83,* 10–15.

Erikson, E. (1950). *Childhood and society.* New York: Norton.

Erikson, E. (1968). *Identity, youth, and crisis.* New York: Norton.

Essex, N. (2000). Classroom harassment: The principal's liability. *Principal, 79* (4), 52–55.

Evans, G. (February/March 2004). The environment of childhood poverty. *American Psychologist, 59* (2), 77–92.

Evertson, C. M., Emmer, E. T., Clements, B. S., & Worsham, M. E. (2000). *Classroom management for elementary teachers* (5th ed.). Boston: Allyn & Bacon.

Fagan, J. (May 2001). There's no place like school. *Principal, 80* (5), 36–37.

Federation for American Immigration Reform: Frequently asked questions. Retrieved June 30, 2006 from http://www.fairus.org/site/PageServer ?pagename=team_team62d3

Feldhusen, J. F. (2000). Gifted and talented children. In R. C. Reynolds & E. Fletcher-Janzen (Eds.), *Encyclopedia of Special Education, Vol. 2* (2nd ed.), pp. 820–821. New York: Wiley.

Fenzel, L. M. (1989). Role strain in early adolescence. *Journal of Early Adolescence, 9,* 13–33.

Fermanich, M. L. (2002). School funding on professional development: A cross case analysis of seven schools in one urban district. *Elementary School Journal, 103* (1), 27–50.

Finn, J. (March 2002). Small classes in American schools: Research, practice, and politics. *Phi Delta Kappan, 83* (7), 551–560.

Fischer, L., Schimmel, D., & Kelly, C. (1999). *Teachers and the law.* NY: Longman.

Fiske, E. (1991). *Smart schools, smart kids: Why do some schools work?* New York: Simon & Schuster.

Five million children: 1992 update. (1992). New York: National Center for Children in Poverty, Columbia University.

Flaxman, S. (2000). Opening bell: Get organized for the first day of school with this handy checklist. *Scholastic Instructor,* 20–21.

Flynt, E. S., & Cooter, R. B., Jr. (May 2005). Improving middle-grades reading in urban schools; the Memphis comprehension framework. *Reading Teacher, 58* (8), 774–780.

Fombonne, E. (1999). The epidemiology of autism: A review. *Psychological Medicine, 29,* 769–786.

Franklin, V. P. (1992). *Black self-determination: A cultural history of African American resistance* (2nd ed.). New York: Lawrence Hill.

Freeland, R. (1998). *Collected wisdom: Strategies & resources for TAs.* Pittsburgh, PA: Eberly Center for Teaching Excellence, Carnegie Mellon.

Freire, P. (1968). *Pedagogy of the oppressed.* New York: Continuum.

Freud, S. (1974). *The ego and the id.* London: Hogarth.

Fulghum, R. (1988). *All I really need to know I learned in kindergarten.* New York: Villard.

Futrell, M. H., Gomez, J., & Bedden, D. (January 2003). Teaching the children of a new America: The challenge of diversity. *Phi Delta Kappan, 84* (5), 381–385.

Gambrell, L. (1983). The occurrence of think-time during reading comprehension instruction. *Journal of Educational Research, 77* (2), 77–80.

Gans, H. (1988). *Middle American individualism.* New York: Free Press.

Garan, E. M. (2002). Beyond the smoke and mirrors; a critique of the national reading panel report on phonics. In R. L. Allington (Ed.), *Big brother and the national reading curriculum: How ideology trumped evidence,* pp. 90–111. Portsmouth, NH: Heinemann.

Garcia, E. E. (1993). Language, culture, and education. In L. Darling-Hammond (Ed.), *Review of research in education,* pp. 51–98. Washington, DC: American Educational Research Association.

Garcia, E. E. (1995). Educating Mexican American students: Past treatment and recent developments in theory, research, policy, and practice. In J. A. Banks

& C. A. McGee Banks (Eds.), *Handbook of research on multicultural education,* pp. 372–387. New York: Macmillan.

Gardiner, S. (October 2001). Cybercheating; a new twist on an old problem. *Phi Delta Kappan, 83* (2), 172–174.

Gardner, H. (1983). *Frames of mind: The theory of multiple intelligences.* New York: Basic Books.

Gardner, H. (1999). *Intelligence reframed: Multiple intelligences for the 21st century.* New York: Basic Books.

Garet, M., Porter, A., Desimone, L. Birman, B., & Yoon, K. (Winter, 2001). What makes professional development effective?: Results from a national sample of teachers. *American Educational Research Journal, 38* (4), 915–945.

Gargiulo, R. (2006). *Special education in contemporary society: An introduction to exceptionality* (2nd ed.). Belmont, CA: Thomson Wadsworth.

Garrett, J. (2006). Characteristics of an honorable teacher. *Kappa Delta Pi Record, 42* (2), 62–63.

Gates, B. (1996). *The road ahead.* New York: Penguin.

Gates, J., & Stuht, A. (May/June 2006). Educational options: The new tradition. *Leadership, 35* (5), 24–38.

Gifford, V., & Dean, M. (1990). Differences in extracurricular activity participation, achievement, and attitudes toward school between ninth-grade students attending junior high school and those attending senior high school. *Adolescence, 25* (100), 799–802.

Gilligan, C. (1982). *In a different voice: Psychological theory and women's development.* Cambridge, MA: Harvard University Press.

Gilroy, M. (October 23, 2001). Bilingual education on the edge. *The Hispanic Outlook on Higher Education, 12,* 37–39.

Glasser, W. (April 1997). A new look at school failure and school success. *Phi Delta Kappan, 78,* 596–602.

Golden, O. (September 2000). The federal response to child abuse and neglect. *American Psychologist, 55* (9), 1050–1053.

Goleman, D. (1995). *Emotional intelligence.* New York: Bantam.

Good, T. L., & Brophy, J. E. (1994). *Looking in classrooms* (6th ed.). New York: HarperCollins.

Goode, S. (December 2006). Assistive technology and diversity issues. *Topics in Early Childhood Special Education, 26* (1), 51–54.

Goodlad, J. I. (1990). *Teachers for our nation's schools.* San Francisco: Jossey-Bass.

Gordon, E. E., & Gordon, E. H. (2003). *Literacy in America: Historic journey and contemporary solutions.* Westport, CT: Praeger.

Gordon, J. A. (2000). Asian American resistance to selecting teaching as a career: The power of community and tradition. *Teachers College Record, 102* (1), 173–196.

Gordon, S. P., & Maxey, S. (2000). *How to help beginning teachers succeed* (2nd ed.). Alexandria, VA: Association for Supervision and Curriculum Development.

Gottfried, A. E., Gottfried, A. W., & Bathurst, K. (1997). Maternal and dual-earner employment status and parenting. In I. Galib & B. Wheaton (Eds.), *Stress and adversity over the life course: Trajectories and turning points,* pp. 139–160. New York: Cambridge University Press.

Gould, M., & Gould, H. (December 2003). A clear vision for equity and opportunity. *Phi Delta Kappan, 85* (4), 324–328.

Greenway, R., & Vanourek, G. (Spring 2006). The virtual revolution: Understanding online schools. *Education Next, 6* (2), 34–41.

Griffin, A. (1982). Land-grant college or university. *The World Book Encyclopedia,* pp. 56–57. Chicago: World Book-Childcraft International.

Guisbond, L., & Neill, M. (September/October 2004). Failing our children. *Clearing House, 78* (1), 12–16.

Halverson, S. (2004). Teaching ethics: The role of the classroom teacher. *Childhood Education, 80* (3), 157–158.

Harris, A. J., & Sipay, E. R. (1980). *How to increase reading ability* (7th ed.). New York: Longman.

Health United States and Prevention Profile. (1992). Washington, DC: United States Department of Health and Human Services.

Helgeson, L. (Summer 2003). New teachers—Last to be hired, first to burn out. *NRTA Live and Learn, 3.*

Hendrie, C. (2005). Court: Class strip-searches unconstitutional. *Education Week, 24* (31), 3, 22.

Henke, R., Chen, X., & Geis, S. (2000). Progress through the pipeline: 1992–1993 college graduates and elementary/secondary school teaching as of 1997. Washington, DC: National Center for Education Statistics.

Henkoff, R. (October 21, 1991). Four states: Reform turns radical. *Fortune Magazine,* 137–144.

Hershey, A. M., Silverberg, M. K., & Haimson, J. (February 1999). *Expanding Options for Students: Report to Congress on the National Evaluation of School-to-Work Implementation.* Princeton, NJ: Mathematica Policy Research.

Hirsch, E. D., Jr. (1988). *Cultural literacy.* New York: Vintage Books.

Hirsch, E. D., Jr. (1996). *The schools we need.* New York: Doubleday.

Holland, A., & Andre, T. (1987). Participation in extracurricular activities in secondary school: What is known, what needs to be known? *Review of Educational Research, 57* (4), 437–466.

Hoover, D. W., & Milich, R. (1994). Effects of sugar ingestion expectancies on mother-child interactions. *Journal of Abnormal Child Psychology, 22,* 501–515.

Hopkins, B. J., & Wendel, F. C. (1997). *Creating school-community-business partnerships.* Bloomington, IN: Phi Delta Kappa Foundation.

Hunsader, P. D. (November/December 2002). Why boys fail—and what we can do about it. *Principal, 82* (2), 52–54.

Hutchins, R. M. (Ed.). (1952). *The great conversation.* Chicago: Encyclopedia Britannica, 25, 30–31.

Hyman, J., & Cohen, S. A. (1979). Learning for mastery: Ten conclusions after 15 years and 3,000 schools. *Educational Leadership, 37,* 104–109.

Hymowitz, K. (Spring 2001). Parenting; the lost art. *American Educator,* 4–6.

Ingersoll, R. (June 2002). The teacher shortage: A case of wrong diagnosis and wrong prescription. *NASSP Bulletin.*

Ingersoll, R. (September 2003). Is there really a teacher shortage?: A research report. Washington, DC: University of Washington: Center for the Study of Teaching and Policy.

Interstate New Teacher Assessment and Support Consortium. (1991). Model standards for beginning teacher licensing and development: A resource for state dialogue. Washington, DC: Council of Chief State School Officers.

Irvine, J. J. (1991). *Black students and school failure.* New York: Praeger.

Ishizuka, K. (May 2005). Have tools, lack skills. *School Library Journal, 51* (5), 24–25.

Ivey, G. (November 2002). Getting started: Manageable literacy practices. *Educational Leadership, 60* (3), 20–23.

Jackson, N. E. (1991). Precocious readers of English: Origin, structure, and predictive significance. In A. J. Tannenbaum & P. Klein (Eds.), *To be young and gifted.* Norwood, NJ: Ablex.

Jencks, C., & Phillips, M. (1998). *The Black-White test score gap.* Washington, DC: Brookings Institution Press.

Jennings, J. (January 26, 2000). Title I—A success. *Education Week.* p. 30.

Johnson, D. W., & Johnson, R. T. (1998). Cultural diversity and cooperative learning. In J. W. Putnam (Ed.), *Cooperative Learning Strategies for Inclusion.* Baltimore, MD: Brooks Publishing.

Johnson, J. (2003). What parents are saying about TV today: A report from public agenda. Available at http://www.publicagenda.org.

Johnson, R. T., & Johnson, D. W. (1986). Action research: Cooperative learning in the science classroom. *Science and Children, 24* (2), 31–32.

Johnston, J. D. (1978). Review of adult literacy education in the United States. *Journal of Reading, 21* (6), 562–563.

Jones, V., & Jones, L. (2001). *Comprehensive classroom management: creating communities of support and solving problems* (6th ed.). Boston: Allyn & Bacon.

Joyner, C. (1998). Head Start: Research insufficient to assess program impact. Testimony before the Subcommittee on Children and Families, Committee on Labor and Human Resources, U.S. Senate, and to Subcommittee on Early Childhood, Youth, and Families, Committee on Education and the Workforce, House of Representatives. ED 420382.

Jurmaine, R. (1994). *Baby Think It Over®.* (Available from Baby Think It Over®, Inc., 2709 Mondovi Road, Eau Claire, WI 54701).

Kann, L., Kinchen, S. A., Williams, B. I., Ross, J. G., Lowry, R., Grunbaum, J., & Kolbe, L. J. (2000). Special report: Youth risk behavior surveillance. United States, 1999. *Journal of School Health, 70* (7), 271–285.

Kant, I. (1960). *Education,* trans. by Annette Charlton. Ann Arbor: University of Michigan Press.

Keca, J., & Cook-Cottone, C. (May 2005). Middle-school and high school programs help beat eating disorders. *Principal Leadership, 5,* 11–15.

Kennen, E., & Lopez, E. (February 14, 2005). Finding alternative degree paths for nontraditional students. *Hispanic Outlook in Higher Education, 15,* 21–22.

Khmelkov, V. (2000). Developing professionalism: Effects of school workplace organization on novice teachers' sense of responsibility and efficacy. Ph.D. dissertation 0165 at University of Notre Dame.

Kids Count Data Book. (1997). *State profiles of child well-being.* Baltimore: Annie E. Casey Foundation.

Kilpatrick, W. (September 1918). The project method. *Teachers College Record,* 319–335.

King-Sears, M. E. (2001). Three steps for gaining access to the general education curriculum for learners with disabilities. *Intervention in School and Clinic, 37* (2), 67–76.

Kirst, M. (1984). Who controls our schools? American values in conflict. New York: Freeman.

Kirst, M. (Summer 1984). Choosing textbooks: Reflections of a state board president. *American Educator, 9.*

Kluckhohn, F., & Strodtbeck, F. (1961). *Variations in value orientations.* Westport, CT: Greenwood Press.

Knight, G. R. (1982). *Issues and alternatives in educational philosophy.* Berrien Springs, MI: Andrews University Press.

Koblinsky, S., Gordon, A., & Anderson, E. (2000). Changes in the social skills and behavior problems of homeless children during the preschool years. *Early Education & Development, 11* (3), 321–338.

Kohn, A. (2003). Almost there, but not quite. *Educational Leadership, 60* (6), 26–29.

Kominski, R., Jamieson, A., & Martinez, G. (June 2001). At-risk conditions of United States school-age children (Working Paper Series 52). [Online]. Washington, DC: United States Bureau of the Census, Population Division.

Korenman, S., Kaestner, R., & Joyce, T. (2001). Unintended pregnancy and the consequences of nonmarital childbearing. In L. Wu & B. Wolfe (Eds.). (2001). *Out of wedlock: Causes and consequences of nonmarital fertility.* NY: Russell Sage Foundation, 259–286.

Kounin, J. (1970). *Discipline and group management in the classroom.* New York: Holt, Rinehart, & Winston.

Kozol, J. (1991). *Savage inequalities: Children in America's schools.* New York: Crown Publishers.

Krashen, S. (1996). Is English in trouble? *Multicultural Education 4* (2), 16–19.

Krashen, S. (2002). More smoke and mirrors: a critique of the national reading panel report on fluency. In R. L. Allington (Ed.), *Big brother and the national reading curriculum: How ideology trumped evidence.* 114–124.

Krathwohl, D., Bloom, B., & Masia, B. (1964). *Taxonomy of educational objectives, handbook II: Affective Domain.* New York: David McKay.

Laczko-Kerr, I., & Berliner, D. (May 2003). In harm's way: How undercertified teachers hurt their students. *Educational Leadership, 60* (8), 34–39.

LaRoche, C. (2005). Student rights associated with disciplinary and academic hearings and sanctions. *College Student Journal, 39* (1), 149–55.

Lasley, T. J., Matczynski, J. J., & Rowley, J. B. (2002). *Instructional models' strategies for teaching in a diverse society.* Belmont, CA: Wadsworth.

The law: What it is, and isn't. (May 2003). *NEA Today, 21* (8), 22, 24.

Lazar, A., & Slostad, F. (March/April 1999). How to overcome obstacles to parent-teacher partnerships. *Clearing House, 72* (4), 206–210.

Lecca, P. J., Quervalú, I., Nunes, J. V., & Gonzales, H. F. (1998). *Cultural competency in health, social, and human services: Directions for the twenty-first century.* New York: Garland.

Lewis, A. (March 1998). Washington scene. *Education Digest, 63* (7), 68–71.

Lewis, A. (March 1999). Washington scene. *Education Digest, 64* (7), 69–73.

Lewis, A. (September 2002). Washington scene. *Education Digest, 68* (1), 67–71.

Lewis, A. (April 2004). Washington scene. *Education Digest, 69* (8), 68–71.

Lewis, A. (November 2004). Washington scene. *Education Digest, 70* (3), 66–70.

Lewis, A. (January 2005). Washington scene. *Education Digest, 70* (5), 68–71.

Lewis, A. (September 2005). Washington scene. *Education Digest, 71* (1), 68–72.

Lewis, A. (November 2005). Washington scene. *Education Digest, 87* (3), 179–180.

Lewis, S., & Allman, C. B. (2000). *Seeing eye to eye: An administrator's guide to students with low vision.* New York: American Foundation for the Blind Press.

Lickona, T. (October 2000). Character-based sexuality education: Bringing parents into the picture. *Educational Leadership, 58* (2), 60–64.

Livingston, A. (ed.) (June 2006). *The condition of education in 2006 in brief.* Washington, DC: National Center for Education Statistics.

Long, N., & Morse, W. (1996). Conflict in the classroom; the education of at-risk and troubled students. Austin, TX: Pro-Ed.

Louv, R. (2005). Last child in the woods: Saving our children from nature-deficit disorder. Chapel Hill, NC: Algonquin Books.

Luckasson, R., Borthwick-Duffy, S., Buntinx, W., Coulter, D., Craig, E., Reeve, A., Schalock, R., Snell, M., Spitalnick, D., Spreat, S., & Tasse, M. (2002). *Mental retardation: Definition, support, and systems of supports* (10th ed.). Washington, DC: American Association on Mental Retardation.

Mager, R. (1975). *Preparing instructional objectives.* Belmont, CA: Fearon.

Major, C., & Pines, R. (1999). *Teaching to teach: New partnerships in teacher education.* Washington, DC: National Education Association.

Majority of youth understand copyright but continue to download illegally. (September 2004). *Reading Teacher, 58* (1), n.p.

Mann, H. (1846). In G. C. Mann (Ed.), *The life and works of Horace Mann, Vol. IV,* pp. 115–117. (1891). Boston: Lee and Shepard.

Manning, M. L., & Baruth, L. G. (1996). *Multicultural education of children and adolescents.* Boston: Allyn & Bacon.

Marshall, P. L. (2002). *Cultural diversity in our schools.* Belmont, CA: Wadsworth.

Maslow, A. (1943). A theory of human motivation. *Psychological Review, 50* (4), 370–396.

Maslow, A. (1954). *Motivation and personality.* New York: Harper & Row.

Maslow, A. H. (1968). *Toward a psychology of being* (2nd ed.). Princeton, NJ: Van Nostrand.

Maslow, A. H. (1987). *Motivation and personality* (3rd ed.). New York: Harper & Row.

Mathews, R. (2000). Cultural patterns of South Asian and Southeast Asian Americans. *Interventions in School & Clinic, 36* (2), 101–104.

Mathis, W. J. (May, 2003). No child left behind: Costs and benefits. *Phi Delta Kappan, 84* (9), 679–686.

McCann, T. M., Johannessen, L. R., & Ricca, B. P. (2005*). Supporting beginning English teachers: research and implications for teacher induction.* Urbana, IL: National Council of Teachers of English.

McCubbin, H., Thompson, E., Thompson, A., & Futrell, J. (Eds.) (1999). *The dynamics of resilient families.* Thousand Oaks, CA: Sage.

McDaniel, T. (1979). The teacher's ten commandments: School law in the classroom. *Phi Delta Kappan, 60* (10), 707.

McEwan, E. (1998). Angry parents & failing schools: What's wrong with the public schools & what you can do about it. Wheaton, Illinois: Harold Shaw.

McGuiness, D. (1997). *Why our children can't read and what we can do about it.* New York: Free Press.

Meier, T. (November 2003). Why can't she remember that? The importance of storybook reading in multilingual, multicultural classrooms. *Reading Teacher, 57* (3), 242–252.

Mercer, C. D., Jordan, L., Allsop, D. H., & Mercer, A. R. (1996). Learning disabilities definitions and criteria used by state education departments. *Learning Disabilities Quarterly, 19,* 217–231.

Miller, J. (May 2004). Rebuilding the food pyramid. *Odyssey,* 16–21.

Million, J. (November 2002). Facts for parents if a school flunks. *Education Digest, 68* (3), 21–22.

Million, J. (2003). Talking to parents. *Education Digest, 68* (5), 52–53.

Miranda, L. C. (1991). *Latino child poverty in the United States.* Washington, DC: Children's Defense Fund.

Mohr, K. A. J. (September, 2004). English as an accelerated language: A call to action for reading teachers. *Reading Teacher, 58* (1), 18–26.

Montessori, M. (1939). *The secret of childhood.* New York: Frederick A. Stokes.

Muther, C. (April 1985). What every textbook evaluator should know. *Educational Leadership, 42* (7).

NAEP 2004 Trends in Academic Progress. (2004). Washington, DC: National Center for Education Progress.

National Board for Professional Teaching Standards. (1997). In *Journal of Research and Development in Education, 34* (1), Fall 2000.

National Board for Professional Teaching Standards. (2006). At http://www.nbpts .org/UserFiles/File/2006_QA_Brochure.pdf.

National Center for Education Statistics. (2004). *The nation's report card: Mathematics Highlights 2003.* Washington, DC: U.S. Department of Education.

National Center for Education Statistics. (2004). *The nation's report card: Reading Highlights 2003.* Washington, DC: U.S. Department of Education.

National Clearinghouse for English Language Acquisition (NCELA), Newsline Bulletin (June 11, 2002. Retrieved June 30, 2006, from http://www.ncela.gwu .edu/enews/2002/0611.htm.

National Coalition for the Homeless. (1999). *Education of homeless children and youth.* (NCH Fact Sheet #10). [Online]. Available at http://nch.ari.net/ edchild.html.

National Health and Nutrition Examination Survey. (1999). Washington, DC: National Center for Health Statistics.

National Household Survey on Drug Abuse. (May 2001). Washington, DC: United States Department of Health and Human Services.

NCES Survey: Over 40% of U.S. teachers teach LEPs. (June 11, 2002). NCELA Newsline Bulletin.

Nehring, J. (1992). *The schools we have: The schools we want.* San Francisco: Jossey-Bass.

Newman, R. (Winter 1997/1998). Parent conferences: A conversation between you and your child's teacher. *Childhood Education, 74* (2), 100–101.

Nidds, J. A., & McGerald, J. (January 1997). How functional is portfolio assessment anyway? *Education Digest, 62* (5), 47–50.

Nieto, S. (2000). *Affirming diversity: The sociopolitical context of multicultural education* (3rd ed.). New York: Addison Wesley.

Nieto, S. (May 2003). What keeps teachers going? *Educational Leadership, 60* (8), 14–18.

No Child Left Behind Act: Guide to "frequently asked questions." (February 17, 2005). Washington, DC: United States Committee on Education and the Workforce.

Northwest Regional Education Lab. (1998). *Catalog of school reform models* (1st ed.). Washington, DC: U.S. Department of Education. Ch. 12, p. 12.

Office of the Federal Register. (1994). *Code of Federal Regulations 34. Parts 300 to 399.* Washington, DC: Author.

Oppenheimer, T. (2004). *The flickering mind: Saving education from the false promise of technology.* New York: Random House.

The Opportunity to Excel. (February 2001). Washington, DC: National Education Association.

Orange, C. (2002). *The quick reference guide to educational innovations: Practices, programs, policies, and philosophies.* Thousand Oaks, CA: Corwin.

Orfield, G. (Ed.). (2004). *Dropouts in America; confronting the graduation rate crisis.* Cambridge, MA: Harvard Education Press.

Orfield, G., & Lee, Chungmei. (January 18, 2004). *Brown at 50: King's dream or Plessy's nightmare?* Cambridge, MA: Harvard Graduate School of Education.

Ornstein, A., & Levine, D. (1997). *Foundations of education* (6th ed.). Boston: Houghton Mifflin.

Oswald, R. F. (May 2002). Resilience within the family networks of lesbians and gay men: Intentionality and redefinition. *Journal of Marriage and Family, 64,* 374–383.

Otto, L. B. (1982). Extracurricular activities. In H. Walberg (Ed.), *Improving Educational Standards and Productivity,* pp. 217–227. Berkeley, CA: McCutchan.

Out, J. W., & Lafreniere, K. D. (Fall 2001). Baby Think It Over®: Using role-playing to prevent teen pregnancy. *Adolescence, 36* (143), 571–582.

Patterson, M. J., & Fiscus, L. (May 2000). School trips without a hitch. *Education Digest, 65* (9), 48–53.

Payne, R. K. (1998). *A framework for understanding poverty.* Baytown, TX: RFT Publishing.

Peirce, C. S. (January 1878). How to make our ideas clear. *Popular Science Monthly.*

Pfeiffer, S., & Reddy, L. (Eds.) (2000). *Inclusion practices with special needs students: Theory, research, and application.* Binghamton, NY: Haworth.

Piaget, J. (1926). *The language and thought of the child.* New York: Harcourt, Brace & World.

Piaget, J. (1985). *The equilibration of cognitive structures: The central problem of intellectual development.* Chicago: University of Chicago Press.

Pitler, H. (May/June 2006). Viewing technology through three lenses. *Principal, 85* (5), 38–42.

Pizzolongo, P. (2005). NAEYC's revised code of ethical and statement of commitment. *Young Children, 60* (5), 64–65.

The politics of IDEA—Revisited. (January 2003). *NEA Today, 10* (4), 11.

Pong, S., Dronkers, J., & Hampden-Thompson, G. (August 2003). Family policies and children's school achievement in single- versus two-parent families. *Journal of Marriage and Family, 65,* 681–699.

Poon-McBrayer, K. F., & Garcia, S. B. (2000). Profiles of Asian American students with LD at initial referral, assessment, and placement in special education. *Journal of Learning Disabilities, 33* (1), 61–71.

President's Advisory Commission on Educational Excellence for Hispanic Americans. (1996). *Our nation on the fault line: Hispanic American education.* Washington, DC: White House Initiative on Educational Excellence for Hispanic Americans. (ERIC Document Reproduction Service No. ED 408 382).

President's Advisory Commission on Educational Excellence for Hispanic Americans. (2000). *Creating the will: Hispanics achieving educational excellence.* Washington, DC: White House Initiative on Educational Excellence for Hispanic Americans. (ERIC Document Reproduction Service No. 446 195).

Professional standards for the accreditation of schools, colleges, and departments of education, 2002 revision. (2002). Washington, DC: NCATE.

Puma, M. J., Karweit, N., Price, C., Ricciuti, A., Thompson, W., & Vaden-Kierman, M. (1997). *Prospects: Final report on student outcomes.* Washington, DC: U.S. Department of Education, Planning and Evaluation Services.

Quinlan, A. (March/April 2004). Six steps for mediating conflicts. *Principal, 83,* 69.

Ravitch, D. (2000). *Left back: A century of failed school reforms.* New York: Simon & Schuster.

Renchler, R. (1993). Poverty and learning. *ERIC Digest, 83.* Eugene, OR: ERIC Clearinghouse on Educational Management.

Report of the National Reading Panel. (December 2000). *Teaching children to read.* Washington, DC: National Reading Panel.

Report of the United States Bureau of the Census. (1998). Washington, DC: Department of Commerce.

Reynolds, C. R. (2000). Pennsylvania Association for Retarded Citizens v. Pennsylvania (1972). In C. R. Reynolds & E. Fletcher-Janzen (Eds.), *Encyclopedia of Special Education, Vol. 3* (2nd ed.), pp. 1338–1339. New York: Wiley.

Riley, J. (1996). *The teaching of reading.* London: Paul Chapman.

Ringstaff, C., & Kelley, L. (2002). The learning return on our educational technology investment: A review of findings from research. San Francisco: WestEd RTEC.

Roan, S. (September 28, 1994). Square pegs? Being rejected by peers is not only hurtful, it can cause emotional problems and bad behavior. *Los Angeles Times Home Edition,* E-1.

Robelen, E. W. (2002). Rules clarify changes on teacher, paraprofessional qualifications. *Education Week, 21* (3), 36.

Rogers, C. (1961). *On becoming a person.* Boston: Houghton Mifflin.

Rogers, C. (1962). The interpersonal relationship: The core of guidance. *Harvard Educational Review, 32,* 416–429.

Rogers, C. (1983). *Freedom to learn for the 80s.* Columbus, OH: Merrill.

Rolon, C. A. (November/December 2005). Helping Latino students learn. *Principal, 85,* 30–34.

Rosenblatt, R., & Helfand, D. (March 23, 2001). Schools feeling the new baby boom. *News & Observer,* p. 14A.

Rosenshine, B. (1983). Teaching functions in instructional programs. *Elementary School Journal, 83* (4), 335–352.

Rosenshine, B. (1998). "Subject: Learning Styles." (E-mail to Joel Stellwagen)

Rosenthal, R., & Jacobson, L. (1968). *Pygmalion in the classroom.* New York: Holt.

Rowe, M. B. (March, 1978). Give students time to respond. *School Science and Mathematics, 78,* 207–216.

Rubin, L. J., & Borgers, S. B. (September 1991). The changing family: Implications for education. *Principal,* 11–13.

Rust, F. (1991). A comparative analysis of beliefs about teaching among preservice teachers. Paper presented at the Annual Meeting of the American Educational Research Association.

Rutherford, F. J., & Ahlgren, A. (1990). *Science for all Americans.* New York: Oxford University Press.

Sartre, J. P. (1947). *Existentialism,* trans. by Bernard Frechtman. New York: Philosophical Library.

Schaeffer, E. (Winter 1997/1998). Character education in the curriculum and beyond. *Middle Matters, 6* (1), 6.

Schlesinger, A. M., Jr., (1998). *The disuniting of America: Reflections on a multicultural society.* New York: W. W. Norton.

School practices to promote the achievement of Hispanic students. (2000). New York: ERIC Clearinghouse on Urban Education. (ERIC Document Reproduction Service No. ED 439 186).

Schroeder, K. (January 1999). Education news in brief. *Education Digest, 44* (5), 73–76.

Schroeder, K. (March 2004). Education news in brief. *Education Digest, 49* (7), 70–74.

Schroeder, K. (April 2005). Education news in brief. *Education Digest, 50* (8), 72–75.

Scott-Little, C., Kagan, S. L., & Frelow, V. S. (November 2005). Inside the content; the breadth and depth of early learning standards: creating the conditions for success with early learning standards. Greensboro, NC: SERVE.

Seastrom, M. M., et al. (May 2002). Qualifications of the public school teacher workforce: Prevalence of out-of-field teachers 1987–88 and 1999–2000: Statistical analysis report. Washington, DC: United States Office of Education, National Center for Education Statistics.

Senge, P. (1990). *The fifth discipline: The art & practice of the learning organization.* New York: Doubleday.

Shank, M. (2002). Making curriculum sparkle for students with AD/HD. Unpublished manuscript.

Shannon, S., & Milian, M. (Fall 2002). Parents choose dual language programs in Colorado: Survey. *Bilingual Research Journal, 26* (3). 681–696.

Sheurer, D., & Parkay, F. (1992). The new Christian right and the public school curriculum: The Florida report. In J. B. Smith & J. G. Coleman Jr. (Eds.), *School library media annual, Vol. 10.* Englewood, CO: Libraries Unlimited.

Should second-career new teachers be required to take methods courses before starting work? (May 2001). *NEA Today, 19* (8), 11.

Shuler, D., et al. (Summer 1998). Beginning teachers' classroom management problems and teacher preparation concerns. *Florida Educational Research Council's Research Bulletin, 29* (2), 11–34.

Significant Features of Fiscal Federalism. (1995). Washington, DC: United States Advisory Commission on Intergovernmental Relations.

Sikorski, J. F. (2004). Teacher of teachers: An interview with James H. Korn. *Teaching of Psychology, 31* (1), 72–76.

Simpson, E. (1972). *The classification of educational objectives: Psychomotor domain.* Urbana, IL: University of Illinois Press.

Sizer, T. R. (1985). *Horace's compromise: The dilemma of the American high school.* Boston: Houghton Mifflin.

Skinner, B. F. (1948). *Walden II.* New York: Macmillan.

Slavin, R. E. (1988). The cooperative revolution in education. *The School Administrator, 45,* 9–13.

Slavin, R. E. (1989). Research on cooperative learning: Consensus and controversy. *Educational Leadership, 47* (4), 52–54.

Slavin, R. E. (1995). *Cooperative learning: Theory, research, and practice* (2nd ed.). Boston: Allyn & Bacon.

Smith, A. C., & Smith, D. I. (2001). Emergency and transitional shelter population: 2000 (Census 2000 special reports). Washington, DC: U.S. Department of Commerce.

Smith, T., & Ingersoll, R. (2003). Reducing teacher turnover: What are the components of effective induction? Paper presented at the annual meeting of the American Educational Research Association.

Spring, J. (2000). *American education* (9th ed.). Boston: McGraw-Hill.

Standards for staff development (rev. ed.). (2001). Oxford, OH: National Staff Development Council.

Statistical Abstract of the United States, 2001. (2001). Washington, DC: U.S. Department of Commerce, Bureau of the Census.

Status of the American public school teacher. (2003). Washington, DC: National Education Association.

Steele, C. M. (April 1992). Race and the schooling of Black Americans. *Atlantic Monthly,* 68–78.

Sternberg, R. J., & Powell, J. S. (1983). The development of intelligence. In P. H. Mussen (Ed.), *Handbook of child psychology, Vol. 3.* New York: Wiley.

Stevens, B., & Tollafield, A. (March 2003). Make the most of parent/teacher conferences. *Phi Delta Kappan, 84,* 521–524.

Stiggins, R. (2001). *Student-involved classroom assessment* (3rd ed.). Upper Saddle River, NJ: Prentice Hall.

Stone, J. (June 6, 2003). When education research lies. *Chronicle of Higher Education, 49,* B12–13.

Stronge, J. (2002). *Qualities of effective teachers.* Alexandria, VA: ASCD.

Students with chronic illnesses: Guidance for families, schools, and students. (April 2003). *Journal of School Health, 73,* 131–32.

Study: High school student smoking rate drops. (November 24, 2003). http://no-smoking.org/nov03/11-24-03-3.html.

Sunal, C. S., & Haas, M. E. (2005). *Social studies for the elementary and middle grades: A constructivist approach* (2nd ed.). Boston: Pearson.

Suppes, P. (April 1968). Computer technology and the future of education. *Phi Delta Kappan.* 420–423.

Sweeney, J. (1990). Classroom practice and educational research. *The Social Studies, 81,* 278–282.

Takona, J. P. (June 2003). Portfolio development for teacher candidates. ERIC Clearinghouse on Assessment and Evaluation. ED 481816.

Tanner, L. (April 9, 2003). Obese kids' suffering profound. *Charlotte (NC) Observer,* 12A.

Tasker, F., & Golombok, S. (1997). Young people's attitudes toward living in a lesbian family: A longitudinal study of children raised by post-divorce lesbian mothers. *Journal of Divorce and Remarriage, 28,* 183–202.

Teacher quality: A report on the preparation and qualifications of public school teachers. (1999). Washington, DC: United States Department of Education, National Center for Education Statistics.

Teachers and ESPs—By the numbers. (September 2003). *NEA Today, 22* (1), 34–35.

Teachers—Kindergarten, elementary, and secondary. Downloaded on July 19, 2006, from http://www.collegegrad.com/career/teachingcareer.shtml.

Teitel, L. (2001). *How professional development schools make a difference: A review of research.* Washington, DC: National Council for Accreditation of Teacher Education.

Terman, L. (1926). *Genetic studies of genius, Vol. I: Mental and physical traits of a thousand gifted students* (2nd ed.). Stanford, CA: Stanford University Press.

Thomas, D. (December 1, 1996). Every child deserves a home. *Parade Magazine,* 8.

Thomson, M., & Caulfield, R. (1998). Teen pregnancy and parenthood: Infants and toddlers who need care. *Early Childhood Education Journal, 25* (3), 203–205.

Toch, T. (February 26, 1996). Why teachers don't teach. *U.S. News and World Report, 120* (8), 62–68.

Tomlinson, C. (August 2000). *Differentiation of instruction in the elementary grades.* EDO-PS-00-7. Washington, DC: Office of Educational Research and Improvement, U.S. Department of Education.

Trueba, H. T., Cheng, L., & Ima, K. (1993). *Myth or reality: Adaptive strategies of Asian Americans in California.* Washington, DC: Falmer.

Turnbull, R., & Cilley, M. (1999). *Explanations and implications of the 1997 amendments to IDEA.* Columbus, OH: Merrill.

Turnbull, R., Turnbull, A., Shank, M., & Smith, S. J. (2004). *Exceptional lives: Special education in today's schools* (4th ed.). Upper Saddle River, NJ: Pearson Education.

Tyack, D., & Cuban, L. (1995). *Tinkering with Utopia: A century of public school reform.* (ERIC Document Reproduction Service No. ED391847).

Tyler, R. (1949). *Basic principles of curriculum and instruction.* Chicago: University of Chicago.

Type of partnership. (November 4, 2005). Washington, DC: NCATE. Downloaded on July 24, 2006, at www.ncate.org/states/TypePartnership.asp?ch=105.

U.S. Department of Education. (2002). Twenty-fourth annual report to Congress on the implementation of the Individuals with Disabilities Education Act. Washington, DC: U.S. Government Printing Office.

U.S. Department of Health and Human Services, Administration on Children, Youth, and Families. (2000). *Child maltreatment 1998: Reports from the states to the National Child Abuse and Neglect Data System.* Washington, DC: U.S. Government Printing Office.

Vail, K. (December 2003). Grasping what kids need to raise performance. *American School Board Journal, 190,* 46–52.

Vail, K. (January 2004). Raising the (salad) bar on obesity. *American School Board Journal, 191,* 22–25.

Vail, K. (April 2005). Helping students through depression. *American School Board Journal, 192,* 34–36.

Veronikas, S., & Shaughnessy, M. (May/June 2006). An interview with Kathy Schrock about teaching and technology. *TechTrends, 50* (3), 8–10.

Viadero, D. (June 11, 2003). Report examines "Authorizers" of charter schools. *Education Week, 22* (40), 15, 17.

Violence in the United States public schools: 2000 school survey on crime and safety. (October, 2003). Washington, DC: National Center for Education Statistics.

Wagner, E. (1992). Time to end the confusion over copying. *Academe, 78,* 27–29.

Walker, H. M., Zeller, R. W., Close, D. W., Webber, J., & Gresham, F. (1999). The present unwrapped: Change and challenge in the field of behavioral disorders. *Behavioral Disorders, 24* (4), 293–304.

Washburne, C. (1926). The philosophy of the Winnetka curriculum. In Harold Rugg (Ed.), *The foundations and technique for the study of education.* National Society for the Study of Education. Bloomington, IN: Public School Publishing.

Watson, J. B. (1924). *Behaviorism.* New York: Norton.

Weber, W. (1990). Classroom management. In *Classroom Teaching Skills* (4th ed.). Lexington, MA: Heath.

Wechsler, D. (1975). Intelligence defined and undefined: A relativistic appraisal. *American Psychologist, 30* (2), 135–139.

Weinberg, W. A., Harper, C. R., Emslie, G. J., & Brumback, R. A. (1995). *Depression and other affective illnesses as a cause of school failure and maladaptation in learning-disabled children, adolescents, and young adults—Secondary education and beyond.* Pittsburgh: Learning Disability Association.

Weintraub, M. (2000). Gifted handicapped. In R. C. Reynolds & E. Fletcher-Janzen (Eds.), *Encyclopedia of Special Education, Vol. 2* (2nd ed.), pp. 824–825. New York: Wiley.

Wenglinski, H. (2000). *How teaching matters: Bringing the classroom back into discussions of teacher quality.* Princeton, NJ: Milken Family Foundation and Educational Testing Service.

What will the new IDEA do? (March/April 2005). *Emphasis* (South Carolina Education Association), 24 (6), 10.

White, C. (February 2005). A better idea. *NEA Today, 23* (5), 34–35.

White-Clark, R. (March/April 2005). Training teachers to succeed in a multicultural classroom. *Principal, 84,* 40–44.

Wildavsky, B. (2000). At least they have high self-esteem. *U.S. News and World Report.* 50.

Willert, H. J., & Lenhardt, A. C. (Winter 2003). Tackling school violence does take the whole village. *The Educational Forum, 67,* 110–118.

Willingham, W., & Cole, N. (1997). *Gender and fair assessment.* Mahwah, NJ: Lawrence Erlbaum Associates.

Winn, M. (2002). *The plug-in drug: Television, computers, and family life.* New York: Penguin Putnam.

Wolkomir, R., & Wolkomir, J. (March 2001). Noise busters. *Smithsonian, 31* (12), 88–92, 94, 96, 98.

Wong, H. K., & Wong, R. T. (1991). *The first days of school.* Sunnyvale, CA: Harry K. Wong Publications.

Worthy, J. (April 2001). A life of learning and enjoyment from literacy. *Reading Teacher, 54* (7), 690–691.

Wright, J. C., & Huston, A. C. (May 1995). *Effects of educational TV viewing of lower-income preschoolers on academic skills, school readiness, and school adjustment one to three years later.* University of Kansas: Center for Research on the Influences of TV on Children.

Yaden, D. B., Jr., et al. (October 2000). Early literacy for inner-city children: Effects of reading and writing interventions in English and Spanish during the preschool years. *Reading Teacher, 54* (2), 186–189.

Yardley, J. (March 25, 2001). Non-Hispanic whites may soon be a minority in Texas. *New York Times,* 18Y.

Yatvin, J., Weaver, C., & Garan, E. (September 2003). Reading first; cautions and recommendations. *Language Arts, 81* (1), 28–33.

Young, J., & Brozo, W. (July/September 2001). Boys will be boys, or will they? Literacy and masculinities. *Reading Research Quarterly, 36,* 316–325.

Zepeda, S., & Ponticell, J. (Spring 1996). Classroom climate and first-year teachers. *Kappa Delta Pi Record,* 91–93.

Zill, N., Resnick, G., Kim, K., McKey, R. H., Clark, C., Par-Samant, S., Connell, D., Vaden-Kierman, M., O'Brien, R., & D'Elio, M. A. (2001). Head Start family and child experiences survey (FACES): Longitudinal findings on program performance. Third report. ED453969.

Zirkel, P. A. (May 2001). Confidentiality of school records. *Principal, 80* (5), 50–51.

Zirkel, P. A. (January/February 2003). Privacy of student records: An update. *Principal, 82* (3), 10, 12–13.

Subject Index

A

Abington School District v. Schempp, 344
Abolitionist Society, 264
Academic freedom, 333–334
Academic language skills, 67
Academic self-concept, 75
Academy of Plato, 255
Accidents, liability for, 329
Accomplished Teaching Validation Study, 132
Accountability movement, 279
Accreditation agency, 105–107
Activity curriculum, 174–175
Add-on certification, 109
Adequate Yearly Progress (AYP), 71, 73–74, 368
 states, role of, 374
ADHD (attention deficit hyperactivity disorder), 90–91
Administration
 communicating with, 19–20
 intervention, administrative, 440
 in nineteenth century, 266
 on purposes of school, 362
 reform, administrative, 437–438
Administrative/supervisory
 organizations, 134
 list of, 137
Adoption states for textbooks, 189–190
Advanced degrees, 131
Advanced placement (AP) credits, 109
Aesthetics and axiology, 291–292
Affective perspective, 169–175, 276
 transfer of learning and, 164
African Americans, 61–62. *See also* Separate but equal doctrine
 at-risk students, 405
 in colonial America, 262
 early years of nation, education in, 264
 measures for working with, 62
 in nineteenth century education, 266–267
 normal schools for, 266–267
 single-parent families, 402
African Free School, 264, 265
Agriculture Department, 381
Alcohol use, 51–52, 335
 abuse of, 413–414
Allergies, 95
All I Really Need to Know I Learned in Kindergarten (Fulghum), 361
All Talk, No Action, 108
Alphabet and kindergarten, 427
Alternative certification, 118–119
 online information, 122
Alternative schooling, 279
Alternative teacher education programs, 118–121
The Amendments to the Individuals with Disabilities Education Act (IDEA), 348

American Association for the Advancement of Science (AAAS), 194
 national education standards and, 191
American Association of University Women (AAUW), 341
American Association on Mental Retardation (AAMR), 83, 85
American Council on the Teaching of Foreign Languages (ACTFL), 197
 national education standards and, 192
American Educator's Encyclopedia (Dejnozka & Kapel), 345
American Federation of Labor/Congress of Industrial Organizations (AFL/CIO), 133
American Federation of Teachers (AFT), 132, 133
 founding of, 271
American Foundation for Vision Awareness, 93
American Psychiatric Association (APA)
 on ADHD (attention deficit hyperactivity disorder), 90
 on emotional disorders, 92
American Sign Language (ASL), 94
American Speech-Language-Hearing Association (ASHA), 93
American Spelling Book (Webster), 264, 265
The Americans with Disabilities Act (ADA) of 1990, 348
Ancestral identity, 67–68
Ancillary businesses, 471–472
Angry students, 76
Anorexia nervosa, 96
Anxiety disorders, 92
Aphasia, developmental, 88
Appearance issues, 334–335
Applications for employment, 125
Arranging experiences, 34–37
Art of teaching, 7–9
Arts standards, 197–198
Asian Americans, 64–66
 nineteenth century education and, 273
Assertive Discipline (Canter & Canter), 225
Assessment, 215–224. *See also* Formative assessments; Grades; Objectives; Summative assessments
 aims of, 215–216
 classroom assessment, 217
 evaluation compared, 217
 instruction and, 218–220
 keys to, 219–220
 prepackaged assessments, 219
 by school districts, 377
 standardized testing, 216–218
Assistive technologies, 459
 for mentally retarded students, 86
Asthma, 95
Athens, education in, 254–255
Athletics. *See* Physical education

At-risk students, 404–406
 cooperative learning and, 172
 latchkey children, 402–403
Attitude
 examining, 14
 and purpose, 12–13
Auditory learning style, 79
Auditory sensory disabilities, 93–94
Autism, 89–90
Autism Society of America, 89
AV (audio-visual) equipment, 35
Axiology, 291–292, 319

B

Baby Think It Over program, 416–417
Back to basics movement, 279, 427
Baptist education, 261
Base salaries for teachers, 127, 128
Behavioral disorders, 91–92
Behaviorism, 308–309, 312, 427
 in classroom, 309
Behaviors. *See also* Classroom management
 ADHD (attention deficit hyperactivity disorder) students, 91
 of autistic students, 90
 home environment and, 408–409
 modeling of, 50–51
Bell curve, 216–217
Bias, gender, 70
Bible readings, 344
Bilingual education, 72, 74
 history of, 278
 teaching positions in, 124–125
The Bilingual Education Act, 349
Bill for the More General Diffusion of Knowledge (Jefferson), 263, 265
Bill of Rights and copyrights, 331
Bill of Rights for Student Teachers, 133, 134–135
Bisexual students, 96
Black History Month, 420
Blacks. *See* African Americans
Blended families, 402–403
Blindness, 92–93
Block grants, 349
Bloom's taxonomy, 17, 38
 synthesis, 41
Board of education
 funding by, 386–387
 state board, role of, 373
Board of Education v. Allen, 344
Bodily kinesthetic intelligence, 83, 84
Books. *See also* Textbooks
 electronic books (e-books), 479–480, 482
 parents' concerns, 184
 special interest groups and, 184
Boston Latin Grammar School, 263
Boston's Mentoring Program, 131
Brain injuries, 88, 95

Branching programs, 167
Breach of contract, 327
Brevity, copyright law and, 332
Broad fields curriculum, 172–173
Brookings Institution charter school studies, 123
Brown v. Board of Education of Topeka, 274, 278, 353, 413
　Warren, Earl, on, 337, 338–339
Buckley Amendment, 342, 346–347
Buddhism, 297
　idealism of, 294
Bulimia nervosa, 96
Bullying, 415
Business
　ancillary businesses, 471–472
　demands of, 432
　funding from, 387
　involvement of, 431–432
　purposes of school, 361
　and reform model, 430–432
　tax funding and, 431

C

California Standards Test, 182
Campus design, 461–466
The Canterbury Tales (Chaucer), 112
Cardinal Principles of Secondary Education, 275
Carnegie units, 158, 272
Categorical funding, 274, 349
Catholic education, 261
CD-ROM, 35
Census Bureau
　on diversity, 60
　on literacy, 80
Center for the Advancement of Ethics and Character, 156
Centers for Disease Control and Prevention, 467
Cerebral palsy, 94–95
Certification, 22. *See also* Licensing
　add-on certification, 109
　alternative certification, 118–119
　comparing requirements, 120
　defined, 109
　examinations, 109
　legal eligibility for, 118
　as National-Board Certified teacher, 131–132
　other fields, use in, 123–124
　Praxis series, 119–120
　teacher testimonial, 110–111
Change, reform and, 427–428
Change agents, 447
Chaperoning functions, 240
Character education, 156, 170, 439–440
Charter schools, 369
　teaching in, 122–123
Chicago Renaissance 2010 project, 369
Child abuse and neglect, 411–412
　reporting, 329–330, 411–412
　signs of, 412
Child Abuse Prevention and Treatment Act, 329, 347, 411
Childhood Education and Development Act, 351

Child Nutrition and WIC (Women, Infants, and Children) Reauthorization Act, 351
Christmas, 420
Church of England, 262
　ethnic minorities, education of, 264
Cigarette smoking, 414
Civil rights
　legislation, 346–347
　Supreme Court cases, 354
The Civil Rights Act of 1964, 346
Classical conditioning, 308
Classical idealism, 294
Classical realism, 295–296
Classroom assessment, 217
Classroom lessons, 34–35, 37
Classroom management, 224–240. *See also* Consequences; Discipline; Procedures; Routines; Rules
　arrangement of classroom for, 239
　concerns, list of, 232
　effective teachers, traits of, 238–239
　expectations, communicating, 233–234
　modeling behavior, 226–227
　perspectives on, 225–227
　planning for, 231–232
　practicing, 232
　Principles of Effective Discipline, 233–234
　procedures, 230–231
　proximity of teacher to students, 239
　teacher behaviors, 238–240
　teacher testimonial, 226–227
　terminology of, 228–231
　traditional perspective, 225
Classroom pragmatics. *See also* Assessment; Classroom management
　defined, 215
Class rules. *See* Rules
Class size
　instructional reform and, 437
　physical plant design and, 464–465
Clinical experiences, 106
Clinical practice, 106
Clubs
　as extracurricular activities, 160
　religious clubs, 344
Codes of ethics, 323–325
Cognitive development model, 17
Cognitive perspective, 276
Cognitive perspective on curriculum, 163–169
Collaboration
　with colleagues, 129
　informed collaboration, 441
Colleagues
　collaboration with, 129
　communicating with, 19–21
　meetings, 380
Colleges and universities
　curriculum, entrance requirements and, 187–188
　land-grant colleges, 272–273, 345
　legislation affecting, 345
　in Middle Ages, 258
　preparation perceptions, 127–128, 129
　and reform model, 429–430
Colonial America, education in, 259–262
Combined (CB) behaviors, 91

Committee for Economic Development, 156
Committee for Public Education v. Regan, 344
Committee of Ten on Secondary Studies, 271–272
Committee of Thirteen on College Entrance Requirements, 272
Committee work, 129, 240–241
　principals assigning, 380
Common School Journal (Mann), 270
Common schools, 267
　advocacy for, 270–271
Communication, 10–11, 17–22. *See also* English language
　Asian American students and, 66
　in classroom management, 227
　of expectations to students, 233–234
　Hispanic students and, 66–67
　with homeless families, 410
Community. *See also* Local governments
　communicating with, 21–22
　design of schools and, 470–471
　global community, 483
　and Internet, 477–478
Compensatory education, 349
Competencies of teachers, 186
Competency-based education (CBE), 167
Competitive students, 78
Comprehensive arts standards, 197–198
Compulsory education, 261
Computer-assisted instruction (CAI), 167–168
Computer-managed instruction (CMI), 168
Computers, 36
　in curriculum, 167–169
　games, influence of, 419, 420
　history of, 456
　mastery learning and, 167
　for mentally retarded students, 86
　programmed instruction and, 309
　reliance on, 35
　standards for curriculum, 199
　voice-recognition computers, 459
Conceptual intervention, 440
Conceptual reform, 437–438
Conditioned stimulus/response, 308
The Condition of Education, 345
Conduct disorders, 92
Conduct with students, 335–336
Conferences
　parent conferences, 240
　problem-solving conferences, 236–237
Confidentiality requirements, 114–115
Confident students, 77
Conflict resolution, 237
Confucianism, 297
Congress, 345
　role in education, 371
Consequences, 230
　academic consequences, 235
　enforcement of, 235–236
　extenuating circumstances, recognizing, 236
　pragmatism and, 298, 299
　problem-solving conferences, 236–237
　protests of, 236
　responding to misbehavior, 235
　students identifying, 235
Consistency in consequences, 230

Constituencies for communication skills, 11
Constructivism, 310–311, 312
Consumables, 466
Content, 10–11, 14–17
    elementary content, 15
    in mastery learning, 166
    multicultural content, 68
    secondary content, 15–16
Continuing education, 22, 131
Contracts, employment, 326–327
Convergent thinking, 41
Conversational language skills, 67
Cooperative learning, 171–172
    activities, 62
Cooperative students, 78
Copyright Act of 1976, 331
Copyright laws, 331–332
Core commonalties, 173
Core curriculum, 165–166
Corporal punishment, 337–338
Corporations. *See* Business
Coursework, 109–111
    continuing coursework, 22, 131
    and field observations, 113
Crack babies, 414
Crack cocaine use, 414
The Cracker Barrel Journal, 50
Creative intelligence, 299
Critical needs areas, 117
Cultural diversity, 59–69
Cultural Literacy (Hirsch), 304–305
Cultural pluralism, 60
Cultural synchronization, 61
Cumulative effect, copyright law and, 332
Curriculum. *See also* Extracurricular activities
    activity curriculum, 174–175
    for ADHD (attention deficit hyperactivity disorder) students, 91
    affective perspective of, 164, 169–175
    alternative certification and, 119
    broad fields curriculum, 172–173
    cognitive perspective, 163–169
    college entrance requirements and, 187–188
    computers in, 167–169
    cooperative learning, 171–172
    core curriculum, 165–166
    cultural diversity and, 60
    defined, 153–156
    ethnic diversity and, 61–62
    experiences and, 154
    explicit curriculum, 158, 318
    and field observation, 114
    four curricula, 157–162
    humanistic education, 170–171
    implicit curriculum, 158–159
    inquiry curriculum, 173–174
    interventions, curricular, 439–440
    in later twentieth century, 279
    legislators and, 191
    mastery learning, 166–167
    for mentally retarded students, 86
    national curriculum debate, 202–204
    national education standards, 191–192
    A Nation at Risk: The Imperative for Educational Reform affecting, 279–280
    in nineteenth century, 266
    null curriculum, 159–160
    outcome-based education (OBE), 167

outcomes and, 154–155, 167
parents and, 183–184, 191
perspectives of, 162–175
problem-solving curriculum, 173–174
purpose of, 156–157
reforms, 436
relevant curriculum, 173–174
schools, influence of, 186–188, 191
school uniforms issue, 206–208
special interest groups and, 184, 191
standardized testing and, 187
state legislatures and, 185–186
student-centered curriculum, 163, 169–170
subject-centered curriculum, 163–165
teacher testimonials, 164–165, 192–193
testing as issue, 200–202
textbooks and, 188–190, 191
Curriculum specialists, 376–377

D

Dame schools, 260
Dance standards, 197–198
Dark Ages, 258
Davis v. Monroe County Board of Education, 341–342
Deductive reasoning, 293
    realism and, 296
Defense Department, 381
Democracy and Education (Dewey), 275–276
Democracy in America (de Tocqueville), 360
Demographics for teaching positions, 124
Den, Idol of the, 296
Depression, 91–92, 96
    suicide and, 418
Design of schools, 461–466
    ancillary businesses and, 471–472
    community activities and, 470–471
    equal access considerations, 463
    expandability issues, 465
    flow of school, 468–469
    layout considerations, 466–469
    modular schools, 465–466
    necessary facilities, 466
    physical education considerations, 466–469
    physical plant design, 463–466
    postfederal design, 462–463
    prefederal design, 461–462
    size requirements, 464–465
    use of facilities and, 469–471
    year-round schools, 469–471
Developmental aphasia, 88
Deviation IQ, 82
Diabetes, 95
Dialogue, 41
Differences in children, recognizing, 226
Digest of Education Statistics, 351, 481
Diplomacy and staff communication, 20–21
Direct instruction, 38–39
    for learning disabled students, 89
    in taxonomy of instructional techniques, 47
Disaggregate analysis, 374
Discipline. *See also* Classroom management; Consequences
    administrators, communicating with, 20
    behaviorism and, 309

corporal punishment, 337–338
defined, 228
parents, communicating with, 18
privacy of disciplinary records, 342
school uniforms and, 207
teaching, 226
violence and, 414–416
Discovery learning, 44–45
    in taxonomy of instructional techniques, 47
Discussion
    Asian American students and, 65–66
    in taxonomy of instructional techniques, 47
    techniques, 41
Dismissal from employment, 328
Distance education, 458–459
District personnel. *See* School districts
Divergent thinking, 41
Diversity, 58
    in academic self-concept, 75
    cultural diversity, 59–69
    empathy for, 96
    gender diversity, 69–71
    in intelligence, 81–83
    of language, 71–74
    learning diversities, 79, 80–96
    in motivation, 74–75
    physical diversities, 80–96
    of reading abilities, 79–80
    religious diversity, 69
    of sensory disorders, 92–96
    sensory diversities, 80–96
    Supreme Court cases, 354
    teacher testimonial, 64–65
Divorce, 402
Donations, asking for, 129
Drama programs, 160
Drill and practice, 39
    in taxonomy of instructional techniques, 47
Dropout rates
    ethnicity and, 405, 406
    for Native American students, 63
Drug use, 335, 413–414
    testing for, 340
Dual attitude, 12–13
Due process
    for handicapped children education, 348
    and students, 336
    and teachers, 326
DVDs, 35, 419–420
Dynamic content, 10–11, 15, 16–17
Dyslexia, 88

E

Early Childhood Today, 136–137
East Asian students, 64
Eastern philosophy, 297
Eating disorders, 92, 96
Echolalia, 90
The Economic Opportunity Act, 345, 346
Economic pragmatics, 482
Economics
    of school uniforms, 207
    of teaching, 9
    textbooks and, 189

Edison Project, 369
Educable mentally retarded (EMR), 85–86
Educational Excellence for All Children
    Act, 350
Educational reforms. *See* Reforms
Educational Research Act, 351
Educational Testing Service (ETS) Praxis
    series, 119–120
Education Amendments of 1974, 351
Education Amendments of the Indian
    Education Act of 1972, 346
Education Consolidation and Improvement
    Act (ECIA), 349
Education Department, 381–383
Education Digest, 136
Education for All Handicapped Children
    Act, 279, 347–348
Education for Economic Security Act, 351
Education management organizations
    (EMO), 369
Education of Mentally Retarded Children
    Act, 347
Education of the Handicapped Act
    Amendments of 1983, 348
Education of the Handicapped Act
    Amendments of 1986, 348
Education Week, 136
Effective teachers, traits of, 238–239
Effort, grade points for, 221–222
Electronic books (e-books), 479–480, 482
Electronic media, copyright law and, 332
Electronic walls, 473–474
Elementary and Secondary Education Act
    (ESEA), 15, 278
    Title VII of, 267, 349
Elementary and Secondary Education
    Amendments of 1968, 347
Elementary and Secondary School
    Improvement Amendments, 349
Elementary School Journal, 136
Elementary schools, 362
    content, 15
    federal legislation, 345–346
    financing for, 383
    purpose of, 366
ELLs (English language learners), 67,
    71–72
    demographic data for, 72–73
    reading abilities and, 79
    teaching strategies, 74
E-mail, English usage and, 460
Emergent literacy programs, 204–206
Emotional behaviors
    disorders, 91–92
    diversity in, 75–78
Emotional Intelligence (Goleman), 76
Empathy, 96
Employment issues, 326–328
Energy Department, 381
Engel v. Vitale, 343, 354
English grammar schools, 263
English language. *See also* ESL (English as a
    second language)
    e-mail and text messaging and, 460
    ESOL (English for speakers of other
        languages), 71
    Hispanic students and, 66–67
Environmental Education Act, 351
Environmental noise, 93

Epilepsy, 95
Epistemology, 292–293
E-publishing, 189
Equal Access Act, 344
Equal access requirements, 344, 463
ERIC (Educational Resources Information
    Center), 138
ESL (English as a second language), 67,
    71–72
    at-risk students and, 405
    teaching positions in, 125
ESOL (English for speakers of other lan-
    guages), 71
Essentialism, 303–305, 312
    social reconstructionism
        compared, 307
Establishment Clause, 344
Ethics, 319–325, 322–323
    articulating ethical beliefs, 320–321
    axiology, 291, 319
    in character education, 170
    codes of, 323–325
    curriculum and, 156
    honorable teachers, 323
    National Education Association (NEA)
        code of, 132–133
    Oath of Ethical Conduct, 325
    personal ethics, 319–320
Ethnicity, 59–71, 402
    and at-risk students, 405
    and charter schools, 123
    early years of nation, education in,
        264–265
    land-grant colleges and, 272–273
    National Board Certification and, 131
    and poverty, 406
    public schools, representation in, 60
    television viewing and, 419–420
Evaluation
    assessment compared, 217
    summative assessment as, 218
Evidence for reform, 442
Evolution as null curriculum, 159
Exceptional children, 81–82
    assistive technology, 459
    equal access requirements, 463
    legislation, 347–348
    Supreme Court cases, 354
Exclusionary criteria for learning disabili-
    ties, 88
Existentialism, 300–301, 301, 312
Expectations
    for behavior, 226
    communication to students,
        233–234
Experiences
    arranging experiences, 34–37
    curriculum and, 154
    experiential education, 476–479
Experimentalism, 299
Explicit curriculum, 158, 318
Expulsion of students, 336–337
Extended family, 402
Extensive support for mentally
    retarded, 86
Extracurricular activities, 160–162
    and character education, 170
    design of schools and, 466–469
    influence of, 418–419

Extrinsic-reward aspect, 309
Extroverted students, 77
Eye contact, 227

F

Facilitating learning, 33–49
Faculty. *See* Colleagues
Families. *See also* Parents
    alternative structures, 403–404
    blended families, 402–403
    extended family, 402
    homelessness, 407–410
    nuclear family, 401–402
    poverty, 406–407
    single-parent families, 402–403
Family Educational Rights and Privacy Act
    (FERPA), 342, 346–347
Federal government
    categorical funding, 274, 349
    in early years of nation, 265
    financing education, 381–383
    national defense and education, 278
    in nineteenth century education, 272
    reform model and, 433
    role in education, 371
Federal laws, 319, 344–355. *See also*
    Legal issues
    challenges to, 353–355
    table of legislation, 352
Fetal alcohol syndrome, 414
Field observations, 112–116. *See also*
    Student teaching
    adjustment by teachers, 48
    attendance during, 115
    curriculum, learning about, 114
    demeanor of students, 78
    policy handbooks, examining, 114
    record/react/reflect in, 115–116
    for specialization courses, 111
    teachers, learning about, 113–114
Field trips, 36–37
    as experiential education, 476
    liability for, 329
    and Progressivist movement, 277
Fifth Amendment and copyrights, 331
The Fifth Discipline (Senge), 483
Fights, legal issues and, 330–331
Financing education, 381–388. *See*
    also Grants
    channeling funds to schools, 385–388
    future and, 481–482
    local governments, 385
    reforms, costs of, 446
    school districts, role of, 377
    states, role of, 383–385
Fingerprinting teachers, 112
Firing of teacher, 328
First Amendment
    copyright laws and, 331
    free speech issues, 333
First-year teachers, 103–104
Flexibility, 48–49
Flexible scheduling, 277
Florida A&M, 273
Flow of school, 468–469
Follow Through, 346
Foreign languages standards, 197
Formal appraisals, 130

Formative assessments, 210, 217–218
  conducting, 219
Forms (Aristotle), 295
Foster care, children in, 404
Foundations, funding from, 387
Four Idols (Bacon), 296
Four-phase learning cycle, 45
Fourteenth Amendment
  free speech issues, 333
  tenured teaches, 328
A Framework for Understanding Poverty
    (Payne), 406, 409
Freedom of expression, 332–334
Freedom of speech, 333, 340–341
Functional academics/curriculum, 86
Functionally blind students, 93
Funding education. *See* Financing education
Fused curriculum, 172
Future. *See also* Technology
  and funding education, 481–482
  and global community, 483

G

Gain scores, 222, 223
Gays and lesbians
  parents, 404
  students, 96
GED (general equivalency degree), 383
Gender
  bias, 70
  cognitive differences and, 70–71
  colonial American, women's education
    in, 262
  defined, 70
  diversity in, 69–71
  dropout rates and, 405, 406
  learning disabilities and, 88
  in nineteenth century education, 267
  and physical education programs,
    198–199
General education courses, 109–110
General welfare clause, 344–345
The GI Bill, 345
Gifted and talented students, 86–87
Global community, 483
Goals. *See* Objectives
Golden Mean, 163, 296
Goss v. Lopez, 354
Government. *See* Federal government;
    Local governments; States
Governor, role of, 373
Grades
  assignment of, 220–224
  at-risk students and, 405
  consequences involving, 235
  effort, points for, 221–222
  gain scores, 222, 223
  humanistic education and, 223
  inflation, 222–224
  normal curve and, 216–217
  objectives, meeting, 221
  principals and policy, 379–380
  responsibility for, 128
Grammar school, 263
Grants
  block grants, 349
  categorical grants, 274, 349
  corporate grant funding, 432

funding from, 387
Title VI grants, 386
writing, 129
Great Books, 427
The Great Conversation (Hutchins), 302–303
Greek role in education, 254–256
Guest speakers, 36, 37

H

Handicapped Children's Early Education
    Assistance Act, 347
*Hanna Perkins School v. Simmons-
    Harris,* 354
Hanukkah, 420
Happiness and classroom management, 227
Happy students, 76
Harvard University
  establishment of, 260
  Project on the Next Generation of
    Teachers, 121
Hazelwood School District v. Kuhlmeier, 354
Hazing, 415
Head Start, 278, 346, 365
  financing, 383
Health and Human Services Department,
    381, 383
  child abuse and death, 411
Health impaired students, 94–96
Hearing disabilities, 93–94
Hebrew role in education, 257
Hidden curriculum, 158
Hierarchy of Needs (Maslow), 17,
    170–171, 310
Higher education. *See* Colleges and
    universities
The Higher Education Act of 1965, 345
High schools, 362
  evolution of, 263
  federal legislation, 345–346
  financing for, 383
  purpose of, 367–368
High-stakes tests, 350
Hinduism, 297
  idealism of, 294
Hispanic American Month, 420
Hispanic Americans, 66–67
  dropout rates for, 405, 406
  as ELLs (English language learners), 72
  nineteenth century education, 267
  single-parent families, 402
History of education
  in America, 259–273
  in early years of nation, 262–265
  Greece, role of, 254–256
  matter of law, education as, 260–261
  in nineteenth century, 265–273
  second half of twentieth century, 278
  of secular education, 260
  in twentieth century America, 273–281
Holiday observances, 420
Holographic displays, 474–475
Homelessness, 407–410
Homeschooling, 279, 369–371
Homosexuals. *See* Gays and lesbians
Honesty, 320
Honig v. Doe, 354
Honorable teachers, 323
Hornbooks, 261

"How to Make Our Ideas Clear"
    (Peirce), 298
Humane treatment of others, 320
Humanism, 170–171, 309–310, 312, 427
  in classroom, 309–310
  in Renaissance, 258–259
Humor and classroom management, 227
Hunger, 409
The Hurried Child (Elkind), 419

I

Idealism, 294–295, 301, 312
  classical idealism, 294
  modern idealism, 294–295
  religious idealism, 294
Idols (Bacon), 296
IEPs (individual education plans), 347
Ill-defined problems, 174
Illinois Standards Achievement Test
    (ISAT), 182
Illiteracy, 80
Illnesses, students with, 95–96
Imitation in social learning theory, 50
Immigration, 273
Implementation of reforms, 445–447
Implicit curriculum, 158–159
Improving America's Schools Act, 349
Improvisation IXV (Kandinsky), 292
Inclusionary criteria for learning
    disabilities, 88
Inclusion model, 89
Indexes of vulnerability, 67
Individuals with Disabilities Education Act
    (IDEA), 348
  on ADHD (attention deficit hyperactivity
    disorder), 90
  on autism, 90
  emotional/behavioral disorders, 91–92
  on learning disabilities, 88
  on physical and health impairments, 95
  on visual sensory disability, 93
Induction period, 327
Inductive reasoning, 293
Inference questions, 44
Inflation of grades, 222–224
Informed collaboration, 441
Ingraham v. Wright, 354
In loco parentis, 325, 434
Inquiry approach, 45–47, 277
  curriculum, 173–174
  in taxonomy of instructional
    techniques, 47
In-service programs, 22–23
Institutio Oratoria (Quintilian), 256
Instructional interventions, 440
Instructional techniques, 37–47, 41. *See
    also* Classroom management
  application of, 46
  assessment and, 218–220
  combination of techniques, applying,
    46–47
  direct instruction, 38–39
  discovery learning, 44–45
  drill and practice, 39
  innovations in, 472–475
  inquiry approach, 45–47
  lecture, 39, 40
  for mentally retarded students, 86

Instructional techniques, continued
   mental modeling, 41–44
   question-and-answer technique, 39–40
   reforms, 436–437
   taxonomy of, 47
Instructor, 136
Integrated curriculum, 172
Integration cases, 353
Intelligence
   defined, 82
   diversities in, 81–83
   intelligence quotient (IQ), 82, 86–87
   multiple intelligences theory, 83, 84
   normal curve representing, 82–83
Intelligence quotient (IQ), 82
   gifted and talented students, 86–87
Intentional torts, 329
Intermittent support for mentally
   retarded, 86
Internalizing disorders, 91–92
International Baccalaureate (IB) credits, 109
International Reading Association (IRA), 21
   on diversity, 58
   standards development, 195–196
Internet
   copyright law and, 332
   distance education, 458–459
   and experiential education, 476–477
   local issues and, 477–478
   teaching positions, looking for, 126
Interpersonal musical intelligence, 83, 84
Interventions, 436, 438–440
   administrative interventions, 440
   character education, 439–440
   curricular interventions, 439–440
   instructional interventions, 440
Interviews
   of decision makers, 435
   for teaching positions, 126–127
Intrapersonal musical intelligence, 83, 84
Introverted students, 77
IRAs (individual retirement accounts), 482
Islam, 297
"I Wonder. . ." model, 41, 42–44

J

Jim Crow laws, 266
Job Corps, 278
Journal of Learning Disabilities, 137
Judiciary, role of, 375
Junior high. *See* Middle school

K

Kappa Delta Pi (KDP), 135
Kentucky Education Reform Act, 372
Keyboarding skills, 168
Kindergarten
   alphabet and, 427
   history of, 266
   purpose of, 365–366
Kinesthetic learning style, 79
Kwaanza, 420

L

Laboratory School of University of
   Chicago, 272
Labor Department, 381, 383

Land-grant colleges, 272–273, 345
Land Ordinance Act, 265
Language. *See also* English language
   curriculum standards, 195–196
   diversity and, 71–74
   foreign languages standards, 197
   Hispanic students and, 66–67
   immersion, 72
   teacher/school expectations, 73–74
Lanham Act, 1950 Amendments to, 346
Latchkey children, 402–403
Latin Grammar Schools, 260, 261
Latino/a Americans. *See* Hispanic
   Americans
Lau v. Nichols, 278, 354
Laws. *See* Federal laws; Legal issues
Layout of facilities, 466–469
Learners, development as, 22–23
Learning disorders, 81, 87–92, 88–89
Learning strategies, 89
Learning styles, 57–58
   diversity of, 79
Least restrictive environment (LRE), 348
Leaving profession, reasons for, 6
Lectures, 39, 40
   in taxonomy of instructional
   techniques, 47
Lee v. Weisman, 343
Legal issues
   for certification eligibility, 118
   child abuse, reporting, 329–330
   conduct with students, 335–336
   contracts, employment, 326–327
   copyright laws, 331–332
   corporal punishment, 337–338
   dismissal from employment, 328
   due process, protection of, 326
   employment issues, 326–328
   expulsion of students, 336–337
   freedom of expression, 332–334
   freedom of speech, 340–341
   induction period, 327
   liability of teachers, 328–329
   lifestyle decisions, 334–335
   marriage of students, 337
   matter of law, education as, 260–261
   parenthood of students, 337
   pregnancy of students, 337
   reasonable force, use of, 330–331
   religion in schools, 343–344
   search and seizure, 338–339
   self-defense, right to, 331
   sexual behavior, private, 335
   sexual harassment, 341–343
   of students, 336–343
   suspension of students, 336–337
   teachers and, 325–336
   tenure, 327
   tort law, 328–329
Legislatures. *See also* Congress
   state legislature, role of, 364
Lemon Test, 344
Lemon v. Kurtzman, 343, 344
LEPs (limited English proficiency), 71, 72
Lesbians. *See* Gays and lesbians
Lesson plans, 118
Letter-sound associations, 205
Levels of school, 362–365
   structure of, 364

Liability insurance coverage, 329
Liability of teachers, 328–329
The Liberal Education of Boys (Erasmus), 258
Library funding, 386
Licensing
   accreditation agency, 105–107
   defined, 109
   other fields, use in, 123–124
   reciprocal licensing agreements, 107
Lifestyle decisions, 334–335
Limited support for mentally retarded, 86
Linear programming, 167
Linguistic intelligence, 83, 84
Lip reading, 94
Litchfield Academy, 267
Literacy, 79. *See also* Reading
   emergent literacy programs, 204–206
   illiteracy, 80
Literature-based instruction, 206
Local community. *See* Community
Local education agency, 184
Local governments, 375–381
   district personnel, 376–378
   financing education, 385
   school boards, 375
Locker searches, 340
Logic, 293
Logical-mathematical intelligence, 83, 84
Logistical innovations, 461
Look-say method, 427–428, 436–437
Lord's Prayer, 344
Lotteries, 385
Low vision students, 93
Loyalty, 320–321
Lunch duty, 240
Lunch subsidies, 382
Lyceum of Aristotle, 256, 295

M

Magazines, influence of, 419–420
Mager objectives, 221
Magnet schools, 368–369
Maieutics, 294
Mailbox Teacher, 137
Mainstreaming, 89
Major premise, 293
Mandated reporters, teachers as, 330
Marijuana use, 414
Marketplace, Idol of the, 296
Marriage of students, 337
Maryland Business Roundtable for
   Education, 457–458
Massachusetts Act of 1642, 261
Massachusetts Act of 1647, 261
Massachusetts Comprehensive Assessment
   System (MCAS), 182
Master's degrees, 22
Mastery learning, 166–167
Materials
   in classroom management, 227
   and curriculum, 155
   for reform programs, 446
   technology and, 479–481
Mathematics
   new math, 427
   standards, 193–194
Mayflower Compact, 260
McGuffey Readers, 266

The McKinney Education of Homeless Children and Youth Act (EHCY), 409–410
Media and Methods, 137
Media influences, 419–420
Mediating conflicts, 416
Melting pot metaphor, 59–60, 274
Mennonite Baptist education, 261
Mental modeling, 41–44
    in taxonomy of instructional techniques, 47
Mental retardation, 83, 85–86
    classification of, 85–86
    levels of support for, 86
Mentoring, 23–24
    as administrative intervention, 440
    being a mentor, 130–131
Metaphysics, 290–291
Methods courses, 110–111
Michigan State University, 272
Mid-continent Research for Education, 457
Middle Ages, education in, 258
Middle school, 362
    purpose of, 367
Mild hearing loss, 94
Mills v. Board of Education of the District of Columbia, 354
Minimal brain dysfunction, 88
Minor premise, 293
Modeling, 49–52. *See also* Mental modeling; Role models
    in social learning theory, 50
Moderate hearing loss, 94
Moderate-severe hearing loss, 94
Modular schools, 465–466
Moments of meditation, 344
Monitoring, 48–49
Montessori methods/materials, 276
Mood disorders, 92
Moral standards, 51, 319
Morrill Act of 1862, 272, 345
Motivation
    and classroom management, 227
    diversity in, 74–75
    of teachers, 5–6
Multiculturalism, 60
    and content, 68
    as reform movement, 438–439
Multidimensional student development, 62
Multimedia presentations, 35–36, 37
Multiple disabilities, 95
Multiple intelligences theory, 83, 84, 87
Multiple situations, supervision of, 238
Music
    programs, 160
    standards, 197–198
Musical intelligence, 83, 84
My Pedagogic Creed (Dewey), 6

N

NAACP (National Association for the Advancement of Colored People), 268, 270
Name-calling by teacher, 320
National Assessment of Educational Progress (NAEP), 202–203
    Assessment Authorization, 351, 353

    on charter schools, 123
    Hispanic students and, 73
National Association for Sport and Physical Education (NASPE), 192, 199
National Association for the Education of Young Children (NAEYC)
    on diversity, 58
    ethics codes from, 323
National-Board Certified teachers, 131–132
National Board for Professional Teaching Standards (NBPTS), 10, 131–132
National Center for Education Statistics, 349
    on ELLs (English language learners), 72
    on homeschooling, 370
    on reading proficiency, 367–368
National Center for History in the Schools (NCHS), 192
National Center for Research in Vocational Education, 199
National Clearinghouse for Bilingual Education, 72
National Coalition for the Homeless, 407
National Commission for Excellence in Education, 279–280
National Commission on Testing and Public Policy, 187
National Council for Accreditation of Teacher Education (NCATE), 24
    on alternative certification, 119
    standards of, 105–107
National Council for the Social Studies (NCSS), 192, 196
National Council of Teachers of English (NCTE), 192, 195–196
National Council of Teachers of Mathematics (NCTM), 21
    curriculum/assessment standards, 193–194, 204
    national education standards and, 191
National curriculum debate, 202–204
National defense, 273, 278
National Defense Education Act (NDEA), 153, 278, 351
National Defense Student Loans (NDSL), 438
National Education Association (NEA), 132–133
    Committee of Ten on Secondary Studies, 271–272
    Committee of Thirteen on College Entrance Requirements, 272
    ethics codes from, 323–324
    Fact Sheet on Teacher Quality, 108
    founding of, 271–272
    Second Curriculum Committee, 274–275
    Teacher Education Initiative, 24
National education standards, 191–192
National Household Survey on Drug Abuse, 414
Nationalism, 304–305
National Joint Committee on Learning Disabilities (NJCLD), 88
National Parent-Teacher Association, 415
National Reading Recovery Center, 440
National Research Council, National Academy of Sciences, 194
The National School Lunch Act, 346

National Science Education Standards, 194–195
National Science Teachers Association (NSTA), 21
    and national curriculum, 204
    national education standards and, 191
    Scope, Sequence, and Coordination Project, 194
National Society for Autistic Children, 89
National Youth Tobacco Survey, 414
A Nation at Risk: The Imperative for Educational Reform, 279–280, 304
Nation's Report Card, 203
Native American Month, 420
Native Americans, 60–61, 63–64
    in colonial America, 262
    depression in, 96
    early years of nation, education in, 264
    philosophy of, 290
The Natural Investigator, 42–43
Naturalistic musical intelligence, 83, 84
Nature-deficit disorder, 461
Nature of reforms, 443–445
Navajo culture, 63
NCBLA. *See* No Child Left Behind Act
Need criteria for learning disabilities, 88
Need for reforms, 442–443
Neglect. *See* Child abuse and neglect
Negligence
    cases, 328–329
    child abuse, reporting, 329–330
Networking for teaching positions, 126
New England Primer, 261, 262
Newspapers, influence of, 419–420
New Teacher Advocate, 135
New World education, 259–262
Nineteenth century, education in, 265–273
No Child Left Behind Act, 15, 108, 187. *See also* Adequate Yearly Progress (AYP)
    charter schools and, 123
    ELLs (English language learners) and, 71, 73–74
    essentialism and, 305
    National Assessment of Educational Progress (NAEP) and, 203
    primary grades, purpose of, 365–366
    standards of, 108–109
    states, role of, 374
    testing and curriculum issues, 200–202
    vouchers and, 368
Noninstructional tasks
    committee work, 240–241
    outside classroom, 240
    substitute teacher, planning for, 241–242
Nonverbal communication
    in classroom management, 227
    cultural preference for, 63
Normal curve, 216–217
Normal hearing, 94
Normal schools, 267
Norm groups, 216
North American Council for Online Learning, 458
The Northwest Ordinances, 345
Northwest Regional Laboratory (NWREL), 444

Northwest Territories, education in, 265
Novelty, appreciation of, 77–78
Nuclear family, 401–402
Null curriculum, 159–160

O

Oath of Ethical Conduct, 325
Objectives
of cooperative learning, 172
grades and, 221
of reform programs, 445
Obsessive-compulsive disorder, 92
Ockham's razor, 35
Office staff, communicating with, 20–21
Ohio State University, National Reading
Recovery Center, 440
The Old Deluder Satan Act, 261
Omnibus Consolidated and Emergency
Supplemental Appropriations Act,
351
On Civil Disobedience (Thoreau), 156
Online learning, 458
Open classroom plans, 186
Open-ended questions, 219
Operant conditioning, 308
Oppositional defiant disorder, 92
Oral/aural methods, 94
Orthopedic impairments, 95
OSHA (Occupational Safety and Health
Administration), 93
Other health impairments, 95
Outcome-based education (OBE), 167
Outcomes and curriculum, 154, 167
Outside classroom tasks, 240
Overweight/obese students, 467
Oxford University, 258

P

Pacific Islander students, 64–66
Paideia Proposal: An Educational Manifesto
(Adler), 303
Parents
autism and, 89
communicating with, 18–19
complaints of, 128
conferences, 240
and curriculum, 183–184, 191
education, lack of, 409
involvement, lack of, 409
pressure from, 419
on purpose of schools, 361
in reform model, 434–435
single-parent families, 402–403
students as, 337
working with, 240–241
Parent-teacher organizations (PTOs/
PTAs), 133
curriculum, influence on, 183
responsibilities for, 240
teachers, responsibilities of, 129
Parochial schools
in colonial America, 261
public funds for, 344
teaching in, 121–122
PDS model, 24
Pedagogues, 256

Pedagogy, 6–10, 429
competencies, 10–11
defined, 6
and higher education, 429–430
Pedagogy of the Oppressed (Freire), 290
*Pennsylvania Association for Retarded
Citizens (PARC) v. Pennsylvania,* 354
People for the American Way, 184
Perceptual disabilities, 88
Perennialism, 163, 302–303, 312
social reconstructionism compared, 307
Performance appraisals, 130
Performance-based education (PBE), 167
Perry Preschool Project, 346
Personal appearance issues,
334–335
Personality
development theories, 17
diversity in, 75–78
Pervasive support for mentally retarded, 86
Phi Delta Kappa (PDK), 135
Phi Delta Kappan, 135
Philadelphia Academy, 263
Phillips v. Lincoln County School District, 329
Philosophy, 288–289, 301–307. *See also*
specific philosophies
axiology, 291–292
conceptual clusters, 290–291
constructivism, 310–311, 312
and curriculum, 186–187
Eastern philosophy, 297
epistemology, 292–293
essentialism, 303–305, 312
existentialism, 300–301, 312
idealism, 294–295, 312
logic, 293
metaphysics, 290–291
perennialism, 302–303, 312
personal philosophy, developing, 289–290
pragmatism, 298–300, 312
purpose and, 11–12
realism, 295–297, 312
schools of, 289, 291, 293–301
social reconstructionism, 306–307
of teaching, 9
word derivation, 289
Phoneme-grapheme correspondence, 205
Phonics, 195, 205, 427, 436–437
and emergent literacy, 204–205
Physical disabilities, 81, 94–96. *See also*
Exceptional children
Physical education
design of schools for, 466–469
as extracurricular program, 160, 161
implications of programs, 468
standards for, 198–199
Physical plant design, 463–466
Pickering v. Board of Education, 333
Pietà (Michelangelo), 292
Pilgrims and education, 259–260
PL 76-849, 346
PL 78-346, 345
PL 79-396, 346
PL 83-531, 351
PL 83-597, 346
PL 85-864, 351
PL 85-926, 347
PL 88-352, 346

PL 88-452, 345, 346
PL 89-10, 349
PL 89-329, 345
PL 90-247, 347, 349
PL 90-538, 347
PL 91-516, 351
PL 92-318, 346
PL 93-112, 347
PL 93-247, 347
PL 93-380, 351
PL 94-142, 347–348
PL 95-561, 351
PL 97-35, 349
PL 98-199, 348
PL 98-377, 351
PL 99-457, 348
PL 100-297, 349
PL 100-407, 348
PL 101-239, 351
PL 101-336, 348
PL 101-542, 347
PL 101-600, 351
PL 103-33, 351, 353
PL 103-227, 347
PL 103-239, 351
PL 103-382, 349
PL 105-17, 348
PL 105-277, 351
PL 105-285, 350
PL 107-110. *See* No Child Left Behind Act
PL 108-265, 351
Planning, 16
for classroom management, 231–232
by school districts, 377
for substitute teacher, 241–242
Pledge of Allegiance, 51
Policy handbooks, 114–115
Politics and reform model, 432–434
Politics (Aristotle), 257
Portable classrooms, 463
Portfolio
preparation, 116
for teaching positions, 125–126
Positive behavior support, 90
Postfederal school design, 462–463
Post-traumatic stress disorders, 92
Poverty, 406–407
extracurricular activities and, 419
language achievement and, 71
learning disabilities and, 88
Power
and reform politics, 434
struggles, 236
Practicing classroom management, 232
Pragmatism, 298–300, 301, 312
foundation for, 298
Prairie View A&M, 273
Praxis series, 119–120
Prayer groups, 344
Prayer in school, 343–344
Predominantly Hyperactive-Impulsive (HI)
behaviors, 91
Predominantly Inattentive (IN) behaviors, 91
Prefederal school design, 461–462
Pregnancy of students, 337, 416–417
Prekindergarten, purpose of, 365–366
President's Advisory Commission, 2000, 66
Pressured children, 419

Pre-vocational education, 199
Primary grades, 362
  purpose of, 365–366
Principals, 378–381
  teacher testimonial, 378–379
Principles of Effective Discipline, 233–234
Principles of Learning Test (PLT), 120
Privacy requirements, 115
  students' rights, 342–343
Private schools, 261. *See also* Parochial schools
  in second part of twentieth century, 279
  teaching in, 121–122
Privatization of public schools, 369
Probable cause and search and seizure, 339–340
Probationary period, 327
  dismissal during, 328
Problem-solving
  conferences, 236–237
  curriculum, 173–174
  Dewey, John on, 299
Procedural due process, 326
Procedures, 230–231
  implementing, 237–238
  practicing, 232
Professional development, 10–11, 22–24, 130–132
  and student teaching, 117
  technology and, 457
Professional education, 110
Professionalism in field observations, 114–115
Professional organizations, 132–138. *See also* specific organizations
  administrative/supervisory organizations, 134, 137
  communication with, 21
  ethics codes from, 323–324
  generalized organizations, 132–133
  and national education standards, 192
  research-oriented organizations, 135
  special service organizations, 138
  subject area organizations, 133–134, 137
Profound hearing loss, 94
Programmed instruction, 309
Progressive Education Association (PEA), 276
Progressivism, 170, 300, 305–306, 312, 427
  challenges to, 276–277
  Dewey, John and, 275–276
Property taxes, 385
Proposals Relating to the Education of Youth in Pennsylvania (Franklin), 263
Protestant vernacular schools, 259
Proximity of teacher to students, 239
Psychology of teaching, 9
Publications, 136–137
Public schools
  privatization of, 369
  religious instruction in, 344
  salaries for teachers, 127
  teaching in, 121
Pull-out programs for ELLs (English language learners), 72, 74
Purdue University, 272
  Placement Manual, 125
Puritan view, 260

Purpose, 10–11, 11–14, 361–362, 363
  attitude and, 12–13
  business demands and, 432
  in classical realism, 296
  of curriculum, 156–157
  levels, purposes of, 365–368
  and philosophy, 11–12
  of reforms, 442–443
  and style, 13–14

Q

Quadrivium, 154, 258
Quaker education, 261, 262
  for slaves, 264
Question-and-answer technique, 39–40
  in taxonomy of instructional techniques, 47
The Quick Reference Guide to Educational Innovations (Orange), 448

R

Race. *See also* specific races
  diversity of, 59–71
  early years of nation, education in, 264–265
  learning disabilities and, 88
Radical empiricism, 298
Reading. *See also* Literacy; Phonics; Whole Language
  curriculum standards, 195–196
  diversity of abilities, 79–80
  emergent literacy programs, 204–206
  instructional intervention, 440
  instructional reform, 436–437
Reading Excellence Act, 351
Reading First program, 71, 350
Reading Recovery, 440
Realism, 295–297, 301, 312
  classical realism, 295–296
  religious realism, 296
Reasonable force, use of, 330–331
Reasonable suspicion and search and seizure, 339–340
Reasons
  for entering profession, 5–7
  for leaving profession, 6
Recall in question-and-answer technique, 40
Reciprocal licensing agreements, 107
Record/react/reflect
  in field observations, 115–116
  in student teaching, 118
Rectification requirements, 22
Reflection. *See also* Record/react/reflect
  in question-and-answer technique, 39–40
Reflexive conditioning, 308
The Reformation, 258–259
Reform model, 429–435
  business and, 430–432
  common purpose, finding, 430
  higher education and, 429–430
  parents in, 434–435
  politics and, 432–434
Reforms, 426–427. *See also* Interventions
  administrative reform, 437–438
  change and, 427–428

claims of program, 444–445
comparable programs, availability of, 443
costs of, 446
curricular reform, 436
development of program, 444
evaluating, 447
exemplary reforms, 441–447
implementation of, 445–447
instructional reform, 436–437
material requirements, 446
nature of program, 443–445
need for program, 442–443
personnel implementing, 445
purpose of, 442–443
teacher testimonial, 438–439
training requirements, 446
Regents of the University of California v. Bakke, 354
Regional issues
  in colonial America, 261–262
  in early twentieth century, 274
Regrouping plans, 34–35
The Rehabilitation Act, Section 504, 347
Relevant curriculum, 173–174
Religion. *See also* specific relitions
  colonial American education and, 261
  diversity of, 69
  early years of nation, education in, 264
  homeschooling and, 370
  idealism, religious, 294
  legal issues, 343–344
  in Middle Ages, 258
  in New World, 260
  prayer in school, 343–344
  realism, religious, 296
  Supreme Court challenges, 354
Remedial education, 350
Renaissance, education in, 258–259
Renaissance 2010 project, Chicago, 369
Replicability of reforms, 444
Representation of school, 21
The Republic (Plato), 255–256
Research
  classroom-based research, 24
  federal legislation, 351, 353
  organizations for, 135
  professional development and, 24
Resegregation trend, 61
Responsibilities as teacher, 127–129
Resumes for teaching positions, 125
The Right Method of Instruction (Erasmus), 258
Roberts v. City of Boston, 266
Role models, 49–50
  away from school, 51–52
  classroom management, modeling in, 226–227
Roman role in education, 256–257
Romantic naturalism, 305
Routines, 230–231
  implementing, 237–238
  practicing, 232
Rules. *See also* Consequences
  defined, 228–229
  drafting of, 234
  enforcement of, 235–236
  expectations, communicating, 233–234

Rules, continued
positive words in, 229
practicing, 232
Principles of Effective Discipline and, 234
teacher's behavior and, 239
tips for making, 229

S

Sad students, 76–77
Safe Schools Act, 347
Safety issues, 333
Salad bowl metaphor, 59, 60
Salaries
base salaries, 127, 128
for National-Board Certified teacher, 131–132
postgraduate work and, 109
Sales taxes, 385
San Antonio v. Rodriguez, 384
Santa Fe Independent School District v. Doe, 343–344
Savage Inequalities: Children in America's Schools (Kozol), 385
Scanners, 168
Schizophrenia, 91, 92
Scholasticism, 258
School assignments, 128
School boards, 183–184
local school boards, 375
School choice, 368
School districts, 376–378
assessment by, 377
curriculum specialist, 376–377
financial management, 377
personnel of, 377–378
planning by, 377
School Dropout Prevention and Basic Skills Improvement Act, 351
The School Milk Program Act, 346
School privatization, 369
Schools. *See also* Purpose
and curriculum, 186–188, 191
options for, 368–371
The Schools We Have: The Schools We Want (Nehring), 58
School-to-Work Opportunities Act, 351, 383
School-to-work programs, 199
School uniforms, 206–208
Science for All Americans (Rutherford & Ahlgren), 155
Science in the Multicultural Classroom: A Guide to Teaching and Learning (Barba), 437
Science of teaching, 9–10
Science standards, 194–195
Scientific management, 266
Search and seizure laws, 338–339
drug tests, 340
probable cause and, 339–340
reasonable suspicion and, 339–340
Secondary content, 15–16
Secondary schools. *See* High schools
Second Curriculum Committee, 274–275
The Secret of Childhood (Montessori), 277
Secular education, 260
Self-concept, 75
Self-defense, right to, 331
Self-determination, 300–301
Self-esteem, 172

Self-fulfilling prophecy, 75
Sensory disorders, 81
diversity of, 92–96
Separate but equal doctrine, 266–267, 413
Brown v. Board of Education of Topeka, 274, 278
challenge to, 268–270
land-grant colleges and, 272–273
The Servicemen's Readjustment Act, 345
Sesame Street, 420
Severe hearing loss, 94
Sex, defined, 70
Sex discrimination, 279
Sex education, 416–417
and null curriculum, 159
Sexism, 70
Sexual behavior, 335
Sexual harassment, 341–343
Sexual stereotyping, 70
Shortage of teachers, 124
Shunning, 415
Single-parent families, 402–403
Site-based management, 122–123, 241
Slaves, education of, 264
Slight hearing loss, 94
Smith v. School District of the Township of Darby, 328
Social interaction, 311
Social learning theory, 50
Social observances, 420
Social promotion, 350
Social reconstructionism, 306–307, 312, 401
Social studies standards, 196
Socioeconomic issues, 401–413. *See also* Poverty
divorce, 402
single-parent families, 402–403
teacher testimonial, 408–409
Sociology of teaching, 9
Socratic method, 294
Software and copyrights, 332
Sophists, 255
The Souls of Black Folk (DuBois), 268–269, 290
South Asian students, 64
South Carolina State University, 273
Southeast Asian students, 64
Soviet Union. *See* Sputnik
Spanish-speaking skills, 66–67
Sparta, 254–255
Spatial intelligence, 83, 84
Special Education in Contemporary Society: An Introduction to Exceptionality (Gargiulo), 83
Special interest groups
and curriculum, 184, 191
and textbook selection, 189
Specialization courses, 110–111
Special needs children. *See* Exceptional children
Special service organizations, 138
Speech
freedom of, 333, 340–341
synthesizers, 459
Spontaneity, copyright law and, 332
Sputnik, 153, 273–274
National Defense Education Act (NDEA) and, 351

progressivism and, 306
reforms and, 438
Standardized tests, 216–218
and at-risk students, 405
and curriculum, 187
high-stakes tests, 350
principals, role of, 380
Standards 2000 for mathematics, 194
Stanford-Binet test, 82
State education agencies (SEAs), 109, 374, 381
States
curriculum, legislatures and, 185–186, 191
financing education, 383–385
governor, role of, 373
grading of schools, 374
judiciary, role of, 374
legislature, role of, 374
per-pupil expenditures by, 383–384
politics of reform, 432–434
reform model and, 433
role in education, 372–375
state education agencies (SEAs), 109, 374, 381
superintendent of education, 372, 373
textbooks, influence over, 188–189
Static content, 10–11, 14, 15–16
Stereotypes
of mental retardation, 83
sexual stereotyping, 70
Strategy of teaching, 33
Strip searches, 340
Structure of education, 157
Student-centered curriculum, 163, 169–170, 290
core curriculum as, 165
progressivism and, 305
Student government/organizations, 160
Student projects, 277
The Student Right-to-Know Campus Security Act, 347
Student teaching, 106, 112, 116–118
Bill of Rights for Student Teachers, 133, 134–135
career objectives and, 116–117
preparation for, 117–118
record/react/reflect in, 118
supervising teacher, requesting, 117
Style
examining, 14
learning styles, 57–58, 70
purpose and, 13–14
Subject area organizations, 133–134
list of, 137
Subject-centered curriculum, 163–165
Subject matter
federal legislation, 351
perennialism and, 303
Substance abuse, 413–414. *See also* Alcohol use; Drug use
Substantive due process, 326
Substitute teachers, 241–242
Success for All, 427
Suicide, 96, 417–418
warning signs for, 418
Summa Theologica (Aristotle), 258
Summative assessments, 218
constructing, 219–220
development of skills, 219

Summerhill, 301
Summer vacations, 5
Superintendent of education for state, 372, 373
Superintendent of schools, local, 376
Supreme Court. *See also* specific cases
    federal law, challenges to, 353–355
Suspension of students, 336–337
Swann v. Charlotte-Mecklenburg (North Carolina) Board of Education, 353
Sweatt v. Painter, 353
Symbolic expression, 333
Synthesis, 41

T

Tactile learning style, 79
Talmud, 257
Taoism, 297
Taxes, 385
    business, tax funding and, 431
    future of funding with, 481–482
Taxonomies
    of educational objectives, 17
    of instructional techniques, 47
Taxonomy of Educational Objectives Handbook I: Cognitive Domain (Bloom et al.), 38, 169
The Taxonomy of Education Objectives: Affective Domain, 169
Taylor v. Simmons-Harris, 354
Teacher, 136–137
Teacher accountability movement, 279
Teacher-centered perspective, 290
Teacher-designed tests, 187
Teacher Education Initiative, 24
Teacher education programs, 105–107
Teachers and the Law (Fischer, Schimmel & Kelly), 326
Teach for America, 119
Teaching positions, 124–125
    demographics of, 124
    geography of, 124–125
    interviewing skills, 126–127
    networking for, 126
    portfolio for, 125–126
    resumes, 125
Teaching Pre-K-8, 136–137
Teasing/taunting, 415
Technology, 35, 455–456. *See also* Computers
    assistive technology, 86, 459
    design of facilities and, 461–466
    distance education, 458–459
    electronic walls, 473–474
    and experiential education, 476–479
    Gates, Bill on, 465
    holographic displays, 474–475
    and instructional techniques, 472–475
    issues, 459–461
    logistical innovations, 461
    and materials, 479–481
    for mentally retarded students, 86
    for professional development, 457
    in schools, 456–459
    standards for curriculum, 199
    for students, 457–458
    for teachers, 457
Technology-Related Assistance for Individuals with Disabilities Act, 348

Teen pregnancy of, 337, 416–417
Television, 35, 419–420
Temperament, diversity in, 75–78
Tenth Amendment, 344
Tenure, 327
    for college professors, 430
    dismissal of tenured teacher, 328
TESOL (teaching English to speakers of other languages), 71
Testing. *See also* Assessment; Standardized tests
    con point of view on, 201–202
    as curriculum issue, 200–202
    high-stakes tests, 350
    pro point of view on, 200–201
    teacher-designed tests, 187
Texas A&M, 272
Texas Assessment of Knowledge and Skills (TAKS), 182
Textbooks
    adoption states, 189–190
    and curriculum, 155, 188–190, 191
    electronic books (e-books), 479–480, 482
    e-publishing and, 189
    homogenization of, 189
    technology and, 480–481
Text messaging, 460
Theater standards, 197–198
Theatre, Idol of the, 296
Tinker v. Des Moines Independent School District, 340
Title I services, 350, 382
Title IX of Education Amendments of 1972, 198–199, 279, 337
    on sexual harassment, 341
Title VI grants, 386
Title VII of ESEA, 267, 349
Tobacco use, 414
Tope Integration for Macro-Learning Experiences (TIME), 478
Tort law, 328–329
Total communication, 49
Totally blind students, 93
Touch-screen capabilities, 168
Traditional schedule, 364–365
Traditional teacher education, 109–118
Trainable mentally retarded (TMR), 85–86
Transfer of learning, 164
Transitions, teachers handling, 238–239
Traumatic brain injury, 95
Tribe, Idol of the, 296
Trivium, 154, 258
Troy Seminary, 267
Truth. *See* Philosophy
TSWBAT (the student with be able to) format, 221
Turnover rate for teachers, 124
Tuskegee University, 267–268, 273
2000 School Survey on Crime and Safety, 415
Tyler rationale, 157

U

Uniforms in schools, 206–208
Unintentional torts, 329
United States Department of Education, 138
The United States v. The Miami University, 343

University of Bologna, 258
University of California, 272
University of Chicago, Laboratory School of, 272
University of Nebraska, 272
University of Paris, 258
University of Pennsylvania, 263
University of Salerno, 258
Upward Bound, 278

V

Values
    of African American students, 61
    -centered education, 170
Vandalism, 414–416
VCRs, 35
Vernacular schools, 259
Vernonica School District v. Acton, 340
Videotapes and copyrights, 332
Violence in schools, 154, 414–416
    mediating conflicts, 416
Violence in the United States Public Schools, 415
Virtual classroom, 371
Virtual schools, 458
VISTA, 346
Visual arts standards, 197–198
Visual learning style, 79
Visual sensory disability, 92–93
Vocalic learning style, 79
Vocational education, 427
    business demands for, 432
    in colonial America, 261
    federal financing, 383
    perennialism and, 303
    standards, 199
Voice-recognition computers, 459
Vouchers, 368

W

Wallace v. Jaffree, 344
War on Poverty, 278
Well-defined problems, 173–174
Westside School District v. Mergens, 344
White American students, 67–69
White House Conferences on Education, 1956, 1964, 163
Whole Language, 195, 205, 427, 436
    and emergent literacy, 206
    look-say method, 427–428
Who's Who Among American High School Students, 405
William and Mary College, 263
Withdrawal disorders, 91–92
"Withitness" of teachers, 238
Women's History Month, 420
World War II, 276–277

Y

Year-round schools, 364–365
    design considerations, 469–471

Z

Zelman v. Simmons-Harris, 354
Zen Buddhism, 297
Zorach v. Clawson, 344

Name Index

A

Abedi, J., 73, 350
Achilles, C. M., 437
Adler, Mortimer, 156, 303, 312
Ahlgren, A., 155
Alba, R., 68
Alber, S., 129
Alcuin, 258
Allen, Julie, 408–409
Allen, R., 405
Allington, R. L., 79, 350
Allman, C. B., 93
Allsop, D. H., 88
Altwerger, B., 205
Amato, P. R., 403
Amschler, D. H., 467
Anderson, E., 409
Anderson, J., 343
Anderson, L. W., 155
Anderson, P. J., 67
Andre, T., 160
Aquinas, St. Thomas, 258, 296, 312
Aristotle, 163, 256, 257, 288, 293, 295–296, 298, 312
Asakawa, K., 65
Ashford, E., 372
Atkins, J., 45
August, D., 79
Augustine, St., 294, 312
Ayers, W., 369

B

Bacon, Francis, 293, 296, 298, 312
Bagley, William C., 303–304, 312, 429
Bandura, Albert, 50
Banks, James A., 59, 438
Barba, Robertta, 437
Barbe, W., 79
Baren, M., 91
Barkley, R., 91
Barone, D., 350
Barton, P., 402, 405
Baruth, L. G., 60
Bathurst, K., 403
Bedden, D., 405
Beller, A., 403
Benezet, Anthony, 264, 265
ben Gamala, Joshua, 257
Bentley, M., 41, 42–44, 311
Berkeley, George, 294–295, 312
Berliner, David, 119, 182, 239
Besharov, D., 346
Best, A. M., 88
Biancarosa, G., 80, 367
Bickerstaff, L., 420
Bielick, S., 370
Biemiller, A., 366

Binet, Alfred, 82
Binkney, R., 350
Bird, G., 403
Birman, B., 23
Black, S., 72, 73, 74, 93, 416
Blackmon, David W., 378–379
Blair, J., 131
Block, James, 166
Bloom, Benjamin, 17, 38, 166, 218, 279
Blow, Susan, 266
Bobo, J., 403
Bobok, B. L., 6
Bode, Boyd, 306, 429
Boers, D., 19
Borgers, S. B., 402
Borich, G. D., 230
Boyer, Ernest, 173
Bracey, G., 123
Brameld, Theodore, 307, 312
Bransford, J., 16, 224
Brendtro, L. K., 92
Brenna-Holmes, Megan, 110–111
Brophy, J. E., 75, 236, 377
Browder, D., 86
Brown, Bradford, 160–161
Brown, W. K., 92
Brozo, W., 88
Bruner, Jerome, 155, 157, 159, 279, 433, 478, 482
Buchanan, B., 467
Bugeja, M., 405
Burden, P. R., 229
Burgess, J., 126
Burmeister, L. E., 79
Burns, M., 439
Burns, R., 239, 469
Bushweller, K., 405
Butterfield, R. A., 63
Butts, R., 274

C

Calvin, John, 258
Cambourne, B., 35
Canedy, D., 405, 406
Cangelosi, J. S., 224–225
Canter, L., 225
Canter, M., 225
Cantor, J., 420
Carbo, M., 79
Carnoy, M., 123
Carrasquillo, A. L., 67
Carroll, John, 166
Carter, R., 68
Caulfield, R., 417
Cetron, K., 461
Cetron, M., 461
Chandler, K., 370
Chao, C. M., 66

Charlemagne, 258
Chaucer, Geoffrey, 112
Chavers, D., 63
Checkley, K., 84
Chen, X., 124
Cheng, L. L., 65, 66
Chung, S., 403
Cilley, M., 88
Cizek, G. J., 405
Clements, B. S., 231
Close, D. W., 91
Cohen, S. A., 166–167
Cole, N., 70
Collier, V., 74, 349, 405
Collins, Marjory, 252
Collins, P. A., 420
Conley, D. T., 188
Cook, G., 374
Cook-Cottone, C., 96
Counts, George, 307, 312
Coutinho, M. J., 88
Crandall, Prudence, 253–254, 266
Crawford, J., 72, 73
Cremin, L., 274
Csikszentmihalyi, M., 65
Cuban, L., 428
Culyer, G., 445
Culyer, R., 23, 41, 201, 445

D

Dalberg, John, 434
Darling, S., 128
Darling-Hammond, L., 16, 24, 224
Dean, M., 161
Dearman, C., 129
Dejnozka, E., 345, 347
Denmark, V., 131
Descartes, Rene, 294–295, 312
Deshler, D., 33, 78
Desimone, L., 23
de Tocqueville, Alexis, 360
Devito, Al, 242
Dewey, Alice, 272
Dewey, John, 6, 163, 169–170, 174–175, 253–254, 272, 275–276, 298–300, 305, 312, 429, 432, 438, 439
Deyhle, D., 63
Dietel, R., 73, 350
Dougherty, J., 329
Dronkers, J., 404
Druck, K., 415
Drucker, M. J., 349
Duarte, A., 60
DuBois, W. E. B., 253–254, 268–270, 290
Duke, N., 366
Dunn, R., 79
Dyer, P. C., 350

E

Ebert, C., 41, 42–44, 311, 455, 478
Ebert, E., 41, 42–44, 311, 455, 478
Edelsky, C., 205
Einstein, Albert, 455
Eisner, E., 159, 160
Eitzen, D. F., 403
Eliot, Charles, 261
Elkind, D., 419
Elliott, Beth, 226–227
Ellis, E., 33
Elmer, J., 403
Emmer, E. T., 231, 238, 239
English, J., 410
Epstein, J., 19
Erasmus, Desiderius, 258
Erikson, E., 17
Essex, N., 342, 347
Evans, G., 407
Evertson, C. M., 231

F

Fagan, Juanita, 407–408
Feldhusen, J. F., 87
Fenzel, L. M., 403
Fermanich, M. L., 4
Finn, J., 464
Fischer, L., 326, 327, 334
Fiscus, L., 37
Fiske, Edward, 187
Flaxman, S., 232
Flores, M., 205
Fombonne, E., 78
Franklin, Benjamin, 263, 264
Franklin, V. P., 61
Freeland, R., 58
Freire, Paulo, 290
Frelow, V. S., 468
Freud, Sigmund, 17
Froebel, Friedrich, 253–254, 266, 297
Fulghum, Robert, 361
Futrell, J., 404
Futrell, M. H., 405

G

Galileo, 293
Gambrell, L., 40
Gans, H., 68
Garan, E. M., 350
Garcia, E. E., 67
Garcia, S. B., 65
Gardiner, S., 405
Gardner, Howard, 83, 84, 87
Garet, M., 23
Gargiulo, Richard M., 83, 85
Garrett, Joyce, 323
Gates, Bill, 475
Gates, J., 368
Geis, S., 124
Gifford, V., 161
Gilchrist, L., 403
Gilligan, Carol, 70
Gilroy, M., 72, 74, 405
Glasser, William, 232

Golden, O., 410
Goleman, Daniel, 76
Golombok, S., 404
Gomez, J., 405
Good, T. L., 75
Goode, S., 460, 461
Goodlad, John I., 104, 122
Gordon, A., 409
Gordon, E. E., 80
Gordon, E. H., 80
Gordon, J. A., 65
Gordon, S. P., 6
Gottfried, A. E., 403
Gottfried, A. W., 403
Gould, H., 93
Gould, M., 93
Greenway, R., 458
Gresham, F., 91
Griffin, A., 345
Guisbond, L., 350

H

Haas, M. E., 172
Hakuta, K., 74, 79
Halverson, S., 322
Hamnuna, R., 257
Hampden-Thompson, G., 404
Hardman, D., 350
Harris, William, 163
Hastings, J. T., 218
Helfand, D., 68
Helgeson, L., 6, 121
Hendrie, C., 340
Henke, R., 124
Henkoff, R., 384
Heraclitus, 427
Herbart, Johann Friedrich, 297
Hirsch, E. D., Jr., 152, 154–155, 156, 166, 304–305, 312
Holland, A., 160
Hoover, D. W., 91
Hopkins, B. J., 387
Huguley, Sally, 192–193
Hunsader, P. D., 405
Huston, A. C., 420
Hutchins, Robert Maynard, 253–254, 302–303, 312
Hyman, J., 166–167
Hymowitz, K., 434

I

Ingersoll, R., 6, 124
Irvine, Jacqueline Jordan, 61
Ishizuka, K., 458, 461
Ivey, G., 366

J

Jackson, N. E., 79
Jacobsen, R., 123
Jacobson, L., 75
James, William, 298, 312
Jamieson, A., 404
Jansorn, N. R., 19
Jefferson, Thomas, 253–254, 263, 265

Jencks, C., 71
Jennings, J., 350
Johannessen, L. R., 6
Johnson, D. W., 171, 172
Johnson, J., 419
Johnson, R. T., 171, 172
Jones, L., 229, 231
Jones, V., 229, 231
Jordan, L., 88
Joyce, T., 403
Joyner, C., 346
Jurmaine, R., 416

K

Kaestner, R., 403
Kagan, S. L., 468
Kandinsky, Wassily, 292
Kann, L., 413
Kapel, D., 345, 347
Kaplowitz, M., 415
Karplus, R., 45
Keca, J., 96
Keith, B., 403
Kelley, L., 457
Kelly, C., 326, 327, 334
Kemerait, L., 403
Kennen, E., 124
Khmelkov, V., 23
Kierkegaard, Soren, 300, 312
Kilpatrick, William, 174–175
King-Sears, M. E., 193
Kirst, Michael, 189
Klonsky, M., 369
Kluckhohn, F., 68
Knight, George, 300
Koblinsky, S., 409
Kohn, A., 225
Kominski, R., 404
Korenman, S., 403
Korn, James H., 11–12
Kounin, Jacob, 238–239
Kozol, Jonathan, 385, 413
Krashen, S., 67, 350
Krathwohl, D., 17
Krathwohl, O. R., 155

L

Laczko-Kerr, I., 119
Lafreniere, K. D., 416
LaRoche, C., 336
Larson, Charyl, 64–65
Lasley, T. J., 38
Lazar, A., 19
Lecca, P. J., 65
Lee, Chungmei, 61
Lenhardt, A. C., 415
Lenz, B., 33
Levine, D., 165
Lewis, A., 4, 19, 79, 119, 348, 350, 372, 374
Lewis, S., 93
Lickona, Thomas, 439
Livingston, A., 121
Locke, John, 292, 296–297, 312

Long, N. J., 92, 224
Lopez, E., 124
Lorain, P., 126
Louv, Richard, 461
Luckasson, R., 85
Luther, Martin, 258

M

Madaus, G. F., 218
Mager, R., 221
Major, C., 24
Mann, Horace, 253–254, 266, 270–271, 303, 318, 432
Manning, M. L., 60
Marshall, Patricia, 62, 64, 66, 67
Marshall, Thurgood, 333
Martinez, G., 404
Maslow, Abraham, 17, 170–171, 310, 312
Matczynski, J. J., 38
Mather, Cotton, 264, 265
Mathews, R., 65, 73
Mathis, W. J., 350
Maxey, S., 6
McCann, T. M., 6
McCarthy, Joseph, 278
McCubbin, H., 404
McDaniel, T., 329
McEwan, Elaine, 429, 434, 438, 440
McGerald, J., 116
McGuffey, William H., 266
McGuiness, D., 80
Meier, T., 60
Mercer, A. R., 88
Mercer, C. D., 88
Michelangelo, 292
Milian, M., 72
Milich, R., 91
Miller, J., 467
Million, J., 18
Miranda, L. C., 406
Mishel, L., 123
Mohr, K. A. J., 74
Montessori, Maria, 253–254, 276, 277, 297, 438
Moore, Roy, 69
Morrill, Justin, 272
Morse, W., 224
Muther, Connie, 189

N

Napoleon, 254
Neau, Elias, 264, 265
Nehring, James, 58
Neill, A. S., 301
Neill, M., 350
Newman, R., 434
Nidds, J. A., 116
Nieto, S., 5, 172
Nietzsche, Friedrich, 300, 312

O

O'Connor, Sandra Day, 340
Oppenheimer, T., 400, 461
Orange, Carolyn, 427, 440, 449

Orfield, G., 61, 405
Ornstein, A., 165
Oswald, D. P., 88
Oswald, R. F., 404
Otto, L. B., 419
Out, J. W., 416

P

Paplia, A., 410
Parkay, F., 184
Parks, E., 68
Patterson, M. J., 37
Pavlov, Ivan, 308, 312
Payne, Ruby, 71, 406, 409
Peabody, Elizabeth, 266
Peirce, Charles Sanders, 298, 312
Penn, William, 264
Pestalozzi, Johann, 266, 270, 297
Phillips, M., 71
Piaget, Jean, 17, 311, 312
Pickering, Marvin, 333
Pierce, Sarah, 267
Pines, R., 24
Pitler, Howard, 456, 457
Pizzolongo, P., 323
Plato, 255–256, 260, 293, 294, 295, 312
Podsen, I., 131
Pong, S., 404
Ponticell, J., 23
Poon-McBrayer, K. R., 65
Porter, A., 23
Powell, J. S., 82
Protagoras, 255
Puffer, Richard, 438–439
Puma, M. J., 350

Q

Qingfeng, Xia, 4
Quinlan, A., 416
Quintilian, 256–257

R

Ravitch, Diane, 426, 428
Renchler, R, 406
Ricca, B. P., 6
Rickover, Hyman, 277
Riley, J., 79
Riley, Richard, 193
Ringstaff, C., 457
Roan, S., 91
Robelen, E. W., 15
Roberts, Sarah, 264
Rogers, Carl, 170, 309–310, 312
Rolon, C. A., 60
Rosenblatt, R., 68
Rosenshine, B., 39
Rosenthal, R., 75
Rothstein, R., 123
Rousseau, Jean-Jacques, 169, 305, 312
Rowe, Mary Budd, 40
Rowley, J. B., 38
Rubin, L. J., 402
Rust, F., 5
Rutherford, F. J., 155

S

Sartre, Jean-Paul, 300, 312
Schimmel, D., 326, 327, 334
Schinke, S., 403
Schlesinger, Arthur, 63
Schroeder, K., 80, 128, 129, 350, 415
Schurz, Margarethe, 253–254, 266
Scott-Little, C., 468
Senge, Peter, 430, 483
Shank, M., 91, 93, 94
Shannon, S., 72
Shaughnessy, M., 456
Sheurer, D., 184
Shuler, D., 225
Shulman, L., 16
Sikorski, J. F., 11
Simon, Theophile, 82
Simpson, E., 17
Sizer, Theodore, 156
Skinner, B. F., 308, 312, 457
Slavin, R. E., 171, 172
Slostad, F., 19
Smith, A. C., 407
Smith, D. I., 407
Smith, S. J., 93, 94
Snell, M., 86
Snow, C., 367
Snow, W., 403
Socrates, 253–254, 255, 293, 294, 312
Souter, David, 340
Spring, Joel, 184
Steele, C. M., 61
Sternberg, R. J., 82
Stevens, B., 18
Stevens, John Paul, 340
Stiggins, R., 187, 218, 219–220, 442
Stone, J., 131
Strodtbeck, F., 68
Stronge, J., 12, 18, 119, 120
Stuht, A., 368
Sunal, C. S., 172
Suppes, Patrick, 167
Swassing, R., 79
Sweeney, J., 440

T

Takona, J. P., 126
Tanner, L., 467
Tasker, F., 404
Taylor, Frederick, 266
Taylor, J., 350
Teitel, L., 24, 117
Terman, Lewis, 82
Thomas, D., 404
Thomas, W., 74, 349, 405
Thompson, A., 404
Thompson, E., 404
Thomson, M., 417
Thoreau, Henry D., 156
Toch, T., 5, 6
Tollafield, A., 18
Tomlinson, C., 33
Trueba, H. T., 64, 65
Turman, Lynette, 42–43
Turnbull, A., 93, 94

Turnbull, R., 88, 93, 94
Twain, Mark, 361
Tyack, D., 428
Tyler, Ralph, 157, 276

V

Vail, K., 407, 467
Vanourek, G., 458
Veronikas, S., 456
Viadero, D., 122
Vygotsky, Lev, 311, 312

W

Waddilove, Joe, 8–9
Wagner, E., 329
Walker, H. M., 91
Warren, Earl, 337, 338–339
Washburne, Carlton, 306
Washington, Booker T., 253–254, 267–268, 269

Washington, George, 361
Watson, John, 308, 312
Weaver, C., 350
Webber, J., 91
Weber, W., 224
Webster, Noah, 253–254, 263–264, 265
Wechsler, David, 82
Weinberg, W. A., 77
Weintraub, M., 87
Wendel, F. C., 387
Wenglinski, H., 23
Westberg, S., 128
White, C., 348
White-Clark, R., 73
Whittle, Christopher, 369, 431
Wildavsky, B., 223
Willard, Emma Hart, 267
Willert, H. J., 415
Willingham, W., 70
Winn, M., 420
Wise, Arthur, 119

Wolkomir, J., 93
Wolkomir, R., 93
Wong, Harry K., 214, 231, 440
Worsham, M. E., 231
Worthy, J., 367
Wright, Clint, 164–165
Wright, J. C., 420

Y

Yaden, D. B., Jr., 66
Yardley, J., 68
Yatvin, J., 350
Yoon, K., 23
Young, J., 88

Z

Zeller, R. W., 91
Zepeda, S., 23
Zill, N., 346
Zirkel, P. A., 20, 347

The National Board for Professional Teaching Standards (NBPTS)

The National Board for Professional Teaching Standards (NBPTS), like INTASC, is committed to the improvement of education by raising the quality of teaching. The NBPTS was also formed in 1987. Its inception followed the 1983 landmark report on the condition of education in the United States, *A Nation at Risk*. The National Board is a nonprofit, nonpartisan organization. The board is comprised primarily of classroom teachers and also includes school administrators, elected officials, teacher union leaders, and business and community leaders.

The NBPTS recognizes five core propositions that reflect accomplished teachers and effective teaching. Each of the five propositions is further detailed in terms of what teachers should know and be able to do. In addition, the NBPTS has described standards for accomplished teaching within every subject area. To pursue National Board certification you will need to have completed a baccalaureate degree and at least three years of teaching in a public or private school. The cost, which many states subsidize for successful candidates, is currently $2,300. The certificate is valid for 10 years. The table on the opposite page correlates each of the core propositions with the chapters in this book. For a more detailed explanation of the propositions and their subheadings, visit the NBPTS Web site at http://www.nbpts.org/the_standards/the_five_core_propositio.